DICTIONARY
GERMAN•ENGLISH
ENGLISH•GERMAN

DICTIONARY
GERMAN • ENGLISH
ENGLISH • GERMAN

TIGER BOOKS INTERNATIONAL
LONDON

This edition published in 1994 by
Tiger Books International PLC, London

ISBN 1-85501-371 1

Printed and bound in Slovenia

	Abbreviations	**Abkürzungen**
abbr	abbreviation	Abkürzung
acc	accusative	Akkusativ
adj	adjective	Adjektiv
adv	adverb	Adverb
art	article	Artikel
auto	automobile	Automobil
aux	auxiliary	Hilfs-
bot	botany	Botanik
chem	chemistry	Chemie
col	colloquial term	umgangssprachlich
com	commerce	Handel
compd	in compounds	Kompositum
comput	computers	Informatik
conj	conjunction	Konjunktion
dat	dative	Dativ
excl	exclamation	Ausruf
f	feminine noun	Femininum
fam	colloquial term	umgangssprachlich
fig	figurative use	übertragen
gr	grammar	Grammatik
imp	impersonal	unpersönlich
inform	computers	Informatik
interj	interjection	Ausruf
invar	invariable	unveränderlich
irr	irregular	unregelmäßig
jur	law term	Rechtswesen
law	law term	Rechtswesen
ling	linguistics	Sprachwissenschaft
m	masculine noun	Maskulinum
mar	marine term	Marine
mat, math	mathematics	Mathematik
med	medicine	Medizin
mil	military term	militärisch
mus	music	Musik

n	noun	Substantiv
n	neuter	Neutrum
nom	nominative	Nominativ
pej	pejorative	abschätzig
pl	plural	Plural
pn	pronoun	Pronomen
prep	preposition	Präposition
rad	radio	radio
rail	railway	Eisenbahn
rel	relative	Relativ-
relig	religion	Religion
sl	slang	Slang
teat	theatre	Theater
tec	technology	Technik
TV	television	Fernsehen
vb	verb	Verb
vi	intransitive verb	intransitives Verb
vr	reflexive verb	reflexives Verb
vt	transitive verb	transitives Verb
zo, zool	zoology	Zoologie

A

Aal *m* eel.
Aasgeier *m* vulture.
ab *prep* from; * *adv* away; down; off.
abändern *vt* to alter.
Abänderung *f* alteration.
Abbau *m* dismantling; decrease; mining; decomposition.
abbauen *vt* to dismantle; to mine, break down.
abbeißen *vt* to bite off.
Abbild *n* image.
abbilden *vt* to portray.
Abbildung *f* illustration.
abblasen *vt* to blow off; to cancel.
abblenden *vt* to dip (headlights).
abbrechen *vt vi* to break off; to stop.
abbrennen *vt* to burn; * *vi* to burn down.
abbringen *vt* to divert; to dissuade.
Abbruch *m* breaking off; demolition.
abbuchen *vt* to debit.
abbürsten *vt* to brush off.
abbüßen *vt* to atone.
abdanken *vi* to resign.
Abdankung *f* resignation.
abdecken *vt* to uncover; to cover; to clear (table).
abdichten *vt* to seal; to tighten.
abdrehen *vt vi* to turn off.
Abdrift *f* drift.
Abdruck *m* reprint.
abdrucken *vt* to reprint.
abdrücken *vt* to mould; to fire (weapon); to hug.
Abend *m* evening; **guten ~** good evening.
Abendanzug *m* evening dress.
Abendblatt *n* evening paper.
Abendessen *n* dinner.
Abendkasse *f* box office.
Abendland *n* the West.

Abendmahl *n* Holy Communion.
abends *adv* in the evening(s).
Abenteuer *n* adventure.
Abenteuergeschichte *f* adventure story.
abenteuerlich *adj* adventurous.
aber *adj* again; * *conj* but, however.
Aberglaube *m* superstition.
abergläubisch *adj* superstitious.
aberkennen *vt* to deny.
Aberkennung *f* denial.
abermals *adv* again.
abfahren *vi* to leave; to cover (distance); * *vt* to remove.
Abfahrt *f* departure; descent.
Abfall *m* waste; slope; decline.
Abfalleimer *m* rubbish bin, garbage can.
Abfalleisen *n* scrap iron.
abfallen *vi* to fall off.
abfallend *adj* sloping.
abfällig *adj* disapproving.
Abfallprodukt *n* by-product.
abfangen *vt* to catch.
abfärben *vi* to fade.
abfassen *vt* to intercept; to write, draft.
abfedern *vt* to pluck.
abfertigen *vt* to dispatch; to clear (customs); to serve (customer).
Abfertigung *f* dispatch, clearance.
abfeuern *vt* to fire.
abfinden *vt* to settle.
Abfindung *f* settlement.
abflachen *vt* to level.
abflauen *vi* to calm down.
abfliegen *vi* to take off, fly off.
abfließen *vi* to flow away.
Abflug *m* departure, take-off.
Abfluß *m* outflow.
abfordern *vt* to demand.
abforsten *vt* to deforest.

Abforstung *f* deforestation.
abfragen *vt* to question.
abfrieren *vi* to freeze off.
Abfuhr *m* removal; defeat.
abführen *vt* to lead away; to pay.
Abführmittel *n* laxative.
Abführung *f* removal; settlement.
abfüllen *vt* to fill.
Abgabe *f* delivery; pass (ball); tax.
abgabenfrei *adj* duty-free.
Abgang *m* departure.
Abgas *n* exhaust (gas).
abgeben *vt* to hand over; to pass (ball).
abgehärtet *adj* hardened.
abgehen *vi* to leave.
abgelegen *adj* isolated.
Abgelegenheit *f* remoteness.
abgelten *vt* to compensate.
abgemacht *adj* fixed.
Abgeordnete(r) *mf* deputy, member of parliament.
abgesehen von apart from.
abgesondert *adj* separate.
abgespannt *adj* exhausted.
abgestanden *adj* stale.
abgestorben *adj* numb; dead.
abgestumpft *adj* blunt.
abgewinnen *vt* to win.
abgewöhnen *vt* to wean off; * *vr* to give up.
Abgott *m* idol.
Abgötterei *f* idolatry.
abgöttisch *adj* idolatrous.
abgrenzen *vt* to demarcate.
Abgrund *m* abyss.
abgründig *adj* abysmal.
abhalten *vt* to hold off.
abhanden *adv* ~ **kommen** *vi* to become lost.
Abhandlung *f* treatise.
Abhang *m* slope.
abhängen *vt* to take down; to detach; * *vi* to hang up (telephone); ~ **von** depend on.
abhängig *adj* dependent; sloping.
Abhängigkeit *f* dependence.
abhärten *vt* to harden.

abhauen *vt* to cut off; * *vi* (*coll*) to clear off.
abheben *vt* to lift; to remove; to cut (cards).
abhelfen *vi* to help.
Abhilfe *f* remedy.
abholen *vt* to collect; to meet.
abhören *vt* to test (pupil); to eavesdrop.
Abhörgerät *n* bug.
Abitur *n* German school-leaving examination.
Abkehr *f* turning away; departure.
abkehren *vt vr* turn away.
abklären *vt* to clarify.
abklingen *vi* to die away.
abknöpfen *vt* to unbutton; * (*coll*) to deprive.
Abkommen *n* agreement.
abkommen *vi* to get away.
abkömmlich *adj* available.
Abkommling *m* descendant.
abkratzen *vt* to scrape off; * *vi* (*coll*) to kick the bucket.
abkühlen *vt vr* to cool down.
abkürzen *vt* to abbreviate.
Abkürzung *f* abbreviation.
abladen *vt* to unload.
Ablage *f* store-room.
ablagern *vt* to store.
Ablaß *m* outlet; reduction.
ablassen *vt* to emit; to reduce; * *vi* to stop.
Ablauf *m* drain; course; expiry.
ablaufen *vi* to drain away; to happen; to expire.
ableben *vi* to expire.
ablecken *vt* to lick off.
ablegen *vt* to put down, take off.
ablehnen *vt vi* to refuse.
ablehnend *adj* critical.
Ablehnung *f* refusal.
ableiten *vt* to divert; to derive; to infer.
Ableitung *f* diversion; deduction; derivation.
ablenken *vt* to turn away, divert.
Ablenkung *f* diversion.
ablesen *vt* to read out.

Ablesung *f* reading.
ableugnen *vt* to deny.
abliefern *vt* to deliver.
Ablieferung *f* delivery.
ablösen *vt* to take off; to take over.
Ablösung *f* loosening; detachment; relief; redemption.
abmachen *vt* to take off; to settle, agree.
Abmachung *f* agreement.
abmagern *vi* to grow thinner.
Abmagerungskur *f* diet.
Abmarsch *m* departure.
abmessen *vt* to measure.
Abmessung *f* measurement.
abmontieren *vt* to dismantle.
abmühen *vr* to tire.
Abnahme *f* removal; purchase; decrease.
abnehmbar *adj* removable.
abnehmen *vt* to remove; to purchase; * *vi* to decrease.
Abnehmer *m* purchaser, customer.
Abneigung *f* reluctance, dislike.
abnorm *adj* abnormal.
abnutzen *vt* to wear out.
Abnutzung *f* wear.
Abonnement *n* subscription.
Abonnent(in) *m(f)* subscriber.
abonnieren *vt* to subscribe.
Abordnung *f* delegation.
Abort *m* lavatory.
abpacken *vt* to pack.
abpassen *vt* to wait for; to adjust.
Abpfiff *m* final whistle.
abplagen *vi* to slave; * *vr* to struggle.
Abprall *m* rebound.
abprallen *vi* to rebound.
abraten *vi* to advise against.
abräumen *vt* to clear up.
abrechnen *vt* to deduct; * *vi* to settle.
Abrechnung *f* settlement; account.
Abrede *f* agreement; **in ~ stellen** to deny, question.
abreden *vi* to advise against.

abregen *vr* to calm down.
abreiben *vt* to rub off.
Abreise *f* departure.
abreisen *vi* to leave.
abreißen *vt vi* to tear off.
abriegeln *vt* to bar.
Abriß *m* demolition; sketch.
abrollen *vt vi* to unroll.
Abruf *m* call.
abrufen *vt* to call away.
abrunden *vt* to round off.
abrüsten *vi* to disarm.
Abrüstung *f* disarmament.
Absage *f* refusal; cancellation.
absagen *vt vi* to call off.
absägen *vt* to saw off.
absatteln *vt* to unsaddle.
Absatz *m* sales; paragraph; ledge, landing; heel.
Absatzgebiet *n* market.
absaugen *vt* to suck off, vacuum.
abschaben *vt* to scrape (off).
abschaffen *vt* to abolish.
Abschaffung *f* abolition.
abschalten *vt vi* to switch off.
abschätzen *vt* to estimate.
Abschätzer *m* assessor.
abschätzig *adj* derogatory.
Abschaum *m* scum.
abschäumen *vt* to skim off.
Abscheu *m* loathing.
abscheulich *adj* horrible.
abschicken *vt* to send off, post.
abschieben *vt* to push away, expel.
Abschied *m* departure; ~ **nehmen** to take one's leave.
abschießen *vt* to shoot (down); to get rid of.
abschirmen *vt* to screen.
abschirren *vt* to unharness.
Abschlag *m* reduction.
abschlagen *vt* to knock off; to take down; to refuse.
abschlägig *adj* negative.
Abschlagsdividende *f* interim dividend.
abschleifen *vt* to grind down.
Abschleppdienst *m* towing service.
Abschleppseil *n* tow rope.

abschließen *vt* to lock; to conclude.

abschließend *adj* final; * *adv* finally.

Abschluß *m* conclusion.

Abschlußprüfung *f* final exams.

abschmieren *vt* to lubricate.

abschneiden *vt* to cut off.

Abschnitt *m* section.

abschnüren *vt* to constrict.

abschöpfen *vt* to skim off.

abschrauben *vt* to unscrew.

abschrecken *vt* to frighten off.

abschreiben *vt* to copy; to write off; to write down, deduct.

Abschreibung *f* depreciation, write-off.

Abschrift *f* copy.

Abschuß *m* firing; shooting down.

abschüssig *adj* steep.

abschütteln *vt* to shake off.

abschwächen *vt* to weaken, lessen.

abschweifen *vi* to deviate, depart.

Abschweifung *f* digression.

abschwellen *vi* to die down.

abschwören *vi* to renounce.

absehbar *adj* foreseeable.

absehen *vt* to foresee; * *vi* to refrain from; to disregard.

abseits *adv* aside, apart, offside.

absenden *vt* to send off.

Absender *m* sender.

absetzen *vt* to put down; to take off; to sell; * *vr* to go away; to be deposited.

absichern *vt* to guard against.

Absicht *f* intention.

absichtlich *adj* deliberate, intentional; * *adv* deliberately, intentionally.

absinken *vi* to sink.

absolut *adj* absolute.

absolvieren *vt* to pass (exam).

absonderlich *adj* strange.

absondern *vt* to separate; to give off.

abspalten *vt* to split off.

abspenstig *adj* unfaithful.

absperren *vt* to block off; to lock.

Absperrung *f* blocking off.

abspielen *vt* to play; to pass (ball); * *vr* to happen.

Absprache *f* agreement, arrangement.

absprechen *vt* to agree, arrange; to deny.

abspringen *vi* to jump down; to come off.

Absprung *m* jump.

abspülen *vt* to rinse; to wash up.

abstammen *vi* to descend, derive.

Abstammung *f* descent, derivation.

Abstand *m* distance; ~ **nehmen** refrain from; **mit ~** by far.

abstatten *vt* to give; to pay.

abstauben *vt vi* to dust; (*coll*) to pinch.

abstehen *vi* to stick out, stand off; to go stale.

absteigen *vi* to get off; to accomodate; to be relegated.

abstellen *vt* to put down; to pull out, switch off; to park.

Abstellgleis *n* siding.

abstempeln *vt* to stamp.

absterben *vi* to die; to go numb.

Abstieg *m* descent, decline; relegation.

abstimmen *vt* to adjust, tune; * *vi* to vote; * *vr* to agree.

Abstimmung *f* harmonising; vote.

Abstinenz *f* abstinence.

Abstinenzler(in) *m(f)* teetotaller.

abstoßen *vt* to push away; to dispose of.

abstoßend *adj* repellent.

abstrakt *adj* abstract; * *adv* abstractly.

abstreiten *vt* to dispute.

Abstrich *m* cut, deduction; (*med*) smear.

abstufen *vt* to grade.

abstumpfen *vt vi* to blunt.

Absturz *m* fall, crash (aircraft).

absuchen *vt* to scour, look everywhere.

absurd *adj* absurd.

Abszeß *m* abscess.

Abt *m* abbot.

abtasten *vt* to feel, palpate, probe.

abtauen *vt vi* to thaw.

Abtei *f* abbey.

Abteil *n* compartment.

abteilen *vt* to divide.

Abteilung *f* department, section.

abtönen *vt* to tone down.

abtransportieren *vt* to remove.

abtreiben *vt* to drive, drift off course; to abort; * *vi* to be driven off course, abort.

Abtreibung *f* abortion.

abtrennen *vt* to separate.

abtreten *vt* to wear out; to hand over; * *vi* to resign.

Abtritt *m* resignation.

abtrocknen *vt vi* to dry.

abtun *vt* to take off, remove.

abverlangen *vt* to demand.

abwägen *vt* to weigh up.

abwandeln *vt* to adapt.

abwandern *vi* to migrate.

Abwanderung *f* migration.

abwarten *vt* to wait for; * *vi* to wait.

abwärts *adv* down(wards).

Abwasch *m* washing-up.

abwaschen *vt* to wash off, wash up.

Abwasser *n* sewage.

abwechseln *vi vr* to alternate.

abwechselnd *adj* alternate.

Abwechslung *f* change.

Abweg *m* detour, wrong way.

abwegig *adj* wrong, misleading.

Abwehr *f* defence.

abwehren *vt* to fend off.

abweichen *vi* to deviate; to differ.

abweisen *vt* to turn away.

abwenden *vt vi* to turn away.

abwerfen *vt* to throw off; to drop; to yield.

abwerten *vt* to devalue.

abwesend *adj* absent.

Abwesenheit *f* absence.

abwickeln *vt* unwind, wind up.

abwiegen *vt* to weigh out.

abwischen *vt* to wipe (off).

Abwurf *m* throwing off.

abwürgen *vt* to strangle; to foil.

abzahlen *vt* to pay off.

Abzahlung *f* repayment, hire purchase.

abzapfen *vt* to draw off; to drain.

abzäunen *vt* to fence off.

Abzeichen *n* badge.

abzeichnen *vt* to copy, draw.

Abziehbild *n* transfer.

abziehen *vt* to take off, withdraw.

Abzug *m* departure, withdrawal; copy; deduction; flue, trigger.

abzüglich *prep* minus, less.

abzweigen *vi* to branch off; * *vt* to put aside.

Abzweigung *f* junction.

ach *excl* oh; ~ **ja!** oh, yes!; ~ **nein?** you don't say?; ~ **so!** I see.

Achse *f* axis, axle.

Achsel *f* shoulder.

Achselhöhle *f* armpit.

acht *num* eight; ~ **Tage** a week.

Acht *f* ban; attention.

achtbar *adj* respectable.

achte *adj* eighth.

Achtel *num* eighth.

achten *vt* to respect; * *vi* to pay attention.

ächten *vt* to ban.

achtlos *adj* careless.

achtsam *adj* careful.

Achtung *f* attention, respect; * *excl* look out!.

achtzehn *num* eighteen.

achtzig *num* eighty.

ächzen *vi* to groan.

Acker *m* field.

Ackerbau *m* agriculture.

Ackerbohne *f* broad bean.

ackern *vt vi* to plough; to work hard.

addieren *vt* to add.

Addition *f* addition.

Adel *m* aristocracy.

adelig, adlig *adj* noble.

Ader *f* vein.

Adler *m* eagle.

Admiral *m* admiral.

adoptieren *vt* to adopt.

Adoption *f* adoption.

Adrenalin *n* adrenalin(e).

Adressant *m* sender, drawer.

Adressat *m* addressee, drawee.

Adresse *f* address.

Adressieren *vt* to address.

Advent *m* Advent.

Aerobic *n* aerobics.

Affäre *f* affair.

Affe *m* monkey.

affektiert *adj* affected.

Afrika *n* Africa.

Afrikaner(in) *m(f)* African.

afrikanisch *adj* African.

After *m* anus.

Agent *m* agent.

Aggression *f* aggression.

aggressiv *adj* aggressive.

Agitation *f* agitation.

Ägypten *n* Egypt.

Ägypter(in) *m(f)* Egyptian.

ägyptisch *adj* Egyptian.

ähneln *vi* resemble; * *vr* to be alike.

ahnen *vt* to suspect.

ähnlich *adj* similar.

Ähnlichkeit *f* similarity.

Ahnung *f* suspicion.

ahnungslos *adj* unsuspecting.

Ahorn *m* maple.

Ähre *f* ear (corn, etc).

Aids *n* Aids.

Akademie *f* academy.

Akademiker(in) *m(f)* graduate.

akademisch *adj* academic.

Akkord *m* chord.

Akkordeon *n* accordion.

Akrobat(in) *m(f)* acrobat.

Akt *m* act; nude.

Akte *f* document, file.

Aktenschrank *m* filing cabi-

net.

Aktentasche *f* briefcase.

Aktie *f* share.

Aktiengesellschaft *f* joint-stock company.

Aktion *f* campaign, action.

Aktionär(in) *m(f)* shareholder.

aktiv *adj* active.

Aktiva *pl* assets.

aktivieren *vt* to activate.

Aktivität *f* activity.

Aktualität *f* topicality.

aktuell *adj* topical, up-to-date.

Akustik *f* acoustics.

akut *adj* acute.

Akzent *m* accent, stress.

akzeptieren *vt* to accept.

Alarm *m* alarm.

Albanien *n* Albania.

albern *adj* absurd.

Album *n* album.

Algebra *f* algebra.

Algerien *n* Algeria.

Algier *n* Algiers.

Alibi *n* alibi.

Alimente *pl* alimony.

Alkohol *m* alcohol.

Alkoholiker(in) *m(f)* alcoholic.

alkoholisch *adj* alcoholic.

All *n* universe.

all (aller, alles) *pn* all; * *adj* all, every, any.

alle *adv* finished.

Allee *f* avenue.

allein *adj* alone; * *conj* only, but.

Alleinerziehende(r) *mf* single parent.

alleinstehend *adj* alone, single.

allemal *adv* always; **ein für ~** once and for all.

allenfalls *adv* in any event; perhaps.

allerbeste *adj* very best.

allerdings *adv* certainly.

Allergie *f* allergy.

allergisch *adj* allergic.

allerhand *adj* all kinds of.

alles *pn* everything.

allgemein *adj* general.

allgemeingültig *adj* generally

accepted.
Allianz f alliance.
allmählich adj gradual.
Alltag m everyday life.
alltäglich adj adv everyday.
allwissend adj omniscient.
allzu adv all too.
Almosen n alms.
Alpen pl (the) Alps.
Alphabet n alphabet.
alphabetisch adj alphabetical.
Alptraum m nightmare.
als conj when; as; than; ~ **ob** as if.
also conj so, therefore.
alt adj old.
Alt m alto.
Altar m altar.
Alteisen n scrap iron.
älter adj older.
Alter n age.
altern vi to age.
Alternative f alternative.
Altersheim n old people's home.
Altersversorgung f old age pension.
Altertum n antiquity.
Altglascontainer m bottle bank.
althergebracht adj traditional.
altmodisch adj old-fashioned.
Altpapier n waste paper.
Altstadt f old town.
Aluminium n aluminium.
am = an dem.
Amateur m amateur.
Amboß m anvil.
ambulant adj outpatient.
Ambulanz f outpatients (department).
Ameise f ant.
Amerika n America.
Amerikaner(in) m(f) American.
amerikanisch adj American.
Ampel f traffic light.
amputieren vt to amputate.
Amsel f blackbird.
Amt n office; post.
amtieren vi to hold office.

amtlich adj official.
Amtsperson f official.
Amtsstunden pl office hours.
Amtszeit f period of office.
amüsant adj amusing.
amüsieren vt to amuse; * vi to enjoy oneself
an prep at, on, near, to.
analog adj analagous.
Analogie f analogy.
Analyse f analysis.
analysieren vt to analyse.
Ananas f pineapple.
Anarchie f anarchy.
Anatomie f anatomy.
Anbau m cultivation; extension.
anbauen vt to cultivate; to extend.
anbehalten vt to keep on.
anbei adv enclosed.
anbeißen vt to bite into; * vi to bite.
anbelangen vt to concern.
anbeten vt to worship.
Anbetracht m in ~ (+ gen) in view of.
anbieten vt to offer; * vi to volunteer.
anbinden vt to tie up.
Anblick m sight.
anblicken vt to look at.
anbrechen vt to break into; * vi to begin (night, day).
anbrennen vi to catch fire.
anbringen vt to bring in or on; to sell; to attach.
Anbruch m beginning.
Andacht f attention.
andächtig adj devout.
andauern vi to continue.
andauernd adj continual.
Anden pl (the) Andes.
Andenken n remembrance.
andere adj other; different.
ändern vt vr to change.
andernfalls adv otherwise.
anders adv differently; else.
andersartig adj different.
andersherum adv the other way round.
anderswo adv somewhere else.

anderthalb *adj* one and a half.
Änderung *f* change.
anderweitig *adj* other; * *adv* otherwise, elsewhere.
andeuten *vt* to indicate.
Andeutung *f* indication.
andrehen *vt* to turn on.
androhen *vt* to threaten.
aneignen *vt* sich (*dat*) etwas ~ to acquire.
aneinander *adv* together.
anekeln *vt* to disgust.
Anemone *f* anemone.
anerkannt *adj* recognised.
anerkennen *vt* to recognise.
Anerkennung *f* recognition.
anfachen *vt* to kindle.
anfahren *vt* to deliver; to collide with; to call at (port); * *vi* to start up; to drive up.
Anfall *m* attack, fit.
anfallen *vt* to attack; * *vi* to occur; to accrue.
anfällig *adj* susceptible.
Anfang *m* beginning.
anfangen *vt* to begin; to do.
Anfänger(in) *m(f)* beginner.
anfänglich *adj* initial.
anfangs *adv* at first.
Anfangsbuchstabe *m* initial letter.
Anfangsstadium *n* initial stages.
anfassen *vt* to touch; *vr* to help.
anfechten *vt* to dispute; to trouble.
anfertigen *vt* to produce.
Anfertigung *f* production.
anfeuern *vt* to spur on.
anflehen *vt* to implore.
anfliegen *vt* to fly to.
Anflug *m* approach (aircraft); trace.
anfordern *vt* to demand, call on; to requisition.
Anfrage *f* inquiry.
anfragen *vi* to inquire.
anfreunden *vr* to become friends.
anfügen *vt* to attach; to add.
anfühlen *vt* to feel.
anführen *vt* to lead; to cite; to mislead.
Anführer *m* leader.
Anführung *f* leadership; quotation.
Anführungszeichen *pl* quotation marks.
Angabe *f* statement; specification; service (tennis, etc); boasting.
angeben *vt* to give; to specify; inform on; * *vi* to serve (tennis, etc); to boast.
Angeber *m* show-off.
Angeberei *f* showing off.
angeblich *adj* alleged.
angeboren *adj* innate,.
Angebot *n* offer, tender; supply; ~ und Nachfrage supply and demand.
angebracht *adj* appropriate.
angehen *vi* to relate to; to tackle; apply to; * *vi* to catch fire, take root; to go bad.
angehören *vi* to belong.
Angehörige(r) *mf* relative.
Angeklagte(r) *mf* defendant.
Angel *f* fishing rod; hinge.
Angelegenheit *f* matter, issue.
Angelhaken *m* fish hook.
angeln *vt* to catch; * *vi* to fish.
Angeln *n* fishing.
Angelrute *f* fishing rod.
angemessen *adj* appropriate.
angenehm *adj* pleasant.
angenommen *adj* assumed, assuming.
angesehen *adj* respected.
angesichts *prep* in view of.
angespannt *adj* tense.
Angestellte(r) *mf* (white-collar) worker, employee.
angetan *adj* clad; impressed, pleased.
angewiesen *adj* dependent.
angewöhnen *vt* become accustomed.
Angewohnheit *f* habit.
angleichen *vt* *vr* to adjust.
Angler *m* angler.
angreifen *vt* to attack; to touch.
Angriff *m* attack.
Angst *f* fear, anxiety.

ängstigen *vt* to frighten; * *vr* to worry.

ängstlich *adj* nervous.

anhaben *vt* to wear; to do against.

Anhalt *m* support.

anhalten *vt* to stop, arrest; * *vi* to stop; to last.

Anhalter *m* hitch-hiker; **per ~ fahren** to hitch-hike.

Anhaltspunkt *m* clue, criterion.

anhand *prep* with.

Anhang *m* appendix; dependants.

anhangen *vt* to hang up, add on.

Anhänger *m* supporter; trailer.

Anhäufung *f* accumulation.

anheben *vt* to raise.

Anhieb *m* **auf ~** straight away.

anhören *vt* to listen to, hear; * *vr* to sound.

animieren *vt* to encourage.

ankaufen *vt* to purchase.

Anker *m* anchor.

Anklage *f* accusation.

Anklagebank *f* dock (in court).

anklagen *vt* to accuse.

Ankläger *m* plaintiff.

Anklang *m* **~ finden** meet with approval.

ankleiden *vt* to dress.

anklopfen *vi* to knock.

anknüpfen *vt* to tie on; to begin; * *vi* to refer.

ankommen *vi* to arrive; **es kommt darauf an** it all depends.

ankündigen *vt* to announce.

Ankündigung *f* announcement.

Ankunft *f* arrival.

ankurbeln *vt* to start; to boost.

Anlage *f* layout, structure; plant, installation, grounds; talent; capital.

Anlagevermögen *n* fixed assets.

Anlaß *m* occasion; reason.

anlassen *vt* to leave on; to start; * *vr* to appear.

Anlasser *m* starter.

anläßlich *prep* on the occasion of.

Anlauf *m* run-up.

anlaufen *vt* to call at; * *vi* to begin; to run up; to increase; to tarnish.

anlegen *vt* to lay, design; to invest; to aim.

anlehnen *vt* to lean; to leave ajar; * *vr* to lean.

Anleihe *f* loan.

anleiten *vt* to instruct.

Anleitung *f* instructions.

anlernen *vt* to teach.

anliegen *vi* to be close to; to cling (clothes).

anlügen *vt* to lie to.

anmachen *vt* to put on.

anmaßen *vt* **sich etwas ~** to claim, usurp.

anmaßend *adj* arrogant.

Anmaßung *f* arrogance.

anmelden *vt* to announce; * *vr* to make an appointment; to register.

Anmeldung *f* appointment, announcement, registration.

anmerken *vt* to note (down).

Anmerkung *f* comment.

Anmut *f* grace, charm.

anmuten *vt* to seem.

anmutig *adj* graceful, charming.

annähern *f* to approach.

annähernd *adj* approximate; * *adv* approximately.

Annäherung *f* approach.

Annahme *f* acceptance.

annehmbar *adj* acceptable.

annehmen *vt* to accept, assume.

anonym *adj* anonymous.

Anonymität *f* anonymity.

Anorak *m* anorak.

anordnen *vt* to arrange; to order.

Anordnung *f* arrangement, order.

anpacken *vt* to grasp; to tackle; **mit ~** to pull one's weight.

anpassen *vt* to fit, adapt; * *vr*

to adapt.

Anpassung f adaptation, adjustment.

Anprall m collision.

anprangern vt to denounce.

anpreisen vt to recommend, extol.

Anprobe f trying-on.

anprobieren vt to try on.

anrechnen vt to charge; to deduct; to allow for.

Anrecht n right.

Anrede f address; salutation.

anreden vt to speak to.

anregen vt to touch; to stimulate.

Anregung f sugggestion; stimulus.

anreichern vt to enrich.

Anreise f journey.

Anreiz m stimulus.

anrichten vt to prepare, serve; to cause.

anrüchig adj disreputable.

anrücken vi to approach.

Anruf m call.

anrufen vt to call; to invoke.

ans = an das.

Ansage f announcement.

Ansager(in) m(f) announcer.

ansässig adj resident, located.

Ansatz m beginning; extension, appendage; mouthpiece; deposit; charge; estimate.

Ansatzpunkt m starting point.

anschaffen vt to buy, acquire.

Anschaffung f purchase, acquisition.

anschalten vt to switch on.

anschauen vt to look at.

anschaulich adj clear; graphic.

Anschauung f opinion, view.

Anschein m appearance; **allem ~ nach** to all apearances.

anscheinend adj apparent; * adv apparently.

Anschlag m impact; advertisement.

anschlagen vt to strike; to affix; to estimate; * vi to hit, affect.

anschließen vt to connect; to

support; * vr to join, agree.

anschließend adj adjacent; subsequent; * adv then.

Anschluß m connection; supply; annexation; **im ~ an** further to.

Anschlußzug m connecting train.

anschnallen vt to buckle up; * vi to fasten one's seat belt.

anschneiden vt to cut; to broach.

anschreiben vt to write (to); to charge.

anschreien vt to shout at.

Anschrift f address.

Anschuldigung f accusation.

ansehen vt to look at.

Ansehen n respect; reputation.

ansehnlich adj imposing.

ansetzen vt to affix; to develop; to prepare; * vi to try; to begin; to prepare.

Ansicht f view; **zur ~** on approval; **meiner ~ nach** in my opinion.

ansiedeln vt vr to settle.

Ansiedler(in) m(f) settler.

anspannen vt to harness; to strain.

Anspannung f tension, exertion.

Anspiel n start (sports); to kick-off.

anspielen vi to lead; to kick off; to serve; to refer to.

Anspielung f allusion.

Ansprache f address, speech.

ansprechen vt to speak to; to appeal to.

ansprechend adj appealing, attractive.

anspringen vt to jump on; * vi to jump, pounce; to start (engine).

Anspruch m claim, right; **in ~ nehmen** occupy, take up.

anspruchslos adj undemanding.

anspruchsvoll adj demanding.

Anstalt f institution; **Anstalten** pl preparations.

Anstand *m* decency.

anständig *adj* decent.

anstandslos *adv* unhesitatingly.

anstarren *vt* to stare at.

anstatt *prep conj* instead of.

anstecken *vt* to stick on; to ignite; to infect; * *vi* to be infectious.

ansteckend *adj* infectious.

Ansteckung *f* infection.

anstehen *vi* queue up, stand in line.

anstelle *prep* in place of.

anstellen *vt* to turn on; to recruit, employ; to do; * *vr* to queue up, stand in line.

Anstellung *f* employment, position.

Anstieg *m* climb, rise.

anstiften *vt* to instigate.

Anstifter *m* instigator.

Anstoß *m* impetus; start (game); kick-off; offence.

anstoßen *vt* push, kick; * *vi* to knock; to drink a toast.

anstößig *adj* objectionable.

anstreichen *vt* to paint.

Anstreicher(in) *m(f)* painter.

anstrengen *vt* to exert; * *vi* to make an effort.

Anstrengung *f* effort.

Anstrich *m* coat of paint.

Ansturm *m* assault.

Antarktis *f* the Antarctic.

antarktisch *adj* antarctic.

antasten *vt* to touch; to encroach; to injure.

Anteil *m* share.

Anteilseigner(in) *m(f)* shareholder.

Antenne *f* antenna.

Antibiotikum *n* antibiotic.

antik *adj* antique.

Antike *f* antique; antiquity.

Antilope *f* antelope.

Antiquar(in) *m(f)* second-hand bookseller.

antiquarisch *adj adv* second-hand.

Antrag *m* application; proposal.

antreffen *vt* to meet.

antreiben *vt* to propel; to wash up; * *vi* to be washed up.

antreten *vt* to begin; to come into; to offer; to line up.

Antrieb *m* drive.

Antritt *m* beginning.

antun *vt* put on; to do to.

Antwerpen *n* Antwerp.

Antwort *f* answer.

antworten *vi* to answer.

anvertrauen *vt* to entrust.

anwachsen *vi* to grow, take root.

Anwalt *m* **Anwältin** *f* lawyer, solicitor.

anweisen *vt* to instruct; to allocate.

Anweisung *f* instruction; remittance.

anwendbar *adj* applicable.

anwenden *vt* to use.

Anwendung *f* use.

anwesend *adj* present.

Anwesenheit *f* presence.

Anzahl *f* number.

anzahlen *vt* pay on account.

Anzahlung *f* deposit.

Anzeichen *n* indication.

Anzeige *f* advertisement.

anzeigen *vt* to advertise, announce.

anziehen *vt* to put on; to dress; to attract; to pull tight; to absorb; * *vr* to get dressed.

Anziehung *f* attraction.

Anziehungskraft *f* attraction; magnetism; gravitation.

Anzug *m* suit; **im ~ sein** to approach.

anzünden *vt* to light, ignite.

Anzünder *m* lighter.

anzweifeln *vt* to doubt.

Apathie *f* apathy.

apathisch *adj* apathetic.

Apfel *m* apple.

Apfelsine *f* orange.

Apfelwein *m* cider.

Apostel *m* apostle.

Apostroph *m* apostrophe.

Apotheke *f* chemist's shop, pharmacy.

Apotheker(in) *m(f)* chemist,

pharmacist.

Apparat *m* item of equipment; telephone; camera; **am ~!** speaking! **am ~ bleiben** hold the line.

Appell *m* roll-call; appeal.

Appetit *m* appetite; **guten ~** enjoy your meal.

appetitlich *adj* appetising.

Applaus *m* applause.

Aprikose *f* apricot.

April *m* April.

Aquarell *n* watercolour.

Aquarium *n* aquarium.

Äquator *m* equator.

äquatorial *adj* equatorial.

Araber *m* **Arabin** *f* Arab.

Arabien *n* Arabia.

arabisch *adj* Arabian.

Arbeit *f* work.

Arbeiter(in) *m(f)* worker.

arbeiten *vt vi* to work.

Arbeitsamt *n* employment office, job centre.

Arbeitsgericht *n* employment tribunal.

Arbeitskräfte *pl* workers, labour.

arbeitslos *adj* unemployed.

Arbeitslosigkeit *f* unemployment.

Arbeitsplatz *m* job; place of work.

arbeitsscheu *adj* workshy.

Arbeitszeit *f* working hours.

Archäologe *m* archaeologist.

Archäologie *f* archaeology.

Architekt(in) *m(f)* architect.

Architektur *f* architecture.

Archiv *n* archive.

arg *adj* bad, evil; * *adv* badly.

Arg *n* malice, harm.

Argentinien *n* Argentina.

Ärger *m* anger; trouble.

ärgerlich *adj* angry; annoying.

ärgern *vt* to annoy; * *vr* to get annoyed.

Ärgernis *n* annoyance.

Arglist *f* cunning, deceit.

arglistig *adj* malicious.

arglos *adj* guileless.

Arglosigkeit *f* innocence.

Argument *n* argument.

Argwohn *m* suspicion, distrust.

Arie *f* aria.

Aristokrat *m* aristocrat.

Aristokratie *f* aristocracy.

Arithmetik *f* arithmetic.

arithmetisch   *adj* arithmetic(al).

Arktis *f* Arctic.

arktisch *adj* arctic.

arm *adj* poor.

Arm *m* arm.

Armaturenbrett *n* instrument panel, dashboard.

Armband *n* bracelet.

Armbanduhr *f* wristwatch.

Armee *f* army.

Ärmel *m* sleeve.

Ärmelkanal *m* (the) English Channel.

ärmlich *adj* poor, shabby.

Ärmlichkeit *f* poverty, shabbiness.

armselig *adj* poverty-stricken.

Armut *f* poverty.

Aroma *n* aroma.

aromatisch *adj* aromatic.

arrangieren *vt* to arrange; * *vr* to reach an arrangement.

Arrest *m* arrest, detention.

arrogant *adj* arrogant.

Arroganz *f* arrogance.

Arsch *m* arse, bum.

Art *f* way; sort; species.

Arterie *f* artery.

artig *adj* well-behaved.

Artikel *m* article.

Artillerie *f* artillery.

Arznei *f* medicine.

Arzneiformel *f* prescription.

Arzneimittel *n* medicine, drug.

Arzt *m* **Ärztin** *f* doctor.

ärztlich *adj* medical.

As *n* ace; A flat.

Asbest *m* asbestos.

Asche *f* ash(es).

Aschenbecher *m* ashtray.

Aschermittwoch   *m* Ash Wednesday.

Asien *n* Asia.

Asiat(in) *m(f)* Asian.

asiatisch *adj* Asian.

asozial *adj* antisocial.
Aspekt *m* aspect.
Assistent(in) *m(f)* assistant.
Assoziation *f* association.
Ast *m* branch.
ästhetisch *adj* aesthetic.
Asthma *n* asthma.
Astrologe *m* astrologer.
Astrologie *f* astrology.
astrologisch *adj* astrological.
Astronaut *m* astronaut.
Astronom *m* astronomy.
Astronomie *f* astronomy.
Asyl *n* asylum.
Asylbewerber *m* asylum-seeker.
Atem *m* breath.
atemlos *adj* breathless.
Atheismus *m* atheism.
Atheist *m* atheist.
Athen *n* Athens.
Äther *m* ether.
Äthiopien *n* Ethiopia.
Athlet *m* athlete.
Atlantik *m* Atlantic (Ocean).
Atlas *m* atlas.
atmen *vt vi* to breathe.
Atmosphäre *f* atmosphere.
Atmosphärendruck *m* atmospheric pressure.
atmosphärisch *adj* atmospheric.
Atmung *f* breathing.
Atom *n* atom.
Atombombe *f* atomic bomb.
Atomenergie *f* atomic or nuclear energy.
Atomforscher *m* nuclear scientist.
Atomkraftwerk *n* nuclear power station.
Atomkrieg *m* nuclear war.
Atommüll *m* atomic waste.
Atomwaffen *pl* nuclear weapons.
atypisch *adj* atypical.
ätzen *vt* to corrode.
Ätzdruck *m* etching.
ätzend *adj* corrosive, caustic.
au! *excl* ow!, ouch!.
auch *adv* also; even; really; ever.

auf *prep + dat* on, in, at; * *prep + acc* on, in, at, to; up; ~ **und ab** up and down; *conj* ~ **daß** so that; * *adj* open.
aufatmen *vi* to breathe deeply, breathe a sigh of relief.
Aufbau *m* building, structure.
aufbauen *vt* to build.
aufbereiten *vt* to prepare.
aufbessern *vt* to increase.
aufbewahren *vt* to keep.
Aufbewahrung *f* storage.
aufbieten *vt* to summon up; to proclaim.
aufblasen *vt* to blow up; * *vr* to puff oneself up.
aufbleiben *vi* stay open, stay up.
aufblicken *vi* to look up.
aufblühen *vi* to blossom, flourish.
aufbrauchen *vt* to use up.
aufbrechen *vt vi* to break open.
aufbringen *vt* to bring up; to open; to produce; to raise; to obtain.
Aufbruch *m* departure; uprising.
aufdecken *vt* to uncover; * *vi* to lay the table.
aufdringlich *adj* pushy.
aufeinander *adv* on top of each other; one by one.
Aufeinanderfolge *f* succession.
aufeinanderfolgend *adj* successive.
aufeinanderhäufen *vt* to heap up.
Aufenthalt *m* stay; stop; delay.
auferlegen *vt* to impose.
auferstehen *vi* to rise from the dead.
Auferstehung *f* resurrection.
aufessen *vt* to eat up.
auffahren *vt* to line up, bring up; * *vi* to rise; to drive up; to crash into; to run aground; to flare up, start up.
auffahrend *adj* bad-tempered.
Auffahrt *f* approach; entry; driveway.

auffallen *vi* to fall, hit; to be conspicuous.

auffallend, auffällig *adj* conspicuous.

auffangen *vt* to collect; to catch; to absorb.

auffassen *vt* to grasp.

Auffassung *f* opinion.

auffinden *vt* to locate.

Auffindung *f* discovery.

auffordern *vt* to ask; to call on; to order.

Aufforderung *f* call; request.

auffrischen *vt vi* to freshen (up).

aufführen *vt* to list; to perform (play, etc).

Aufführung *f* list; performance.

Aufgabe *f* job; homework; giving up; handing over; posting.

Aufgang *m* ascent; stairway; germination.

aufgeben *vt* to give up; to send; to hand in; to post; to serve (tennis); to inform.

aufgeblasen *adj* inflated; arrogant.

Aufgebot *n* announcement; banns (of marriage).

aufgehen *vi* to rise; to open; to grow.

aufgeklärt *adj* enlightened.

aufgelegt *adj* disposed, inclined.

aufgeregt *adj* excited.

aufgeschlossen *adj* open(-minded).

Aufgeschlossenheit *f* open-mindedness.

aufgeweckt *adj* intelligent, alert.

aufgreifen *vt* to pick up.

aufgrund *prep* on the basis of, because of.

aufhaben *vt* to wear; to have to do.

aufhalten *vt* to hold open; to stop; to stay. * *vr* to live, stay.

aufhängen to hang up; * *vr* to hang oneself

Aufhänger *m* peg, hook.

aufheben *vt* to lift; to cancel; * *vr* to offset, cancel out.

Aufheben(s) *n* fuss.

aufheitern *vt vr* to brighten; to cheer up.

aufhellen *vt vr* see aufheitern.

aufhetzen *vt* to incite.

aufholen *vt* to make up (lost time); * *vi* to catch up.

aufhorchen *vi* to listen closely.

aufhören *vi* to stop.

aufkaufen *vt* to buy up.

aufklären *vt* to clarify; to enlighten.

Aufklärung *f* enlightenment.

aufkleben *vt* to stick on.

Aufkleber *m* sticker.

aufknöpfen *vt* to unbutton.

aufkommen *vi* to come up; to pay for.

aufladen *vt* to load.

Auflage *f* edition; circulation; imposition; tax.

auflassen *vt* to leave open; to leave on.

auflauern *vt* to lie in wait for.

Auflauf *f* crowd; riot; soufflé.

auflaufen *vi* to rise; to swell.

aufleben *vi* to revive.

auflecken *vt* to lick up.

auflegen *vt* to put on; to hang up (telephone).

auflehnen *vt* to lean on; * *vr* to rebel.

Auflehnung *f* rebellion.

auflesen *vt* to pick up, gather.

aufleuchten *vi* to light up.

auflockern *vt* to loosen; to relax.

auflösen *vt* to dissolve, disintegrate; to solve.

Auflösung *f* solution; break-up; termination.

aufmachen *vt* to open; * *vr* to set off for.

Aufmachung *f* format; layout; outfit.

aufmerksam *adj* alert; **auf etwas ~ machen** to point out.

Aufmerksamkeit *f* alertness.

aufmuntern *vt* to encourage.

Aufnahme *f* absorption; beginning; inclusion; photograph; recording.

aufnehmen *vt* to lift; to absorb; to begin; to photograph; to record.

aufopfern *vt vr* to sacrifice (oneself).

aufopfernd *adj* self-sacrificing.

aufpassen *vi* to listen, watch, pay attention.

aufprägen *vt* to emboss.

Aufprall *m* impact.

aufprallen *vi* to bounce.

aufpumpen *vt* to pump up.

aufraffen *vt* to snatch up.

aufräumen *vt vi* to clear away.

aufrechnen *vt* to calculate; to charge; to settle.

aufrecht *adj adv* upright.

aufrechterhalten *vt* to maintain, keep up.

aufregen *vt* to excite; * *vr* to get excited.

aufregend *adj* exciting.

Aufregung *f* excitement.

aufreißen *vt* to tear up; to fling open; * *vi* to open; to split.

aufreizen *vt* to incite.

aufreizend *adj* provocative.

Aufreizung *f* provocation.

aufrichten *vt* to raise; to comfort; * *vr* to arise, stand up.

aufrichtig *adj* sincere.

Aufrichtigkeit *f* honesty.

aufriegeln *vt* to unbolt.

Aufriß *m* draft; sketch; elevation.

aufrollen *vt vi* to roll up.

aufrücken *vi* to advance; to be promoted.

Aufruf *m* call, summons.

aufrufen *vt* to call up; to call out.

Aufruhr *m* uproar; revolt.

aufrühren *vt* to stir up.

aufrunden *vt* to round off.

aufrüsten *vt vi* to arm.

aufs = auf das.

aufsammeln *vt* to gather up.

Aufsatz *m* essay.

aufsaugen *vt* to suck up.

aufschauen *vi* to look up.

aufschieben *vt* to push open; to postpone.

Aufschlag *m* cuff; turn-up; lapel; surcharge; impact; serv(ic)e (tennis).

aufschließen *vt* to open, unlock; * *vr* to close ranks.

Aufschluß *m* information.

aufschneiden *vt* to cut up; * *vi* to boast.

Aufschnitt *m* cold meat.

aufschrauben *vt* to screw onto; to unscrew.

aufschrecken *vt* to frighten; * *vi* to give a start.

Aufschrei *m* cry.

aufschreien *vi* to cry out.

Aufschrift *f* inscription; label.

Aufschub *m* postponement, delay.

Aufschwung *n* upturn.

aufsehen *vi* to look up.

Aufsehen *n* sensation, stir.

Aufseher *m* supervisor.

aufsetzen *vt* to put on; to draw up; * *vi* to touch down.

Aufsicht *f* supervision.

aufsitzen *vi* to sit up; to get onto.

aufspalten *vt vr* to split up.

aufsparen *vt* to save (up).

aufsperren *vt* to unlock.

aufspielen *vt vi* to strike up; * *vr* to show off.

aufsprengen *vt* to force open; to blow up.

aufspringen *vi* to jump up; to burst; to fly open.

aufspüren *vt* to track down.

Aufstand *m* rebellion.

aufständisch *adj* rebellious.

aufstecken *vt* to put up; to give up.

aufstehen *vi* to be open; to stand up; to rebel.

aufsteigen *vi* to get onto; to climb.

aufstellen *vt* to put up; to display; to prepare; to set up.

Aufstellung *f* arrangement; preparation; list.

Aufstieg *m* ascent.

aufstoßen *vt* to push open; to knock against; * *vi* to belch.

Aufstrich *m* upstroke; spread; layer.

aufstützen *vt* to support.

aufsuchen *vt* to seek out; to visit.

auftanken *vt vi* to refuel.

auftauchen *vi* rise up; to crop up.

aufteilen *vt* to divide.

Aufteilung *f* division.

Auftrag *m* job; order; **im ~ von** on behalf of.

auftragen *vt* to serve (food); to apply (paint, etc); to wear out.

Auftraggeber(in) *m(f)* customer.

auftreten *vi* to step; to appear; to enter; to occur.

Auftreten *n* appearance, occurrence.

Auftritt *m* entrance; appearance; scene.

auftrocknen *vt vi* to dry up.

auftun *vt vr* to open.

aufwachen *vi* to wake up.

aufwachsen *vi* to grow.

Aufwand *m* expenditure; extravagance.

aufwärmen *vt* to warm up.

aufwärts *adv* upwards.

aufwecken *vt* to wake up.

aufweisen *vt* to display.

aufwenden *vt* to spend; to devote.

aufwendig *adj* expensive.

aufwerfen *vt* to throw open; to raise.

aufwerten *vt* to revalue.

aufwinden *vt* to wind up; to lift.

aufwischen *vt* to wipe up.

aufzählen *vt* to list.

aufzeichnen *vt* to draw; to record.

Aufzeichnung *f* note; recording.

aufzeigen *vt* to show.

aufziehen *vt* to raise; to pull open; to wind up; to tease.

Aufzug *m* lift, elevator; procession.

Augapfel *m* eyeball; apple of one's eye.

Auge *n* eye; bud.

Augenblick *m* moment.

augenblicklich *adj* momentary; present.

Augenbraue *f* eyebrow.

Augenheilkunde *f* ophthalmology.

Augenmerk *n* attention.

Augenschein *m* appearance.

augenscheinlich *adj* obvious.

Augenstern *m* pupil.

Augentäuschung *f* optical illusion.

Augenwimper *f* eyelash.

Augenzeuge *m* eye witness.

August *m* August.

Auktion *f* auction.

Auktionator(in) *m(f)* auctioneer.

Aula *f* hall, auditorium.

aus *prep* out of, from; made of; * *adv* finished, over.

ausarbeiten *vt* to work out.

ausarten *vi* to degenerate.

ausatmen *vi* to breathe out.

Ausbau *m* extension, enlargement.

ausbauen *vt* to extend; to remove.

ausbessern *vt* to repair.

Ausbeute *f* profit.

ausbeuten *vt* to exploit.

Ausbeutung *f* exploitation.

ausbezahlen *vt* to pay off.

ausbilden *vt* to develop; to train; to educate.

Ausbildung *f* education, training.

ausblasen *vt* to blow out.

ausbleiben *vi* to stay away, fail to turn up/happen.

Ausblick *m* outlook.

ausbrechen *vt* to break out; to vomit; * *vi* to break out.

ausbreiten *vt* to expand.

ausbrennen *vt* to burn; * *vi* burn out.

ausbringen *vt* to bring out; to yield.

Ausbruch *m* outbreak; breakout; eruption.

ausbrüten *vt* to hatch.

Ausdauer *f* endurance.

ausdauern *vi* to endure.

ausdehnen *vt vr* to extend.

ausdenken *vt* to think out.

Ausdruck *m* expression; print-out.

ausdrucken *vt* to print out.

ausdrücken *vt* to express; to squeeze; to stub out.

ausdrücklich *adj* express.

auseinander *adv* apart.

auseinanderbrechen *vt vi* to break apart.

auseinanderbringen *vt* to separate.

auseinanderfallen *vi* to disintegrate.

auseinandergehen *vi* to part company.

auseinanderhalten *vt* keep apart; to tell apart.

auseinandernehmen *vt* to take to pieces.

auseinandersetzen *vt* to put asunder; to explain; to argue; to agree.

Auseinandersetzung *f* disagreement.

auseinandertreiben *vi* to drift apart.

auserlesen *adj* selected.

auserwählen *vt* to select.

Ausfahrt *f* departure; excursion; exit.

Ausfall *m* falling out; loss; shortage; fallout.

ausfallen *vi* to fall out; to be missing; to be cancelled; to break down; to stop.

ausfegen *vt* to sweep out.

ausfertigen *vt* to draw up.

Ausfertigung *f* drawing up.

ausfindig machen *vt* to discover.

ausfliegen *vi* to fly out.

ausfließen *vi* to flow out.

Ausflucht *f* pretext.

Ausflug *m* excursion.

Ausfluß *m* outflow.

ausfragen *vt* to question.

Ausfuhr *f* export(s).

ausführbar *adj* feasible.

ausführen *vt* to take out, carry out; to export.

ausführlich *adj* detailed * *adv* in detail.

Ausführung *f* execution, implementation.

ausfüllen *vt* to fill in.

Ausgabe *f* expenditure; edition, issue.

Ausgang *m* exit.

Ausgangspunkt *m* starting point, basis.

ausgeben *vt* to spend; to distribute; * *vr* to pass oneself off.

ausgebildet *adj* qualified.

ausgefallen *adj* exceptional.

ausgeglichen *adj* balanced.

ausgehen *vi* to go out; to end; **davon ~** to assume.

Ausgehverbot *n* curfew.

ausgelassen *adj* high-spirited.

ausgelastet *adj* fully occupied.

ausgelernt *adj* trained.

ausgemacht *adj* settled; complete.

ausgenommen *prep* except.

ausgeprägt *adj* prominent.

ausgerechnet *adv* precisely.

ausgereift *adj* mature.

ausgeschaltet *adj* out of action; switched off.

ausgeschlossen *adj* excluded.

ausgesprochen complete; distinct; * *adv* distinctly.

Ausgestoßene(r) *mf* outcast.

ausgesucht *adj* select(ed).

ausgewogen *adj* well-balanced.

ausgezeichnet *adj* excellent.

ausgiebig *adj* generous; ample.

Ausgleich *m* balance; equalisation.

ausgleichen *vt* to reconcile; * *vi* to equalise.

ausgraben *vt* to dig up.

Ausguck *m* lookout.

aushalten *vt* to bear; * *vi* to hold out.

aushändigen *vt* to hand over.

aushängen *vt* to display; * *vi* to

be on display.

ausheben vt to lift out; to clear out.

aushelfen vi to help out.

Aushilfe f help.

Aushilfskraft f temporary employee.

aushöhlen vt to hollow out.

auskennen vr know very well.

auskleiden vr undress.

ausklingen vi to die away.

auskochen vt to boil.

auskommen vi to manage.

auskömmlich adj adequate.

Auskunft f information.

auslachen vt to laugh at.

ausladen vt to unload.

Ausladung f unloading.

Auslage f expenditure; window display.

Ausland n im ~ abroad.

Ausländer(in) m(f) foreigner.

ausländisch adj foreign.

Auslandskorrespondent(in) m(f) foreign correspondent.

Auslaß m outlet.

auslassen vt to leave out; to let out.

auslasten vt to balance; to make full use of.

Auslauf m outlet; run (for animals).

auslaufen vi to run out; to leak.

Ausläufer m spur; ridge; runner (plant).

ausleben vr to enjoy life to the full.

auslecken vt to lick out.

ausleeren vt to empty.

auslegen vt to lay out; to put down; to lend; to explain.

Auslegung f explanation, interpretation.

ausleihen vt to lend.

Auslese f selection.

auslesen vt to select.

ausliefern vt to hand over.

Auslieferung f delivery.

auslöffeln vt to spoon out.

auslosen vt to draw lots.

auslöschen vt to extinguish; to eradicate.

auslösen vt to spark off; to redeem; to ransom.

Auslosung f draw(ing).

ausmachen vt to turn off; to make out, distinguish; to agree; to represent, constitute; to matter.

Ausmarsch m departure.

Ausmaß n size, scale.

ausmerzen vt to weed out.

Ausnahme f exception.

Ausnahmefall m special case.

Ausnahmezustand m state of emergency.

ausnahmslos adv without exception.

ausnahmsweise adv for once.

ausnehmen vt to take out; to clean out; * vr to look.

ausnützen vt to make use of.

auspacken vt to unpack.

auspflanzen vt to plant out.

auspressen vt to press out.

ausprobieren vt to try out.

Auspuff m exhaust.

Auspuffrohr n exhaust pipe.

Auspufftopf m silencer (car).

auspumpen vt to pump out.

ausräuchern vt to smoke out, fumigate.

ausräumen vt to empty, clear away.

ausrechnen vt to calculate, work out.

Ausrede f excuse.

ausreden vt to dissuade; * vi to have one's say.

ausreichen vi to suffice.

ausreichend adj sufficient.

ausreigen vi to ripen.

Ausreise f departure.

Ausreiseerlaubnis f exit visa.

ausreißen vt to tear out; * vi to get torn; to run away.

ausrenken vt to dislocate.

ausrichten vt to arrange; to hand over; to line up.

ausrollen vt to roll out.

ausrotten vt to eradicate.

Ausrottung f eradication.

Ausruf m cry; announcement.

ausrufen vt to call out, to

proclaim.

Ausrufungszeichen *n* exclamation mark.

ausrüsten *vt* to equip, fit.

Ausrüstung *f* equipment.

Aussaat *f* sowing.

aussäen *vt* to sow.

Aussage *f* statement.

aussagen *vt vi* to state.

Aussatz *m* leprosy.

Aussätzige(r) *f(m)* leper.

aussaugen *vt* to suck out.

ausschalten *vt* to switch off; to eliminate.

ausschauen *vi* to look out.

ausscheiden *vt* to separate; to excrete; to secrete; to depart.

Ausscheidung *f* separation; excretion; secretion; departure.

ausschenken *vt vi* to pour.

ausschicken *vt* to send out.

ausschießen *vt* to shoot out.

ausschimpfen *vt* to tell off.

ausschlafen *vi* to sleep in.

Ausschlag *m* rash; swing; **den ~ geben** to tip the balance.

ausschlagen *vt* to knock out; to reject; * *vi* to kick out; to germinate.

ausschlaggebend *adj* decisive; **~e Stimme** casting vote.

ausschließen *vt* to exclude.

ausschließlich *adj* exclusive; * *adv* exclusively; * *prep* excluding.

Ausschluß *m* exclusion.

ausschneiden *vt* to cut out.

Ausschnitt *m* extract; section.

ausschnitzen *vt* to carve out.

ausschöpfen *vt* to drain; to exhaust.

ausschreiben *vt* to write out; to advertise.

Ausschreibung *f* announcement; call for tenders.

Ausschuß *m* committee; waste.

ausschütten *vt* to pour out; to pay.

ausschweifen *vt* to wash; * *vi* to stray.

aussehen *vi* to look.

Aussehen *n* appearance.

außen *adv* outside.

Außenbilanz *f* balance of payments.

Außenbordmotor *m* outboard motor.

Außendienst *m* sales force.

Außenhandel *m* foreign trade.

Außenminister *m* foreign minister, foreign secretary (Brit); Secretary of State (US).

Außenministerium *n* foreign ministry, foreign office (Brit); Department of State (US).

Außenpolitik *f* foreign policy.

Außenseite *f* outside.

Außenseiter *m* outsider.

außer *prep* out of, except; **~ sich** beside oneself; * *conj* except.

außerdem *conj* besides, moreover.

äußere *adj* outer.

außerehelich *adj* illegitimate; extramarital.

außergerichtlich *adj* extrajudicial.

außergewöhnlich *adj* unusual.

außerhalb *adv prep* outside.

äußerlich *adj* external, outward.

Äußerlichkeit f superficiaty.

äußern *vt* to utter; * *vr* to express one's opinion.

außerordentlich *adj* unusual.

äußerst *adv* extremely; * *adj* utmost.

Äußerung *f* utterance.

Aussetzen *n* interruption.

aussetzen *vt* to put out; to postpone; to expose; * *vi* to stop.

Aussicht *f* view.

aussichtslos *adj* hopeless.

Aussichtspunkt *m* viewpoint.

aussichtsreich *adj* promising.

aussöhnen *vt* to reconcile; * *vr* to be reconciled.

Aussöhnung *f* reconciliation.

aussondern *vt* to separate.

aussortieren *vt* to sort out.

ausspannen *vt* to spread out; to unharness; * *vr* to relax.

aussperren *vt* to lock out.

ausspielen *vt* to lead; to play off.

Aussprache *f* pronunciation; discussion.

aussprechen *vt* to pronounce; * *vr* to speak; to discuss; * *vi* to finish speaking.

Ausspruch *m* utterance.

ausspucken *vt vi* to spit out.

ausspülen *vt* to rinse out.

ausstatten *vt* to equip.

Ausstattung *f* equipment; outfit; appearance.

ausstechen *vt* to dig out, cut out.

ausstehen *vt* to endure; * *vi* to stand out.

aussteigen *vi* to get out.

ausstellen *vt* to exhibit.

Ausstellung *f* exhibition.

aussterben *vi* to die out.

Aussteuer *f* dowry.

Ausstieg *m* exit.

ausstoßen *vt* to emit; to expel.

ausstrahlen *vt vi* to radiate; to emit; to broadcast.

ausstrecken *vt vr* to stretch out.

ausstreichen *vt* to delete; to smooth.

ausströmen *vt vi* to pour out.

aussuchen *vt* to pick out, select.

Austausch *m* exchange.

austauschen *vt* to exchange.

austeilen *vt* to distribute.

Auster *f* oyster.

austoben *vr* to run wild; * *vi* to calm down.

Austrag *m* decision; settlement.

austragen *vt* to deliver; to settle; to organise.

Australien *n* Australia.

Australier(in) *m(f)* Australian.

australienisch *adj* Australian.

austreiben *vt* to drive out.

austreten *vt* to wear out; * *vi* to leave.

austrinken *vt vi* to drink up.

Austritt *m* emission; withdrawal.

austrocknen *vt vi* to dry up.

ausüben *vt* to exercise, perform.

Ausverkauf *m* (clearance) sale.

ausverkaufen *vt* to sell out, sell up.

ausverkauft *adj* sold out.

auswachsen *vi* to grow.

Auswahl *f* selection.

auswählen *vt* to select.

Auswanderer(in) *m(f)* emigrant.

auswandern *vi* to emigrate.

Auswanderung *f* emigration.

auswärtig *adj* foreign, external.

auswärts *adv* outside; outwards; away.

auswaschen *vt* to wash out.

auswechseln *vt* to exchange.

Auswechslung *f* exchange.

Ausweg *m* way out.

ausweichen *vi* to move aside.

ausweiden *vt* to gut.

Ausweis *m* passport, identity card.

ausweisen *vt* to expel; * *vr* to prove one's identity.

ausweiten *vt vr* extend.

auswendig *adv* by heart.

auswerfen *vt* to throw out.

auswerten *vt* to evaluate.

auswickeln *vt* to unwrap.

auswiegen *vt* to weigh out.

auswirken *vt* to effect; * *vr* to have an effect.

Auswirkung *f* effect.

auswischen *vt* to wipe out.

Auswuchs *m* outgrowth.

Auswurf *m* ejection.

auszahlen *vt* to pay out; to pay off; * *vr* to pay for itself.

auszeichnen *vt* to distinguish, decorate.

ausziehbar *adj* removable.

ausziehen *vt* to take out; * *vi* to leave; * *vr* to undress.

Auszug *m* departure; extract; removal.

Auto *n* car.

Autobahn *f* motorway, freeway.

Autobiographie *f* autobiography.

autobiographisch *adj* autobiographical.

Autobus *m* bus, coach.

Autofähre *f* car ferry.

Autofahrer(in) *m(f)* motorist.

Autogramm *n* autograph.

Autohändler *m* car dealer.

Autokrat *m* autocrat.

Automat *m* vending or slot machine.

automatisch *adj* automatic.

Autor(in) *m(f)* author.

Autorennen *n* motor racing.

autorisieren *vt* to authorise.

Autorität *f* authority.

Autostopp *m* hitch-hiking.

Autovermietung *m* car rental.

Autowäsche *f* car wash.

Axt *f* axe.

B

Baby *n* baby.

Babysitter *m* babysitter.

Bach *m* stream.

Backbord *n* port (ship).

Backe *f* cheek.

backen *vt vi* to bake.

Bäcker *m* baker.

Bäckerei *f* bakery, baker's shop.

Backofen *m* oven.

Backpulver *n* baking powder.

Backstein *m* brick.

Bad *n* bath; swim.

Badeanzug *m* swimming costume.

Badehose *f* swimming trunks.

baden *vt vi* to bathe, bath.

Badewanne *f* bathtub.

Badezimmer *n* bathroom.

Bahn *f* railway; road; track.

bahnen *vt* to clear.

Bahnhof *m* station.

Bahnsteig *m* platform.

Bahnübergang *m* level (US grade) crossing.

Bahre *f* barrow; stretcher.

Baisse *f* fall (market).

Bajonett *n* bayonet.

Bakterie *f* bacterium; **Bakterien** *pl* bacteria.

bald *adv* soon.

baldig *adj* early; rapid.

baldigst, baldmöglichst *adv* as soon as possible.

Balgen *pl* bellows.

Balken *m* beam.

Balkon *m* balcony.

Ball *m* ball.

ballen *vt vr* to ball, clench.

Ballett *n* ballet.

Ballkeid *n* ballgown.

Ballon *m* balloon.

Bambus *m* bamboo.

Banane *f* banana.

Band *m* band; tape; volume.

Bandage *f* bandage.

bandagieren *vt* to bandage.

Bande *f* band, gang (of thieves, thugs etc).

Bandit *m* bandit.

Bandmaß *m* tape measure.

bang(e) *adj* worried, afraid.

bangen *vi* to worry.

Bangigkeit *f* anxiety.

Bank *f* bench; bank.

Bankett *n* banquet; shoulder (of road).

Bankier *m* banker.

Bankkonto *m* bank account.

Banknote *f* banknote.

Bankraub *m* bank robbery.

Bankräuber *m* bank robber.

bankrott *adj* bankrupt.

Bankrott *m* bankruptcy; ~ **machen** to be declared bankrupt.

Bankwesen *n* banking.

Bann *m* ban; spell; excommunication.

bannen *vt* to prevent; to banish; to exorcise.

Banner *n* banner.

Bar *f* bar.

bar *adj* devoid; sheer; bare; in cash.

Bär *m* bear.

barbarisch *adj* barbaric.

barfuß *adj* **barfüßig** *adv* barefoot.

Bargeld *n* cash.

bargeldlos *adj* cashless.

Bariton *m* baritone.

Barkeeper *m* barman, bartender.

barmherzig *adj* compassionate.

Barmherzigkeit *f* compassion.

barock *adj* **Barock** *n* baroque.

Barometer *n* barometer.

barometrisch *adj* barometric.

Baron *m* baron.

Baronesse *f* baroness.

Barrikade *f* barricade.

Bart *m* beard.

Base *f* base; female cousin.

Basel *n* Basle.

basieren *vt* to base; * *vi* to be based.

Basis *f* base, basis.

Baß *m* bass (voice).

Bastelarbeit *f* handicrafts; do-it-yourself.

basteln *vt* to make; * *vi* to practise a hobby; to potter.

Bastler *m* hobbyist.

Batterie *f* battery.

batteriegespeist *adj* battery operated.

Batterieladgerät *n* battery charger.

Bau *m* building; structure; **im ~** under construction.

Bauarbeiter *m* construction worker.

Bauch *m* stomach.

Bauchschmerzen *pl* stomach ache.

bauen *vt vi* to build; to cultivate.

Bauer *m* farmer; peasant; pawn (chess); cage.

Bäuerin *f* farmer; farmer's wife.

Bauernhaus *n* farmhouse.

Bauernhof *m* farmyard.

Baum *m* tree.

Baumgarten *m* orchard.

Baumstamm *m* tree trunk.

Baumwolle *f* cotton.

Bauplatz *m* building site.

Bausch *m* pad.

bauschen *vi vr* to swell.

Bausparkasse *f* building society.

Baustelle *f* building site.

Baustoff *m* building material.

Bayern *n* Bavaria.

bayrisch *adj* Bavarian.

beabsichtigen *vt* to intend.

beachten *vt* to comply with.

beachtlich *adj* considerable.

Beachtung *f* notice, compliance.

Beamte(r) *m* **Beamtin** *f* official, civil servant.

beängstigen *vt* to worry.

beängstigend *adj* worrying.

beanspruchen *vt* to take up; to claim.

beanstanden *vt* to complain.

Beanstandung *f* complaint.

beantworten *vt* to answer.

Beantwortung *f* answer.

bearbeiten *vt* to work on; to cultivate.

Bearbeitung *f* treatment; cultivation.

beargwohnen *vt* to suspect.

beaufsichtigen *vt* to supervise.

Beaufsichtigung *f* supervision.

beauftragen *vt* to order; to entrust.

bebauen *vt* to build on; to cultivate.

beben *vi* to shake.

Becher *m* mug.

Becken *n* basin; cymbal; pelvis.

Bedacht *m* consideration.

bedächtig *adj* thoughtful.

bedanken *vr* to thank.

Bedarf *m* need, demand; **bei ~** if necessary.

bedauerlich *adj* regrettable.

bedauern *vt* to regret; to pity.

Bedauern *n* regret.

bedecken *vt* to cover.

bedenken *vt* to consider.

Bedenken *n* consideration; doubt.

bedenklich *adj* dubious.

bedeuten *vt* to mean.

bedeutend *adj* important.

Bedeutung *f* meaning.

bedeutungslos *adj* insignificant.

bedeutungsvoll *adj* significant.

bedienen *vt* to serve; to operate; * *vr* to help oneself; ~ **Sie sich!** help yourself.

Bedienung *f* service; serving staff.

Bedienungsanleitung, - anweisung *f* instructions for use.

bedingen *vt* to require.

Bedingung *f* condition.

bedingungslos *adj* unconditional.

bedrohen *vt* to threaten.

bedrohlich *adj* threatening.

Bedrohung *f* threat.

bedrücken *vt* to pressurise.

bedürfen *vi* to need.

Bedürfnis *n* need.

Bedürfnisanstalt *f* public convenience (US rest room).

bedürftig *adj* needing; needy.

Bedürftigkeit *f* neediness.

beehren *vt* to honour.

beeidigen *vt* to swear.

Beeidigung *f* swearing.

beeilen *vr* hurry; ~ **Sie sich!** hurry up!.

beeindrücken *vt* to impress.

beeinflußbar *adj* impressionable.

beeinflussen *vt* to influence.

beeinträchtigen *vt* to limit.

beendigen *vt* to end.

beengen *vt* to oppress.

beerben *vt* to inherit.

beerdigen *vt* to bury.

Beerdigung *f* burial.

Beerdigungsunternehmer *m* undertaker.

Beere *f* berry.

Beet *n* bed (in garden).

befähigen *vt* to enable.

befahrbar *adj* passable.

befangen *adj* shy; biased.

Befangenheit *f* shyness; bias.

befassen *vr* to handle, deal with.

Befehl *m* order.

befehlen *vt* to order; * *vi* to give orders.

befehlerisch *adj* imperious.

befestigen *vt* to fasten; to strengthen.

Befestigung *f* fastening; strengthening.

befeuchten *vt* to moisten.

befiedert *adj* feathered.

befinden *vt* to deem; * *vi* to decide; * *vr* to be (located); to feel.

Befinden *n* health; condition; opinion.

beflecken *vt* to stain.

befluten *vt* to flood.

befördern *vt* to send; to promote.

Beförderung *f* dispatch; promotion.

befragen *vt* to question.

befreien *vt* to release.

Befreiung *f* liberation.

befremden *vt* to surprise.

befreunden *vr* to make friends.

befriedigen *vt* to satisfy.

befriedigend *adj* satisfactory.

Befriedigung *f* satisfaction.

befristet *adj* time-limited.

befruchten *vt* to fertilise.

Befruchtung *f* fertilisation, insemination.

befugen *vt* to authorise.

Befugnis *f* authority.

befugt *adj* authorised.

Befund *m* findings.

befürworten *vt* to support, advocate.

Befürworter *m* advocate.

begabt *adj* gifted.

Begabung *adj* talent.

begeben *vr* to proceed; to occur.

begegnen *vi* to meet.

Begegnung *f* meeting.

begehen *vt* to go along; to commit; to celebrate.

begehren *vt* to covet.

begehrenswert *adj* desirable.

begehrlich *adj* covetous.

Begehrlichkeit *f* greed.
Begehung *f* inspection; celebration.
begeistern *vt* to excite.
begeisternd *adj* exciting.
Begeisterung *f* enthusiasm.
Begierde *f* desire.
begießen *vt* to sprinkle.
Beginn *m* beginning.
beginnen *vt vi* to begin.
beglaubigen *vt* to certify.
beglaubigt *adj* certified.
Beglaubigung *f* certification.
Begleitbrief *n* covering letter.
begleiten *vt* to accompany.
Begleiter *m* companion.
Begleitung *f* company, accompaniment.
beglücken *vt* to make happy.
beglückwünschen *vt* to congratulate.
Beglückwünschung *f* congratulation.
begnadet *adj* gifted.
begnadigen *vt* to pardon.
Begnadigung *f* pardon.
begnügen *vr* to be satisfied.
begraben *vt* to bury.
Begräbnis *n* burial, funeral.
begreifen *vt* to understand.
begreiflich *adj* understandable.
begreiflicherwise *adv* understandably.
begrenzen *vt* to delineate; to limit.
begrenzt *adj* limited.
Begrenzung *f* limitation.
Begriff *m* concept; **im ~ sein** to be about to.
begründen *vt* to establish; to justify.
begründet *adj* justified.
begrüßen *vt* to greet.
Begrüßung *f* greeting.
begünstigen *vt* to favour; to promote.
Begünstigung *f* promotion; favour.
begutachten *vt* to appraise.
begütert *adj* well off.
begütigen *vt* to calm.

behaart *adj* hairy.
behäbig *adj* sedate, portly.
behaftet *adj* afflicted.
behagen *vi* to please.
behaglich *adj* comfortable.
Behaglichkeit *f* comfort.
behalten *vt* to keep.
Behälter *m* container.
behandeln *vt* to handle.
Behandlung *f* handling.
beharren *vi* to insist.
beharrlich *adj* steadfast.
Beharrlichkeit *f* perseverance.
behaupten *vt* to assert; * *vr* to assert oneself
Behauptung *f* claim.
Behausung *f* housing.
beheben *vt* to remove.
Behebung *f* removal.
beheizen *vt* to heat.
behelfen *vr* to manage, make do.
behelligen *vt* to harrass.
beherbergen *vt* to accommodate.
behend *adj* agile.
beherrschen *vt* to control; to master; * *vr* to control oneself
Beherrschung *f* control.
beherzigen *vt* to take to heart.
beherzt *adj* courageous.
Beherztheit *f* courage.
behindern *vt* to hinder.
Behinderte(r) *mf* handicapped person.
Behinderung *f* hindrance; handicap.
Behörde *f* official body; **die Behörden** *pl* the authorities.
behördlich *adj* official.
behüten *vt* to protect; **Gott behüte!** God forbid.
behutsam *adj* careful.
bei *prep* near; by; at; at the home of; among; in; during.
beibehalten *vt* to keep.
Beibehaltung *f* retention.
beibringen *vt* to bring forward; to provide.
Beichte *f* confession.
beichten *vt vi* to confess.
Beichtsuhl *m* confessional.

beide *adj* both.
beiderseitig *adj* mutual.
beiderseits *adv* mutually;
  * *prep* on both sides of.
beiderseitig *adj* mutual.
beidhändig *adj* ambidextrous.
beieinander *adv* together.
Beifahrer *m* passenger.
Beifall *m* applause.
beifügen *vt* to add, enclose.
Beifügung *f* enclosure.
beige *adj* beige.
beigeben *vt* to add; to give; * *vr*
  to give in.
Beihilfe *f* assistance; subsidy.
beikommen *vt* to reach; to
  tackle.
Beil *n* axe.
Beilage *f* enclosure; vegetables;
  garnish.
beiläufig *adj* incidental; * *adv*
  incidentally.
beilegen *vt* to add; to enclose;
  to ascribe; to settle.
beileibe *adv* certainly.
beiliegend *adj* enclosed.
beimessen *vt* to attribute.
beimischen *vt* to mix in.
Beimischung *f* addition.
Bein *n* leg; bone.
beinah(e) *adv* nearly.
Beiname *m* nickname.
beinhalten *vt* to contain.
Beirat *m* adviser; supervisory
  board.
beirren *vt* to confuse.
beisammen *adv* together.
Beischlaf *m* sexual intercourse.
Beisein *n* presence.
beiseite *adv* aside.
beisetzen *vt* to bury.
Beisetzung *f* burial.
beisitzen *vt* to attend.
Beispiel *n* example; **zum ~** for
  example.
beispielhaft *adj* exemplary.
beispielsweise *adv* for example.
beißen *vt vi* to bite; to burn.
Beistand *m* support.
beistehen *vi* to assist.
beistimmen *vi* to agree with.

Beitrag *m* contribution.
beitragen *vt* to contribute.
beitreten *vi* to join.
Beitritt *m* joining.
beiwohnen *vi* to attend.
Beize *f* corrosion.
beizen *vt* to corrode; to stain.
bejahen *vt* to say yes to.
bejahrt *adj* elderly.
Bejahung *f* affirmation.
bekämpfen *vt vr* to fight.
bekannt *adj* (well-)known; acquainted.
Bekannte(r) *mf* acquaintance.
bekanntgeben *vt* to announce.
bekanntlich *adv* as you know.
bekanntmachen *vt* to announce.
Bekanntmachung *f* announcement.
Bekanntschaft *f* acquaintance.
bekanntwerden *vi* to become
  known, acquainted.
bekehren *vt vi* to convert.
bekennen *vt* to admit.
Bekenntnis *n* admission; confession.
beklagen *vt* to lament; * *vr* to
  complain.
Beklagte(r) *mf* defendant; respondent.
bekleiden *vt* to clothe; to occupy.
Bekleidung *f* clothing.
bekommen *vt* to receive.
bekräftigen *vt* to confirm.
Bekräftigung *f* confirmation.
bekümmern *vt* to afflict.
bekunden *vt* to state.
belächeln *vt* to smile at.
belachen *vt* to laugh at.
beladen *vt* to load.
Belag *m* covering, coating.
belagern *vt* to besiege.
Belagerung *f* siege.
Belang *m* importance; **~e** *pl* interests.
belangen *vt* to sue.
belanglos *adj* unimportant.
Belanglosigkeit *f* insignifi-
  cance.
belangreich *adj* important.

Belangung *f* legal action.
belassen *vt* to leave.
belasten *vt* to burden; to charge.
belästigen *vt* to annoy.
Belästigung *f* annoyance.
Belastung *f* load; charge.
belaufen *vr* to amount.
beleben *vt* to enliven.
belebend *adj* invigorating.
belebt *adj* busy.
Belebung *f* animation.
Beleg *m* receipt; proof.
belegen *vt* to cover; to prove.
Belegschaft *f* personnel.
belehren *vt* to teach.
Belehrung *f* teaching.
beleidigen *vt* to insult.
Beleidigung *f* insult; libel; slander.
belesen *adj* well-read.
beleuchten *vt* to illuminate.
Beleuchtung *f* illumination.
Belgien *n* Belgium.
Belgier(in) *m(f)* Belgian.
belgisch *adj* Belgian.
Belgrad *n* Belgrade.
belichten *vt* to expose (film).
Belichtung *f* exposure.
Belieben *n* nach ~ as you wish.
beliebig *adj* any; as you like.
beliebt *adj* popular.
Beliebtheit *f* popularity.
beliefern *vt* to supply.
bellen *vi* to bark.
belohnen *vt* to reward.
Belohnung *f* reward.
belüften *vt* to ventilate.
Belüftung *f* ventilation.
belustigen *vt* to amuse.
Belustigung *f* amusement.
bemalen *vt* to paint.
bemannen *vt* to staff.
bemerkbar *adj* noticeable.
bemerken *vt* to notice; to remark.
bemerkenswert *adj* remarkable.
Bemerkung *f* remark.
bemessen *vt* to measure; to assess.
bemühen *vr* to endeavour.

Bemühung *f* effort.
benachbart *adj* neighbouring.
benachrichtigen *vt* to notify.
Benachrichtigung *f* notification.
benachteiligen *vt* to discriminate against.
benehmen *vr* to take away; to behave.
Benehmen *n* behaviour.
beneiden *vt* to envy.
beneidenswert *adj* enviable.
benennen *vt* to name.
Benennung *f* naming.
benötigen *vt* to need.
benummern *vt* to number.
benutzen, benützen *vt* to use.
Benutzer *m* user.
Benutzung *f* use.
Benzin *n* petrol, gas(oline).
Benzintank *m* petrol or gas tank.
beobachten *vt* to watch.
Beobachter *m* observer.
Beobachtung *f* observation.
bepacken *vt* to pack.
bepflanzen *vt* to plant.
bequem *adj* comfortable; lazy.
Bequemlichkeit *f* convenience, comfort; laziness.
beraten *vt* to advise; to discuss.
Berater *m* adviser.
Beratung *f* advice; consultation.
berauben *vt* to rob.
berechnen *vt* to calculate; to charge.
Berechnung *f* calculation; charge.
berechtigen *vt* to entitle.
berechtigt *adj* justified.
Berechtigung *f* entitlement.
bereden *vt* to discuss.
Bereich *m* area.
bereichern *vt* to enrich; * *vr* to get rich.
bereinigen *vt* to settle.
bereit *adj* ready; willing.
bereiten *vt* to prepare.
bereithalten *vt* to keep ready.
bereitmachen *vt vr* to prepare.
Bereitschaft *f* readiness.

bereitstellen *vt* to provide.
bereuen *vt* to regret.
Berg *m* mountain, hill.
bergab *adv* downhill.
bergauf *adv* uphill.
Bergbau *m* mining.
bergen *vt* to shelter; to save; to hide.
bergig *adj* mountainous.
Bergmann *m* miner.
Bergsteigen *n* mountaineeering.
Bergsteiger(in) *m(f)* mountaineer.
Bergwerk *n* mine.
Bericht *m* report.
berichten *vt vi* to report.
Berichterstatter *m* reporter.
berichtigen *vt* to correct.
Berichtigung *f* correction.
beriechen *vt* to smell.
bersten *vi* to burst.
berücksichtigen *vt* to consider.
Berücksichtigung *f* consideration.
Beruf *m* occupation.
berufen *vt* to appoint; * *vr* to appeal.
beruflich *adj* professional.
Berufung *f* calling.
beruhen *vi* to be based.
beruhigen *vt* to calm; * *vr* to calm down.
Beruhigung *f* calming.
berühmt *adj* famous.
Berühmtheit *f* fame.
berühren *vt* to touch; to affect; * *vr* to come into contact.
Berührung *f* contact.
besagen *vt* to mean.
besagt *adj* in question.
Besatzung *f* garrison; crew; occupation.
beschädigen *vt* to damage.
Beschädigung *f* damage.
beschaffen *vt* to obtain; * *adj* constituted, conditioned.
Bechaffenheit *f* nature.
Beschaffung *f* acquisition.
beschäftigen *vt* to occupy; * *vr* to occupy oneself

beschäftigt *adj* occupied.
Beschäftigung *f* occupation; concern.
beschämen *vt* to shame.
beschämend *adj* shameful, shaming.
beschämt *adj* ashamed.
beschatten *vt* to shade; to shadow.
bechauen *vt* to look at.
Bescheid *m* information; directions; ~ **wissen** to be well aware.
bescheiden *vr* to make do; * *adj* modest, shy.
bescheinigen *vt* to confirm.
Bescheinigung *f* certificate, confirmation.
bescheren *vt* to present.
Bescherung *f* presentation; problem.
beschießen *vt* to fire at.
beschimpfen *vt* to insult.
Beschimpfung *f* abuse.
beschirmen *vt* to protect.
Beschlag *m* metal fittings; tarnish; damp; seizure; **in ~ nehmen** to confiscate, take over.
Beschlagnahme *f* confiscation.
beschlagnahmen *vt* to confiscate.
beschleunigen *vt vi* to accelerate.
Beschleunigung *f* acceleration.
beschließen *vt* to decide; conclude.
Beschluß *m* decision, conclusion.
beschmutzen *vt* to dirty.
beschränken *vt* to confine; * *vr* to confine oneself
beschränkt *adj* confined.
Beschränkung *f* limitation.
beschreiben *vt* to describe; to write on.
Beschreibung *f* description.
beschreiten *vt* to walk on.
beschriften *vt* to inscribe.
beschuldigen *vt* to accuse.
Beschuldigung *f* accusation.

Beschwerde f complaint.

beschweren vt to weigh down; * vr to complain.

beschwindeln vt to cheat.

beschwören vt to swear to; to implore; to conjure up.

beseelen vt to inspire.

besehen vt to inspect.

beseitigen vt to remove.

Beseitigung f removal.

Besen m broom.

Besenschrank m broom cupboard.

Besenstiel m broomstick.

besessen adj possessed.

besetzen vt to occupy; to fill.

besetzt adj occupied.

Besetzung f occupation.

besichtigen vt to inspect.

Besichtigung f inspection, visit.

besiegen vt to conquer.

besinnen vr to consider; **sich ander(e)s ~** to change one's mind.

Besinnung f consideration; consciousness.

besinnungslos adj unconscious.

Besitz m possession.

besitzen vt to possess.

Besitzer(in) m(f) owner.

besoffen adj drunk.

besolden vt to pay.

Besoldung f pay.

besonder adj particular, special.

Besonderheit f pecularity.

besonders adv particularly.

besonnen adj sensible.

besonnt adj sunny.

besorgen vt to provide, acquire.

Besorgnis f concern.

besorgt adj concerned.

Besorgtheit f concern.

Besorgung f acquisition.

besprechen vt vr to discuss.

Besprechung f discussion, meeting.

bespritzen vt to spray.

besser adj adv better.

bessern vt to improve.

Besserung f improvement; **gute ~!** get well soon.

Bestand m durability; stock, supply.

beständig adj lasting.

Bestandsaufnahme f stocktaking.

Bestandteil m component.

bestärken vt to strengthen.

bestätigen vt to confirm.

Bestätigung f confirmation.

bestatten vt to bury, cremate.

Bestatter m undertaker.

Bestattung f funeral.

beste(r,s) adj best; **am besten** best.

bestechen vt to bribe.

Bestechung f bribery.

Besteck n cutlery.

bestehen vi to exist; * vt to pass (exam, etc); **~ auf** to insist on; **~ aus** to consist of.

besteigen vt to ascend, climb.

bestellen vt to order; to appoint; to cultivate.

Bestellung f order.

bestenfalls adv at best.

bestens adv very well, best.

besteuern vt to tax.

bestimmen vt to determine; to decide; to specify.

bestimmt adj definite, specific; * adv definitely.

Bestimmung f determination; destination.

bestrafen vt to punish.

bestrahlen vt to shine on; to irradiate.

Bestrahlung f irradiation; radiotherapy.

bestreben vr to strive.

bestreiten vt to dispute; to pay for.

bestreuen vt to sprinkle.

bestürmen vt to attack; to pester.

Besuch m visit.

besuchen vt to visit, attend.

Besucher(in) m(f) visitor.

betätigen vt to operate, control.

Betätigung f activity.

betäuben vt to deafen; to stun.

Betäubungsmittel *n* anaesthetic.
Bete *f* beetroot.
beteiligen *vt* to involve; * *vr* to participate.
Beteiligung *f* participation.
beten *vt vi* to pray.
Beton *m* concrete.
betonen *vt* to emphasise.
Betonung *f* emphasis.
Betracht *m* consideration; **in ~ kommen** to be concerned; **in ~ ziehen** to consider.
betrachten *vt* to consider.
beträchtlich *adj* considerable.
Betrachtung *f* consideration.
Betrag *m* amount.
betragen *vt* to amount to; * *vr* to behave.
betrauen *vt* to entrust.
betrauern *vt* to mourn.
betreffen *vt* to relate, affect.
betreffend *adj* relevant.
betreiben *vt* to operate; to practise.
betreten *vt* to enter; ~ **verboten** no entry; * *adj* confused, embarrassed.
betreuen *vt* to look after.
Betrieb *m* company; factory; operation; **außer ~** out of order.
Betriebsanleitung *f* operating instructions.
Betriebsrat *m* works council.
betrinken *vr* to get drunk.
betroffen *adj* affected; shocked.
betrüben *vt vr* to grieve.
betrübt *adj* grieved.
Betrug *m* deception; fraud.
betrügen *vt* to deceive.
Betrüger(in) *m(f)* cheat.
betrügerisch *adj* fraudulent.
betrunken *adj* drunk.
Bett *n* bed.
betteln *vi* to beg.
betten *vt* to put to bed; to embed.
Bettflasche *f* hot water bottle.
Bettlaken *n* sheet.
Bettler(in) *m(f)* beggar.
Beuge *f* bend.

beugen *vt* to bend; * *vr* to bow.
Beule *f* bump, lump.
beunruhigen *vt vr* to worry.
beurkunden *vt* to certify.
beurteilen *vt* to judge.
Beurteilung *f* judgment.
Beute *f* loot.
Beutel *m* bag; purse.
Bevölkerung *f* population.
bevollmächtigen *vt* to authorise.
Bevollmächtigte(r) *mf* authorised representative.
Bevollmächtigung *f* authorisation; power of attorney.
bevor *conj* before.
bevorstehen *vi* to be forthcoming.
bevorstehend *adj* imminent.
bevorzugen *vt* to prefer.
Bevorzugung *f* preference.
bewachen *vt* to watch.
Bewachung *f* guard.
bewaffnen *vt vr* to arm (oneself).
bewahren *vt* to keep.
bewähren *vt* to prove; * *vr* to prove oneself
bewährt *adj* tried and tested.
Bewährung *f* probation.
bewaldet *adj* wooded.
bewältigen *vt* to overcome, manage.
Bewältigung *f* conquest.
bewässern *vt* to water.
Bewässerung *f* irrigation.
bewegen *vt vr* to move.
beweglich *adj* movable.
bewegt *adj* rough (sea); moved.
Bewegung *f* movement.
Beweis *m* proof.
beweisen *vt* to prove.
bewerben *vr* to apply.
Bewerber(in) *m(f)* applicant.
Bewerbung *f* application.
bewerkstelligen *vt* to achieve.
bewerten *vt* to evaluate.
bewilligen *vt* to allow.
Bewilligung *f* permission.
bewirken *vt* to cause.
bewirten *vt* to entertain.
bewirtschaften *vt* to cultivate;

to manage.
Bewirtung f entertainment.
bewohnen vt to inhabit.
Bewohner(in) m(f) inhabitant.
bewölkt adj cloudy.
Bewunderer(in) m(f) admirer.
bewundern vt to admire.
bewundernswert, bewundernswürdig adj admirable.
Bewunderung f admiration.
bewußt adj conscious; deliberate.
bewußtlos adj unconscious.
Bewußtsein n consciousness.
bezahlen vt vi to pay (for).
Bezahlung f payment.
bezähmen vt to tame; to restrain.
bezaubern vt to enchant.
bezaubernd adj charming.
Bezauberung f enchantment.
bezeichnen vt to describe; to mark; to call; to label.
Bezeichnung f description; name.
beziehen vt to refer; to occupy; to cover; to obtain; * vr to refer.
Beziehung f connection, relationship.
beziehungsweise adv or; respectively.
beziffern vt to number.
Bezirk m district.
Bezug m covering; purchase; income; reference; **in ~ auf** with reference to; **~ nehmen auf** to refer to.
bezüglich prep adj concerning.
Bezugnahme f reference.
bezweifeln vt to doubt.
Bibel f bible.
Bibliographie f bibliography.
Bibliothek f library.
Bibliothekar(in) m(f) librarian.
biblisch adj biblical.
bieder adj adj respectable.
biegen vt vr to bend; vi to turn (corner).
biegsam adj flexible.
Biegung f bend.

Biene f bee.
Bienenkorb m beehive.
Bier n beer.
Bierkrug m beer mug.π
Bierkeller m Bierkeller, beer cellar.
bieten vt to offer, bid; * vr to present oneself
Bieter(in) m(f) bidder.
Bigamie f bigamy.
Bikini m bikini.
Bilanz f balance; balance sheet.
Bild n picture.
bilden vt to form; to educate; * vr to develop.
Bildhauer(in) m(f) sculptor.
Bildschirm m TV screen.
Bildung f formation; education.
Billard n billiards.
billig adj cheap; reasonable.
billigen vt to approve.
Billigkeit f fairness; cheapness.
Billigung f approval.
Binde f band, bandage; sanitary towel.
binden vt to tie.
Bindestrich m hyphen.
Bindewort n conjunction.
Bindfaden m string.
Bindung f connection; compound.
binnen prep within.
Binnenhandel m domestic trade.
Biographie f biography.
Biologe m biologist.
Biologie f biology.
biologisch adj biological.
Birke f birch.
Birne f pear; lightbulb.
bis prep until; by; to, as far as; up to; **~ morgen** by tomorrow, until tomorrow, see you tommorrow; **~ auf** except for; * conj to; until.
Bischof m bishop.
bisexuell adj bisexual.
bisher adv hitherto.
bisherig adj previous.
bislang adv hitherto.
Biskuit n biscuit, (US) cracker.
Biß m bite.

bißchen *adj adv*: **ein ~** a bit, a little.

bissig *adj* biting.

bisweilen *adv* sometimes.

Bitte *f* request.

bitte *excl* please; **(wie) bitte?** pardon?; **bitte (schön)** don't mention it.

bitten *vt vi* to ask.

bitter *adj* bitter.

Bitterkeit *f* bitterness.

blank *adj* bright; bare; broke.

Blase *f* bubble; blister; bladder.

blasen *vt vi* to blow.

Blasphemie *f* blasphemy.

blaß *adj* pale.

Blässe *f* paleness.

Blatt *n* leaf; page; sheet; newspaper.

blättern *vi*: **~ in** to leaf through.

blau *adj* blue; drunk; **blaues Auge** black eye; **Fahrt ins Blaue** mystery tour.

blaumachen *vi* to play truant.

Blech *n* tin; sheet metal.

Blei *n* lead.

bleiben *vi* to remain.

bleifrei *adj* unleaded.

Bleistift *m* pencil.

Blende *f* blind; blinker; aperture (camera).

blenden *vt* to blind.

Blick *m* look.

blicken *vt* to look.

blind *adj* blind.

Blindheit *f* blindness.

blinken *vi* to flash; to sparkle.

blinzeln *vi* to blink, wink.

Blitz *m* lightning; flash.

blitzschnell *adj adv* quick as a flash.

Block *m* block; notepad.

Blockflöte *f* recorder.

blockieren *vt* to block.

Blockschrift *f* block letters.

blöd *adj* stupid.

Blödsinn *m* nonsense.

blond *adj* blond(e).

bloß *adj* naked; sheer; * *adv* only.

Blöße *f* bareness.

bloßlegen, bloßstellen *vt* to reveal.

blühen *vi* to flower; to flourish.

Blume *f* flower; bouquet (wine).

Blumenkohl *m* cauliflower.

Bluse *f* blouse.

Blut *n* blood.

Blüte *n* blossom.

bluten *vi* to bleed.

blutig *adj* bloody.

Bö *f* gust.

Bock *m* buck; ram; support.

Boden *m* ground, floor, soil.

Bodensee *m* Lake Constance.

Bogen *m* bow; arch; curve.

Bohle *f* board.

Böhmen *n* Bohemia.

Bohne *f* bean.

bohren *vt* to drill.

Bohrer *m* drill.

Bolivien *n* Bolivia.

Bolzen *m* bolt.

Bombe *f* bomb.

Bonbon *m* sweet.

Boot *n* boat.

Bord *n* shelf; edge; **an ~** on board.

Bordell *n* brothel.

borgen *vt* to borrow; to lend.

Börse *f* purse; stock exchange.

bös *adj* angry; bad.

bösartig *adj* malicious.

Bösartigkeit *f* malice.

boshaft *adj* malicious.

Bosheit *f* malice.

böswillig *adj* malicious.

Botanik *f* botany.

Botaniker *m* botanist.

botanisch *adj* botanical.

Bote *m* messenger.

Botschaft *f* message; embassy.

Botschafter(in) *m(f)* ambassador.

boxen *vi* to box.

Boxen *n* boxing.

Boxer *m* boxer.

Branche *f* (sector of) industry.

Brand *m* fire; gangrene.

branden *vi* to surge; to break.

brandmarken *vt* to brand; to denounce.

Brandstifter *m* arsonist.

Branntwein *m* brandy, spirits.
Brasilien *n* Brazil.
braten *vt* to roast; to bake; to fry.
Bratpfanne *f* frying pan.
Bratwurst *f* grilled sausage.
brauchbar *adj* usable.
brauchen *vt* to use; to need.
Braue *f* brow.
brauen *vt* to brew.
Brauerei *f* brewery.
braun *adj* brown.
Bräune *f* brownness; tan.
braunen *vt* to brown.
Braunschweig *n* Brunswick.
Braut *f* bride, fiancée.
Brautigam *m* bridegroom, fiancé.
brav *adj* good.
brechen *vt vi* to break; to vomit.
Brechreiz *m* nausea.
Brei *m* porridge, oatmeal; pulp.
breit *adj* wide.
Breite *f* width; latitude.
breiten *vt* to spread.
Bremse *f* brake.
bremsen *vt vi* to brake.
brennbar *adj* (in)flammable..
brennen *vr vi* to burn.
Brennessel *f* (stinging) nettle.
Brett *n* board.
Brief *m* letter.
Briefkasten *m* letter box.
Briefmarke *f* stamp.
Briefträger(in) *m(f)* postman, mailman (mailwoman).
Briefumschlag *m* envelope.
Brille *f* glasses; goggles; toilet seat.
bringen *vt* to bring; to present; to cause; to achieve.
Brise *f* breeze.
bröckeln *vt vi* to crumble.
Brocken *m* crumb, lump.
brodeln *vi* to bubble, simmer.
Brombeere *f* blackberry.
Bronze *f* bronze.
Brosche *f* brooch.
Broschüre *f* brochure.
Brot *n* bread; loaf.
Brötchen *n* (bread) roll.
Bruch *m* break.

brüchig *adj* fragile.
Bruchteil *m* fraction.
Brücke *f* bridge; rug.
Bruder *m* brother.
brüderlich *adj* brotherly.
brüllen *vi* to roar.
brummen *vi* to hum; to grumble.
Brunnen *m* well; spring; fountain.
Brüssel *n* Brussels.
Brust *f* breast, chest.
brüsten *vr* to boast.
Brustschwimmen *n* breaststroke.
Brustwarze *f* nipple.
Brut *f* brood; hatching.
brutal *adj* brutal.
Brutalität *f* brutality.
brüten *vi vt* to hatch, brood.
brutto *adv* gross.
Bube *m* lad; jack (cards).
bübisch *adj* mischievous.
Buch *n* book.
Buche *f* beech.
buchen *vt* to book.
Buchführung *f* book-keeping.
Buchhandlung *f* bookshop.
Büchse *f* box; can; rifle.
Büchsenöffner *m* can opener.
Buchstabe *m* letter; character.
buchstabieren *vt* to spell.
buchstäblich *adj* literal; * *adv* literally.
Bucht *f* bay.
Buckel *m* hump.
buck(e)lig *adj* hump-backed.
Buckelige(r) *mf* hunchback.
bücken *vt vr* to bend.
Bückling *m* kipper; bow.
Bude *f* booth; stall.
Büfett *n* sideboard; buffet.
Büffel *m* buffalo; oaf.
Bug *m* bow (ship); nose (aircraft).
Bügel *m* clothes hanger; stirrup.
Bügelbrett *n* ironing board.
Bügeleisen *n* iron.
bügeln *vt vi* to iron.
Bühne *f* stage, platform.
Bühnenbild *n* scenery.

Bukarest *n* Bucharest.
Bulgarien *n* Bulgaria.
Bulldogge *f* bulldog.
Bulldozer *m* bulldozer.
Bulle *m* bull; seal (letter).
Bummel *m* stroll.
bummeln *vi* to stroll, dawdle.
Bund *n* bundle; band; * *m* tie; alliance; federation.
Bündel *n* bundle.
bundeln *vt* to bundle.
Bundes- *prefix* federal, German.
Bundesbahn *f* German Railways.
Bundeskanzler *m* Chancellor.
Bundesland *n* Land, state.
Bundesliga *f* football league.
Bundespräsident *m* German president.
Bundesrat *m* upper house of German parliament.
Bundesregierung *f* federal government.
Bundesrepublik *f* Federal Republic (of Germany).
Bundesstaat *m* federal state.
Bundestag *m* lower house of German parliament.
Bundeswehr *f* German armed forces.
bündig *adj* binding; concise.
Bündnis *n* alliance.
Bunker *m* bunker.
bunt *adj* colourful.
Buntstift *m* crayon.
Burg *f* castle.
Bürge *m* guarantor.
bürgen *vt* to guarantee.
Bürger(in) *m(f)* citizen; middle-class person.
Bürgerkrieg *m* civil war.
bürgerlich *adj* middle-class; civil; **Bürgerliches Gesetzbuch** *n* Civil Code; **bürgerliches Recht** *n* civil law.
Bürgermeister *m* mayor.
Bürgerschaft *f* populace.
Bürgersteig *m* pavement, sidewalk (US).
Bürgschaft *f* security, guarantee.

Büro *n* office.
Büroangestellte(r) *mf* office worker.
Büroklammer *f* paperclip.
Bürokrat *m* bureaucrat.
Bürokratie *f* bureaucracy.
bürokratisch *adj* bureaucratic.
Bursche *m* lad; guy; servant.
Bürste *f* brush.
bürsten *vt* to brush.
Bus *m* bus.
Busch *m* bush.
Büschel *n* bunch; tuft.
Buschholz *n* brushwood.
buschig *adj* bushy.
Busen *m* bosom; bay.
Buße *f* penance; fine.
büßen *vt vi* to atone.
Büßer(in) *m(f)* penitent.
Bußgeld *n* fine.
Büste *f* bust.
Büstenhalter *m* bra.
Butter *f* butter.
Butterblume *f* buttercup.
Butterbrot *n* bread and butter.
Butterbrotpapier *n* greaseproof paper.

C

Café *n* café.
Cafeteria *f* cafeteria.
Camp *n* camp.
campen *vi* to camp.
Camper *m* camper.
Campingkocher *m* camping stove.
Campingplatz *m* camping site.
Caravan *m* caravan.
CD-Spieler *m* CD player.
Cellist *m* cellist.
Cello *n* cello.
Celcius *n* Celsius.
Chamäleon *n* chameleon.
Champagner *m* Champagne.
Champignon *m* button mushroom.

Chance *f* chance, opportunity.
Chaos *n* chaos.
chaotisch *adj* chaotic.
Charakter *m* character.
charakterfest *adj* of firm character.
charakterisieren *vt* to characterise, depict, portray.
charakteristisch *adj* characteristic, typical.
charakterlos *adj* unprincipled.
Charakterlosigkeit *f* lack of principle.
Charakterschwäche *f* weakness of character.
Charakterstärke *f* strength of character.
Charakterzug *m* charactistic, trait.
charmant *adj* charming, delightful.
Charme *m* charm.
Charterflug *m* charter flight.
Chauffeur *m* chauffeur.
Chauvinist *m* chauvinist.
Chef(in) *m(f)* boss, head (of firm).
Chefarzt *m* senior consultant.
Chemie *f* chemistry.
Chemiefaser *f* man-made fibre.
Chemikalie *f* chemical.
Chemiker(in) *m(f)* chemist.
chemisch *adj* chemical; **~e Reinigung** dry cleaning.
Chiffre *f* cipher; box number.
Chile *n* Chile.
chilenisch *adj* Chilean.
China *n* China.
Chinese *m* Chinese.
Chinesin *f* Chinese.
chinesisch *adj* Chinese.
Chinin *n* quinine.
Chirurg *m* surgeon.
Chirurgie surgery.
chirurgisch *adj* surgical.
Chlor *n* chlorine.
Chloroform *n* chloroform.
Cholera *f* cholera.
cholerisch *adj* choleric.
Chor *m* choir; chorus.
Choral *m* chorale.
Choregraph *m* choreographer.

Chorknabe *m* choirboy.
Christ(in) *m(f)* Christian.
Christbaum *m* Christmas tree.
Christenheit *f* Christianity.
christlich *adj* Christian.
Christus *m* Christ.
Chrom *n* chromium; chrome.
Chronik *f* chronicle.
chronisch *adj* chronic.
Chronologie *f* chronology.
chronologisch *adj* chronological.
Chrysantheme *f* chrysanthemum.
circa *adv* about, approximately.
Clown *m* clown.
Cocktail *m* cocktail.
Computer *m* computer.
Computerspiel *n* computer game.
Container *m* container.
Cord *m* cord, corduroy.
Couch *f* couch.
Cousin *m* cousin.
Cousine *f* cousin.
Creme *f* cream; polish; (tooth)paste.
cremig adj creamy.
Curry *m/n* curry powder.
Cursor *m* cursor.
cutten *vt* to edit (of film).
Cutter *m* (film) editor.

D

da *adv* there; here; then; so; * *conj* as.
dabei *adv* nearby; in the process of.
dabeisein *vi* to be present.
dabeistehen *vi* to stand around.
Dach *n* roof.
Dachboden *m* attic.
Dachrinne *f* gutter.
Dachs *m* badger.
dadurch *adv* through there; by it; **~ daß** because.

dafür *adv* for it.

dagegen *adv* against it; however; * *conj* whereas.

daheim *adv* at home.

daher *adv* from there; hence.

daherum *adv* thereabouts.

dahin *adv* there; then; gone.

dahinauf *adv* up there.

dahinaus *adv* out there.

dahinein *adv* in there.

dahingegen *conj* on the other hand.

dahingehend *vi* to pass by.

dahingehend *adv* such that.

dahinstehen *vi* to be uncertain.

dahinten *adv* back there.

dahinter *adv* behind it.

dahinunter *adv* down there.

Dahlie *f* dahlia.

daliegen *vi* to lie around.

damalig *adj* then; **der damalige Präsident** the then president.

damals *adv* then.

Dame *f* lady; queen (cards, chess); draughts.

damit *adv* with it; by it; * *conj* so that.

Damm *m* dam, embankment; jetty.

dämmen *vt* to dam; to stem.

Dämmer *m* dusk.

dämmerig *adj* dim.

dämmern *vi* to dawn; to grow dusky.

Dämmerung *f* dawn; dusk.

Dämon *m* demon.

dämonisch *adj* demonic.

Dampf *m* steam; vapour.

dampfen *vi* to steam.

dämpfen *vt* to steam; to dampen.

Dampfer *m* steamer.

Dampfkochtopf *m* pressure cooker.

danach *adv* after that; accordingly.

daneben *adv* beside it; also.

danebengehen *vi* to miss.

Däne *m* **Dänin** *f* Dane.

Dänemark *n* Denmark.

dänisch *adj* Danish.

dank *prep* thanks to.

Dank *m* thanks.

dankbar *adj* grateful.

Dankbarkeit *f* gratitude.

danke (schön) *excl* thank you, thanks.

danken *vt* to thank.

dann *adv* then.

daran *adv* on it; of it; about it.

darauf *adv* on it; to it; afterwards.

darauffolgend *adj* subsequent.

daraufhin *adv* afterwards.

daraus *adv* from it.

darbieten *vt* to present.

Darbietung *f* presentation.

darin *adv* in there; in it.

darlegen *vt* to explain.

Darlegung *f* explanation.

Darleh(e)n *n* loan.

Darm *m* intestine.

darstellen *vt* to depict.

Darsteller(in) *m(f)* actor, actress.

Darstellung *f* presentation.

darüber *adv* over it; about it; ~ **hinaus** in addition, furthermore.

darum *adv* around it; therefore.

darunter *adv* under it.

das *def art* the; * *pron* that.

Dasein *n* existence.

daß *conj* that.

dasselbe *art pron* the same.

dastehen *vi* to stand there.

Daten *pl* data.

Datenbank *f* database.

Datenverarbeitung *f* data processing.

datieren *vt* to date.

Dattel *f* date (fruit).

Datum *n* date.

Dauer *f* duration.

dauerhaft *adj* lasting.

dauern *vi* to last.

Dauerwelle *f* perm.

Daumen *m* thumb.

Daune *f* down.

Daunendecke *f* eiderdown.

davon *adv* of that/it; away.

davongehen *vi* to leave.

davor *adv* before it, in front of it.

dazu *adv* to that, to it; also.

dazugehören *vi* belong to it.

dazukommen *vi* come along.

dazwischen *adv* between (them).

dazwischenkommen *vi* to get caught up in; to occur.

dazwischenliegend *adj* intermediate.

dazwischentreten *vi* to intervene.

Debatte *f* debate.

debattieren *vt vi* to debate.

Deck *n* deck.

Decke *f* covering; table cloth; blanket; ceiling.

Deckel *m* lid.

decken *vt* to cover; to lay (table); * *vr* to cover oneself; to coincide.

Deckname *m* alias.

Deckung *f* covering.

Defekt *m* defect.

defekt *adj* defective.

definieren *vt* to define.

Definition *f* definition.

definitiv *adj* definit(iv)e.

Defizit *n* deficit.

deftig *adj* heavy; rude.

Degen *m* sword.

degradieren *vt* to degrade; to demote.

dehnbar *adj* elastic.

Dehnbarkeit *f* elasticity.

dehnen *vt vr* to stretch.

Deich *m* dyke.

dein(e) *poss adj* your.

deine(r,s) *poss pron* yours.

dekadent *adj* decadent.

Dekadenz *f* decadence.

dekorieren *vt* to decorate.

Delegation *f* delegation.

delegieren *vt* to delegate.

Delegierte(r) *mf* delegate.

delikat *adj* delicate; delicious.

Delikatesse *f* delicacy; delicatessen.

Delikt *n* offence.

Delphin *m* dolphin.

dementieren *vt* to deny.

dementsprechend, demgemäß *adv* accordingly.

demgegenüber *adv* on the other hand.

Demission *f* resignation.

demnach *adv* therefore.

demnächst *adv* soon.

Demokratie *f* democracy.

demokratisch *adj* democratic.

demolieren *vt* to demolish.

Demonstrant(in) *m(f)* demonstrator.

Demonstration *f* demonstration.

demonstrieren *vt vi* to demonstrate.

Demut *f* humility.

demütig *adj* humble.

demüten *vt* to humiliate.

Demütung *f* humiliation.

demzufolge *adv* accordingly.

den *art* acc of **der**.

denen *pron* dat pl of **der, die, das**.

denkbar *adj* conceivable.

denken *vt vi vr* to think.

Denken *n* thinking.

Denker *m* thinker.

Denkmal *n* monument.

denn *conj* as; than; * *adv* then; **es sei ~, daß** unless; **was ~?** what is it now?.

dennoch *adv conj* however.

deponieren *vt* to deposit.

deportieren *vt* to deport.

Depot *n* deposit; warehouse.

Depression *f* depression.

deprimieren *vt* to depress.

der *m* **die** *f* **das** *n* **die** *pl def art* the.

derart *adv* such that.

derb *adj* solid, sturdy, course, (uncouth).

dergleichen *pron* such.

derjenige *pron* he, she, it; the one (who); that (which).

derselbe *art pron* the same.

derzeitig *adj* current.

des *art gen of* **der**.

desgleichen *pron* the same.

deshalb *adv* therefore.

Desinfektion *f* disinfection.

Desinfektionsmittel *n* disinfectant.

desinfizieren *vt* to disinfect.

dessen *pron gen of* der, das.

Dessert *n* dessert.

desto *adv* all the, so much the.

deswegen *conj* therefore.

Detail *n* detail.

Detektiv *m* detective.

deuten *vt* to interpret; * *vi* to point.

deutlich *adj* clear.

Deutlichkeit *f* clarity.

deutsch *adj* German.

Deutsch *n* German (language).

Deutsche(r) *mf* German (person).

Deutschland *n* Germany.

Deutung *f* interpretation.

Devise *f* motto; foreign currency.

Dezember *m* December.

dezent *adj* unobtrusive.

dezimal *adj* decimal.

Diagnose *f* diagnosis.

diagonal *adj* diagonal.

Diagonale *f* diagonal.

Dialekt *m* dialect.

Dialog *m* dialogue.

Diamant *m* diamond.

Diapositiv *n* slide.

Diät *f* diet.

dich *pron acc of* du you, yourself.

dicht *adj* tight; dense; * *adv* close.

Dichte *f* density, thickness; tightness.

dichten *vt* to seal.

Dichter(in) *m(f)* poet(ess).

dichterisch *adj* poetic(al).

dichthalten *vi* to keep quiet.

Dichtung *f* seal; poetry.

dick *adj* thick; fat.

Dicke *f* thickness; fatness.

die *def art* the.

Dieb(in) *m(f)* thief.

Diebstahl *m* theft.

dienen *vi* to serve.

Diener(in) *m(f)* servant.

Dienst *m* service; duty; **außer ~** retired.

Dienstag *m* Tuesday.

Dienstleistung *f* service.

dies *pron* this; these.

diesbezüglich *adj* relevant.

dieselbe *pron art* the same.

Dieselmotor *m* diesel engine.

diese(r,s) *pron* this (one).

diesmal *adv* this time.

diesseitig *adj* on this side.

diesseits *adv prep* on this side.

Differenz *f* difference.

differenzieren *vt* to differentiate.

Diktat *n* dictation.

Diktator *m* dictator.

Diktatur *f* dictatorship.

diktieren *vt* to dictate.

Dilemma *n* dilemma.

Dimension *f* dimension.

Ding *n* thing.

Dings(bums) *n* thingamajig.

Diözese *f* diocese.

Diplom *n* diploma.

Diplomat *m* diplomat.

Diplomatie *f* diplomacy.

diplomatisch *adj* diplomatic.

dir *pron dat of* **du** (to) you.

direkt *adj* direct.

Direktion *f* management.

Direktor *m* director.

Dirigent *m* conductor.

Dirne *f* prostitute.

Diskette *f* diskette.

Diskothek *f* disco(theque).

diskret *adj* discreet.

Diskretion *f* discretion.

Diskussion *f* discussion.

diskutieren *vt vi* to discuss.

Dissertation *f* dissertation.

Dissident(in) *m(f)* dissident.

Distanz *f* distance.

Distel *f* thistle.

Disziplin *f* discipline.

Dividende *f* dividend.

dividieren *vt* to divide.

Division *f* division.

doch *conj* however; * *adv* after all, yet.

Dock *n* dock(yard).

Doktor(in) *m(f)* doctor.

Dokument *n* document.

Dokumentarfilm *m* documentary (film).

Dolch m dagger.

Dollar m dollar.

dolmetschen vt vi to interpret.

Dolomien pl (the) Dolomites.

Dometscher m interpreter.

Dom m cathedral.

dominieren vt vi to dominate.

Donau f Danube.

Donner m thunder.

donnern vi to thunder.

Donnerstag m Thursday.

doof adj dull.

Doppelbett n double bed.

Doppeldecker m double-decker.

Doppelfenster n double glazing.

Doppelgänger m double.

doppeln vt to double.

Doppelpunkt m colon.

doppelt adj double.

Doppelzimmer n double room.

Dorf n village.

Dorn m thorn.

dorren vi to dry up.

dörren vt to dry.

Dorsch m cod.

dort adv there.

dorther adv from there, hence.

dorthin adv (to) there.

dorthinaus adv out there.

dorthinein adv in there.

dortig adj there.

dösen vi to doze.

Dose f box, can.

Dosenöffner m can opener.

dosieren vt to dose, measure out.

dösig adj dozy.

Dosis f dose.

Dozent m lecturer.

Drache m dragon.

Drachen m kite.

Draht m wire; **auf ~ sein** to be in good form.

Drahtzange f pliers.

Drall m twist, spin.

Dramá n drama.

Dramatiker m dramatist.

dramatisch adj dramatic; * adv dramatically.

Drang m pressure; impulse.

drängeln vi to jostle.

drängen vt to push; * vi to be urgent.

dränieren vt to drain.

drastisch adj drastic; * adv drastically.

draußen adv outside.

Dreck m filth.

dreckig adj filthy.

drehbar adj revolving.

Drehbuch n script.

drehen vt vi to turn.

Drehung f turn.

drei num three.

Dreibein n tripod.

Dreieck n triangle.

dreieckig adj triangular.

Dreieinigkeit f Trinity.

dreifach adj, adv triple.

Dreikönigsfest n Epiphany.

dreimonatlich adj adv quarterly.

dreißig num thirty.

dreiviertel num three quarters.

Dreiviertelstunde f three quarters of an hour.

dreizehn num thirteen.

Drill m (mil) drill.

drillen vt to drill.

dringen vi to penetrate; to insist.

dringlich adj urgent.

drinnen adv inside.

dritte(r,s) adj third.

Dritte(r) m third (party).

Drittel n third.

droben adv up there.

Droge f drug.

Drogenhändler m drug dealer.

Drogerie f drugstore.

drohen vi to threaten.

dröhnen vi to rumble.

Drohung f threat.

Drossel f thrush; throttle.

drosseln vt to throttle.

drüben adv over there.

Druck m pressure; printing.

drücken vt to press; to oppress; * vi to press, touch; * vr to get out of.

Drucker *m* printer.

Drücker *m* button; latch; trigger.

Druckerei *f* printing press.

drunten *adv* down there.

Drüse *f* gland.

Dschungel *m* jungle.

du *pron* you.

ducken *vt vr* to duck, crouch.

Duell *n* duel.

Duett *n* duet.

Duft *m* scent.

duften *vi* to smell (pleasant).

duftig *adj* fragrant; delicate.

dulden *vt* to tolerate.

dumm *adj* stupid.

Dummheit *f* stupidity.

Dummkopf *m* idiot.

dumpf *adj* dull.

Düne *f* dune.

Düngemittel *n* fertiliser.

düngen *vt* to fertilise.

dunkel *adj* dark.

Dunkelheit *f* darkness.

dunkeln *vi* to darken.

Dünkirchen *n* Dunkirk.

dünn *adj* thin.

Dunst *m* vapour.

dünsten *vt vi* to steam.

dunstig *adj* hazy.

Dur *n* (*mus*) major.

durch *prep* through, by means of.

durchaus *adv* completely.

Durchblick *m* view.

durchblicken *vi* to look through; to become apparent.

durchbrechen *vt vi* to break through.

durchbringen *vt* to bring through; * *vr* to manage.

Durchbruch *m* breakthrough.

durchdenken *vt* to think through.

durchdringen *vi* to penetrate; to succeed.

Durchdringung *f* penetration.

durcheinander *adv* higgledy-piggledy.

Durcheinander *n* confusion.

durchfahren *vt vi* to travel through.

Durchfahrt *f* passage.

Durchfall *m* diarrhoea.

durchfallen *vi* to fall through; to fail.

durchführbar *adj* feasible.

durchführen *vt* to carry through.

Durchführung *f* completion.

Durchgang *m* passage.

durchgeben *vt* to pass on.

durchgehen *vt* to go though; * *vi* to run away.

durchgehend *adj* through (train); continuous; * *adv* usually.

durchgreifend *adj* drastic.

durchhalten *vt vi* to hold out.

durchkommen *vi* to get through.

durchlassen *vt* to let in.

durchlässig *adj* permeable.

durchmachen *vt* to go though.

Durchmesser *m* diameter.

durchnehmen *vt* to go though.

durchschauen *vt* to see through; * *vi* to look through.

durchscheinend *adj* translucent.

Durchschlag *m* colander; (carbon) copy.

durchschlagen *vt* to split; * *vi* tobecome apparent; * *vr* to manage.

durchschlagend *adj* decisive.

durchschneiden *vt* to cut through.

Durchschnitt *m* average.

durchschnittlich *adj* average; * *adv* on average.

durchsehen *vt vi* to look through.

durchsetzen *vt* to carry though; * *vr* to assert oneself

durchsichtig *adj* transparent.

durchstoßen *vt vi* to break through.

durchtrieben *adj* cunning.

durchweg *adv* throughout.

dürfen *vi* to be allowed.

dürftig *adj* needy.

dürr *adj* arid.

Dürre *f* aridity.

Durst *m* thirst; **~ haben** to be thirsty.
dürstig *adj* thirsty.
Dusche *f* shower.
duschen *vt vi* to shower.
Düse *f* nozzle; jet.
Düsenflugzeug *n* jet (aircraft).
Düsentriebwerk *n* jet engine.
düster *adj* dark.
Düsterheit, Düsterkeit *f* gloom.
Dutzend *n* dozen.
duzen *vt* to call so **du**, be familiar.
dynamisch *adj* dynamic.
Dynamit *n* dynamite.
Dynamo *m* dynamo.

E

Ebbe *f* low tide.
eben *adj* level; * *adv* exactly.
Ebene *f* plain.
ebenfalls *adv* also.
ebenso *adv* equally.
ebensogut *adv* just as well.
ebensehr, ebenviel *adv* just as much.
ebensowenig *adv* just as little.
ebnen *vt* to level.
Echo *n* echo.
echt *adj* genuine.
Ecke *f* corner; angle.
edel *adj* noble; precious.
Efeu *m* ivy.
Effekten *pl* effects; securities.
effektiv *adj* effective.
egal *adj* equal; **das ist mir ~** it's all the same to me.
Egoismus *m* egotism.
Egoist(in) *m(f)* egotist.
egoistisch *adj* selfish.
ehe *conj* before.
Ehe *f* marriage.
Ehebrecher(in) *m(f)* adulterer.
ehebrecherisch *adj* adulterous.
Ehebruch *m* adultery.

Ehefrau *f* wife.
ehelich *adj* matrimonial.
ehemalig *adj* former.
ehemals *adv* formerly.
Ehemann *m* husband.
Ehepaar *n* married couple.
eher *adv* sooner; rather.
Ehering *m* wedding ring.
Ehescheidung *f* divorce.
ehestens *adv* as soon as possible.
ehrbar *adj* honourable.
Ehre *f* honour.
ehren *vt* to honour.
Ehrengast *m* guest of honour.
ehrenhaft, ehrenvoll *adj* honourable.
Ehrenwort *n* word of honour.
Ehrfurcht *f* reverence.
ehrfürchtig *adj* reverential.
Ehrgeiz *m* ambition.
ehrgeizig *adj* ambitious.
ehrlich *adj* honest; * *adv* honestly.
Ehrlichkeit *f* honesty.
ehrlos *adj* dishonourable.
Ei *n* egg.
Eibe *f* yew.
Eiche *f* oak.
Eichel *f* acorn.
eichen *vt* to standardise.
Eichhörnchen *n* squirrel.
Eid *m* oath.
Eidechse *f* lizard.
eidgenössisch *adj* Swiss.
Eidotter *n* egg yolk.
Eierbecher *m* eggcup.
Eierkuchen *m* omelette, pancake.
Eierschale *f* eggshell.
Eierstock *m* ovary.
Eifer *m* enthusiasm.
eifern *vi* to be eager for.
Eifersucht *f* jealousy.
eifersüchtig *adj* jealous.
eiförmig *adj* egg-shaped, oval.
eifrig *adj* eager.
Eigelb *n* egg yolk.
eigen *adj* own; particular; unusual.
Eigenart *f* peculiarity.
eigenartig *adj* peculiar.

Eigenheit *f* peculiarity.
Eigenliebe *f* egotism.
eigenmächtig *adj* high-handed; independent.
eigens *adv* deliberately.
Eigenschaft *f* characteristic.
Eigenschaftswort *n* adjective.
Eigensinn *m* stubbornness.
eigensinning *adj* stubborn.
eigenständig *adj* independent.
eigentlich *adj* actual, real; * *adv* actually, really.
Eigentor *n* own goal.
Eigentum *n* property, ownership.
Eigentümer(in) *m(f)* owner.
eigentümlich *adj* special, particular.
Eigentümlichkeit *f* peculiarity.
Eigentumswohnung *f* freehold flat, apartment.
Eigenwille *m* wilfulness.
eigenwillig *adj* self-willed.
eignen *vr* to suit.
Eigner *m* owner.
Eignung *f* suitability.
Eilbote *m* courier.
Eilbrief *m* express letter.
Eile *f* hurry.
eilen *vi vr* to hurry.
eilig *adj* hurried; **es ~ haben** to be in a hurry.
Eimer *m* bucket.
ein(e) *num* one; * *indef art* a, an; * *pron* **eine(r,s)** one.
einander *adv* each other, one another.
einarbeiten *vr* familiarise oneself
einarmen *vt* to inhale.
Einbahnstraße *f* one-way street.
Einbau *m* installation.
einbauen *vt* to install.
einberufen *vt* to convene.
Einberufung *f* convocation.
einbeziehen *vt* to include.
Einbeziehung *f* inclusion.
einbiegen *vi* to turn.
einbilden *vr* to imagine.
Einbildung *f* imagination.

Einblick *m* view; insight.
einbrechen *vi* to break into; to collapse; to invade; to fall (night).
einbringen *vt* to bring in.
Einbruch *m* break-in; invasion; arrival (night).
Einbuße *f* loss.
einbüßen *vt* to lose.
einchecken *vt vi* to check in.
eindeutig *adj* clear.
eindringen *vi* to break in; to invade; to penetrate.
Eindruck *m* impression.
eindrucksvoll *adj* impressive.
eineinhalb *num* one and a half.
einerlei *adj* (one and) the same.
einerseits *adv* on the one hand.
einfach *adj* single; simple; * *adv* simply.
Einfachheit *f* simplicity.
einfahren *vt* to bring in; * *vi* to come in.
Einfahrt *f* entrance.
Einfall *m* idea; incursion.
einfallen *vi* to raid; to occur; to fall in.
einfassen *vt* to enclose.
Einfassung *f* enclosure.
einfinden *vr* to turn up.
einfließen *vi* to flow in.
EInfluß *m* influence.
einflußreich *adj* influential.
einförmig *adj* uniform.
Einförmigkeit *f* uniformity.
einfrieren *vt vi* to freeze.
einfügen *vt* to insert.
Einfuhr *f* import(s).
einführen *vt* to introduce; to import.
Einführung *f* introduction.
Eingabe *f* application.
Eingang *m* entrance; arrival; receipt.
eingangs *adv* first of all.
eingeben *vt* to give in; to enter; to inspire.
Eingebung *f* inspiration.
eingebildet *adj* imaginary; arrogant.
Eingeborene(r) *mf* native.
eingeboren *adj* innate.

eingehen *vt* to enter into, incur; * *vi* to come in; to be understood; to die.

eingenommen *adj* partial, biased.

Eingenommenheit *f* bias.

eingestehen *vt* to admit.

Eingeweide *pl* entrails.

eingewurzelt *adj* deep-rooted.

eingliedern *vt* to incorporate.

Eingliederung *f* incorporation.

eingreifen *vi* to intervene.

Eingriff *m* intervention; surgery.

einhalten *vt* to comply with; * *vi* to stop.

Einhaltung *f* compliance.

einhändigen *vt* to hand in.

einhängen *vt vi* to hang (up).

Einheit *f* unit; unity.

einheitlich *adj* uniform.

Einheitlichkeit *f* uniformity.

einholen *vt vi* to bring in; to catch up; * *vi* ~ **gehen** to go shopping.

einig *adj* united; agreed.

einige(r,s) *adj pron* some.

einigen *vt* to unite; * *vr* to agree.

einigermaßen *adv* somewhat.

Einigkeit *f* unity.

Einigung *f* agreement; unification.

Einkauf *m* purchase.

einkaufen *vt* to buy; * *vi* to shop.

Einkaufszentrum *n* shopping centre.

Einklang *m* harmony.

einkommen *vi* to apply; to come in.

Einkommen *n* income.

Einkommen(s)steuer *f* income tax.

Einkünfte *pl* income.

einladen *vt* to invite.

Einladung *f* invitation.

Einlage *f* enclosure; deposit; support.

einlagern *vt* to store.

Einlaß *m* admission.

einlassen *vt* to admit; * *vr* to become involved.

Einlauf *m* entry; enema.

einlaufen *vi* to come in.

einleben *vr* to become accustomed.

einlegen *vt* to insert; to make; to have.

einleiten *vt* to introduce.

Einleitung *f* introduction.

einliefern *vt* to deliver.

Einlieferung *f* delivery.

einlösen *vt* to cash (cheque); to redeem.

einmal *adv* once; one day; even; **auf** ~ suddenly.

einmalig *adv* unique.

Einmarsch *m* entry; invasion.

einmauern *vt* to immure.

einmengen, einmischen *vt* to mix in; * *vr* to interfere.

einmütig *adj* unanimous.

Einmütigkeit *f* unanimity.

Einnahme *f* capture; income.

einnehmen *vt* to take (in, up).

einnicken *vi* to nod off.

Einöde *f* desert.

einordnen *vt* to arrange; * *vr* to adjust; to get into lane.

einpacken *vt vi* to pack.

einpassen *vt* to fit in(to).

einpflanzen *vt* to plant.

einprägen *vt* to imprint.

einrahmen *vt* to frame.

einräumen *vt* to put away; to concede.

einreden *vt* to persuade.

einreichen *vt* to hand in.

einreihen *vt* to classify; to enrol.

Einreise *f* entry.

einrichten *vt* to arrange.

Einrichtung *f* furnishings; installation; institution.

eins *num* one.

Eins *f* one.

einsam *adj* lonely.

Einsamkeit *f* loneliness.

Einsatz *m* insert; inset; stake, risk; use; effort.

einschalten *vt* to switch on; to insert; to bring in; * *vr* to intervene.

einschätzen *vt* estimate.

einschenken *vt vi* to pour out.

einschicken *vt* to send in.

einschlafen *vi* to fall asleep.

Einschlag *m* impact; hint.

einschlagen *vt* to break in; to wrap; to take (road); * *vi* to hit; to agree, succeed.

einschlägig *adj* relevant.

einschleichen *vi* to creep in.

einschließen *vt* to lock up; to enclose.

einschließlich *adv* inclusive; * *prep* including.

Einschluß *m* inclusion.

einschmelzen *vt* to melt.

einschneiden *vt* to cut into.

einschneidend *adj* incisive.

Einschnitt *m* cut.

einschränken *vt* to restrict.

Einschränkung *f* restriction.

einschreiben *vt* to write in; to register.

Einschreiben *n* recorded delivery.

einschüchtern *vt* to intimidate.

Einschüchterung *f* intimidation.

einsehen *vt* to look at; to realise.

Einsehen *n* understanding.

einseitig *adj* one-sided.

einsenden *vt* to send in.

einsetzen *vt* to put in; to use; to install; * *vi* to set in; to come in; * *vr* to work hard.

Einsicht *f* inspection; insight.

einsparen *vt* to save.

Einsparung *f* saving(s).

einsperren *vt* to lock in.

einspielen *vt* to bring in; to play in; * *vr* to practise.

einspringen *vi* to help out.

Einspruch *m* objection.

einst *adv* once.

einstehen *vi* to guarantee.

einsteigen *vi* to get in.

einstellbar *adj* adjustable.

einstellen *vt* to adjust; to stop; to employ; * *vr* to adapt.

Einstellung *f* adjustment; ces-

sation; recruitment; attitude.

Einstieg *m* entry.

einstig *adj* former.

einstimmen *vi* to join in.

einstimmig *adj* unanimous.

Einstimmigkeit *f* unanimity.

einstufen *vt* to classify.

Einsturz *m* collapse.

einstürzen *vi* to collapse.

einstweilen *adv* meanwhile.

einstweilig *adj* temporary.

eintauchen *vt* to dip in; * *vi* to dive in.

einteilen *vt* to divide.

Einteilung *f* division.

eintönig *adj* monotonous.

Eintönigkeit *f* monotony.

Eintrag *m* entry.

eintragen *vt* to record.

eintreffen *vi* to arrive.

eintreten *vi* to enter; to join; to occur.

Eintritt *m* entrance.

Eintrittskarte *f* (entrance) ticket.

Einvernehmen *n* agreement.

einverstanden *adj* agreed.

Einverständnis *n* agreement.

Einwand *m* objection.

Einwanderer *m* immigrant.

einwandern *vi* to immigrate.

Einwanderung *f* immigration.

einwandfrei *adj* impeccable; * *adv* absolutely.

einwärts *adv* inward(s).

einweihen *vt* to inaugurate.

Einweihung *f* inauguration.

einweisen *vt* to install.

einwenden *vt* to object.

Einwendung *f* objection.

einwerfen *vt* to throw in; to put in; to post; to smash.

einwickeln *vt* to wrap.

einwilligen *vt* to agree.

einwirken *vi* to affect.

Einwirkung *f* effect.

Einwohner(in) *m(f)* inhabitant.

Einwurf *m* throw-in; objection.

einzahlen *vt* pay in.

Einzahlung *f* (in)payment.

Einzelfall *m* individual case.

Einzelhandel *m* retailing.
Einzelhändler *m* retailer.
Einzelheit *f* detail.
einzeln *adj* single; * *adv* individually.
Einzelzimmer *n* single room.
einziehen *vt* to draw in; to withdraw; to collect; * *vi* to move into; to arrive.
einzig *adj* single; only.
einzigartig *adj* unique.
Einzug *m* entrance.
Eis *n* ice (cream).
Eisbahn *f* skating rink.
Eisbär *m* polar bear.
Eisberg *m* iceberg.
Eisen *n* iron.
Eisenbahn *f* railway, railroad.
eisern *adj* iron.
Eishockey *n* ice hockey.
eisig *adj* icy.
eiskalt *adj* ice-cold.
Eislauf *m* skating.
eislaufen *vi* to skate.
Eisläufer(in) *m(f)* skater.
Eisschrank *m* fridge.
eitel *adj* vain.
Eitelkeit *f* vanity.
Eiweiß *n* egg white; protein.
Ekel *m* disgust.
ekelhaft, ek(e)lig *adj* disgusting.
ekeln *vt* to disgust.
Ekstase *f* ecstasy.
ekstatisch *adj* ecstatic.
elastisch *adj* elastic.
Elefant *m* elephant.
elegant *adj* elegant.
Elektriker *m* electrician.
elektrisch *adj* electrical.
Elektrizität *f* electricity.
Elektronik *f* electronics.
elektronisch *adj* electronic.
Element *n* element.
elementar *adj* elementary.
Elend *n* misery.
elend *adj* miserable.
elf *adj* eleven.
Elf *f* eleven; * *m* elf.
Elfenbein *n* ivory.
eliminieren *vt* to eliminate.
Elite *f* elite.

Ellenbogen *m* elbow.
Elsaß *n* Alsace.
Eltern *pl* parents.
Empfang *m* reception; receipt.
empfangen *vt* to receive; * *vi* to conceive, become pregnant.
Empfänger *m* receiver, recipient.
Empfängnis *f* conception.
Empfängnisverhütung *f* contraception.
Empfangsherr (-dame) *m(f)* receptionist.
empfehlen *vt* to recommend; * *vr* to take one's leave.
Empfehlung *f* recommendation.
empfinden *vt* to feel.
empfindlich *adj* sensitive.
Emfindlichkeit *f* sensitivity.
empfindsam *adj* sentimental.
Emfindsamkeit *f* sentimentality.
Empfindung *f* feeling.
empfindungslos *adj* insensitive.
Emphase *f* emphasis.
empor *adv* upwards.
empören *vt* to anger.
Empörung *f* indignation; rebellion.
Ende *n* end.
enden *vi* to end.
endgültig *adj* final.
endlich *adj* final; * *adv* finally, at last.
endlos *adj* endless.
Endspiel *n* final.
Endstation *f* terminus.
Endung *f* ending.
Energie *f* energy.
energisch *adj* energetic.
eng *adj* narrow; close; tight.
Engel *m* angel.
engelhaft *adj* angelic.
engherzig *adj* narrow-minded.
England *n* England.
Engländer(in) *m(f)* Englishman(woman).
Englisch *n* English (language).
englisch *adj* English.
Engpaß *m* bottleneck.

Enkel(in) *m(f)* grandson, (grandaughter).
enorm *adj* enormous.
entarten *vi* to degenerate.
entartet *adj* degenerate.
entbehren *vt* to manage without.
entbehrlich *adj* non-essential.
entbinden *vt* to release; * *vi* to give birth.
entblößen *vt* to bare.
entdecken *vt* to discover.
Entdeckung *f* discovery.
Ente *f* duck.
entehren *vt* to dishonour.
enteignen *vt* to expropriate.
enteisen *vt* to defrost.
entfallen *vi* to fall; to escape.
entfalten *vt* unfold.
entfernen *vt* to remove.
entfernt *adj* distant.
Entfernung *f* distance.
entführen *vt* to abduct.
Entführer *m* kidnapper.
Entführung *f* abduction.
entgegen *adv prep* against, contrary to.
entgegengesetzt *adj* opposite.
entgegenkommen *vi* to meet, comply with.
entgehen *vi* to escape.
Entgelt *n* compensation, reward.
enthalten *vt* to contain; * *vr* to refrain from.
Enthaltung *f* abstention.
enthaltsam *adj* abstemious.
enthüllen *vt* to uncover.
entkleiden *vt vr* to undress.
entkommen *vi* to escape.
entkräften *vt* to weaken.
entladen *vt* to unload; to set off; * *vr* to discharge.
entlang *adv prep* along.
entlarven *vt* to expose.
entlassen *vt* to dismiss.
Entlassung *f* dismissal.
entlasten *vt* to unburden.
Entlastung *f* relief.
entleeren *vt* to empty.
Entleerung *f* emptying.
entlegen *adj* distant.

entlehnen *vt* to borrow.
entmachten *vt* to deprive of power.
entmutigen *vt* to discourage.
Entnahme *f* withdrawal.
entnehmen *vt* to remove.
entrüsten *vt* to enrage.
entschädigen *vt* to compensate.
Entschädigung *f* compensation.
entscheiden *vt vi* to decide.
entscheidend *adj* decisive.
Entscheidung *f* decision.
entschieden *adj* decided.
Entschiedenheit *f* determination.
entschließen *vr* to decide.
entschlossen *adj* determined.
Entschlossenheit *f* determination.
Entschluß *m* decision.
entschlüsseln *vt* to decipher.
entschuldigen *vt* to excuse; * *vr* to apologise.
Entschuldigung *f* excuse; ~! excuse me!; sorry!.
entsenden *vt* to send off.
entsetzen *vt* to dismiss; to frighten; to appal.
Entsetzen *n* terror; dismay.
entsetzlich *adj* appalling.
entsetzt *adj* appalled.
Entsetzung *f* dismissal.
entsinnen *vr* to remember.
entspannen *vt vr* to relax.
Entspannung *f* relaxation.
entsprechen *vi* to correspond with; to be equivalent to.
entsprechend *adj* appropriate; * *adv* appropriately.
entspringen *vi* to arise from; to escape from.
entstehen *vi* to come into existence.
Entstehung *f* beginning.
entstellen *vt* to deface.
enttäuschen *vt* to disappoint.
Enttäuschung *f* disappointment.
entwaffnen *vt* to disarm.
Entwaffnung *f* disarmament.

entwässern vt to drain.
entweder conj: ~ ... **oder** ... either ... or ....
entwerfen vt to design.
entwerten vt to devalue; to cancel (ticket).
Entwertung f devaluation.
entwickeln vt vr to develop.
Entwicklung f development.
Entwurf m design.
entwurzeln vt to uproot.
entziehen vt to withdraw; * vr to escape.
Entziehung f withdrawal.
entziffern vt to decipher.
entzücken vt to delight.
entzückend adj delightful.
entzünden vt to light; * vr to catch light; to become inflamed.
entzwei adv in two.
entzweibrechen vt vi to break in two.
Enzyklopädie f encyclopedia.
Epidemie f epidemic.
Episode f episode.
Epoche f epoch.
er pron he.
erachten vi to consider.
Erachten n opinion; **meines Erachtens** in my opinion.
erarbeiten vt to acquire.
erbarmen vt have pity on.
Erbarmen n pity.
erbärmlich adj pitiful.
erbarmungslos adj pitiless.
erbarmungsvoll adj compassionate.
erbauen vt to build; to edify.
Erbauung f construction; edification.
Erbe m heir.
erben vt to inherit.
erbeuten vt to capture.
Erbin f heiress.
erbitten vt to ask for.
erbittern vt to embitter.
erbittert adj bitter.
erblassen, erbleichen vi to pale.
erblich adj hereditary.
erblicken vt to see.

erbrechen vt vr to vomit.
erbringen vt to provide.
Erbschaft f inheritance, estate.
Erbse n pea.
Erbstück n heirloom.
Erdbeben n earthquake.
Erdbeere f strawberry.
Erde f earth.
erdenken vt to think out.
erdenklich adj conceivable.
Erdgas n natural gas.
Erdgeschoß n ground floor.
Erdkunde f geography.
Erdnuß f peanut.
Erdöl n petroleum.
erdrosseln vt to strangle.
erdrücken vt to crush.
Erdrutsch m landslide.
ereignen vr to occur.
Ereignis n event.
erfahren vt to experience; to discover; * adj experienced.
Erfahrung f experience.
erfassen vt to grasp; to understand; to record; to include.
Erfassung f registration.
erfinden vt to discover, invent.
Erfinder m inventor.
Erfindung f invention.
Erfolg m result; success; ~ **haben** to succeed.
erfolgen vi to result; to happen.
erfolglos adj unsuccessful.
erfolgreich adj successful.
erforderlich adj necessary.
erfordern vt to require.
erforschen vt to explore; to investigate.
Erforschung f exploration; investigation.
erfragen vt to ascertain, inquire.
erfreuen vt to please; * vr to enjoy.
erfreulich adj pleasing.
erfreulicherweise adv fortunately.
erfrieren vi to freeze to death; to be frostbitten.
erfrischen vt to refresh.
Erfrischung f refreshment.
erfüllen vt to fill; to comply

with; * *vr* to be fulfilled.
Erfüllung *f* fulfilment.
ergänzen *vt* to supplement;
* *vr* to complement one another.
ergänzend *adj* additional.
Ergänzung *f* completion; supplement.
Ergänzungsfarbe *f* complementary colour.
ergeben *vt* to result in; to produce; to yield; * *vr* to surrender; to result; * *adj* loyal.
Ergebnis *n* result.
ergehen *vi* to be issued; to to
come out; ~ **lassen** to issue;
über sich ~ lassen to endure.
ergiebig *adj* productive.
ergreifen *vt* to grasp.
ergriffen *adj* moved.
erhaben *adj* raised; lofty.
erhalten *vt* to receive; to maintain.
erhältlich *adj* available.
Erhaltung *f* maintenance;
preservation.
erheben *vt* to raise; * *vr* to rise.
erheblich *adj* considerable;
* *adv* considerably.
Erhebung *f* elevation; raising;
collection.
erhitzen *vt* to heat; * *vr* to heat
up.
erhoffen *vt* to hope for.
erhöhen *vt* to raise.
erholen *vr* to recover.
Erholung *f* recovery.
erhören *vt* to hear; to grant.
erinnern *vt* to remind; * *vr* to
remember.
Erinnerung *f* memory.
erkälten *vr* to catch cold;
erkältet sein to have a cold.
Erkältung *f* cold.
erkennbar *adj* recognisable.
erkennen *vt* to recognise; to realise.
erkenntlich *adj* perceptible;
grateful.
Erkenntlichkeit *f* gratitude.
Erkenntnis *f* knowledge; realisation; acknowledgment.

Erkennung *f* recognition.
erklären *vt* to explain; to declare.
Erklärung *f* explanation.
erklettern, erklimmen *vt* to
climb.
erkranken *vi* to fall ill.
Erkrankung *f* sickness.
erkunden *vt* to explore.
erkundigen *vr* to inquire.
Erkundigung *f* inquiry.
erlangen *vt* to reach.
Erlaß *m* exemption; decree.
erlassen *vt* to issue; to exempt.
erläßlich *adj* allowable.
erlauben *vt* to allow.
Erlaubnis *f* permission.
erlaubt *adj* allowed.
erläutern *vt* to explain.
Erläuterung *f* explanation.
erleben *vt* to experience.
Erlebnis *n* experience.
erledigen *vt* to carry out; to finish.
erledigt *adj* done.
Erledigung *f* settlement; handling.
erleichtern *vt* to facilitate; to
relieve.
erleichtert *adj* relieved.
Erleichterung *f* enlightenment; relief.
erleiden *vt* to suffer.
erlernen *vt* to learn.
erlesen *vt* to select; * *adj* select.
erliegen *vi* to succumb.
Erlös *m* proceeds.
erlöschen *vi* to be extin-
guished.
erlösen *vt* to save.
Erlösung *f* redemption.
ermächtigen *vt* to authorise.
Ermächtigung *f* authorisation.
ermahnen *vt* to admonish.
ermangeln *vi* to lack.
ermäßigen *vt* to reduce.
Ermäßigung *f* reduction.
ermessen *vt* to assess.
Ermessen *n* judgment; **nach
meinem ~** in my opinion.
ermitteln *vt* to determine.
Ermittlung *f* determination.

ermöglichen *vt* to make possible.

ermorden *vt* to murder.

Ermordung *f* murder.

ermüden *vt vi* to tire.

ermunten, ermutigen *vt* to encourage.

ernähren *vt* to feed; * *vr* to earn a living.

Ernährung *f* nutrition.

ernennen *vt* to appoint.

erneuern *vt* to renew.

Erneuerung *f* renewal, renovation.

erneut *adj* renewed; * *adj* again.

Ernst *m* seriousness; **im ~** in earnest.

ernst *adj* serious.

Ernstfall *m* emergency.

ernsthaft *adj* serious.

ernstlich *adj* serious; * *adv* seriously.

Ernte *f* harvest.

ernten *vt vi* to harvest.

Eroberer *m* conqueror.

erobern *vt* to conquer.

Eroberung *f* conquest.

eröffnen *vt* to open; * *vr* to present itself.

erörtern *vt* to discuss.

erotisch *adj* erotic.

erpressen *vt* to extort; to blackmail.

erproben *vt* to try, test.

errechnen *vt* to calculate.

erregbar *adj* excitable.

erregen *vt* to excite; to inspire.

erregend *adj* exciting.

erregt *adj* excited.

erreichbar *adj* accessible.

erreichen *vt* to reach.

errichten *vt* to erect.

erringen *vt* to achieve.

erröten *vi* to blush.

Ersatz *m* compensation; alternative, substitute.

Ersatzreifen *m* spare tyre.

Ersatzteil *n* spare part.

erscheinen *vi* to appear.

Erscheinung *f* appearance.

erschießen *vt* to shoot (dead).

Erschießung *f* shooting, execution.

erschlagen *vt* to kill.

erschließen *vt* to open up; to develop.

erschöpfen *vt* to exhaust.

erschöpft *adj* exhausted.

Erschöpfung *f* exhaustion.

erschrecken *vt* to frighten; * *vi vr* to be frightened.

erschrocken *adj* frightened.

erschüttern *vt* to shake; to upset.

erschütternd *adj* shocking.

Erschütterung *f* shock.

erschweren *vt* to make more difficult, complicate.

ersehen *vt* to see, note.

ersetzbar *adj* replaceable, reparable.

ersetzen *vt* to replace.

ersichtlich *adj* obvious.

ersinnen *vt* to devise.

ersparen *vt* to spare, save.

erst *adj* first; only; not until.

erstatten *vt* to repay; to notify.

erstaunen *vt* to astonish; * *vi* to be astonished.

erstaunlich *adj* astonishing.

erste *adj* first.

erstechen *vt* to stab (to death).

erstehen *vt* to buy; * *vi* to arise.

ersteigen *vt* to climb.

erstellen *vt* to provide; to construct.

erstens *adv* firstly.

erstklassig *adj* first-class.

erstmalig *adj* first.

erstmals *adv* for the first time.

erstreben *vt* to strive for.

erstrecken *vr* to extend.

ersuchen *vt* to request.

Ersuchen *n* request.

erteilen *vt* to give, grant.

Ertrag *m* yield, profit.

ertragen *vt* to endure.

erträglich *adj* bearable.

ertrinken *vi* to drown.

erwachen *vi* to awake.

erwachsen *adj* grown-up.

Erwachsene(r) *mf* adult.

erwägen *vt* to consider.

Erwägung *f* consideration.
erwähnen *vt* to mention.
Erwähnung *f* mention.
erwärmen *vt* to warm, heat;
 * *vr* to heat up.
erwarten *vt* to expect.
Erwartung *f* expectation.
erwartungsvoll *adj* expectant;
 * *adv* expectantly.
erwecken *vt* to wake, stir up.
erweisen *vt* to prove.
erweitern *vt vr* to widen, expand.
Erweiterung *f* expansion.
Erwerb *m* acquisition; occupation.
erwerben *vt* to acquire; to earn.
erwidern *vt* to return; to reply.
Erwiderung *f* reply.
erwünscht *adj* desired.
erwürgen *vt* to strangle.
Erz *n* ore.
erzählen *vt* to tell.
Erzählung *f* story.
Erzbischof *m* archbishop.
erzeugen *vt* to produce.
Erzeugnis *n* product.
Erzeugung *f* production.
erziehen *vt* to bring up; to educate.
Erziehung *f* bringing up; education.
erzielen *vt* to achieve.
erzwingen *vt* to force.
es *pron nom, acc* it.
Esche *f* ash (tree).
Esel *m* donkey.
eßbar *adj* edible.
essen *vt vi* to eat.
Essen *n* food; meal.
Essig *m* vinegar.
Eßlöffel *m* tablespoon.
Estland *n* Estonia.
etablieren *vt vr* to establish.
Etage *f* floor, storey.
ethisch *adj* ethical.
Etikett *n* label.
Etikette *f* etiquette.
etliche *pron pl* some, several.
Etui *n* case.
etwa *adv* about, approximately;
 for example.

etwaig *adj* any; possible.
etwas *pron* something; anything; * *adj* some, a little.
euch *pron* (*acc dat of* **ihr**) you,
 to you; yourselves.
euer *pron* (*gen of* **ihr**) of you;
 * *poss adj* your.
Eule *f* owl.
eure(r,s) *poss pron* yours.
Europa *n* Europe.
Europäer(in) *m(f)* European.
europäisch *adj* European.
eventuell *adj* possible; * *adv*
 possibly, if necessary.
ewig *adj* eternal.
Ewigkeit *f* eternity.
Examen *n* examination.
Exemplar *n* sample; copy (of
 book).
Exil *n* exile.
Existenz *f* existence; livelihood.
existieren *vi* to exist.
exklusiv *adj* exclusive.
exklusive *adv* excluding.
Exkursion *f* excursion.
exotisch *adj* exotic.
Expansion *f* expansion.
Expedition *f* dispatch; expedition.
Experiment *n* experiment.
experimentell *adj* experimental.
experimentieren *vi* to experiment.
Experte *m* **Expertin** *f* expert.
explodieren *vi* to explode.
Explosion *f* explosion.
explosiv *adj* explosive.
Export *m* export.
Exporteur *m* exporter.
exportieren *vt* to export.
expreß *adv* express(ly).
extensiv *adj* extensive.
extern *adj* external.
extra *adj adv* extra.
extravagant *adj* extravagant.
extrem *adj* extreme.
exzentrisch *adj* eccentric.
Exzeß *m* excess.

F

Fabel f fable.
fabelhaft adj fabulous.
Fabrik f factory.
Fabrikant m manufacturer.
Fach n compartment; subject.
fächeln vt to fan.
Fächer m fan.
Fachhochschule f technical college.
fachlich adj technical, professional.
Fachmann m expert.
fachmännisch adj professional.
Fackel f torch.
fade adj dull.
Faden m thread.
fähig adj capable.
Fähigkeit f ability.
Fahne f flag.
Fähre f ferry.
fahren vt vi to travel; to drive.
Fahrer(in) m(f) driver.
Fahrgast m passenger.
Fahrgeld n fare.
Fahrkarte f ticket.
fahrlässig adj negligent.
Fahrlässigkeit f negligence.
Fahrlehrer(in) m(f) driving instructor.
Fahrplan m timetable.
Fahrprüfung f driving test.
Fahrrad n bicycle.
Fahrt f journey; **gute ~** have a good trip.
Fahrzeug n vehicle.
faktisch adj factual; * adv actually, de facto.
Faktor m factor.
Falke m falcon.
Fall m fall; case; **auf jeden ~, auf alle Fälle** in any case; **auf keinen ~** by no means.
Falle f trap.
fallen vi to fall; **~ lassen** to drop.
fällen vt to fell (tree); to pronounce (judgment).

fällig adj due.
Fälligkeit f expiry.
falls conj in case.
Fallschirm m parachute.
falsch adj wrong; false.
fälschen vt to falsify.
Falschheit f falsity.
fälschlich adv falsely.
Fälschung f fake.
Falte f fold; wrinkle.
falten vt to fold.
Familie f family.
Familienname m surname, last name.
Fanatiker m fanatic.
fanatisch adj fanatic(al).
Fang m catch.
fangen vt to catch.
Farbe f colour; dye; paint.
Farbfernsehen n colour television.
farbig adj coloured.
farblos adj colourless.
Farbstoff m dye, colouring.
Farn m fern.
Faser f fibre.
Faß n barrel.
fassen vt to grasp; to understand.
Fassung f frame; version; composure.
fast adv nearly.
fasten vi to fast.
Fastzeit f Lent.
faszinieren vt to fascinate.
fatal adj fatal; awkward.
fatalistisch adj fatalistic.
faul adj rotten; lazy.
faulen vi to rot.
faulenzen vi to laze around.
Faulheit f laziness.
Fäulnis f decay.
Faust f fist; **auf eigene ~** on one's own initiative.
Februar m February.
fechten vi to fence; to fight.
Feder f feather; spring; nib.
Fee f fairy.
fegen vt vi to sweep.
fehlen vi to be absent; to lack; **sie fehlt mir** I miss her.
Fehler m mistake; fault.

fehlerfrei *adj* faultless.
fehlerhaft *adj* faulty.
Fehlschlag *m* miss; failure.
fehlschlagen *vi* to fail.
Feier *f* celebration.
feierlich *adj* festive; ceremonious.
feiern *vt* to celebrate.
Feiertag *m* holiday.
feig(e) *adj* cowardly.
Feige *f* fig.
Feigheit *f* cowardice.
Feigling *m* coward.
Feile *f* file.
feilen *vt* to file.
feilschen *vi* to bargain, haggle.
fein *adj* fine.
Feind *m* enemy.
feindlich *adj* hostile.
Feindlichkeit, Feindschaft, Feindseligkeit *f* hostility.
Feinheit *f* fineness, refinement.
Feinkost *f* delicatessen.
Feld *n* field.
Feldwebel *m* sergeant.
Fell *n* skin, hide.
Fels *m* rock.
Felsen *m* cliff.
Fenster *n* window.
Fensterbrett *n* windowsill.
Fensterputzer *m* window cleaner.
Ferien *pl* holidays, vacation.
Ferkel *n* piglet.
fern *adj adv* far, distant.
Fernbedienung *f* remote control.
Ferne *f* distance.
ferner *adj* further; * *adv* furthermore.
Fernglas *n* binoculars.
fernhalten *vt* to keep away.
Fernrohr *n* telescope.
Fernsehen *n* television.
fernsehen *vi* to watch television.
Fernseher *m* television (set).
Fernsprecher *m* telephone.
Ferse *f* heel.
fertig *adj* ready; complete.
Fertigkeit *f* skill.
fertigmachen *vt* to complete.

Fertigung *f* production.
fesseln *vt* to bind.
fest *adj* firm; solid; fixed.
Fest *n* festival; party.
festbinden *vt* to fasten.
festhalten *vt* to hold; to arrest.
festigen *vt* to strengthen.
Festigkeit *f* strength.
festlegen *vt* to fix.
festlich *adj* festive.
festmachen *vt* to fix; * *vi* to moor.
Festnahme *f* capture.
festnehmen *vt* to capture, arrest.
feststehen *vi* to be certain.
feststellen *vt* to establish; to state.
Festung *f* fortress.
Fett *n* fat, grease.
fett *adj* fat, greasy.
fetten *vt* to grease.
Fettnäpfchen *n* ins ~ treten to put one's foot in it.
feucht *adj* damp.
Feuchtigkeit *f* damp, humidity.
Feuer *n* fire; **haben Sie ~?** have you got a light?.
Feueralarm *n* fire alarm.
feuergefährlich   *adj* (in)flammable.
Feuerlöscher *m* fire extinguisher.
Feuermann *m* -**frau** *f* fireman, firewoman, firefighter.
feuern *vt vi* to fire.
Feuerversicherung *f* fire insurance.
Feuerwehr *f* fire brigade.
Feuerwehrwagen *n* fire engine, fire truck.
Feuerwerk *n* fireworks.
Feuerzeug *n* cigarette lighter.
feurig *adj* fiery.
Fichte *f* spruce, pine.
Fieber *n* fever.
fieberhaft *adj* feverish.
Figur *f* figure; chess piece.
Fiktion *f* fiction.
fiktiv *adj* fictitious.
Filiale *f* branch; subsidiary.

Film *m* film.
filmen *vt vi* to film.
Filter *m* filter.
filtern *vt* to filter.
Filz *m* felt.
Filzstift *m* felt-tip (pen).
Finanz *f* finance.
Finanzamt *n* Inland (US Internal) Revenue.
finanziell *adj* financial.
finanzieren *vt* to finance.
Finanzminister *m* finance minister; Chancellor of the Exchequer (Brit); Treasury Secretary (US).
Finanzministerium *n* finance ministry; Exchequer (Brit); Treasury Department (US).
finden *vt* to find; to think, believe; * *vr* to be (located).
Finger *m* finger.
Fingerabdruck *m* fingerprint.
Fingerhut *m* thimble, foxglove.
Fingernagel *m* fingernail.
Finke *f* finch.
Finne *m* **Finnin** *f* Finn.
finnisch *adj* Finnish.
Finnland *n* Finland.
finster *adj* dark, gloomy.
Finsternis *f* darkness.
Firma *f* company.
Fisch *m* fish.
fischen *vt vi* to fish.
Fischermann *m* fisherman.
Fischfang *m* fishing.
Fischhändler *m* fishmonger.
fischig *adj* fishy.
fix *adj* fixed; clever.
flach *adj* flat; shallow.
Fläche *f* surface; area.
flackern *vi* to flicker; to flare.
Flagge *f* flag.
Flamme *f* flame.
flammen *vi* to blaze.
Flanke *f* flank; wing (football, etc).
Flasche *f* bottle.
Flaschenöffner *m* bottle opener.
flattern *vi* to flutter.
flau *adj* weak.
Flaute *f* calm; recession.

Fleck *m* spot; stain.
Fledermaus *f* bat.
flehen *vi* to implore.
Fleisch *n* flesh; meat.
fleißig *adj* hard-working.
Flieder *m* lilac.
Fliege *f* fly; bow tie.
fliegen *vt vi* to fly.
Fliegenpilz *m* toadstool.
Flieger *m* flier.
fliehen *vt vi* to flee.
Fliese *f* tile.
Fließband *n* conveyor belt.
fließen *vi* to flow.
fließend *adj* flowing; fluent.
flimmern *vi* to glitter.
flink *adj* quick, agile.
Flinte *f* rifle.
Flitterwochen *pl* honeymoon.
Flocke *f* flake.
Floh *m* flea.
Florenz *n* Florence.
Flöte *f* flute.
Fluch *m* curse.
fluchen *vi* to curse, swear.
Flucht *f* flight.
flüchten *vi* to flee.
flüchtig *adj* fugitive; fleeting.
Flüchtling *m* refugee.
Flug *m* flight.
Flugblatt *n* leaflet.
Flügel *m* wing; grand piano.
Fluggast *m* (air) passenger.
Fluggesellschaft *f* airline.
Flughafen *m* airport.
Flugzeug *n* aircraft.
Flugzeugträger *m* aircraft carrier.
Flur *m* hall.
Fluß *m* river; flow.
flüssig *adj* liquid.
Flüssigkeit *f* liquid, fluid.
flüstern *vi vt* to whisper.
Flut *f* flood; high tide.
fluten *vi* to flood.
Folge *f* result; series; sequence.
folgen *vi* to follow.
folglich *adv* consequently.
folgsam *adj* obedient.
Folie *f* foil, film.
Folter *f* torture.
foltern *vt* to torture.

Fön m hair drier.
Fonds m fund.
Fontäne f fountain.
Förderband n conveyor belt.
fordern vt to demand.
fördern vt to promote, encourage.
Forderung f demand.
Förderung f promotion, encouragement.
Forelle f trout.
Form f form, shape; mould.
Formalität f formality.
Format n format; importance.
formatieren vt to format.
Formation f formation.
Formel f formula.
formell adj formal.
formen vt to form.
förmlich adj formal; literal.
formlos adj shapeless; informal.
Formular n form.
formulieren vt to formulate.
forschen vi to investigate, research.
Forscher(in) m(f) researcher, scientist.
Forschung f research.
Forst m forest.
fort adv away; gone; on(wards).
fortan adv from now on.
Fortbestand m continuance.
fortbestehen vi to continue, survive.
fortbewegen vt to move on, away.
Fortbildung f further education.
fortdauern vi to continue.
fortfahren vi to drive on; to leave.
fortgehen vi to go away, continue.
fortgeschritten adj advanced.
fortleben vi to survive.
fortpflanzen vt vr to reproduce.
Fortschritt m progress.
fortsetzen vt to continue.
Fortsetzung f continuation.
Foto n photo(graph).

Fotoapparat m camera.
Fotograf(in) m(f) photographer.
Fotografie f photograph(y).
fotografieren vt to photograph; * vi to take photographs.
fotografisch adj photographic.
Fotokopie f photocopy.
fotokopieren vt to photocopy.
Fracht f freight.
Frack m tails.
Frage f question.
fragen vt vi to ask.
Fragezeichen n question mark.
fraglich adj questionable, doubtful.
fragwürdig adj questionable, dubious.
Fraktion f parliamentary group.
frankieren vt to frank.
franko adv post-paid.
Frankreich n France.
Franzose m Frenchman.
Französin f Frenchwoman.
französisch adj French.
Frau f woman; wife; Mrs, Ms.
Fräulein n young woman; Miss, Ms.
frech adj cheeky.
Frechheit f cheek.
frei adj free; freelance.
freigebig adj generous.
freihalten vt keep free.
Freihandel m free trade.
Freiheit f freedom.
Freikörperkultur f nudism.
freilassen vt to release.
Freilassung f release.
freilich adv certainly.
freimachen vt to frank.
Freimaurer m freemason.
freisprechen vt to acquit.
Freispruch m acquittal.
freistellen vt to exempt.
Freitag m Friday.
freiwillig adj voluntary; * adv voluntarily.
Freiwillige(r) mf volunteer.
Freizeit f free time.

fremd *adj* strange, foreign.

Fremde(r) *mf* stranger, foreigner.

Fremdsprache *f* foreign language.

Frequenz *f* frequency.

fressen *vt vi* to eat, guzzle.

Freude *f* joy.

freudig *adj* joyful.

freuen *vt* to please; **es freut mich** I am glad; * *vr* to be happy; to look forward.

Freund *m* friend, boyfriend.

Freundin *f* friend, girlfriend.

freundlich *adj* friendly.

Freundschaft *f* friendship.

Frieden *m* peace.

Friedhof *m* cemetery.

friedlich *adj* peaceful.

frieren *vt vi* to freeze.

Frikadelle *f* meatball.

frisch *adj* fresh.

Frische *f* freshness.

Friseur *m* **Friseuse** *f* hairdresser.

Frist *f* period; time limit, deadline.

fristlos *adj* without notice.

froh, fröhlich *adj* happy.

fromm *adj* devout, pious.

Frömmigkeit *f* piety.

Front *f* front.

Frosch *m* frog.

Frost *m* frost.

frostig *adj* frosty.

Frucht *f* fruit; corn.

fruchtbar *adj* fruitful.

fruchtlos *adj* fruitless.

Fruchtsaft *m* fruit juice.

früh *adj adv* early; in the morning.

Frühjahr *n* **Frühling** *m* spring.

Frühstück *n* breakfast.

frühzeitig *adj* early, premature.

Frustration *f* frustration.

frustrieren *vt* to frustrate.

Fuchs *m* fox.

Füchsin *f* vixen.

fügen *vt* to place; to ordain; * *vr* to comply, adapt.

fügsam *adj* obedient.

fühlbar *adj* tangible.

fühlen *vt vi vr* to feel.

führen *vt vi* to lead; to manage; * *vr* to behave.

Führer *m* leader.

Führerschein *m* driver's licence.

Führung *f* leadership, management.

füllen *vt* to fill.

Fund *m* find.

Fundbüro *n* lost property office.

fünf *num* five.

fünfte(r,s) *adj* fifth.

Fünftel *n* fifth.

fünfzehn *num* fifteen.

fünfzig *num* fifty.

Funk *m* radio.

Funke *m* spark.

funkeln *vi* sparkle.

Funkgerät *n* radio (set).

Funkstation *f* radio station.

Funktion *f* function.

funktionell *adj* functional.

funktionieren *vi* to function.

für *prep* for; **Tag ~ Tag** day after day; **was ~** what kind of; **das Für und Wider** the pros and cons.

Furcht *f* fear.

furchtbar *adj* fearful, dreadful.

fürchten *vt* to fear; * *vr* to be afraid.

fürchterlich *adj* terrible.

furchtlos *adj* fearless.

furchtsam *adj* timid.

fürs = **für das**.

Fürsorge *f* care; welfare.

Fürsprache *f* recommendation, advocacy.

Fürst *m* prince.

Fürstentum *n* principality.

Fürstin *f* princess.

Fusion *f* fusion, merger.

Fuß *m* foot.

Fußball *m* football.

Fußboden *m* floor.

Fußgänger(in) *m(f)* pedestrian.

Fußnote *f* footnote.

Fußspur *f* footprint.
Fußtritt *m* footstep; kick.
füttern *vt* to feed.

G

Gabe *f* gift.
Gabel *f* fork.
Gabelung *f* fork (in road).
gaffen *vi* to gape.
gähnen *vi* to yawn.
galant *adj* gallant.
Galerie *f* gallery.
Galgen *m* gallows.
Galopp *m* gallop.
galoppieren *vi* to gallop.
Gang *m* walk; operation; corridor; gangway; aisle; gear; **in ~ bringen/setzen** start up; **in ~ sein** be underway.
gängig *adj* current.
Gans *f* goose.
Gänseblümchen *n* daisy.
ganz *adj* all; whole; * *adv* very; completely.
gänzlich *adj* complete; * *adv* completely.
ganztägig *adj* all-day, full-time.
gar *adj* well cooked; *adv* absolutely; **~ nicht** not at all; **~ nichts** nothing at all.
Garage *f* garage.
Garantie *f* guarantee.
garantieren *vt* to guarantee.
Garbe *f* sheaf.
Garde *f* guard.
Garderobe *f* wardrobe; cloakroom.
Gardine *f* curtain.
gären *vi* to ferment.
Garten *m* garden.
Gartenarbeit *f* gardening.
Gärtner(in) *m(f)* gardener.
Gärung *f* fermentation.
Gas *n* gas; **~ geben** to accelerate.
Gasmaske *f* gasmask.
Gaspedal *n* accelerator, gas pedal.

Gasse *f* street, alley.
Gast *f* guest.
Gastarbeiter(in) *m(f)* foreign worker.
gastfreundlich *adj* hospitable.
Gastfreundschaft *f* hospitality.
Gastgeber(in) *m(f)* host, hostess.
Gasthaus *n*, **Gasthof** *m* hotel.
gastronomisch *adj* gastronomic.
Gaststätte *f* restaurant.
Gastwirt *m* landlord, hotelier.
Gaswerk *n* gasworks.
Gaszähler *m* gas meter.
Gatte *m* **Gattin** *f* spouse.
Gattung *f* type, genus.
gaukeln *vi* to juggle, do tricks.
Gauner *m* swindler.
Gebäck *n* pastry.
Gebärde *f* gesture.
gebärden, gebaren *vr* to behave.
gebären *vt* to give birth to.
Gebärmutter *f* womb.
Gebäude *n* building.
geben *vt* to give; to deal (cards); **es gibt** there is/are; * *vr* to behave.
Geber(in) *m(f)* giver.
Gebet *n* prayer.
Gebiet *n* area.
gebieten *vt* to command.
Gebilde *n* object; structure.
gebildet *adj* educated.
Gebinde *n* bundle.
Gebirge *n* mountains.
Gebiß *n* teeth; dentures.
geboren *adj* born; née.
geborgen *adj* safe.
Geborgenheit *f* safety.
Gebot *n* commandment; bid.
Gebrauch *m* use; custom.
gebrauchen *vt* to use.
gebräuchlich *adj* customary.
Gebrauchsanweisung *f* instructions (for use).
gebrauchsfertig *adj* ready for use, instant.
gebraucht *adj* used.
gebrochen *adj* broken.

Gebrüder *pl* brothers.
Gebühr *f* fee.
Geburt *f* birth.
Geburtenbeschränkung, - kontrolle *f* birth control.
Geburtsdatum *n* date of birth.
Geburtsort *m* place of birth.
Geburtstag *m* birthday.
Geburtsurkunde *f* birth certificate.
Gedächtnis *n* memory.
Gedanke *m* thought.
gedeihen *vi* to thrive, flourish.
gedenken *vi* to think of.
Gedicht *n* poem.
gedrängt *adj* crowded, compressed.
gedrückt *adj* depressed.
Geduld *f* patience.
geduldig *adj* patient.
geehrt *adj* honoured; **sehr geehrte Herr ...** Dear Mr ....
geeignet *adj* suitable.
Gefahr *f* danger; risk.
gefährden *vt* to endanger.
gefährlich *adj* dangerous.
Gefalle *n* slope.
Gefallen *m* favour, kindness; * *n* pleasure.
gefallen *vi* to please; **es gefällt mir** I like it.
gefällig *adj* pleasant.
gefangen *adj* captive.
Gefangene(r) *mf* prisoner.
gefangenhalten *vt* to keep prisoner.
Gefangenschaft *f* captivity.
Gefängnis *n* prison.
Gefängnisstrafe *f* prison sentence.
Gefängniszelle *f* prison cell.
Gefäß *n* container.
gefaßt *adj* calm; *prep*ared.
Gefecht *n* fight(ing).
Geflügel *n* poultry.
gefräßig *adj* greedy.
gefrieren *vi* to freeze.
Gefrierpunkt *m* freezing point.
Gefrierschutzmittel *n* antifreeze.
Gefriertruhe *f* deep-freeze.
Gefüge *n* joints; structure.

gefügig *adj* pliable; docile.
Gefühl *n* feeling.
gefühlsmäßig *adj* emotional; instinctive.
gegebenenfalls *adv* if necessary.
gegen *prep* towards; against; about; in return for; versus.
Gegend *f* area.
gegeneinander *adv* against one another.
Gegensatz *m* contrast; contrary.
gegensätzlich *adj* contrary.
gegenseitig *adj* mutual.
Gegenspieler *m* opponent.
Gegenstand *m* object.
Gegenteil *n* opposite; **im ~ on** the contrary.
gegenüber *adv* opposite; * *prep* opposite, towards, in the face of.
Gegenwart *f* present.
gegenwärtig *adj* present.
Gegner *m* opponent.
gegnerisch *adj* opposing.
Gegnerschaft *f* opposition.
Gehackte(s) *n* mince.
Gehalt *m* contents; salary.
Gehäuse *n* case.
geheim *adj* secret.
Geheimdienst *m* secret service.
geheimhalten *vt* to keep secret.
Geheimhaltung *f* confidentiality.
Geheimnis *n* secret.
gehen *vt vi* to go; to walk; ~ **um** to be about, relate to; **wie geht's?** how are you?.
Gehilfe *m* Gehilfin *f* assistant.
Gehirn *n* brain.
Gehölz *n* wood, copse.
Gehör *n* hearing.
gehorchen *vi* to obey.
gehören *vi* to belong to.
gehörig *adj* belonging to; appropriate.
gehorsam *adj* obedient.
Gehorsam *m* obedience, submission.

Gehsteig, Gehweg m pavement.
Geier m vulture.
Geige f violin.
Geiger(in) m(f) violinist.
geil adj randy.
Geisel f hostage.
Geist m spirit, mind; ghost.
geistkrank adj mentally ill.
geistig adj intellectual.
geistlich adj spiritual.
Geistliche(r) mf priest.
Geistlichkeit f clergy.
Geiz m meanness.
Geizhals m miser.
geizig adj mean.
gekonnt adj clever.
Gelächter n laughter.
geladen adj loaded; live (wire).
Gelände n (area of) land.
Geländer n railings, banisters.
gelangen vi to reach.
gelassen adj calm.
Gelassenheit f calmness.
geläufig adj fluent; common.
gelaunt adj: **gut/schlecht ~** in a good/bad mood.
gelb adj yellow.
Geld n money.
Geldautomat m cashpoint.
Geldbeutel m Geldbörse f purse.
Geldstrafe f fine.
Geldstück n coin.
Gelee m or n jelly.
gelegen adj located; convenient.
Gelegenheit f opportunity; occasion.
Gelegenheitsarbeit f casual work.
gelegentlich adj occasional; * dv occasionally.
gelehrt adj learned.
Gelehrte(r) mf scholar.
Geleit n escort.
geleiten vt to escort.
Gelenk n joint.
gelernt adj skilled.
gelingen vi to succeed; **es gelang mir** I succeeded.
geloben vt to promise.

Gelöbnis n promise.
gelten vt to be worth; * vi to be valid, apply.
Geltung f validity.
gelungen adj successful.
Gemälde n painting.
gemäß prep in accordance with.
gemäßigt adj moderate.
gemein adj common.
Gemeinde f district.
Gemeindewahl f local election.
gemeinsam adj joint, common.
Gemeinschaft f community.
Gemisch n mixture.
gemischt adj mixed.
Gemüse n vegetables.
Gemüt n nature, temperament.
gemütlich adj cosy, comfortable.
Gemütlichkeit f cosiness, comfort.
Gen n gene.
genau adj exact; * adv exactly.
Genauigkeit f accuracy.
genauso adv just the same.
genehm adj acceptable.
genehmigen vt to approve, allow.
Genehmigung f approval, authorisation.
geneigt adj inclined.
Generation f generation.
Generator m generator.
generell adj general.
genesen vi to recover.
Genf n Geneva; **~er See** Lake Geneva.
genial adj brilliant.
Genick n neck.
Genie n genius.
genießen vt to enjoy; to eat.
Genosse m **Genossin** f companion.
Genossenschaft f cooperative (society).
Genua n Genoa.
genug adj adv enough.
genügen vi to suffice.
Genugtuung f satisfaction.
Genuß m pleasure; enjoyment; consumption.
genußreich adj enjoyable.

Geograph *m* geographer.
Geographie *f* geography.
geographisch *adj* geographical.
Geologe *m* geologist.
Geologie *f* geology.
geologisch *adj* geological.
Gepäck *n* baggage.
Gepäckausgabe, Gepäckaufbewahrung *f* left luggage.
Gepäckträger *m* porter.
gepflegt *adj* smart.
Gepflogenheit *f* habit.
gerade *adj* straight; * *adv* exactly; especially; even (number); just (about).
geradeaus *adv* straight on.
geradezu *adv* almost.
Gerät *n* tool, (item of) equipment.
geraten *vi* toturn out; to come; to prosper.
geraum *adj*: **geraume Zeit** a long time.
geräumig *adj* spacious.
Geräusch *n* noise.
geräuschlos *adj* noiseless.
geräuschvoll *adj* noisy.
gerecht *adj* fair.
Gerechtigkeit *f* justice.
Gerede *n* talk.
geregelt *adj* regular.
gereizt *adj* irritated.
Gereiztheit *f* irritation.
Gericht *n* dish, course; court.
gerichtlich *adj* judicial.
Gerichtshof *m* court.
gering *adj* little, slight.
geringfügig *adj* minor, slight.
gern(e) *adv* willingly; ~ **haben, mögen, tun** to like; **ich schwimme** ~ I like swimming.
Gerste *f* barley.
Geruch *m* smell.
Gerücht *n* rumour.
Gerüst *n* scaffolding, frame(work).
gesamt *adj* whole; total.
Gesamtheit *f* totality.
Gesamtschule *f* comprehen-

sive school.
Gesandte(r) *m* **Gesandtin** *f* envoy.
Gesang *m* singing, song.
Geschäft *n* business; transaction; shop.
geschäftig *adj* busy.
geschäftlich *adj* commercial, business.
Geschäftsanteil *m* share.
Geschäftsfrau *f* businesswoman.
Geschäftsführer *m* director.
Geschäftsführung *f* management.
Geschäftsjahr *n* financial year.
Geschäftsleiter *m* manager.
Geschäftsleitung *f* management.
Geschäftsmann *m* businessman.
Geschäftsverkehr *m* business (dealings).
Geschäftszeichen *n* reference number.
Geschäftszeit *f* business or opening hours.
geschehen *vi* to happen.
gescheit *adj* clever.
Geschenk *n* gift.
Geschichte *f* story; history.
geschichtlich *adj* historic(al); * *adv* historically.
Geschick *n* destiny; skill.
geschickt *adj* skilful.
geschieden *adj* divorced.
Geschirr *n* crockery, kitchen utensils; harness.
Geschirrspülmaschine *f* dishwasher.
Geschirrtuch *n* dishcloth.
Geschlecht *n* sex, gender; species.
geschlechtlich *adj* sexual.
Geschlechtskrankheit *f* venereal disease.
Geschlechtsverkehr *m* sexual intercourse.
geschlossen *adj* closed.
Geschmack *m* taste.
geschmacklos *adj* tasteless.
geschmacksvoll *adj* tasteful.

Geschöpf *n* creature.
Geschoß *n* projectile; floor, storey.
Geschrei *n* shouting.
Geschütz *n* gun.
Geschwader *n* squadron.
geschweige *adj conj* ~ **denn** not to mention.
Geschwindigkeit *f* speed.
Geschwindigkeitsgrenze *f* speed limit.
Geschwindigkeitsmesser *m* speedometer.
Geschwister *pl* brother(s) and sister(s).
Geschworene(r) *mf* juror; **die Geschworenen** *pl* the jury.
Geselle *m* companion.
gesellig *adj* sociable.
Geselligkeit *f* sociability.
Gesellschaft *f* company; society.
gesellschaftlich *adj* social.
Gesetz *n* law.
Gesetzgebung *f* legislation.
gesetzlich *adj* legal, statutory.
gesetzlos *adj* lawless.
gesetzmäßig *adj* legal.
gesetzwidrig *adj* illegal.
Gesicht *n* face.
Gesichtspunkt *m* point of view.
gesinnt *adj* disposed.
Gesinnung *f* disposition.
Gespann *n* team.
gespannt *adj* tight; in suspense.
Gespenst *n* ghost.
gespensterhaft *adj* ghostly.
Gespinst *n* tissue, fabric.
Gespött *n* mockery.
Gespräch *n* talk, conversation.
gesprächig *adj* talkative.
Gesprechspartner *m* interlocutor.
Gestalt *f* shape; figure.
gestalten *vt* to form; to design; * *vr* to turn out.
Gestalter(in) *m(f)* designer.
Gestaltung *f* formation; arrangement.
Geständnis *n* confession.
gestatten *vt* to allow.

Geste *f* gesture.
gestehen *vt vi* to confess.
Gestein *n* rock.
Gestell *n* frame.
gestern *adv* yesterday.
Gestirn *n* star; constellation.
gestrichen *adj* cancelled.
Gesuch *n* request.
gesucht *adj* sought-after.
gesund *adj* healthy.
Gesundheit *f* health.
Gesundung *f* recovery.
Getränk *n* drink.
Getreide *n* corn; grain, cereals.
Getriebe *n* gears, gearbox.
geübt *adj* experienced.
Geübtheit *f* skill, experience.
Gewächs *n* growth; plant.
Gewächshaus *n* greenhouse.
gewagt *adj* daring.
gewählt *adj* selected.
gewahren *vt* to perceive.
Gewähr *f* guarantee.
gewähren *vt* to grant.
gewährleisten *vt* to guarantee.
Gewährleistung *f* guarantee.
Gewahrsam *m/n* safekeeping; custody.
Gewalt *f* power; violence.
gewaltig *adj* huge.
gewalttätig *adj* violent.
gewandt *adj* agile, skilful.
Gewebe *n* fabric, tissue.
Gewehr *n* gun.
Gewerbe *n* occupation; industry.
gewerblich *adj* commercial, industrial.
Gewerkschaft *f* trade union.
Gewicht *n* weight.
gewichtig *adj* heavy.
gewiegt *adj* experienced.
gewillt *adj* willing.
Gewinn *n* profit.
gewinnbringend *adj* profitable.
gewinnen *vt vi* to win.
Gewinner(in) *m(f)* winner.
Gewinnung *f* winning; extraction.
gewiß *adj* certain; * *adv* certainly.

Gewissen n conscience.

gewissenhaft adj conscientious.

gewissenlos adj unscrupulous.

gewissermaßen adv as it were; to an extent.

Gewißheit f certainty.

Gewitter n (thunder)storm.

gewöhnen vt to accustom; * vr to become used to.

Gewohnheit f habit.

gewöhnlich adj usual: * adv usually.

gewohnt adj usual; used to.

gewollt adj deliberate.

Gewürz n spice.

Gezeiten pl tide.

gezielt adj deliberate; specific.

Gier f greed, eagerness.

gierig adj greedy.

gießen vt vi to pour.

Gießkanne f watering can.

Gift m poison.

giftig adj poisonous.

Gigant m giant.

Gipfel m summit.

Gips m gypsum; plaster.

gipsen vt to plaster.

Gipser m plasterer.

Giraffe f giraffe.

Giro n giro.

Girobank f clearing bank.

Girokonto n current account.

Gitarre f guitar.

Gitter n grille, grating.

Glanz m brightness; glory.

glänzen vt to polish; * vi to gleam.

glänzend adj briliant.

Glas n glass.

Glaser m glazier.

gläsern adj glassy.

glatt adj smooth; * adv smoothly.

Glatteis n (black) ice.

Glatze f bald patch, bald head.

Glauben m belief.

glauben vt vi to believe.

glaubhaft adj credible.

gläubig adj believing.

Gläubiger(in) m(f) creditor.

glaublich, glaubwürdig adj credible.

gleich adj same; * adv equally; immediately; * prep like.

gleichartig adj similar.

gleichbedeutend adj synonymous.

gleichberechtigt adj having equal rights.

Gleichberechtigung f equality.

gleichdenkend adj likeminded.

gleichen vi to be equal to; to resemble.

gleichfalls adv also.

gleichgesinnt adj like-minded.

Gleichgewicht n balance.

gleichgültig adj indifferent; **das ist mir ~** it's all the same to me.

Gleichgültigkeit f indifference.

Gleichheit f equality.

gleichkommen vi to equal.

gleichlautend adj similar.

gleichmachen vt to equalise.

gleichmäßig adj proportionate; uniform.

Gleichmäßigkeit f uniformity.

gleichmütig adj even-tempered.

gleichsam adv as it were.

gleichsehen vi to resemble.

Gleichstrom m direct current.

Gleichung f equation.

gleichwertig adj equivalent.

gleichzeitig adj simultaneous.

Gleis n track; platform.

gleiten vi to glide; to slide.

Gletscher m glacier.

Glied n member; limb.

Gliederung f structure; classification.

glimmen vi to smoulder, glimmer.

Globus m globe.

Glocke f bell.

Glück n luck; happiness; ~ **haben** to succeed; **viel ~** good luck.

glücklich adj fortunate; happy; * adv fortunately.

glücklicherweise *adv* fortunately.

glückselig *adj* ecstatic.

Glückwunsch *m* best wishes.

Glückwunschkarte *f* greetings card.

Glühbirne *f* light bulb.

glühen *vi* to glow.

glühend *adj* glowing.

Glühwein *m* mulled wine.

Gnade *f* grace, favour; mercy.

gnädig *adj* gracious.

Gold *n* gold.

golden *adj* golden.

goldfarbig *adj* gold(-coloured).

Goldfisch *m* goldfish.

Goldschmied *m* goldsmith.

Golf *m* gulf; * *n* golf.

Golfball *m* golfball.

Golfplatz *m* golf course.

Golfschläger *m* golf club.

Golfspieler(in) *m(f)* golfer.

gönnen *vt* to allow.

Gorilla *m* gorilla.

Gott *m* god, God; **Grüß ~** hallo.

Gottesdienst *m* service.

Göttin *f* goddess.

göttlich *adj* divine.

Götze *m* idol.

Grab *n* grave.

graben *vt vi* to dig.

Graben *m* ditch.

Grabstein *m* gravestone.

Grad *m* degree.

Graf *m* count; earl.

Gräfin *f* countess.

Gram *m* grief.

grämen *vt vr* to grieve.

Gramm *n* gramme.

Grammatik *f* grammar.

grammatisch *adj* grammatical.

Gran *n* grain.

Granate *f* grenade.

Granit *m* granite.

Graphik *f* graphics.

graphisch *adj* graphic; * *adv* graphically.

Gras *n* grass.

grasen *vi* to graze.

gräßlich *adj* horrible.

Grat *m* ridge.

Gräte *f* fishbone.

gratulieren *vi* to congratulate.

grau *adj* grey.

grausam *adj* cruel.

Grausamkeit *f* cruelty.

gravieren *vt* to engrave.

Gravitation *f* gravitation.

Gravüre *f* engraving.

greifbar *adj* tangible.

greifen *vt* to grip.

Greis *m* old man.

grell *adj* shrill; garish.

Gremium *n* body, group.

Grenze *f* boundary, frontier, edge.

grenzen *vi* to adjoin.

grenzenlos *adj* boundless.

Greuel *m* horror.

greulich *adj* horrible.

Griecher *m* **Griechin** *f* Greek.

Griechenland *n* Greece.

griechisch *adj* Greek.

Griff *m* grasp, hold; lever; handle.

Grill *m* grill.

Grille *f* cricket; whim.

grillen *vt* to grill.

Grinsen *n* grin.

grinsen *vi* to grin.

Grippe *f* flu.

grob *adj* coarse; gross.

Groll *m* grudge.

grollen *vi* to sulk.

Gros *n* gross; majority.

Groschen *m* 10-pfenning coin.

groß *adj* great; large; tall; *adj* greatly, highly.

großartig *adj* great.

Großbritannien *n* (Great) Britain.

Großbuchstabe *m* capital (letter).

Größe *f* size; quantity.

Großeltern *pl* grandparents.

großenteils *adv* largely.

Großhandel *m* wholesale (trade).

Großhändler, Grossist *m* wholesaler.

Großmut *f* generosity.

großmütig *adj* generous.

Großmutter *f* grandmother.

Großstadt *f* city.
größtenteils *adv* mainly.
großtun *vi* to boast.
Großvater *m* grandfather.
großzügig *adj* large-scale; generous.
Großzügigkeit *f* grandness; generosity.
grotesk *adj* grotesque.
Grube *f* pit, mine.
grün *adj* green.
Grund *m* ground; reason.
Grundbesitz *m* property.
gründen *vt* to establish; * *vr* ~ **auf** to be based on.
Gründer(in) *m(f)* founder.
Grundgesetz *n* constitution.
Grundlage *f* basis.
grundlegend *adj* fundamental.
gründlich *adj* thorough.
grundlos *adj* groundless.
Grundriß *m* ground-plan, layout.
Grundsatz *m* principle.
grundsätzlich *adj* fundamental; * *adv* fundametally.
Grundschule *f* primary school.
Grundstück *n* (piece of) land.
Gründung *f* foundation.
grunzen *vt vi* to grunt.
Gruppe *f* group.
gruppieren *vt* to group.
Gruß *m* greeting; salute; **mit freundlichen Grüßen** yours sincerely; **viele Grüße** best wishes.
grüßen *vt* to greet, welcome; to salute.
gucken *vi* to look, peep.
gültig *adj* valid.
Gültigkeit *f* validity.
Gummi *m* or *n* rubber.
Gummiband *n* rubber band; elastic.
Gunst *f* favour.
günstig *adj* favourable.
Gurgel *f* throat.
gurgeln *vt vi* to gurgle, gargle.
Gurke *f* cucumber, gherkin.
Gurt, Gürtel *m* belt.
Guß *m* founding, casting; downpour.
Gußeisen *n* cast iron.
gut *adj* good; **also** ~ OK then; * *adv* well; **gut 30 Minuten** a good 30 minutes; **na** ~ alright then; **laß es** ~ **sein** that will do; ~ **so!** well done!; **schon** ~! never mind.
Gut *n* good(s); property.
Gutachten *n* assessment, valuation.
gutartig *adj* good-natured.
gutaussehend *adj* good-looking.
Güte *f* goodness.
Güterzug *m* goods train.
guterhalten *adj* well-preserved.
gutgelaunt *adj* cheerful.
gutgemeint *adj* well-meant.
Guthaben *n* credit balance; account.
gutheißen *vt* to approve of.
gutherzig *adj* good-natured.
gütig *adj* kind.
gütlich *adj* amicable.
gutmachen *vt* to repair; to compensate.
gutmütig *adj* good-natured.
Gutschein *m* voucher; credit note.
gutschreiben *vt* to credit.
Gutschrift *f* credit.
guttun *vi* to do good.
Gymnasium *n* secondary school.
Gymnastik *f* gymnastics.
Gynäkologe *m* gynaecologist.
Gynäkologie *f* gynaecology.

H

Haag: Den ~ The Hague.
Haar *n* hair.
Haarbürste *f* hairbrush.
haarig *adj* hairy.
Haarschnitt *m* haircut.
haben *vt v aux* to have.

hacken *vt vi* to chop.
Hackfleisch *n* mince.
Hafen *m* port, harbour.
Hafer *m* oats.
Haft *f* custody.
haftbar *adj* liable.
Haftbarkeit *f* liability.
haften *vi* to stick, persist; to be liable.
Haftpflicht *f* liability.
Haftschalen *pl* contact lenses.
Haftung *f* adhesion; liability.
Hagel *m* hail.
Hahn *m* cock, rooster; tap.
Hähnchen *n* cockerel; chicken.
Hai *m* shark.
Hain *m* copse.
Haken *m* hook.
Hakenkreuz *n* swastika.
halb *adj adv* half; **~ vier** half past three.
Halbfinale *n* semi-final.
halbieren *vt* to halve.
Halbinsel *f* peninsula.
halbjährig *adj* six-monthly.
Halbkreis *m* semicircle.
Halbkugel *f* hemisphere.
Halbmond *m* half-moon, crescent.
halboffen *adj* half-open, ajar.
halbrund *adj* semicircular.
Halbtagsarbeit *f* part-time work.
Halbton *m* semitone.
halbwegs *adv* halfway.
halbwüchsig *adj* adolescent.
Halbwüchsige(r) *mf* adolescent, teenager.
Hälfte *f* half.
Halle *f* hall.
hallen *vi* to echo.
Hals *m* neck, throat.
Halskette *f* necklace.
Halsschmerzen *pl* sore throat.
Halstuch *n* scarf.
Halt *m* hold; stop.
halt *adv* just; * *excl* ~! stop!
haltbar *adj* lasting.
Haltbarkeit *f* durability.
halten *vt* to hold; to keep; to contain; **~ für** to consider; **~ von** to think of; * *vi* to stop;

to last; * *vr* to last.
Haltestelle *f* stop.
haltlos *adj* unstable.
Haltlosigkeit *f* instability.
haltmachen *vi* to stop.
Haltung *f* attitude; posture.
Hammer *m* hammer.
hämmern *vt vi* to hammer.
Hand *f* hand.
Handarbeit *f* manual work; needlework.
Handbremse *f* handbrake.
Handbuch *n* manual.
Händedruck *m* handshake.
Handel *m* trade, commerce; deal.
handeln *vi* to act; to trade; * *vr* **sich ~ um** to be a matter of.
Handelsbilanz *f* balance of trade.
Handelsgericht *n* commercial court.
Handelsgesetzbuch *n* commercial code.
Handelskammer *f* Chamber of Commerce.
Handelsrecht *n* commercial law.
Handelsregister *n* companies register.
Handgelenk *n* wrist.
handgemacht *adj* handmade.
Handgepäck *n* hand baggage.
handhaben *vt* to handle.
Händler(in) *m(f)* dealer; shopkeeper.
handlich *adj* handy.
Handlung *f* action; shop.
Handschrift *f* handwriting.
Handschuh *m* glove.
Handtasche *f* handbag.
Handtuch *n* towel.
Handvoll *f* handful.
Handwerk *n* craft, trade.
Handwerker *m* artisan.
Hang *m* slope.
hängen *vt vi* to hang.
Hannover *n* Hanover.
Harfe *f* harp.
Harke *f* rake.
harmlos *adj* harmless.
Harmonie *f* harmony.

harmonisch *adj* harmonious.
Harn *m* urine.
harnen *vi* to urinate.
harren *vi* to wait.
hart *adj* hard.
Härte *f* hardness.
härten *vt vi* to harden.
hartgekocht *adj* hard-boiled.
hartherzig *adj* hard-hearted.
harthörig *adj* hard of hearing.
hartnäckig *adj* obstinate.
Hase *m* hare.
Haß *m* hatred.
hassen *vt* to hate.
häßlich *adj* ugly, unpleasant.
Hast *f* haste.
hasten *vi* to hurry.
hastig *adj* hurried; * *adv* hurriedly.
Haube *f* hood; bonnet.
Hauch *m* breath; trace.
hauchen *vi* to breathe.
hauen *vt* to cut; to thrash.
häufeln *vt vi* to pile (up).
Haufen *m* pile.
häufen *vt vr* to pile (up).
häufig *adj* frequent; * *adv* frequently, often.
Häufigkeit *f* frequency.
Haupt *n* head; chief.
Haupt- *in compounds* chief, main.
Hauptbahnhof *m* main station.
Hauptmann *m* captain.
Hauptrolle *f* leading role.
Hauptsache *f* main thing.
hauptsächlich *adj* main; * *adv* mainly.
Hauptschule *f* secondary school.
Hauptstadt *f* capital city.
Hauptstrasse *f* main street, major road.
Hauptwort *n* noun.
Haus *n* house; building; **nach ~e** home; **zu ~e** (at) home.
Hausangestellte *f* servant.
Hausarbeit *f* housework; homework.
Hausarzt *m* general practitioner.

Hausaufgabe *f* homework.
Häusermakler *m* estate agent.
Hausfrau *f* housewife.
Hausgarten *m* back garden.
hausgemacht *adj* home-made.
Haushalt *m* household; budget.
häuslich *adj* domestic.
Hausschuh *m* slipper.
Haustier *n* pet.
Hauswirt *m* landlord.
Haut *f* skin.
Hebel *m* lever.
heben *vt* to lift.
Hecke *f* hedge.
Heer *n* army.
Hefe *f* yeast.
Heft *n* handle; notebook; issue.
heften *vt* to attach.
heftig *adj* strong, intense.
Heftklammer *f* paper clip.
Heftmaschine *f* stapler.
Heftpflaster *n* sticking plaster.
Heftzwecke *f* drawing pin.
hegen *vt* to tend; to harbour (grudge, etc).
Heide *m* **Heidin** *f* heathen.
Heide *f* heath, heather.
heikel *adj* fussy; difficult.
Heil *n* well-being.
heil *adj* safe, uninjured.
heilen *vt* to cure; * *vi* to heal.
heilig *adj* holy.
Heilige(r) *mf* saint.
Heiligabend *m* Christmas Eve.
Heiligkeit *f* holiness.
heilsam *adj* beneficial.
Heilung *f* cure.
Heim *n* home.
heim *adv* home.
Heimarbeit *f* homework.
Heimat *f* home(land).
heimisch *adj* home, native.
heimlos *adj* homeless.
heimfahren *vi* to drive (or go) home.
Heimfahrt *f* return journey.
heimgehen *vi* to go home; to pass on (die).
heimisch *adj* home, native; * **sich ~ fühlen** to feel at home.
Heimkehr *f* homecoming.

Heimkunft *f* homecoming.
heimlich *adj* secret; * *adv* secretly.
Heimlichkeit *f* secrecy.
heimsuchen *vt* to afflict; to haunt.
heimwärts *adv* homeward.
Heimweh *n* homesickness.
Heirat *f* marriage.
heiraten *vt vi* to marry.
Heiratsurkunde *f* marriage certificate.
heiser *adj* hoarse.
Heiserkeit *f* hoarseness.
heiß *adj* hot.
heißen *vt* to call; * *vi* to be called; **ich heiße Bob** my name is Bob; to mean; **das heißt** that is (to say).
heißlaufen *vi* to overheat.
heiter *adj* bright; cheerful; sunny.
Heiterkeit *f* cheerfulness.
heizen *vt* to heat.
Heizkörper *m* radiator.
Heizöl *n* fuel oil.
Heizung *f* heating.
hektisch *adj* hectic.
Held(in) *m(f)* hero.
heldenhaft *adj* heroic; * *adv* heriocally.
Heldentum *n* heroism.
helfen *vi* to help.
Helfer(in) *m(f)* helper.
Helium *n* helium.
hell *adj* clear; bright; light (colour).
Helle, Helligkeit *f* brightness.
hellwach *adj* wide awake.
Helm *m* helmet; rudder.
Hemd *m* shirt.
Hemisphäre *f* hemisphere.
hemmen *vt* to obstruct.
Hemmung *f* hindrance; inhibition.
hemmungslos *adj* uninhibited.
Henkel *m* handle.
henken *vt* to hand.
Henker *m* hangman.
Henne *f* hen.
her *adv* here; from; ago.
herab *adv* down(wards).

herabkommen *vi* come down.
herabsetzen *vt* to reduce.
heran *adv* this way; here; near.
herankommen, herannahen *vi* to approach.
heranwachsen *vi* to grow up.
herauf *adv* up(wards), up here.
heraus *adv* out(wards); from.
herausfordern *vt* to challenge.
Herausforderung *f* challenge.
herausgeben *vt* to give up; to publish.
Herausgeber *m* publisher.
herb *adj* bitter.
herbei *adv* here.
herbeiführen *vt* to cause.
Herberge *f* hostel, inn.
Herbst *m* autumn.
Herd *m* hearth; cooker.
Herde *f* herd.
herein *adv* in (here); into; **~!** come in!.
hereingeben *vt* to give.
hereinlassen *vt* to let in.
Hering *m* herring.
herkommen *vi* to approach; **komm her!** come here!; **wo kommen Sie her?** where are you from?
herkömmlich *adj* traditional.
Herkunft *f* origin.
herleiten *vt* to derive, deduce.
hernach *adv* after(wards).
hernehmen *vt* to take (from).
Herr *m* lord; Mr; gentleman; **mein ~** sir.
herrlich *adj* magnificent.
Herrschaft *f* domination; rule.
herrschen *vi* to rule; to prevail.
Herrscher(in) *m(f)* ruler.
herstellen *vt* to produce.
Hersteller(in) *m(f)* manufacturer.
Herstellung *f* production.
herüber *adv* over (here).
herum *adv* around; **um den Tisch ~** round the table.
herunter *adv* down.
hervor *adv* forth, out.
hervorheben *vt* to emphasise.
hervorragend *adj* outstanding.

Herz *n* heart.
Herzanfall, Herzinfarkt *m* heart attack.
herzlich *adj* cordial; **herzliche Grüße** best wishes.
herzlos *adj* heartless.
Herzog *m* duke.
Herzogin *f* duchess.
hetzen *vt* to hunt; * *vi* to hurry.
Heu *n* hay.
Heuchelei *f* hypocrisy.
heucheln *vt* to pretend; * *vi* to be a hypocrite.
heulen *vi* to howl; to hoot; to cry.
Heuschnupfen *m* hay fever.
heute *adv* today.
heutig *adj* present-day.
heutzutage *adv* nowadays.
Hexagon *m* hexagon.
Hexe *f* witch.
Hexerei *f* witchcraft.
Hieb *m* blow; cut.
hier *adv* here; **~ oben** up here; **~ unten** down here.
hierauf *adv* thereupon.
hieraus *adv* from this.
hierbei *adv* at this, herewith.
hierdurch *adv* through here.
hierfür *adv* for this.
hierher *adv* here.
hierin *adv* in this.
hiermit *adv* herewith.
hiernach *adv* after this.
hierüber *adv* over here; about this.
hierum *adv* about this.
hierunter *adv* under this.
hiervon *adv* of this.
hierzu *adv* to this; moreover.
Hilfe *f* help; **erste ~** first aid.
hilflos *adj* helpless.
hilfreich *adj* helpful.
Hilfskraft *f* assistant.
Hilfsmittel *n* aid, means.
Himbeere *f* raspberry.
Himmel *m* sky; heaven.
Himmelfahrt *f* ascension.
hin *adv* there; away; gone; **~ und zurück** there and back; **~ und her** to and fro.
hinauf *adv* up(wards).

hinaufsteigen *vi* to climb.
hinaus *adv* out.
hinausgehen *vi* to leave.
hinauskommen *vi* to come out.
hinauslehnen *vr* to lean out.
hinausschieben *vt* to postpone.
Hinblick *m* **in ~ auf** in view of.
hindern *vt* to hinder.
Hindernis *n* **Hinderung** *f* obstacle.
hindeuten *vi* to point.
hindurch *adv* through.
hinein *adv* in(to).
hineinfallen *vi* to fall in.
hineingehen *vi* to go in.
hineinpassen *vi* to fit in.
hineinreden *vi* to interfere.
hinfahren *vi* to go (there).
hinfallen *vi* to fall.
hinfällig *adj* decrepit.
hinführen *vt vi* to lead (there).
Hingabe *f* devotion.
hingeben *vr* to devote oneself.
hingehen *vi* to go (by).
hinhalten *vt* to hold out.
hinken *vi* to limp.
hinkommen *vi* to arrive (there).
hinlegen *vt* to put down; * *vr* to lie down.
hinnehmen *vt* to accept.
hinreichen *vi* to suffice.
hinreichend *adj* sufficient.
hinreißen *vt* to carry off; to enchant.
hinrichten *vt* to execute.
Hinrichtung *f* execution.
hinschreiben *vt* to write down.
hinsetzen *vt* to put down.
Hinsicht *f* respect, regard.
hinsichtlich *adv* with regard to.
hinten *adv* behind.
hinter *prep* behind.
hintere *adj* rear.
hintereinander *adv* one by one.
hintergehen *vt* to deceive.
Hintergehung *f* deception.
Hintergrund *m* background.
hinterher *adv* behind;

aftwerwards.
hinterlassen *vt* to leave (behind).
Hintertür *f* back door.
hinüber *adv* across.
hinübergehen *vi* to go across.
hinunter *adv* down.
hinunterfahren, hinuntergehen *vi* to go down.
hinweg *adv* away; off.
hinweggehen *vi* to go away.
hinwegkommen *vi* to get over.
hinwegsetzen *vr* to ignore.
Hinweis *m* reference; instruction.
hinweisen *vt* to refer to; * *vi* to point at.
hinwenden *vt vr* to turn (to).
hinzu *adv* there; also.
hinzufügen *vt* to enclose.
Hirn *n* brain.
Hirsch *m* stag.
Hirt *m* herdsman.
hissen *vt* to hoist.
Historiker *m* historian.
historisch *adj* historic; * *adv* historically.
Hitze *f* heat.
Hitzewelle *f* heatwave.
hitzig *adj* hot-headed.
Hobby *n* hobby.
Hobel *m* plane.
hoch *adj* high.
Hochachtung *f* respect.
hochachtungsvoll *adj* yours faithfully.
Hochdeutsch *n* High German.
Hochebene *f* plateau.
hochentwickelt *adj* highly developed.
Hochfrequenz *f* high frequency.
hochgehen *vi* to rise.
hochhalten *vt* to hold up; to respect.
hochheben *vt* to lift.
Hochmut *m* pride.
hochmütig *adj* haughty.
Hochschule *f* college.
Hochsprung *m* high jump.
Hochspringer(in) *m(f)* high-jumper.

höchst *adj* highest; * *adv* highly.
höchstens *adv* at most.
höchstwahrscheinlich *adv* most probably.
Hochwasser *n* high water; flood.
hochwertig *adj* high-quality.
Hochzeit *f* wedding.
Hochzeitskleid *n* wedding dress.
Hochzeitskuchen *m* wedding cake.
Hochzeitsreise *f* honeymoon.
hochziehen *vt* to raise.
hocken *vi* to crouch.
Hocker *m* stool.
Höcker *m* hump.
Hockey *n* hockey.
Hoden *m* testicle.
Hof *n* court(yard); farm.
hoffen *vt vi* to hope.
hoffentlich *adv* hopefully.
Hoffnung *f* hope.
hoffnungslos *adj* hopeless.
hoffnungsvoll *adj* hopeful.
höflich *adj* polite; * *adv* politely.
Höflichkeit *f* politeness.
Höhe *f* height; amount.
Hoheit *f* Highness; sovereignty.
Höhepunkt *m* climax.
höher *adj adv* higher.
hohl *adj* hollow.
Höhle *f* cave.
Hohn *m* scorn.
höhnen *vi* to mock.
höhnisch *adj* scornful.
holen *vt* to fetch, get
Holland *n* Holland.
Holländer(in)   *m(f)* Dutchman(woman).
holländisch *adj* Dutch.
Hölle *f* hell.
höllisch *adj* hellish.
holp(e)rig *adj* bumpy.
holpern *vi* to stumble.
Holz *n* wood.
hölzern *adj* wooden.
Holzfäller *m* woodcutter.
holzig *adj* woody.
Holzkohle *f* charcoal.

homosexuell *adj* homosexual.
Honig *m* honey.
Hopfen *m* hop(s).
Hörapparat *m* hearing aid.
hörbar *adj* audible.
horchen *vi* to listen.
hören *vt vi* to hear; to listen.
Hörer(in) *m(f)* listener; receiver.
Horizont *m* horizon.
horizontal *adj* horizontal.
Hormon *n* hormone.
Hörmuschel *f* earpiece.
Horn *n* horn.
Horoskop *n* horoscope.
Hörsaal *m* lecture hall.
Hörspiel *n* radio play.
horten *vt* to hoard.
Hose *f* trousers.
Hoseträger *m* braces.
Hotel *n* hotel.
hübsch *adj* pretty.
Hubschrauber *m* helicopter.
Huf *m* hoof.
Hufeisen *n* horseshoe.
Hüfte *f* hip.
Hügel *m* hill.
Huhn *n* hen, chicken.
huldigen *vi* to pay homage to.
Hülle *f* covering; wrapping.
hüllen *vt* to wrap.
Hülse *f* husk.
Hummel *f* bumblebee.
Hummer *m* lobster.
Humor *m* humour.
humoristisch, humorvoll *adj* humorous.
Hund *m* dog.
hundert *num* hundred.
hundertprozentig *adj* a hundred per cent.
Hündin *f* bitch.
Hunger *m* hunger; ~ **haben** to be hungry.
hungern *vi* to starve.
hungrig *adj* hungry.
Hupe *f* horn.
hupern *vi* to hoot.
hüpfen *vi* to hop.
Hürde *f* hurdle.
Hure *f* whore.
husten *vi* to cough.

Husten *m* cough.
Hut *m* hat; * *f* care.
hüten *vt* to guard; * *vr* to take care.
Hütte *f* hut; foundry.
Hygiene *f* hygiene.
hygienisch *adj* hygienic; * *adv* hygienically.
Hymne *f* hymn; anthem.
Hypnose *f* hypnosis.
hypnotisch *adj* hypnotic.
Hypothek *f* mortgage.
Hypothese *f* hypothesis.
hypothetisch *adj* hypothetical.
Hysterie *f* hysteria.
hysterisch *adj* hysterical.

I

ich *pron* I.
Ich *n* ego.
ideal *adj* ideal.
Ideal *n* ideal.
Idee *f* idea.
identifizieren *vt vr* to identify.
Identifizierung *f* identification.
identisch *adj* identical.
Identität *f* identity.
Ideologie *f* ideology.
ideologisch *adj* ideological.
Idiot *m* idiot.
idyllisch *adj* idyllic.
Igel *m* hedgehog.
ignorieren *vt* to ignore.
ihm *pron* (to) him, (to) it.
ihn *pron* him, it.
ihnen *pron* (to) them.
Ihnen *pron* (to) you.
ihr *pron* you; her, it; * *poss adj* her, its, their.
ihrerseits *adv* on her/their/your part.
illegal *adj* illegal.
Illumination *f* illumination.
illuminieren *vt* to illuminate.
Illusion *f* illusion.
Illustration *f* illustration.

illustrieren *vt* to illustrate.
Illustrierte *f* magazine.
Imbiß *m* snack.
Imitation *f* imitation.
imitieren *vt* to imitate.
immer *adv* always, ever; **noch**
  ~ still; ~ **wieder** repeatedly;
  ~ **größer** bigger and bigger.
immerhin *adv* after all.
immergrün *adj* evergreen.
Immobilien *pl* property.
immun *adj* immune.
immunisieren *vt* to immunise.
Immunität *f* immunity.
Imperialismus *m* imperialism.
imperialistisch *adj* imperialistic.
impfen *vt* to vaccinate.
Import *m* import.
importieren *vt* to import.
impotent *adj* impotent.
Impotenz *f* impotence.
Impuls *m* impulse.
impulsiv *adj* impulsive.
imstande *adj* able.
in *prep* in, into.
indem *conj* as; while.
Inder(in) *m(f)* Indian.
Indianer(in) *m(f)* (Red) Indian.
indianisch *adj* (Red) Indian.
Indien *n* India.
Indier(in) *m(f)* Indian.
indirekt *adj* indirect.
indisch *adj* Indian.
individuell *adj* individual.
Individuum *n* individual.
Indonesien *n* Indonesia.
Industrie *f* industry.
industriell *adj* industrial.
ineinander *adv* into each other
  or one another.
Infektion *f* infection.
infizieren *vt* to infect; * *vr* to
  become infected.
Inflation *f* inflation.
infolge *prep* due to.
infolgedessen *adv* as a result.
Information *f* information.
informieren *vt* to inform.
Ingenieur *m* engineer.
Ingwer *m* ginger.
Inhaber(in) *m(f)* owner.

Inhalt *m* content(s).
Initiative *f* initiative.
inklusive *adv* including.
Inland *n* home country.
inmitten *prep* in the middle of.
innehaben *vt* to hold.
innehalten *vt* to comply with;
  * *vi* to pause.
innen *adv* inside.
Innenminister *m* minister of
  the interior; home secretary
  (Brit); secretary of the interior
  (US).
Innenstadt *f* town (or city) centre
inner *adj* inner, interior.
innerhalb *adv prep* within.
innerlich *adj* inner; mental.
innig *adj* warm; sincere.
inoffiziell *adj* unofficial.
Insasse *m* occupant.
insbesondere *adv* in particular.
Inschrift *f* inscription.
Insekt *n* insect.
Insel *f* island.
insgesamt *adv* altogether.
insofern, insoweit *adv* in so
  far, in this respect; * *conj* if;
  so.
Inspektion *f* inspection.
Inspektor, Inspekteur *m* inspector.
Inspiration *f* inspiration.
inspirieren *vt* to inspire.
instandhalten *vt* to maintain,
  service.
instandsetzen *vt* to repair.
Instanz *f* authority; court.
Instinkt *m* instinct.
instinktiv *adj* instinctive.
Institut *n* institution.
Instrument *n* instrument.
intellektuell *adj* intellectual.
Intellektuelle(r) *mf* intellectual.
intelligent *adj* intelligent.
Intelligenz *f* intelligence.
intensiv *adj* intensive.
interessant *adj* interesting.
Interesse *n* interest
interessieren *vt* to interest;

* *vr* to be interested.
intern *adj* internal.
international *adj* international.
Interpretation *f* interpretation.
interpretieren *vt* to interpret.
Intervall *n* interval.
Interview *n* interview.
interviewen *vt* to interview.
intim *adj* intimate; cosy.
Intimität *f* intimacy.
Intrige *f* intrigue.
Invalide(r) *mf* invalid.
Invasion *f* invasion.
Inventar *n* inventory.
Inventur *f* stocktake.
investieren *vt* to invest.
Investition *f* investment.
inwendig *adv* inward.
inwiefern, inwieweit *adv* to what extent.
inzwischen *adv* meanwhile; since.
Irak *m* Iraq.
Iran *n* Iran.
irdisch *adj* earthly.
Ire *m* Irishman.
irgend *adv* some, any; at all; ever; **wer ~** whoever; **~ etwas** something, anything.
irgendein *adj* some, any.
irgendeiner *adj* somebody.
irgendwann *adv* sometime.
irgendwie *adv* somehow.
irgendwo *adv* somewhere.
irgendwohin *adv* somewhere.
Irin *f* Irishwoman.
Iris *f* iris.
irisch *adj* Irish.
Irland *n* Ireland.
Irländer(in) *m(f)* Irishman, Irishwoman.
Ironie *f* irony.
ironisch *adj* ironic.
irre *adj* mad.
Irre(r) *mf* lunatic.
irreführen *vt* to mislead.
irren *vi vr* to get lost; to make a mistake.
irritieren *vt* to irritate.
Irrtum *m* error.

irrtümlich *adj* wrong.
Island *n* Iceland.
islandisch *adj* Icelandic.
Isolation *f* isolation; insulation.
isolieren *vt* to isolate; to insulate.
Israel *n* Israel.
Israeli *m* Israeli.
israelisch *adj* Israeli.
Italien *n* Italy.
Italiener(in) *m(f)* Italian.
italienisch *adj* Italian.

J

ja *adv* yes; after all; well; **komm ja!** do come!.
Jacht *f* yacht.
Jacke *f* jacket.
Jagd *f* hunt(ing).
Jagdflugzeug *n* fighter (aircraft).
jagen *vt* to hunt; to expel; * *vi* to hunt; to race.
Jäger *m* hunter.
jäh *adj* sudden; steep.
Jahr *n* year.
jahrelang *adv* for years.
Jahreszeit *f* season.
Jahrhundert *n* century.
jährlich *adj* annual; * *adv* annually.
Jahrmarkt *m* fair.
Jahrzent *n* decade.
Jammer *m* misery.
jämmerlich *adj* lamentable.
jammern *vt* to arouse pity; * *vi* to lament.
Januar, Jänner *m* January.
Japan *n* Japan.
Japaner(in) *m(f)* Japanese (person).
japanisch *adj* Japanese.
jauchzen *vt vi* to cheer.
jawohl *adv* yes (certainly).
Jazz *m* jazz.
je *adv* ever, every; each; * *conj* **~ nach** according to; **~**

nachdem it depends; ~ **größer, desto besser** the bigger the better.

jede *pron* each, every(one).
jedenfalls *adv* in any case.
jedermann *pron* everyone.
jederzeit *adv* at any time.
jedesmal *adv* every time.
jedoch *adv* however.
jeher *adv* **seit** ~ since time immemorial.
jemals *adv* ever.
jemand *pron* somebody, anybody.
jene *adv* that; * *pron* that one.
jenseits *prep* beyond.
jetzt *adv* now.
jeweilig *adj* respective.
jeweils *adv* respectively.
Jordanien *n* Jordan.
Journalist(in) *m(f)* journalist.
Jubel *m* jubilation.
jubeln *vi* to rejoice.
Jubiläum *n* jubilee; anniversary.
jucken *vi* to itch.
Juckreiz *m* itch.
Jude *m* **Jüdin** *f* Jew, Jewess.
jüdisch *adj* Jewish.
Jugend *f* youth.
Jugendherberge *f* youth hostel.
jugendlich *adj* youthful.
Jugendliche(r) *mf* young person.
Jugoslawien *n* Yugoslavia.
Juli *m* July.
jung *adj* young.
Junge *m* boy.
Jungfer *f* spinster.
Jungfrau *f* virgin.
Junggeselle *m* bachelor.
jüngst *adv* recently.
jüngste *adv* youngest; latest.
Juni *m* June.
Jurist *m* lawyer.
Justiz *f* justice.
Juwel *n* jewel.
Juwelier *m* jeweller.

K

Kabarett *n* cabaret.
Kabel *n* cable.
Kabeljau *m* cod.
Kabine *f* cabin; cubicle.
Kabinett *n* cabinet.
Kachel *f* tile.
Käfer *m* beetle.
Kaffee *m* coffee.
Käfig *m* cage.
kahl *adj* bare, bald.
Kai *m* quay.
Kaiser *m* emperor.
Kaiserin *f* empress.
Kakao *m* cocoa.
Kaktus *m* cactus.
Kalb *n* calf.
Kalbfleisch *n* veal.
Kalender *m* calendar.
Kalk *m* calcium, chalk.
kalkulieren *vt* to calculate.
kalt *adj* cold; **mir ist** ~ I am cold.
Kälte *f* cold.
Kamel *n* camel.
Kamera *f* camera.
Kamerad(in) *m(f)* comrade.
Kameradschaft *f* comradeship.
Kamin *m* chimney; fireplace.
Kamm *m* comb; crest.
kämmen *vt vi* to comb; * *vr* to comb one's hair.
Kammer *f* chamber.
Kampagne *f* campaign.
Kampf *m* fight; battle.
kämpfen *vi* to fight.
Kämpfer *m* fighter.
kämpferisch, kampflustig *adj* belligerent.
Kanada *n* Canada.
Kanadier(in) *m(f)* Canadian.
kanadisch *adj* Canadian.
Kanal *m* channel; canal.
Kanalisation *f* drain.
Kanarienvogel *m* canary.
Kandidat(in) *m(f)* candidate.
Känguruh *n* kangaroo.
Kaninchen *n* rabbit.
Kanne *f* can; pot.

Kanone f cannon.
Kante f edge.
Kantine f canteen.
Kanton m canton.
Kanu n canoe.
Kanzel f pulpit.
Kanzler m chancellor.
Kap n cape.
Kapazität f capacity.
Kapelle f chapel.
kapieren vt vi to understand.
Kapital n capital.
Kapitalismus m capitalism.
Kapitalist m capitalist.
kapitalistisch adj capitalist.
Kapitän m captain.
Kapitel n chapter.
Kappe f cap.
Kapsel f capsule.
Kapstadt n Cape Town.
kaputt adj broken.
Karawane f caravan.
Karfreitag m Good Friday.
karg, kärglich adj meagre.
karibisch adj Caribbean.
Karneval m carnival.
Kärnten n Carinthia.
Karo n square; diamonds
(cards).
Karotte f carrot.
Karriere f career.
Karte f card; chart; map; ticket;
menu.
Kartell n cartel.
Kartenspiel n card-playing;
pack.
Kartoffel f potato.
Karton m cardboard.
Karussell n roundabout.
Käse m cheese.
Kaserne f barracks.
Kasino n casino; club; officer's
mess.
Kaskade f cascade.
Kasse f cashbox, cash register;
cash desk; booking office.
Kassette f cassette; box.
kassieren vt vi to collect
(money).
Kassierer(in) m(f) cashier.
Kastanie f chestnut.
Kasten m box.

kastrieren vt to castrate.
Katalog m catalogue.
Katapult m catapult.
katastrophal adj catastrophic.
Katastrophe f catastrophe.
Kategorie f category.
kategorisch adj categorical.
Kater m tom-cat; hangover.
Katholik(in) m(f) Catholic.
katholisch adj Catholic.
Katze f cat.
Katzenjammer m hangover.
Katzensprung m stone's throw.
kauen vt vi to chew.
Kauf m purchase; **ein guter ~**
a bargain; **in ~ nehmen** take
into account.
kaufen vt vi to buy.
Käufer(in) m(f) buyer.
Kaufhaus n department store.
Kaufleute pl tradespeople.
käuflich adj for sale.
Kaufmann m businessman;
tradesman.
kaufmännisch adj commer-
cial; * adv commercially.
Kaugummi m chewing gum.
kaum adv hardly.
Kegel m skittle; cone.
Kegelbahn f bowling alley.
Kehle f throat.
Kehlkopf m larynx.
Kehre f turn, bend.
kehren vt vi to turn; to sweep.
Keil m wedge.
Keim m germ; bud.
keimen vi to germinate.
kein adj no, not any.
keine pron none; no-one; nothing.
keinerlei adj none at all.
keinesfalls, keineswegs adv
not at all.
keinmal adv never.
Keks m/n biscuit.
Kelch m goblet.
Kelle f ladle.
Keller m cellar.
Kellner(in) m(f) waiter, waitress.
kennbar adj recognisable.
kennen vt to know.

kennenlernen vt to get to know; to meet.

Kenner(in) m(f) connoisseur, expert.

kenntlich adj recognisable.

Kenntnis f knowledge; **in ~ nehmen** to note, notice.

Kenntnisnahme f notice.

Kennwort n motto; password.

Kennzeichen n sign; characteristic.

kennzeichnen vt to characterise.

kennzeichnend adj characteristic.

Kennziffer f reference number.

Keramik f ceramics.

Kerbe f notch.

Kerl m chap, guy.

Kern m kernel; nucleus.

Kernenergie f nuclear energy.

Kernkraftwerk n nuclear power station.

Kernwaffen pl nuclear weapons.

Kerze f candle; spark plug.

Kessel m kettle; boiler.

Kette f chain.

keusch adj chaste.

Keuschheit f chastity.

kichern vi to giggle.

Kiefer m jaw; * f pine.

Kies m gravel.

Kiesel(stein) m pebble.

Kilogramm n kilogram.

Kilometer m kilometre.

Kind n child.

Kindergarten m nursery school.

Kinderwagen m pram.

Kindheit f childhood.

kindisch adj childish.

kindlich adj childlike.

Kinn n chin.

Kino n cinema.

Kiosk m kiosk.

Kippe f cigarette end.

kippen vt vi to tip, tilt.

Kirche f church.

Kirchenlied n hymn.

Kirchturm m steeple.

Kirsche f cherry.

Kissen n cushion.

Kiste f box, chest.

Kitsch m kitsch, trash.

kitschig adj trashy.

Kitt m putty.

kitzeln vt to tickle.

Klage f complaint; lawsuit.

klagen vi to complain.

Kläger(in) m(f) plaintiff.

kläglich adj lamentable.

Klang m sound.

Klappe f flap; valve.

klappen vt vi to tip; * vi to click; to work; **das klappt nicht** it doesn't work.

klappern vi to rattle.

klar adj clear; ready; **na ~!** of course!.

klären vt to clarify.

Klarheit f clarity.

Klarinette f clarinet.

klarlegen vt to explain.

klarmachen vt make clear; to prepare.

klarstellen vt to clarify.

klarwerden vi to become clear; * vr to realise.

Klärung f clarification.

Klasse f class.

Klassenzimmer n classroom.

klassifizieren vt to classify.

Klassifizierung f classification.

Klassik f classical period.

Klassiker m classic.

klassisch adj classical; traditional.

Klatsch m clap; smack; gossip.

klatschen vi to clap; to smack; to gossip.

klatschnaß adj soaking wet.

Klaue f claw.

klauen vt (coll) to pinch, nick.

Klausel f clause.

Klavier n piano.

Klavierspieler(in) m(f) pianist.

kleben vt vi to stick.

klebrig adj sticky.

Klebestreifen m sticky tape.

Kleb(e)stoff m glue.

Klecks m blot.

klecksen *vt vi* to blot.
Klee *m* clover.
Kleid *n* dress; * *pl* **Kleider** clothes.
kleiden *vt* to clothe; * *vr* to dress.
Kleiderbügel *m* coat hanger.
Kleiderbürste *f* clothes brush.
Kleiderhaken *m* clothes peg.
Kleiderschrank *m* wardrobe.
Kleidung *f* clothing.
klein *adj* small.
kleinbürgerlich *adj* petty-bourgeois, small-minded.
Kleingeld *n* change.
Kleinigkeit *f* trifle.
Kleinkind *n* infant.
kleinlich *adj* paltry.
Kleinod *n* jewel, treasure.
Kleinstadt *f* small town.
klemmen *vt* to clamp; to squeeze, pinch; * *vi* to jam.
Klempner *m* plumber.
Kleriker *m* clergyman.
Klerus *m* clergy.
klettern *vi* to climb.
Klient(in) *m(f)* client.
Klima *n* climate.
Klimaanlage *f* air conditioning.
klimatisch *adj* climatic.
klimmen *vi* to climb.
Klinge *f* blade, sword.
Klingel *f* bell.
klingeln *vi* to ring.
Klinik *f* clinic.
Klinke *f* handle.
Klippe *f* cliff; reef; obstacle.
klirren *vi* to clink, clatter.
Klo *n* loo.
klopfen *vt vi* to knock.
Kloster *n* monastery; convent.
Klotz *m* log.
Klub *m* club.
Kluft *f* gap; chasm.
klug *adj* clever.
Klugheit *f* cleverness.
Klumpen *m* lump.
knabbern *vt vi* to nibble.
Knabe *m* boy.
knacken *vt vi* to crack
Knall *m* bang.
knallen *vi* to bang.

knapp *adj* tight; scarce; brief; * *adv* just under.
Knappheit *f* tightness; scarcity; brevity.
knarren *vi* to creak.
Knauf *m* knob.
Kneipe *f* bar.
Knick *m* crack; fold.
knicken *vt vi* to crack.
Knie *n* knee.
knien *vi* to kneel.
knirschen *vi* to grind.
knistern *vi* to crackle.
Knitter *m* crease.
Knoblauch *m* garlic.
Knöchel *m* knuckle; ankle.
Knochen *m* bone.
Knochengerüst *n* skeleton.
Knödel *m* dumpling.
Knolle *f* bulb.
Knopf *m* button.
knöpfen *vt* to button.
Knopfloch *n* buttonhole.
Knospe *f* bud.
Knoten *m* knot; lump.
knüpfen *vt* to tie.
Knüppel *m* club, truncheon.
knusperig *adj* crisp.
Koalition *f* coalition.
Koch *m* (male) cook.
kochen *vt vi* to cook; to boil.
Kocher *m* cooker.
Köchin *f* (female) cook.
Kochtopf *m* saucepan.
Koffer *m* (suit)case.
Kofferraum *m* boot (of vehicle).
Kognak *m* brandy.
Kohl *m* cabbage.
Kohle *f* coal; charcoal; carbon.
Kohlendioxyd *n* **Kohlensäure** *f* carbon dioxide.
Kokosnuß *f* coconut.
Kollege *m* **Kollegin** *f* colleague.
kollektiv *adj* collective.
Köln *n* Cologne.
Kolonie *f* colony.
Kolonne *f* column.
Kolumbien *n* Colombia.
Kolumbus *m* Columbus.
Kombination *f* combination.

kombinieren vt vi to combine; * vi to deduce.

Kombi(wagen) m estate car, station wagon.

Komfort m comfort.

Komik f comedy.

Komiker(in) m(f) comedian.

komisch adj funny; strange.

Komma n comma; decimal point.

Kommandant m commander.

kommandieren vt vi to command.

Kommando n command; squad.

kommen vi to come.

Kommentar m commentary; **kein ~** no comment.

Kommentator m commentator.

kommentieren vt to comment upon.

kommerziell adj commercial.

Kommissar m commissioner; (police) inspector.

Kommission f commission; committee.

Kommode f chest of drawers.

Kommunikation f communication.

Kommunion f communion.

Kommunismus m communism.

Kommunist(in) m(f) communist.

kommunistisch adj communist.

kommunizieren vi to communicate.

Komödie f comedy.

Kompaß m compass.

kompensieren vt to compensate.

kompetent adj competent; responsible.

Kompetenz f competence; jurisdiction.

komplett adj complete.

Kompliment n compliment.

komplimentieren vt to compliment.

kompliziert adj complicated.

Komponente f component.

komponieren vt to compose.

Komponist m composer.

Komposition f composition.

Kompromiß m compromise.

Kondensation f condensation.

kondensieren vt to condense.

Konditorei f café; cake shop.

Kondom n condom.

Konferenz f conference.

Konfession f religion; denomination.

Konfirmation f confirmation.

konfirmieren vt to confirm.

konfiszieren vt to confiscate.

Konfiszierung f confiscation.

Konfitüre f jam.

Konflikt m conflict.

konform adj in accordance with.

konfrontieren vt to confront.

Konfusion f confusion.

Kongreß m congress.

König m king.

Königin f queen.

königlich adj royal.

Königreich n kingdom.

Konjunktur f (state of the) economy.

konkret adj concrete.

Konkurrent(in) m(f) competitor.

Konkurrenz f competition.

konkurrieren vi to compete.

Konkurs m bankruptcy.

können vi to be able to; **ich kann** I can; **ich kann Deutsch** I speak German.

Können n ability.

konsequent adj consistent.

Konsequenz f consistency; consequence.

konservativ adj conservative.

Konservative(r) mf conservative.

Konserve(n) f tinned food.

konservieren vt to preserve.

Konservierung f preservation.

konsolidieren vt vr to consolidate.

Konsolidierung f consolidation.

Konsonant *m* consonant.
konstant *adj* constant.
konstatieren *vt* to state; to establish.
Konstanz *n* Constance.
Konstellation *f* constellation.
konstruieren *vt* to construct.
Konstruktion *f* construction.
Konsul *m* consul.
Konsulat *n* consulate.
konsultieren *vt* to consult.
Konsum *m* consumption.
Konsumgüter *pl* consumer goods.
Konsument(in) *m(f)* consumer.
Kontakt *m* contact.
kontaktarm *adj* unsociable.
kontaktfreudig *adj* sociable.
Kontaktlinsen *pl* contact lenses.
Kontinent *m* continent.
kontinental *adj* continental.
kontinuierlich *adj* continuous.
Konto *n* account.
Kontoauszug *m* statement.
Kontrabaß *m* double bass.
Kontrast *m* contrast.
Kontrolle *f* control; check.
Kontrolleur *m* inspector.
kontrollieren *vt* to check.
Kontroverse *f* controversy.
Konvention *f* convention.
konventionell *adj* conventional.
Konversation *f* conversation.
konvertieren *vt vi* to convert.
Konzentration *f* concentration.
Konzentrationslager *n* concentration camp.
konzentrieren *vt vr* to concentrate.
Konzept *n* draft.
Konzern *m* group (of companies).
Konzert *n* concert; concerto.
Konzertsaal *m* concert hall.
Konzession *f* concession.
Kooperation *f* cooperation.
kooperativ *adj* cooperative.
koordinieren *vt* to coordinate.
Koordinierung *f* coordination.

Kopenhagen *n* Copenhagen.
Kopf *m* head.
Kopfhörer *m* headphones.
Kopfkissen *n* pillow.
Kopfkissenbezug *m* pillow case.
kopflos *adj* panic-stricken.
Kopfschmerzen *pl* headache.
Kopftuch *n* headscarf.
Kopfzeile *f* headline.
Kopie *f* copy.
kopieren *vt* to copy.
Koppel *f* leash; couple; enclosure; * *n* belt.
koppeln *vt* to link.
Koralle *f* coral.
Korb *m* basket; **einen ~ bekommen** to be turned down.
Korbball *m* basketball.
Kordel *f* cord.
Kork *m* cork.
Korkenzieher *m* corkscrew.
Korn *n* corn; grain; (gun)sight.
Körper *m* body.
körperbehindert *adj* physically handicapped.
körperlich *adj* physical.
Körperschaft *f* corporation.
Körperschaftssteuer *f* corporation tax.
korrekt *adj* correct.
Korrektur *f* correction; proof; proof-reading.
Korrespondent(in) *m(f)* correspondent.
Korrespondenz *f* correspondence.
Korridor *m* corridor.
korrigieren *vt* to correct.
Korrosion *f* corrosion.
Korruption *f* corruption.
Kosmetik *f* cosmetics.
kosmetisch *adj* cosmetic.
Kosmos *m* cosmos.
Kost *f* food; accommodation.
kostbar *adj* precious; costly.
Kosten *pl* costs.
kosten *vt vi* to cost; to taste.
kostlos *adj adv* free (of charge).
köstlich *adj* precious; delicious.
Kostüm *n* costume.

Kot *m* excrement.
Kotelett *n* cutlet.
Krabbe *f* shrimp.
krabbeln *vi* to crawl.
Krach *m* crash; noise; argument.
krachen *vi* to crash; * *vr* to have a row.
krächzen *vi* to croak.
Kraft *f* strength, force, power; **in ~ treten** to come into force.
Kraftfahrer(in) *m(f)* driver.
Kraftfahrzeug *n* motor vehicle.
kräftig *adj* strong; * *adv* strongly.
kräftigen *vt* to strengthen.
kraftlos *adj* powerless.
kraftvoll *adj* strong.
Kraftwagen *m* motor vehicle.
Kraftwerk *n* power station.
Kragen *m* collar.
Krähe *f* crow.
Kralle *f* claw.
Kram *m* stuff, odds and ends.
Krampf *m* cramp; spasm.
Kran *m* crane; tap.
krank *adj* ill.
Kranke(r) *mf* sick person, patient.
kranken *vi* to suffer.
kränken *vt* to hurt.
Krankenhaus *n* hospital.
Krankenschwester *f* nurse.
Krankenwagen *m* ambulance.
Krankheit *f* illness, disease.
kränklich *adj* sickly.
Kränkung *f* insult.
Kranz *m* wreath.
kratzen *vt vi* to scratch.
Kratzer *m* scratch.
kraus *adj* curly.
Kraut *n* cabbage; herb; plant.
Krawall *m* uproar.
Krawatte *f* tie.
Krebs *m* crab; cancer.
Kredit *m* credit.
Kreditkarte *f* credit card.
Kreditgeber *m* lender.
Kreditnehmer *m* borrower.
Kreide *f* chalk.
Kreis *m* circle; district.
kreischen *vi* to scream.

Kreisel *m* top; roundabout.
kreisen *vi* to rotate.
kreisförmig *adj* circular.
Kreislauf *m* circulation.
Krematorium *n* crematorium.
kremieren *vt* to cremate.
Kreml *m* (the) Kremlin.
krepieren *vi* (*coll*) to kick the bucket.
Kreuz *n* cross; clubs (cards); small of the back.
kreuz *adv* ~ **und quer** back and forth.
kreuzen *vt vi vr* to cross.
Kreuzfahrt *f* cruise.
kreuzigen *vt* to crucify.
Kreuzigung *f* crucifixion.
Kreuzung *f* crossing.
Kreuzweg *m* crossroads; Stations of the Cross.
Kreuzworträtsel *n* crossword (puzzle).
Kreuzzug *m* crusade.
kriechen *vi* to creep, crawl.
Krieg *m* war.
kriegen *vt* to get, receive.
Krieger *m* warrior.
kriegerisch *adj* warlike.
Kriegsgefangene(r) *m* prisoner of war.
Kriegsgericht *n* court martial.
Kriegsschiff *n* warship.
Kriegsverbrecher *m* war criminal.
Krimi *m* thriller.
kriminell *adj* criminal.
Kriminelle(r) *m* criminal.
Krise *f* crisis; recession.
Kristall *m* crystal; * *n* crystal (glass).
Kritik *f* criticism.
Kritiker *m* critic.
kritisch *adj* critical.
kritisieren *vt vi* to criticise.
kritzeln *vt vi* to scribble.
Krokodil *n* crocodile.
Krone *f* crown.
krönen *vt* to crown.
Kronjuwelen *pl* crown jewels.
Kronleuchter *m* chandelier.
Krönung *f* coronation.
Kröte *f* toad.

Krug *m* jug.
Krümel *m* crumb.
krümeln *vi vr* to crumble.
krumm *adj* crooked.
Krümmung *f* curve.
Krüppel *m* cripple.
Kruste *f* crust; scab.
Kübel *m* tub, bucket.
Küche *f* kitchen; cooking.
Kuchen *m* cake.
Kuckuck *m* cuckoo.
Kugel *f* ball; sphere; bullet.
kugelförmig *adj* spherical.
Kugellager *n* ball bearing.
Kugelschreiber *m* ballpoint pen.
Kuh *f* cow.
kühl *adj* cool.
Kühle *f* coolness.
kühlen *vt* to cool.
Kühler *m* radiator (car).
Kühlschrank *m* refrigerator.
Kühltruhe *f* freezer.
kühn *adj* bold.
Kulisse *f* wings, scenery (theatre).
kultivieren *vt* to cultivate.
Kultur *f* culture; cultivation.
kulturell *adj* cultural.
Kummer *m* sorrow.
kümmerlich *adj* wretched.
kümmern *vt* to concern; * *vr* to look after, deal with.
Kunde *f* information; * *m* customer.
kundgeben *vt* to announce.
Kundgebung *f* announcement; demonstration.
kundig *adj* familiar, experienced.
kündigen *vt* to terminate, cancel; * *vi* to give notice.
Kündigung *f* notice.
Kundschaft *f* customers.
künftig *adj* future; * *adv* in future.
Kunst *f* art; skill.
Künstler(in) *m(f)* artist.
künstlich *adj* artificial.
kunstvoll *adj* artistic; skilful.
Kunstwerk *n* work of art.
Kupfer *n* copper.

Kuppe *f* hilltop; fingertip.
Kuppel *f* dome.
kuppeln *vt* to join; * *vi* to pimp; to operate the clutch.
Kupplung *f* clutch (car); coupling.
Kur *f* cure; stay in a health resort.
Kurbel *f* crank.
Kürbis *m* pumpkin.
kurieren *vt* to cure.
kurios *adj* curious.
Kurort *m* health resort.
Kurs *m* price; exchange rate.
Kurse, Kursus *m* course (of teaching).
Kursiv *f* italics.
Kurve *f* curve.
kurz *adj* short; * *adv* shortly.
Kürze *f* shortness.
kürzen *vt* to shorten, reduce.
kurzfristig *adj* short-term.
Kurzgeschichte *f* short story.
kürzlich *adv* recently.
Kurzschluß *m* short circuit.
Kurzschrift *f* shorthand.
kurtzsichtig *adj* short-sighted.
Kurzwelle *f* shortwave.
Kusine *f* cousin.
Kuß *m* kiss.
küssen *vt vr* to kiss.
Küste *f* coast.
Küstenwache *f* coastguard.
Kutsche *f* coach.

L

Labor *n* lab.
Laboratorium *n* laboratory.
lächeln *vi* to smile.
Lächeln *n* smile.
lachen *vi* to laugh.
lächerlich *adj* ridiculous.
Lachs *m* salmon.
Lack *m* varnish; paint.
lackieren *vt* to varnish; to paint.
laden *vt* to load; to charge; to

invite; to summons.
Laden *m* shop.
Ladendieb(in) *m(f)* shoplifter.
Ladendiebstahl *m* shoplifting.
Ladentisch *m* counter.
Ladung *f* load; loading; invitation; summons.
Lage *f* position; layer.
Lager *n* camp; warehouse; bearing.
Lagerbestand *m* stock.
Lagerhaus *n* warehouse.
lagern *vt* to store; * *vi* to lie down; to camp.
Lagerraum *m* store-room.
Lagune *f* lagoon.
lahm *adj* lame.
lähmen, lahmlegen *vt* to cripple, paralyse.
Lähmung *f* paralysis.
Laib *m* loaf.
Laibach *n* Ljubljana.
Laie *m* layman, lay person.
Laken *n* sheet.
lallen *vt vi* to babble.
Lamm *n* lamb.
Lampe *f* lamp.
Lampenschirm *m* lampshade.
Land *n* land; country; countryside; state (of Germany).
Landhaus *n* country house.
landen *vi* to land.
ländlich *adj* rural.
Landschaft *f* countryside; landscape.
Landstraße *f* country road.
Landtag *m* state parliament.
Landung *f* landing.
Landwirt *m* farmer.
Landwirtschaft *f* agriculture.
lang *adj* long; tall
lange *adv* for a long time.
Länge *f* length; height; longitude.
Längegrad *m* (degree of) longitude.
langen *vt* to grasp; * *vi* to suffice.
länger *adj adv* longer; **~e Zeit** for some time.
Langeweile *f* boredom.
langfristig *adj* long-term.

langhaarig *adj* long-haired.
langjährig *adj* lasting many years.
länglich *adj* elongated; longish.
längs *adv prep* along.
langsam *adj* slow.
Langsamkeit *f* slowness.
längst *adv* for a long time; long ago.
langweilen *vt* to bore; * *vr* to be bored.
langweilig *adj* boring.
Langwelle *f* long wave.
langwierig *adj* protracted.
Lanze *f* lance.
Lappen *m* rag; lobe.
Lärm *m* noise.
lärmen *vi* to make a noise.
Laser *m* laser.
lassen *vt* to let; to leave; to stop; * *v aux* to cause to be; **etw machen ~** to get something done.
lässig *adj* lazy, lax.
Last *f* load; trouble; tax, charge.
lasten *vi* to burden.
Laster *n* vice.
lästig *adj* burdensome.
Lastkraftwagen *m* lorry.
Latein *n* Latin.
Lateinamerika *n* Latin America.
lateinisch *adj* Latin.
latent *adj* latent.
Laterne *f* lantern.
Laternenpfahl *m* lamppost.
Latte *f* lath, slat.
Lattich *m* lettuce.
Laub *n* foliage.
lauern *vi* to lurk.
Lauf *m* run; race; course.
Laufbahn *f* career.
laufen *vt vi* to run; to walk.
Laufen *n* running, walking.
laufend *adj* continuous; current.
Läufer(in) *m(f)* runner.
Laune *f* mood.
lauschen *vi* to eavesdrop.
laut *adj* loud; * *adv* loudly; * *prep* according to.
Laut *m* sound.

lauten *vi* to sound; to say.
läuten *vt vi* to ring.
lauter *adj* pure, sheer.
Lautheit *f* loudness.
Lautsprecher *m* loudspeaker.
lauwarm *adj* lukewarm.
Lawine *f* avalanche.
Leben *n* life.
leben *vt vi* to live.
lebendig *adj* alive, lively.
Lebensalter *n* age.
Lebensgefahr *f* danger (of death).
Lebenslauf *m* life; curriculum vitae.
Lebensmittel *pl* food.
Lebensraum *m* living space.
Lebensversicherung *f* life insurance.
Lebenszeit *f* lifetime.
Leber *f* liver.
lebhaft *adj* lively.
leblos *adj* lifeless.
Leck *n* leak.
lecken *vt* to lick; * *vi* to leak.
lecker *adj* delicious.
Leder *n* leather.
ledig *adj* unmarried; empty.
lediglich *adv* only, merely.
leer *adj* empty.
Leere *f* emptiness.
leeren *vt vr* to empty.
legal *adj* legal.
legalisieren *vt* to legalise.
Legalität *f* legality.
legen *vt* to lay, place; * *vr* to lie down, abate.
legendar *adj* legendary.
Legende *f* legend.
legitim *adj* legitimate.
legitimieren *vt* to legitimise; * *vr* to prove one's identity.
Legitimität *f* legitimacy.
Lehne *f* support; arm(rest), back(rest).
lehnen *vt vr* to lean.
Lehnstuhl *m* armchair.
Lehrbuch *n* textbook.
Lehre *f* teaching.
lehren *vt* to teach,
Lehrer(in) *m(f)* teacher.
Lehrgang *m* course.

Lehrling *m* apprentice.
Leib *m* body.
leiblich *adj* bodily.
Leibwache *f* bodyguard.
Leiche *f* corpse.
Leichenwagen *m* hearse.
Leichnam *m* corpse.
leicht *adj* light; easy.
Leichtathletik *f* athletics.
leichthin *adv* lightly, casually.
Leichtigkeit *f* lightness, ease.
Leichtsinn *m* carelessness.
leichtsinnig *adj* careless.
leid *adj*: **es tut mir ~** I am sorry.
Leid *n* pain, sorrow.
leiden *vt vi* to suffer.
Leiden *n* suffering.
Leidenschaft *f* passion.
leidenschaftlich *adj* passionate.
leider *adv* unfortunately.
leihen *vt* to lend; * *vr* to borrow.
Leim *m* glue.
Leine *f* cord; leash.
Leinen *n* linen.
Leinwand *f* canvas.
leise *adj* soft, quiet.
Leiste *f* ledge, edge.
leisten *vt* to perform; * *vr* to afford.
Leistung *f* performance; output.
leistungsfähig *adj* efficient.
Leistungsfähigkeit *f* efficiency.
leiten *vt* to lead, manage.
Leiter *m* leader; * *f* ladder.
Leitmotiv *n* leitmotiv, recurring theme.
Leitung *f* management; pipe; cable.
Lektion *f* lesson.
lenken *vt* to steer.
Lenkrad *n* steering wheel.
Leopard *m* leopard.
Lerche *f* lark.
lernen *vt vi* to learn.
lesbar *adj* legible.
Lesbarkeit *f* legibility.
Lesbierin *f* lesbian.
lesbisch *adj* lesbian.
lesen *vt vi* to read; to pick.

Leser(in) *m(f)* reader.
letzte(r,s) *adj* last; latest.
letztens *adv* recently.
letztlich *adv* recently; ultimately.
Leuchte *f* light.
leuchten *vi* to shine.
Leuchtturm *m* lighthouse.
leugnen *vt vi* to deny.
Leute *pl* people.
Leutnant *m* lieutenant.
Libanon *m* Lebanon.
liberal *adj* liberal.
liberalisieren *vt* to liberalise.
Libyen *n* Libya.
Licht *n* light.
Lichtbild *n* photograph.
lichten *vt* to clear; to weigh (anchor).
Lichtschalter *m* light switch.
Lid *n* eyelid.
lieb *adj* dear; pleasant.
Liebe *f* love.
lieben *vt vi* to love; to like.
liebenswert *adj* lovable.
liebenswürdig *adj* kind.
lieber *adv* rather.
liebevoll *adj* loving.
liebhaben *vt* to like.
Liebhaber(in) *m(f)* lover.
liebkosen *vt vi* to caress.
lieblich *adj* lovely.
Liebling *m* darling; favourite.
Liebschaft *f* love affair.
liebste(r,s) *adj* favourite.
Lied *n* song.
liederlich *adj* careless.
Lieferant *m* supplier.
liefern *vt vi* to deliver, supply.
Lieferschein *m* delivery note.
Lieferung *f* delivery.
liegen *vi* to lie.
Liegestuhl *m* deckchair.
Lift *m* lift, elevator.
Liga *f* league.
Likör *m* liqueur.
lila(farben) *adj* lilac, purple.
Lilie *f* lily.
Limonade *f* lemonade.
Linde *f* lime (tree).
lindern *vt* to soothe.
Linie *f* line.

Linke *f* left (side).
links *adv* (on/to the) left.
linkshändig *adj* left-handed.
Linoleum *n* lino(leum).
Linse *f* lens; lentil.
Lippe *f* lip.
Lippenstift *m* lipstick.
lispeln *vi* to lisp.
Lissabon *n* Lisbon.
List *f* cunning; trick.
Liste *f* list.
listig *adj* cunning.
Litauen *n* Lithuania.
litauisch *adj* Lithuanian.
Liter *m/n* litre.
literarisch *adj* literary.
Literatur *f* literature.
Lizenz *f* licence.
Lob *n* praise.
lobenswert, löblich *adj* praiseworthy.
Loch *n* hole.
Locke *f* lock; curl.
locken *vt* to entice; to curl.
locker *adj* loose.
lockern *vt* to loosen.
Löffel *m* spoon.
Logik *f* logic.
logisch *adj* logical.
Lohn *m* wages; reward.
lohnen *vt vi* to reward; * *vr* to be worth (doing).
lokal *adj* local.
Lokal *n* bar.
Lokomotive *f* locomotive.
London *n* London.
Los *n* lot; lottery ticket.
los *adj* loose; separate; **was ist ~** what's the matter?.
losbinden *vt* to untie.
löschen *vt* to extinguish; to delete; to unload.
Löschpapier *n* blotting paper.
lose *adj* loose.
Lösegeld *n* ransom.
Losen *n* draw, ballot.
lösen *vt* to loosen; to detach; to cancel; to dissolve; * *vr* to undo, dissolve.
losfahren, losgehen *vi* to leave.
loskommen *vi* to come off, es-

cape.
loslassen *vt* to release.
löslich *adj* soluble.
losmachen *vt* to undo.
Losung *f* password, slogan.
Lösung *f* solution.
loswerden *vt* to get rid of.
löten *vt* to solder.
Lothringen *n* Lorraine.
Löwe *m* lion; (*astrol*) Leo.
Löwenzahn *m* dandelion.
Lücke *f* gap.
lückenhaft *adj* incomplete.
lückenlos *adj* complete.
Luft *f* air.
luftdicht *adj* airtight.
lüften *vt* to ventilate.
Luftfahrt *f* aviation.
luftig *adj* airy.
Luftkissenfahrzeug *n* hover-
  craft.
Luftpost *f* airmail.
Lüftung *f* ventilation.
Luftwaffe *f* air force.
Luftzug *m* draught.
Lüge *f* lie.
lügen *vi* to lie.
Lügner(in) *m(f)* liar.
Lumpen *m* rag.
lumpig *adj* ragged.
Lunge *f* lung.
Lungenkrebs *m* lung cancer.
Lupe *f* magnifying glass.
Lust *f* pleasure; willingness; ~
  haben to feel like.
lüstern *adj* lustful.
lustig *adj* cheerful.
lustlos *adj* listless.
Lustspiel *n* comedy.
Luxus *m* luxury.
lyrisch *adj* lyrical.

M

machbar *adj* feasible.
machen *vt* to make, do; **das**
  macht nichts it doesn't matter.
Macht *f* power.

Machthaber *m* ruler.
mächtig *adj* powerful; strong;
  huge.
machtlos *adj* powerless.
machtvoll *adj* powerful.
Mädchen *n* girl.
Magazin *n* magazine.
Magen *m* stomach.
mager *adj* meagre, thin.
Magie *f* magic.
Magier *m* magician.
magisch *adj* magical.
Magnet *m* magnet.
magnetisch *adj* magnetic.
mähen *vt vi* to mow.
Mahl *n* meal.
mahlen *vt vi* to grind.
Mahlzeit *f* meal.
mahnen *vt vi* to warn; to remind.
Mahnung *f* warning; reminder.
Mai *m* May.
Mailand *n* Milan.
Mais *m* maize; corn.
Majestät *f* majesty.
Major *m* major.
Makel *m* stain, spot.
makellos *adj* spotless.
Makler(in) *m(f)* broker.
Mal *n* mark; time, occasion;
  zum ersten ~ for the first
  time.
mal *adv* times; once.
malen *vt vi* to paint.
Maler(in) *m(f)* painter.
malerisch *adj* picturesque.
Malz *n* malt.
man *pron* one; you; ~ **hat es**
  getan it's been done.
Manager *m* manager.
Management *n* management.
manche *adj* many; * *pron* some.
manchmal *adv* sometimes.
Mandel *f* almond; tonsil.
Mangel *m* defect; shortage.
mangelhaft *adj* defective; incomplete.
mangeln *vt* to mangle; *vi* to be
  missing.
mangels *prep* in the absence of.
Manier *f* manner.
Manifest *n* manifesto.

Manipulation *f* manipulation.
manipulieren *vt* to manipulate.
Mann *m* man; husband.
männlich *adj* male, masculine.
Mannschaft *f* team.
Manöver *n* manoeuvre.
manövrieren *vt vi* to manoeuvre.
Mantel *m* coat; casing.
Mappe *f* file, briefcase.
Märchen *n* fairytale.
märchenhaft *adj* fairytale.
Margarine *f* margarine.
Marge *f* margin.
Marine *f* navy.
marineblau *adj* navy blue.
Mark *n* marrow; boundary; (deutsch)mark.
markant *adj* striking.
Marke *f* mark; brand(name).
Markt *m* market.
Marktforschung *f* market research.
Marmelade *f* jam.
Marmor *m* marble.
Marokko *n* Morocco.
Marsch *m* march; * *f* marsh.
marschieren *vi* to march.
marschig *adj* marshy.
Marxismus *m* Marxism.
März *m* March.
Masche *f* mesh; stitch.
Maschine *f* machine.
Maschinenbau *m* mechanical engineering.
Maschinengewehr *n* machine gun.
maschineschreiben *vi* to type.
Maschineschreiber(in) *m(f)* typist.
Maske *f* mask.
maskieren *vt* to mask.
Maß *n* measure; extent; * *f* litre (of beer).
Massage *f* massage.
Masse *f* mass.
Maßgabe *f* proportion; **nach ~** according to.
maßgebend, maßgeblich *adj* authoritative.
mäßig *adj* moderate.

Mäßigkeit *f* moderation.
Maßnahme *f* measure.
Mast *m* mast.
Material *n* material.
Materialismus *m* materialism.
materialistisch *adj* materialistic.
materiell *adj* material.
Mathematik *f* mathematics.
Matratze *f* mattress.
Matrose *m* sailor.
matt *adj* matte; dull; mate (chess).
Matte *f* mat.
Mauer *f* wall.
mauern *vt vi* to lay bricks.
Maul *n* mouth.
Maulwurf *m* mole.
Maurer *m* bricklayer.
Maus *f* mouse.
Maximum *n* maximum.
Mechaniker *m* mechanic.
mechanisch *adj* mechanical.
Medaille *f* medal.
Medizin *f* medicine.
Meer *n* sea.
Meeresspiegel *m* sea level.
Meerrettich *m* horseradish.
Meerschweinchen *n* guinea pig.
Mehl *n* flour.
mehr *adj adv* more.
Mehrarbeit *f* overtime.
mehrere *adj* several.
mehrfach *adj* multiple; * *adv* repeatedly.
Mehrheit *f* majority.
mehrjährig *adj* several years old; perennial.
mehrmals *adv* several times.
Mehrwertsteuer *f* value added tax.
Mehrzahl *f* majority.
Meile *f* mile.
Meilenstein *m* milestone.
mein(e) *poss adj* my.
meine(r,s) *poss pron* mine.
meinen *vt vi* to think, be of the opinion.
meinerseits *adv* for my part.
Meinung *f* opinion.
Meißen *n* Meissen.

meist *adj* most; * *adv* mostly;
am meisten the most.
meistens *adv* usually, generally.
Meister *m* master; champion.
meisterhaft *adj* masterly.
Meisterschaft *f* mastery;
championship.
Meisterstück, Meisterwerk *n*
masterpiece.
Melancholie *f* melancholy.
melancholisch *adj* melancholic.
melden *vt vi* to report; * *vr* to
present oneself
Meldung *f* report.
melken *vt vi* to milk.
Melodie *f* melody.
Menge *f* crowd; quantity.
mengen *vt* to mix; * *vr* to interfere.
Mensch *m* human being; person.
Menschheit *f* humanity.
menschlich *adj* human.
Menstruation *f* menstruation.
Mentalität *f* mentality.
Menü *n* menu.
merkbar *adj* noticeable.
merken *vt* to notice.
merklich *adj* noticeable.
Merkmal *n* characteristic.
Merkur *f* Mercury.
merkwürdig *adj* noteworthy;
remarkable.
Messe *f* mass; (trade) fair.
messen *vt* to measure; * *vr* to
compete.
Messer *n* knife.
Messing *n* brass.
Metall *n* metal.
metallisch *adj* metallic.
Meter *m/n* metre.
Methode *f* method.
Metzger *m* butcher.
Metzgerei *f* butcher's (shop).
Mexiko *n* Mexico.
mich *pron* (*acc*) me, myself.
Miete *f* rental.
mieten *vt* to rent, hire.
Mieter(in) *m(f)* tenant.
Mikrofilm *m* microfilm.

Mikrophon *n* microphone.
Mikrofon *n* microphone.
Mikroskop *n* microscope.
mikroskopisch *adj* micro-
scopic.
Mikrowellenherd *m* micro-
wave (oven).
Milch *f* milk.
Milchflasche *f* milk bottle.
Milchkaffee *m* white coffee.
mild *adj* mild, soft.
Milde *f* mildness, softness.
mildern *vt* to soften, alleviate.
Milieu *n* environment.
militärisch *adj* military.
Milliarde *f* billion.
Millimeter *m n* millimetre.
Million *f* million.
Millionär(in)   *m(f)*
millionaire(ss).
minder *adj* inferior; * *adv* less.
Minderheit *f* minority.
minderjährig *adj* minor, under
age.
mindern *vt vr* to decrease, di-
minish.
Minderung *f* decrease.
minderwertig *adj* inferior.
Minderwertigkeit *f* inferiority.
Minderwertigkeitskomplex
m inferiority complex.
Mindestalter *n* minimum age.
Mindestbetrag *m* minimum
amount.
mindeste(r,s) *adj* least.
mindestens *adv* at least.
Mindestlohn *m* minimum
wage.
Mindestmaß *n* minimum.
Mine *f* mine; lead; refill.
Minenfeld *n* minefield.
Mineral *n* mineral.
mineralisch *adj* mineral.
Mineralwasser *n* mineral wa-
ter.
minimal *adj* minimal.
Minimum *n* minimum.
Minister *m* minister.
Ministerium *n* ministry.
Ministerpräsident *m* prime
minister.
minus *adj* minus.

Minute f minute.
Minze f mint.
mir pron (dat) (to) me, (to) myself.
mischen vt vr to mix.
Mischung f mixture.
mißachten vt to ignore.
Mißbehagen n discomfort, displeasure.
mißbilligen vt to disapprove.
Mißbilligung f disapproval.
Mißbrauch m misuse, abuse.
mißbrauchen vt to misuse, abuse.
missen vt to miss.
Mißerfolg m failure.
mißfallen vi to displease.
Mißfallen n displeasure.
mißglücken vi to fail.
mißhandeln vt to maltreat.
Mission f mission.
Missionar m missionary.
Mißklang m discord.
mißlich adj inconvenient, unpleasant.
mißlingen vi to fail.
mißtrauen vi to distrust.
Mißtrauen n distrust.
mißtrauisch adj distrustful.
Mißverständnis n misunderstanding.
mißverstehen vt to misunderstand.
Mist m manure.
mit prep with; * adv **darf ich** ~? can I come too?.
Mitarbeit f cooperation.
mitarbeiten vi to cooperate.
Mitarbeiter(in) m(f) colleague.
mitbringen vt to bring along; to produce.
miteinander adv together; simultaneously.
mitfahren, mitgehen vi to accompany.
Mitglied n member.
Mitgliedschaft f membership.
mithelfen vi to help.
Mithilfe f assistance.
mitkommen vi to come along; to follow.
Mitleid n pity.

mitmachen vi to join in.
mitnehmen vt to take along; to pick up.
mitspielen vt vi to join in, play.
Mittag m midday.
Mittagessen n lunch.
Mittagspause f lunch break.
Mitte f middle.
mitteilen vt to inform.
Mitteilung f communication.
Mittel n means, resources; average.
Mittelalter n (the) Middle Ages.
mittelalterlich adj medieval.
Mittelamerika n Central America.
mittelbar adj direct.
Mitteleuropa n central Europe.
mittelfristig adj medium-term.
mittelgroß adj medium-sized.
mittelmäßig adj middling, mediocre.
Mittelmeer n Mediterranean (Sea).
Mittelpunkt m centre.
Mittelstand m middle class; small business.
Mittelwelle f medium wave.
mitten adv in the middle.
Mitternacht f midnight.
mittlere(r,s) adj middle; average; medium.
Mittwoch m Wednesday.
mitunter adv sometimes.
mitwirken vi to cooperate.
Mitwirkende(r) mf performer.
Mitwirkung f cooperation, participation.
Möbel n (item of) furniture.
Möbelwagen m removal van.
Mode f fashion.
Modell n model.
Modenschau f fashion show.
modern adj modern.
modernisieren vt to modernise.
Modernisierung f modernisation.
mögen vt vi to want, like; **ich möchte** I would like.

möglich *adj* possible.
möglicherweise *adv* possibly.
Möglichkeit *f* possibility.
Mohn *m* poppy.
Möhre, Mohrrübe *f* carrot.
Moldau *f* Vltava.
Molekül *n* molecule.
Molkerei *f* dairy.
Moll *n* (*mus*) minor.
mollig *adj* comfortable; plump.
Moment *m* moment; ~**!** just a moment!
momentan *adj* momentary; present; * *adv* at (for) the moment.
Monarchie *f* monarchy.
Monat *m* month.
monatlich *adj* monthly.
Mönch *m* monk.
Mond *m* moon.
Mondlicht *n*, **Mondschein** *m* moonlight.
Monitor *m* monitor.
monogam *adj* monogamous.
Monogamie *f* monogamy.
Monolog *m* monologue.
Monopol *n* monopoly.
monoton *adj* monotonous.
Monotonie *f* monotony.
Monsun *m* monsoon.
Montag *m* Monday.
Montage *f* assembly, installation; montage.
Moor *n* moor(land).
Moos *n* moss.
Moped *n* moped.
Moral *f* moral; morality; morale.
Mord *m* murder.
morden *vt vi* to murder.
Mörder(in) *m(f)* murderer.
mörderisch *adj* murderous.
Morgen *m* morning; **guten ~** good morning.
morgen *adv* tomorrow; ~ **früh** tomorrow morning.
Morgenrock *m* dressing gown.
morgens *adv* in the morning(s).
morsch *adj* rotten.
Mosaik *n* mosaic.
Moschee *f* mosque.
Mosel *m* Moselle.

Moskau *n* Moscow.
Moskito *m* mosquito.
Moslem *m* Moslem.
Motel *n* motel.
Motiv *n* motif; motive.
motivieren *vt* to motivate.
Motivierung *f* motivation.
Motor *m* motor, engine.
Motorboot *n* motor boat.
Motorrad *n* motorcycle.
Motte *f* moth.
Motto *n* motto.
Möwe *f* seagull.
Mücke *f* gnat, mosquito.
müde *adj* tired.
Müdigkeit *f* fatigue.
Mühe *f* trouble, effort; **der ~ wert** worth the trouble.
mühelos *adj* easy.
mühevoll *adj* difficult.
Mühle *f* mill.
Mühlstein *m* millstone.
mühsam, mühselig *adj* troublesome.
Müll *m* rubbish, refuse.
Mülleimer *m* dustbin.
Müllwagen *m* dustcart.
Multiplikation *f* multiplication.
multiplizieren *vt* to multiply.
Mumie *f* mummy.
München *n* Munich,
Mund *m* mouth.
mündig *adj* of age.
Mündigkeit *f* majority.
mündlich *adj* oral, verbal.
Mündung *f* mouth (of river).
Mundwasser *n* mouthwash.
Munition *f* ammunition.
munter *adj* lively.
Munterkeit *f* liveliness.
Münze *f* coin.
murmeln *vt vi* to murmur.
murren *vi* to grumble.
Muschel *f* mussel; shell(fish); earpiece.
Museum *n* museum.
Musik *f* music.
musikalisch *adj* musical.
Musiker *m* musician.
Muskel *m* muscle.
müssen *vi v aux* to have to; **ich**

muß I must.
müßig *adj* idle.
Muster *n* pattern, sample.
mustergültig, musterhaft *adj* exemplary.
Musterung *f* inspection.
Mut *m* courage.
Mutation *f* mutation.
mutig *adj* courageous.
mutlos *adj* despondent.
Mutlosigkeit *f* despondency.
mutmaßen *vt* to assume.
mutmaßlich *adj* probable.
Mutter *f* mother.
Muttergesellschaft *f* parent company.
mütterlich *adj* motherly, maternal.
Mutterschaft *f* maternity.
Muttersprache *f* mother tongue.
Muttertag *m* Mother's Day.
Mutti *f* mum(my).
mutwillig *adj* deliberate.
Mütze *f* cap.
mysteriös *adj* mysterious.
Mythe *f* myth.
Mythologie *f* mythology.
mythologisch *adj* mythological.

N

na *excl* now, well; ~ **also!** there you are; ~ **und?** so what?
Nabel *m* navel.
nach *prep* after; to; according to; ~ **und** ~ little by little.
nachahmen *vt vi* to imitate.
Nachahmung *f* imitation.
Nachbar(in) *m(f)* neighbour.
Nachbarschaft *f* neighbourhood.
Nachbau *m* reproduction.
nachbessern *vt* to improve.
nachbilden *vt* to copy.
nachbleiben *vi* to remain behind, lag.

nachdem *adv* afterwards; * *conj* after; **je** ~ it depends.
nachdenken *vi* to think about.
Nachdruck *m* emphasis.
nachdrücklich *adj* express; * *adv* expressly.
nacheinander *adv* in succession.
Nachfahr *m* descendant.
Nachfolge *f* succession; emulation.
nachfolgen *vi* to succeed; to emulate.
Nachfolger(in) *m(f)* successor.
Nachfrage *f* inquiry; demand.
nachfragen *vi* to inquire.
nachfühlen *vt* to sympathise with.
nachgeben *vi* to give way; give in.
nachgehen *vi* to follow.
nachgiebig *adj* soft, flexible.
nachhaltig *adj* lasting.
nachhelfen *vi* to help.
Nachhilfe *f* help.
nachholen *vt* to catch up.
Nachkomme *m* descendant.
nachkommen *vi* to follow.
Nachkriegszeit *f* post-war period.
Nachlaß *m* discount; estate.
nachlassen *vt vi* to decrease.
nachlässig *adj* negligent.
Nachlässigkeit *f* negligence.
nachlaufen *vi* to follow, chase.
nachmachen *vt* to copy.
nachmals *adv* afterwards.
Nachmittag *m* afternoon.
nachmittags *adv* in the afternoon(s).
Nachnahme *f* cash on delivery.
nachprüfen *adj* to verify.
Nachricht *f* (item of) news, message.
Nachrichten *pl* news.
Nachrichtensprecher(in) *m(f)* newsreader.
Nachruf *m* obituary.
nachschreiben *vt vi* to write down.
Nachschrift *f* postscript.
Nachschub *m* supplies; rein-

forcements.
nachsehen *vt vi* to inspect; to forgive.
nachsenden *vt* to forward.
Nachsicht *f* tolerance.
nachsichtig *adj* tolerant.
Nachspeise *f* dessert.
nächst *prep* next to.
nächste(r,s) *adj* next; nearest.
nächstens *adv* soon.
nachstreben *vi* to strive for.
Nacht *f* night.
Nachteil *m* disadvantage.
Nachtigall *f* nightingale.
Nachtklub *m* nightclub.
Nachtrag *m* supplement.
nachtragen *vt* to carry; add.
nachträglich *adj* subsequent; * *adv* subsequently.
nachts *adv* at night(s).
Nachweis *m* proof, evidence.
nachweisbar *adj* demonstrable.
nachweisen *vt* to prove.
Nachwuchs *m* offspring; recruits.
Nacken *m* nape (of the neck).
nackt *adj* naked.
Nacktheit *f* nakedness.
Nadel *f* needle; pin; brooch.
Nagel *m* nail.
Nagelbürste *f* nail brush.
Nagellack *m* nail varnish.
nageln *vt vi* to nail.
Nagelschere *f* nail scissors.
nagen *vt vi* to gnaw.
nah(e) *adj* near(by); close; * *adv* near(by); close; closely; * *prep* near (to), close to; **der Nahe Osten** the Middle East.
Nähe *f* nearness, proximity; vicinity; **in der ~** close by.
nahebei *adv* nearby.
nahekommen *vi* to approach.
naheliegen *vi* to be obvious.
naheliegend *adj* nearby; obvious.
nahen *vi vr* to approach.
nähen *vt vi* to sew.
näher *adj* nearer; more specific.
nähern *vt vr* to approach.
nahestehend *adj* close.

nahezu *adv* nearly.
Nähmaschine *f* sewing machine.
nähren *vt* to feed.
nahrhaft *adj* nutritious.
Nahrung *f*, **Nahrungsmittel** *n* food.
Naht *f* seam; stitch.
naiv *adj* naive.
Naivität *f* naivety.
Name *m* name.
namens *adv* called; * *prep* on behalf of.
namentlich *adj adv* by name; in particular.
namhaft *adj* renowned.
nämlich *adv* namely.
Narbe *f* scar.
Narkose *f* anaesthetic.
narkotisch *adj* narcotic.
Narr *m* fool.
Narrheit *f* folly.
närrisch *adj* foolish.
Narzisse *f* daffodil.
naschen *vt vi* to nibble.
Nase *f* nose.
Nasenbluten *n* nosebleed.
Nasenloch *n* nostril.
Nashorn *n* rhinoceros.
naß *adj* wet.
Nässe *f* wetness.
nässen *vt* to wet.
Nation *f* nation.
national *adj* national.
Nationalhymne *f* national anthem.
nationalisieren *vt* to nationalise.
Nationalisierung *f* nationalisation.
Nationalismus *m* nationalism.
Nationalist *m* nationalist.
nationalistisch *adj* nationalistic.
Nationalität *f* nationality.
Nationalsozialismus *m* national socialism, Nazism.
Nativität *f* nativity.
Natrium *n* sodium.
Natron *n* soda, sodium hydroxide.
Natur *f* nature.

Naturalismus *m* naturalism.
Naturalist *m* naturalist.
naturalistisch *adj* naturalistic.
natürlich *adj* natural; * *adv* naturally, of course.
Naturschutz *m* conservation.
Naturwissenschaftler(in) *m(f)* (natural) scientist.
Nazi *m* Nazi.
Nazismus *m* Nazism.
Neapel *n* Naples.
Nebel *m* mist, fog.
neb(e)lig *adj* misty, foggy.
neben *prep* beside.
nebenan *adv* next door.
nebenbei *adv* by the way.
nebeneinander *adv* side by side.
nebenher *adv* also; alongside.
Nebenkosten *pl* extra costs.
Nebenprodukt *n* by-product.
Nebenrolle *f* minor role.
nebensächlich *adj* secondary, incidental.
nebst *prep* in addition to.
necken *vt* to tease.
nee *adv* no.
Neffe *m* nephew.
negativ *adj* negative.
Negative *n* negative.
Neger(in) *m(f)* negro.
nehmen *vt* to take.
Neid *m* envy, jealousy.
neidisch *adj* envious, jealous.
neigen *vt* to incline; to bow; * *vi* to tend.
Neigung *f* inclination, tendency; like.
nein *adv* no.
Nektar *m* nectar.
Nelke *f* pink, carnation; clove.
nennen *vt* to name, call.
Nenner *m* denominator.
Neon *n* neon.
Nerv *m* nerve.
nervenkrank *adj* mentally ill.
Nervensystem *n* nervous system.
Nervenzusammenbruch *m* nervous breakdown.
nervös *adj* nervous.

Nessel *f* nettle.
Nest *n* nest.
nett *adj* nice.
netto *adv* net.
Nettogewicht *n* net weight.
Nettogewinn *m* net profit.
Netz *n* net; network.
Netzhaut *f* retina.
neu *adj* new.
neuartig *adj* novel.
Neubau *m* rebuilding, new building
neuerdings *adv* recently.
Neuerung *f* innovation.
Neufundland *n* Newfoundland.
neugeboren *adj* new-born.
neugestalten *vt* reorganise, redesign.
Neugestaltung *f* reorganisation, redevelopment.
Neugier(de) *f* curiosity.
neugierig *adj* curious.
Neuheit *f* newness.
Neuigkeit *f* news.
Neujahr *n* New Year.
neulich *adv* recently.
Neumond *m* new moon.
neun *num* nine.
neunzehn *num* nineteen.
neunzig *num* ninety.
Neuordnung *f* reorganisation.
neureich *adj* nouveau riche.
Neurose *f* neurosis.
neurotisch *adj* neurotic.
Neuseeland *n* New Zealand.
neutral *adj* neutral.
Neutrum *n* neuter.
nicht *adv* not.
Nichte *f* niece.
nichtig *adj* futile; invalid.
Nichtraucher(in) *m(f)* nonsmoker.
nichts *pron* nothing.
nichtsdestoweniger *adv* nevertheless.
nichtsnutzig *adj* useless.
Nickel *n* nickel.
nicken *vi* to nod.
nie *adv* never.
nieder *adj* low; inferior; * *adv* down.

niederfallen *vi* to fall down.
Niedergang *m* descent, decline.
niedergedrückt *adj* dejected, depressed.
niedergehen *vi* to go down; to descend.
niedergeschlagen *adj* downcast.
Niederlage *f* defeat.
Niederlande *pl* the Netherlands.
Niederländer(in) *m(f)* Dutchman(woman).
niederländisch *adj* Dutch.
niederlassen *vr* to settle.
Niederlassung *f* settlement; branch (bank, etc).
niederlegen *vt* to put down; to resign.
Niedersachsen *n* Lower Saxony.
Niederschlag *m* precipitation.
niederschlagen *vt* to knock down; to lower.
niederschreiben *vt* to write down.
niederwärts *adv* downwards.
niedrig *adj* low; lowly.
niemals *adv* never.
niemand *pron* no one.
Niere *f* kidney.
nieseln *vi* to drizzle.
Nieselregen *m* drizzle.
niesen *vi* to sneeze.
Nikotin *n* nicotine.
nimmer *adv* never.
nirgendwo(hin) *adv* nowhere.
Niveau *n* level.
nivellieren *vt* to level.
noch *adv* yet; still; also; even; else; **immer ~** still; **~ nicht** not yet; **~ besser** even better; **~ einmal** once again.
nochmals *adv* once again.
Nominativ *m* (*gr*) nominative.
nominieren *vt* to nominate.
Nonne *f* nun.
Nord(en) *m* north.
Nordamerika *n* North America.
Nordeuropa *n* northern Europe.

Nordirland *n* Northern Ireland.
nordisch *adj* northern.
nördlich *adj* northern, northerly.
Nordlicht *n* northern lights, aurora borealis.
Nordost(en) *m* mortheast.
Nordpol *m* North Pole.
Nordrhein-Westfalen *n* North Rhine-Westphalia.
Nordsee *f* North Sea.
Nord-Süd-Gefälle *n* north-south divide.
nordwärts *adv* northwards.
Nordwest(en) *m* northwest.
nörgeln *vt* to nag, carp.
Nörgler *m* faultfinder.
Norm *f* standard, norm.
normal *adj* normal.
normalerweise *adv* normally.
Normalfall *m*: **im ~** normally.
Normandie *f* Normandy.
Norwegen *n* Norway.
Norweger(in) *m(f)* Norwegian.
norwegisch *adj* Norwegian.
Not *f* need; emergency; poverty.
Notar *m* notary.
Notausgang *m* emergency exit.
Note *f* note; mark.
Notfall *m* emergency.
notfalls, nötigenfalls *adv* if necessary.
notieren *vt* to note; to quote; * *vi* to be quoted.
Notierung *f* quotation, price.
nötig *adj* necessary; **~ haben** to need.
Notiz *f* note, notice.
Notlandung *f* emergency landing.
notleidend *adj* needy.
Notlüge *f* white lie.
notorisch *adj* notorious.
Notstand *m* state of emergency.
Notwehr *f* self-defence.
notwendig *adj* necessary.
Notwendigkeit *f* necessity.
Notzucht *f* rape.
Novelle *f* short novel; amendment.

November *m* November.
nüchtern *adj* sober, sensible.
Nüchternheit *f* sobriety.
Nudel *f* noodle.
Null *f* zero, nought.
null *adj*: ~ **und nichtig** null and void.
numerisch *adj* numerical.
Nummer *f* number.
Nummernschild *n* number plate.
nun *adv* now; * *excl* well.
nur *adv* only.
Nürnberg *n* Nuremberg.
Nuß *f* nut.
Nußbaum *m* walnut tree.
Nußknacker *m* nutcracker.
nutzbar *adj* useful, usable.
Nutzen *m* use; benefit.
nutzen, nützen *vt* to use; * *vi* to be useful.
nützlich *adj* useful.
nutzlos *adj* useless.
Nylon *n* nylon.

O

Oase *f* oasis.
ob *conj* if, whether.
obdachlos *adj* homeless.
Obdachlose(r) *mf* homeless person.
Obdachlosenasyl *n* shelter for the homeless.
Obduktion *f* post-mortem.
obduzieren *vt* to do a post-mortem on.
oben *adv* above; upstairs.
obenan *adv* at the top.
obenauf *adv* up above, on the top; * *adj* in form.
obenerwähnt, obengenannt *adj* above mentioned.
Ober *m* waiter.
Oberarm *m* upper arm.
Oberarzt *m* senior physician.
Oberaufsicht *f* supervision.
Oberbayern *n* Upper Bavaria.

Oberbefehl *m* supreme commander.
Oberbefehlshaber *m* commander-in-chief.
Oberfläche *f* surface.
oberflächlich *adj* superficial.
Obergeschoß *n* upper storey.
oberhalb *adv prep* above.
Oberherrschaft *f* supremacy, sovereignty.
Oberin *f* matron; Mother Superior.
Oberkellner *m* head waiter.
Oberleutnant *m* first lieutenant.
Oberlicht *n* skylight.
Oberlippe *f* upper lip.
Oberst *m* colonel.
oberste(r,s) *adj* very top, topmost.
obgleich *conj* although.
Obhut *f* care, protection.
obig *adj* above.
Objekt *n* objective.
Objektiv *n* lens.
objektiv *adj* objective.
Objektivität *f* objectivity.
Oblate *f* wafer; host.
obligatorisch *adj* obligatory, mandatory.
Oboe *f* oboe.
Obrigkeit *f* authorities, administration; government.
obschon *conj* although.
Observatorium *n* observatory.
obskur *adj* obscure; dubious.
Obst *n* fruit.
Obstbaum *m* fruit tree.
Obstgarten *m* orchard.
Obstsalat *m* fruit salad.
obszön *adj* obscene.
Obszönität *f* obscenity.
obwohl *conj* although.
Ochse *m* ox.
ochsen *vt vi* to cram, swat.
Ochsenschwanzsuppe *f* oxtail soup.
Ochsenzunge *f* oxtongue.
öd(e) *adj* waste, barren; chill.
Öde *f* desert, waste(land); tedium.
oder *conj* or.

Ofen m stove; oven; fire, heater; furnace; cooker.

Ofenrohr n stovepipe.

offen adj open; frank; vacant; ~ **gesagt** to be honest.

offenbar adj obvious.

offenbaren vt to reveal, manifest.

Offenbarung f revelation.

offenbleiben vi to stay open; to remain open.

offenhalten vi to keep open.

Offenheit f candour, frankness.

offenherzig adj candid, frank; revealing.

offenkundig adj well-known; evident.

offenlassen vi to leave open.

offensichtlich adj obvious, evident.

offensiv adj offensive.

Offensive f offensive.

offenstehen vi to be open; to be unpaid.

öffentlich adj public; ~**er Feiertag** m bank holiday.

Öffentlichkeit f public; the general public.

offiziell adj official.

Offizier m officer.

Offizierskasino n officers' mess.

öffnen vt vr to open.

Öffner m opener.

Öffnung f opening.

oft adv often.

öfter adv more often, more frequently.

öfters adv often, frequently.

ohne prep conj without; ~ **weiteres** without a second thought.

ohnedies adv anyway.

ohnegleichen adj unsurpassed, without equal.

ohnehin adv anyway, in any case.

Ohnmacht f faint; impotence; **in ~ fallen** to faint.

ohnmächtig adj in a faint, unconscious; weak, impotent.

Ohr n ear; hearing.

Ohrenarzt m ear specialist.

ohrenbetäubend adj deafening.

Ohrenschmalz n earwax.

Ohrenschmerzen pl earache.

ohrfeigen vt: **jdn ~** to slap sb's face; to box sb's ears.

Ohrläppchen n ear lobe.

Ohrring m earring.

Ohrwurm m earwig.

Ökologe m **Ökologin** f ecologist.

Ökologie f ecology.

ökologisch adj ecological.

ökonomisch adj economical.

Oktan n octane.

Oktave f octave.

Oktober m October.

ökumenisch adj ecumenical.

Öl n oil.

Ölbaum m olive tree.

ölen vt to fuel, lubricate.

Ölfarbe f oil paint.

Ölfeld n oilfield.

Ölheizung f oil-fired central heating.

ölig adj oily.

Ölindustrie f oil industry.

oliv adj olive-green.

Olive f olive.

Ölsardine f sardine.

Öltanker m oil tanker.

Ölung f lubrication; oiling; anointment.

olympisch adj Olympic.

Oma f granny.

Omelett n omelette.

Omen n omen.

ominös adj ominous.

Omnibus m bus, omnibus.

Onanie f masturbation.

onanieren vi to masturbate.

Onkel m uncle.

Opa m grandpa.

Opal m opal.

Oper f opera; opera house.

Operation f operation.

Operationssaal m operating theatre.

Operette f operetta.

operieren vt to operate on; * vi to operate.

Opernglas *m* opera glasses.
Opernhaus *n* opera house.
Opernsänger(in) *m(f)* opera singer.
Opfer *n* sacrifice; victim.
opfern *vt* to sacrifice.
Opferung *f* sacrifice.
Opium *n* opium.
opponieren *vi*: **gegen jdn/etw ~** to oppose sb/something.
Opportunist *m* opportunist.
Opposition *f* opposition.
oppositionell *adj* opposing.
Optik *f* optics.
Optiker *m* optician.
optimal *adj* optimal, optimum.
Optimismus *m* optimism.
Optimist *m* optimist.
optimistisch *adj* optimistic.
Optimum *n* optimum.
optisch *adj* optical.
Orakel *n* oracle.
oral *adj* (*med*) oral.
Orange *f* orange.
orange *adj* orange.
Orangenmarmelade *f* marmalade.
Orchester *n* orchestra.
Orchidee *f* orchid.
Orden *m* order; decoration.
Ordensschwester *f* nun.
ordentlich *adj* decent, respectable; neat, tidy; not bad; real, proper; * *adv* properly.
Ordentlichkeit *f* respectability; neatness, tidiness.
ordinär *adj* common, vulgar.
ordnen *vt* to order, put in order.
Ordner *m* steward; file.
Ordnung *f* order; ordering; tidiness; **in ~!** okay!.
ordnungsgemäß *adj* proper, according to the rules.
ordnungsliebend *adj* orderly, methodical.
ordnungswidrig *adj* irregular, contrary to the rules.
Ordnungszahl *f* ordinal number.
Organ *n* organ; voice.
Organisation *f* organisation.

Organisator *m* organiser.
organisch *adj* organic.
organisieren *vt* to organise, arrange; * *vr* to organise.
Organismus *m* organism.
Organist *m* organist.
Orgasmus *m* orgasm.
Orgel *f* organ.
Orgie *f* orgy.
Orient *m* Orient, east.
Orientale *m* Oriental.
orientalisch *adj* oriental.
orientieren *vt* to locate; to inform; * *vr* to find one's bearings.
Orientierung *f* orientation.
Orientierungssinn *m* sense of direction.
original *adj* original.
Original *n* original.
Originalität *f* originality.
originell *adj* original.
Orkan *m* hurricane.
orkanartig *adj* gale-force; thunderous.
Ornament *n* decoration, ornament.
Ort *m* place; **an ~ und Stelle** on the spot.
orten *vt* to locate.
orthodox *adj* orthodox.
Orthographie *f* spelling orthography.
orthographisch *adj* orthographic.
Orthopädie *f* orthopaedics.
orthopädisch *adj* orthopaedic.
örtlich *adj* local.
Örtlichkeit *f* locality.
Ortschaft *f* village, small town.
ortsfremd *adj* non-local.
Ortszeit *f* local time.
Ortung *f* locating.
Öse *f* loop, eye.
Ostasien *n* Eastern Asia.
Osten *m* east.
Ostende *n* Ostend.
Osterei *n* Easter egg.
Osterfest *n* Easter.
Osterglocke *f* daffodil.
Osterhase *m* Easter bunny.
Ostermontag *m* Easter Mon-

day.

Ostern n Easter.

Österreich n Austria,

Österreicher(in) m(f) Austrian.

österreichisch adj Austrian,

östlich adj eastern, easterly.

Ostsee f Baltic Sea.

Otter m otter; * f adder.

Ouvertüre f overture.

oval adj oval.

Ovation f ovation.

Oxyd n oxide.

oxydieren vt vi to oxidise.

Oxydierung f oxidisation.

Ozean m ocean.

Ozon n ozone.

Ozonloch n ozone hole.

Ozonschicht f ozone layer.

P

Paar n pair; couple; **ein paar** a few.

paaren vt vr to couple; to mate.

Paarung f combination; mating.

paarweise adv in pairs, in couples.

Pacht f lease.

pachten vt to lease.

Pächter m leaseholder, tenant.

Pachtvertrag m lease.

Pack m pack, bundle; * n mob, rabble.

Päckchen n small package; packet; small parcel.

packen vt to pack; to grasp, seize; to grip.

Packen m bundle.

Packesel m packhorse.

Packung f packet; box; (med) compress.

Pägadoge m teacher.

pädagogisch adj educational, pedagogic.

Paddel n paddle.

paddeln vi to paddle.

Paket n parcel; packet.

Paketpost f parcel post.

Pakt m pact.

Palast m palace.

Palästina n Palestine.

Palme f palm; palm tree.

Palmsonntag m Palm Sunday.

Pampelmuse f grapefruit.

panieren vt to bread.

Panik f panic.

panisch adj panic stricken.

Panne f breakdown.

Pannenhilfe f breakdown service.

panschen vi to splash about; * vt to water down.

Panther m panther.

Pantoffel m slipper.

Pantomime f mime.

Panzer m tank; armour.

panzern vt to armour; * vr to arm oneself

Papagei m parrot.

Papier n paper.

Papiergeld n paper money.

Papierhändler m stationer.

Pappe f cardboard.

Pappel f poplar.

pappen vt vi to stick.

Paprika m paprika; pepper.

Papst m pope.

päpstlich adj papal.

Paradies n paradise.

paradiesisch adj heavenly.

Paradox n paradox.

Paragraph m paragraph; section.

parallel adj parallel.

Parameter m parameter.

Paranuß f Brazil nut.

Parasit m parasite.

Parfüm n perfume, scent.

parfümieren vt to perfume, scent.

parfümiert adj perfumed, scented.

Paris n Paris.

Park m park, public garden.

parken vt vi to park.

Parkett n (theatre) stalls.

Parkhaus n multi-storey car

park.

Parkplatz *m* car park; parking space.

Parkuhr *f* parking meter.

Parlament *n* parliament.

parlametarisch *adj* parliamentary.

Parodie *f* parody.

parodieren *vt* to parody.

Partei *f* party.

Parteitag *m* party conference.

Parterre *n* ground floor; (theatre) stalls.

Partie *f* part; game; outing.

Partisan *m* partisan.

Partitur *f* (*mus*) score.

Partizip *n* participle.

Partner(in) *m(f)* partner.

Partnerschaft *f* partnership.

Party *f* party.

Paß *m* pass; passport.

passabel *adj* passable, reasonable.

Passagier *m* passenger.

Paßamt *n* passport office.

passen *vi* to fit; to suit, be convenient.

passieren *vt* to pass; to strain; * *vi* to happen.

Passion *f* passion.

passioniert *adj* passionate, enthusiastic.

Passionsspiel *n* Passion Play.

passiv *adj* passive.

Passiv *n* passive.

Passiva *pl* liabilities.

Passivität *f* passiveness.

Paßkontrolle *f* passport control.

Paßstelle *f* passport office.

Paste *f* paste.

Pastell *n* pastel.

Pastete *f* pie, pastry.

pasteurisieren *vt* to pasteurise.

Pastor *m* pastor, minister

Pate *m* godfather.

Patenkind *n* godchild.

Patent *n* patent; (*mil*) commission.

patent *adj* clever.

Patentamt *n* patent office.

Patentante *f* godmother.

patentieren *vt* to patent.

Patentinhaber *m* patentee.

pathetisch *adj* emotional; bombastic.

Pathologe *m* pathologist.

pathologisch *adj* pathological.

Pathos *n* emotiveness, emotionalism.

Patient(in) *m(f)* patient.

Patin *f* godmother.

Patina *f* patina.

Patriot *m* patriot.

patriotisch *adj* patriotic.

Patriotismus *m* patriotism.

Patrone *f* cartridge.

Patrouille *f* patrol.

patrouillieren *vi* to patrol.

patsch *excl* splash.

Patsche *f* mess, jam.

patschen *vi* to smack, slap.

patzig *adj* cheeky, saucy.

Pauke *f* kettledrum; **auf die ~ hauen** to live it up.

pauken *vt vi* (*coll*) to swot.

pauschal *adj* inclusive; sweeping.

Pauschalpreis *m* all-in price.

Pauschalsumme *f* lump sum.

Pause *f* interval; break; pause.

pausen *vt* to trace.

Pavian *m* baboon.

Pazifik *m* Pacific (Ocean).

Pech *n* pitch; bad luck; **~ haben** to be unlucky.

Pedal *n* pedal.

Pedant *m* pedant.

pedantisch *adj* pedantic.

peilen *vt* to get a fix on.

Pein *f* pain, agony.

peinigen *vi* to torture; to torment.

peinlich *adj* awkward, painful; painstaking.

Peitsche *f* whip.

peitschen *vt* to whip.

Pelikan *m* pelican.

Pelle *f* skin.

pellen *vi* to skin, peel.

Pelz *m* fur.

Pendel *n* pendulum.

pendeln *vi* to commute; to op-

erate a shuttle service.
Pendler *m* commuter.
Penis *m* penis.
pennen *vi* to kip.
Penner *m* tramp.
Pension *f* pension; retirement; guest-house.
Pensionär(in) *m(f)* pensioner.
pensionieren *vt* to pension off.
pensioniert *adj* retired.
Pensionierung *f* retirement.
per *prep* by, per.
perfekt *adj* perfect.
perforieren *vt* to perforate.
Pergament *n* parchment.
Pergamentpapier *n* greaseproof paper.
Periode *f* period.
periodisch *adj* periodic; recurring.
Perle *f* pearl.
perlen *vi* to sparkle; to trickle.
Perlmutt *n* mother-of-pearl.
perplex *adj* dumbfounded.
Perser *m* Persian.
Persien *n* Persia.
persisch *adj* Persian.
Person *f* person.
Personal *n* personnel, staff.
Personalausweis *m* identity card.
Personalcomputer *m* personal computer.
Personalien *pl* particulars.
Personenaufzug *m* lift, elevator.
Personenkraftwagen *m* car.
Personenzug *m* passenger train.
personifizieren *vt* to personify.
persönlich *adj* personal; * *adv* personally; in person.
Persönlichkeit *f* personality.
Perspektive *f* perspective.
Perücke *f* wig.
Pessimismus *m* pessimism.
Pessimist *m* pessimist.
pessimistisch *adj* pessimistic.
Pest *f* plague.
Petersilie *f* parsley.
Pfad *m* path.
Pfadfinder *m* boy scout.

Pfadfinderin *f* girl guide.
Pfahl *m* post, stake.
Pfand *n* pledge, security.
pfänden *vt* to seize, distrain.
Pfändung *f* seizure, distraint.
Pfanne *f* frying pan.
Pfannkuchen *m* pancake.
Pfarrer *m* vicar; priest.
Pfarrhaus *n* vicarage.
Pfau *m* peacock.
Pfeffer *m* pepper.
Pfefferkorn *n* peppercorn.
Pfefferkuchen *m* gingerbread.
Pfefferminz *n* peppermint.
pfeffern *vt* to pepper; (*coll*) to fling.
Pfeife *f* whistle.
pfeifen *vi vt* to whistle.
Pfeiler *m* pillar.
Pfeilschütze *m* archer.
Pferd *n* horse.
Pferdestall *m* stable.
Pfingsten *pl* Whitsuntide.
Pfingstsonntag *m* Whitsunday, Pentecost.
Pfirsich *m* peach.
pflanzen *vt* to plant.
Pflanzenwuchs *m* vegetation.
Pflaume *f* plum; prune.
pflegen *vt* to nurse, look after.
Pfleger *m* orderly; male nurse.
Pflegerin *f* nurse.
Pflicht *f* duty.
pflücken *vt* to pick, pluck, gather.
Pflug *m* plough.
pflügen *vt* to plough.
Pforte *f* gate; door.
Pförtner *m* porter, doorman.
Pfote *f* paw.
pfropfen *vt* to cram; to graft.
pfui *excl* ugh!.
Pfund *n* pound.
pfuschen *vi* to be sloppy.
Pfuscher *m* sloppy worker.
Pfütze *f* puddle.
Phänomen *n* phenomenal.
phänomenal *adj* phenomenal.
Phantasie *f* fancy, imagination.
phantasieren *vi* to fantasise.
phantasievoll *adj* imaginative.
phantastisch *adj* fantastic.

Philippinen *pl* (the) Philippines.

Philologe *m* philologist.

Philologie *f* philology.

Philosoph *m* philosopher.

Philosophie *f* philosophy.

philosophisch *adj* philosophical.

Phonetik *f* phonetics.

phonetisch *adj* phonetic.

Phosphor *m* phosphorus.

Phrase *f* phrase.

Physik *f* physics.

physikalisch *adj* of physics.

Physiker(in) *m(f)* physicist.

Physiologie *f* physiology.

physisch *adj* physical.

Pianist(in) *m(f)* pianist.

picken *vi* to pick, peck.

Picknick *n* picnic.

piepen *vi* to chirp.

piepsen *vi* to chirp.

Pigment *n* pigment.

Pilger(in) *m(f)* pilgrim.

Pilgerfahrt *f* pilgrimage.

Pille *f* pill.

Pilot *m* pilot.

Pilz *m* fungus; mushroom; toadstool.

Pinguin *m* penguin.

Pinie *f* pine.

pinkeln *vi* to pee.

Pinsel *m* paintbrush.

Pionier *m* pioneer; (*mil*) sapper.

Pirat *m* pirate.

Piratensender *m* pirate radio station.

Pistole *f* pistol.

Pizza *f* pizza.

plädieren *vi* to plead.

Plädoyer *n* speech for the defence; plea.

Plage *f* plague; nuisance.

plagen *vt* to torment; * *vr* to toil, slave.

Plakat *n* placard; poster.

Plan *m* plan; map.

planen *vt* to plan; plot.

Planer *m* planner.

Planet *m* planet.

Planetenbahn *f* orbit.

planieren *vt* to plane, level.

Planke *f* plank.

Plankton *n* plankton.

planmäßig *adj* systematic; according to plan.

planschen *vi* to splash.

Plantage *f* plantation.

Planung *f* planning.

Planwirtschaft *f* planned economy.

plappern *vi* to chatter.

plärren *vi* to cry, whine; to blare.

Plasma *n* plasma.

Plastik *f* sculpture; * *n* plastic.

Plastiktüte *f* plastic bag.

plastisch *adj* plastic.

Platane *f* plane (tree).

Platin *n* platinum.

platonisch *adj* platonic.

platschen *vi* to splash.

plätschern *vi* to babble.

platschnaß *adj* drenched.

platt *adj* flat.

plattdeutsch *adj* Low German.

Platte *f* plate; flag; record; tile.

Plattenspieler *m* record-player.

Plattenfuß *m* flat foot.

Platz *m* place; seat; space, room; square: ~ **nehmen** to take a seat.

Platzanweiser(in) *m(f)* usher(ette).

platzen *vi* to burst; to explode.

Platzkarte *f* seat reservation.

Platzmangel *m* lack of space.

Plauderei *f* chat, conversation.

plaudern *vi* to chat, talk.

plausibel *adj* plausible.

plazieren *vt* to place; * *vr* to be placed; to be seeded.

Pleite *f* bankruptcy.

pleite *adj* (*coll*) broke.

Plenum *n* plenum.

Plombe *f* lead seal; (tooth) filling.

plombieren *vt* to seal; to fill (tooth).

plötzlich *adj* sudden; * *adv* suddenly.

plump *adj* clumsy; heavy-look-

ing, shapeless.
plumpsen *vt* to plump down, fall.
Plunder *m* rubbish.
plündern *vt* to plunder; to sack; * *vi* to plunder.
Plünderung *f* plundering, pillage, sack.
Plural *m* plural.
Plus *n* plus; advantage; profit.
Plutonium *n* plutonium.
Po *m* (*coll*) bottom, bum.
Pöbel *m* mob, rabble.
pochen *vi* to knock; to pound.
Pocken *pl* smallpox.
Podium *n* podium.
Poesie *f* poetry.
Poet *m* poet.
poetisch *adj* poetic.
pökeln *vt* to pickle, salt.
Poker *n/m* poker.
Pol *m* pole.
polar *adj* polar.
Polarkreis *m* Arctic circle.
Pole *m* Pole.
Polen *n* Poland.
Police *f* insurance policy.
polieren *vt* to polish.
Polin *f* Pole.
Politik *f* politics; policy.
Politiker(in) *m(f)* politician.
politisch *adj* political.
Politur *f* polish.
Polizei *f* police.
Polizeibeamte(r) *m* police officer.
Polizeistaat *m* police state.
Polizeiwache *f* police station.
Polizist(in) *m(f)* policeman (woman).
polnisch *adj* Polish.
Polster *n* cushion; upholstery; padding.
Polsterer *m* upholsterer.
polstern *vt* to upholster; to pad.
Polterabend *m* party on eve of wedding.
poltern *vi* to crash; to rant.
Pomp *m* pomp.
pompös *adj* showy, ostentatious.
Popmusik *f* pop music.

poppig *adj* gaudy.
populär *adj* popular.
Popularität *f* popularity.
Pore *f* pore.
Pornographie *f* pornography.
pornographisch *adj* pornography.
porös *adj* porous.
Porree *f* leek.
Portefeuille *n* portfolio.
Portemonnaie *n* purse.
Portier *m* porter; doorman.
Porto *n* postage.
portofrei *adv* post free, carriage free.
Porträt *n* portrait.
porträtieren *vt* to paint, portray.
Portugal *n* Portugal.
Portugiese *m* Portuguese.
Portugiesin *f* Portuguese.
portugiesisch *adj* Portuguese.
Porzellan *n* china, porcelain.
Posaune *f* trombone.
Pose *f* pose.
Position *f* position.
positiv *adj* positive.
possessiv *adj* possessive.
Post *f* post (office); mail.
Postamt *n* post office.
Postanweisung *f* postal order.
Postbeamte(r) *m* post office clerk.
Postbote *m* postman.
Poster *n* poster.
Postfach *n* PO box.
Postkarte *f* postcard.
postlagernd *adv* poste restante.
Postleitzahl *f* post code.
Postsparkasse *f* post office savings bank.
Poststempel *m* postmark.
potent *adj* potent.
Potential *n* potential.
potentiell *adj* potential.
Potenz *f* power; potency.
Pracht *f* splendour, magnificence.
prächtig *adj* splendid.
Prachtstück *n* showpiece.
prachtvoll *adj* magnificent,

splendid.
Prädikat *n* title; predicate.
Prag *n* Prague.
prägen *vt* to stamp; to mint; to coin; to form.
prägnant *adj* precise, terse.
Prägung *f* minting; forming.
prahlen *vi* to boast, brag.
Prahlerei *f* boasting.
Praktik *f* practice.
praktikabel *adj* practicable.
Praktikant(in) *m(f)* trainee.
praktisch *adj* practical, handy.
praktizieren *vt vi* to practise.
Praline *f* chocolate.
prall *adj* taut; firmly rounded; plump.
prallen *vi* to bounce, rebound; to blaze.
Prämie *f* premium; prize, award.
prämieren *vt* to give an award to.
Präparat *n* preparation; medicine.
Präposition *f* preposition.
Prärie *f* prairie.
Präsens *n* present tense.
präsentieren *vt* to present.
Präservativ *n* contraceptive.
Präsident(in) *m(f)* president.
Präsidentschaft *f* presidency.
Präsidium *n* presidency, chairmanship.
prasseln *vi* to crackle; to drum.
Praxis *f* practice; surgery; office.
präzis *adj* precise.
Präzision *f* precision.
predigen *vt vi* to preach.
Predigt *f* sermon.
Preis *m* prize; price.
preisbewußt *adj* price-conscious.
Preiselbeere *f* cranberry.
preisen *vi* to praise.
preisgeben *vt* to abandon; to sacrifice; to expose.
Preisklasse *f* price range.
Preisliste *f* price list.
prekär *adj* precarious.
prellen *vt* to bump; to cheat,

swindle.
Prellung *f* bruise.
Premiere *f* premiere.
Premierminister *m* prime minister, premier.
Presse *f* press, newspapers.
Pressekonferenz *f* press conference.
pressen *vt* to press.
pressieren *vi* to (be in a) hurry.
Preßburg *n* Bratislava.
Preßluft *f* compressed air.
Prestige *n* prestige.
Preuße *m* Prussian.
Preußen *n* Prussia.
preußisch *adj* Prussian.
prickeln *vt vi* to tingle; to tickle.
Priester *m* priest.
prima *adj* excellent, first-class.
primär *adj* primary.
Primel *f* primrose.
primitiv *adj* primitive.
Prinz *m* prince.
Prinzessin *f* princess.
Prinzip *n* principle.
Priorität *f* priority.
Prisma *n* prism.
privat *adj* private.
Privatgesellschaft *f* private company.
privatisieren *vt* to privatise.
Privatisierung *f* privatisation.
pro *prep* per.
Probe *f* test; sample; rehearsal.
proben *vt* to try; to rehearse.
probeweise *adv* on approval.
Probezeit *f* trial period; probationary period.
probieren *vt* to try; to taste, sample; * *vi* to try; to taste.
Problem *n* problem.
problematisch *adj* problematical.
Produkt *n* product; produce.
Produktion *f* production; output.
produktiv *adj* productive.
Produktivität *f* productivity.
Produzent(in) *m(f)* manufacturer; producer.
produzieren *vt* to produce.

Professor *m* professor.
Profil *n* profile; image.
Profit *m* profit.
profitieren *vi* to profit.
Prognose *f* prognosis, prediction.
Programm *n* programme; program.
programmieren *vt* to program.
Programmier(in) *m(f)* programmer.
Projekt *m* project.
progressiv *adj* progressive.
Projektion *f* projection.
Projektor *m* projector.
proklamieren *vt* to proclaim.
Prokurist(in) *m(f)* company secretary.
Proletarier *m* proletarian.
Prolog *m* prologue.
Promenade *f* promenade.
Promotion *f* doctorate.
promovieren *vi* to do a doctorate.
prompt *adj* prompt.
Pronomen *n* pronoun.
Propaganda *f* propaganda.
Prophet *m* prophet.
prophezieren *vt* to prophesy.
Prophezierung *f* prophecy.
Proportion *f* proportion.
Prosa *f* prose.
prosaisch *adj* prosaic.
Prospekt *m* prospectus; brochure, leaflet.
prost *excl* cheers.
Prostituierte *f* prostitute.
Prostitution *f* prostitution.
Protein *n* protein.
Protest *m* protest.
Protestant(in) *m(f)* Protestant.
protestantisch *adj* Protestant.
protestieren *vi* to protest.
Protokoll *n* protocol; minutes.
protokollieren *vt* to take down in the minutes.
protzen *vi* to show off.
protzig *adj* ostentatious.
Provinz *f* province.
provinziell *adj* provincial.
Provision *f* commission; bank charges.

provisorisch *adj* provisional.
Provokation *f* provocation.
provozieren *vt* to provoke.
Prozent *n* per cent, percentage.
Prozeß *m* lawsuit, action, trial.
Prozession *f* procession.
prüde *adj* prudish.
Prüderie *f* prudery.
prüfen *vt* to examine, test; to check.
Prüfer *m* examiner.
Prüfung *f* test, examination; checking.
prügeln *vt* to beat; * *vr* to fight.
Psalm *m* psalm.
Psychiater *m* psychiatrist.
psychiatrisch *adj* psychiatric.
psychisch *adj* mental.
Psychoanalyse *f* psychoanalysis.
Psychologe *m* psychologist.
Psychologie *f* psychology.
psychologisch *adj* psychological.
Pubertät *f* puberty.
Publikum *n* crowd; audience.
publizieren *vt* to publish, publicise.
Pudel *m* poodle.
Puder *m* powder.
Puderdose *f* powder compact.
pudern *vt* to powder.
Puffer *m* buffer.
Puls *m* pulse.
Pulsader *f* artery.
pulsieren *vi* to throb, pulsate.
Pult *n* desk.
Pulver *n* powder.
pulverig *adj* powdery.
pummelig *adj* chubby.
Pumpe *f* pump.
pumpen *vt* to pump; (*coll*) to lend; to borrow.
Punkt *m* point; dot; full stop.
punktieren *vt* to dot; (*med*) aspirate.
pünktlich *adj* punctual.
Pünktlichkeit *f* punctuality.
Punktzahl *f* score.
Pupille *f* pupil.
Puppe *f* doll; puppet; chrysalis.

Puppentheater *n* puppet theatre.

pur *adj* pure; sheer; neat.

purpurn *adj* purple, crimson.

purzeln *vi* to tumble.

pusten *vi* to puff, blow.

Pute *f* turkey-hen.

Puter *m* turkey-cock.

Putz *m* plaster, roughcast.

putzen *vt* to clean; * *vr* to clean oneself

Putzfrau *f* charwoman.

putzig *adj* quaint, funny.

Pyjama *m* pyjamas.

Pyramide *f* pyramid.

Pyrenäen *pl* (the) Pyrenees.

Q

Quacksalber *m* quack (doctor).

Quader *m* square stone; cuboid.

Quadrat *n* square.

quadratisch *adj* square.

Quadratmeter *m* square metre.

quaken *vi* to croak; to quack.

quäken *vi* to screech.

Qual *f* pain, agony; anguish.

quälen *vt* to torment; * *vr* to struggle; to torment oneself.

Qualifikation *f* qualification.

qualifizieren *vt* to qualify; to label; * *vr* to qualify.

Qualität *f* quality.

Qualitätsware *f* article of high quality.

Qualle *f* jellyfish.

Qualm *m* dense smoke.

qualmen *vt vi* to smoke.

qualmig *adj* smoky, full of smoke.

qualvoll *adj* agonising, excruciating.

Quantentheorie *f* quantum theory.

Quantität *f* quantity.

quantitativ *adj* quantitative.

Quantum *n* quantity, amount.

Quarantäne *f* quarantine.

Quark *m* curd cheese.

Quartal *n* quarter (year).

Quartett *n* quartet.

Quartier *n* quarters; accommodation; district.

Quarz *m* quartz.

quasseln *vi* (*coll*) to natter.

Quatsch *m* nonsense, rubbish.

quatschen *vi* to chat, natter.

Quecksilber *n* mercury.

Quelle *f* spring; source.

quellen *vi* to well up; to stream.

Quellwasser *n* spring water.

quer *adv* crosswise; at right angles.

Querbalken *m* crossbeam.

querfeldein *adv* across country.

Querflöte *f* flute.

Querschnitt *m* cross-section.

Querstraße *f* intersecting road.

quetschen *vt* to squash, crush; to bruise.

Quetschung *f* bruise.

quiecken *vi* to squeak.

quietschen *vt* to screech.

Quintessenz *f* quintessence.

Quintett *n* quintet.

quitt *adj* quits, even.

Quitte *f* quince.

quittieren *vt* to give a receipt for.

Quittung *f* receipt.

Quiz *n* quiz.

Quote *f* rate, number.

Quotient *m* quotient.

R

Rabatt *m* discount; rebate.

Rabe *f* raven.

Rache *f* revenge, vengeance.

rächen *vt* to avenge; * *vr* to take (one's) revenge; **das wird sich ~** you'll pay for that.

Rad *n* wheel; bike.

Radar *m/n* radar.

radebrechen *vi*: **deutsch** *etc*
  ~ to speak broken German *etc*.
radeln *vi* to cycle.
radfahren *vi* to cycle.
Radfahrer(in) *m(f)* cyclist.
radieren *vt* to rub out, erase;
  to etch.
Radiergummi *m* rubber,
  eraser.
Radierung *f* etching.
Radieschen *n* radish.
radikal *adj* radical.
Radio *n* radio.
radioaktiv *adj* radioactive.
Radioaktivität *f* radioactivity.
Radius *m* radius.
Radkappe *f* hub cap.
Radrennen *n* cycling race.
raffen *vt* to snatch, pick up;
  gather up.
ragen *vi* to tower, rise.
Rahm *m* cream.
Rahmen *m* frame(work); **im ~
  von** within the framework of.
rahmen *vt* to frame.
Rakete *f* rocket.
rammen *vt* to ram.
Rampe *f* ramp.
ramponieren *vt* (*coll*) to damage.
Ramsch *m* junk.
Rand *m* edge; rim; margin.
randalieren *vi* to (go on the)
  rampage.
Rang *m* rank; standing; quality.
rangieren *vt* (*rail*) to shunt;
  * *vi* to rank, be classed.
Ranke *f* tendril, shoot.
ranzig *adj* rancid.
rar *adj* rare.
Rarität *f* rarity; curio.
rasch *adj* quick, swift.
rascheln *vi* to rustle.
Rasen *m* lawn; grass.
rasen *vi* to rave; to race.
rasend *adj* furious.
Rasenmäher *m* lawnmower.
Rasierapparat *m* shaver.
rasieren *vt vr* to shave.
Rasierklinge *f* razor blade.
Rasierpinsel *m* shaving brush.

Rasse *f* race; breed.
Rassenhund *m* thoroughbred
  dog.
rasseln *vi* to clatter.
Rassenhaß *m* race hatred.
Rassismus *m* racism.
Rast *f* rest.
rasten *vi* to rest.
rastlos *adj* tireless; restless.
Rasur *f* shaving.
Rat *m* councillor; counsellor;
  counsel, advice.
Rate *f* instalment.
raten *vt vi* to guess; **jdm ~** to
  advise sb.
Ratenzahlung *f* hire purchase.
Ratgeber *m* adviser.
Rathaus *n* town hall.
ratifizieren *vt* to ratify.
Ratifizierung *f* ratification.
Ration *f* ration.
rational *adj* rational.
rationalisieren *vt* to rational-
  ise.
Rationalisierung *f* rationali-
  sation.
rationieren *vt* to ration.
ratsam *adj* advisable.
Ratschlag *m* piece of advice.
Rätsel *n* puzzle; riddle.
rätselhaft *adj* mysterious.
Ratte *f* rat.
Rattenfänger *m* ratcatcher.
Raub *m* robbery.
rauben *vt* to rob; to kidnap, abduct.
Räuber *m* robber.
raubgierig *adj* rapacious.
Raubkopie *f* pirate copy.
Raubtier *n* predator.
Raubvogel *m* bird of prey.
Rauch *m* smoke.
rauchen *vt vi* to smoke.
Raucher(in) *m(f)* smoker.
räuchern *vt* to smoke, cure.
rauchig *adj* smoky.
raufen *vt* to pull out (hair); * *vi*
  vr to fight.
Rauferei *f* brawl.
rauh *adj* rough, coarse; harsh.
Raum *m* room; space.
räumen *vt* to clear; to vacate;

to put away.
Raumfähre f space shuttle.
Raumfahrt f space travel.
räumlich adj spatial.
Räumlichkeiten fpl premises.
Räumung f evacuation; clearing away.
raunen vi to whisper, murmur.
Raupe f caterpillar.
Raupenschlepper m caterpillar tractor.
Rausch m intoxication.
rauschen vi to rush; to rustle; to hiss.
rauschend adj thunderous; sumptuous.
Rauschgift n drug.
Rauschgiftsüchtige(r) mf drug addict.
räuspern vr to clear one's throat.
Razzia f raid.
reagieren vi to react.
Reaktion f reaction.
Reaktor m reactor.
real adj real, material.
realisieren vi to carry out.
Realismus m realism.
realistisch adj realistic.
Rebe f vine.
rebellieren vi to rebel.
Rebellion f rebellion.
rebellisch adj rebellious.
Rebhuhn n partridge.
rebooten vt to reboot.
Rechen m rake.
rechen vt vi to rake.
Rechenfehler m miscalculation.
rechnen vt vi to calculate.
Rechnen n arithmetic.
Rechner m calculator; computer.
Rechnung f calculation(s); bill, invoice.
Rechnungsjahr n financial year.
Rechnungsprüfer m auditor.
Rechnungswesen n accountancy.
Recht n right, law; **das ~ verletzen** to break the law.

recht adj right; * adv really, quite; **~ haben** to be right.
Rechte f right (hand); (political) Right.
rechte(r,s) adj right; right-wing.
Rechteck n right angle.
rechten vi to argue, dispute.
rechtfertigen vt to justify; * vr to justify oneself
Rechtfertigung f justification.
rechtlich adj legal.
rechtlos adj with no rights.
rechtmäßig adj legal, lawful.
rechts adv on/to the right.
Rechtsabteilung f legal department.
Rechtsanwalt   m
Rechtsanwältin f lawyer.
Rechtshänder m right-handed person.
rechtsverbindlich adj legally binding.
rechtswidrig adj illegal.
Rechtswissenschaft f jurisprudence.
rechtzeitig adj timely; * adv on time.
Reck n horizontal bar.
recken vt vr to stretch.
recyceln vt to recycle.
Redakteur m editor.
Redaktion f editing; editorial staff.
Rede f talk;, speech.
Redefreiheit f freedom of speech.
redegewandt adj eloquent.
reden vi to talk, speak: * vt to say; to talk.
redlich adj honest.
Redner(in) m(f) orator, speaker.
redselig adj talkative.
reduzieren vt to reduce.
Reede f protected anchorage.
Reeder m shipowner.
Reederei f shipping company.
referieren vi: **~ über** +acc to speak/talk on.
reflektieren vt to reflect.
Reflex m reflex.

reflexiv *adj* (*gr*) reflexive.
Reform *f* reform.
Reformation *f* reformation.
reformieren *vt* to reform.
Regal *n* shelves, bookcase; stand, rack.
rege *adj* lively; keen.
Regel *f* rule; (*med*) period; **in der ~** as a rule.
regelmäßig *adj* regular.
Regelmäßigkeit *f* regularity.
regeln *vt* to regulate, control; settle; * *vr* **sich von selbst ~** to take care of itself.
Regelung *f* regulation; settlement; ruling.
regelwidrig *adj* irregular, against the rules.
regen *vt vr* to move, stir.
Regen *m* rain.
Regenbogen *m* rainbow.
Regenguß *m* shower.
Regenmantel *m* raincoat.
Regenschirm *m* umbrella.
Regenwald *m* rainforest.
Regenwurm *m* earthworm.
Regenzeit *f* rainy season.
Regie *f* direction (of film, etc); (theatre) production.
regieren *vt* to govern, rule.
Regierung *f* government; reign.
Regierungswechsel *m* change of government.
Regiment *n* regiment.
Region *f* region.
Regisseur *m* producer; film director.
Register *n* register; table of contents, index.
registrieren *vt* to register.
Regler *m* regulator, governor.
reglos *adj* motionless.
regnen *vi* to rain.
regnerisch *adj* rainy.
regulär *adj* regular.
regulieren *vt* to regulate; to settle; to adjust.
Regung *f* motion; feeling, impulse.
Reh *n* roe, deer.
Rehbock *m* roebuck.

Rehkitz *n* fawn.
Reibe *f* grater.
reiben *vt* to rub; grate.
Reibung *f* friction.
Reich *n* realm; kingdom, empire; **das Dritte ~** the Third Reich.
reich *adj* rich.
reichen *vi* to reach; to be enough; * *vt* to hold out; to pass, hand out.
Reichtum *m* wealth, riches.
reif *adj* ripe; mature.
Reif *m* ring, hoop.
Reife *f* ripeness; maturity.
reifen *vi* to ripen; to mature.
Reifen *m* ring, hoop; tyre.
Reifendruck *m* tyre pressure.
Reifenpanne *f* puncture.
Reihe *f* row; series.
Reihenfolge *f* sequence.
Reihenhaus *n* terraced house.
Reiher *m* heron.
Reim *m* rhyme.
reimen *vt* to rhyme.
rein *adj* clean; pure; * *adv* purely.
Reinfall *m* let-down.
Reingewinn *m* net profit.
Reinheit *f* purity; cleanness.
reinigen *vt* to clean, purify.
Reinigung *f* cleaning.
Reinigungsanstalt *f* dry cleaner's.
Reinigungsmittel *n* detergent.
Reis *m* rice.
Reise *f* journey; voyage.
Reisebüro *n* travel agency.
Reisebus *m* coach.
Reiseführer *m* guide; guidebook.
Reiseindustrie *f* travel industry.
Reiseleiter *m* courier.
reisen *vi* to travel.
Reisende *m* traveller.
Reisepaß *m* passport.
Reiseversicherung *f* travel insurance.
reißen *vt* to tear; to pull, drag; * *vi* to tear; to pull, drag.
reißend *adj* raging.

Reißnagel *m* drawing pin.
Reißverschluß *m* zip, zip fastener.
reiten *vt vi* to ride (horse).
Reiter(in) *m(f)* rider.
Reiz *m* charm; attraction; stimulus.
reizbar *adj* irritating.
Reizbarkeit *f* irritability.
reizen *vt* to stimulate; to irritate; to appeal to, attract.
reizend *adj* charming.
reizevoll *adj* attractive.
rekeln *vr* to stretch out; to lounge about.
Reklamation *f* complaint.
Reklame *f* advertisement; advertising.
reklamieren *vt* to demand back; to put in a claim.
rekonstruieren *vt* to reconstruct.
Rekord *m* record.
Rektor *m* rector; headteacher.
Rektorat *n* rectorate; headship.
Rekrut *m* recruit, conscript.
Relais *n* relay.
relativ *adj* relative.
Relativität *f* relativity.
relevant *adj* relevant.
Religion *f* religion.
religiös *adj* religious.
Rendezvous *n* rendezvous.
Rendite *f* rate of return.
Rennbahn *f* racecourse; race track.
rennen *vi* to run, race.
Rennen *n* race; running.
Rennfahrer *m* racing driver.
Rennpferd *n* racing horse.
Rennwagen *m* racing car.
renommiert *adj* renowned.
renovieren *vt* to renovate, refurbish.
Renovierung *f* renovation, refurbishment.
rentabel *adj* profitable, lucrative.
Rentabilität *f* profitability.
Rente *f* pension.
Rentier *n* reindeer.
rentieren *vr* to pay, be profit-
able.
Rentner(in) *m(f)* pensioner.
Reparatur *f* repair; repairing.
reparieren *vt* to repair.
Reportage *f* report; live coverage.
Reporter *m* reporter, commentator.
repräsentativ *adj* representative; impressive.
repräsentieren *vt* to represent; to constitute; * *vi* to perform official duties.
reprivatisieren *vt* to denationalise.
Repravitisierung *f* denationalisation.
Reproduktion *f* reproduction.
reproduzieren *vt* to reproduce.
Reptil *n* reptile.
Republik *f* republic.
Republikaner *m* Republican.
republikanisch *adj* republican.
Reservat *n* reservation.
Reserve *f* reserve.
Reserverad *n* spare wheel.
reservieren *vt* to reserve.
Reservoir *n* reservoir.
Reservierung *f* reservation.
Residenz *f* residence, seat.
resignieren *vi* to resign.
resolut *adj* resolute.
Resonanz *f* resonance; response.
Resozialisierung *f* rehabilitation.
Respekt *m* respect.
respektieren *vt* to respect.
respektlos *adj* disrespectful.
respektvoll *adj* respectful.
Ressort *n* departure.
Rest *m* rest, remainder; remains.
Restaurant *n* restaurant.
restaurieren *vt* to restore.
Restbetrag *m* outstanding sum, remainder.
restlich *adj* remaining.
Resultat *n* result.
retten *vt* to save, rescue.
Retter(in) *m(f)* rescuer.

Rettich *m* radish.

Rettung *f* help; **seine letzte ~** his last hope.

Rettungsboot *n* lifeboat.

Rettungswagen *m* ambulance.

retuschieren *vt* to retouch (photos).

Reue *f* remorse; regret.

reuen *vt*: **es reut ihn** he regrets it.

reuig *adj* penitent.

Revanche *f* revenge.

revanchieren *vr* to get one's own back, have one's revenge; to return the compliment.

Revier *n* district; police station; beat.

Revolte *f* revolt.

revoltieren *vi* to rebel.

Revolution *f* revolution.

Revolutionär *m* revolutionary.

revolutionieren *vt* to revolutionise.

Revolver *m* revolver.

rezensieren *vt* to review.

Rezension *f* review.

Rezept *n* recipe; (*med*) prescription.

Rezeption *f* reception.

Rezession *f* recession.

rezitieren *vt* to recite.

R-Gespräch *n* reverse charge call.

Rhabarber *m* rhubarb.

Rhein *m* Rhine.

rhetorisch *adj* rhetorical.

Rheuma *n* rheumatism.

rheumatisch *adj* rheumatic.

Rheumatismus *m* rheumatism.

Rhinozeros *n* rhinoceros.

rhythmisch *adj* rhythmical.

Rhythmus *m* rhythm.

richten *vt* to adjust; to direct; to aim; * *vr*: **sich ~ an** +*acc* to direct at.

Richter(in) *m(f)* judge, magistrate.

richterlich *adj* judicial.

Richtlinie *f* guideline.

Richtung *f* direction; tendency.

riechen *vt vi* to smell.

Riese *m* giant.

rieseln *vt* to trickle; to fall gently.

Riesenrad *n* big wheel.

riesig *adj* gigantic.

Riesenschlange *f* boa constrictor.

Riff *n* reef.

Rind *n* ox; cow; cattle; beef.

Rinde *f* bark; crust; rind.

Rindfleisch *n* beef.

Ring *m* ring.

Ringeinatter *f* grass snake.

ringen *vi* to wrestle; to struggle.

Ringen *n* wrestling.

Ringfinger *m* ring finger.

Ringkämpfer *m* wrestler.

ringsherum *adv* round about.

Ringstraße *f* ring road.

Rinne *f* gutter, drain.

rinnen *vi* to run, trickle.

Rippe *f* rib.

Risiko *n* risk; venture.

riskant *adj* risky, hazardous.

riskieren *vt* to risk.

Riß *m* tear; crack; scratch.

rissig *adj* torn; cracked; scratched.

Ritt *m* ride.

Ritter *m* knight.

ritterlich *adj* chivalrous.

Rivale *m* rival.

Rivalität *f* rivalry.

Robbe *f* seal.

Roboter *m* robot.

robust *adj* robust.

Rock *m* skirt; jacket; tunic.

Rodel *m* toboggan.

Rodelbahn *f* toboggan run.

rodeln *vi* to toboggan.

roden *vi* to clear.

Rogen *m* roe, spawn.

Roggen *m* rye.

Roggenbrot *n* rye bread.

roh *adj* raw; coarse, crude.

Rohmaterial *n* raw material.

Rohöl *n* crude oil.

Rohr *n* pipe, tube; cane; reed; barrel.

Röhre *f* tube, pipe; valve; oven.

Rohrleitung *f* pipeline.

Rohrzucker m cane sugar.
Rohstoff m raw material.
Rokoko n rococo.
Rolladen m shutter.
Rollbahn f runway.
Rolle f roll; role; spool; **keine ~ spielen** not to matter.
rollen vt vi to roll; to taxi.
Rollschuh m roller skate.
Rollstuhl m wheelchair.
Rolltreppe f escalator.
Rom n Rome.
Roman m novel.
Romantik f romanticism.
romantisch adj romantic.
Romanze f romance.
Römer m Roman.
römisch adj Roman.
römisch-katholisch adj Roman Catholic.
röntgen vt to X-ray.
Röntgenstrahlen pl X-rays.
rosa adj pink.
Rose f rose.
Rosenholz n rosewood.
Rosenkohl m Brussels sprouts.
Rosenkranz m rosary.
Rosenstock m rose bush.
rosig adj rosy.
Rosine f raisin, currant.
Roß n horse, steed.
Roßkastanie f horse chestnut.
Rost m rust; grill.
rosten vi to rust.
rösten vt to roast; to toast; to grill.
rostfrei adj rust-free; rust-proof; stainless.
rostig adj rusty.
rot adj red.
Röte f redness.
Röteln pl German measles.
röten vt vr to redden.
rothaarig adj red-haired.
Rotkehlchen n robin.
rötlich adj reddish.
Rotwein m red wine.
Route f route.
Routine f experience; routine.
Rube f turnip.
Rubin m ruby.
Rubrik f heading; column.

Ruck m jerk, jolt.
Rückantwort f reply.
rückbezüglich adj reflexive.
rückdatieren vt to backdate.
rücken vt to move.
Rücken m back; ridge.
Rückenmark n spinal cord.
Rückenschwimmen n backstroke.
Rückerstattung f return, restitution.
Rückfahrkarte f return ticket.
Rückfahrt f return journey.
Rückfall m relapse.
rückfällig adj relapsing.
Rückflug m return flight.
Rückfrage f question.
rückfragen vi to check, enquire (further).
Rückgabe f return.
Rückgang m decline, fall.
Rückgrat n spine, backbone.
Rückhalt m backing, support.
rückkaufen vt to repurchase; to surrender.
Rückkehr f return.
Rücklage f reserves.
Rücklicht n back light.
rücklings adv from behind; backwards.
Rücknahme f taking back.
Rückporto n return postage.
Rückreise f return journey; home voyage.
Rückruf m recall.
Rucksack m rucksack.
Rückschau f reflection.
Rückschlag m setback.
Rückschluß m conclusion.
Rückschritt m retrogression.
rückschrittlich adj retrograde; reactionary.
Rückseite f back; reverse (of coin, etc).
Rücksicht f consideration.
rücksichtslos adj inconsiderate; reckless; ruthless.
rücksichtsvoll adj considerate.
Rücksitz m back seat.
Rückspiegel m rear-view mirror.

Rückspiel n return match.
Rücksprache f further discussion.
Rückstand m arrears.
rückständig adj out-of-date; in arrears.
Rückstellung f provision.
Rückstrahler m rear reflector.
Rücktritt m resignation.
Rückvergütung f repayment; refund.
rückvermieten vt to lease back.
rückversichern vt to reinsure.
Rückversicherung f reinsurance.
rückwärtig adj rear.
rückwärts adv back, backwards.
Rückwärtsgang m reverse gear.
Rückweg m return journey, way back.
rückwirkend adj retroactive.
Rückwirkung f retroactive effect.
Rückzahlung f repayment.
Rückzug m retreat.
Rudel n pack; herd.
Ruder n oar; rudder.
Ruderboot n rowing boat.
rudern vt vi to row.
Rudersport m rowing.
Ruf m shout, call; reputation.
rufen vi to call, cry.
rügen vt to rebuke.
Ruhe f rest; peace, quiet; calm; silence.
ruhelos adj restless.
ruhen vi to rest.
Ruhestand m retirement; **in den ~ treten** to retire.
ruhig adj quiet; still; steady.
Ruhm m glory, fame.
rühmen vt to praise; * vr to boast.
Ruhr f dysentery.
Rührei n scrambled eggs.
rühren vt vr to stir; * vr: **~ von** to come from.
rührend adj moving, touching.
Rührung f emotion.

Ruin m ruin.
Ruine f ruin.
ruinieren vt to ruin.
rülpsen vi to burp, belch.
Rumäne m Romanian.
Rumänien n Romania.
Rumänin f Romanian.
rumänisch adj Romanian.
Rummel m hubbub; fair.
Rummelplatz m fair, fairground.
Rumpf m trunk, torso; fuselage; hull.
rund adj round; * adv around.
Rundbrief m circular.
Runde f round; lap; circle.
Rundfahrt f round trip.
Rundfunk m broadcasting.
Rundfunkgerät n wireless set.
Rundfunksender m transmitter.
Rundfunksendung f broadcast, radio programme.
rundheraus adv straight out, bluntly.
rundherum adv round about; all round.
rundlich adj plump, rounded.
Rundreise f round trop.
Rundschreiben n circular.
Runzel f wrinkle.
runzeln vt to wrinkle.
rupfen vt to pluck.
Ruß m spot.
Russe m Russian.
Rüssel m snout; (elephant's) trunk.
rußig adj sooty.
Russin f Russian.
russisch adj Russian.
Rußland n Russia.
rüsten vt to prepare; * vi to prepare; to arm; * vr to prepare oneself; to arm oneself
Rüstung f preparation; arming; armour; armaments.
Rute f rod.
Rutsch m slide; landslide.
Rutschbahn f slide.
rutschen vi to slide; to slip.
rutschig adj slippery.
rütteln vt vi to shake, jolt.

S

Saal *m* hall; room.
Saat *f* seed; sowing; crop.
Säbel *m* sabre, sword.
Sabotage *f* sabotage.
Sache *f* thing, object; affair, business; matter.
Sachkunde *f* expert knowledge.
sachkundig *adj* expert.
sachlich *adj* objective; matter-of-fact.
sächlich *adj* neuter.
Sachse *m* Saxon.
Sachsen *n* Saxony.
sächsisch *adj* Saxon.
Sachverständige(r) *m* expert, specialist.
Sack *m* sack.
Sadismus *m* sadism.
Sadist *m* sadist.
säen *vt vi* to sow.
Saft *m* juice; sap.
saftig *adj* juicy.
Sage *f* saga.
Säge *f* saw.
Sägemehl *n* sawdust.
sagen *vt vi* to say, tell.
sägen *vt vi* to saw.
sagenhaft *adj* legendary; (*coll*) smashing, great.
Sahne *f* cream.
Saison *f* season.
Saite *f* string, chord.
Saiteninstrument *n* string instrument.
Sakrament *n* sacrament.
Sakristei *f* sacristy.
Salat *m* salad; lettuce.
Salatsoße *f* salad dressing.
Salbe *f* ointment/
Saldo *n* balance of an account.
Salon *m* drawing room.
salopp *adj* casual.
Salpeter *m* saltpetre.
Salpetersäure *f* nitric acid.
Salz *n* salt.
salzen *vt* to salt.
salzig *adj* salty.

Salzsäure *f* hydrochloric acid.
Salzwasser *n* salt water.
Samen *m* seed; sperm.
sammeln *vt* to collect; * *vr* to assemble, gather; to concentrate.
Sammlung *f* collection; assembly, gathering; concentration.
Samstag *m* Saturday.
Samt *m* velvet.
samt *prep* (along) with, together with.
sämtlich *adj* all (the), entire.
Sand *m* sand.
Sandgrube *f* bunker.
sandig *adj* sandy.
Sandpapier *n* sandpaper.
sandstrahlen *vt vi* to sandblast.
Sanduhr *f* hourglass.
sanft *adj* gentle, soft.
Sänger(in) *m* (*f*) singer.
sanieren *vt* to redevelop; to make financially sound; * *vr* to line one's pockets; to become financially sound.
Sanierung *f* redevelopment.
sanktionieren *vt* to sanction.
Saphir *m* sapphire.
Sardelle *f* anchovy.
Sardine *f* sardine.
Sardinien *n* Sardinia.
Sarg *m* coffin.
Sarkasmus *m* sarcasm.
Satan *m* Satan, devil.
Satellit *m* satellite.
Satellitenfernsehen *n* satellite television.
Satire *f* satire.
satirisch *adj* satirical.
satt *adj* full; rich; deep; ~ **machen** to be filling.
Sattel *m* saddle.
satteln *vt* to saddle.
sättigen *vt* to satisfy; (*chem*) to saturate.
Sattler *m* saddler.
Satz *m* sentence; clause; (*mus*) movement; set; jump.
Satzlehre *f* syntax.
Satzung *f* by-law, statute.
Satzzeichen *n* punctuation

mark.

Sau f sow.

sauber adj clean, neat; fine.

säubern vt to clean; to purge.

Säuberung f cleaning; purge.

saubhalten vt to keep clean.

Sauce f sauce, gravy.

sauer adj sour; acid.

Sauerei f (coll) scandal, rotten state of affairs.

säuerlich adj sour; dour.

Sauerkraut n sauerkraut, pickled cabbage.

Sauermilch f sour milk.

Sauerstoff m oxygen.

saufen vt vi to drink, booze.

Säufer m (coll) boozer.

saugen vt vi to suck.

säugen vi to suckle.

Sauger m dummy; teat; vacuum cleaner.

Säugetier n mammal.

Säugling m infant, baby.

Säule f pillar, column.

Saum m hem; seam.

säumen vt to hem; to seam; * vi to hesiate, delay.

Sauna f sauma.

Säure f sourness, acidity.

sausen vt to blow; to buzz.

Saxophon n saxophone.

schaben vt to scrape.

schäbig adj shabby.

Schablone f stencil; pattern.

Schach n chess; check.

schachmatt adj checkmate.

Schachspiel n game of chess.

Schacht m shaft.

Schachtel f box.

schade adj a pity/shame; * excl (wie) ~! (what a) pity/shame.

Schädel m skull.

Schaden m harm, damage; injury.

schaden vi +dat to hurt.

Schadenersatz m damages.

Schadenfreude f malicious glee.

schädigen to damage; to do harm to.

schädlich adj injurious.

Schaf n sheep.

Schafbock m ram.

Schäfer(in) m(f) shepherd(ess).

Schäferhund m sheepdog.

schaffen vt to create; to make; to manage; * vi to work.

Schaffner(in) m(f) guard; bus conductor.

Schakal m jackal.

Schal m scarf.

Schale f shell, peel, skin, pod, husk.

schälen vt to peel; to shell; * vr to peel.

Schall m sound.

Schalldämpfer m silencer.

schalldicht adj soundproof.

Schallmauer f sound barrier.

Schallplatte f gramophone player.

schalten vt to switch; * vi to change gear.

Schalter m ticket office; (bank, etc) counter; switch.

Schaltjahr n leap year.

Scham f shame; modesty.

schämen vr to be ashamed.

schamlos adj shameless.

Schande f shame, disgrace.

schändlich adj shameful, disgraceful.

Schanze f entrenchment, fortification.

scharen vt to assemble, rally.

scharf adj sharp; spicy, hot.

Schärfe f sharpness.

schärfen vt to sharpen.

scharfmachen vt to stir up.

Scharfach m scarlet fever.

Scharnier n hinge.

scharren vt vi to scrape, scratch.

Schatten m shadow, shade.

schattieren vt vi to shade.

schattig adj shady.

Schatz m treasure; darling.

schätzen vt to estimate; to value; to think highly of.

schauen vi to look.

Schauer m shower; shudder.

Schaufel f shovel; scoop.

Schaukel f swing.

schaukeln vi to swing, rock.

Schaukelpferd *n* rocking horse.

Schaukelstuhl *m* rocking chair.

Schaum *m* foam; froth.

schäumen *vi* to foam.

schaumig *adj* frothy, foamy.

Schauplatz *m* scene.

schaufig *adj* dreadful, horrible.

Schauspiel *n* spectacle; play.

Schauspieler(in) *m(f)* actor (actress).

Schauspielhaus *n* theatre.

Scheck *m* cheque.

Scheckheft *m* chequebook.

Scheckkarte *f* cheque (guarantee) card.

scheffeln *vt* to amass.

Scheibe *f* pane; disc; slice; target.

Scheibenwischer *m* windscreen wiper.

Scheide *f* sheath; boundary; vagina.

scheiden *vt* to separate; to dissolve; * *vi* to depart; to part.

Scheidung *f* divorce.

Schein *m* light; appearance; banknote; certificate.

scheinbar *adj* apparent.

scheinen *vi* to shine; to look, seem, appear.

scheinheilig *adj* hypocritical.

Scheinwerfer *m* spotlight; searchlight; headlamp.

Scheiße *f* (*coll*) shit.

Scheitel *m* top; (hair) parting.

scheiteln *vt* to part.

scheitern *vi* to fail.

schellen *vi* to ring.

Schellfisch *m* haddock.

Scheim *m* rogue.

scheimisch *adj* roguish, mischievous.

Schelte *f* scolding.

schelten *vt* to scold.

Schema *n* scheme, plan.

schematisch *adj* schematic.

Schenkel *m* thigh.

schenken *vt* to give; to pour.

Schere *f* scissors.

scheren *vt* to cut; to shear; * *vr* to care.

Scherz *m* joke, jest.

scherzen *vi* to jest, be joking.

Scheu *f* shyness.

scheuen *vr:* **sich ~ vor** +*dat* to be afraid of, shrink from; * *vi* to shy (of horse).

Scheuerlappen *m* floor cloth.

scheuern *vt* to scrub, scour.

Scheune *f* barn.

Scheusal *n* monster.

Schicht *f* layer; shift.

Schichtarbeit *f* shift work.

schichten *vt* to heap, layer.

schicken *vt* to send.

Schicksal *n* fate, destiny.

schieben *vt* to push; to put; * *vi* to push.

Schiebetür *f* sliding door.

Schiedsrichter *m* referee, umpire.

schief *adj* crooked; sloping; leaning.

Schiefer *m* slate.

schiefgehen *vi* (*coll*) to go wrong.

schielen *vi* to squint.

Schiene *f* rail.

schienen *vt* to put in splints.

schier *adj* sheer; * *adv* nearly, almost.

schießen *vt vi* to shoot.

Schiff *m* vessel, boat, ship; nave.

Schiffahrt *f* shipping; voyage.

Schiffsbau *m* shipbuiding.

Schiffsschraube *f* ship's propeller.

Schikane *f* dirty trick; harassment.

schikanieren *vt* to harass, torment.

Schild *m* shield; sign, nameplate.

schildern *vt* to depict, portray.

Schildkröte *f* tortoise; turtle.

Schilf *n* reed.

schillern *vt* to shimmer.

Schilling *m* schilling.

Schimmel *m* mould; white horse.

schimmeln *vi* to get mouldy.

Schimmer *m* shimmer; glimmer.

schimmern *vi* to shimmer, glimmer.

Schimpanse *f* chimpanzee.

schimpfen *vt* to scold; * *vi* to curse, complain.

schinden *vt* to maltreat.

Schinken *m* ham.

Schippe *f* shovel.

schippen *vt* to shovel.

Schirm *m* umbrella; parasol; screen.

schizophren *adj* schizophrenic.

Schlacht *f* battle; **eine ~ liefern** to give battle.

schlachten *vt* to slaughter, kill.

Schlachter *m* butcher.

Schlachtfeld *n* battlefield.

Schlachthof *m* slaughterhouse, abattoir.

Schlaf *m* sleep, doze.

schlafen *vi* to sleep; **~ gehen** to go to bed.

Schlafengehen *n* going to bed.

Schlafenszeit *f* bedtime.

schlaff *adj* slack; limp; exhausted.

Schlafgelegenheit *f* sleeping accommodation.

Schlaflied *n* lullaby.

schlaflos *adj* sleepless.

Schlaflosigkeit *f* sleeplessness, insomnia.

Schlafmittel *n* sleeping pill.

schläfrig *adj* sleepy.

Schlafsaal *m* dormitory.

Schlafsack *m* sleeping bag.

Schlaftablette *f* sleeping pill.

Schlafwagen *m* sleeping car, sleeper.

schlafwandeln *vi* to sleepwalk.

Schlafzimmer *n* bedroom.

Schlag *m* blow; stroke; beat; **mit einem ~** all at once; **~ auf ~** in rapid succession.

Schlagader *f* artery.

Schlaganfall *m* stroke.

schlagartig *adj* sudden, without warning.

Schlagbaum *m* barrier.

schlagen *vt vi* to beat; to strike, hit; * *vr* to fight.

Schlager *m* hit.

Schläger *m* brawler; racket; bat.

Schlägerei *f* fight, punch-up.

Schlagersuanger(in) *m(f)* pop singer.

schlagfertig *adj* quick-witted.

Schlagfertigkeit *f* ready wit.

Schlagloch *n* pothole.

Schlagobers *n* whipped cream.

Schlagsahne *f* whipped cream.

Schlagseite *f* list.

Schlagwort *n* catch phrase, slogan.

Schlagzeug *n* percussion; drums.

Schlagzeuger *m* drummer.

Schlamassel *m* mess.

Schlamm *m* mud.

schlammig *adj* muddy.

Schlampe *f* (*coll*) slut.

schlampen *vi* (*coll*) to be sloppy.

Schlamperei *f* (*coll*) sloppy work; disorderliness.

schlampig *adj* (*coll*) sloppy, messy.

Schlange *f* snake, serpent; queue; **~ stehen** to (form a) queue.

schlängeln *vr* to wind; to twist.

Schlangengebiß *m* snake bite.

Schlangengift *n* snake venom.

schlank *adj* slim, slender.

Schlankheit *f* slimness, slenderness.

Schlankheitskur *f* diet.

schlapp *adj* limp.

Schlaraffenland *n* land of milk and honey.

schlau *adj* sly, cunning.

Schlauch *m* hose; (flexible) tube.

Schlauchboot *n* rubber dinghy.

schlauchen *vt* to exhaust.

schlauchlos *adj* tubeless (of tyre).

Schlaufe *f* loop; hanger.

Schlauheit *f* cunning.

Schläue *f* cunning.

Schlaukopf *m* clever dick.

schlecht *adj* bad; * *adv* badly.
Schlechtigkeit *f* badness, wickedness.
schlechtmachen *vt* to run down.
schlecken *vt vi* to lick.
Schlegel *m* (drum)stick; mallet, hammer.
schleichen *vi* to crawl, creep.
schleichend *adj* gradual; creeping.
Schleichwerbung *f* (*commercial*) plug.
Schleier *m* veil.
Schleife *f* bow; loop.
schleifen *vt* to drag; to grind.
Schleifstein *m* grindstone.
Schleim *m* slime; (*med*) mucus; gruel.
Schleimhaut *f* mucous membrane.
schleimig *adj* slimy.
schlemmen *vi* to feast.
Schlemmer *m* gourmet.
Schlemmerei *f* feasting, gluttony.
schlendern *vi* to stroll.
schlenkern *vt vi* to dangle, swing.
Schleppe *f* train.
schleppen *vt* to tow; drag; haul.
Schlepper *m* tug; tractor.
Schlesien *n* Silesia.
Schleuder *f* catapult; spindrier; centrifuge.
schleudern *vt* to hurl; * *vi* to skid.
Schleuderpreis *m* give-away price.
Schleudersitz *m* ejector seat.
Schleuderware *f* cut-price goods.
schleunigst *adv* straight away.
Schleuse *f* lock; sluice.
schlicht *adj* simple, plain.
schlichten *vt* to smooth; to settle.
Schlichter *m* mediator, arbitrator.
Schlichtung *f* settlement; arbitration.
Schlick *m* mud; (oil) slick.

Schließe *f* fastener.
schließen *vt* to close, shut; to enter into; * *vi vr* to close, shut.
Schließfach *n* locker.
schließlich *adv* finally.
Schliff *m* cut(ting).
schlimm *adj* bad.
schlimmer *adj* worse.
schlimmste(r,s) *adj* worst.
schlimmstenfalls *adv* at (the) worst.
Schlinge *f* loop; noose; sling.
schlingen *vt* to wind; to gobble, bolt; * *vi* to gobble, bolt one's food.
schlingern *vi* to roll.
Schlips *m* tie.
Schlitten *m* sledge.
Schlittenfahren *n* tobogganing.
schlittern *vi* to slide.
Schlittschuh *m* skate; ~ **laufen** to skate.
Schlittschuhbahn *f* skating rink.
Schlittschuhläufer(in) *m(f)* skater.
Schlitz *m* slit; slot.
schlitzäugig *adj* slant-eyed.
schlitzen *vt* to slit.
Schloß *n* lock; castle.
Schlosser *m* locksmith; fitter, mechanic.
Schlosserei *f* metal working shop.
Schlott *m* chimney; funnel.
schlottern *vi* to shake, tremble.
Schlucht *f* ravine, gorge.
schluchzen *vi* to sob.
Schluck *m* swallow.
Schluckauf *m* hiccups.
schlucken *vt vi* to swallow.
schludern *vi* to skimp.
Schlummer *m* slumber.
schlummern *vi* to slumber.
schlüpfen *vi* to slip.
Schluß *m* end, conclusion.
Schlußbilanz *f* balance sheet.
Schlüssel *m* key.
Schlüsselblume *f* cowslip, primrose.

schmachten *vi* to languish.
schmal *adj* narrow.
Schmalz *n* dripping lard.
schmecken *vt vi* to taste; **gut (schlecht)** ~ to taste good (bad).
schmeißen *vt* to fling.
schmelzen *vi* to melt.
Schmerz *m* pain, grief.
schmerzen *vi* to hurt, be painful, grieve.
schmerzhaft *adj* painful, sore.
schmerzlich *adj* painful; grievous.
schmerzlos *adj* painless.
Schmetterling *m* butterfly.
Schmied *m* smith, blacksmith.
Schmiede *f* forge, smithy.
Schmiedeeisen *n* wrought iron.
schmieden *vt* to forge.
schmieren *vt* to smear.
schmollen *vi* to pout.
Schmuck *m* jewellery; adornment.
schmücken *vt* to decorate.
schmucklos *adj* unadorned.
Schmuggel *m* smuggling.
schmuggeln *vt vi* to smuggle.
Schmuggler *m* smuggler.
schmunzeln *vi* to smile benignly.
schmusen *vi* to cuddle.
Schmutz *m* filth, dirt.
Schmutzfleck *m* stain.
schmutzig *adj* dirty.
Schnabel *m* bill, beak.
Schnake *f* cranefly; gnat.
Schnalle *f* buckle, clasp.
schnallen *vt* to buckle.
schnappen *vt* to catch, grab; * *vi* to snap.
Schnappschloß *n* spring lock.
Schnappschuß *m* snapshot.
Schnaps *m* spirits; schnaps.
schnarchen *vi* to snore.
schnattern *vi* to gabble (of geese); to quack.
schnauben *vi* to snort; * *vr* to blow one's nose.
schnaufen *vi* to puff, pant.
Schnauze *f* snout, muzzle; spout.

Schnecke *f* snail.
Schneckenhaus *n* snail's shell.
Schnee *m* snow.
Schneeball *m* snowball.
Schneeflocke *f* snowflake.
Schneeglöckchen *n* snowdrop.
Schneekette *f* snow chain.
Schneemann *n* snowman.
Schneepflug *m* snowplough.
Schneeschmelze *f* thaw.
Schneide *f* edge; blade.
schneiden *vt* to cut; * *vr* to cut oneself; to intersect.
Schneider *m* tailor.
Schneiderei *f* tailor's.
Schneiderin *f* dressmaker.
schneidern *vt* to make; * *vi* to be a tailor.
Schneidezahn *m* incisor.
schneien *vi* to snow.
Schneise *f* clearing.
schnell *adj* quick, rapid, fast; * *adv* quickly, fast.
Schnellhefter *m* loose-leaf binder.
Schnelligkeit *f* speed.
Schnellimbiß *m* snack bar.
Schnellkochtopf *m* pressure cooker.
Schnellreinigung *f* dry cleaner's.
schnellstens *adv* as quickly as possible.
Schnellstraße *f* expressway.
Schnellzug *m* express train.
schneuzen *vr* to blow one's nose.
schnippeln *vt* to snip.
schnippisch *adj* sharp-tongued.
Schnitt *m* cut(ting); intersection; section; average; pattern.
Schnitte *f* slice.
Schnittfläche *f* section.
Schnittlauch *m* chive.
Schnittstelle *f* (*computer*) interface.
Schnittwunde *f* cut.
Schnitzarbeit *f* wood carving.
Schnitzel *n* chip; escalope.
schnitzen *vt* to carve.
Schnitzer *m* carver.

Schnitzerei f carving.
Schnorchel m snorkel.
Schnörkel m flourish; scroll.
schnorren vt to cadge.
schnüffeln vt to sniff.
Schnüffler m snooper.
Schnuller m dummy.
Schnupfen m cold.
schnuppern vt to sniff.
Schnur f string, cord, twine; flex.
schnüren vt to tie.
schnurgerade adj straight (as a die).
Schnurrbart m moustache.
schnurren vi to purr; to hum.
Schnursenkel m shoelace.
schnurstracks adv straight (away).
Schock m shock.
schockieren vt to shock, outrage.
Schöffe m lay magistrate.
Schöffin f lay magistrate.
Schokolade f chocolate.
Scholle f clod; ice floe; plaice.
schon adv already; all right; just.
schön adj beautiful; nice.
schonen vt to look after; * vi to take it easy.
schonend adj careful, gentle.
Schönheit f beauty.
Schönheitsfehler m flaw, blemish.
Schönheitsoperation f cosmetic surgery.
Schonkost f special diet.
schönmachen vr to make oneself look nice.
Schonung f good care; consideration.
schonungslos adj harsh, unsparing.
Schonzeit f close season.
schöpfen vt to scoop, ladle; to breathe in.
Schöpfer m creator; founder.
schöpferisch adj creative.
Schöpfkelle f ladle.
Schöpfung f creation; genesis.
Schorf m scab.

Schornstein m chimney; funnel.
Schornsteinfeger m chimney sweep.
Schotte m Scot, Scotsman.
Schottin f Scot, Scotswoman.
schottish adj Scottish.
Schottland n Scotland.
schraffieren vt to hatch.
schräg adj slanting.
Schräge f slant.
Schrägstrich m oblique stroke.
Schramme f scratch.
schrammen vt to scratch.
Schrank m cupboard; wardrobe.
Schranke f barrier.
Schrankenwärter m level crossing attendant.
Schrankkoffer m trunk.
Schraube f screw.
schrauben vt to screw.
Schraubenschlüssel m spanner.
Schraubenzieher m screwdriver.
Schraubstock m (tech) vice.
Schreck m terror; fright.
schrecken vt to frighten, scare.
Schreckgespenst n spectre, nightmare.
schreckhaft adj jumpy, easily frightened.
schrecklich adj terrible, awful.
Schrei m shout; scream.
Schreibblock m writing pad.
schreiben vt vi to write; to spell.
schreibfaul adj lazy about writing letters.
Schreibkraft f typist.
Schreibmaschine f typewriter.
Schreibpapier n notepaper.
Schreibtisch m desk.
Schreibung f spelling.
Schreibwaren pl stationery.
Schreibzentrale f typing pool.
Schreibzeug n writing materials.
schreien vt vi to scream, cry out.
schreiend adj loud; glaring.

Schrein *m* shrine.

Schreiner *m* joiner; carpenter.

Schreinerei *f* joiner's workshop.

schreiten *vi* to stride.

Schrift *f* (hand)writing; script; typeface, font; pamphlet.

Schriftdeutsch *n* written German.

Schriftführer *m* secretary.

schriftlich *adj* written; * *adv* in writing.

Schriftsteller(in) *m(f)* writer, author.

Schriftstück *n* document.

Schriftwechsel *m* correspondence.

schrill *adj* shrill.

Schritt *m* step; walk; pace.

Schrittmacher *m* pacemaker.

schroff *adj* steep; brusque.

schröpfen *vt* to fleece.

Schrott *m* scrap metal.

Schrotthaufen *m* scrap heap.

schrottreif *adj* ready for the scrap heap.

schrubben *vt* to scrub.

Schrubber *m* scrubbing brush.

schrumpfen *vi* to shrink; to shrivel.

Schubfach *n* drawer.

Schubkarren *m* wheelbarrow.

Schublade *f* drawer.

schüchtern *adj* shy, timid.

Schüchternheit *f* shyness, timidity.

Schuh *m* shoe.

Schuhband *n* shoe lace.

Schuhcreme *f* shoe polish.

Schuhgröße *f* shoe size.

Schuhlöffel *m* shoehorn.

Schuhmacher *m* shoemaker.

Schularbeit *f* homework.

Schulaufgaben *pl* homework.

Schulbesuch *m* school attendance.

Schulbuch *n* school book.

Schuld *f* guilt, fault; **~en** *pl* debts; **in ~en geraten** to get into debt.

schuldig *adj* guilty.

Schuldner(in) *m(f)* debtor.

Schule *f* school.

schulen *vt* to train.

Schüler(in) *m(f)* pupil.

Schulkamerad *m* schoolmate.

Schulter *f* shoulder.

schultern *vt* to shoulder.

Schulung *f* schooling, education.

Schuppe *f* (fish) scale; **~n** *pl* dandruff.

Schuppen *m* shed.

Schurke *m* rogue.

Schürze *f* apron.

Schuß *m* shot.

Schüssel *f* dish.

Schutt *m* rubbish; rubble.

schütteln *vt* to shake.

Schutz *m* shelter; protection.

Schutzblech *n* mudguard.

Schütze *m* gunman; marksman; (*astrol*) Sagittarius.

schützen *vt* to protect.

Schutzmarke *f* trade mark.

Schwaben *n* Swabia.

schwach *adj* weak, feeble.

Schwäche *f* weakness.

schwächen *vt* to weaken.

Schwachheit *f* weakness.

Schwächling *m* weakling.

Schwachsinn *m* imbecility.

Schwager *m* brother-in-law.

Schwägerin *f* sister-in-law.

Schwalbe *f* swallow.

Schwamm *m* sponge.

Schwan *m* swan.

schwanger *adj* pregnant.

Schwangerschaft *f* pregnancy.

schwanken *vi* to sway; to fluctuate; to stagger.

Schwankung *f* fluctuation.

Schwanz *m* tail.

schwänzen *vt* to skip, cut; * *vi* to play truant.

Schwarm *m* swarm.

schwarz *adj* black.

Schwarze(r) *mf* black (man/woman).

schwärzen *vt* to blacken, slander.

schwärzlich *adj* blackish.

Schwarzmarkt *m* black market.

Schwarzwald *m* (the) Black Forest.

Schwarzweißfilm *m* black and white film.

schwatzen *vi* to chatter.

schweben *vi* to soar; to drift, float.

Schwede *m* Swede.

Schweden *n* Sweden.

Schwedin *f* Swede.

schwedisch *adj* Swedish.

Schwefel *m* sulphur.

Schwefelsäure *f* sulphuric acid.

Schweigen *n* silence.

schweigen *vi* to be silent.

schweigsam *adj* silent, taciturn.

Schweigsamkeit *f* quietness.

Schwein *n* pig.

Schweinefleisch *n* pork.

Schweinestall *m* pigsty.

Schweiß *m* sweat.

schweißen *vt vi* to weld.

Schweißer *m* welder.

Schweiz *f* Switzerland.

Schweizer(in) *m(f)* Swiss.

schweizerisch *adj* Swiss.

Schwelle *f* doorstpe, threshold.

schwellen *vi* to swell.

Schwellung *f* swelling.

Schwemme *f* surplus.

schwenken *vt* to swing; to wave; * *vi* to swivel.

schwer *adj* heavy; difficult, hard; serious; * *vi* very seriously.

Schwerarbeiter *m* labourer, manual worker.

Schwere *f* heaviness; gravity.

Schwergewicht *n* heavyweight; emphasis.

Schwerindustrie *f* heavy industry.

schwerlich *adv* hardly.

Schwerpunkt *m* centre of gravity; emphasis.

Schwert *n* sword.

Schwester *f* sister; nurse.

schwesterlich *adj* sisterly.

Schwiegereltern *pl* parents-in-law.

Schwiegermutter *f* mother-in-law.

Schwiegersohn *m* son-in-law.

Schwiegertochter *f* daughter-in-law.

Schwiegervater *m* father-in-law.

schwierig *adj* difficult.

Schwierigkeit *f* difficulty.

Schwimmbad *n* swimming baths.

schwimmen *vi* to swim.

Schwimmveste *f* life jacket.

schwinden *vi* to disappear;to decline.

schwingen *vt vi* to swing.

Schwingung *f* vibration; oscillation.

schwitzen *vi* to sweat, perspire.

schwören *vt vi* to swear.

schwul *adj* (*coll*) gay, queer.

schwül *adj* stuffy, close.

Schwung *m* swing; momentum.

Schwur *m* oath.

schwürzen *vi* to swear.

sechs *num* six.

sechste(r,s) *adj* sixth.

Sechstel *n* sixth.

sechzehn *num* sixteen.

sechzig *num* sixty.

See *m* lake; * *f* sea.

Seebad *n* seaside resort.

Seehund *m* seal.

Seeigel *m* sea urchin.

seekrank *adj* seasick.

Seekrankheit *f* seasickness.

Seelachs *m* rock salmon.

Seele *f* soul.

Seeleute *pl* seamen.

seelisch *adj* mental.

Seelöwe *m* sea lion.

Seelsorger *m* clergyman.

Seemacht *f* naval power.

Seemann *m* sailor, seaman.

Seemeile *f* nautical mile.

Seemöwe *f* seagull.

Seenot *f* distress.

Seepolyp *m* octopus.

Seeräuber *m* pirate.

Seereise *f* voyage.

Seerose *f* water lily.
Seestern *m* starfish.
Seetang *m* seaweed.
seetüchtig *adj* seaworthy.
Seeweg *m* sea route.
Seezunge *f* sole.
Segel *n* sail.
Segelboot *n* yacht.
Segelfliegen *n* gliding.
Segelflugzeug *n* glider.
segeln *vt vi* to sail.
Segelschiff *n* sailing vessel.
Segelsport *m* sailing.
Segen *m* blessing.
segensreich *adj* beneficial.
Segler *m* sailor, yachtsman.
segnen *vt* to bless.
sehen *vt vi* to see; to look.
sehenswert *adj* worth seeing.
Sehenswürdigkeiten *pl* sights.
Seher *m* seer.
Sehfehler *m* sight defect.
Sehne *f* sinew; string.
sehnen *vr*: **sich ~ nach** to yearn for.
sehnig *adj* sinewy.
sehnlich *adj* ardent.
Sehnsucht *f* longing.
sensüchtig *adj* longing.
sehr *adv* very; a lot, much.
seicht *adj* shallow.
Seide *f* silk.
seiden *adj* silk.
Seidenpapier *n* tissue paper.
Seidenraupe *f* silkworm.
seidig *adj* silky.
Seife *f* soap.
Seifenlauge *f* soapsuds.
Seifenschale *f* soap dish.
Seifenschaum *m* lather.
seihen *vt* to filter, strain.
Seil *n* rope, cable.
Seilbahn *f* cable railway.
Seilhüpfen *n* skipping.
Seiltänzer(in) *m(f)* tightrope walker.
sein *vi v aux* to be.
sein(e) *poss adj* his; its.
seine(r,s) *poss pron* his; its.
Seismograph *m* seismograph.
seit *prep conj* since.

seitdem *adv conj* since.
Seite *f* side; page.
seitens *prep* on the part of.
Seitenstraße *f* side road.
seither *adv conj* since (then).
seitlich *adj* on one/the side.
seitwärts *adv* sidewards.
Sekretär(in) *m(f)* secretary.
Sekretariat *n* secretariat.
Sekt *m* champagne.
Sekte *f* sect.
Sekunde *f* second.
selber = selbst.
Selbst *n* self.
selbst *pron*: **ich ~** myself, **wir ~** ourselves, etc; alone, on one's own; * *adv* even.
selbständig *adj* independent; self-employed.
Selbständigkeit *f* independence; self-employment.
Selbstbedienung *f* self-service.
Selbstbedienungsgeschäft *n* self-service store.
Selbstbefriedung *f* masturbation.
selbstbewußt *adj* self-confident.
selbstgemacht *adj* homemade.
selbstlos *adj* selfless, unselfish.
Selbstmord *m* suicide; **~ begehen** to commit suicide.
Selbstmörder(in) *m(f)* suicide.
selbstmörderisch *adj* suicidal.
selbstsicher *adj* self-assured.
Selbstsucht *f* selfishness.
selbstsüchtig *adj* selfish.
selbstverständlich *adj* obvious; * *adv* naturally.
Selbstverteidigung *f* self-defence.
selig *adj* blessed; blissful; deceased, late.
Sellerie *m/f* celery.
selten *adj* rare, scarce; * *adv* seldom, rarely.
Seltenheit *f* rairty.
Selterwasser *n* soda water.
seltsam *adj* strange.
Seltsamkeit *f* strangeness.

Semikolon *n* semicolon.
Seminar *n* seminary; seminar.
Senat *m* senate.
Sendefolge *f* series.
senden *vt* to send; to transmit, broadcast; * *vi* to transmit, broadcast.
Sender *m* station; transmitter.
Sendung *f* consignment; broadcast, transmission; programme.
Senf *m* mustard.
senil *adj* senile.
Senior(in) *m(f)* pensioner.
Senkblei *n* plumb.
Senke *f* depression.
senken *vt* to lower; * *vr* to sink.
senkrecht *adj* vertical, perpendicular.
Senkrechtstarter *m* vertical takeoff plane.
Sensation *f* sensation.
sensationell *adj* sensational.
Sense *f* scythe.
September *m* September.
Serie *f* series.
serienweise *adv* in series.
seriös *adj* serious.
Service *n* set, service; * *m* service.
servieren *vt vi* to serve.
Serviererin *f* waitress.
Serviette *f* serviette, napkin.
Sessel *m* armchair.
Sessellift *m* chairlift.
setzen *vt* to put, set; to plant* *vr* to settle; to sit down; * *vi* to leap; to bet.
Seuche *f* epidemic.
seufzen *vi* to sigh.
Seufzer *m* sigh.
Sex *m* sex.
Sexualität *f* sexuality.
Sexualkunde *f* sex education.
sexuell *adj* sexual.
Shampoo *n* shampoo.
Sibieren *n* Siberian.
sibirisch *adj* Siberian.
sich *pron* oneself, himself, herself, itself, themselves.
Sichel *f* sickle; crescent.
sicher *adj* safe; certain; secure.

sichergehen *vi* to make sure.
Sicherheit *f* certainty; safety; security.
Sicherheitsgurt *m* safety belt.
Sicherheitsnadel *f* safety pin.
Sicherheitsschloß *n* safety lock.
sicherlich *adj* surely, certainly.
sichern *vt* to protect; secure.
sicherstellen *vt* to impound; (*computer*) to save.
Sicherung *f* fuse; safety catch.
Sicherungskopie back-up copy.
Sicht *f* sight; view; **auf ~ zahlbar** payable at sight; **in ~ kommen** to come into sight.
sichtbar *adj* visible.
sichten *vt* to sight; to sort out.
sichtlich *adj* obvious.
Sichtverhältnisse *pl* visibility.
Sichtvermerk *m* visa.
sickern *vi* to seep, trickle.
sie *pron* (*nom*) she, it, they; (*acc*) her, it, them.
Sie *pron* you.
Sieb *n* sieve; strainer.
sieben *num* seven; * *vt* to sift; to strain.
Siebensachen *pl* belongings.
siebzehn *num* seventeen.
siebzig *num* seventy.
sieden *vt* to boil, simmer.
Siedepunkt *m* boiling point.
Siedler *m* settler.
Siedlung *f* settlement; housing estate.
Sieg *m* victory, triumph.
Siegel *m* seal.
Siegelring *m* signet ring.
siegen *vi* to win; be victorious.
Sieger *m* victor; winner.
siegreich *adj* victorious.
Signal *n* signal, call.
Silbe *f* syllable.
Silber *n* silver.
silbern *adj* silver.
Silhouette *f* silhouette.
Silo *n/m* silo.
Silvester, Silvesterabend *m* New Year's Eve.
simpel *adj* simple.

Sims *n* mantelpiece; sill.
simulieren *vt* to simulate; * *vi* to feign illness.
simultan *adj* simultaneous.
Sinfonie *f* symphony.
singen *vt vi* to sing.
Singular *m* singular.
Singvogel *m* songbird.
sinken *vi* to sink; to fall.
Sinn *m* sense; mind; meaning.
sinnen *vi* to ponder.
Sinnestäuschung *f* illusion.
sinngemäß *adj* faithful.
sinnlich *adj* sensual; sensory.
Sinnlichkeit *f* sensuality.
sinnlos *adj* senseless; meaningless.
Sinnlosigkeit *f* senselessness; meaninglessness.
sinnvoll *adj* sensible.
Sirene *f* siren.
Sirup *m* syrup.
Sitte *f* custom,; ~**n** *pl* morals.
Sittenpolizei *f* vice squad.
sittlich *adj* moral.
Sittlichkeit *f* morality.
Situation *f* situation.
Sitz *m* seat.
sitzen *vi* to sit.
sitzend *adj* sedentary.
Sitzplatz *m* seat.
Sitzung *f* meeting.
Sizilien *n* Sicily.
Skala *f* scale.
Skalpell *n* scalpel.
Skandal *m* scandal.
skandalös *adj* scandalous.
Skandinavien *n* Scandinavia.
Skandinavier(in) *m(f)* Scandinavian.
skandinavisch *adj* Scandinavian.
Skelett *n* skeleton.
Skepsis *f* scepticism.
skeptisch *adj* sceptical.
Ski *m* ski; ~ **laufen** to ski.
Skiläufer *m* skier.
Skilehrer *m* ski instructor.
Skilift *m* ski-lift.
Skispringen *n* ski-jumping.
Skistock *m* ski-pole.
Skizze *f* sketch.

skizzieren *vt vi* to sketch.
Sklave *m* slave.
Sklaverei *f* slavery.
Sklavin *f* slave.
Skonto *m* discount.
Skorpion *m* scorpion; (*astrol*) Scorpio.
Skrupel *m* scruple.
skrupellos *adj* unscrupulous.
Skulptur *f* (piece of) sculpture.
Smaragd *m* emerald.
Smoking *m* dinner jacket.
so *adv* so; like this; ~ **daß** *conj* so that; *excl* **so?** really?.
Socke *f* sock.
Sockel *m* pedestal.
Sodawasser *n* soda water.
Sodbrennen *n* heartburn.
soeben *adv* just (now).
Sofa *m* sofa,.
sofern *conj* if, provided (that).
sofort *adv* immediately, at once.
sofortig *adj* immediate.
Software *f* software.
sogar *adv* even.
sogenannt *adj* so-called.
sogleich *adv* straight away.
Sohle *f* sole.
Sohn *m* son.
Solarzelle *f* solar cell.
solch *pron* such.
solche(r,s) *adj*: **ein** ~ such a.
Soldat *m* soldier.
Söldner *m* mercenary.
solidarisch *adj* in solidarity.
Solidarität *f* solidarity.
solid(e) *adj* solid; respectable.
Solist(in) *m(f)* soloist.
Soll *n* debit.
sollen *v aux* to be supposed to, should.
Solo *n* solo.
somit *conj* and so, therefore.
Sommer *m* summer.
sommerlich *adj* summer; summery.
Sommerschlußverkauf *m* summer sale.
Sommersprossen *pl* freckles.
Sonate *f* sonata.
Sonde *f* probe.
Sonderangebot *m* special offer

sonderbar *adj* odd, strange.
Sonderfahrt *f* special trip, excursion.
Sonderfall *m* special case.
sonderlich *adj* particular; peculiar; remarkable.
sondern *conj* but; * *vt* to separate; **nicht nur ... ~ auch** not only ... but also.
Sonderzug *m* special train.
Sonnabend *m* Saturday.
Sonne *f* sun.
sonnen *vt* to sun oneself
Sonnenaufgang *m* sunrise.
sonnenbaden *vi* to sunbathe.
Sonnenbrand *m* sunburn.
Sonnenbrille *f* sunglasses.
Sonnenkreme *f* suntan lotion.
Sonnenenergie *f* solar energy.
Sonnenfinsternis *f* solar eclipse.
Sonnenkollektor *m* solar panel.
Sonnenschein *m* sunshine.
Sonnenschirm *m* sunshade, parasol.
Sonnenstich *m* sunstroke.
Sonnenuntergang *m* sunset.
Sonnenwende *f* solstice.
sonnig *adj* sunny.
Sonntag *m* Sunday.
sonst *adv* else, otherwise; * *conj* otherwise; **~ noch etwas?** anything else?; **~ nichts** nothing else.
sonstjemand *pron* anybody (at all).
sonstwo *adv* somewhere else.
sonstwoher *adv* from somewhere else.
sonstwohin *adv* (to) somewhere else.
sooft *conj* whenever.
Sopran *m* soprano.
Sorge *f* care, worry.
sorgen *vi*: **für jdn ~** to look after sb; * *vr*: **sich ~ (um)** to worry (about).
sorgenfrei *adj* carefree.
sorgenvoll *adj* worried.
Sorgerecht *n* custody (of a child).

Sorgfalt *f* carefulness.
sorgfältig *adj* careful.
sorglos *adj* careless; carefree.
sorgsam *adj* careful.
Sorte *f* sort; brand.
sortieren *vt* to sort (out).
Sortiment *n* assortment.
sosehr *conj* as much as.
Soße *f* sauce; gravy.
soufflieren *vt vi* to prompt.
Souterrain *n* basement.
souverän *adj* sovereign.
soviel *conj* as far as (I know, etc).
soweit *conj* as far as.
sowenig *conj* as little as.
sowie *conj* as soon as; as well as.
sowieso *adv* anyway.
sowohl *conj*: **~ ... als auch** both ... and.
sozial *adj* social.
Sozialabgaben *pl* social security contributions.
Sozialarbeiter(in) *m(f)* social worker.
sozialisieren *vi* to socialise.
Sozialismus *m* socialism.
Sozialist *m* socialist.
sozialistisch *adj* socialist.
Sozialpolitik *f* social welfare policy.
Sozialprodukt *n* (net) national product.
Sozialstaat *m* welfare state.
Sozialwohnung *f* council flat.
sozialogisch *adj* sociological.
sozusagen *adv* so to speak.
Spachtel *m* spatula.
spähen *vi* to peep.
Spalt *m* crack; chink.
Spalte *f* crack, fissure; column (in newspaper, etc).
spalten *vt vr* to split.
Spaltung *f* splitting.
Span *m* shaving.
Spange *f* clasp; buckle.
Spanien *n* Spain.
Spanier(in) *m(f)* Spaniard.
spanisch *adj* Spanish.
Spannbeton *m* pre-stressed concrete.

Spanne *f* space; gap.

spannen *vt* to tighten; * *vi* to be tight.

spannend *adj* exciting, gripping.

Spannung *f* tension; voltage; suspense.

Sparbuch *n* savings book.

sparen *vt vi* to save, economise.

Sparer *m* saver.

Spargel *m* asparagus.

Sparkasse *f* savings bank.

Sparkonto *n* savings account.

spärlich *adj* meagre; scanty.

sparsam *adj* economical, thrifty.

Sparsamkeit *f* thrift.

Sparschwein *n* piggy bank.

Sparte *f* line of business.

Spaß *m* joke; fun; **jdm ~ machen** to be fun (for sb).

spaßen *vi* to joke.

spaßhaft *adj* jocular, funny.

Spaßverderber *m* spoilsport.

spät *adj adv* late; **wie ~ ist es?** what time is it?.

Spaten *m* spade.

später *adj adv* later.

spätestens *adv* at the latest.

Spatz *m* sparrow.

spazieren *vi* to stroll, walk.

spazierenfahren *vi* to go for a drive.

spazierengehen *vi* to go for a walk.

Spaziergang *m* walk.

Spazierstock *m* walking stick.

Specht *m* woodpecker.

Speck *m* bacon.

Spediteur *m* carrier; furniture remover.

Spedition *f* carriage; road haulage contractor; removal firm.

Speer *m* spear; javelin.

Speerwerfen *n* throwing the javelin.

Speiche *f* spoke.

Speichel *m* saliva, spit, spittle.

Speicher *m* storehouse; loft; tank; (*computer*) memory.

speichern *vt* to store; (*computer*) to save.

speien *vt vi* to spit; to vomit.

Speise *f* food.

Speisekammer *f* larder, pantry.

speisen *vt* to feed; to eat; * *vi* to dine.

Speiseröhre *f* gullet, oesophagus.

Speisewagen *m* dining car.

Spekulant *m* speculator.

Spekulation *f* speculation.

spekulieren *vi* to speculate.

Spelunke *f* dive.

Spende *f* donation.

spenden *vt* to give, donate.

Spender *m* donor.

Sperling *m* sparrow.

Sperma *n* sperm.

Sperre *f* barrier; ban.

sperren *vt* to block; to bar; * *vr* to baulk.

Sperrgebiet *n* prohibited area.

Sperrholz *n* plywood.

sperrig *adj* bulky.

Sperrstunde *f* closing time.

Spiegel *m* mirror.

Spiegelei *n* fried egg.

Spiel *n* play, game, match; **die Olympischen ~e** the Olympic Games.

spielen *vt vi* to play; to gamble.

Spieler *m* player; gambler.

Spielfeld *m* playing field; playground.

Spielkarte *f* playing card.

Spielzeug *n* toy, plaything.

Spinat *m* spinach.

Spinn(en)gewebe *m* cobweb.

Spinne *f* spider.

spinnen *vt* to spin.

Spinnerei *f* spinning-mill.

Spion *m* spy.

Spionage *f* espionage, spying.

spionieren *vi* to spy.

spitz *adj* acute, pointed.

Spitzen *pl* lace.

Spitzhacke *f* pickaxe.

sponsern *vt* to sponsor.

Sporn *m* spur.

Sport *m* sport.

Spott *m* mockery, sneer.

Sprache *f* language.

sprechen *vt vi* to speak.

sprengen *vt* to blow up; to sprinkle, water.

Sprengstoff *m* explosive.

Sprichwort *n* proverb, saying.

sprießen *vt* to sprout.

Springbrunnen *m* fountain.

springen *vi* to jump.

spritzen *vt* to squirt.

sprühen *vi* to sparkle.

spucken *vi* to spit.

spülen *vt* to wash up, rinse.

Spülküche *f* scullery.

Spülstein *m* sink.

spüren *vt* to perceive.

Staat *m* state.

Staatsanwalt *m* public prosecutor.

Staatsstreich *m* coup d'état.

Stabhochsprung *m* pole vault.

Stachel *m* sting, prickle; thorn.

Stachelbeere *f* gooseberry.

Stadt *f* town.

Städter *m* citizen, townsman.

städtlich *adj* urban.

Stadtrat *m* town council; town councillor.

Staffelei *f* easel.

Staffellauf *m* relay race.

Stahl *m* steel.

Stamm *m* trunk, stem.

stampfen *vt* to mash, crush.

Stand *m* state, position, situation.

Standbild *m* statue.

Standesamt *n* registry office.

starr *adj* stiff; rigid; staring.

starren *vi* to stare.

Starrheit *f* rigidity.

starrköpfig *adj* stubborn.

Starrsinn *m* obstinacy.

Start *m* start; takeoff.

Startbahn *f* runway.

starten *vt* to start; * *vi* to take off.

Starter *m* starter.

Station *f* station; hospital ward.

stationieren *vt* to station.

Statistik *m* statistician.

statistisch *adj* statistical.

Stativ *n* tripod.

statt *conj prep* instead of.

Stätte *f* place.

stattfinden *vi* to take place.

statthaft *adj* admissible.

stattlich *adj* imposing, handsome.

Statue *f* statue.

Status *m* status.

Statussymbol *n* status symbol.

Stau *m* blockage; (traffic) jam.

Staub *m* dust.

stauben *vi* to be dusty.

staubig *adj* dusty.

staubsaugen *vi* to vacuum.

Staubsauger *m* vacuum cleaner.

Staubtuch *n* duster.

Staudamm *m* dam.

Staude *f* shrub.

stauen *vt* to dam up; to stop the flow of; * *vr* to become dammed up; to become congested.

Staunen *n* astonishment, surprise.

staunen *vi* to be astonished, surprised (**über** at).

Stausee *m* reservoir, manmade lake.

Stauung *f* damming-up; congestion.

Steak *n* steak.

stechen *vt* to prick; to stab; to poke; to sting.

stechend *adj* piercing, stabbing; pungent.

Stechpalme *f* holly..

Steckdose *f* wall socket.

stecken *vt* to put, insert; to stick; * *vi* to be; to be stuck.

steckenbleiben *vi* to get stuck.

steckenlassen *vt* to leave in.

Steckenpferd *n* hobby-horse.

Stecker *m* plug.

Stecknadel *f* pin.

Steckrübe *f* turnip.

Steg *m* small bridge; landing stage.

stehen *vi* to stand; to be; to have stopped.

stehenbleiben *vi* to stop; to stay as it is.

stehenlassen *vt* to leave; to

grow.

Stehlampe *f* standard lamp.

stehlen *vt* to steal.

steif *adj* stiff.

Steifheit *f* stiffness.

Steigbügel *m* stirrup.

steigen *vi* to climb; to rise.

steigern *vt* to raise; to compare; * *vi* to bid; * *vr* to increase.

Steigerung *f* raising; comparison.

Steigung *f* incline, gradient, rise.

steil *adj* steep.

Stein *m* stone; jewel.

Steinbock *m* (*astrol*) Capricorn.

Steinbruch *m* quarry.

steinern *adj* made of stone.

Steingarnele *f* prawn.

Steingut *n* stoneware.

steinig *adj* stony.

steinigen *vt* to stone.

Steinkohle *f* mineral coal.

Steinmetz *m* stone-cutter.

Steinzeit *f* Stone Age.

Stelle *f* place; post, job; office.

stellen *vt* to put; to set; to supply; * *vr* to stand; to present oneself

Stellenangebot *n* offer of a post.

Stellengesuch *n* application for a post.

Stellenvermittlung *f* employment agency.

Stellung *f* position.

Stellungnahme *f* comment.

stellvertretend *adj* deputy, acting.

Stellvertreter *m* deputy.

Steize *f* stilt.

stemmen *vt* to lift (up); to press.

Stempel *m* stamp.

stempeln *vt* to stamp; to cancel.

Stengel *m* stalk, stem.

Stenographie *f* shorthand.

stenographieren *vt vi* to write (in) shorthand.

Stenotypist(in) *m(f)* shorthand typist.

Steppdecke *f* quilt.

Steppe *f* steppe, prairie.

steppen *vt* to stitch; * *vi* to tap-dance.

Sterbefall *m* death.

Sterbehilfe *f* euthanasia.

sterben *vi* to die.

sterblich *adj* mortal.

Sterblichkeit *f* mortality.

Stereoanlage *f* stereo (system).

stereotyp *adj* stereotype.

steril *adj* sterile.

sterilisieren *vt* to sterilise.

Sterilisierung *f* sterilisation.

Stern *m* star.

Sternbild *n* constellation.

Sternkunde *f* astronomy.

Sternschnuppe *f* meteor, falling star.

Sternwarte *f* observatory.

stet *adj* steady.

stetig *adj* constant, continual.

stets *adv* continually, always.

Steuer *f* tax; * *n* helm; rudder; steering wheel.

Steuerberater(in) *m(f)* tax consultant.

Steuerbord *n* (*mar*) starboard.

Steuererklärung *f* tax return.

Steuermann *m* helmsman.

steuern *vt* to steer; to pilot; to control.

Steuerrad *n* steering wheel.

Steuerung *f* steering; piloting; control.

Steuerzahler *m* taxpayer.

Steward *m* steward.

Stewardeß *f* stewardess; air hostess.

Stich *m* sting; stab; stitch; tinge.

sticheln *vi* to jibe.

stichhaftig *adj* sound, tenable.

Stichprobe *f* spot check.

Stichstraße *f* cul-de-sac.

Stichwort *n* cue; headword; note.

sticken *vt vi* to embroider.

Stickerei *f* embroidery.

stickig *adj* stuffy, close.

Stickstoff *m* nitrogen.

Stiefel *m* boot.

Stiefkind *n* stepchild.
Stiefmutter *f* stepmother.
Stiefmütterchen *n* pansy.
Stiefvater *m* stepfather.
Stiege *f* staircase.
Stiel *m* handle; stalk.
Stier *m* bull; (*astrol*) Taurus.
stier *adj* staring, fixed.
stieren *vi* to stare.
Stierkampf *m* bullfight.
Stierkampfarena *f* bullring.
Stierkämpfer *m* bullfighter.
Stift *m* peg; tack; crayon; pencil; * *n* foundation; religious institution.
stiften *vt* to found; to cause; to contribute.
Stifter(in) *m(f)* founder.
Stiftung *f* donation; foundation.
Stil *m* style.
still *adj* quiet; still; secret.
Stille *f* stillness, quietness.
stillen *vt* to stop; to satisfy; to breast-feed.
stillhalten *vi* to keep still.
stil(l)legen *vt* to close down.
stillschweigen *vt* to be silent.
Stillschweigen *n* silence.
stillschweigend *adj* silent; tacit; * *adv* silently; tacitly.
Stillstand *m* standstill.
stillstehen *vi* to stand still.
Stimmbänder *pl* vocal chords.
stimmberechtigt *adj* entitled to vote.
Stimme *f* voice; vote.
stimmen *vt* to tune; * *vi* to be right.
Stimmenmehrheit *f* majority of votes.
Stimmenthaltung *f* abstention.
Stimmgabel *f* tuning fork.
Stimmrecht *n* right to vote.
Stimmung *f* mood.
stimmungsvoll *adj* enjoyable.
Stimmzettel *m* ballot paper.
stinken *vi* to stink.
Stipendium *n* grant.
Stirn *f* forehead; brow.
Stirnband *n* headband.
Stirnhöhle *f* sinus.

Stöberhund *m* retriever.
stöbern *vi* to rummage.
stochern *vi* to poke (about).
Stock *m* (walking) stick; storey, floor.
stocken *vt* to stop, pause.
stockend *adj* halting.
Stockung *f* stoppage.
Stockwerk *n* storey, floor.
Stoff *m* material, cloth; matter; subject.
stofflich *adj* material.
Stofftier *n* soft toy.
Stoffwechsel *m* metabolism.
stöhnen *vi* to groan.
stoisch *adj* stoical.
Stellen *m* gallery; stud.
stolpern *vi* to stumble, trip.
Stolz *m* pride, arrogance.
stolz *adj* proud.
stolzieren *vi* to strut.
stopfen *vt* to stuff; to fill (up); to darn; * *vi* to cause constipation.
Stopfgarn *n* darning thread.
Stoppel *f* stubble.
stoppen *vt* to stop; to time; * *vi* to stop.
Stoppschild *n* stop sign.
Stoppuhr *f* stopwatch.
Stöpsel *m* plug; stopper.
Storch *m* stork.
stören *vt* to disturb; to interfere with; * *vr*: **sich an etw** *dat* ~ to let something bother one.
störend *adj* disturbing, annoying.
Störenfried *m* troublemaker.
störrisch *adj* stubborn, perverse.
Störung *f* disturbance; interference.
Stoß *m* push; blow; knock.
Stoßdämpfer *m* shock absorber.
stoßen *vt* to push, shove; to knock, bump; * *vr* to get a knock; * *vi* ~ **an/auf** +*acc* to bump into; to come across.
Stoßstange *f* bumper.
stottern *vt vi* to stutter.
Strafanstalt *f* prison, penal-

institution.

Strafarbeit *f* punishment (in school).

strafbar *adj* punishable.

Strafe *f* punishment; penalty; sentence.

strafen *vt* to punish.

straff *adj* tight; strict; concise.

straffen *vt* to tighten, tauten.

Strafgefangene(r) *mf* prisoner, convict.

Strafgesetzbuch *n* criminal code.

sträflich *adj* criminal.

Sträfling *m* convict.

Strafporto *n* excess postage (charge).

Strafpredigt *f* telling-off.

Strafraum *m* penalty area (in sport).

Strafrecht *n* criminal code.

Strafstoß *m* penalty (kick).

Straftat *f* punishable act.

Strahl *m* ray, beam; jet.

strahlen *vi* to radiate; to beam.

Strahlung *f* radiation.

Strähne *f* strand.

stramm *adj* tight; robust; erect.

strampeln *vi* to kick (about), fidget.

Strand *m* shore, strand; beach.

Strandbad *n* open-air swimming pool.

stranden *vi* to run aground; to fail.

Strandgut *n* flotsam.

Strandkorb *m* beach chair.

Strang *m* cord, rope.

Strapaze *f* strain, exertion.

strapazieren *vt* to treat roughly, punish; to wear out.

strapazierfähig *adj* hardwearing.

strapaziös *adj* tough, exhausting.

Straßburg *n* Strasbourg.

Straße *f* street, road.

Straßenbahn *f* tram(way).

Straßenbahnwagen *m* tram car.

Straßenbeleuchtung *f* street lighting.

Straßenkarte *f* street amp.

Straßenkehrer *m* roadsweeper.

Straßenreinigung *f* street cleaning.

Straßensperre *f* road block.

Straßenübergang *m* pedestrian crossing.

Straßenverkehrsordnung *f* highway code.

Stratege *m* strategist.

Strategie *f* strategy.

strategisch *adj* strategic.

sträuben *vt* to ruffle; * *vr* to bristle.

Strauch *m* shrub, bush.

Strauß *m* ostrich; bouquet, bunch.

streben *vi* to strive, endeavour; ~ **nach** to strive for.

Streber *m* pusher, climber.

strebsam *adj* industrious.

Strecke *f* stretch; distance.

strecken *vt* to stretch; to lay down (weapons); * *vr* to stretch (oneself).

Streich *m* trick, prank; blow.

streicheln *vt* to stroke.

streichen *vt* to stroke; to spread; to paint; to delete; to cancel; * *vi* to brush; to prowl.

Streichholz *n* match.

Streichinstrument *n* string instrument.

Streife *f* patrol.

streifen *vt* to brush against; to touch on; to take off; * *vi* to roam.

Streifen *m* strip; stripe; film.

Streifschuß *m* graze, grazing shot.

Streifzug *m* scouting trip.

Streik *m* strike.

Streikbrecher *m* strikebreaker, blackleg.

streiken *vi* to strike.

Streikposten *m* picket.

Streit *m* argument; dispute.

streiten *vi* to argue; to dispute.

Streitfrage *f* point at issue.

Streitkräfte *pl* armed forces.

streng *adj* strict; severe.

Strenge *f* strictness, severity.
strenggenommen *adv* strictly
speaking.
strenggläubig *adj* strict, orthodox.
strengstens *adv* strictly.
Streß *m* stress.
stressen *vt* to put under stress.
streuen *vt* to strew, scatter.
Streuung *f* dispersion.
Strich *m* line; stroke; **auf den
~ gehen** (*coll*) to walk the
streets.
Strichkode *m* barcode.
Strichmädchen *n* street-
walker.
Strichpunkt *m* semicolon.
strichweise *adv* here and
there.
Strick *m* rope.
stricken *vt vi* to knit.
Strickjacke *f* cardigan.
Strickleiter *f* rope ladder.
Stricknadel *f* knitting needle.
Strickwaren *pl* knitwear.
striegeln *vt* to groom.
strikt *adj* strict.
strittig *adj* in dispute, disputed.
Stroh *n* straw.
Strohblume *f* everlasting
flower.
Strohdach *n* thatched roof.
Strohhelm *m* (drinking) straw.
Strom *m* river; (electric) current; stream.
stromabwärts *adv* down-
stream.
stromaufwärts *adv* upstream.
strömen *vt* to stream, pour.
Stromkreis *m* circuit.
stromlinienförmig stream-
lined.
Stromsperre *f* power cut.
Strömung *f* current.
Strophe *f* verse, stanza.
strotzen *vi*: **~ vor/von** to
abound in.
Strudel *m* whirlwind, vortex;
strudel.
Struktur *f* structure.
Strumpf *m* stocking.

Strumpfband *n* garter.
Strumpfhose *f* (pair of) tights.
Stube *f* room.
Stubenarrest *m* (*mil*) confine-
ment to barracks.
Stubenhocker *m* (*coll*) stay-at-
home.
stubenrein *adj* house-trained.
Stuck *m* stucco.
Stück *n* play; piece, part.
Stückchen *n* little piece.
Stücklohn *m* piecework wages.
stückweise *adv* piecemeal, bit
by bit.
Student(in) *m(f)* student.
studentisch *adj* student, aca-
demic.
Studie *f* study.
studieren *vt vi* to study.
Studio *n* studio.
Studium *n* studies.
Stufe *f* step; stage.
stufenweise *adv* gradually.
Stuhl *m* chair.
Stuhlgang *m* bowel movement.
stülpern *vt* to turn upside
down.
stumm *adj* silent; dumb.
Stummel *m* stump; stub.
Stummfilm *m* silent film.
Stümper *m* incompetent.
stümperhaft *adj* incompetent,
bungling.
stümpern *vi* to bungle.
Stumpf *m* stump.
stumpf *adj* blunt; dull; obtuse
(of angle).
Stumpfsinn *m* tediousness.
stumpfsinnig *adj* dull.
Stunde *f* hour; lesson.
Stundengeschwindigkeit *f*
average speed per hour.
Stundenkilometer *pl* kilome-
tres per hour.
stundenlang *adj* for hours.
Stundenlohn *m* hourly wage.
Stundenplan *m* timetable.
stundenweise *adv* by the hour;
every hour.
stündlich *adj* hourly.
Stups *m* push.
Stupsnase *f* snub nose.

stur *adj* pigheaded, obstinate.

Sturm *m* storm, gale, tempest; attack, assault.

stürmen *vi* to rage; to storm; * *vt* (*mil*) to storm.

Stürmer *m* forward, striker (in sport).

stürmisch *adj* stormy.

Sturmwarnung *f* storm warning.

Sturz *m* fall; overthrow.

stürzen *vt* to overthrow; to overturn; * *vr* to rush; to plunge; * *vi* to fall; to dash; to dive.

Sturzflug *m* nose-dive.

Sturzhelm *m* crash helmet.

Stute *f* mare.

Stützbalken *m* brace, joist.

Stütze *f* support; help.

stutzen *vt* to trim; to clip; * *vi* to hesitate, become suspicious.

stützen *vt* to support; to prop up.

stutzig *adj* perplexed; suspicious.

Stützpunkt *m* point of support; fulcrum.

Subjekt *n* subject.

subjektiv *adj* subjective.

Subjektivität *f* subjectivity.

Substantiv *n* noun, substantive.

Substanz *f* substance.

subtil *adj* subtle.

subtrahieren *vt* to subtract, deduct.

Subtraktion *f* subtraction.

subtropisch *adj* subtropical.

Subvention *f* subsidy.

subventionieren *vt* to subsidise.

Suchaktion *f* search.

Suche *f* search.

suchen *vt* to seek, look for; * *vi* to seek, search.

Sucher *m* seeker, searcher; viewfinder.

Sucht *f* mania; addiction, craving.

süchtig *adj* addicted.

Süchtige(r) *mf* addict.

Südamerika *n* South America.

Südafrika *n* South Africa.

Süden *m* south.

Südfrüchte *pl* citrus fruits, tropical fruits.

südlich *adj* southern, southerly.

Südost(en) *m* southeast.

südöstlich *adj* southeastern.

Südpol *m* South Pole.

südwärts *adv* southwards.

Südwest(en) *m* southwest.

südwestlich *adj* southwestern.

süffig *adj* pleasant to the taste.

süffisant *adj* smug.

suggerieren *vt* to suggest.

Sühne *f* atonement, expiation.

sühnen *vt* to atone for, expiate.

Sultan *m* sultan.

Sultanine *f* sultana.

Sülze *f* brawn.

Summe *f* sum, total.

summen *vt vi* to buzz; to hum.

Sumpf *m* marsh, swamp.

sumpfig *adj* marshy.

Sünde *f* sin.

Sündenbock *m* scapegoat.

Sünder(in) *m(f)* sinner.

sündigen *vi* to sin.

Super *n* four star (petrol).

Superlativ *m* superlative.

Supermacht *f* superpower.

Supermarkt *m* supermarket.

Suppe *f* soup, broth.

Suppenteller *m* soup plate.

süß *adj* sweet.

Süße *f* sweetness.

süßen *vt* to sweeten.

Süßigkeit *f* sweetness, sweet.

süßlich *adj* sweetish; sugary.

süßsauer *adj* pickled; sweet-and-sour.

Süßspeise *f* sweet, pudding.

Süßstoff *m* sweetener.

Süßwaren *pl* confectionery.

Süßewasser *n* fresh water.

Symbol *n* symbol.

symbolisch *adj* symbolic.

Symmetrie *f* symmetry.

symmetrisch *adj* symmetrical.

Sympathie *f* sympathy, liking.

sympathisch *adj* likeable.

sympathisieren *vi* to sympathise.
Symptom *n* symptom.
symptomatisch *adj* symptomatic.
Synagoge *f* synagogue.
synchron *adj* synchronous.
Synchrongetriebe *n* synchromesh (gears).
synchronisieren *vt* to synchronise; to dub (film).
Synonym *n* synonym.
synonym *adj* synonymous.
Synthese *f* synthesis.
synthetisch *adj* synthetic.
Syphilis *f* syphilis.
Syrien *n* Syria.
System *n* system.
systematisch systematic.
systematisieren *vt* to systematise.
Szene *f* scene.
Szenerie *f* scenery.

T

Tabak *m* tobacco.
tabellarisch *adj* tabular.
Tabelle *f* table.
Tablett *n* tray.
Tablette *f* tablet, pill.
Tabu *n* taboo.
tabu *adj* taboo.
Tachometer *m* speedometer.
Tadel *m* censure; scolding; fault, blemish.
tadellos *adj* faultless, irreproachable.
tadeln *vt* to scold.
Tafel *f* table; board; blackboard.
Taft *m* taffeta.
Tag *m* day, daylight; **guten ~!** good morning/afternoon.
Tagdienst *m* day duty.
Tagebuch *n* diary, journal.
tagelang *adv* for days.
tagen *vi* to sit, meet.
Tagesanbruch *m* daybreak.

Tagesfahrt *f* day trip.
Tagesordnung *f* agenda.
täglich *adj* daily.
tagsüber *adv* during the day.
Tagung *f* conference.
Taille *f* waist.
Takt *m* tact; (*mus*) time.
Taktik *f* tactics.
taktisch *adj* tactical.
taktlos *adj* tactless.
Taktlosigkeit *f* tactlessness.
taktvoll *adj* tactful.
Tal *n* valley.
Talent *n* talent.
Talsperre *f* dam.
Tang *m* seaweed.
Tank *m* tank.
tanken *vi* to fill up with petrol; to refuel.
Tanker *m* tanker.
Tankstelle *f* service station.
Tanne *f* spruce, fir.
Tannenbaum *m* fir tree.
Tannenzapfen *m* fir cone.
Tante *f* aunt.
Tanz *m* dance.
tanzen *vt vi* to dance.
Tänzer(in) *m(f)* dancer.
Tanzsaal *m* dance hall, ballroom.
Tapete *f* wallpaper.
tapezieren *vt* to wallpaper.
Tapezierer *m* (interior) decorator.
tapfer *adj* gallant, brave.
Tapferkeit *f* courage, bravery.
Tarif *m* tariff, scale of charges.
tarnen *vt* to camouflage; to disguise.
Tasche *f* pocket; handbag.
Taschenbuch *n* paperback.
Taschendieb *m* pickpocket.
Taschengeld *n* pocket money.
Taschenlampe *f* torch.
Taschenmesser *m* penknife.
Taschentuch *n* handkerchief.
Tasse *f* cup.
Tastatur *f* keyboard.
Taste *f* key.
tasten *vt* to feel, touch; * *vi* to feel, grope; * *vr* to feel one's way.

Tat *f* deed, act, action; **in der ~** as a matter of fact, indeed.

tatenlos *adj* inactive.

Täter(in) *m(f)* perpetrator, culprit.

tätig *adj* active, busy.

Tätigkeit *f* activity; occupation.

tätlich *adj* violent.

Tätlichkeit *f* violence.

tätowieren *vt* to tattoo.

Tatsache *f* fact.

tatsächlich *adj* actual; * *adv* really.

Tatze *f* paw.

Tau *n* rope; * *m* dew.

taub *adj* deaf.

Taube *f* pigeon; dove.

Taubheit *f* deafness.

taubstumm *adj* deaf-and-dumb.

tauchten *vt* to dip; * *vi* to dive; to submerge.

tauen *vt vi* to thaw.

Taufbecken *n* font.

Taufe *f* baptism, christening.

taufen *vt* to christen, baptise.

Taufschein *m* certificate of baptism.

taugen *vi* to be of use.

Taugenichts *m* good-for-nothing.

tauglich *adj* suitable; (*mil*) fit.

Taumel *m* dizziness; frenzy.

taumeln *vi* to reel, stagger.

Tausch *m* exchange.

tauschen *vt* to exchange, swap.

täuschen *vt* to deceive; * *vi* to be deceptive; * *vr* to be wrong.

täuschend *adj* deceptive.

Täuschung *f* deception.

tausend *num* thousand.

Tauwetter *n* thaw.

Taxi *n* taxi.

Taxifahrer(in) *m(f)* taxi driver.

Taxistand *m* taxi rank.

Technik *f* technology; technique.

Techniker *m* technician.

technisch *adj* technical.

Technologie *f* technology.

technologisch *adj* technological.

Tee *m* tea.

Teebeutel *m* tea bag.

Teekanne *f* teapot.

Teelöffel *m* teaspoon.

Teer *m* tar.

teeren *vt* to tar.

Teich *m* pond.

Teig *m* dough.

Teil *m/n* part; share; component; **zum ~** partly.

teilbar *adj* divisible.

Teilchen *n* (atomic) particle.

teilen *vt vr* to divide; to share.

teilhaben *vi*: **~ an** +*dat* to share in.

Teilnahme *f* participation.

teilnehmen *vi*: **~ an** +*dat* to take part in.

teilweise *adv* partially, in part.

Teint *m* complexion.

Telefax *n* fax.

Telefon *n* telephone.

Telefonbuch *n* telephone directory.

Telefonhörer *m* receiver.

telefonieren *vi* to telephone.

Telefonist(in) *m(f)* telephonist.

Telefonkarte *f* phonecard.

Telefonnummer *f* phone number.

Telefonzelle *f* telephone kiosk, callbox.

Telefonzentrale *f* telephone exchange.

Telegraf *m* telegraph.

telegrafieren *vt vi* to telegraph, wire.

Telegramm *n* telegram, cable.

Teleobjektiv *n* telephoto lens.

telepathisch *adj* telepathic.

Teleskop *n* telscope.

Telex *n* telex; telex machine.

Teller *m* plate.

Tempel *m* temple.

Temperament *n* temperament; liveliness.

temperamentvoll *adj* high-spirited, lively.

Temperatur *f* temperature.

Tempo *n* speed, pace; (*mus*) tempo.

Tendenz *f* tendency; intention.

tendieren vi: ~ **zu** to show a tendency to, incline towards.

Tennis n tennis.

Tennisball m tennis ball.

Tennisplatz m tennis court.

Tennisschläger m tennis racket.

Tennisspieler(in) m(f) tennis player.

Tenor m tenor.

Teppich m carpet.

Termin m date; time limit, deadline; appointment.

Termite f termite.

Terpentin n turpentine, turps.

Terrasse f terrace.

Terrine f tureen.

Territorium m territory.

Terror m terror.

terrorisieren vt to terrorise.

Terrorismus m terrorism.

Terrorist m terrorist.

Terz f (mus) third.

Terzett n trio.

Test m test.

Testament n will; (rel) Testament.

Testamentsvollstrecker m executor (of will).

testen vt to test.

teuer adj expensive, dear.

Teufel m devil.

teuflisch adj devilish, diabolical.

Text m text.

textil adj textile.

Textilien pl textiles.

Textilindustrie f textile industry.

Textverarbeitung f word processing.

Theater n theatre; **ins ~ gehen** to go to the theatre.

Theaterbesucher m playgoer.

Theaterkasse f box office.

Theaterstück n (stage-)play.

Thema n theme, subject, topic.

Themse f Thames.

Theologe m theologian.

Theologie f theology.

theologisch adj theological.

Theoretiker m theorist.

theoretisch adj theoretical.

Theorie f theory.

Therapeut m therapist.

theraupeutisch adj therapeutic.

Therapie f therapy.

Thermometer m thermometer.

Thermostat m thermostat.

These f thesis.

Thrombose f thrombosis.

Thron m throne.

Thronfolge f succession to the throne.

Thunfisch m tuna.

Thymian m thyme.

Tick m tic; quirk.

ticken vi to tick.

tief adj deep; profound; low/

Tiefe f depth.

Tiefebene f plain.

Tiefgarage f underground garage.

tiefgekühlt adj frozen.

tiefgreifend adj far-reaching.

Tiefkühlfach n deep-freeze compartment.

Tiefkühlkost f frozen food.

Tiefkühltruhe f freezer.

Tiefpunkt m low point; low ebb.

Tiefsee f deep sea.

Tier n animal.

Tierarzt n vet, veterinary surgeon.

Tiergarten m zoo.

tierisch adj animal; brutish.

Tierkreis m zodiac.

Tierkunde f zoology.

Tierquälerei f cruelty to animals.

Tiger(in) m(f) tiger (tigress).

tilgen vt to erase; to pay off, redeem (debts).

Tilgung f redemption.

Tinte f ink.

Tintenfaß n inkwell, inkstand.

Tintenfisch m cuttlefish.

Tip m tip.

tippen vi vt to touch, tap; to type.

Tippfehler m typing error.

Tirol n the Tyrol.

Tiroler(in) m(f) Tyrolean.

tirolisch *adj* Tyrolean.
Tisch *m* table.
Tischdecke *f* tablecloth.
Tischler *m* joiner, carpenter.
tischlern *vi* to do carpentry.
Tischrede *f* after-dinner speech.
Tischtennis *n* table tennis.
Tischtuch *n* tablecloth.
Titel *m* title.
Titelbild *n* cover (picture); frontispiece.
Titelrolle *f* title role.
Toast *m* toast.
Toaster *m* toaster.
toben *vi* to rage.
tobsüchtig *adj* maniacal.
Tochter *f* daughter.
Tochtergesellschaft *f* subsidiary (company).
Tod *m* death.
todernst *adj* deadly serious; * *adv* in dead earnest.
Todesangst *f* mortal fear.
Todesanzeige *f* obituary.
Todesfall *m* death.
Todesstrafe *f* death penalty.
Todesursache *f* cause of death.
todkrank *adj* dangerously ill.
tödlich *adj* fatal, deadly.
todmüde *adj* dead tired.
Toilette *f* toilet, lavatory.
Toilettenartikel *pl* toiletries.
Toilettenpapier *n* toilet paper.
Toilettentisch *m* dressing table.
tolerant *adj* tolerant.
Toleranz *f* tolerance.
tolerieren *vt* to tolerate.
toll *adj* mad; wild.
tollen *vi* to romp.
Tollkirsche *f* deadly nightshade.
Tollwut *f* rabies.
Tomate *f* tomato.
Tombola *f* tombola.
Ton *m* clay; sound; note; tone; shade.
Tonart *f* (musical) key.
Tonband *n* sound-recording tape.
Tonbandgerät *n* tape recorder.

tönen *vi* to sound; * *vt* to shade; to tint.
tönern *adj* clay.
Tonfall *m* intonation.
Tonleiter *f* (*mus*) scale.
tonlos *adj* soundless/
Tonne *f* barrel; ton. tonne.
Tontaube *f* clay pigeon.
Topas *m* topaz.
Topf *m* pot.
Topfblume *f* pot plant.
Töpfer *m* potter.
Töpferscheibe *f* potter's wheel.
Tor *m* fool; gate; goal.
Torbogen *m* archway.
Torf *m* peat.
Torheit *f* foolishness.
töricht *adj* foolish.
torkeln *vi* to reel, stagger.
Torpedo *m* torpedo.
Torte *f* tart; cake.
Tortur *f* ordeal.
Torwart *m* goalkeeper.
tosen *vi* to roar.
tot *adj* dead.
total *adj* total.
totalitär *adj* totalitarian.
Tote(r) *mf* dead man.
töten *vt vi* to kill.
Totenbett *n* death bed.
totenblaß *adj* deadly pale.
Totenkopf *m* skull.
Totenschein *m* death certificate.
totfahren *vt* to run over.
totgeboren *adj* stillborn.
Totschlag *m* manslaughter.
totschlagen *vt* to kill.
totstellen *vr* to pretend to be dead.
Tötung *f* killing.
Toupet *n* toupee.
Tour *f* tour, excursion; revolution.
Tourenzähler *m* rev counter.
Tourist *m* tourist.
Touristenklasse *f* tourist class.
Trab *m* trot.
Trabantenstadt *f* satellite town.
traben *vi* to trot.
Tracht *f* costume, dress.

trachten *vi*: ~ **(nach)** to strive (for).
trächtig *adj* pregnant.
Tradition *f* tradition.
traditionell *adj* traditional.
Tragbahre *f* stretcher.
tragbar *adj* portable; wearable; bearable.
träge *adj* sluggish; inert.
tragen *vt* to wear; to carry; to bear; * *vi* to be pregnant.
Träger *m* carrier; wearer; bearer.
Trägerrakete *f* launch vehicle.
Tragetasche *f* carrier bag.
Tragfläche *f* (*aviation*) wing.
Tragflügelboot *n* hydrofoil.
Trägheit *f* laziness; inertia.
Tragik *f* tragedy.
tragisch *adj* tragic.
Tragödie *f* tragedy.
Tragweite *f* range; scope.
Trainer *m* trainer, coach; (football) manager.
trainieren *vt* to train, coach.
Training *n* training.
Trainingsanzug *m* track suit.
Traktor *m* tractor; tractor feed.
trällern *vt vi* to trill, sing.
Tram *f* tram.
trampeln *vt vi* to trample.
trampen *vi* to hitch-hike.
Tramper(in) *m(f)* hitch-hiker.
tranchieren *vt* to carve.
Träne *f* tear.
tränen *vi* to water.
Tränengas *n* teargas.
tränken *vt* to water.
Transformator *m* transformer.
Transistor *m* transistor.
Transitverkehr *m* transit traffic.
Transitvisum *n* transit visa.
transparent *adj* transparent.
Transparent *n* transparency.
Transplantation *f* transplantation; graft.
Transport *m* transport.
transportieren *vt* to transport.
Transportunternehmen *n* carrier.
Trapez *n* trapeze.

Traube *f* grape; bunch of grapes.
Traubenzucker *m* glucose.
trauen *vi*: **jdm/etw** ~ to trust sb/something; * *vr* to dare; * *vt* to marry.
Trauer *f* sorrow; mourning; **in** ~ **sein (um)** to be in mourning (for).
Trauerfall *m* death, bereavement.
Trauerfeier *f* funeral service.
Trauerkleidung *f* mourning.
trauern *vi* to mourn.
Trauerspiel *n* tragedy.
traulich *adj* cosy, intimate.
Traum *m* dream.
Trauma *n* trauma.
träumen *vt vi* to dream.
Träumer *m* dreamer.
Träumerei *f* dreaming.
träumerisch *adj* dreamy.
traumhaft *adj* dreamlike.
traurig *adj* sad.
Traurigkeit *f* sadness.
Trauring *m* wedding ring.
Trauschein *m* marriage certificate.
Trauung *f* wedding ceremony.
Trauzeuge *m* witness (to a marriage).
Trauzeugin *f* witness (to a marriage).
Trecker *m* tractor.
treffen *vi vt* to meet; to strike, hit; * *vi* to hit; * *vr* to meet.
Treffen *n* meeting.
treffend *adj* pertinent.
Treffpunkt *m* meeting place.
Treibeis *n* drift ice.
treiben *vt* to drive; to do, go in for; to pursue; * *vi* to drift; to sprout.
Treibhaus *n* greenhouse.
Treibhauseffekt *m* greenhouse effect.
Treibhausgas *n* greenhouse gas.
Treibstoff *m* fuel.
trennbar *adj* separable.
trennen *vt* to separate; to divide; * *vr* to separate.

Trennung *f* separation.
Trennungsstrich *m* hyphen.
Trennwand *f* partition wall.
treppab *adv* downstairs.
treppauf *adv* upstairs.
Treppe *f* stairs, staircase.
Treppenabsatz *m* landing.
Treppengeländer *n* banisters.
Tresor *m* safe; bank vault.
Tretboot *n* pedal boat.
treten *vt* to step; to appear; * *vt* to kick; to trample.
treu *adj* faithful, loyal.
Treubruch *m* breach of faith.
Treue *f* faithfulness, loyalty.
Treuhand *f* trust.
Treuhandanstalt *f* trustreeship.
Treuhänder *m* trustee.
Treuhandgesellschaft *f* trust company.
treulos *adj* unfaithful, disloyal.
Tribüne *f* grandstand; platform.
Trichter *m* funnel.
triefen *vi* to drip, be dripping.
triftig *adj* good, convincing.
trimmen *vi* to do keep fit exercises.
trinkbar *adj* drinkable.
trinken *vt vi* to drink.
Trinker *m* drinker.
Trinkgeld *n* tip, gratuity.
Trinkhalle *f* refreshment kiosk.
Trinkwasser *n* drinking water.
Tripper *m* gonorrhoea.
Tritt *m* step; kick.
Triumph *m* triumph.
Triumphbogen *m* triumphal arch.
triumphieren *vi* to triumph; to exult.
trocken *adj* dry.
Trockenelement *n* dry cell.
Trockenhaube *f* hair-dryer.
trockenlegen *vt* to drain.
Trockenmilch *f* dried milk.
Trockenrasur *f* dry/electric shave.
trocknen *vt vi* to dry.
Trödel *m* junk.

Trödelmarkt *m* flea market.
trödeln *vi* (*coll*) to dawdle.
Trog *m* trough.
Trommel *f* drum.
Trommelfell *n* eardrum.
trommeln *vt vi* to drum.
Trompete *f* trumpet.
Trompeter *m* trumpeter.
Tropen *pl* tropics.
Tropenhelm *m* sun helmet.
tröpfeln *vi* to drop, trickle.
Tropfen *m* drop.
tropfen *vt vi* to drip.
tropfenweise *adv* in drops.
tropisch *adj* tropical.
Trost *m* comfort, consolation.
trösten *vt* to comfort, console.
trolstlos *adj* bleak; wretched.
Trostpreis *m* consolation prize.
trostreich *adj* comforting.
Trott *m* trot; routine.
Trottel *m* (*coll*) dope, fool.
trotten *vi* to trot.
Trottoir *n* pavement.
Trotz *m* pigheadedness.
trotz *prep* in spite of, despite.
trotzdem *adv* nevertheless, all the same; * *conj* although.
trotzen *vt* to defy; to brave.
trotzig *adj* pigheadedness.
Trotzkopf *m* obstinate child.
trüb *adj* dull; gloomy; cloudy.
Trubel *m* hurly-burly.
trüben *vt* to cloud; * *vr* to become clouded.
Trübheit *f* dullness; cloudiness; gloom.
Trübsal *f* distress.
Trübsinn *m* depression.
trübsinnig *adj* gloomy, depressed.
Trüfel *f* truffle.
trügen *vt* to deceive; * *vi* to be deceptive.
trügerisch *adj* deceptive.
Trugschluß *m* false conclusion.
Truhe *f* chest.
Trümmer *pl* wreckage; ruins.
Trümmerhaufen *m* heap of rubble.
Trumpf *m* trump.
trumpfen *vt vi* to trump.

Trunk *m* drink.
trunken *adj* intoxicated.
Trunkenheit *f* intoxication.
Trunkensucht *f* alcoholism.
Trupp *m* troop.
Truppe *f* troop; force; troupe.
Truppen *pl* troops.
Truthahn *m* turkey.
Tscheche *m* Czech.
Tschechin *f* Czech.
tschechisch *adj* Czech.
tschüs *excl* cheerio.
T-Shirt *n* T-shirt.
Tube *f* tube.
Tuberkulose *f* tuberculosis.
Tuch *n* cloth; scarf; towel/
Tuchfabrik *f* cloth mill.
tüchtig *adj* efficient, able, capable.
Tüchtigkeit *f* efficiency, ability.
Tücke *f* malice; problem.
tückisch *adj* malicious.
Tugend *f* virtue.
tugendhaft *adj* virtuous.
Tüll *m* tulle.
Tüle *f* spout.
Tulpe *f* tulip.
Tumor *m* tumour.
Tümpel *m* pond, pool.
Tumult *m* tumult.
tun *vt* to do; * *vi* to act.
tünchen *vt* to whitewash.
Tunke *f* sauce.
tunken *vt* to dunk.
tunlichst *adv* if at all possible.
tunlichstbald *adv* as soon as possible.
Tunnel *m* tunnel.
Tupfen *m* dot, spot.
tupfen *vt vi* to dot.
Tür *f* door.
Turban *m* turban.
Turbine *f* turbine.
Türke *m* Turk.
Türkei *f* Turkey.
Türkin *f* Turk.
Türkis *m* turquoise.
türkis *adj* turquoise.
türkisch *adj* Turkish.
Turm *m* tower; steeple; rook, castle (in chess).
türmen *vr* to tower up; * *vi* to

heap up.
turnen *vi* to do gymnastics; * *vt* to perform.
Turnen *n* gymnastics; physical education, PE.
Turner(in) *m(f)* gymnast.
Turnhalle *f* gym, gymnasium.
Turnier *n* tournament.
Turnverein *m* gymnastics club.
tuscheln *vt vi* to whisper.
Tüte *f* bag.
tuten *vi* to hoot.
Typ *m* type.
Type *f* type.
Typhus *m* typhoid.
typisch *adj* typical.
Tyrann *m* tyrant.
Tyrannei *f* tyranny.
tyrannisch *adj* tyrannical.
tyrannisieren *vt* to tyrannise.

U

U-Bahn *f* underground, tube.
übel *adj* bad, wicked.
Übel *n* evil.
übelgelaunt *adj* bad-tempered.
Übelkeit *f* nausea.
üben *vt vi* to exercise, practise.
über *prep* over, above; via; about.
überall *adv* everywhere.
überanstrengen *vt* to overexert; * *vr* to overexert oneself
überarbeiten *vt* to rework, revise; * *vr* to overwork (oneself).
überaus *adv* exceedingly.
überbieten *vt* to outbid; to surpass; to break (record).
Überblick *m* view; overview, survey.
überblicken *vt* to survey.
überbringen *vt* to deliver, hand over.
überbuchen *vt* to overbook.
überdauern *vt* to outlast.

überdenken *vt* to think over.

überdies *adv* besides.

Überdruß *m* weariness.

übereilt *adj* premature, over-hasty.

übereinander *adv* one upon the other; about each other.

übereinkommen *vi* to agree.

Übereinkunft *f* agreement.

übereinstimmen *vi* to agree.

Übereinstimmung *f* agreement.

überfahren *vt* to run over; to walk all over.

Überfahrt *f* passage, crossing.

Überfall *m* assault.

überfallen *vt* to attack; to raid.

überfällig *adj* overdue.

überfliegen *vt* to fly over, overfly.

Überfluß *m* superabundance, excess.

überflüssig *adj* superfluous.

Übergepäck *n* excess baggage.

überfließen *vi* to overflow.

Übergabe *f* handing over; (*mil*) surrender.

Übergang *m* crossing; transition.

übergeben *vt* to hand over; (*mil*) to surrender; * *vr* to be sick.

übergehen *vi* to pass; to go over, defect.

Übergewicht *n* excess weight.

überhaupt *adv* at all; in general; especially; ~ **nicht** not at all.

überheblich *adj* arrogant.

Überheblichkeit *f* arrogance.

überholen *vt* to overtake; to overhaul.

überholt *adj* obsolete, out-of-date.

überhören *vt* not to hear; to ignore.

überirdisch *adj* unearthly, supernatural.

überladen *vt* to overload; * *adj* cluttered.

überlasten *vt* to overload; to overtax.

überlaufen *vi* to flow over; to go over, defect.

Überläufer *m* defector.

überleben *vi* to survive.

Überlebende(r) *m* survivor.

überlegen *vt* to consider; * *adj* superior.

Überlegenheit *f* superiority.

Überlegung *f* consideration, deliberation.

überliefern *vt* to hand down, transmit.

Überlieferung *f* tradition.

überlisten *vt* to outwit.

überm = **über dem**.

Übermacht *f* superior force.

übermächtig *adj* superior; overpowering.

übermannen *vt* to overcome.

Übermaß *n* excess.

übermäßig *adj* excessive.

Übermensch *m* superman.

übermenschlich *adj* superhuman.

übermitteln *vt* to convey.

Übermittlung *f* transmission.

übermorgen *adv* the day after tomorrow.

übermüdet *adj* overtired.

Übermüdung *f* (over)fatigue.

Übermut *m* overenthusiasm.

übermütig *adj* overenthusiastic.

übernächste(r,s) *adj* one after next.

übernachten *vi*: (**bei jdm**) ~ to spend the night (at sb's place).

Übernahme *f* takeover; adoption.

übernatürlich *adj* supernatural.

übernehmen *vt* to take over; to adopt; * *vr* to take on too much.

überprüfen *vt* to check, examine.

überquellen *vi* to overflow.

überqueren *vt* to cross.

überragen *vt* to tower above.

überragend *adj* superior.

überraschen *vt* to surprise.

Überraschung *f* surprise.

überreden *vt* to persuade.
Überredung *f* persuasion.
überreichen *vt* to present, hand over.
Überrest *m* remains, remnants.
übers = **über das**.
Überschallgeschwindigkeit *f* supersonic speed.
überschätzen *vt* to overestimate.
Überschlag *m* (financial) estimate; somersault.
überschlagen *vt* to estimate; * *vr* to somersault.
überschreiben *vt* to provide with a heading.
überschreiten *vt* to cross/step over; to exceed.
Überschrift *f* heading, title.
Überschuß *m* surplus.
überschüssig *adj* surplus, excessive.
überschwemmen *vt* to flood.
Überschwemmung *f* flood.
Übersee *f*: **nach/im ~** overseas.
überseeisch *adj* overseas.
übersehen *vt* to look over.
übersetzen *vt* to translate; * *vi* to cross.
Übersetzer(in) *m(f)* translator.
Übersetzung *f* translation.
Übersicht *f* overall view.
übersichtlich *adj* clear; open.
Übersichtlichkeit *f* clarity, lucidity.
überstehen *vt* to get over, overcome.
übersteigen *vt* to climb over; to exceed.
Überstunden *pl* overtime.
Übertrag *m* amount brought forward.
übertragbar *adj* transferable; (*med*) infectious.
übertragen *vt* to transfer; to broadcast; to transmit (illness); * *vr* to spread.
Übertragung *f* broadcast; transmission.
übertreiben *vt* to exaggerate.
Übertreibung *f* exaggeration.

übertreten to cross, to break; to step (over).
Übertretung *f* transgression.
übervoll *adj* overfull.
überwachen *vt* to supervise; to keep under surveillance.
Überwachung *f* supervision; surveillance.
überwältigen *vt* to overpower.
überwältigend *adj* overwhelming.
überweisen *vt* to transfer.
Überweisung *f* transfer.
überwiegen *vi* to predominate.
überwiegend *adj* predominant.
überwinden *vt* to overcome; * *vr* to make an effort (to do something).
Überwindung *f* effort, strength of mind.
überzeugen *vt* to convince, persuade.
überzeugend *adj* convincing.
Überzeugung *f* conviction, belief.
üblich *adj* usual.
U-Boot *n* submarine.
übrig *adj* remaining.
übrigbleiben *vi* to remain, be left (over).
übrigens *adv* besides; by the way.
übriglassen *vt* to leave (over).
Übung *f* practice; exercise; **~ macht den Meister** practice makes perfect.
Ufer *n* bank; shore.
Uhr *f* watch; clock; **20 ~ 8** o'clock; **wieviel ~ ist es?** what time is it?.
Uhrband *n* watch strap.
Uhrmacher *m* watchmaker.
Uhrwerk *n* clockwork.
Uhu *m* eagle owl.
UKW *abbr* (= **Ultrakurzwelle**) VHF.
ulkig *adj* funny.
Ulme *f* elm.
Ultimatum *n* ultimatum.
Ultraschall *m* ultrasound.
ultraviolett *adj* ultraviolet.

um *prep* (a)round; at (of time); by; * *adv* about; ~ ... **zu** in order to.
umändern *vt* to alter.
Umänderung *f* alteration.
umarbeiten *vt* to remodel; to revise, rework.
umarmen *vt* to embrace.
Umbau *m* reconstruction.
umbauen *vt* to reconstruct.
umbilden *vt* to reorganise; to reshuffle (cabinet).
umbinden *vt* to put on.
umblättern *vt* to turn over.
umblicken *vr* to look round.
umbringen *vt* to kill.
umbuchen *vi* to change one's flight/reservation; * *vt* to change.
umdenken *vi* to adjust one's views.
umdrehen *vi* *vr* to turn (round).
Umdrehung *f* revolution; rotation.
umeinander *adv* round one another.
umfahren *vt* to run over; to drive round.
umfallen *vi* to fall down/over.
Umfang *m* extent; range; area.
umfangreich *adj* extensive; voluminous.
umfassen *vt* to embrace; to surround; to include.
umfassend *adj* comprehensive, extensive.
umformatieren *vt* to reformat.
umformen *vi* to transform.
Umformer *m* transformer, converter.
Umfrage *f* poll.
umfüllen *vt* to trasnfer; to decant.
umfunktionieren *vt* to transform, convert.
Umgang *m* company; way of behaving; dealings.
umgänglich *adj* sociable.
Umgangsformen *pl* manners.
Umgangssprache *f* colloquial language.

umgeben *vt* to surround.
Umgebung *f* surroundings; environment.
umgehen *vi* to go round, bypass; to circumvent; to avoid; **im Schlosse** ~ to haunt the castle.
umgehend *adj* immediate.
Umgehung *f* bypassing; circumvention; avoidance.
Umgehungsstraße *f* bypass.
umgekehrt *adj* reverse(d); opposite; * *adv* vice versa, the other way round.
umgraben *vt* to dig up.
Umhang *m* wrap, cape.
umhauen *vt* to fell; to bowl over.
umher *adv* about, around.
umhergehen *vi* to walk about.
umherziehen *vi* to wander from place to place.
umhören *vr* to ask around.
Umkehr *f* turning back; change.
umkehren *vi* to turn back; * *vt* reverse; to turn inside out.
umkippen *vt* to tip over; * *vi* to overturn; to keel over; to change one's mind.
Umkleidekabine *f* changing cubicle.
Umkleideraum *m* changing room.
umkommen *vi* to die; to go bad.
Umkreis *m* neighbourhood; **im ~ von** within a radius of.
umladen *vt* to tranship.
Umlage *f* share of the costs.
Umlauf *m* circulation.
Umlaufbahn *f* orbit.
Umlaut *m* umlaut.
umlegen *vt* to put on; to move, shift; to share out; to tip over.
umleiten *vt* to divert.
Umleitung *f* diversion.
umliegend *adj* surrounding.
umrahmen *vt* to frame.
umranden *vt* to border, edge.
umrechnen *vt* to convert.
Umrechnung *f* conversion.
Umrechnungsskurs *m* rate of

exchange.

umreißen *vt* to sketch, outline.

Umriß *m* outline.

umrühren *vt vi* to stir.

ums = um das.

Umsatz *m* turnover.

Umsatzsteuer *f* sales tax.

umschalten *vt* to switch.

Umschau *f* look(ing) round.

umschauen *vr* to look round.

Umschlag *n* envelope.

umschlagen *vi* to change; to capsize; * *vt* to knock over; to turn over.

umschreiben *vt* to rewrite; to transfer.

umschulen *vt* to retrain.

Umschwung *m* change (around), revolution.

umsehen *vr* to look around/about.

umseitig *adv* overleaf.

umsichtig *adj* cautious, prudent.

umsonst *adv* for nothing; in vain.

Umstand *m* circumstance.

umständlich *adj* cumbersome; long-winded.

Umstandskleid *n* maternity dress.

umsteigen *vi* to change (train, etc).

umstellen *vt* to rearrange; to convert; * *vr* to adapt (oneself).

Umstellung *f* change; conversion.

umstritten *adj* disputed.

Umsturz *m* overthrow.

umstürzen *vt* to overturn; * *vi* to collapse, fall down.

Umtausch *m* exchange.

umtauschen *vt* to exchange.

Umweg *m* detour.

Umwelt *f* environment.

umweltfeindlich *adj* ecologically harmless.

umweltfreundlich *adj* environment-friendly.

Umweltschützer *m* environmentalist.

Umweltverschmutzung *f* environmental pollution.

umwenden *vt vr* to turn (around).

umwerfen *vt* to overturn, upset.

umziehen *vt vr* to change; * *vi* to move.

Umzug *m* procession; move, removal.

unabänderlich *adj* irreversible.

unabhängig *adj* independent, autonomous.

Unabhängigkeit *f* independence, autonomy.

unachtsam *adj* careless.

Unachtsamkeit *f* carelessness.

unangenehm *adj* unpleasant.

Unnehmlichkeit *f* inconvenience.

unanständig *adj* indecent, improper.

Unart *f* bad manners; bad habit.

unartig *adj* badly behaved; naughty.

unaufmerksam *adj* inattentive.

unaufrichtig *adj* insincere.

unbeabsichtigt *adj* unintentional.

unbedeutend *adj* unimportant, insignificant.

unbegrenzt *adj* unlimited.

unbegründet *adj* unfounded.

unbekannt *adj* unknown.

unbequem *adj* uncomfortable; inconvenient.

unberührt *adj* untouched, intact.

unbeschlossen *adj* undetermined, undecided.

unbeständig *adj* inconstant; unstable.

unbeweglich *adj* motionless.

unbewohnt *adj* unoccupied, vacant.

unbewußt *adj* unconscious.

unbezahlt *adj* outstanding; unpaid.

und *conj* and; ~ **so weiter** and

so on.

Undank *m* ingratitude.
undankbar *adj* ungrateful.
undeutich *adj* indistinct.
undicht *adj* leaky.
Unding *n* absurdity.
uneben *adj* uneven.
unehelich *adj* illegitimate.
Unehre *f* dishonour.
uneinig *adj* disunited.
unendlich *adj* endless, infinite.
unerfahren *adj* inexperienced.
unfähig *adj* incapable, incompetent.
unfair *adj* unfair.
Unfall *m* accident.
Unfallversicherung *f* accident insurance.
unfreundlich *adj* unfriendly, unkind.
Unfreundlichkeit *f* unfriendliness.
unfruchtbar *adj* infertile; unfruitful.
Unfruchtbarkeit *f* infertility; unfruitfulness.
Ungar(in) *m(f)* Hungarian.
ungarisch *adj* Hungarian.
Ungarn *n* Hungary.
Ungeduld *f* impatience.
ungeduldig *adj* impatient.
ungefähr *adj* rough, approximate; * *adv* about, approximately.
ungeheuer *adj* huge; * *adv* enormously.
Ungeheuer *m* monster.
ungeheuerlich *adj* monstrous.
ungehorsam *adj* disobedient.
Ungehorsam *m* disobedience.
ungenau *adj* inaccurate, inexact.
Ungenauigkeit *f* inaccuracy, inexactitude.
ungepflegt *adj* untended; unkempt; neglected.
ungerade *adj* odd, uneven.
ungeschickt *adj* unskilled, clumsy.
ungesetzlich *adj* illegal.
ungewandt *adj* clumsy, awkward.

ungewiß *adj* uncertain.
Ungewißheit *f* uncertainty.
ungewöhnlich *adj* unusual.
ungezogen *adj* impertinent, rude.
Ungezogenheit *f* impertinence, rudeness.
ungläubig *adj* unbelievable.
unglaublich *adj* incredible.
ungleich *adj* dissimilar; unequal; * *adv* incomparably.
Ungleichheit *f* dissimilarity; inequality.
Unglück *n* bad luck; misfortune; calamity; accident.
unglücklich *adj* unhappy; unlucky; unfortunate.
unglücklicherweise *adv* unfortunately.
Unglücksfall *m* accident, calamity.
ungültig *adj* invalid.
Ungültigkeit *f* invalidity.
ungünstig *adj* unfavourable.
unhaltbar *adj* untenable.
Unheil *n* evil; misfortune.
unheilbar *adj* incurable.
unhöflich *adj* impolite.
Unhöflichkeit *f* impoliteness.
Uni *f* (*coll*) university.
Uniform *f* uniform.
uninteressant *adj* uninterested.
Universität *f* university.
Universum *n* universe.
Unkenntnis *f* ignorance.
unklar *adj* unclear.
Unklarheit *f* unclarity.
Unkosten *pl* expense(s).
Unkraut *n* weed(s).
unleserlich *adj* illegible.
unlösbar *adj* insoluble.
Unlust *m* lack of enthusiasm.
unmäßig *adj* immoderate, intemperate.
Unmensch *m* ogre, brute.
unmenschlich *adj* inhuman, brutal; awful.
unmerklich *adj* imperceptible.
unmittelbar *adj* immediate.
unmöglich *adj* impossible.
Unmöglichkeit *f* impossibility.

unmoralisch *adj* immoral.

Unmut *m* ill humour.

unnötig *adj* unnecessary.

unnütz *adj* useless.

unordentlich *adj* untidy.

Unordnung *f* disorder.

unpassend *adj* inappropriate; inopportune.

unpersönlich *adj* impersonal.

unrecht *adj* wrong.

Unrecht *m* wrong.

unrechtsmäßig *adj* unlawful.

unregelmäßig *adj* irregular.

Unregelmäßigkeit *f* irregularity.

unreif *adj* unripe; immature.

unrein *adj* unclean.

Unruhe *f* unrest.

unruhig *adj* restless.

uns *pron* us; ourselves.

unschädlich *adj* harmless.

Unschuld *m* innocence.

unschuldig *adj* innocent.

unser(e) *poss adj* our.

unsere(r,s) *poss pron* ours.

unsicher *adj* uncertain; insecure.

Unsicherheit *f* uncertainty; insecurity.

unsichtbar *adj* invisible.

Unsinn *m* nonsense.

unsinnig *adj* nonsensical.

Unsitte *f* deplorable habit.

unsittlich *adj* indecent.

unsre = **unsere**.

unsterblich *adj* immortal.

Unstimmigkeit *f* disagreement; inconsistency.

unsympatisch   *adj* uncongenial.

untätig *adj* idle.

unteilbar *adj* indivisible.

unten *adv* below; downstairs; at the bottom.

unter *prep* under; underneath, below; among(st).

Unterarm *m* forearm.

Unterbewußtsein *n* subconscious.

unterbieten *vt* to undercut; to lower.

unterbrechen *vt* to interrupt.

Unterbrechung *f* interruption.

unterbringen *vt* to stow; to accommodate.

unterdessen *adv* meanwhile.

Unterdruck *m* low pressure.

unterdrücken *vt* to suppress; to oppress.

untere(r,s) *adj* lower.

untereinander *adv* with each other, among one another, *etc.*

unterentwickelt *adj* underdeveloped.

unterernährt *adj* underfed, undernourished.

Unterernährung *f* malnutrition.

Untergang *m* downfall, decline; sinking.

untergeben *adj* subordinate.

untergehen *vi* to go down; to set (of the sun); to fall; to perish.

Untergeschoß *n* basement.

Untergewicht *n* underweight.

Untergrund *m* foundation; underground.

Untergrundbahn *f* underground, tube.

unterhalb *prep adv* below.

Unterhalt *m* maintenance.

unterhalten *vt* to maintain; to entertain; * *vt* to talk; to enjoy oneself

unterhaltend *adj* entertaining, amusing.

Unterhaltung *f* maintenance; talk; amusement, entertainment.

Unterhemd *n* vest.

Unterhose *f* underpants.

unterkommen *vi* to find shelter; to find work.

Unterkunft *f* accommodation.

Unterlage *f* foundation; document.

unterlassen *vt* to refrain from; to fail t do.

Unterleib *m* abdomen.

unterliegen *vi* to be subject to.

unternehmen *vi* to undertake.

Unternehmen *n* undertaking, enterprise.

Unternehmer *m* businessman, entrepreneur.
Unterricht *m* instruction, lessons.
unterrichten *vt* to instruct; to teach.
untersagen *vt* to forbid.
unterschätzen *vt* to underestimate.
unterscheiden *vt* to distinguish; * *vr* to differ.
Unterscheidung *f* distinction; differentiation.
Unterschied *m* difference.
unterschlagen *vt* to embezzle.
Unterschlagung *f* embezzlement.
unterschreiben *vt* to sign.
Unterschrift *f* signature.
Unterseeboot *m* submarine.
untersetzt *adj* stocky.
unterste(r,s) *adj* lowest, bottom.
unterstützen *vt* to support.
Unterstützung *f* support, backing.
untersuchen *vt* to examine; to investigate.
Untersuchung *f* examination; investigation.
Untertan *m* subject (of a country).
Untertasse *f* saucer.
Untertitel *m* subtitle.
Unterwäsche *f* underwear.
unterwegs *adv* on the way.
unterwerfen *vt* to subject; to subjugate; * *vr* (+*dat*) to submit (to).
unterzeichnen *vt* to sign.
untragbar *adj* intolerable.
untreu *adj* unfaithful.
Untreue *f* unfaithfulness.
untüchtig *adj* incapable, unqualified.
unveränderlich *adj* unchangeable.
unverschämt *adj* shameless.
unversöhnlich *adj* irreconcilable.
unverständlich *adj* unintelligible.

unvollkommen *adj* imperfect.
unvollständig *adj* incomplete.
unwahr *adj* untrue.
unwahrscheinlich *adj* improbable, unlikely.
Unwetter *n* thunderstorm.
unwiderruflich *adj* irrevocable.
unwirklich *adj* unreal.
unwohl *adj* unwell, ill.
unwürdig *adj* unworthy.
Unze *f* ounce.
Unzucht *f* sexual offence.
unzüchtig *adj* immoral; lewd.
unzufrieden *adj* dissatisfied.
Unzufriedenheit *f* discontent.
uralt *adj* very old, ancient.
Ural *m* (the) Urals.
Uran *n* uranium.
Urbild *n* original.
Urgroßmutter *f* great-grandmother.
Urgroßvater *m* great-grandfather.
Urin *m* urine.
Urkunde *f* deed, document.
Urlaub *m* holiday(s), leave.
Urlauber *m* holiday-maker.
Urlaubsort *m* holiday resort.
Urne *f* urn.
Ursache *f* cause.
Ursprung *m* origin, source.
ursprünglich *adj* original; * *adv* originally.
Urteil *m* judgment, sentence.
urteilen *vt* to judge.
Urwald *m* primeval forest; jungle.
Urzeit *f* prehistoric times.
usw (= **und so weiter**) etc.
Utopie *f* illusion, pipedream.
utopisch *adj* utopian.

V

vag(e) *adj* vague.
Vagina *f* vagina.
Vakuum *n* vacuum.
Vampir *m* vampire.

Vanille *f* vanilla.
Variation *f* variation.
variieren *vt vi* to vary.
Vase *f* vase.
Vater *m* father.
Vaterland *n* native country, fatherland.
väterlich *adj* fatherly.
Vaterschaft *f* paternity.
Vaterunser *n* Lord's Prayer.
Vati *m* daddy.
Vatikan *m* (the) Vatican.
Vegetarier(in) *m(f)* vegetarian.
Veilchen *n* violet.
Vene *f* vein.
Venedig *n* Venice.
Ventil *n* valve.
Ventilator *m* ventilator.
verabreden *vt* to agree, arrange.
Verabredung *f* arrangement; appointment.
verabscheuen *vt* to abhor, detest.
verabschieden *vt* say goodbye to; to discharge; * *vr* to take one's leave.
Verabschiedung *f* leave-taking; discharge.
verachten *vt* to despise, scorn.
verächtlich *adj* contemptible, despicable.
Verachtung *f* contempt, scorn.
verallgemeinen *vt* to generalise.
Verallgemeinerung *f* generalisation.
veralten *vi* to become obsolete.
Veranda *f* veranda.
veränderlich *adj* changeable, unsettled.
verändern *vt vr* to change, alter.
Veränderung *f* change, alteration.
Veranlagung *f* disposition.
veranlassen *vt* to cause.
veranschaulichen *vt* to illustrate.
veranschlagen *vt* to estimate.
veranstalten *vt* to arrange, organise.

Veranstaltung *f* organising; function, event.
verantworten *vt* to answer for ; * *vr* to justify oneself
verantwortlich *adj* responsible.
Verantwortung *f* responsibility.
verantwortungsbewußt *adj* responsible.
verantwortungslos *adj* irresponsible.
verarbeiten *vt* to process; to assimilate.
Verarbeitung *f* processing; assimilation.
verärgern *vt* to annoy.
verausgaben *vr* to run out of money; to exhaust oneself
Verb *n* verb.
Verband *m* association, society; (*med*) bandage.
Verbandkasten *m* first-aid box.
Verbandzeug *n* bandage.
verbannen *vt* to banish.
Verbannung *f* exile.
verbergen *vt vr*: (**sich**) ~ (**vor** +*dat*) to hide (from).
verbessern *vt vr* to improve; to correct (oneself).
Verbesserung *f* improvement; correction.
verbeugen *vr* to bow.
Verbeugung *f* bow.
verbiegen *vi* to bend.
verbieten *vt* to forbid, prohibit.
verbinden *vt* to connect; to combine; * *vr* to combine, join.
verbindlich *adj* binding.
Verbindung *f* connection; combination; (*chem*) compound; club.
verbissen *adj* bitter; grim.
Verbleib *m* whereabouts.
verbleiben *vi* to remain.
verbleit *adj* leaded (of petrol).
verblüffen *vt* to amaze, stagger.
Verblüffung *f* amazement.
verblühen *vi* to fade, wither.
verbluten *vi* to bleed to death.

verborgen *adj* hidden.

Verbot *n* ban, prohibition.

verboten *adj* forbidden; **Rauchen ~!** no smoking.

Verbotsschild *n* prohibitory sign.

Verbrauch *m* consumption.

verbrauchen *vt* to use up.

Verbraucher *m* consumer.

verbraucht *adj* finished, used up; stale; worn-out.

Verbrechen *n* crime, offence.

verbrechen *vi* to commit a crime.

Verbrecher *m* criminal.

verbrecherisch *adj* criminal.

verbreiten *vt vr* to spread.

verbreitern *vt* to broaden.

Verbreitung *f* spread, propagation.

verbrennbar *adj* combustible.

verbrennen *vt* to burn; to cremate.

Verbrennung *f* burning; combustion; cremation.

Verbrennungsmotor *m* internal combustion engine.

verbringen *vt* to spend (of time).

verbrühen *vt* to scald.

verbuchen *vt* to register; to suffer; to enjoy.

verbunden *adj* connected.

verbünden *vr* to ally oneself

Verbündete(r) *mf* ally.

Verdacht *f* suspicion.

verdächtig *adj* suspicious, suspect.

verdächtigen *vt* to suspect.

verdammen *vt* to damn, condemn.

verdammt *adj adv* damned.

verdampfen *vi* to evaporate, vaporise.

verdanken *vt*: **jdm etw ~** to owe sb something.

verdauen *vt* to digest.

verdaulich *adj* digestible.

Verdauung *f* digestion.

Verdeck *m* hood (of car); deck.

verdecken *vt* to cover (up); to hide.

Verderben *n* ruin.

verderben *vt* to ruin; to spoil to corrupt; * *vi* to rot.

verderblich *adj* perishable; pernicious.

verdeutlichen *vt* to make clear.

verdichten *vt* to condense.

verdienen *vt* to earn; to deserve.

Verdienst *m* earnings; * *n* merit.

verdient *adj* well-earned; deserving of esteem.

verdoppeln *vt* to double.

verdorben *adj* ruined; spoilt; corrupt.

verdrängen *vt* to oust, displace; to repress.

verdrehen *vt* to twist; to roll (one's eyes).

verdreifachen *vt* to treble.

verdrießen *vt* to annoy.

verdrießlich *adj* annoyed.

Verdruß *m* annoyance.

verdummen *vt* to make stupid; * *vi* to grow stupid.

verdunkeln *vt vi* to darken.

Verdunk(e)lung *f* blackout.

verdünnen *vt* to dilute.

verdunsten *vt* to evaporate.

verdursten *vi* to die of thirst.

verdutzt *adj* taken aback, nonplussed.

verehren *vt* to venerate, worship.

Verehrer(in) *m(f)* admirer, worshipper.

verehrt *adj* esteemed.

Verehrung *f* respect; worship.

Verein *m* association, club.

vereinbar *adj* compatible.

vereinbaren *vt* to agree upon.

Vereinbarung *f* agreement.

vereinen *vt* to unite; to reconcile.

vereinfachen *vt* to simplify.

vereinigen *vt vr* to unite.

Vereinigte Staaten (von Amerika) *pl* United States of America.

Vereinigung *f* union.

vereint *adj* united.

Vereinte Nationen *pl* United Nations.

vereinzelt *adj* isolated.

vereiteln *vt* to frustrate.

vereitern *vt* to fester.

verengen *vr* to narrow.

vererben *vt* to bequeath; (*biol*) to transmit; * *vr* to be hereditary.

vererblich *adj* hereditary.

Vererbung *f* bequeathing; (*biol*) transmission; heredity.

verewigen *vt* to immortalise.

verfahren *vi* to act; * *vr* to get lost; * *adj* tangled.

Verfahren *n* procedure; process; (*jur*) proceedings.

Verfall *m* decline; dilapidation; expiry.

verfallen *vi* to decline; to lapse.

Verfallsdatum *n* expiry date; sell-by date.

verfänglich *adj* tricky, awkward.

verfärben *vr* to change colour.

verfassen *vt* to prepare, work out.

Verfasser(in) *m(f)* writer, author.

Verfassung *f* constitution.

Verfassungsgericht *n* constitutional court.

verfassungswidrig *adj* unconstitutional.

verfaulen *vi* to rot.

verfehlen *vt* to miss.

verfeinern *vt* to refine.

verfilmen *vt* to film.

verflixt *adj* (*coll*) damn, damned.

verfluchen *vt* to curse.

verfolgen *vt* to pursue; to prosecute; to persecute.

Verfolger *m* pursuer.

Verfolgung *f* pursuit; prosecution; persecution.

verfrüht *adj* premature.

verfügbar *adj* available.

verfügen *vt* to direct, order; * *vr* to proceed.

Verfügung *f* direction, order;

zur ~ at one's disposal.

verführen *vt* to tempt; to seduce.

Verführer *m* tempter; seducer.

verführerisch *adj* seductive.

Verführung *f* temptation; seduction.

vergammeln *vi* to go off; to go to seed.

vergangen *adj* past.

Vergangenheit *f* past.

vergänglich *adj* fleeting, transitory.

Vergänglichkeit *f* fleetingness, transitoriness.

vergasen *vt* to gas.

Vergaser *m* carburettor.

vergeben *vt* to forgive.

vergebens *adv* in vain.

vergeblich *adv* in vain; * *adj* vain, futile.

Vergebung *f* forgiveness.

Vergehen *n* offence.

vergehen *vi* to pass away; * *vr* to commit an offence.

vergelten *vi*: **jdm etw ~** to pay sb back for something.

Vergeltung *f* retaliation, reprisal.

Vergeltungsschlag *m* (*mil*) reprisal.

vergessen *vt* to forget.

Vergessenheit *f* oblivion.

vergeßlich *adj* forgetful.

Vergeßlichkeit *f* forgetfulness.

vergeuden *vt* to waste, squander.

vergewaltigen *vt* to rape; to violate.

Vergewaltigung *f* rape.

vergewissern *vr* to make sure.

vergießen *vt* to shed.

vergiften *vt* to poison.

Vergiftung *f* poisoning.

Vergißmeinnicht *n* forget-me-not.

Vergleich *m* comparison; (*jur*) settlement.

vergleichbar *adj* comparable.

vergleichen *vt* to compare; * *vr* to reach a settlement.

vergnügen *vt* to enjoy oneself.

Vergnügen *n* pleasure.
vergnügt *adj* cheerful.
Vergnügung *f* amusement, pleasure.
Vergnügungspark *m* amusement park.
vergolden *vr* to gild.
vergöttern *vt* to idolise.
vergraben *vt* to bury.
vergriffen *adj* out of print; out of stock.
vergrößern *vt* to increase; to enlarge; to magnify.
Vergrößerung *f* increase; enlargement; magnification.
Vergrößerungsglas *n* magnifying glass.
Vergünstigung *f* privilege, concession.
Vergütung *f* compensation.
verhaften *vt* to arrest.
Verhaftung *f* arrest.
verhallen *vi* to die away.
verhalten *vr* to be, stand; to behave; * *vt* to hold back.
Verhalten *n* behaviour.
Verhältnis *n* relationship; proportion, ratio; ~**se** *pl* conditions.
verhältnismäßig *adj* relative, comparative; * *adv* relatively, comparatively.
verhandeln *vi* to negotiate; (*jur*) to hold proceedings; * *vt* to discuss; (*jur*) to hear.
Verhandlung *f* negotiation; (*jur*) proceedings, trial.
Verhandlungsbasis *f* basis for negotiations.
verhängen *vt* to impose, inflict.
Verhängnis *n* fate, doom.
verhängnisvoll *adj* fatal, disastrous.
verharmlosen *vt* to make light of, play down.
verhärten *vr* to harden.
verhaßt *adj* hateful, odious.
verhauen *vt* (*coll*) to beat up.
verheerend *adj* disastrous, devastating.
verhehlen *vt* to conceal.
verheiraten *vr* to get married.

verheiratet *adj* married.
verhexen *vt* to bewitch.
verhindern *vt* to prevent, hinder.
verhöhnen *vt* to mock, sneer at.
Verhör *m* interrogation; (cross-)examination.
verhören *vt* to interrogate; to (cross-)examine: * *vr* to mishear, misunderstand.
verhungern *vi* to starve, die of hunger.
verhüten *vt* to prevent, avert.
Verhütung *f* prevention.
Verhütungsmittel *n* contraceptive.
verirren *vr* to go astray.
verjagen *vt* to drive away/out.
verkalken *vi* to calcify; (*coll*) to become senile.
verkannt *adj* unappreciated.
Verkauf *m* sale.
verkaufen *vt* to sell.
Verkäufer(in) *m(f)* seller; salesman(woman); shop assistant.
Verkehr *m* traffic; circulation.
verkehren *vi* to ply, run; * *vt* *vr* to turn, transform.
Verkehrsampel *pl* traffic lights.
Verkehrsamt *n* tourist office.
Verkehrsdelikt *n* traffic offence.
verkehrsgünstig *adj* convenient.
Verkehrsmittel *n* means of transport.
Verkehrsschild *n* road sign.
Verkehrsstauung *f* traffic jam.
Verkehrsstockung *f* traffic jam.
Verkehrsunfall *m* traffic accident.
Verkehrsverein *m* tourist information office.
Verkehrszeichen *m* traffic sign.
verkehrt *adj* wrong; the wrong way round.
verkennen *vt* to misjudge.

verklagen *vt* to sue, take to court.

verklären *vt* to transfigure.

verkleiden *vr* to disguise (oneself); to get dressed up; * *vt* to cover.

Verkleidung *f* disguise; wainscoting.

verkleinern *vt* to make smaller.

verklemmt *adj* inhibited.

verknüpfen *vt* to tie (up), knot.

verkommen *vi* to decay, deteriorate; to come down in the world; * *adj* dissolute, depraved.

verkörpern *vt* to embody, personify.

verkraften *vt* to cope with.

verkriechen *vr* to creep away.

Verkrümmung *f* bend, warp; curvature.

verkrüppelt *adj* crippled.

verkühlen *vi* to get a chill.

verkümmern *vi* to waste away.

verkünden *vt* to proclaim; to pronounce (judgment).

verkürzen *vt* to shorten; to abbreviate.

Verkürzung *f* abbreviation.

verladen *vt* to load; to embark.

Verlag *m* publishing house.

verlangen *vt* to demand; to desire.

Verlangen *n* desire.

verlängern *vt* to extend; to lengthen.

Verlängerung *f* extension; extra time (in sport).

Verlängerungsschnur *f* extension cable.

verlangsamen *vi* to decelerate, slow down.

verlassen *vt* to leave; * *vr*: **sich ~ auf** +*acc* to depend on; * *adj* desolate; abandoned.

verläßlich *adj* reliable.

Verlauf *m* course.

verlaufen *vi* to pass; to run; * *vr* to get lost; to disperse.

verlegen *vt* to move; to mislay; to publish; * *adj* embarrassed.

Verleger *m* publisher.

Verleih *m* hire service.

verleihen *vt* to lend; to confer, bestow; to award.

Verleihung *f* lending; bestowal; award.

verleiten *vt* to lead astray.

verlernen *vt* to unlearn, forget.

verlesen *vt* to read out; to sort out; * *vr* to make a mistake in reading.

verletzen *vt* to injure; to violate (law, etc).

verletzend *adj* hurtful.

verletzlich *adj* vulnerable, sensitive.

Verletzte(r) *mf* injured person.

Verletzung *f* injury; infringement, violation.

verleugnen *vt* to belie; to disown.

verleumden *vt* to slander, defame.

Verleumdung *f* slander, libel.

verlieben *vr*: **sich ~ (in** +*acc*) to fall in love (with).

verliebt *adj* in love.

verlieren *vt vi* to lose; * *vr* to get lost.

Verlierer *m* loser.

verloben *vr* to get engaged (to).

Verlobte(r) *mf* fiancé(e).

Verlobung *f* engagement.

verlocken *vt* to entice, lure.

Verlockung *f* attraction, enticement.

verlogen *adj* untruthful.

verloren *adj* lost; poached (of eggs).

verlosen *vt* to raffle, draw lots for.

Verlosung *f* raffle, lottery.

verlottern *vi* (*coll*) to go to the dogs.

verludern *vi* (*coll*) to go to the dogs.

Verlust *m* loss; (*mil*) casualty.

vermachen *vt* to bequeath.

Vermächtnis *n* legacy.

Vermählten *pl* bride and bridegroom.

Vermählung *f* marriage, wedding.

vermarkten *vt* to market.

vermehren *vi vr* to increase; to multiply.

Vermehrung *f* increase; multiplying.

vermeiden *vt* to avoid.

vermeintlich *adj* supposed.

Vermerk *m* note; endorsement.

vermerken *vt* to note.

vermessen *vt* to survey; * *adj* presumptuous.

Vermessenheit *f* presumptuousness.

Vermessung *f* surveying.

vermieten *vt* to let, rent (out); to hire (out).

Vermieter(in)   *m(f)* landlord(lady).

Vermietung *f* letting, renting (out); hiring (out).

vermindern *vt vr* to decrease, reduce; to diminish.

Verminderung *f* reduction.

vermischen *vt vr* to mix, blend.

vermissen *vt* to miss.

vermitteln *vi* to mediate; * *vt* to connect.

Vermittler *m* agent, mediator.

Vermittlung *f* procurement; agency; mediation.

vermögen *vi* to be capable of.

Vermögen *n* wealth; property; ability; **ein ~ kosten** to cost a fortune.

vermögend *adj* wealthy, opulent.

vermuten *vt* to suppose; to suspect.

vermutlich *adj* supposed, presumed; * *adv* probably.

Vermutung *f* supposition; suspicion.

vernachlässigen *vt* to neglect.

vernehmen *vt* to perceive, hear; to learn; to (cross-)examine.

Vernehmung *f* (cross-)examination.

verneigen *vr* to bow.

verneinen *vi* to deny; to answer in the negative.

verneinend *adj* negative.

Verneinung *f* negation.

vernichten *vt* to annihilate, destroy.

vernichtend *adj* scathing; crushing.

Vernunft *f* reason, judgement.

vernünftig *adj* reasonable, judicious.

veröffentlichen *vt* to publish.

Veröffentlichung *f* publication.

verordnen *vt* (*med*) to prescribe.

Verordnung *f* order, decree; (*med*) prescription.

verpachten *vt* to (lease) out.

verpacken *vt* to pack.

Verpackung *f* packing, wrapping.

Verpackungsmaterial *n* packing, wrapping.

verpassen *vt* to miss.

verpfänden *vt* to mortgage.

verpflanzen *vt* to transplant.

Verpflanzung *f* transplant.

verpflegen *vt* to feed, cater for.

Verpflegung *f* feeding, catering; food.

verpflichten *vt* to bind, oblige; to engage; * *vr* to undertake; (*mil*) to sign on; * *vi* to carry obligations.

Verpflichtung *f* duty, obligation.

verpönt *adj* disapproved (of), taboo.

verprügeln *vt* to do over, beat up.

Verputz *m* plaster, roughcast.

verputzen *vt* to plaster.

Verrat *m* treason; treachery.

verraten *vt* to betray; * *vr* to give oneself away.

Verräter *m* traitor.

verräterisch *adj* treacherous.

verrechnen *vi*: **~ mit** to set off against; * *vr* to miscalculate.

Verrechnungsscheck   *m* crossed cheque.

verregnet *adj* spoilt by rain.

verrecken *vi* to die.

verreisen *vi* to go away (on a journey).

verrenken *vt* to comfort; (*med*) to dislocate.

verrichten *vt* to perform, carry out.

verriegeln *vt* to lock, bolt up.

verringern *vt* to reduce; * *vr* to diminish.

Verringerung *f* reduction; lessening.

verrinnen *vi* to run out/away; to elapse.

verrosten *vi* to rust.

verrotten *vi* to rot.

verrücken *vt* to shift, move.

verrückt *adj* mad, crazy.

Verrückte(r) *mf* lunatic.

Verrücktheit *f* madness, lunacy.

verrufen *adj* notorious; disreputable.

Vers *m* verse.

versagen *vi* to fail.

Versagen *n* failure.

Versager *m* failure.

versalzen *vt* to put too much salt in; to spoil.

versammeln *vt vr* to assemble, gather.

Versammlung *f* meeting, gathering.

Versand *m* dispatch, forwarding; dispatch department.

Versandhaus *n* mail-order firm.

versäumen *vt* to miss; to neglect.

verschämt *adj* bashful.

verschandeln *vt* (*coll*) to spoil.

verschärfen *vt vr* to intensify.

verschätzen *vr* to be out in one's reckoning.

verschenken *vt* to give away.

verscheuchen *vt* to chase off/away.

verschicken *vt* to send off.

verschieben *vt* to shift; to shunt; to postpone.

verschieden *adj* different; various.

verschiedentlich *adv* several times.

verschimmeln *vi* to go mouldy.

verschlafen *vt* to sleep through; to miss; * *vi vr* to oversleep; * *adj* sleepy.

Verschlag *m* shed.

verschlagen *vt* to board up; * *adj* cunning.

verschlechtern *vt* to make worse; * *vr* to get worse, deteriorate.

Verschlechterung *f* deterioration.

Verschleiß *m* wear and tear.

verschleißen *vt* to wear out.

verschleppen *vt* to carry off, abduct; to drag out.

verschleudern *vt* squander.

verschließbar *adj* lockable.

verschließen *vt* to close, lock.

verschlimmern *vt* to make worse, aggravate; * *vr* to get worse, deteriorate.

verschlingen *vt* to devour, swallow up.

verschlossen *adj* locked; reserved.

Verschlossenheit *f* reserve.

verschlucken *vt* to swallow; * *vr* to choke.

Verschluß *m* lock; fastener; shutter; plug.

verschlüsseln *vt* to encode.

verschmähen *vt* to disdain, scorn.

verschmerzen *vt* to get over.

verschmieren *vt* to apply, spread on; to smear.

verschmutzen *vt* to soil; to pollute.

verschneit *adj* covered in snow.

verschollen *adj* lost, missing.

verschonen *vt*: **jdn mit etw ~** to spare sb something.

verschönern *vt* to decorate; to improve.

verschreiben *vt* (*med*) to prescribe; * *vr* to make a mistake (in writing).

verschreibungspflichtig *adj* (*med*) available on prescription only.

verschroben *adj* eccentric, odd.

verschrotten *vt* to scrap.

verschulden *vt* to be guilty of.

Verschulden *n* fault, guilt.

verschuldet *adj* in debt.

Verschuldung *f* fault; debts.

verschütten *vt* to spill; to fill, bury.

verschweigen *vt* to keep secret.

verschwenden *vt* to squander.

Verschwender *m* spendthrift.

verschwiegen *adj* discreet; secluded.

Verschwiegenheit *f* discretion; seclusion.

verschwimmen *vi* to become blurred, grow hazy.

verschwinden *vi* to disappear, vanish.

Verschwinden *n* disappearance.

verschwitzt *adj* sweaty.

verschwommen *adj* vague, hazy.

verschwören *vr* to plot, conspire.

Verschwörer *m* conspirator.

Verschwörung *f* plot, conspiracy.

versehen *vt* to supply, provide; to carry out (duty, etc); * *vr* to make a mistake.

Versehen *n* oversight; **aus ~** by mistake.

versehentlich *adv* by mistake.

versehren *vt* to wound.

Versehrte(r) *mf* disabled person.

versenden *vt* to forward, dispatch.

versenken *vt* to sink.

versetzen *vt* to transfer; to pawn.

Versetzung *f* transfer.

verseuchen *vt* to contaminate.

versichern *vt* to assure; to insure.

Versicherung *f* assurance; insurance.

Versicherungsgesellschaft *f* insurance company.

Versicherungspolice *f* insurance policy.

versiegen *vi* to dry up.

versinken *vi* to sink.

versöhnen *vt* to reconcile; * *vr* to become reconciled.

versöhnlich *adj* forgiving, conciliatory.

Versöhnung *f* reconciliation.

versorgen *vt* to provide, supply; to look after.

Versorgung *f* provision; assistance, benefit.

verspäten *vr* to be late.

verspätet *adj* late; belated.

Verspätung *f* delay; **~ haben** to be late.

versperren *vt* to bar, obstruct.

verspielt *adj* playful.

verspotten *vt* to mock, scoff at, deride.

versprechen *vt* to promise.

Versprechen *n* promise.

verstaatlichen *vt* to nationalise.

Verstand *m* intelligence; mind.

verständig *adj* sensible.

verständigen *vt* to inform; * *vr* to communicate; to come to an understanding.

Verständigung *f* communication; agreement.

verständlich *adj* understandable.

Verständlichkeit *f* intelligibility.

Verständnis *n* understanding.

verständnislos *adj* uncomprehending.

verständnisvoll *adj* understanding, sympathetic.

verstärken *vt vr* to intensify.

Verstärker *m* amplifier.

Verstärkung *f* strengthening; amplification.

verstauchen *vt* to sprain.

verstauen *vt* to stow away.

Versteck *m* hiding (place).

verstecken *vt vr* to hide; * *adj* hidden.

verstehen *vt* to understand;

* *vr* to get on.
versteigern *vt* to auction.
Versteigerung *f* auction.
verstellbar adj adjustable, variable.
verstellen *vt* to shift, move; to adjust; to block; to disguise; * *vr* to pretend.
Verstellung *f* pretence.
versteuern *vt* to pay tax on.
verstiegen *adj* exaggerated.
verstimmt *adj* out of tune; put out; upset (of stomach).
verstohlen *adj* stealthy.
verstopfen *vt* to block; to constipate.
Verstopfung *f* obstruction; constipation.
verstorben *adj* late, deceased.
verstört *adj* distraught.
Verstoß *m* infringement, violation.
verstoßen *vt* to disown, reject; * *vi:* ~ **gegen** to offend against.
verstreichen *vt* to spread; * *vi* to elapse.
verstreuen *vt* to scatter.
verstricken *vt* to entangle.
verstümmeln *vt* to maim, mutilate.
verstummen *vi* to go silent; to die away.
Versuch *m* attempt; experiment.
versuchen *vi* to try; to tempt.
Versuchskaninchen *n* guinea-pig (in experiment, etc).
Versuchung f temptation.
versunken *adj* sunken.
vertagen *vt vi* to adjourn.
vertauschen *vt* to exchange; to mix up.
verteidigen *vt* to defend.
Verteidiger *m* defender; (*jur*) defence counsel.
Verteidigung *f* defence.
verteilen *vt* to distribute; to assign.
Verteilung *f* distribution, allotment.
vertiefen *vt* to deepen.

Vertiefung *f* depression.
vertikal *adj* vertical.
vertilgen *vt* to exterminate.
vertonen *vt* to set to music.
Vertrag *m* contract, agreement; treaty.
vertragen *vt* to tolerate, stand; * *vr* to get along.
vertraglich *adj* contractual.
verträglich *adj* sociable, good-natured.
Verträglichkeit *f* sociability; good nature.
Vertragsbruch *m* breach of contract.
Vertragspartner *m* party to a contract.
vertragswidrig *adj* contrary to contract.
Vertrauen *n* trust, confidence.
vertrauen *vi:* **jdm** ~ to trust sb; ~ **auf** +*acc* to rely on.
vertrauenerweckend *adj* inspiring trust.
vertrauensvoll *adj* trustful.
vertrauenswürdig *adj* trustworthy.
vertraulich *adj* familiar; confidential.
vertraut *adj* familiar.
Vertrautheit *f* familiarity.
vertreiben *vt* to drive away; to expel; to sell.
vertreten *vt* to represent; to advocate.
Vertreter *m* representative; advocate.
Vertretung *f* representation; advocacy.
Vertrieb *m* marketing (department).
vertrocknen *vi* to dry up.
vertrösten *vt* to put off.
vertun *vt* to waste; * *vr* (*coll*) to make a mistake.
vertuschen *vt* to hush/cover up.
verüben *vt* to commit.
verunglimpfen *vt* to disparage.
verunglücken *vi* to have an accident.

verunreinigen *vt* to pollute; to soil.

verunsichern *vt* to rattle.

veruntreuen *vt* to embezzle.

verursachen *vt* to cause.

verurteilen *vt* to sentence, condemn.

Verurteilung *f* sentence; condemnation.

vervielfachen *vt* to multiply.

vervielfältigen *vt* to copy, duplicate.

Vervielfältigung *f* copying, duplication.

vervollkommen *vt* to perfect.

vervollständigen *vt* to complete.

verwackeln *vt* to blur.

verwählen *vr* to dial the wrong number.

verwahren *vt* to lock away; * *vr* to protest.

verwalten *vt* to administer; to manage.

Verwalter *m* manager; trustee.

Verwaltung *f* administration; management.

verwandeln *vt* to change, transform; * vr to change; to be transformed.

Verwandlung *f* change, transformation.

verwandt *adj* related.

Verwandte(r) *mf* relation.

Verwandtschaft *f* relationship; relations.

verwarnen *vt* to caution.

Verwarnung *f* caution.

verwechseln *vt* to confuse.

Verwechslung *f* confusion.

verwegen *adj* bold, daring.

Verwehung *f* snowdrift.

verweichlicht *adj* effeminate.

Verweigerung *f* refusal.

verweilen *vi* to linger.

Verweis *m* rebuke, reprimand; reference.

verweisen *vt* to refer.

verwelken *vi* to fade.

verwendbar *adj* usable.

verwenden *vt* to use; to spend; * *vr* to intercede.

Verwendung *f* use.

verwerfen *vt* to reject.

verwerflich *adj* reprehensible.

verwerten *vt* to utilise.

Verwertung *f* utilisation.

verwesen *vi* to decay.

verwickeln *vt* to tangle; to involve; * *vr* to get tangled.

verwickelt *adj* difficult, complicated.

verwildern *vi* to run wild.

verwinden *vt* to get over.

verwirklichen *vt* to realise, put into effect.

Verwirklichung *f* realisation.

verwirren *vt* to tangle; to confuse.

Verwirrung *f* confusion.

verwittern *vt* to weather.

verwitwet *adj* widowed.

verwöhnen *vt* to spoil, pamper.

verworfen *adj* depraved.

verworren *adj* confused.

verwundbar *adj* vulnerable.

verwunden *vt* to wound.

verwunderlich *adj* surprising.

Verwunderung *f* astonished.

Verwundete(r) *mf* wounded person, casualty.

Verwundung *f* wound.

verwünschen *vt* to curse.

verwüsten *vt* to devastate.

verzagen *vi* to despair.

verzählen *vr* to miscount.

verzehren *vt* to consume.

verzeichnen *vt* to list; to register.

Verzeichnis *n* list; index.

verzeihen *vt vi* to forgive.

verzeihlich *adj* pardonable.

Verzeihung *f* pardon, forgiveness; ~! excuse me!, sorry!.

verzichten *vi*: ~ **auf** +*acc* to give up, forgo.

verziehen *vi* to move; * *vt* to put out of shape; to spoil; * *vr* to go out of shape; to contort.

verzieren *vi* to decorate, ornament.

Verzierung *f* decoration.

verzinsen *vt* to pay interest on.

verzögern *vt* to delay.

Verzögerung *f* delay.
Verzögerungstaktik *f* delaying tactics.
verzollen *vt* to pay duty on; **haben Sie etwas zu ~?** do you have anything to declare?.
verzückt *adj* enraptured.
Verzug *m* delay.
verzweifeln *vi* to despair.
verzweifelt *adj* desperate.
Verzweiflung *f* despair, desperation.
verzwickt *adj* awkward, complicated.
Vesuv *m* Vesuvius.
Veto *n* veto.
Vetter *m* cousin.
vibrieren *vi* to vibrate.
Video *n* video.
Videogerät *n* video recorder.
Videorecorder *m* video recorder.
Vieh *n* cattle.
viehisch *adj* bestial.
viel *adj* much, a lot of; * *adv* much, a lot.
vielerlei *adj* a great variety of.
vieles *pron* a lot.
vielfach *adj adv* many times.
Vielfalt *f* variety.
vielfältig *adj* varied, many-sided.
vielleicht *adv* perhaps, maybe.
vielmal(s) *adv* many times; **danke vielmals** many thanks.
vielmehr *adv* rather, on the contrary.
vielsagend *adj* significant.
vielseitig *adj* many-sided.
vielversprechend *adj* promising.
vier *num* four.
Viereck *n* quadrilateral; square.
viereckig *adj* four-sided; square.
Viertaktmotor *m* four-stroke engine.
vierte(r,s) *adj* fourth.
Viertel *n* quarter.
Vierteljahr *n* quarter.

vierteljährlich *adj* quarterly.
vierteln *vt* to divide into four/quarters.
Viertelnote *f* crotchet.
Viertelstunde *f* quarter of an hour.
Vierwaldstätter See *m* Lake Lucerne.
vierzehn *num* fourteen.
vierzehntägig *adj adv* fortnightly.
vierzig *num* forty.
Villa *f* villa.
Violine *f* violin.
Violinschlüssel *m* treble clef.
Virus *m/n* virus.
Visier *n* gunsight; visor.
Visite *f* (*med*) visit.
Visitenkarte *f* visiting card.
Visum *n* visa.
vital *adj* lively, vital.
Vitamin *n* vitamin.
Vogel *m* bird.
Vogelbauer *n* birdcage.
Vogelhäuschen *n* bird house.
Vogelperspektive *f* bird's-eye view.
Vogelscheuche *f* scarecrow.
Vokabel *f* word.
Vokabular *n* vocabulary.
Vokal *m* vowel.
Volk *n* people; nation.
Völkerrecht *n* international law.
völkerrechtlich *adj* according to international law.
Völkerverständigung *f* international understanding.
Volksentscheid *m* referendum.
Volksfest *n* fair.
Volkslied *n* folksong.
Volkstanz *m* folk dance.
Volkswirtschaft *f* economics.
Volkszählung *f* census.
voll *adj* full; * *adv* fully.
vollauf *adv* amply.
Vollbart *m* full beard.
vollbringen *vt* to accomplish.
vollenden *vt* to finish, complete.
vollendet *adj* completed.
vollends *adv* completely.

Vollendung *f* completion.
voller *adj* fuller.
Volleyball *m* volleyball.
völlig *adj* complete; * *adv* completely.
volljährig *adj* of age.
Vollkaskoversicherung *f* fully comprehensive insurance.
vollkommen *adj* perfect.
Vollkommenheit *f* perfection.
Vollkornbrot *n* wholemeal bread.
Vollmacht *f* authority, full powers.
Vollmilch *f* full-cream milk.
Vollmond *m* full moon.
Vollpension *f* full board.
vollständig *adj* complete.
vollstrecken *vt* to execute.
volltanken *vt vi* to full up.
Vollwertkost *f* whole-food.
vollzählig *adj* complete; in full number.
vollziehen *vt* to carry out; * *vr* to happen.
Vollzug *m* execution.
Volt *n* volt.
Volumen *n* volume.
vom = von dem
von *prep* of; from; by; about.
voneinander *adv* from each other.
vor *prep* in front of; before; with; ~ **allem** most of all; ~ **3 Tagen** 3 days ago.
Vorabend *m* eve, evening before.
voran *adv* before, ahead.
vorangehen *vi* to go ahead.
vorankommen *vi* to come along, make progress.
Voranschlag *m* estimate.
Vorarbeiter *m* foreman.
voraus *adv* ahead; in advance.
vorausgehen *vi* to go (on) ahead; to precede.
Voraussage *f* prediction.
voraussagen *vt* to predict.
voraussehen *vt* to foresee.
voraussetzen *vt* to assume; **vorausgesetzt, daß ...** provided that ....

Voraussetzung *f* prerequisite, requirement.
Voraussicht *f* foresight.
voraussichtlich *adv* probably.
Vorbehalt *m* reservation, proviso.
vorbehaltslos *adj* unconditional; * *adv* unconditionally.
vorbei *adv* by, past.
vorbeigehen *vi* to go past, pass by.
vorbelastet *adj* handicapped.
vorbereiten *vt* to prepare.
Vorbereitung *f* preparation.
vorbestraft *adj* previously convicted.
vorbeugen *vt vr* to prevent; * *vi*: ~ +dat to prevent.
vorbeugend *adj* preventive.
Vorbeugung *f* prevention.
Vorbild *n* model, pattern.
vorbildlich *adj* model, ideal.
vorbringen *vt* to advance, state.
Vorderachse *f* front axle.
vordere(r,s) *adj* front.
Vordergrund *m* foreground.
Vordermann *m* man in front.
Vorderseite *f* front (side).
vorderste(r,s) *adj* front.
vordrängen *vt* to push to the front.
voreilig *adj* rash, hasty.
voreindander *adv* in front of each other.
voreingenommen *adj* biased.
Voreingenommenheit *f* bias.
vorenthalten *vt*: **jdm etw** ~ to withhold something from sb.
vorerst *adv* for the moment.
Vorfahr *m* ancestor.
vorfahren *vi* to drive (on) ahead.
Vorfahrt *f* right of way.
Vorfahrtsregel *f* right of way.
Vorfahrtsschild *n* give way sign.
Vorfall *m* incident.
vorfallen *vi* to occur.
vorfinden *vt* to find.
Vorfreude *f* (joyful) anticipation.

vorführen *vt* to show, display.

Vorgabe *f* start, handicap (in sport); (*computer*) default.

Vorgang *m* course of events; process.

Vorgänger(in) *m(f)* predecessor.

vorgeben *vt* to pretend, use as a pretext; to give an advantage of (in sport).

Vorgebirge *n* cape, promontory.

vorgefaßt *adj* preconceived.

vorgefertigt *adj* prefabricated.

vorgehen *vi* to go (on) ahead; to act, proceed; to take precedence.

Vorgehen *n* action.

Vorgeschichte *f* past history.

Vorgeschmack *m* foretaste.

Vorgesetzte(r) *mf* superior.

vorgestern *adv* the day before yesterday.

vorhaben *vt* to intend.

Vorhaben *n* intention.

Vorhalle *f* entrance hall.

vorhalten *vt* to hold up; * *vi* to last.

vorhanden *adj* existing; available.

Vorhang *m* curtain.

Vorhängeschloß *m* padlock.

vorher *adv* before(hand).

vorherstimmen *vt* to preordain.

vorhergehen *vi* to precede.

vorherig *adj* previous.

Vorherrschaft *f* supremacy, predominance.

vorherrschen *vi* to predominate.

Vorhersage *f* forecast.

vorhersagen *vt* to forecast, predict.

vorhersehbar *adj* predictable.

vorhersehen *vt* to foresee.

vorhin *adv* just now, not long ago.

vorig *adv* last, previous.

Vorkämpfer(in) *m(f)* pioneer.

Vorkaufsrecht *n* purchase option.

Vorkehrung *f* precaution.

vorkommen *vi* to come forward; to happen, occur.

Vorkommen *n* occurrence.

Vorladung *f* summons.

Vorlage *f* pattern, model; bill (for a law).

vorlassen *vt* to admit.

vorläufig *adj* temporary, provisional.

vorlaut *adj* cheeky, impertinent.

vorlesen *vt* to read (out).

Vorleser(in) *m(f)* lecturer, reader.

Vorlesung *f* lecture; **eine ~ halten** to give a lecture.

vorletzte(r,s) *adj* last but one.

Vorliebe *f* preference, partiality.

vorliegen *vi* to be (here).

vorliegend *adj* present, at issue.

Vormachtstellung *f* supremacy.

Vormarsch *m* advance.

vormerken *vt* to book.

Vormittag *m* morning.

vormittags *adv* in the morning, before noon.

Vormund *m* guardian.

vorn *adv* in front.

Vorname *m* first/Christian name.

vornehm *adj* refined; distinguished; aristocratic.

vornehmen *vt* to carry out.

Vorort *m* suburb.

Vorrang *m* precedence, priority.

vorranging *adj* of prime importance.

Vorrat *m* stock, supply.

vorrätig *adj* in stock.

Vorratskammer *f* pantry.

Vorrecht *n* privilege.

Vorrichtung *f* device, contrivance.

vorrücken *vi* to advance; * *vt* to move forward.

Vorsatz *m* intention; (*jur*) intent.

vorsätzlich *adj* intentional;

(*jur*) premeditated; * *adv* intentionally.

Vorschau *f* (TV, etc) preview; (film) trailer.

Vorschlag *m* suggestion, proposal.

vorschlagen *vi* to suggest, propose.

vorschreiben *vt* to prescribe, specify.

Vorschrift *f* regulation(s); rule(s); instruction(s).

vorschriftsmäßig *adj* as per regulations/instructions.

Vorschuß *m* advance.

vorsehen *vt* to plan, provide for; * *vr* to be careful, take care; * *vi* to be visible.

Vorsehung *f* providence.

Vorsicht *f* caution, care.

vorsichtig *adj* cautious, careful.

vorsichtshalber *adv* just in case.

Vorsilbe *f* prefix.

vorsingen *vt* to sing (to); to audition (for); * *vi* to sing.

Vorsitz *m* chair(manship).

Vorsitzende(r) *mf* chairman(woman).

Vorsorge *f* precaution(s), provision(s).

vorsorgen *vi*: ~ **für** to make provision for.

Vorsorgeuntersuchung *f* check-up.

vorsorglich *adj* as a precaution.

Vorspeise *f* hors d'œuvre.

Vorspiel *n* prelude.

vorsprechen *vt* say out loud, recite.

Vorsprung *m* projection; advantage, start.

Vorstadt *f* suburbs.

Vorstand *m* executive committee; board (of directors).

vorstehen *vi* to project.

vorstellbar *adj* conceivable.

vorstellen *vt* to introduce; to represent; * *vr*: **sich** *dat* **etw** ~ to imagine something.

Vorstellung *f* introduction; performance; idea, thought.

vorstoßen *vi* to venture (forth).

Vorstrafe *f* previous conviction.

vortäuschen *vt* to pretend, feign.

Vorteil *m* advantage.

vorteilhaft *adj* advantageous.

Vortrag *m* lecture, talk.

vortragen *vt* to carry forward; to perform (song, etc).

vortrefflich *adj* excellent.

vortreten *vi* to step forward; to protrude.

vorüber *adv* past, over.

vorübergehen *vi* to pass (by).

vorübergehend *adj* temporary, passing.

Vorurteil *n* prejudice.

Vorverkauf *m* advance booking.

Vorwahl *f* preliminary election; dialling code.

Vorwand *m* pretext.

vorwärts *adv* forward.

Vorwärtsgang *m* forward gear.

vorwärtsgehen *vi* to progress.

vorwärtskommen *vi* to get on, make progress.

Vorwäsche *f* prewash.

vorweg *adv* in advance.

vorwegnehmen *vt* to anticipate.

vorweisen *vt* to show, produce.

vorwerfen *vi*: **jdm etw** ~ to reproach sb for something.

vorwiegend *adj* predominant; * *adv* predominantly.

vorwitzig *adj* cheeky.

Vorwort *n* preface.

Vorwurf *m* reproach.

vorwurfsvoll *adj* reproachful.

vorzeigen *vt* to show, produce.

vorzeitig *adj* premature.

vorziehen *vt* to pull forward; to prefer.

Vorzimmer *n* outer office.

Vorzug *m* preference; advantage.

vorzüglich *adj* excellent.

vulgär *adj* vulgar.

Vulkan *m* volcano.

W

Waage *f* scale(s); balance;
(*astrol*) Libra.
Wabe *f* honeycomb.
wach *adj* awake.
wachen *vi* to watch; to be
awake.
wachhalten *vt* to keep awake.
wachhaltend *adj* on duty.
Wacholder *m* juniper.
Wachposten *m* guard, sentry.
wachrütteln *vt* to rouse; to
shake up.
Wachs *n* wax.
wachsam *adj* watchful, on one's
guard, vigilant.
wachsen *vi* to grow; to increase.
wachsen *vt* to wax.
wächsern *adj* waxy.
Wachstum *n* growth; increase.
Wachtel *f* quail.
Wächter *m* guard.
Wachtturm *m* watchtower.
wackelig *adj* shaky; loose.
wackeln *vi* to shake; to wobble,
be loose.
Wade *f* calf.
Waffe *f* weapon.
Waffel *f* waffle; wafer.
Wagemut *m* daring.
wagen *vt* to dare; to risk.
Wagen *m* car; truck, lorry; cart,
wag(g)on, carriage.
wägen *vt* to weigh (one's words,
etc).
Waggon *m* wag(g)on.
waghalsig *adj* foolhardy.
Wagnis *n* risk.
Wahl *f* choice; option; selection;
election; vote.
wählbar *adj* eligible.
wählen *vt vi* to choose, pick, select; to vote, elect.
Wähler(in) *m(f)* voter.
wählerisch *adj* fastidious, particular.
Wählerschaft *f* electorate.
Wahlgang *m* ballot.
Wahlkabine *f* polling booth.

Wahlkreis *m* constituency.
wahllos *adj* at random.
Wahlspruch *m* motto.
Wahlurne *f* ballot box.
Wahn *m* delusion; folly.
wähnen *vt* to believe (to be).
Wahnsinn *m* madness, insanity.
wahnsinnig *adj* mad, insane;
* *adv* incredibly.
wahr *adj* true; real; genuine.
wahren *vt* to keep (secret, etc);
to protect (interests, etc).
währen *vi* to last.
während *prep* during; * *conj*
while; whereas.
währenddessen *adv* meanwhile.
wahrhaben *vt* to refuse to admit something.
wahrhaft *adv* truly.
wahrhaftig *adj* true, real;
* *adv* really.
Wahrheit *f* truth.
wahrlich *adv* really, certainly.
wahrnehmen *vt* to perceive,
notice.
Wahrnehmung *f* perception.
wahrsagen *vi* to tell fortunes,
prophesy.
Wahrsager(in) *m(f)* fortune-
teller.
wahrscheinlich *adj* probable;
* *adv* probably.
Wahrscheinlichkeit *f* probability, likelihood.
Wahrung *f* protection; safe-
guarding.
Währung *f* currency.
Wahrzeichen *n* landmark.
Waise *f* orphan.
Waisenhaus *n* orphanage.
Wal *m* whale.
Wald *m* wood(s), forest.
Walfang *m* whaling.
Wall *m* dam, embankment;
rampart.
Wallach *m* gelding.
wallen *vi* to flow.
Wallfahrer(in) *m(f)* pilgrim.
Wallfahrt *f* pilgrimage.
Walnuß *f* walnut.

Walroß *n* walrus.
walten *vi* to rule.
Walze *f* roller; cylinder.
walzen *vt* to roll.
wälzen *vt* to roll; to hunt through; * *vr* to wallow; to roll about.
Walzer *m* waltz.
Wand *f* wall; partition; precipice.
Wandalismus *m* vandalism.
Wandel *m* change.
wandelbar *adj* changeable, variable.
wandeln *vt vr* to change; * *vi* to walk.
Wanderer *m* hiker, rambler.
wandern *vi* to hike; to ramble, roam, wander.
Wanderschaft *f* travels.
Wandgemälde *n* mural.
Wandlung *f* change, transformation.
Wandtafel *f* blackboard.
Wandteppich *m* tapestry.
Wange *f* cheek.
wankelmütig *adj* inconstant, fickle.
wanken *vi* to stagger, reel; to rock; to waver.
wann *inter adv* when, at what time.
Wanne *f* tub; bathtub.
Wanze *f* bedbug.
Wappen *n* (coat of) arms, crest.
Ware *f* goods; article; product.
Warenhaus *n* department store.
Warenlager *n* stock, store.
Warenzeichen *n* trade mark.
warm *adj* warm; hot.
Wärme *f* warmth; heat.
wärmen *vt* to warm (up).
Warmwasserbereiter *m* water heater.
Warmwasserversorgung *f* hot-water supply.
warnen *vt* to warn, caution.
Warnung *f* warning, caution.
Warschau *n* Warsaw.
Warte *f* point of view; level.
warten *vi* to wait; to await.

warten *vt* to service, maintain.
Wärter *m* attendant; keeper.
Wartesaal *m* waiting room.
Wartung *f* maintenance.
warum *adv* why.
Warze *f* wart.
was *inter pron* what; * *rel pron* what.
waschbar *adj* washable.
Waschbecken *n* washbasin.
Wäsche *f* wash(ing), laundry; linen; underwear.
waschen *vt vr* to wash.
Wäscherei *f* laundry.
Waschmaschine *f* washing machine.
Wasser *n* water.
Wasserdampf *m* steam.
wasserdicht *adj* waterproof; watertight.
Wasserfall *m* waterfall; falls.
Wasserkessel *m* kettle.
Wasserlauf *m* watercourse.
Wasserkraftwerk *n* hydroelectric power station.
Wassermann *m* (*astrol*) Aquarius.
Wassermelone *f* water melon.
wassern *vi* to land on water; to splash down.
wässern *vt* to soak; to water; * *vi* water (of eyes, etc).
Wasserrohr *n* water pipe.
Wasserski *m* water ski(ing).
Wasserspiegel *m* water level.
Wassersport *m* water sports, aquatics.
Wasserstoff *m* hydrogen.
Wasserstoffbombe *f* hydrogen bomb, H-bomb.
Wasserstraße *f* waterway.
Wasserversorgung *f* water supply.
Wasserzeichen *n* watermark.
wäßrig *adj* watery.
waten *vi* to wade.
watscheln *vi* to waddle.
Watt *n* watt.
Watte *f* cotton wool.
wau *excl* woof.
weben *vt* to weave.
Weber *m* weaver.

Weberei *f* weaving mill.

Webstuhl *m* loom.

Wechsel *m* change; bill of exchange.

Wechselgeld *n* change.

wechselhaft *adj* variable.

Wechselkurs *m* rate of exchange.

wechseln *vt vi* to change.

Wechselstrom *m* alternating current.

Wechselwirkung *f* interaction.

wecken *vt* to wake (up).

Wecker *m* alarm clock.

wedeln *vi* to wag; to wave.

weder *conj*: ~ ... **noch** ... neither ... nor ....

Weg *m* way; path; route.

weg *adv* away, off.

wegbleiben *vi* to stay away.

wegen *prep* because of.

wegfallen *vi* to be left out.

weggehen *vi* to go away; to leave.

weglassen *vt* to leave out.

weglegen *vt* to put aside.

wegmachen *vt* to get rid of.

wegnehmen *vt* to take away.

wegtun *vt* to put away.

Wegweiser *m* road sign, signpost.

wegwerfen *vt* to throw away.

wegwerfend *adj* disparaging.

weh *adj* sore; ~ **tun** to hurt.

wehen *vt vi* to blow.

wehmütig *adj* melancholy.

Wehrdienst *m* military service.

Wehrdienstverweigerer *m* conscientious objector.

wehren *vr* to restrain oneself

wehrlos *adj* defenceless.

Wehrpflicht *f* compulsory military service.

wehrpflichtig *adj* liable for military service.

Weib *n* woman, female, wife.

Weibchen *n* feminine.

weiblich *adj* female.

weich *adj* soft.

weichen *vi* to yield.

Weichheit *f* softness.

Weichling *m* weakling.

Weichsel *f* Vistula.

Weide *f* willow; pasture.

weiden *vi* to graze.

weidlich *adv* thoroughly.

weigern *vt* to refuse.

Weigerung *f* refusal.

Weihe *f* consecration; ordination.

weihen *vt* to consecrate; ordain.

Weiher *m* pond.

Weihnachten *n* Christmas.

weihnachtlich *adj* Christmas.

Weihnachtsabend *m* Christmas Eve.

Weihnachtslied *n* Christmas carol.

Weinachtsmann *m* Father Christmas, Santa Claus.

Weihnachtstag *m* Christmas Day.

Weihrausch *m* incense.

Weihwasser *n* holy water.

weil *conj* because.

Weile *f* while, short time.

Wein *m* wine; vine.

Weinberg *m* vineyard.

Weinbrand *m* brandy.

weinen *vt vi* to cry.

Weinglas *n* wine glass.

Weinkarte *f* wine list.

Weinlese *f* vintage.

Weinprobe *f* wine-tasting.

Weinrebe *f* vine.

Weinstock *m* vine.

Weintraube *f* grape.

weise *adj* wise.

Weise *m* way, manner; tune; **auf diese** ~ in this way.

weisen *vt* to show.

Weisheit *f* wisdom.

Weisheitszahn *m* wisdom tooth.

weiß *adj* white.

Weißbrot *n* white bread.

weißen *vt* to whitewash.

Weißglut *f* incandescence.

Weißwein *m* white wine.

weit *adj* wide; broad; long.

weitaus *adv* by far.

weitblickend *adj* far-seeing.

Weite *f* width; space; distance.

weiten *vt vi* to widen.

weiter *adj* wider; broader; farther; further; * *adv* further; **ohne ~es** without further ado.

weiterarbeiten *vi* to go on working.

weiterbilden *vr* to continue one's education.

Weiterfahrt *f* continuation of the journey.

weitergehen *vi* to go on.

weiterkommen *vi* to make progress.

weiterläufig *adj* spacious; lengthy; distant.

weiterleiten *vt* to pass on.

weitermachen *vt vi* to continue.

weitgehend *adj* considerable; * *adv* largely.

weitreichend *adj* long-range; far-reaching.

weitschweifig *adj* long-winded.

weitsichtig *adj* long-sighted; far-sighted.

Weitsprung *m* long jump.

weitverbreitet *adj* widespread.

Weitwinkelobjektiv *n* wide-angle lens.

Weizen *m* wheat.

welche(r,s) *inter pron* which; * *indef pron* some; any; * *rel pron* who; which, that.

welk *adj* withered.

welken *vi* to wither.

Wellblech *n* corrugated iron.

Welle *f* wave; shaft.

Wellenbereich *m* waveband.

Wellenlänge *f* wavelength.

Wellensittich *m* budgerigar.

Welt *f* world.

Weltall *n* universe,

Weltanschauung *f* philosophy of life.

weltberühmt *adj* world-famous.

Weltkrieg *m* world war.

weltlich *adj* worldly; secular.

Weltmacht *f* world power.

Weltmeister *m* world champion.

Weltraum *m* space.

weltweit *adj* worldwide.

wem *pron* (*dat of* **wer**) to whom.

wen *pron* (*acc of* **wer**) whom.

Wende *f* turn; change.

Wendekreis *m* tropic.

Wendeltreppe *f* spiral staircase.

wenden *vt vi vr* to turn.

Wendepunkt *m* turning point.

Wendung *f* turn; idiom.

wenig *adj adv* little.

wenige *pron pl* few.

weniger *adj* less; fewer; * *adv* less.

wenigste(r,s) *adj* least.

wenigstens *adv* at least.

wenn *conj* if; when.

wer *pron* who.

Werbefernsehen *n* commercial television.

werben *vt* to win; to recruit; * *vi* to advertise.

Werbung *f* advertisement; recruitment.

werden *vi v aux* to become.

werfen *vt* to throw.

Werft *f* shipyard.

Werk *n* work; job; works.

Werkstatt *f* workshop.

Werktag *m* working day.

werktätig *adj* working.

Werkzeug *n* tool.

Wert *m* worth; value.

wert *adj* worth; dear; worthy.

werten *vt* to rate.

Wertgegenstände *pl* valuables.

wertlos *adj* worthless.

Wertpapier *n* security.

wertvoll *adj* valuable.

Wesen *n* being; nature.

wesentlich *adj* significant; considerable.

weshalb *adv* why.

Wespe *f* wasp.

wessen *pron* (*gen of* **wer**) whose.

Weste *f* waistcoat.

Westen *m* west.

Westeuropa *n* western Europe.

Westindien *n* (the) West Indies.

westlich *adj* western; * *adv* to the west.

weswegen *adv* why.

wett *adj* even.

Wettbewerb *m* competition.

Wette *f* wager, bet.

wetten *vt vi* to bet.

Wetter *n* weather.

Wetterbericht *m* weather report.

Wetterdienst *m* meteorological service.

Wettervorhersage *f* weather forecast.

Wettkampf *m* contest.

wettmachen *vt* to make good.

wetzen *vt* to whet, sharpen.

wichtig *adj* important.

Wichtigkeit *f* importance.

Widder *m* ram; (*astrol*) Aries.

wider *prep* against.

widerlegen *vt* to refute.

widerlich *adj* repulsive.

widerrechtlich *adj* unlawful.

Widerrede *f* contradiction.

Widerruf *m* retraction.

widerrufen *vt* to retract.

widerspiegeln *vt* to mirror, reflect; * *vr* to be reflected.

widersprechen *vt* to contradict.

Widerspruch *m* contraction.

Widerstand *m* resistance.

widerstandsfähig *adj* resistant.

widerstehen *vi*: **jdm/etw ~** to withstand sb/something.

widmen *vt* to dedicate; to devote; * *vr* to devote oneself

widrig *adj* adverse.

wie *adv* how; * *conj*: **so schön ~** as beautiful as.

wieder *adv* again.

Wiederaufbau *m* rebuilding.

wiederaufnehmen *vt* to resume.

wiederbekommen *vt* to get back.

wiederbringen *vt* to bring back.

wiedererkennen *vt* to recognise.

Wiedergabe *f* reproduction.

wiedergeben *vt* to return; to repeat.

wiedergutmachen *vt* to make up for.

Wiedergutmachung *f* reparation.

wiederherstellen *vt* to restore.

wiederholen *vt* to repeat.

Wiederholung *f* repeat.

Wiederkehr *f* return; recurrence.

wiedersehen *vt* to see again; **auf Wiedersehen** goodbye.

wiederum *adv* again; on the other hand.

wiedervereinigen to reunite; to reunify.

Wiederwahl *f* re-election.

Wiege *f* cradle.

wiegen *vt* to rock; *vt vi* to weigh.

wiehern *vi* to neigh, whinny.

Wien *n* Vienna.

Wiese *f* meadow.

Wiesel *n* weasel.

wieso *adv* why.

wieviel *adj* how much.

wieweit *adv* to what extent.

wild *adj* wild.

Wild *n* game.

Wilde(r) *mf* savage.

wildern *vi* to poach.

wildfremd *adj* (*coll*) quite strange/unknown.

Wildheit *f* wildness.

Wildleder *n* suede.

Wildnis *f* wilderness.

Wildschwein *n* (wild) boar.

Wille *m* will.

willen *prep* +*gen* **um ... willen** for the sake of ....

willenstark *adj* strong-willed.

willig *adj* willing.

Willkommen *n* welcome.

willkommen *adj* welcome.

willkürlich *adj* arbitrary; voluntary.

wimmeln *vi*: **~ (von)** to swarm (with).

wimmern *vi* to whimper.

Wimper *f* eyelash.

Wimperntusche *f* mascara.

Wind *m* wind.
Windbeutel *m* cream puff; rake.
Winde *f* winch, windlass; (bot) bindweed.
Windel *f* nappy, diaper.
winden *vi* to be windy; * *vt* to wind; to wave; to twist.
Windenergie *f* wind energy.
Windhund *m* greyhound; fly-by-night.
windig *adj* windy; dubious.
Windmühle *f* windmill.
Windpocken *pl* chickenpox.
Windschutzscheibe *f* windscreen.
Windstärke *f* wind-force.
windstill *adj* still, windless.
Windstille *f* calm.
Windstoß *m* gust of wind.
Wink *m* wave; nod; hint.
Winkel *m* angle; set square; corner.
winkeln *vt vi* to wave.
winseln *vi* to whine.
Winter *m* winter.
winterfest *adj* (bot) hardy.
Wintergarten *m* conservatory.
winterlich *adj* wintry.
Winterreifen *m* winter tyre.
Wintersport *m* winter sports.
Winzer *m* vine grower.
winzig *adj* tiny.
Wipfel *m* treetop.
wir *pron* we.
Wirbel *m* whirl, swirl; fuss; vertebra.
wirbeln *vi* to whirl, swirl.
Wirbelsäule *f* spine.
wirken *vi* to have an effect; to work; to seem; * *vt* to work.
wirklich *adj* real; * *adv* really.
Wirklichkeit *f* reality.
wirksam *adj* effective.
Wirkung *f* effect.
wirkungslos *adj* ineffective.
wirr *adj* confused, wild.
Wirrwarr *m* chaos, disorder.
Wirt(in) *m(f)* landlord (landlady).
Wirtschaft *f* pub; economy.
wirtschaftlich *adj* economical; economic.
Wirtschaftskrise *f* economic crisis.
Wirtschaftspolitik *f* economic policy.
Wirtschaftswunder *n* economic miracle.
Wirtshaus *n* inn.
wischen *vt* to wipe.
Wischer *m* wiper.
wispern *vi* to whisper.
wissen *vt* to know.
Wissen *n* knowledge.
Wissenschaft *f* science.
Wissenschaftler(in) *m(f)* scientist.
wissenschaftlich *adj* scientific.
wissenswert *adj* worth knowing.
wissentlich *adj* knowing.
wittern *vt* to scent; to suspect.
Witterung *f* weather; scent.
Witwe *f* widow.
Witwer *m* widower.
Witz *m* joke.
witzig *adj* funny,
wo *adv* where; somewhere.
woanders *adv* elsewhere.
wobei *adv* by/with which.
Woche *f* week.
Wochenende *n* weekend.
wochenlang *adj adv* for weeks.
Wochenschau *f* newsreel.
wöchentlich *adj adv* weekly.
wodurch *adv* through which.
wofür *adv* for which.
wogegen *adv* against which.
woher *adv* where … from.
wohin *adv* where … to.
wohl *adv* well; probably; certainly; perhaps.
Wohl *n* welfare.
Wohlfahrt *f* welfare.
Wohlfahrtsstaat *m* welfare state.
wohlhabend *adj* wealthy.
Wohlstand *m* prosperity.
Wohltat *f* relief; act of charity.
Wohltäter(in) *m(f)* benefactor.
wohltätig *adj* charitable.
Wohltun *vi* to do good.

Wohlwollen *n* good will.
wohlwollend *adj* benevolent.
wohnen *vi* to live, dwell, reside.
wohnhaft *adj* resident.
Wohnheim *n* hall of residence; home; hostel.
Wohnort *m* domicile.
Wohnsitz *m* place of residence.
Wohnung *f* house; flat, apartment.
Wohnwagen *m* caravan.
Wohnzimmer *n* living room, front room, lounge.
wölben *vt vr* to curve.
Wölbung *f* curve.
Wolf *m* wolf.
Wolke *f* cloud.
Wolkenkratzer *m* skyscraper.
wolkig *adj* cloudy.
Wolle *f* wool.
wollen *adj* woollen.
wollen *vt vi v aux* to want.
wollüstig *adj* lusty, sensual.
womit *adv* with which.
wonach *adv* after/for which.
woran *adv* on/at which.
worauf *adv* on which.
woraus *adv* from/out of which.
worin *adv* in which.
Wort *n* word.
Wörterbuch *n* dictionary.
Wortlaut *m* wording.
wortlos *adj* mute.
wortreich *adv* wordy, verbose.
Wortschatz *m* vocabulary.
Wortspiel *n* play on words, pun.
worüber *adv* over/about which.
worum *adv* about/round which.
worunter *adv* under which.
wovon *adv* from which.
wovor *adv* in front of/before which.
wozu *adv* to/for which.
Wrack *n* wreck.
wringen *vt* to wring.
Wucher *m* profiteering.
Wucherer *m* profiteer.
wuchern *vi* to grow wild.
Wucherung *f* growth, tumour.
Wuchs *m* growth; build.
Wucht *f* force.
wühlen *vi* to scrabble; to root;

to burrow; * *vt* to dig.
Wulst *m* bulge; swelling.
wund *adj* sore, raw.
Wunde *f* wound.
Wunder *n* miracle.
wunderbar *adj* wonderful, marvellous.
Wunderkind *n* infant prodigy.
wunderlich *adj* odd, peculiar.
wundern *vr* to be surprised; * *vt* to surprise.
wunderschön *adj* beautiful.
wundervoll *adj* wonderful.
Wundstarrkrampf *m* tetanus, lockjaw.
Wunsch *m* wish
wünschen *vt* to wish, desire.
wünschenswert *adj* desirable.
Würde *f* dignity; honour.
würdevoll *adj* dignified.
würdig *adj* worthy.
würdigen *vt* to appreciate.
Wurf *m* throw; litter.
Würfel *m* dice; cube.
würfeln *vi* to play dice; * *vt* to dice.
würgen *vi vt* to choke.
Wurm *m* worm.
wurmstichig *adj* worm-ridden.
Wurst *f* sausage; **das ist mir ~** (*coll*) I don't care, I don't give a damn.
Würze *f* seasoning, spice.
Würzel *f* root.
würzen *vt* to season, spice.
würzig *adj* spicy.
wüst *adj* untidy, messy; wild; waste.
Wüste *f* desert.
Wut *f* rage, fury.
Wutanfall *m* fit of rage.
wüten *vi* to rage.
wütend *adj* furious.

X

X-Beine *pl* knock-knees.
xerokopieren *vt* to xerox, photocopy.
x-mal *adv* any number of times, n times.
Xylophon *n* xylophone.

Y

Yacht *f* yacht.
Ypsilon *n* the letter Y.

Z

Zacke *f* point; jagged peak; tooth; prong.
zackig *adj* jagged.
zaghaft *adj* timid.
Zaghaftigkeit *f* timidity.
zäh *adj* tough; tenacious.
Zähigkeit *f* toughness; tenacity.
Zahl *f* number.
zahlbar *adj* payable.
zahlen *vt vi* to pay; **zahlen bitte!** the bill please!.
zählen *vt vi* to count.
Zahlenschloß *n* combination lock.
Zähler *m* meter; numerator.
zahllos *adj* countless.
zahlreich *adj* numerous.
Zahltag *m* pay-day.
Zahlung *f* payment.
zahm *adj* tame.
zähmen *vt* to tame; to curb.
Zahn *m* tooth.
Zahnarzt *m* **Zahnärztin** *f* dentist.
Zahnbürste *f* toothbrush.
Zahnfleisch *n* gums.

Zahnpasta *f* toothpaste.
Zahnrad *n* cog.
Zahnschmerzen *pl* toothache.
Zahnstein *m* tartar.
Zange *f* pliers; tongs; pincers; forceps.
zanken *vi vr* to quarrel.
zänkisch *adj* quarrelsome.
Zapfen *m* plug; cone; icicle.
zappeln *vi* to wriggle; to fidget.
zart *adj* soft; tender; delicate.
Zartheit *f* softness; tenderness.
zärtlich *adj* tender, affectionate.
Zauber *m* magic; spell.
Zauberei *f* magic.
zauberhaft *adj* magical, enchanting.
Zauberkünstler *m* conjuror.
zaubern *vi* to conjure, practise magic.
zaudern *vi* to hesitate.
Zaum *m* bridle.
Zaun *m* fence.
Zaunkönig *m* wren.
z.B. (= **zum Beispiel**) e.g.
Zebra *n* zebra.
Zebrastreifen *m* zebra crossing.
Zeche *f* bill; mine.
Zeh *m* toe.
Zehe *f* toe; clove.
zehn *num* ten.
zehnte(r,s) *adj* tenth.
Zehntel *n* tenth.
Zeichen *n* sign.
zeichnen *vt* to draw; to mark; to sign; * *vi* to draw; to sign.
Zeichner *m* artist.
Zeichnung *f* drawing; markings.
Zeigefinger *m* index finger.
zeigen *vt* to show; * *vi* to point; * *vr* to show oneself
Zeiger *m* pointer; hand (of clock).
Zeile *f* line; row.
Zeit *f* time; (*gr*) tense; **zur ~** at the moment.
Zeitalter *n* age.
Zeitarbeit *f* temporary work.
zeitgemäß *adj* in keeping with

the times.

Zeitgenosse *m* contemporary.

zeitig *adj* early.

zeitlich *adj* temporal.

Zeitlupe *f* slow motion.

Zeitraum *m* period.

Zeitrechnung *f* time, era; **nach/vor unserer ~** AD/BC.

Zeitschrift *f* periodical.

Zeitung *f* newspaper.

Zeitvertreib *m* pastime, diversion.

zeitweilig *adj* temporary.

zeitweise *adv* for a time.

Zeitwort *n* verb.

Zeitzünder *m* time fuse.

Zelle *f* cell; callbox.

Zellstoff *m* cellulose.

Zelt *n* tent.

zelten *vi* to camp.

Zeltplatz *m* campsite.

Zement *m* cement.

zementieren *vt* to cement.

zensieren *vt* to censor.

Zentimeter *m/n* centimetre.

Zentner *m* hundredweight.

Zensur *f* censorship.

zentral *adj* central.

Zentrale *f* central office; (telephone) exchange.

Zentralheizung *f* central heating.

Zentrum *n* centre.

zerbrechen *vt vi* to break.

zerbrechlich *adj* fragile.

zerdrücken *vt* to smash, crush; to mash (of potatoes).

Zeremonie *f* ceremony.

Zerfall *m* decay.

zerfallen *vi* to disintegrate, decay.

zergehen *vi* to melt, dissolve.

zerkleinern *vt* to reduce to small pieces.

zerlegbar *adj* able to be dismantled.

zerlegen *vi* to take to pieces; to carve.

zermürben *vt* to wear down.

zerquetschen *vt* to squash.

Zerrbild *n* caricature.

zerreißen *vt* to tear to pieces;

* *vi* to tear, rip.

zerren *vt* to drag; * *vi:* **~ (an** +*dat*) to tug (at).

zerrinnen *vi* to melt away.

zerrissen *adj* torn, tattered.

Zerrissenheit *f* tattered state.

Zerrung *f* (*med*) pulled muscle.

zerrütten *vt* to wreck, destroy.

zerrüttet *adj* wrecked, shattered.

zerschlagen *vt* to shatter, smash; * *vr* to fall through.

zerschneiden *vt* to cut up.

zersetzen *vt vr* to decompose.

zerspringen *vi* to shatter, burst.

Zerstäuber *m* atomiser.

zerstören *vt* to destroy.

Zerstörung *f* destruction.

zerstreuen *vt* to scatter, disperse; to dispel; * *vr* to scatter, disperse; to be dispelled.

zerstreut *adj* scattered; absentminded.

Zerstreutheit *f* absentmindedness.

Zerstreuung *f* dispersion.

zerteilen *vt* to divide into parts.

Zertifikat *n* certificate.

zertreten *vt* to crush underfoot.

zertrümmern *vt* to demolish, to shatter.

zetern *vi* to shout; to shriek.

Zettel *m* slip of paper; note; form.

Zeug *n* stuff; gear; **das ~ haben zu** to have the makings of.

Zeuge *m* witness.

Zeugenaussage *f* evidence.

Zeugin *f* witness.

zeugen *vi* to testify, bear witness; * *vt* to father.

Zeugnis *n* certificate; report; evidence, testimony.

Zickzack *m* zigzag.

Ziege *f* goat.

Ziegel *m* brick; tile.

ziehen *vt* to draw; to pull; to move; * *vi* to draw; to move; to drift.

Ziehharmonika *f* concertina; accordion.

Ziehung f drawing.

Ziel n destination; finish; target; goal.

ziemlich adj quite a, fair; * adv rather; quite a bit.

zieren vi to act coy.

zierlich adj dainty.

Ziffer f figure, digit.

zig adj (coll) umpteen.

Zigarette f cigarette.

Zigarettenautomat m cigarette machine.

Zigarre f cigar.

Zigeuner(in) m(f) gypsy.

Zimmer n room.

Zimmermädchen n chambermaid.

Zimmerpflanze f indoor plant.

zimperlich adj squeamish.

Zimt m cinnamon.

Zink n zinc.

Zinn n tin; pewter.

Zinnsoldat m tin soldier.

Zins m interest.

Zinseszins m compound interest.

Zinsfuß m rate of interest.

zinslos adj interest-free.

Zinssatz m rate of interest.

Zipfel m corner; tip.

zirka adv (round) about.

Zirkel m circle; pair of compasses.

Zirkus m circus.

zischen vi to hiss.

Zitat n quotation, quote.

zitieren vt to quote.

Zitrone f lemon.

Zitronenlimonade f lemonade.

Zitronensaft m lemon juice.

zittern vi to tremble.

zivil adj civil; moderate.

Zivil n plain clothes.

Zivilbevölkerung f civil population.

Zivilisation f civilisation.

zivilisieren vt to civilise.

Zivilist m civilian.

zögern vi to hesitate.

Zoll m customs; duty.

Zollamt n customs office.

Zollbeamte(r) m customs officer.

Zollerklärung f customs declaration.

zollfrei adj duty-free.

Zollkontrolle f customs check.

zollpflichtig adj liable to duty.

Zone f zone.

Zoo m zoo.

Zoologe m zoologist.

Zoologie f zoology.

zoologisch adj zoological.

Zopf m plait; pigtail.

Zorn m anger.

zornig adj angry.

zottig adj shaggy.

zu prep to; at; with; for; into; * conj to; * adv too; towards; shut, closed.

zuallererst adv first of all.

zuallerletzt adv last of all.

Zubehör n accessories.

zubereiten vt to prepare.

zubilligen vt to grant.

zubinden vt to tie up.

zubringen vt to spend.

Zucchini pl courgette.

Zucht f breeding; cultivation; breed; discipline.

züchten vt to breed; to cultivate; to grow.

Züchter m breeder; grower.

Zuchthaus n prison.

züchtigen vt to chastise.

Züchtung f breed; variety.

zucken vi to jerk, twitch; to flicker; * vi to shrug.

Zucker m sugar; (med) diabetes.

Zuckerguß m icing.

zuckerkrank adj diabetic.

Zuckerkrankheit (med) diabetes.

zuckern vt to sugar.

Zuckerrohr n sugar cane.

Zuckerrübe f sugar beet.

Zuckung f convulsion, spasm; twitch.

zudecken vt to cover (up).

zudem adv in addition.

zudringlich adj forward, pushing, obtrusive.

zudrücken vt to close.
zueinander adv to one another; together.
zuerkennen vt to award.
zuerst adv first; at first.
Zufahrt f approach.
Zufahrtsstraße f approach road; slip road.
Zufall m chance; coincidence; **durch ~** by accident.
zufallen vi to close, shut; to fall.
zufällig adj chance; * adv by chance.
Zuflucht f recourse; refuge.
zufolge prep judging by; according to.
zufrieden adj content(ed), satisfied.
zufriedengeben vr to be content/satisfied (with).
zufriedenstellen vt to satisfy.
zufrieren vi to freeze up.
zufügen vt to add.
Zug m train; draught; pull; feature; move, stroke; breath; procession.
Zugabe f extra; encore.
Zugang m access, approach.
zugänglich adj accessible; approachable.
zugeben vt to add; to admit; to permit.
zugehen vi to shut.
Zugehörigkeit f membership; belonging (to).
Zügel m rein(s); curb.
Zugeständnis n concession.
zugestehen vt to admit; to concede.
Zugführer m guard.
zugig adj draughty.
zügig adj swift, speedy.
zugreifen vi to seize/grab at; to help.
zugrunde adv: **~ gehen** to collapse; **einer Sache** dat **etw ~ legen** to base something on something; **~ richten** to destroy, ruin.
zugunsten prep in favour of.
Zugvogel m migratory bird.
zuhalten vt to keep closed; * vi:

auf jdn/etw ~ to make a beeline for somebody or something.
Zuhälter m pimp.
Zuhause n home.
zuhören vi to listen.
Zuhörer m listener.
zukleben vi to paste up.
zukommen vi to come up.
Zukunft f future.
zukünftig adj future; * adv in future.
Zulage f bonus.
zulassen vt to admit; to permit; to license.
zulässig adj permissible.
Zulassung f authorisation; licensing.
zulaufen vi: **~ auf jdn/etw** to run up to somebody or something; **~ auf** to lead towards.
zuletzt adv finally, at last.
zum = **zu dem**.
zumachen vt to shut; to do up, fasten; * vi to shut; to hurry up.
zumal conj especially (as).
zumindest adv at least.
zumutbar adj reasonable.
zumuten vt: **(jdm) etw ~** to expect/ask something (of sb).
Zumutung f unreasonable expectation, impertinence.
zunächst adv first of all.
Zunahme f increase.
Zuname m surname.
zünden vi to light, ignite; to fire.
zündend adj fiery.
Zünder m fuse; detonator.
Zündholz n match.
Zündkerze f spark plug.
Zündschlüssel m ignition key.
Zündung f ignition.
zunehmen vi to increase, grow; to put on weight.
Zuneigung f affection.
Zunft f guild.
zünftig adj proper; decent.
Zunge f tongue.
zuoberst adv at the top.
zupfen vt to pull, pick, pluck.

zur = **zu der**.
zurechnungsfähig *adj* accountable; responsible.
zurechtfinden *vr* to find one's way (about).
zurechtkommen *vi* to cope, manage.
zurechtlegen *vt* to get ready; to have ready.
zurechtmachen *vt* to prepare; * *vi* to get ready.
zurechtweisen *vt* to reprimand.
Zurechtweisung *f* reprimand, rebuff.
zureden *vi*: **jdm ~** to persuade/urge s.o.
Zürich *n* Zurich.
zurück *adv* back.
zurückbehalten *vt* to keep back.
zurückbekommen *vt* to get back.
zurückbleiben *vi* to remain behind; to fall behind.
zurückbringen *vt* to bring back.
zurückfahren *vt* to drive back; * *vi* to travel back; to recoil.
zurückfinden *vi* to find one's way back.
zurückfordern *vt* to demand back.
zurückführen *vt* to lead back.
zurückgeben *vt* to give back.
zurückgeblieben *adj* retarded.
zurückgehen *vi* to go back.
zurückgezogen *adj* retired, withdrawn.
zurückhalten *vt* to hold back; to restrain; * *vr* to be reserved.
zurückhaltend *adj* reserved.
Zurückhaltung *f* reserve.
zurückkehren *vi* to return.
zurückkommen *vi* to come back.
zurücklassen *vt* to leave behind.
zurücknehmen *vt* to take back.
zurückweisen *vt* to reject; to

turn down.
zurückziehen *vt* to pull back; to withdraw; * *vr* to retire.
Zuruf *f* cry, shout.
Zusage *f* promise; consent.
zusagen *vt* to promise; * *vi* to accept.
zusammen *adv* together.
Zusammenarbeit *f* cooperation.
zusammenarbeiten *vi* to cooperate.
zusammenbrechen *vt* to collapse; to break down.
Zusammenbruch *m* collapse, breakdown.
zusammenfassen *vt* to summarise; to unite.
Zusammenfassung *f* summary.
Zusammenhang *m* connection.
zusammenkommen *vi* to assemble; to occur at once.
zusammenschließen *vt vi* to join (together).
Zusammenschluß *m* amalgamation.
zusammensetzen *vr* to be composed of; to get together.
Zusammensetzung *f* composition.
Zusammenstoß *m* collision.
zusätzlich *adj* additional; * *adv* in addition.
zuschauen *vt* to look on, watch.
Zuschauer(in) *m(f)* spectator.
Zuschlag *m* extra charge, surcharge.
zuschlagen *vt* to slam; to hit; * *vi* to shut; to hit, punch.
zuschreiben *vt* to ascribe, attribute.
Zuschrift *f* letter, reply.
Zuschluß *m* subsidy, allowance.
zusehen *vi* to watch; to take care.
zusehends *adv* visibly.
zusenden *vt* to forward, send on.
zuspielen *vt vi* to pass.
zuspitzen *vt* to sharpen; * *vr* to become critical.

zusprechen *vt* to award; * *vi* to speak.

Zustand *m* state, condition.

zustande *adv*: ~ **bringen** to be-ing about; ~ **kommen** to come about.

zuständig *adj* responsible.

Zuständigkeit *f* responsibility.

zustehen *vi*: **jdm** ~ to be sb's right.

zustellen *vt* to send; to block.

zustimmen *vi* to agree.

Zustimmung *f* agreement, con-sent.

zustoßen *vi* to happen.

zutage *adv*: ~ **bringen** to bring to light; ~ **treten** to come to light.

Zutaten *pl* ingredients.

zuteilen *vt* to designate, assign; to allocate.

zutiefst *adv* deeply.

zutragen *vt* to bring; to tell; * *vr* to happen.

Zutrauen *n* trust.

zutrauen *vt*: **jdm etw** ~ to credit sb with something.

zutraulich *adj* trusting, friendly.

zutreffen *vi* to be correct; to ap-ply.

zutreffend *adj* accurate.

Zutritt *m* access, admittance.

Zutun *n* assistance.

zuverlässig *adj* reliable.

Zuverlässigkeit *f* reliability.

zuviel *adv* too much.

zuvor *adv* before, previously.

zuvorkommen *vt* (+*dat*) to an-ticipate.

zuvorkommend *adj* courteous, obliging.

Zuwachs *m* growth, increase.

zuwachsen *vi* to become over-grown; to heal (of wound).

zuwenig *adv* too little.

zuweilen *adv* at times, now and then.

zuwenden *vt* (+*dat*) to turn (to-wards).

zuziehen *vt* to draw, close; to call in (experts, etc); * *vi* to move in.

zuzüglich *prep* plus, with the addition of.

Zwang *m* compulsion, coercion.

zwängen *vt vr* to squeeze.

zwanglos *adj* informal.

zwanzig *num* twenty.

zwar *adv* indeed, to be sure.

Zweck *m* purpose, aim.

zwecklos *adj* pointless.

zwei *num* two.

zweideutig *adj* ambiguous.

zweifach *adj* double.

Zweifel *m* doubt.

zweifelhaft *adj* doubtful.

zweifellos *adj* doubtless.

zweifeln *vi*: ~ (**an etw** *dat*) to doubt (something).

Zweig *m* branch.

zweimal *adv* twice.

zweite(r,s) *adj* second.

Zwerg *m* dwarf.

Zwetsch(g)e *f* plum.

Zwieback *m* rusk.

Zwiebel *f* onion.

Zwilling *m* twin; **~e** *pl* (*astrol*) Gemini.

zwingen *vt* to force, compel.

zwingend *adj* compulsive.

Zwirn *m* thread.

zwischen *prep* between.

Zwischenfall *m* incident.

Zwischenzeit *f* interval; **in der ~** meanwhile, in the interim.

zwitschern *vt vi* to chirp, twit-ter.

zwo *num* two.

zwölf *num* twelve.

Zyklus *m* cycle.

Zylinder *m* cylinder; top hat.

Zyniker *m* cynic.

zynisch *adj* cynical.

Zypern *n* Cyprus.

Zyste *f* cyst.

English-German

A

a *art* ein, eine; per, pro, je.

aback: to be taken ~ (*fig*) überrascht, verblüfft, bestürzt.

abacus *n* Abakus *m*, Rechengestell *n*.

abandon *vt* auf-, preisgeben; im Stich lassen, verlassen; * *n* Hemmungslosigkeit *f*.

abandonment *n* Auf-, Preisgabe *f*; Hingabe *f*; Hemmungslosigkeit *f*.

abase *vt* erniedrigen, demütigen.

abasement *n* Erniedrigung *f*; Demütigung *f*.

abash *vt* beschämen, verlegen machen.

abate *vt* verringern, vermindern; * *vi* abnehmen, nachlassen.

abatement *n* Verminderung *f*, Abschaffung *f*.

abbess *n* Äbtissin *f*.

abbey *n* Abtei *f*.

abbot *n* Abt *m*.

abbreviate *vt* (ab)kürzen.

abbreviation *n* Abkürzung *f*.

abdicate *vt* niederlegen, entsagen; *vi* abdanken.

abdication *n* Abdankung *f*; Verzicht *m*.

abdomen *n* Unterleib *m*, Bauch *m*.

abdominal *adj* Unterleibs-, Bauch-.

abduct *vt* entführen.

abduction *n* Entführung *f*.

abductor *n* Entführer *m*.

aberrant *adj* anomal; (ab)irrend.

aberration *n* Abweichung *f*; (*fig*) Verirrung *f*.

abet *vt* anstiften, aufhetzen; **to aid and ~** Vorschub leisten.

abeyance *n* Unentschiedenheit *f*.

abhor *vt* verabscheuen.

abhorrence *n* Abscheu *m*.

abhorrent *adj* zuwider, verhaßt; abstoßend.

abide *vt* ertragen, aushalten; ausstehen; *vi* bleiben; **~ by** treu bleiben, festhalten an.

ability *n* Fähigkeit *f*; **abilities** *pl* geistige Anlagen *fpl*.

abject *adj*, **~ly** *adv* verworfen; verächtlich; hoffnungslos; (*fig*) tiefst(er, e, es).

abjure *vt* abschwören; entsagen.

ablaze *adj* in Flammen, lodernd.

able *adj*, **ably** *adv* fähig, tüchtig, geschickt; **to be ~** imstande sein, können.

able-bodied *adj* körperlich leistungsfähig, kerngesund; tauglich.

ablution *n* (*relig*) Waschung *f*.

abnegation *n* Ableugnung *f*.

abnormal *adj* abnormal, ungewöhnlich.

abnormality *n* Abnormalität *f*; Anomalie *f*.

aboard *adv* an Bord.

abode *n* Aufenthalt *m*; Wohnung *f*, Wohnsitz *m*.

abolish *vt* abschaffen, aufheben.

abolition *n* Abschaffung *f*, Aufhebung *f*.

abominable *adj* **~bly** *adv* abscheulich.

abomination *n* Abscheu *m*; Greuel *n*.

aboriginal *adj* einheimisch, eingeboren, Ur-.

aborigines *npl* Ureinwohner *mpl*, Urbevölkerung *f*.

abort *vi* eine Fehlgeburt haben.

abortion *n* Fehl-, Frühgeburt *f*; Abtreibung *f*.

abortive *adj* vorzeitig; erfolglos, fehlgeschlagen; verkümmert.

abound *vi* reichlich vorhanden sein; **to ~ with** wimmeln von.

about *prep* über; von; um... herum; bei; im Begriff, dabei;

* *adv* herum, umher; in der Nähe, da; auf den Beinen; etwa, ungefähr; **to be ~ to** im Begriff sein zu; **to go ~** herumlaufen; **to go ~ a thing** etwas in Angriff nehmen, tun; **all ~** überall.

above *prep* über, oberhalb; * *adv* oben, darüber; **~ all** vor allem; **~ mentioned** oben erwähnt.

aboveboard *adj* ehrlich, offen, einwandfrei.

abrasion *n* Abreiben *n*, Abschleifung *f*; Abrieb *m*, Verschleiß *m*; Hautabschürfung *f*, Schramme *f*.

abrasive *adj* abreibend, Schleif-; schroff, abweisend; * *n* Schleifmittel *n*.

abreast *adv* nebeneinander, Seite an Seite.

abridge *vt* (ab-, ver)kürzen; be-, einschränken.

abridgment *n* Kürzung *f*; Kurzfassung *f*; Beschränkung *f*.

abroad *adv* im Ausland; **to go ~** ins Ausland reisen.

abrogate *vt* abschaffen, aufheben.

abrogation *n* Abschaffung, Aufhebung *f*.

abrupt *adj* **~ly** *adv* plötzlich; schroff.

abscess *n* Geschwür *n*.

abscond *vi* flüchten; durchbrennen.

absence *n* Abwesenheit *f*; Mangel *m*.

absent *adj* abwesend; fehlend; zerstreut; * *vi* fernbleiben; sich entfernen.

absentee *n* Abwesende(r) *f(m)*.

absenteeism *n* häufiges, unentschuldigtes Fehlen *n*.

absent-minded *adj* zerstreut.

absolute *adj* **~ly** *adv* uneingeschränkt; vollkommen; entschieden.

absolution *n* Freisprechung *f*; Sündenerlaß *m*.

absolutism *n* Absolutismus *m*.

absolve *vt* freisprechen; die Absolution erteilen.

absorb *vt* aufsaugen; aufnehmen; (*fig*) fesseln.

absorbent *adj* aufsaugend, saugfähig.

absorption *n* Aufnahme *f*; Vertieftsein *n*.

abstain *vi* sich enthalten.

abstemious *adj* **~ly** *adv* mäßig, enthaltsam; bescheiden.

abstemiousness *n* Mäßigkeit *f*, Enthaltsamkeit *f*.

abstinence *n* Enthaltung *f*; Enthaltsamkeit *f*.

abstinent *adj* enthaltsam; mässig.

abstract *adj* **~ly** *adv* abstrakt; * *n* Auszug *m*; Übersicht *f*; **in the ~** rein theoretisch.

abstraction *n* Abstraktion *f*.

abstruse *adj* **~ly** *adv* abstrus.

absurd *adj* **~ly** *adv* absurd; lächerlich.

absurdity *n* Unsinn *m;* Lächerlichkeit *f*.

abundance *n* Überfluß *m*.

abundant *adj* reichlich (vorhanden); reich; **~ly** *adv* reichlich, völlig.

abuse *vt* mißbrauchen; beleidigen; * *n* Mißbrauch *m*; Mißhandlung *f*; Beleidigungen *fpl*.

abusive *adj* **~ly** *adv* Mißbrauch treibend; ausfallend.

abut *vi* stoßen; grenzen; sich berühren.

abysmal *adj* abgrundtief; miserabel.

abyss *n* Abgrund *m*.

acacia *n* Akazie *f*.

academic *adj* akademisch; allgemeinbildend.

academician *n* Mitglied *n* einer Akademie.

academy *n* Akademie *f*; Hochschule *f*.

accede *vi* zustimmen.

accelerate *vt* beschleunigen.

acceleration *n* Beschleunigung *f*.

accelerator *n* Gaspedal *n*.

accent *n* Akzent *m*; Betonung

f; * *vt* betonen.
accentuate *vt* betonen.
accentuation *n* Betonung *f.*
accept *vt* annehmen; akzeptieren.
acceptability *n* Erträglichkeit *f.*
acceptable *adj* annehmbar; erträglich; willkommen.
acceptance *n* Annahme *f;* Aufnahme *f;* Anerkennung *f.*
access *n* Zugang *m;* Zutritt *m;* Zugriff *m.*
accessible *adj* zugänglich.
accession *n* Gelangen *n,* Eintritt *m;* Antritt *m;* Zuwachs *m.*
accessory *n* Zubehör(teil) *n;* (*law*) Komplize *m,* Komplizin *f.*
accident *n* Zufall *m;* Unfall *m.*
accidental *adj* ~ly *adv* zufällig; versehentlich; Unfalls-.
acclaim *vt* loben; mit Beifall begrüßen.
acclamation *n* lauter Beifall *m;* Lob *n.*
acclimate *vt* eingewöhnen.
accommodate *vt* anpassen; einen Gefallen tun; unterbringen; versorgen.
accommodating *adj* entgegenkommend; anpassungsfähig.
accommodation *n* Unterkunft *f;* Versorgung *f;* Beilegung *f.*
accompaniment *n* (*mus*) Begleitung *f.*
accompanist *n* (*mus*) Begleiter(in) *m(f).*
accompany *vt* begleiten.
accomplice *n* Komplize *m,* Komplizin *f.*
accomplish *vt* ausführen, zustande bringen; erreichen.
accomplished *adj* vollendet; kultiviert.
accomplishment *n* Ausführung *f;* Leistung *f;* ~s *pl* Talente *npl,* Bildung *f.*
accord *n* Übereinstimmung *f,* Abkommen *n;* **with one ~** einstimmig; **of one's own ~** aus eigenem Antrieb.
accordance *n:* **in ~ with** in

Übereinstimmung mit, gemäß.
according *prep* gemäß, entsprechend; **~ as** je nachdem wie; **~ly** *adv* demnach, entsprechend.
accordion *n* (*mus*) Akkordeon *n.*
accost *vt* ansprechen; sich nähern.
account *n* Rechnung *f;* Konto *n;* **~s** *pl* Geschäftsbücher *npl;* Rechenschaft *f;* Bericht *m;* Verzeichnis *n;* Erwägung *f;* Bedeutung *f;* **on no ~** auf keinen Fall; **on ~ of** wegen; **to call to ~** zur Rechenschaft ziehen; **to turn to ~** zunutze machen; * *vi* **to ~ for** erklären.
accountability *n* Verantwortlichkeit *f.*
accountable *adj* verantwortlich.
accountancy *n* Buchhaltung *f.*
accountant *n* Buchhalter(in) *m(f),* Steuerberater(in) *m(f).*
account book *n* Kontobuch *n.*
account number *n* Kontonummer *f.*
accrue *vi* erwachsen, entstehen; anwachsen.
accumulate *vt* ansammeln; anhäufen; * *vi* anwachsen; sich anhäufen.
accumulation *n* Ansammlung *f;* Anhäufung *f.*
accuracy *n* Genauigkeit *f.*
accurate *adj* ~ly *adv* genau; richtig.
accursed *adj* verflucht.
accusation *n* Anschuldigung *f;* Vorwurf *m;* (*law*) Anklage *f.*
accusative *n* (*gr*) Akkusativ *m.*
accusatory *adj* anklagend.
accuse *vt* anklagen; beschuldigen.
accused *n* Angeklagte *m/f.*
accuser *n* Ankläger(in) *m(f).*
accustom *vt* gewöhnen.
accustomed *adj* gewohnt, üblich; gewöhnt.
ace *n* As *n;* **within an ~ of** um ein Haar.
acerbic *adj* scharf; verbittert.

acetate *n* (*chem*) Acetat *n*.

ache *n* Schmerz *m*; * *vi* schmerzen, weh tun; sich sehnen.

achieve *vt* leisten; erlangen; erreichen.

achievement *n* Leistung *f*; Ausführung *f*; Erreichung *f*.

acid *adj* sauer; scharf; (*fig*) bissig; * *n* Säure *f*; LSD *n*.

acidity *n* Säure *f*, Schärfe *f*; Säuregrad *m*.

acknowledge *vt* anerkennen; zugeben; bestätigen.

acknowledgment *n* Anerkennung *f*; Bestätigung *f*; Eingeständnis *n*.

acme *n* Gipfel *m*; Höhepunkt *m*.

acne *n* Akne *f*.

acorn *n* Eichel *f*.

acoustics *n* Akustik *f*.

acquaint *vt* bekannt machen, vertraut machen.

acquaintance *n* Bekanntschaft *f*; Bekannte(r) *f(m)*; Kenntnis *f*.

acquiesce *vi* einwilligen; sich fügen, dulden.

acquiescence *n* Einwilligung *f*; Duldung *f*.

acquiescent *adj* ergeben.

acquire *vt* erwerben, erlangen.

acquisition *n* Erwerb *m*, Anschaffung *f*; Errungenschaft *f*.

acquit *vt* freisprechen.

acquittal *n* Freispruch *m*.

acre *n* Acre *m* (=4047qm).

acrid *adj* scharf, beißend.

acrimonious *adj* bitter; erbittert; scharf; beißend.

acrimony *n* Bitterkeit *f*, Schärfe *f*.

across *adv* hinüber; querdurch; im Durchmesser; drüben; überkreuz; waagerecht; * *prep* über; (mitten) durch; auf der anderen Seite von; **to come ~** zufällig sehen; in den Sinn kommen.

act *vt* darstellen; spielen; * *vi* handeln; sich benehmen; (*Theater*) spielen; wirken; * *n* Tat *f*, Werk *n*; Maßnahme *f*; Akt *m*; Gesetz *n*; **~s of the apostles** Apostelgeschichte *f*.

acting *adj* wirkend; geschäftsführend; Bühnen-.

action *n* Handlung *f*; Funktion *f*; Mechanismus *m*; (Ein)Wirkung *f*; (*law*) Klage *f*; (*mil*) Gefecht *n*, Einsatz *m*.

action replay *n* (Zeitlupen)Wiederholung *f*.

activate *vt* aktivieren.

active *adj* **~ly** *adv* aktiv; lebhaft; wirksam.

activity *n* Aktivität *f*; Tätigkeit *f*.

actor *n* Schauspieler *m*.

actress *n* Schauspielerin *f*.

actual *adj* ; tatsächlich; effektiv; gegenwärtig; **~ly** *adv* tatsächlich; eigentlich; momentan.

actuary *n* Versicherungsstatistiker *m*.

acumen *n* Scharfsinn *m*.

acute *adj* **~ly** *adv* scharf; heftig; akut; scharfsinnig; **~ accent** *n* Accent *m* aigu; **~ angle** *n* spitzer Winkel *m*.

acuteness *n* Schärfe *f*; Scharfsinn *m*.

ad *n* Anzeige *f*.

adage *n* Sprichwort *n*.

adamant *adj* unnachgiebig.

adapt *vt* anpassen; umstellen; bearbeiten.

adaptability *n* Anpassungsfähigkeit *f*.

adaptable *adj* anpassungsfähig.

adaptation *n* Anpassung *f*; Bearbeitung *f*.

adaptor *n* Adapter *m*; Bearbeiter *m*.

add *vt* hinzufügen; **to ~ up** addieren.

addendum *n* Anhang *m*.

adder *n* Natter *f*; Viper *f*; Otter *f*.

addict *n* Süchtige(r) *f(m)*.

addiction *n* Sucht *f*.

addictive *adj* suchterzeugend.

addition *n* Zusatz *m*; Vermehrung *f*, Zuwachs *m*.

additional *adj*, **~ly** *adv* zusätzlich.

additive n Zusatz m.

address vt richten; ansprechen; adressieren; widmen; * n Anschrift f; Rede f.

adduce vt anführen, liefern.

adenoids npl Polypen mpl.

adept adj erfahren, geschickt.

adequacy n Angemessenheit f.

adequate adj ~ly adv angemessen; ausreichend.

adhere vi kleben, haften; festhalten an; angehören; verwachsen sein.

adherence n Kleben n; Haften n; Festhalten n.

adherent n Anhänger(in) m(f).

adhesion n Adhäsion f; Haftvermögen n.

adhesive adj haftend, klebend, Kleb(e)-.

adhesive tape n (med) Heftpflaster n.

adhesiveness n Klebrigkeit f; Haftvermögen n.

adieu adv lebe wohl; * n Lebewohl n.

adipose adj fettig, Fett-.

adjacent adj angrenzend; benachbart.

adjectival adj, ~ly adv adjektivisch.

adjective n Adjektiv n.

adjoin vi angrenzen an.

adjoining adj angrenzend, benachbart, Neben-.

adjourn vt verschieben, vertagen; verlegen.

adjournment n Vertagung f; Verschiebung f; Verlegung f.

adjudicate vt entscheiden; zuerkennen.

adjunct n Zusatz m; Mitarbeiter(in) m(f); Attribut n.

adjust vt anpassen; in Ordnung bringen; einstellen.

adjustable adj verstellbar.

adjustment n Anpassung, Einstellung f.

adjutant n (mil) Adjutant m.

ad lib vt improvisieren; * adv nach Belieben; aus dem Stegreif.

administer vt verwalten; ver-

abreichen; **to ~ an oath** einen Eid abnehmen.

administration n Verwaltung f; Verabreichung f.

administrative adj Verwaltungs-.

administrator n Verwaltungsbeamte(r) f(m).

admirable adj, ~bly adv bewundernswert, großartig.

admiral n Admiral m.

admiralship n Admiralswürde f.

admiralty n Admiralität f; Admiralswürde f.

admiration n Bewunderung f.

admire vt bewundern; verehren.

admirer n Bewunderer m; Verehrer(in) m(f).

admiring adj, ~ly adv bewundernd.

admissible adj zulässig; erlaubt.

admission n Eintritt m; Einlaß m; Eingeständnis n; Zulassung f.

admit vt einlassen; aufnehmen; zulassen; zugeben; **to ~ to** zugeben.

admittance n Zutritt m; Aufnahme f.

admittedly adj zugegebenermaßen.

admixture n Zusatz m.

admonish vt ermahnen; warnen.

admonition n Ermahnung f; Warnung f.

admonitory adj ermahnend, warnend.

ad nauseam adv bis zum Überdruß.

ado n Aufheben n.

adolescence n Jugendalter n.

adolescent n Jugendliche(r) f(m).

adopt vt adoptieren; annehmen.

adopted adj Adoptiv-; angenommen.

adoption n Adoption f; Annahme f.

adoptive *adj* Adoptiv-; ange-nommen.

adorable *adj*, **adorably** *adv* an-betungswürdig; entzückend.

adoration *n* Anbetung *f*.

adore *vt* anbeten; verehren.

adorn *vt* schmücken.

adornment *n* Schmuck *m*; Ver-zierung *f*.

adrift *adv* treibend.

adroit *adj* geschickt; gewandt.

adroitness *n* Geschicklichkeit *f*; Gewandtheit *f*.

adulation *n* Schmeichelei *f*.

adulatory *adj* schmeichlerisch.

adult *adj* erwachsen; * *n* Er-wachsene(r) *f*(*m*).

adulterate *vt* verfälschen; * *adj* verfälscht; ehebrecherisch.

adulteration *n* Verfälschung *f*.

adulterer *n* Ehebrecher *m*.

adulteress *n* Ehebrecherin *f*.

adulterous *adj* ehebrecherisch.

adultery *n* Ehebruch *m*.

advance *vt* vorrücken; vorbrin-gen; (be)fördern; vorstrecken; * *vi* vorrücken;* *n* Vorrücken *n*; Fortschritt *m*; Vorsprung *m*; Vorschuß *m*.

advanced *adj* fortgeschritten.

advancement *n* Fortschritt *m*; (Be)Förderung *f*.

advantage *n* Vorteil *m*; **to take ~ of** ausnutzen.

advantageous *adj*, **~ly** *adv* vorteilhaft.

advent *n* Kommen *n*; **Advent** *n* Advent *m*.

adventitious *adj* zufällig.

adventure *n* Abenteuer *n*.

adventurer *n* Abenteurer *m*.

adventurous *adj* **~ly** *adv* aben-teuerlich; verwegen; aben-teuerlustig.

adverb *n* Adverb *n*.

adverbial *adj*, **~ly** *adv* adver-bial.

adversary *n* Gegner(in) *m*(*f*).

adverse *adj* widrig; gegnerisch; nachteilig.

adversity *n* Unglück *n*.

advertise *vt* ankündigen; wer-ben für; * *vi* inserieren.

advertisement *n* Anzeige *f*.

advertising *n* Werbung *f*.

advice *n* Rat *m*; Nachricht *f*.

advisability *n* Ratsamkeit *f*.

advisable *adj* ratsam, empfeh-lenswert.

advise *vt* (be)raten; benachrich-tigen.

advisedly *adv* mit Bedacht, ab-sichtlich.

advisory *adj* beratend.

advocacy *n* Verteidigung *f*; Eintreten *n* (für).

advocate *n* Anwalt *m* Anwältin *f*; Verfechter(in) *m*(*f*); * *vt* ver-teidigen; befürworten.

aerate *vt* (be)lüften.

aerial *n* Antenne *f*; * *adj* luftig; Luft-.

aeroplane *n* Flugzeug *n*.

aerosol *n* Aerosol *n*; Sprühdose *f*.

aerostat *n* Luftfahrzeug *n*.

afar *adv* fern, weit (weg); **from ~** von weit her.

affability *n* Freundlichkeit *f*.

affable *adj*, **~bly** *adv* leutselig; freundlich.

affair *n* Angelegenheit *f*; Sache *f*; Affäre *f*.

affect *vt* betreffen; (ein)wirken auf; beeinflussen.

affectation *n* Affektiertheit *f*; Heuchelei *f*.

affected *adj* **~ly** *adv* betroffen; gerührt; befallen; affektiert; vorgetäuscht.

affectingly *adv* rührend.

affection *n* Liebe *f*; Zuneigung *f*; Gefühl *n*.

affectionate *adj* **~ly** *adv* liebe-voll, zärtlich, herzlich.

affidavit *n* beeidigte Erklärung *f*.

affiliate *vt* (*als Mitglied*) auf-nehmen; angliedern; zuschrei-ben.

affiliation *n* Aufnahme (*als Mitglied*) *f*; Zuschreibung *f*; Angliederung *f*; Mitgliedschaft *f*.

affinity *n* Verwandtschaft *f*; Verschwägerung *f*; Neigung *f*.

affirm *vt* versichern; bestätigen.

affirmation *n* Versicherung *f*; Bestätigung *f*; (*law*) eidesstattliche Erklärung *f*.

affirmative *adj*, **~ly** *adv* bejahend; positiv.

affix *vt* befestigen, anheften; hinzufügen; * *n* (*gr*) Affix *n*; Anhang *m*.

afflict *vt* betrüben; plagen; quälen.

affliction *n* Kummer *m*; Gebrechen *n*; Elend *n*.

affluence *n* Überfluß *f*; Wohlstand *m*.

affluent *adj* reich.

afflux *n* Zufluß *m*; Zustrom *m*.

afford *vt* sich leisten; aufbringen; gewähren.

affray *n* (*law*) Schlägerei *f*.

affront *n* Beleidigung *f*; * *vt* beleidigen; verletzen.

afire *adv* in Flammen.

aflame *adv* in Flammen; (*fig*) leuchtend.

afloat *adv* flott, schwimmend; in Umlauf; überschwemmt.

afraid *adj* **to be ~** Angst haben, sich fürchten; **I am ~** ich fürchte, leider.

afresh *adv* von neuem, von vorn.

aft *adv* (*mar*) achtern.

after *prep* hinterher; nach; * *adv* nachher; darauf; **~ all** schließlich.

afterbirth *n* Nachgeburt *f*.

after-crop *n* Nachernte *f*.

after-effects *npl* Nachwirkung *f*.

afterlife *n* Leben *n* nach dem Tode.

aftermath *n* Folgen *fpl*.

afternoon *n* Nachmittag *m*.

afterpains *npl* Nachwehen *fpl*.

aftershave *n* Rasierwasser *n*.

aftertaste *n* Nachgeschmack *m*.

afterward *adv* später, hinterher.

again *adv* wieder; außerdem; **~ and ~** immer wieder; **as much ~** noch einmal soviel.

against *prep* gegen; **~ the grain** gegen den Strich.

agate *n* Achat *m*.

age *n* Alter *n*; Zeit *f*; **under ~** minderjährig; * *vi* altern.

aged *adj* alt, betagt; -jährig.

agency *n* Agentur *f*; Tätigkeit *f*.

agenda *n* Tagesordnung *f*.

agent *n* Agent(in) *m(f)*; Mittel *n*; Urheber(in) *m(f)*.

agglomerate *vt* anhäufen.

agglomeration *n* Anhäufung *f*.

aggrandizement *n* Vergrößerung *f*; Aufstieg *m*.

aggravate *vt* erschweren, verschlimmern; verärgern.

aggravation *n* Erschwerung *f*; Verschlimmerung *f*; Ärger *m*.

aggregate *n* Anhäufung *f*.

aggregation *n* Anhäufung *f*.

aggression *n* Agression *f*; Angriff *m*.

aggressive *adj* aggressiv.

aggressor *n* Angreifer *m*.

aggrieved *adj* betrübt; gekränkt.

aghast *adj* entsetzt.

agile *adj* beweglich, flink.

agility *n* Beweglichkeit *f*; Behendigkeit *f*.

agitate *vt* schütteln; aufregen; aufwiegeln.

agitation *n* Bewegung *f*; Aufregung *f*.

agitator *n* Agitator *m*.

ago *adv* vor; **how long ~?** wie lange... her? wann?

agog *adj* gespannt.

agonizing *adj* qualvoll.

agony *n* (Höllen)Qual(en) *f(pl)*; (Todes)Kampf *m*.

agrarian *adj* landwirtschaftlich, Agrar-.

agree *vt* zugeben; bereit sein; vereinbaren; * *vi* zustimmen; sich einigen; bekommen.

agreeable *adj*, **~bly** *adv* angenehm; nett; **~ with** einverstanden sein.

agreeableness *n* Liebenswürdigkeit *f*; Bereitschaft *f*.

agreed *adj* einig; **~!** *adv* einverstanden!

agreement *n* Vereinbarung *f*, Abkommen *n*; Übereinstimmung *f*.

agricultural *adj* landwirtschaftlich, Agrar-.

agriculture *n* Landwirtschaft *f*.

agriculturist *n* Landwirt(in) *m(f)*.

aground *adv* (*mar*) gestrandet.

ah! *excl* ah! ach!

ahead *adv* vorn; voraus.

ahoy! *excl* (*mar*) ahoi!

aid *vt* helfen; fördern; **to ~ and abet** Beihilfe leisten; * *n* Hilfe *f*; Beistand *m*; Helfer(in) *m(f)*.

aide-de-camp *n* (*mil*) Adjutant *m*.

AIDS *n* AIDS *n*.

ail *vt* schmerzen; *vi* kränkeln.

ailing *adj* kränkelnd.

ailment *n* Krankheit *f*; Leiden *n*.

aim *vt* zielen; richten; * *vi* zielen; beabsichtigen; * *n* Ziel *n*; Absicht *f*.

aimless *adj* **~ly** ziellos.

air *n* Luft *f*; Brise *f*; Miene *f*;* *vt* lüften; äußern.

airborne *adj* in der Luft.

air-conditioned *adj* klimatisiert.

air-conditioning *n* Klimaanlage *f*.

aircraft *n* Flugzeug *n*; Luftfahrzeug *n*.

air cushion *n* Luftkissen *n*.

air force *n* Luftwaffe *f*.

air freshener *n* Raumspray *n*.

air gun *n* Luftgewehr *n*.

air hole *n* Luftloch *n*.

airiness *n* Luftigkeit *f*; Leichtigkeit *f*.

airless *adj* luftlos; stickig.

airlift *n* Luftbrücke *f*.

airline *n* Fluggesellschaft *f*; Luftschlauch *m*.

airmail *n*: **by ~** per Luftpost *f*

airplane *n* Flugzeug *n*.

airport *n* Flughafen *m*.

air pump *n* Luftpumpe *f*.

airsick *adj* luftkrank.

airstrip *n* Start- und Landebahn *f*.

air terminal *n* Flughafenabfertigungsgebäude *f*.

airtight *adj* luftdicht.

airy *adj* luftig; phantastisch.

aisle *n* Gang *m*; Seitenschiff *n*.

ajar *adj* angelehnt.

akimbo *adj* in die Seite gestemmt (*Arme*).

akin *adj* verwandt; ähnlich.

alabaster *n* Alabaster *m*; * *adj* alabastern.

alacrity *n* Munterkeit *f*; Bereitwilligkeit *f*.

alarm *n* Alarm *m*; Wecker *m*; Alarmanlage *f*; Besorgnis *f*; * *vt* alarmieren; beunruhigen.

alarm bell *n* Alarmglocke *f*.

alarmist *n* Panikmacher(in) *m(f)*.

alas *adv* o weh! leider!

albeit *conj* obwohl, wenn auch.

album *n* Album *n*; Langspielplatte *f*; Sammlung *f*.

alchemist *n* Alchimist *m*.

alchemy *n* Alchimie *f*.

alcohol *n* Alkohol *m*.

alcoholic *adj* alkoholisch; Alkohol-; * *n* Alkoholiker(in) *m(f)*.

alcove *n* Alkoven *m*; Nische *f*.

alder *n* Erle *f*.

ale *n* Ale *n* (*Bier*).

alert *adj* wachsam; munter; aufgeweckt; * *n* Alarmbereitschaft *f*; Alarm *m*.

alertness *n* Wachsamkeit *f*; Munterkeit *f*; Aufgewecktheit *f*.

algae *npl* Alge *f*.

algebra *n* Algebra *f*.

algebraic *adj* algebraisch.

alias *adj* alias.

alibi *n* (*law*) Alibi *n*.

alien *adj* fremd; ausländisch; außerirdisch; * *n* Ausländer(in) *m(f)*; außerirdisches Wesen *n*.

alienate *vt* entfremden; veräußern.

alienation *n* Entfremdung *f*; Veräußerung *f*.

alight *vi* ab-, aussteigen;

landen; * *adj* in Flammen; erleuchtet.

align *vt* (aus)richten; anschließen.

alike *adj adv* gleich; ähnlich.

alimentation *n* Ernährung *f*; Unterhalt *m*.

alimony *n* Unterhalt *m*.

alive *adj* lebendig; am Leben; lebhaft; wimmelnd; stromführend.

alkali *n* Alkali *n*.

alkaline *adj* alkalisch, basisch.

all *adj* all, ganz; jede(r, -s); völlig; * *adv* ganz, völlig; ~ **at once**, ~ **of a sudden** plötzlich; ~ **the same** trotzdem; ~ **the better** umso besser; **not at ~!** überhaupt nicht; **once and for ~** ein für allemal; * *n* Alles *n*.

allay *vt* beruhigen, beschwichtigen; mildern.

all clear *n* Entwarnung *f*; grünes Licht *n*.

allegation *n* Behauptung *f*; Aussage *f*.

allege *vt* behaupten; angeben.

allegiance *n* Treue *f*; Loyalität *f*.

allegorical *adj* ~**ly** *adv* allegorisch, (sinn)bildlich.

allegory *n* Allegorie *f*.

allegro *n* (*mus*) Allegro *n*.

allergy *n* Allrgie *f*.

alleviate *vt* vermindern, lindern.

alleviation *n* Linderung *f*; Milderung *f*.

alley *n* Gasse *f*; Bahn *f*.

alliance *n* Bund *m*; Bündnis *n*; Verwandtschaft *f*.

allied *adj* verbündet; verwandt.

alligator *n* Alligator *m*.

allitteration *n* Stabreim *m*.

all-night *adj* die ganze Nacht (geöffnet).

allocate *vt* verteilen; zuweisen.

allocation *n* Verteilung *f*; Zuweisung *f*.

allot *vt* zuteilen; zuschreiben; auslosen.

allow *vt* erlauben; bewilligen;

zugeben, anerkennen; lassen; **to ~ for** nachlassen, vergüten.

allowable *adj* erlaubt, zulässig.

allowance *n* Erlaubnis *f*; Zuschuß *m*; Taschengeld *n*; Vergütung *f*; Nachlaß *m*; Abschreibung *f*; Nachsicht *f*.

alloy *n* Legierung *f*; (Bei)Mischung *f*.

all-right *adv* schon gut, in Ordnung.

all-round *adj* vielseitig; Gesamt-.

allspice *n* Piment *m*.

allude *vt* anspielen.

allure *vt vi* verlocken; anziehen.

allurement *n* (Ver)Lockung *f*; Anziehungskraft *f*.

alluring *adj*, ~**ly** *adv* (ver)lockend; verführerisch.

allusion *n* Anspielung *f*.

allusive *adj*, ~**ly** *adv* anspielend.

alluvial *adj* alluvial, angeschwemmt.

ally *n* Verbündete(r) *f*(*m*); * *vi* sich verbünden.

almanac *n* Almanach *m*.

almighty *adj* (all)mächtig; riesig.

almond *n* Mandel *f*.

almond milk *n* Mandelmilch *f*.

almond tree *n* Mandelbaum *m*.

almost *adv* fast, beinahe.

alms *n* Almosen *n*.

aloft *prep* (hoch) oben; empor.

alone *adj adv* allein; **to leave ~** in Ruhe lassen.

along *prep* entlang; * *adv* vorwärts, weiter; mit; ~ **side** Seite an Seite.

aloof *adv*, *adj* fern, abseits; zurückhaltend.

aloud *adj* laut.

alphabet *n* Alphabet *n*; ABC *n*.

alphabetical *adj*, ~**ly** *adv* alphabetisch.

alpine *adj* alpin, Gebirgs-.

already *adv* schon, bereits.

also *adv* auch, außerdem.

altar *n* Altar *m*.

altarpiece *n* Altarbild *n*.

alter *vt* (ver)ändern.

alteration n Änderung f; Umbau m.

altercation n Streit m.

alternate vt abwechseln (lassen); * adj, ~ly adv abwechselnd.

alternating adj abwechselnd, Wechsel-.

alternation n Abwechslung f; Wechsel m.

alternative n Alternative f, Wahl f; * adj alternativ, wahlweise; ander(er, e, es); ~ly adv im anderen Falle, wahlweise.

alternator n Wechselstromgenerator m.

although conj obwohl, wenn auch.

altitude n Höhe f.

altogether adv insgesamt; ganz.

alum n Alaun m.

aluminium n Aluminium n.

aluminous adj alaunhaltig; aluminiumhaltig.

always adv immer, jederzeit.

a.m. adv vormittags.

amalgam n Amalgam n; Mischung f.

amalgamate vt vi (sich) vereinigen; zusammenschließen; amalgamieren.

amalgamation n Vereinigung f; Fusion f.

amanuensis n Sekretär(in) m(f).

amaryllis n (bot) Amaryllis f.

amass vt anhäufen.

amateur n Amateur m; Liebhaber(in) m(f); Dilettant(in) m(f).

amateurish adj dilettantisch.

amatory adj sinnlich, erotisch, Liebes-.

amaze vt überraschen, in Staunen versetzen.

amazement n Staunen n; Überraschung f.

amazing adj ~ly adv erstaunlich; unglaublich.

amazon n Amazone f.

ambassador n Botschafter m; Gesandte(r) f(m).

ambassadress n Botschafterin f; Gattin eines Botschafters f.

amber n Bernstein m; Gelb n; * adj Bernstein-; bernsteinfarben; gelb.

ambidextrous adj beidhändig.

ambient adj umgebend, Umgebungs-.

ambiguity n Zwei-, Vieldeutigkeit f.

ambiguous adj ~ly adv zwei-, vieldeutig, unklar; ungewiß.

ambition n Ehrgeiz m; Ziel n.

ambitious adj ~ly adv ehrgeizig; anspruchsvoll.

amble vi schlendern.

ambulance n Krankenwagen m.

ambush n (überfall aus dem) Hinterhalt m; **to lie in ~** auflauern; * vt aus dem Hinterhalt überfallen.

ameliorate vt verbessern.

amelioration n Verbesserung f.

amenable adj zugänglich; gefügig; verantwortlich.

amend vt verbessern; abändern, ergänzen.

amendable adj verbesserungsfähig.

amendment n (Ver)Besserung f; Ergänzung f; Änderungsantrag m.

amends npl (Schaden)Ersatz m; Wiedergutmachung f.

amenities npl Annehmlichkeiten fpl; Vorzüge mpl.

America n Amerika n.

American adj amerikanisch.

amethyst n Amethyst m.

amiability n Liebenswürdigkeit f.

amiable adj liebenswürdig; angenehm.

amiably adv liebenswürdig; angenehm.

amicable adj ~bly adv freundschaftlich, gütlich.

amid(st) prep inmitten, unter.

amiss adv verkehrt, übel; **something's ~** etwas stimmt nicht.

ammonia n Ammoniak m.

ammunition n Munition f.

amnesia n Gedächtnisverlust m.

amnesty n Amnestie f.

among(st) prep unter, inmitten.

amoral adj amoralisch.

amorous adj ~ly adv verliebt, Liebes-, erotisch, sinnlich.

amorphous adj amorph; formlos.

amount n Betrag m; Menge f; * vi betragen; hinauslaufen auf, bedeuten.

amp(ere) n Ampere n.

amphibian n Amphibie f.

amphibious adj amphibisch, Amphibien-.

amphitheatre n Amphitheater n.

ample adj weit, groß, geräumig; reichlich, genügend.

ampleness n Weite f; Geräumigkeit f; Fülle f.

amplification n Erweiterung f; Verstärkung f.

amplifier n Verstärker m.

amplify vt erweitern, verstärken.

amplitude n Größe f; Fülle f; Amplitude f.

amply adv weit, groß, geräumig; reichlich, genügend.

amputate vt amputieren.

amputation n Amputation f.

amulet n Amulett n.

amuse vt amüsieren, unterhalten.

amusement n Unterhaltung f, Vergnügen n, Zeitvertreib m.

amusing adj ~ly adv amüsant.

an art ein, eine; per, pro, je.

anachronism n Anachronismus m.

analog adj (comput) Analog-.

analogous adj analog, entsprechend.

analogy n Entsprechung f.

analysis n Analyse f; Untersuchung f; Auswertung f.

analyst n (Psycho)Analytiker(in) m(f).

analytical adj, ~ly adv analytisch.

analyse vt analysieren; untersuchen; auswerten.

anarchic adj anarchistisch.

anarchist n Anarchist(in) m(f).

anarchy n Anarchie f.

anatomical adj ~ly adv anatomisch.

anatomize vt sezieren.

anatomy n Anatomie f.

ancestor n: ~s pl Vorfahren mpl.

ancestral adj ererbt, Stamm-.

ancestry n Abstammung f; Vorfahren mpl.

anchor n Anker m; * vi ankern.

anchorage n Ankerplatz m; Verankerung f.

anchovy n Sardelle f.

ancient adj ~ly adv (ur)alt.

ancillary adj untergeordnet; Neben-.

and conj und.

anecdotal adj anekdotenhaft.

anecdote n Anekdote f.

anemia n Anämie f.

anemic adj (med) anämisch.

anemone n (bot) Anemone f

anesthetic n Betäubungsmittel n.

anew adv von neuem.

angel n Engel m.

angelic adj engelhaft.

anger n Ärger m; Wut f; * vt verärgern, erzürnen.

angle n Winkel m; Ecke f; Gesichtspunkt m; * vt (ab)biegen; angeln.

angled adj winkelförmig.

angler n Angler(in) m(f).

anglicism n Anglizismus m; englische Eigenart f.

angling n Angeln n.

angrily adv verärgert; stürmisch.

angry adj verärgert; stürmisch.

anguish n Qual f; Schmerz m.

angular adj Winkel-; eckig; knochig.

angularity n Winkligkeit f; Steifheit f.

animal n Tier n.

animate vt beleben, aufmuntern; * adj lebendig, lebhaft.

animated *adj* lebendig, lebhaft.
animation *n* Lebhaftigkeit *f*; Belebung *f*; Zeichentrickfilm *m*.
animosity *n* Feindseligkeit *f*.
animus *n* Animus *m*.
anise *n* Anis *m*.
aniseed *n* Anissamen *m*.
ankle *n* (Fuß)Knöchel *m*; Fessel *f*; ~ **bone** Sprungbein *n*.
annals *n* Annalen *pl*.
annex *vt* beifügen, anhängen; annektieren; * *n* Anhang *m*; Anlage *f*.
annexation *n* Anfügung *f*; Annexion *f*.
annihilate *vt* vernichten.
annihilation *n* Vernichtung *f*.
anniversary *n* Jahrestag *m*; Jubiläum *n*.
annotate *vi* mit Anmerkungen versehen.
annotation *n* Anmerkung *f*.
announce *vt* ankündigen; bekanntgeben.
announcement *n* Ankündigung *f*; Ansage *f*.
announcer *n* Ansager(in) *m(f)*.
annoy *vt* ärgern; belästigen.
annoyance *n* Ärgernis *n*; Belästigung *f*.
annoying *adj* ärgerlich; lästig.
annual *adj* ~**ly** *adv* jährlich, Jahres-.
annuity *n* Rente *f*; Jahreszahlung *f*.
annul *vt* annullieren.
annulment *n* Annullierung *f*; Aufhebung *f*.
annunciation *n* Ankündigung *f*.
anodyne *adj* schmerzstillend.
anoint *vt* salben; einreiben.
anomalous *adj* abnorm; ungewöhnlich.
anomaly *n* Anomalie *f*; Abweichung *f*.
anon *adv* bald; sogleich.
anonymity *n* Anonymität *f*.
anonymous *adj* ~**ly** *adj* anonym.
anorexia *n* Magersucht *f*.
another *adj* ein anderer; noch

ein(er, e, es); **one** ~ einander.
answer *vt* (be)antworten; verantworten; entsprechen; **to** ~ **for** verantwortlich sein; **to** ~ **to** hören auf; * *n* Antwort *f*; Lösung *f*.
answerable *adj* verantwortlich.
answering machine *n* Anrufbeantworter *m*.
ant *n* Ameise *f*.
antagonism *n* Widerstand *m*; Feindschaft *f*; Wechselwirkung *f*.
antagonist *n* Gegner(in) *m(f)*.
antagonize *vt* bekämpfen; zum Feind machen.
antarctic *adj* antarktisch.
anteater *n* Ameisenbär *m*.
antecedent *n*: ~**s** *pl* Vorleben.
antechamber *n* Vorzimmer *n*.
antedate *vt* vorausgehen; (zu)rückdatieren.
antelope *n* Antilope *f*.
antenna *npl* Antenne *f*; Fühler *m*.
anterior *adj* vorder; früher.
anthem *n* Hymne *f*.
ant-hill *n* Ameisenhaufen *m*.
anthology *n* Anthologie *f*; (Gedicht)Sammlung *f*.
anthracite *n* Anthrazit *m*.
anthropology *n* Anthropologie *f*
anti-aircraft *adj* Fliegerabwehr-, Flak-.
antibiotic *n* Antibiotikum *n*.
antibody *n* Antikörper *m*.
Antichrist *n* Antichrist *m*.
anticipate *vt* voraussehen; erwarten; vorwegnehmen; zuvorkommen.
anticipation *n* (Vor)Ahnung *f*; Voraussicht *f*; Vorfreude *f*; Erwartung *f*; Vorwegnahme *f*; Zuvorkommen *n*.
anticlockwise *adv* gegen den Uhrzeigersinn.
antidote *n* Gegengift, Gegenmittel *n*.
antifreeze *n* Frostschutzmittel *n*.
antimony *n* Antimon *n*.

antipathy n Abneigung f.

antipodes npl Antipoden pl.

antiquarian n Altertumsforscher(in) m(f); Antiquitätenhändler(in) m(f).

antiquated adj veraltet.

antique n Antiquität f; adj antik.

antiquity n Altertum n; Antike f.

antiseptic adj antisseptisch.

antisocial adj asozial; ungesellig.

antithesis n Antithese f; Gegensatz m.

antler n Geweih n.

anvil n Amboß m.

anxiety n Angst f; Beklemmung f.

anxious adj ~ly adv ängstlich, besorgt; gespannt.

any adj pn (irgend)eine(r); (irgend)welche; jeder, jede, jedes; ~body irgend jemand; jeder(mann); ~how irgendwie; trotzdem; wie dem auch sei; ~more mehr; ~place irgendwo; überall; ~thing etwas; alles.

apace adv schnell, rasch.

apart adv für sich; getrennt.

apartment n Zimmer n; Wohnung f.

apartment house n Wohnhaus n.

apathetic adj teilnahmslos.

apathy n Teilnahmslosigkeit f.

ape n (Menschen)Affe m; * vt nachäffen.

aperture n Öffnung f; Blende f.

apex n Spitze f; Gipfel m.

aphorism n Aphorismus m.

apiary n Bienenhaus n.

apiece adv pro Stück; pro Person; je.

aplomb n selbstsicheres Auftreten n.

Apocalypse n Apokalypse f.

apocrypha npl Apokryphen pl.

apocryphal adj apokryphisch; zweifelhaft.

apologetic adj rechtfertigend;

entschuldigend; reumütig.

apologist n Verteidiger m.

apologize vt sich entschuldigen; sich rechtfertigen.

apology n Entschuldigung f; Rechtfertigung f.

apoplexy n Schlaganfall m.

apostle n Apostel m.

apostolic adj apostolisch.

apostrophe n Apostroph m.

apotheosis n Vergötterung f.

appall vt erschrecken, entsetzen.

appalling adj entsetzlich.

apparatus n Apparat m.

apparel n Kleidung f.

apparent adj, ~ly adv offensichtlich; scheinbar.

apparition n Erscheinung f, Gespenst n.

appeal vi Berufung einlegen; sich berufen; appellieren; gefallen; * n (law) Berufung f; Appell m; Anziehungskraft f.

appealing adj flehend; ansprechend.

appear vi (er)scheinen.

appearance n Erscheinen n; Auftreten n; Erscheinung f; Anschein m.

appease vt beschwichtigen; stillen.

appellant n (law) Berufungskläger(in) m(f).

append vt anhängen; beifügen.

appendage n Anhängsel n.

appendicitis n Blinddarmentzündung f.

appendix n Blinddarm m.

appertain vi gehören; zustehen.

appetite n Appetit m.

appetizing adj appetitlich, lekker.

applaud vi applaudieren; begrüßen.

applause n Beifall m.

apple n Apfel m.

apple pie n gedeckter Apfelkuchen; **in ~ order** in bester Ordnung.

apple tree n Apfelbaum m.

appliance n Gerät n.

applicability *n* Anwendbarkeit *f*.

applicable *adj* anwendbar.

applicant *n* Bewerber(in) *m(f)*; Antragssteller(in) m(f).

application *n* Anwendung *f*; Antrag *m*; Bewerbung *f*.

applied *adj* angewandt.

apply *vt* anwenden; auftragen; widmen; * *vi* zutreffen; sich anwenden lassen; sich wenden; beantragen; sich bewerben.

appoint *vt* ernennen; bestimmen; ausstatten.

appointee *n* Ernannte(r) *f(m)*.

appointment *n* Ernennung *f*; Bestimmung *f*; Verabredung *f*.

apportion *vt* zuteilen.

apportionment *n* Zuteilung *f*.

apposite *adj* passend.

apposition *n* Beifügung *f*.

appraisal *n* Schätzung *f*; Beurteilung *f*.

appraise *vt* schätzen; beurteilen.

appreciable *adj* merklich.

appreciably *adv* merklich.

appreciate *vt* (ein)schätzen; zu schätzen wissen; einsehen.

appreciation *n* (Ein)Schätzung *f*; Anerkennung *f*; Verständnis *n*.

appreciative *adj* anerkennend; verständnisvoll; dankbar.

apprehend *vt* festnehmen; (be)fürchten.

apprehension *n* Festnahme *f*; Auffassungsvermögen *n*; Befürchtung *f*.

apprehensive *adj* besorgt; schnell begreifend.

apprentice *n* Lehrling *m*; * *vt* in die Lehre geben.

apprenticeship *n* Lehre *f*.

apprise *vt* benachrichtigen.

approach *vt vi* sich nähern; nahekommen; sich wenden an; herangehen an; * *n* Nahen *n*; Annäherung *f*; Methode *f*.

approachable *adj* zugänglich.

approbation *n* Genehmigung *f*; Beifall *m*.

appropriate *vt* verwenden; sich aneignen; * *adj* passend, angemessen.

approval *n* Billigung *f*; Beifall *m*.

approve (of) *vt* billigen; gutheißen.

approximate *vi* sich nähern; * *adj* **~ly** *adv* annähernd.

approximation *n* Annäherung *f*.

apricot *n* Aprikose *f*.

April *n* April *m*.

apron *n* Schürze *f*; Schurz *m*.

apse *n* Apsis *f*.

apt *adj* **~ly** *adv* passend; geneigt; geschickt.

aptitude *n* Neigung *f*; Talent *n*.

aqualung *n* (Unterwasser)Atmungsgerät *n*.

aquarium *n* Aquarium *n*.

Aquarius *n* Wassermann *m*.

aquatic *adj* Wasser-.

aqueduct *n* Aquädukt *m*.

aquiline *adj* Adler-.

arabesque *n* Arabeske *f*.

arable *adj* pflügbar, Acker-.

arbiter *n* Schiedsrichter *m*; Gebieter *m*.

arbitrariness *n* Willkür *f*; Eigenmächtigkeit *f*.

arbitrary *adj* willkürlich; eigenmächtig.

arbitrate *vt* entscheiden, schlichten.

arbitration *n* Schlichtung *f*.

arbitrator *n* Schiedsrichter *m*.

arbor *n* Laube *f*.

arcade *n* Arkade *f*; Passage *f*.

arch *n* Bogen *m*; * *vt vi* (sich)wölben.

arch *adj*, **archly** *adv* Haupt-, Erz-; schalkhaft; schlau.

archaeological *adj* archäologisch.

archaeology *n* Archäologie *f*.

archaic *adj* archaisch.

archangel *n* Erzengel *m*.

archbishop *n* Erzbischof *m*.

archbishopric *n* Erzbistum *n*.

archer *n* Bogenschütze *m*.

archery *n* Bogenschießen *n*.

architect *n* Architekt(in) *m(f)*.

architectural *adj* architektonisch.

architecture *n* Architektur *f*.

archives *npl* Archiv *n*.

archivist *n* Archivar(in) *m(f)*.

archway *n* Bogen(gang) *m*.

arctic *adj* arktisch; eisig.

ardent *adj* ~**ly** *adv* heiß; leidenschaftlich; eifrig.

ardour *n* Eifer *m*; Leidenschaft *f*; Glut *f*.

arduous *adj* schwierig; hart; zäh.

area *n* Fläche *f*; Gebiet *n*.

arena *n* Arena *f*; Schauplatz *m*.

arguably *adv* fraglich; wohl.

argue *vi* argumentieren; streiten; * *vt* erörtern; beweisen; behaupten; überreden.

argument *n* Auseinandersetzung *f*; Argument *n*; Debatte *f*.

argumentation *n* Beweisführung *f*.

argumentative *adj* streitlustig; hinweisend.

aria *n* (*mus*) Arie *f*.

arid *adj* dürr, trocken; unfruchtbar.

aridity *n* Dürre *f*; Trockenheit *f*; Unfruchtbarkeit *f*.

Aries *n* Widder *m*.

aright *adv* recht, richtig; **to set ~** richtigstellen.

arise *vi* entstehen; sich erheben.

aristocracy *n* Aristokratie *f*.

aristocrat *n* Aristokrat(in) *m(f)*.

aristocratic *adj*, ~**ally** *adv* aristokratisch; adlig.

arithmetic *n* Rechnen *n*.

arithmetical *adj* ~**ly** *adv* arithmetisch.

ark *n* Arche *f*.

arm *n* Arm *m*; Armlehne *f*; Waffe *f*; * *vt* (*vi*) sich (be)waffnen.

armament *n* Streitmacht *f*; Bewaffnung *f*; Rüstung *f*.

armchair *n* Sessel *m*.

armed *adj* bewaffnet.

armful *n* Armvoll *m*.

armhole *n* Ärmelloch *n*.

armistice *n* Waffenstillstand *m*.

armour *n* Rüstung *f*; Panzer *m*.

armoured car *n* gepanzertes Fahrzeug *n*.

armoury *n* Waffenkammer *f*; Waffenfabrik *f*.

armpit *n* Achselhöhle *f*.

armrest *n* Armlehne *f*.

army *n* Armee *f*; Heer *n*; Militär *n*.

aroma *n* Duft *m*.

aromatic *adj* aromatisch.

around *prep* um...herum; etwa; * *adv* (rund)herum.

arouse *vt* (auf)wecken; erregen.

arraign *vt* anklagen.

arraignment *n* (Vernehmung zur) Anklage *f*.

arrange *vt* arrangieren; (ein)richten; vereinbaren.

arrangement *n* Arrangement *n*; (An)Ordnung *f*; Vereinbarung *f*.

arrant *adj* völlig; ausgesprochen.

array *n* (Schlacht)Ordnung *f*; Aufgebot *n*; Kleidung *f*.

arrears *npl* Rückstand *m*.

arrest *n* Festnahme *f*; Aufhalten *n*; * *vt* aufhalten; festnehmen.

arrival *n* Ankunft *f*; Ankömmling *m*.

arrive *vi* (an)kommen.

arrogance *n* Überheblichkeit *f*.

arrogant *adj*, ~**ly** *adv* überheblich.

arrogate *vt* anmaßen; in Anspruch nehmen.

arrogation *n* Anmaßung *f*.

arrow *n* Pfeil *m*.

arsenal *n* (*mil*) Arsenal *n*.

arsenic *n* Arsen *n*.

arson *n* Brandstiftung *f*.

art *n* Kunst *f*; Verschlagenheit *f*.

arterial *adj* Schlagader-.

artery *n* Schlagader *f*.

artesian well *n* artesischer Brunnen *m*.

artful *adj* verschlagen; gewandt.

artfulness n Verschlagenheit f; Gewandtheit f.

art gallery n Kunstgalerie f.

arthritis n Arthritis f.

artichoke n Artischocke f.

article n Artikel m.

articulate vt artikulieren.

articulated adj gegliedert; artikuliert.

articulation n Aussprache f.

artifice n Kunstgriff m.

artificial adj ~ly adv künstlich, Kunst-.

artificiality n Künstlichkeit f.

artillery n Artillerie f.

artisan n (Kunst)Handwerker(in) m(f).

artist n Künstler(in) m(f).

artistic adj Kunst-, künstlerisch.

artistry n Kunstfertigkeit f.

artless adj ~ly adv arglos; ungekünstelt; stümperhaft.

artlessness n Arglosigkeit f; Einfachheit f; Kunstlosigkeit f.

art school n Kunstakademie f.

as conj (so) wie; als; obwohl; weil; daß; ~ for, ~ to was... betrifft.

asbestos n Asbest m.

ascend vi (auf)steigen; reichen.

ascendancy n Überlegenheit f; Herrschaft f.

ascension n Besteigung f; Himmelfahrt f.

ascent n Aufstieg m; Besteigung f; Steigung f.

ascertain vt feststellen; sich vergewissern.

ascetic adj asketisch; * n Asket(in) m(f).

ascribe vt zuschreiben.

ash n (bot) Esche f

ashcan n Mülleimer m.

ashamed adj beschämt.

ashore adv am Land, ans Land; **to go** ~ an Land gehen.

ashtray n Aschenbecher m.

Ash Wednesday n Aschermittwoch m.

aside adv beiseite; abgesehen.

ask vt fragen; bitten; verlangen; **to** ~ **after** sich erkundigen nach; **to** ~ **for** bitten um; **to** ~ **out** einladen.

askance adv von der Seite; schief.

askew adv schief.

asleep adj schlafend; **to fall** ~ einschlafen.

asparagus n Spargel m.

aspect n Aspekt m; Aussehen n; Hinsicht f; Lage f; Seite f; Ansicht f.

aspen n Espe f.

aspersion n Verleumdung f.

asphalt n Asphalt m.

asphyxia n (med) Erstickung f.

asphyxiate vt ersticken.

asphyxiation n Erstickung f.

aspirant n Aspirant(in) m(f); Bewerber(in) m(f).

aspirate vt aspirieren; * n Hauchlaut m.

aspiration n Atmen n; Streben n; ~s pl Ambitionen fpl; Aspiration f.

aspire vi streben; aufsteigen.

aspirin n Aspirin n.

ass n Esel m; **she** ~ Eselin f.

assail vt angreifen; bestürmen.

assailant n Angreifer(in) m(f).

assassin n Attentäter(in) m(f).

assassinate vt ermorden.

assassination n Attentat.

assault n Angriff m; * vt angreifen.

assemblage n Versammlung f; Ansammlung f.

assemble vt versammeln; zusammenstellen; zusammenbauen; * vi sich versammeln.

assembly n Versammlung f; Montage f.

assembly line n Fließband n.

assent n Zustimmung f; * vi zustimmen.

assert vt behaupten; durchsetzen.

assertion n Behauptung f.

assertive adj bestimmt; positiv.

assess vt festsetzen; (ab)schätzen; besteuern.

assessment n Veranlagung f; (Ab)Schätzung f; Beurteilung f.

assessor *n* Steuereinschätzer(in) *m*(*f*); Sachverständige(r) *f*(*m*).

asset *n* Vorzug *m; * Gewinn *m;* Vermögenswert *m;* **~s** *pl* Vermögen *n*.

assiduous *adj,* **~ly** *adv* fleißig; beharrlich; aufmerksam.

assign *vt* zuweisen; bestimmen.

assignation *n* Zuweisung *f;* Bestimmung *f*.

assignment *n* Zuweisung *f;* Bestimmung *f;* Aufgabe *f*.

assimilate *vt* assimilieren; anpassen; aufnehmen.

assimilation *n* Assimilation *f;* Anpassung *f;* Aufnahme *f*.

assist *vt* helfen; unterstützen.

assistance *n* Hilfe *f;* Unterstützung *f*.

assistant *n* Assistent(in) *m*(*f*); Angestellte(r) *f*(*m*).

associate *vt* verbinden; anschließen; * *adj* verbunden; beigeordnet; Mit-; * *n* Partner *m;* Genosse *m*.

association *n* Vereinigung *f;* Verein *m;* Umgang *m;* Assoziation *f*.

assonance *n* Assonanz *f*.

assorted *adj* sortiert; gemischt.

assortment *n* Sortieren *n;* Auswahl *f*.

assuage *vt* lindern; besänftigen.

assume *vt* annehmen; voraussetzen; übernehmen; sich anmaßen.

assumption *n* Annahme *f;* Voraussetzung *f;* Anmaßung *f;* **Assumption** *n* Mariä Himmelfahrt *f*.

assurance *n* Zu-, Versicherung *f;* Selbstsicherheit *f*.

assure *vt* (ver)sichern; zusichern; beruhigen.

assuredly *adv* (selbst)sicher; gewiß.

asterisk *n* Sternchen *n*.

astern *adv* (*mar*) achtern.

asthma *n* Asthma *n*.

asthmatic *adj* asthmatisch.

astonish *vt* in Erstaunen setzen; verblüffen.

astonishing *adj* **~ly** *adv* erstaunlich.

astonishment *n* (Er)Staunen *n*.

astound *vt* verblüffen; überraschen.

astraddle *adv* rittlings; (quer) über.

astray *adv:* **to go ~** auf Abwege geraten; irregehen; **to lead ~** irreführen; verleiten.

astride *adv* rittlings; (quer) über.

astringent *adj* zusammenziehend.

astrologer *n* Astrologe *m*.

astrological *adj* astrologisch.

astrology *n* Astrologie *f*.

astronaut *n* Astronaut *m*.

astronomer *n* Astronom *m*.

astronomical *adj* astronomisch.

astronomy *n* Astronomie *f*.

astute *adj* scharfsinnig; schlau.

asylum *n* Asyl *n;* (Irren)Anstalt *f*.

at *prep* in; an; bei; zu; auf; nach; gegen; um; mit; für; über; unter; aus; **~ once** auf einmal; augenblicklich; **~ all** überhaupt; **~ all events** auf alle Fälle; **~ first** zuerst; **~ last** endlich.

atheism *n* Atheismus *m*.

atheist *n* Atheist *m*.

athlete *n* (Leicht)Athlet(in) *m*(*f*); Sportler(in) *m*(*f*).

athletic *adj* Sport-; sportlich; muskulös.

atlas *n* Atlas *m*.

atmosphere *n* Atmosphäre *f*.

atmospheric *adj* Luft-; Wetter-; stimmungsvoll.

atom *n* Atom *n*.

atom bomb *n* Atombombe *f*.

atomic *adj* Atom-.

atone *vt* büßen; sühnen.

atonement *n* Buße *f;* Sühne *f*.

atop *adv* oben.

atrocious *adj* **~ly** *adv* abscheulich; grauenhaft.

atrocity *n* Abscheulichkeit *f;* Greueltat *f*.

atrophy *n* (*med*) Atrophie *f*.

attach *vt* befestigen; beifügen; verbinden.

attaché *n* Attaché *m*.

attachment *n* Befestigung *f*; Anhängsel *n*; Zuneigung *f*; Zugehörigkeit *f*.

attack *vt* angreifen; in Angriff nehmen; * *n* Angriff *m*; Anfall *m*.

attacker *n* Angreifer(in) *m(f)*.

attain *vt* erreichen; erlangen.

attainable *adj* erreichbar.

attempt *vt* versuchen; in Angriff nehmen; * *n* Versuch *m*; Bemühung *f*; Anschlag *m*.

attend *vt vi* (be)achten; bedienen; pflegen; begleiten; teilnehmen an; anwesend sein; **to ~ to** sich kümmern um; erledigen; bedienen.

attendance *n* Dienst *m*; Bedienung *f*; Pflege *f*; Anwesenheit *f*; Teilnahme *f*; Begleitung *f*.

attendant *n* Begleiter(in) *m(f)*; Diener(in) *m(f)*; Wart *m*.

attention *n* Aufmerksamkeit *f*; Beachtung *f*.

attentive *adj* ~ly *adv* aufmerksam.

attenuate *vt* verdünnen; vermindern; schlank machen.

attest *vt* bezeugen; bescheinigen; beglaubigen.

attic *n* Dachgeschoß *n*; Mansarde *f*.

attire *n* Kleidung *f*.

attitude *n* Haltung *f*; (Ein)Stellung *f*.

attorney *n* Anwalt *m*; Bevollmächtigte(r) *f(m)*; Vollmacht *f*.

attract *vt* anziehen; gewinnen; erregen.

attraction *n* Anziehungskraft *f*; Attraktion *f*.

attractive *adj* anziehend; attraktiv.

attribute *vt* zuschreiben; zurückführen; * *n* Attribut *n*; Eigenschaft *f*.

attrition *n* Abnutzung *f*.

auburn *adj* kastanienbraun.

auction *n* Versteigerung *f*.

auctioneer *n* Auktionator *m*.

audacious *adj* ~ly *adv* kühn; dreist.

audacity *n* Kühnheit *f*; Dreistigkeit *f*.

audible *adj* ~ly *adv* hörbar; vernehmlich.

audience *n* Publikum *n*; Audienz *f*; Gehör *n*.

audit *n* Rechnungsprüfung *f*; Bilanz *f*; * *vt* prüfen.

auditor *n* Rechnungsprüfer *m*.

auditory *adj* (Ge)Hör-.

augment *vt* vermehren; vergrößern; * *vi* zunehmen.

augmentation *n* Vergrößerung *f*; Zunahme *f*.

August *n* August *m*.

august *adj* erhaben.

aunt *n* Tante *f*.

au pair *n* Au-pair-Mädchen *n*.

aura *n* Aura *f*.

auspices *npl* Schirmherrschaft *f*.

auspicious *adj*, ~ly *adv* günstig; glücklich.

austere *adj* ~ly *adv* streng; karg; hart.

austerity *n* Strenge *f*; Kargheit *f*.

authentic *adj* ~ly *adv* authentisch; echt.

authenticate *vt* beglaubigen; die Echtheit bescheinigen.

authenticity *n* Echtheit *f*; Glaubwürdigkeit *f*.

author *n* Urheber *m*; Verfasser *m*; Schriftsteller *m*.

authoress *n* Urheberin *f*; Verfasserin *f*; Schriftstellerin *f*.

authoritarian *adj* autoritär.

authoritative *adj* ~ly *adv* herrisch; maßgebend.

authority *n* Autorität *f*; Vollmacht *f*.

authorization *n* Bevollmächtigung *f*.

authorize *vt* ermächtigen; genehmigen.

authorship *n* Urheberschaft *f*.

auto *n* Auto *n*.

autocrat *n* Autokrat *m*.

autocratic *adj* unumschränkt.

autograph *n* Autogramm *n*.

automated *adj* vollautomatis-
iert.

automatic *adj* automatisch.

automaton *n* Roboter *m*.

autonomy *n* Autonomie *f*; Selbständigkeit *f*.

autopsy *n* Autopsie *f*.

autumn *n* Herbst *m*.

autumnal *adj* herbstlich.

auxiliary *adj* Hilfs-.

avail *vt*: to ~ **oneself of** sich zunutze machen; * *n*: **to no** ~
vergeblich.

available *adj* verfügbar; vorhanden.

avalanche *n* Lawine *f*.

avarice *n* Geiz *m*.

avaricious *adj* geizig.

avenge *vt* rächen.

avenue *n* Weg *m*; Allee *f*; Boule-
vard *m*.

aver *vt* behaupten; beweisen.

average *vt* durchschnittlich betragen, ~ haben, ~ schaffen,
etc; * *n* Durchschnitt *m*.

aversion *n* Abneigung *f*.

avert *vt* abwenden.

aviary *n* Vogelhaus *n*.

avoid *vt* (ver)meiden.

avoidable *adj* vermeidbar.

await *vt* erwarten.

awake *vt* wecken; * *vi* aufwachen; erwachen; * *adj*
wach; sich bewußt.

awakening *n* Erwachen *n*;
Wecken *n*.

award *vt* zusprechen; verleihen; * *n* Urteil *n*; Zuerken-
nung *f*; Auszeichnung *f*.

aware *adj* bewußt.

awareness *n* Bewußtsein *n*.

away *adv* weg; fort; entfernt;
abwesend; drauflos; ~! fort!
far and ~ bei weitem.

away game *n* Auswärtsspiel *n*.

awe *n* (Ehr)Furcht *f*.

awe-inspiring, awesome *adj*
ehrfurchtgebietend; furchteinflößend.

awful *adj*, **~ly** *adv* furchtbar;
schrecklich.

awhile *adv* eine Weile.

awkward *adj*, **~ly** *adv* unge-

schickt; unangenehm; un-
handlich.

awkwardness *n* Ungeschicklichkeit *f*; Unannehmlichkeit
f; Unhandlichkeit *f*.

awl *n* Ahle *f*.

awning *n* (*mar*) Sonnensegel *n*;
Plane *f*; Markise *f*.

awry *adv* schief.

ax *n* Axt *f*; * *vt* rücksichtslos
kürzen; abschaffen; entlassen.

axiom *n* Axiom *n*.

axis *n* Achse *f*.

axle *n* Achse *f*.

ay(e) *excl* ja.

B

baa *n* Blöken *n*; * *vi* blöken.

babble *vi* stammeln; plappern;
~, **babbling** *n* Gestammel *n*;
Geplapper *n*.

babbler *n* Schwätzer(in) *m(f)*.

babe, baby *n* Baby *n*; Säugling
m; kleines Kind *n*.

baboon *n* Pavian *m*.

babyhood *n* Säuglingsalter *n*.

babyish *adj* kindisch; kindlich.

baby carriage *n* Kinderwagen
m.

bachelor *n* Junggeselle *m*; Bak-
kalaureus *m*.

bachelorhood *n* Junggesellen-
stand *m*; Bakkalaureat *n*.

back *n* Rücken *m*; Rückseite *f*;
Rückenlehne *f*; * *adj* Hinter-;
Rück-; rückwärtig * *adv* zurück; **a few years** ~ vor einigen Jahren; * *vt* unterstützen;
decken; zurückbewegen;
setzen auf; hinten grenzen an.

backbite *vt* verleumden.

backbiter *n* Verleumder(in)
m(f).

backbone *n* Wirbelsäule *f*;
Rückgrat *n*.

backdate *vt* rückdatieren.

backdoor *n* Hintertür *f.*
backer *n* Unterstützer(in) *m(f)*; Hintermann *m.*
backgammon *n* Backgammon *n.*
background *n* Hintergrund *m.*
backlash *n* Rückschlag *m*; (heftige) Reaktion *f.*
backlog *n* Rückstand *m.*
back number *n* alte Nummer (*einer Zeitung*) *f.*
backpack *n* Rucksack *m.*
back payment *n* Nachzahlung *f.*
backside *n* Rückseite *f*; Hintern *m.*
back-up lights *npl* (*auto*) Rückfahrscheinwerfer *mpl.*
backward *adj* Rück(wärts)-; rückständig; zurückgeblieben; * *adv* rückwärts; zurück.
bacon *n* Speck *m.*
bad *adj* ~**ly** *adv* schlecht; böse; schlimm; unanständig; ungültig.
badge *n* Abzeichen *n.*
badger *n* Dachs *m*; * *vt* hetzen; zusetzen.
badminton *n* Federball *m.*
badness *n* Schlechtigkeit *f*; Verdorbenheit *f.*
baffle *vt* verblüffen; vereiteln.
bag *n* Tasche *f*; Sack *m*; Beutel *m*; Tüte *f.*
baggage *n* Gepäck *n.*
bagpipe *n* Dudelsack *m.*
bail *n* Kaution *f*; Bürge *m*; Bürgschaft *f*; * *vt* gegen Kaution freilassen; heraushelfen; ausschöpfen.
bailiff *n* Gerichtsvollzieher *m*; Gerichtsdiener *m*; (Guts)Verwalter *m.*
bait *vt* mit einem Köder versehen; ködern; hetzen; piesacken; * *n* Köder *m.*
baize *n* Boi *m.*
bake *vt* backen; braten; dörren; brennen.
bakery *n* Bäckerei *f.*
baker *n* Bäcker *m*; ~**s dozen** dreizehn.
baking *n* Backen *n.*

baking powder *n* Backpulver *n.*
balance *n* Waage *f*; Gleichgewicht *n*; Ausgleich *m*; Ausgewogenheit *f*; Kontostand *m*; **to lose one's** ~ das Gleichgewicht verlieren; * *vt* abwägen; balancieren; ausgleichen.
balance sheet *n* Bilanz *f.*
balcony *n* Balkon *m.*
bald *adj* kahl; dürftig.
baldness *n* Kahlheit *f*; Dürftigkeit *f.*
bale *n* Ballen *m*; * *vt* in Ballen verpacken; ausschöpfen.
baleful *adj* ~**ly** *adv* unheilvoll; verderblich; bösartig.
ball *n* Ball *m*; Kugel *f*; Ballen *m*; Knäuel *n*; Klumpen *m*; Kloß *m.*
ballad *n* Ballade *f.*
ballast *n* Ballast *m*; Schotter *m*; * *vt* mit Ballast beladen; beschottern.
ballerina *n* Ballerina *f.*
ballet *n* Ballett *n.*
ballistic *adj* ballistisch.
balloon *n* Ballon *m.*
ballot *n* (geheime) Wahl *f*; Abstimmung *f*; * *vi* (geheim) abstimmen, wählen; losen.
ballpoint (pen) *n* Kugelschreiber *m.*
ballroom *n* Ballsaal *m.*
balm, balsam *n* Balsam *m*; Melisse *f.*
balmy *adj* balsamisch; mild.
balustrade *n* Balustrade *f*; Geländer *n.*
bamboo *n* Bambus *m.*
bamboozle *vt* (*fam*) prellen; verwirren.
ban *n* Verbot *n*; Sperre *f*; Ächtung *f*; * *vt* verbieten; sperren.
banal *adj* banal; abgedroschen.
banana *n* Banane *f.*
band *n* Gruppe *f*; Bande *f*; Kapelle *f*; Band *f*; Band *n*; Ring *m*; Streifen *m.*
bandage *n* Bandage *f*, Verband *m*; * *vt* verbinden.
bandaid *n* Pflaster *n.*
bandit *n* Bandit *m*; Räuber *m.*

bandstand *n* Musikpavillion *m*.

bandy *vt* sich zuwerfen; sich erzählen; austauschen.

bandy-legged *adj* O-beinig.

bang *n* Knall *m*; * *vt* dröhnend (zu) schlagen; knallen; (an)stoßen.

bangle *n* Armreif *m*.

bangs *npl* Pony *m*.

banish *vt* verbannen; ausweisen.

banishment *n* Verbannung *f*; Ausweisung *f*.

banister(s) *n(pl)* Treppengeländer *n*.

banjo *n* Banjo *n*.

bank *n* Bank *f*; (Erd)Wall *m*; Damm *m*; Böschung *f*; Ufer *n*; * *vt* bei einer Bank einzahlen; eindämmen; **to ~ on** sich verlassen auf.

bank account *n* Bankkonto *n*.

bank card *n* Scheckkarte *f*.

banker *n* Bankier *m*.

banking *n* Bancwesen *n*; Bankgeschäft *n*.

banknote *n* Geldschein *m*.

bankrupt *adj* bankrott; * *n* Bankrotteur *m*; Zahlungsunfähige(r) *f(m)*.

bankruptcy *n* Bankrott *m*; Konkurs *m*.

bank statement *n* Kontoauszug *m*.

banner *n* Banner *n*; Standarte *f*; Transparent *n*.

banquet *n* Bankett *n*; Festessen *n*.

baptism *n* Taufe *f*.

baptismal *adj* Tauf-.

baptistry *n* Taufkapelle *f*; Taufbecken *n*.

baptize *vt* taufen.

bar *n* Stange *f*; Riegel *m*; Schranke *f*; Barren *m*; Hindernis *n*; Streifen *m*; Takt *m*; Bar *f*; (*law*) Gericht *n*; Anwaltschaft *f*; * *vt* verriegeln; versperren; (ver)hindern; verbieten; ausschließen.

barbarian *n* Barbar(in) *m(f)*; * *adj* barbarisch; grausam.

barbaric *adj* barbarisch; grausam.

barbarism *n* (*gr*) Sprachwidrigkeit *f*; Barbarei *f*.

barbarity *n* Barbarei *f*; Unmenschlichkeit *f*.

barbarous *adj* barbarisch; grausam.

barbecue *n* Grillfest *n*; Grill *m*.

barber *n* (Herren)Friseur *m*.

bar code *n* Strichcode *m*.

bard *n* Barde *m*.

bare *adj* bloß; nackt; kahl; * *vt* entblößen; enthüllen.

barefaced *adj* frech; schamlos.

barefoot(ed) *adj* barfuß.

bareheaded *adj* barhäuptig.

barelegged *adj* mit nackten Beinen.

barely *adv* kaum; knapp.

bareness *n* Blöße *f*; Dürftigkeit *f*.

bargain *n* Abmachung *f*; Geschäft *n*; Gelegenheitskauf *m*; Sonderangebot *n*; * *vi* (ver)handeln; feilschen; vereinbaren; **to ~ for** rechnen mit.

barge *n* Barkasse *f*; Hausboot *n*; Flußboot *n*; Lastkahn *m*.

baritone *n* (*mus*) Bariton *m*.

bark *n* Rinde *f*; Bellen *n*; * *vi* bellen.

barley *n* Gerste *f*.

barmaid *n* Bardame *f*.

barman *n* Barmann *m*.

barn *n* Scheune *f*; Stall *m*.

barnacle *n* Entenmuschel *f*.

barometer *n* Barometer *n*.

baron *n* Baron *m*.

baroness *n* Baroness *f*.

baronial *adj* Barons-; prunkvoll.

barracks *npl* Kaserne *f*.

barrage *n* (Stau)Damm *m*; Sperrfeuer *n*; (*fig*) Hagel *m*; Schwall *m*.

barrel *n* Faß *n*; Tonne *f*; (Gewehr) Lauf *m*; Walze *f*; Trommel *f*.

barrelled *adj* (*of firearms*)... läufig.

barrel organ *n* Drehorgel *f*.

barren *adj* unfruchtbar; öde.

barricade *n* Barrikade *f*; Hindernis *n*; * *vt* verbarrikadieren.

barrier *n* Barriere *f*; Schranke *f*; Hindernis *n*.

barring *adv* ausgenommen; abgesehen von.

barrow *n* Karren *m*; Hügel(grab) *m(n)*.

bartender *n* Barmann *m*.

barter *vi* Tauschhandel treiben; verhandeln; * *vt* tauschen.

base *n* Basis *f*; Grundlage *f*; Fundament *n*; Sockel *m*; Stützpunkt *m*; * *vt* stützen; gründen; stationieren; * *adj* Grund-; gemein; niedrig; unecht.

baseball *n* Baseball *m*.

baseless *adj* grundlos.

basement *n* Keller(geschoß) *m(n)*.

baseness *n* Gemeinheit *f*; Niedrigkeit *f*; Unechtheit *f*.

bash *vt* heftig schlagen; verprügeln.

bashful *adj* ~ly *adv* schüchtern; verschämt.

basic *adj*, ~ally *adv* grundlegend; Grund-.

basilisk *n* Basilisk *m*.

basin *n* Becken *n*; Schale *f*.

basis *n* Basis *f*; Grundlage *f*; Fundament *n*.

bask *vi* sich aalen; sich sonnen.

basket *n* Korb *m*.

basketball *n* Basketball *m*.

bass *n* (*mus*) Baß *m*.

bassoon *n* Fagott *n*.

bass viol *n* Gambe *f*.

bass voice *n* Baßstimme *f*.

bastard *n* Bastard *m*; (*sl*) Schwein *n*; * *adj* unehelich; Bastard-.

bastardy *n* uneheliche Geburt *f*.

baste *vt* (*Braten*) mit Fett begießen; (ver)prügeln; (an)heften.

basting *n* Prügel *pl*; Heftnaht *f*.

bastion *n* (*mil*) Bastion *f*.

bat *n* Fledermaus *f*; Schläger *m*.

batch *n* Schub *m*; Stapel *m*; Partie *f*.

bath *n* Bad *n*.

bathe *vt* (*vi*) baden.

bathing suit *n* Badeanzug *m*.

bathos *n* Abgleiten vom Erhabenen ins Lächerliche; Gemeinplatz *m*.

bathroom *n* Badezimmer *n*.

baths *npl* Badeanstalt *f*.

bathtub *n* Badewanne *f*.

baton *n* Stab *m*; Taktstock *m*; Schlagstock *m*.

battalion *n* (*mil*) Bataillon *n*.

batter *vt* (wiederholt) schlagen; argmitnehmen; * *n* Eierkuchenteig *m*.

battering ram *n* (*mil*) Sturmbock *m*.

battery *n* Batterie *f*; tätlicher Angriff *m*.

battle *n* Schlacht *f*; Gefecht *n*; Kampf *m*; * *vi* kämpfen; streiten.

battle array *n* Schlachtordnung *f*.

battlefield *n* Schlachtfeld *n*.

battlement *n* Brustwehr *f*; Zinnen *fpl*.

battleship *n* Schlachtschiff *n*.

bawdy *adj* unzüchtig; obszön.

bawl *vi* schreien; brüllen.

bay *n* Bucht *f*; Lorbeer *m*; * *vi* bellen; * *adj* kastanienbraun.

bayonet *n* Bajonett *n*.

bay window *n* Erkerfenster *n*.

bazaar *n* Basar *m*.

be *vi* sein.

beach *n* Strand *m*.

beacon *n* Leuchtturm *m*; Leuchtfeuer *n*; Bake *f*.

bead *n* Perle *f*; Tropfen *m*; ~s *npl* Rosenkranz *m*.

beagle *n* Beagle *m*.

beak *n* Schnabel *m*; Tülle *f*.

beaker *n* Becher *m*.

beam *n* Strahl *m*; Balken *m*; * *vi* strahlen.

bean *n* Bohne *f*; **French ~** grüne Bohne *f*.

beansprouts *npl* Sojasprossen *fpl*.

bear[1] *vt* (er)tragen; gebären;

führen; ausstehen; * *vi* tragen; lasten; drücken; Einfluß haben.

bear² *n* Bär *m*; **she ~** Bärin *f*.

bearable *adj* erträglich.

beard *n* Bart *m*.

bearded *adj* bärtig.

bearer *n* Träger(in) *m(f)*; Überbringer(in) *m(f)*.

bearing *n* (Er)Tragen *n*; Verhalten *n*; (Körper)Haltung *f*; Bezug *m*; Tragweite *f*; Position *f*.

beast *n* Tier *n*; Bestie *f*; Vieh *n*; **~ of burden** Lasttier *n*.

beastliness *n* Bestialität *f*; Gemeinheit *f*; Scheußlichkeit *f*.

beastly *adj adv* bestialisch; tierisch; gemein; scheußlich.

beat *vt* schlagen; (ver)prügeln; * *vi* schlagen; * *n* Schlag *m*; Takt *m*; Revier *n*.

beatific *adj* selig; beseligend.

beatify *vt* seligsprechen; glücklich machen.

beating *n* Schlagen *n*; Prügel *pl*; Niederlage *f*.

beatitude *n* Seligkeit *f*.

beautiful *adj* **~ly** *adv* schön; wunderbar.

beautify *vt* verschönern.

beauty *n* Schönheit *f*; (*das*) Schöne *n*; Prachtexemplar *n*; **~ salon** *n* Schönheitssalon *m*; **~ spot** *n* schönes Fleckchen Erde; Leberfleck *n*.

beaver *n* Biber *m*.

because *conj* weil; da.

beckon *vt* (herbei)winken; ein Zeichen geben.

become *vt* (an)stehen; sich schicken für; * *vi* werden.

becoming *adj* kleidsam; schicklich.

bed *n* Bett *n*; Lager *n*; Beet *n*.

bedclothes *npl* Bettwäsche *f*.

bedding *n* Bettzeug *n*; Streu *f*.

bedecked *adj* geschmückt.

bedlam *n* Tumult *m*; Irrenhaus *n*.

bed-post *n* Bettpfosten *m*.

bedridden *adj* bettlägerig.

bedroom *n* Schlafzimmer *n*.

bedspread *n* Tagesdecke *f*.

bedtime *n* Schlafenszeit *f*.

bee *n* Biene *f*.

beech *n* Buche *f*.

beef *n* Rindfleisch *n*; Mastrind *n*.

beefburger *n* Hamburger *m*.

beefsteak *n* Beefsteak *n*.

beehive *n* Bienenstock *m*.

beeline *n* kürzester Weg *m*.

beer *n* Bier *n*.

beeswax *n* Bienenwachs *n*.

beet *n* Bete *f*; Runkelrübe *f*.

beetle *n* Käfer *m*.

befall *vt* zustoßen; widerfahren.

befit *vt* anstehen; sich geziemen für.

before *adv* vorn; vorher; * *prep* vor; * *conj* bevor; ehe.

beforehand *adv* zuvor; (im) voraus.

befriend *vt* behilflich sein.

beg *vt* erbetteln; (er)bitten; * *vi* betteln; bitten; flehen; sich erlauben.

beget *vt* (er)zeugen.

beggar *n* Bettler(in) *m(f)*; (*fam*) Kerl *m*.

begin *vt, vi* beginnen, anfangen.

beginner *n* Anfänger(in) *m(f)*.

beginning *n* Anfang *m*; Beginn *m*; Ursprung *m*.

begrudge *vt* mißgönnen.

behalf *n*: **on ~ of** zugunsten von; für; im Namen von; im Auftrag von.

behave *vi* sich benehmen; sich verhalten.

behaviour *n* Benehmen *n*; Verhalten *n*.

behead *vt* enthaupten; köpfen.

behind *prep* hinter; * *adv* (nach) hinten; hinterher.

behold *vt* sehen; anschauen; erblicken.

behove *vi* erforderlich sein für; sich schicken für.

beige *adj* beige.

being *n* (Da)Sein *n*; Existenz *f*; Wesen *n*.

belated *adj* verspätet.

belch *vi* aufstoßen; rülpsen; * *n* Rülpser *m*.

belfry *n* Glockenturm *m*.

belie *vt* Lügen strafen; enttäuschen.

belief *n* Glaube *m*; Meinung *f*; Religion *f*.

believable *adj* glaubhaft.

believe *vt* glauben; meinen; * *vi* glauben; vertrauen; viel halten.

believer *n* Gläubige(r) *f(m)*.

belittle *vt* verkleinern; (*fig*) herabsetzen.

bell *n* Glocke *f*; Klingel *f*; Läuten *n*.

bellicose *adj* kriegslustig.

belligerent *adj* kriegführend; (*fig*) streitlustig, aggressiv.

bellow *vi* brüllen; grölen; * *n* Brüllen *n*.

bellows *npl* Blasebalg *m*.

belly *n* Bauch *m*; Magen *m*.

bellyful *n* **to have a ~ of** sich den Bauch vollschlagen mit; die Nase voll haben von.

belong *vi* gehören.

belongings *npl* Habseligkeiten *fpl*.

beloved *adj* geliebt.

below *adv* unten; hinunter; (dar)unter. * *prep* unter; unterhalb.

belt *n* Gürtel *m*; Gurt *m*; Riemen *m*.

bemoan *vt* beklagen.

bemused *adj* verwirrt; betäubt.

bench *n* Bank *f*; Sitz *m*; Gericht *n*.

bend *vt* biegen; krümmen; beugen; spannen; richten; * *vi* sich krümmen; sich (ver)beugen; (sich) neigen; * *n* Kurve *f*; Krümmung *f*.

beneath *adv* unten; darunter. * *prep* unter; unterhalb.

benediction *n* Segen *m*.

benefactor *n* Wohltäter *m*.

benefice *n* Pfründe *f*; Lehen *n*.

beneficent *adj* wohltätig; nützlich; wohltuend.

beneficial *adj* nützlich; wohltuend; nutznießend.

beneficiary *n* Nutznießer(in) *m(f)*; Empfänger(in) *m(f)*.

benefit *n* Vorteil *m*; Nutzen *m*; Leistung *f*; Unterstützung *f*; Wohltätigkeitsveranstaltung *f*; * *vt* nützen; zugute kommen; begünstigen; * *vi* Nutzen ziehen.

benevolence *n* Wohltätigkeit *f*; Wohlwollen *n*.

benevolent *adj* wohltätig; gütig; wohlwollend.

benign *adj* gütig; freundlich; vorteilhaft; (*med*) gutartig.

bent *n* Neigung *f*; Hang *m*; Veranlagung *f*.

benzine *n* (*chem*) Leichtbenzin *n*.

bequeath *vt* (*law*) vermachen; (*fig*) überliefern.

bequest *n* Vermächtnis *n*; Erbe *n*.

bereave *vt* berauben.

bereavement *n* schmerzlicher Verlust *m*; Trauerfall *m*.

beret *n* Baskenmütze *f*; Felduniformmütze *f*.

berm *n* Bankett *n*.

berry *n* Beere *f*.

berserk *adj* rasend; wütend.

berth *n* (*mar*) Ankerplatz *m*; Koje *f*; Seeraum *m*.

beseech *vt* inständig bitten (um); anflehen.

beset *vt* bedrängen; (*fig*) heimsuchen.

beside(s) *prep* neben; dicht bei; außer(halb); * *adv* außerdem; sonst.

besiege *vt* belagern; (*fig*) bedrängen.

best *adj* best(er, e, es); größt(er, e, es); * *adv* am besten; am meisten; * *n* (*der, die, das*) Beste *m, f, n*.

bestial *adj*, **~ly** *adv* tierisch; bestialisch; gemein.

bestiality *n* Bestialität *f*; Greueltat *f*.

bestow *vt* schenken; verleihen.

bestseller *n* Bestseller *m*.

bet *n* Wette *f*; * *vt* wetten.

betray *vt* verraten; hintergehen.

betrayal *n* Verrat *m*.

betroth *vt* verloben.

betrothal *n* Verlobung *f*.

better *adj, adv* besser; **so much the ~** desto besser; * *vt* verbessern; übertreffen.

betting *n* Wetten *n*.

between *prep* zwischen; unter.

bevel *n* Schrägung *f*; * *vt* abschrägen; facettieren.

beverage *n* Getränk *n*.

bevy *n* Schwarm *m*.

beware *vi* sich hüten; sich in acht nehmen.

bewilder *vt* verwirren; verblüffen; bestürzen.

bewilderment *n* Verwirrung *f*.

bewitch *vt* verhexen; bezaubern.

beyond *prep* jenseits; außer; über... hinaus.

bias *n* Neigung *f*; Vorliebe *f*; Vorurteil *n*; schräge Seite *f*.

bib *n* Latz *m*; Lätzchen *n*.

Bible *n* Bibel *f*.

biblical *adj* biblisch.

bibliography *n* Bibliographie *f*.

bicarbonate of soda *n* doppeltkohlensaures Natron *n*.

bicker *vi* zanken.

bicycle *n* Fahrrad *n*.

bid *vt* bieten; gebieten; * *n* Gebot *n*; Angebot *n*; Versuch *m*.

bidding *n* Geheiß *n*; Bieten *n*; Gebot *n*.

bide *vt* abwarten.

biennial *adj* zweijährlich.

bifocals *npl* Zweistärkenbrille *f*.

bifurcated *adj* gegabelt.

big *adj* groß; erwachsen; schwanger; dick.

bigamist *n* Bigamist(in) *m(f)*.

bigamy *n* Bigamie *f*.

big dipper *n* Achterbahn *f*.

bigheaded *adj* eingebildet.

bigness *n* Größe *f*; Umfang *m*.

bigot *n* selbstgerechte Person *f*; Frömmler(in) *m(f)*.

bigoted *adj* selbstgerecht; bigott.

bike *n* Fahrrad *n*; Motorrad *n*.

bikini *n* Bikini *m*.

bilberry *n* Heidelbeere *f*.

bile *n* Galle *f*.

bilingual *adj* zweisprachig.

bilious *adj* Gallen-; (*fig*) gereizt.

bill *n* Schnabel *m*; Rechnung *f*; Wechsel *m*; Gesetzesvorlage *f*; Klageschrift *f*; Liste *f*; Bescheinigung *f*; Plakat *n*; Programm *n*.

billboard *n* Reklamefläche *f*.

billet *n* (*mil*) Quartier *n*; Unterkunft *f*; Scheit *n*.

billiards *npl* Billard *n*.

billiard-table *n* Billardtisch *m*.

billion *n* Milliarde *f*.

billy-goat *n* Ziegenbock *m*.

bin *n* Kasten *m*; Behälter *m*.

bind *vt* (ver)binden; fesseln; verpflichten.

binder *n* Binder *m*; Bindfaden *m*; Einband *m*; Hefter *m*; Bindemittel *n*.

binding *n* Einband *m*; Bindung *f*.

binge *n* (*fam*) Sauftour *f*; Freßgelage *n*.

bingo *n* Bingo *n*.

binoculars *npl* Fernglas *n*.

biochemistry *n* Biochemie *f*.

biographer *n* Biograph *m*.

biographical *adj* biographisch.

biography *n* Biographie *f*.

biological *adj* biologisch.

biology *n* Biologie *f*.

biped *n* Zweifüßer *m*.

birch *n* Birke *f*.

bird *n* Vogel *m*.

bird's-eye view *n* Vogelschau *f*.

bird-watcher *n* Vogelbeobachter *m*.

birth *n* Geburt *f*; Abstammung *f*; Entstehung *f*.

birth certificate *n* Geburtsurkunde *f*.

birth control *n* Geburtenregelung *f*.

birthday *n* Geburtstag *m*.

birthplace *n* Geburtsort *m*.

birthright *n* (Erst)Geburtsrecht *n*.

biscuit *n* Keks *m*.

bisect *vt* halbieren; in zwei Teile schneiden.

bishop *n* Bischof *m*.

bison *n* Bison *m*; Wisent *m*.

bit *n* Gebiß *n*; Mundstück *n*; Bohrer *m*; Bissen *m*; Stück *n*; Stückchen *n*; Moment *m*.

bitch *n* Hündin *f*; (*fig*) Miststück *n*.

bite *vt* beißen; schneiden in; ~ **the dust** (*fam*) ins Gras beißen; * *n* Biß *m*; Bissen *m*; Schärfe *f*.

bitter *adj* ~**ly** *adv* bitter; (v)erbittert; scharf.

bitterness *n* Bitterkeit *f*; (V)Erbitterung *f*.

bitumen *n* Bitumen *n*; Asphalt *m*.

bizarre *adj* bizarr; absonderlich.

blab *vi* plappern; (aus)plaudern.

black *adj* schwarz; dunkel; düster; * *n* Schwarz *n*; Schwarze(r) *f(m)*.

blackberry *n* Brombeere *f*.

blackbird *n* Amsel *f*.

blackboard *n* Tafel *f*.

blacken *vt* schwärzen; (*fig*) schlechtmachen; schwarzmalen.

black ice *n* Glatteis *n*.

blackjack *n* Siebzehnundvier *n*.

blackleg *n* Falschspieler *m*; Streikbrecher *m*.

blacklist *n* schwarze Liste *f*.

blackmail *n* Erpressung *f*; * *vt* erpressen.

black market *n* Schwarzmarkt *m*.

blackness *n* Schwärze *f*.

black pudding *n* Blutwurst *f*.

black sheep *n* (*fig*) schwarzes Schaf.

blacksmith *n* Schmied *m*.

blackthorn *n* Schlehdorn *m*.

bladder *n* Blase *f*.

blade *n* Klinge *f*; Blatt *n*; Halm *m*.

blame *vt* tadeln; die Schuld geben; * *n* Tadel *m*; Schuld *f*.

blameless *adj*, ~**ly** *adv* untadelig; schuldlos.

blanch *vt* bleichen; blanchieren; * *vi* erbleichen.

bland *adj* mild; verbindlich; fad; langweilig.

blank *adj* blank; leer; Blanko-; verblüfft; * *n* Leere *f*; Lücke *f*; freier Raum *m*; Leerblatt *n*; Vordruck *m*; Niete *f*; Platzpatrone *f*.

blank check *n* Blankoscheck *m*.

blanket *n* Decke *f*.

blare *vi* schmettern; plärren; dröhnen; grell leuchten.

blase *adj* gleichgültig; blasiert.

blaspheme *vt* lästern; schmähen.

blasphemous *adj* (gottes)lästerlich.

blasphemy *n* Blasphemie *f*; (Gottes)Lästerung *f*.

blast *n* Windstoß *m*; Ton *m*; Explosion *f*; Sprengung *f*; Druckwelle *f*; (*bot*) Mehltau *m*; * *vt* sprengen; (*fig*) zunichte machen.

blast-off *n* Start *m*.

blatant *adj* lärmend; aufdringlich; eklatant.

blaze *n* loderndes Feuer *n*; heller Schein *m*; (*fig*) Ausbruch *m*; * *vi* lodern; leuchten; brennen.

bleach *vt vi* bleichen; * *n* Bleichmittel *n*.

bleached *adj* (aus)gebleicht.

bleak *adj* öde; rauh; (*fig*) trostlos.

bleakness *n* Öde *f*; Rauhheit *f*; Trostlosigkeit *f*.

bleary(-eyed) *adj* trübe; verschwommen.

bleat *n* Blöken *n*; * *vi* blöken.

bleed *vi* bluten; *vt* zur Ader lassen; abzapfen; schröpfen.

bleeding *n* Blutung *f*; Aderlaß *m*.

bleeper *n* Piepser *m*.

blemish *vt* entstellen; beflekken; * *n* Makel *m*; (Schönheits)Fehler *m*.

blend *vt* mischen.

bless *vt* segnen; (lob)preisen.

blessing n Segen m.

blight vt vernichten; verderben.

blind adj blind; ziellos; geheim; **~ alley** n Sackgasse f; * vt (ver) blenden; * n Rolladen m; **Venetian ~** Jalousie f.

blindfold vt die Augen verbinden; **~ed** adj mit verbundenen Augen.

blindly adv blindlings.

blindness n Blindheit f; (fig) Verblendung.

blind side n schwache Seite f.

blind spot n toter Winkel m; (fig) wunder Punkt m.

blink vi blinzeln; zwinkern; schimmern.

blinkers npl Scheuklappen fpl; Blinklicht n.

bliss n (Glück)Seligkeit f.

blissful adj **~ly** adv (glück)selig.

blissfulness n (Glück)Seligkeit f.

blister n Blase f; Bläschen n; * vi Blasen werfen.

blitz n heftiger (Luft)Angriff m; Blitzkrieg m.

blizzard n Schneesturm m.

bloated adj aufgeblasen; geschwollen.

blob n Klecks m.

bloc n Block m.

block n Block m; Klotz m; Verstopfung f; **~ (up)** vt sperren; blockieren; verstopfen.

blockade n Blockade f; Sperre f; * vt blockieren; eine Blockade verhängen.

blockage n Blockierung f; Verstopfung f.

blockbuster n (fam) Knüller m.

blockhead n Dummkopf m.

blond adj blond; hell; * n Blondine f.

blood n Blut n.

blood donor n Blutspender(in) m(f).

blood group n Blutgruppe f.

bloodhound n Bluthund m.

bloodiness n Blutrünstigkeit f.

bloodless adj blutleer; unblutig; (fig) leblos.

blood poisoning n Blutvergiftung f.

blood pressure n Blutdruck m.

bloodshed n Blutvergießen n.

bloodshot adj blutunterlaufen.

bloodstream n Blutkreislauf m.

bloodsucker n Blutsauger m.

blood test n Blutprobe f.

bloodthirsty adj blutdürstig.

blood transfusion n Blutübertragung f.

blood vessel n Blutgefäß n.

bloody adj, adv blutig; grausam; (sl) verdammt; **~ minded** adj stur; boshaft.

bloom n Blüte f; Reif m; Flaum m; (also fig); * vi (er)blühen.

blossom n Blüte f.

blot vt beklecksen; beflecken; durchstreichen; (aus)löschen; * n Klecks m; Fleck m; Makel m.

blotchy adj fleckig.

blotting pad n Schreibunterlage f.

blotting paper n Löschpapier n.

blouse n Bluse f.

blow vi blasen; wehen; schnaufen; durchbrennen; * vt blasen; wehen; **to ~ up** sprengen; aufblasen; explodieren; * n Blasen n; Schlag m; Stoß m.

blowout n Zerplatzen n; Reifenpanne f.

blowpipe n Schweißbrenner m; Blasrohr n.

blubber n Tran m; Speck m; Flennen n; * vi flennen; schluchzen.

bludgeon n Keule f; Totschläger m.

blue adj blau.

bluebell n Glockenblume f; Sternhyazinthe f.

bluebottle n (bot) Kornblume f; (zool) Schmeißflege f.

blueness n Bläue f.

blueprint n Blaupause f; (fig) Plan m; Entwurf m.

bluff n Bluff m; Steilufer n; * vt bluffen.

bluish *adj* bläulich.

blunder *n* Fehler *m*; Schnitzer *m*; Fauxpas *m*; * *vi* einen Fehler machen; einen Fauxpas begehen; stolpern.

blunt *adj* stumpf; ungehobelt; offen; * *vt* abstumpfen.

bluntly *adv* mit schonungsloser Offenheit.

bluntness *n* Stumpfheit *f*; Grobheit *f*.

blur *n* Fleck *m*; verschwommener Eindruck *m*; Schleier *m*; * *vt* verwischen; * *vi* verschwimmen.

blurt out *vt* herausplatzen mit.

blush *n* Erröten *n*; Röte *f*; * *vi* erröten; rot werden.

blustery *adj* stürmisch; prahlerisch.

boa *n* Boa *f*.

boar *n* Eber *m*; **wild ~** Keiler *m*.

board *n* Brett *n*; Tisch *m*; Tafel *f*; Verpflegung *f*; Amt *n*; Ausschuß *m*; Pappe *f*; Bord *m*; * *vt* an Bord gehen; beköstigen; mit Brettern vernageln.

boarder *n* Kostgänger(in) *m(f)*; Internatsschüler(in) *m(f)*.

boarding card *n* Bordkarte *f*.

boarding house *n* Pension *f*.

boarding school *n* Internat *n*.

boast *vi* prahlen; sich rühmen; * *n* Prahlerei *f*.

boastful *adj* prahlerisch.

boat *n* Boot *n*; Schiff *n*.

boating *n* Bootsfahrt *f*; Rudersport *m*; Segelsport *m*.

bobsleigh *n* Bob *m*.

bode *vt* bedeuten; ahnen lassen.

bodice *n* Mieder *n*; Oberteil *n*.

bodily *adj, adv* körperlich; physisch; leibhaftig.

body *n* Körper *m*; Person *f*; Leiche *f*; Rumpf *m*; Hauptteil *m*; Masse *f*; Gesamtheit *f*; Körperschaft *f*; **any ~** irgendjemand; jeder; **every ~** jeder einzelne.

body-building *n* Bodybuilding *n*.

bodyguard *n* Leibwächter *m*.

bodywork *n* Karosserie *f*.

bog *n* Sumpf *m*; Moor *n*; Morast *m*.

boggy *adj* sumpfig; morastig.

bogus *adj* falsch; Schwindel-.

boil *vi* kochen; brodeln; * *vt* kochen; * *n* Kochen *n*; Brodeln *n*; Furunkel *m*.

boiled egg *n* gekochtes Ei *n*.

boiled potatoes *npl* gekochte Kartoffeln *fpl*.

boiler *n* Kessel *m*; Boiler *m*.

boiling point *n* Siedepunkt *m*.

boisterous *adj*, **~ly** *adv* stürmisch; lärmend; ausgelassen.

bold *adj* **~ly** *adv* kühn; mutig; dreist; deutlich; steil.

boldness *n* Kühnheit *f*; Mut *m*; Dreistigkeit *f*; Steilheit *f*.

bolster *n* Polster *n*; Kissen *n*; Unterlage *f*; * *vt* polstern; (unter)stützen.

bolt *n* Bolzen *m*; Riegel *m*; (Blitz)Strahl *m*; plötzlicher Satz *m*; * *vt* verriegeln; verschrauben; herausplatzen mit; hinunterschlingen; * *vi* stürmen; ausreißen; durchgehen.

bomb *n* Bombe *f*; **~ disposal** Bombenräumung *f*.

bombard *vt* bombardieren.

bombardier *n* Artillerieunteroffizier *m*; Bombenschütze *m*.

bombardment *n* Bombardement *n*.

bombshell *n* (*fig*) Bombe *f*.

bond *n* Bund *m*; (Ver)Bindung *f*; Fessel *f*; Zollverschluß *m*; Schuldschein *m*; Anleihe *f*.

bondage *n* Leibeigenschaft *f*; Gefangenschaft *f*; Fesseln *n*.

bond holder *n* Obligationsinhaber *m*.

bone *n* Knochen *m*; Gräte *f*; * *vt* ausbeinen; entgräten.

boneless *adj* ohne Knochen; (*fig*) rückgratlos.

bonfire *n* (Freuden)Feuer *n*.

bonnet *n* Haube *f*; Mütze *f*.

bonny *adj* hübsch.

bonus *n* Bonus *m*; Prämie *f*.

bony *adj* knochig; knöchern.

boo *vt* ausbuhen.

booby trap n versteckte Sprengladung f; (fig) grober Scherz m.

book n Buch n; Heft n; Liste f; Vorschrift f; **to bring to ~** vt zur Rechenschaft ziehen.

bookbinder n Buchbinder(in) m(f).

bookcase n Bücherschrank m.

bookkeeper n Buchhalter(in) m(f).

bookkeeping n Buchhaltung f; Buchführung f.

bookmaking n Buchmacherei f.

bookmarker n Lesezeichen n.

bookseller n Buchhändler(in) m(f).

bookshop n Buchhandlung f.

bookworm n Bücherwurm m.

boom n Dröhnen n; Boom m; * vi dröhnen; rapide ansteigen; florieren.

boon n (fig) Segen m.

boor n ungehobelter Kerl m.

boorish adj ungehobelt.

boost n Förderung f; Auftrieb m; Steigerung f; * vt nachhelfen; steigern.

booster n Verstärkung f; Zusatz m; Wiederholungsimpfung f.

boot n Stiefel m; Kofferraum m; **to ~** adv obendrein.

booth n Bude f; Zelle f; Kabine f.

booty n Beute f.

booze vi saufen; * n (fam) Alkohol m.

border n Rand m; Grenze f; Borte f; Beet n; * vt einfassen; säumen; grenzen an.

borderline n Grenzlinie f; (fig) Grenze f.

bore vt langweilen; bohren; * n Langweiler m; langweilige Sache; Bohrung f; Bohrloch n; Kaliber n.

boredom n Langeweile f.

boring adj langweilig.

born adj geboren; angeboren.

borrow vt borgen; leihen; entlehnen.

borrower n Entleiher(in) m(f);

Darlehensnehmer(in) m(f).

bosom n Busen m; (fig) Schoß m.

bosom friend n Busenfreund(in) m(f).

boss n Boß m; Chef m; Vorgesetzer m.

botanic(al) adj botanisch.

botanist n Botaniker(in) m(f).

botany n Botanik f.

botch vt zusammenschustern; verpfuschen.

both adj beide, beides; * conj sowohl...als.

bother vt belästigen; beunruhigen; * n Belästigung f; Ärger m; Aufregung f.

bottle n Flasche f; * vt in Flaschen abfüllen; einwecken.

bottleneck n Flaschenhals m; Engpaß m.

bottle-opener n Flaschenöffner m.

bottom n Boden m; Fuß m; Sohle f; Grund m; Unterseite f; Unterteil n; Hintern m; * adj unterst(er, e, es); Grund-.

bottomless adj bodenlos.

bough n Ast m; Zweig m.

boulder n Geröllblock m; Findling m.

bounce vi aufprallen; springen; federn; * n Aufprall m; Sprung m; Elastizität f.

bound n Grenze f; Sprung m; * vi begrenzen; springen; * adj gebunden; verpflichtet; zwangsläufig tun müssen; bestimmt; unterwegs.

boundary n Grenze f.

boundless adj grenzenlos; übermäßig.

bounteous, bountiful adj freigebig; reichlich.

bounty n Freigiebigkeit f; Gabe f; Prämie f; Belohnung f.

bouquet n Blumenstrauß m; Blume f.

bourgeois adj bourgeois.

bout n Anfall m; Runde f.

bovine adj Rinder-; (fig) schwerfällig.

bow[1] vt biegen; beugen; neigen;

* *vi* sich (ver)beugen; * *n* Verbeugung *f*.

bow² *n* Bogen *m*; Bügel *m*; Schleife *f*; Bug *m*.

bowels *npl* Eingeweide *pl*; Darm *m*.

bowl *n* Schüssel *f*; Schale *f*; Becken *n*; Kugel *f*; * *vi* kegeln; Bowling spielen.

bowling *n* Bowling *n*; Kegeln *n*.

bowling alley *n* Kegelbahn *f*.

bowling green *n* Rasenplatz *m* (*zum Bowling*).

bowstring *n* Bogensehne *f*.

bow tie *n* Fliege *f*.

box *n* Kiste *f*; Kasten *m*; Dose *f*; Gehäuse *n*; Loge *f*; Box *f*; Buchsbaum; ~ **on the ear** Ohrfeige *f*; * *vt* in eine Schachtel packen; einschließen * *vi* boxen.

boxer *n* Boxer *m*.

boxing *n* Boxen *n*.

boxing gloves *npl* Boxhandschuhe *mpl*.

boxing ring *n* Boxring *m*.

box office *n* Kasse *f*.

box-seat *n* Logenplatz *m*.

boy *n* Junge *m*; Bursche *m*.

boycott *vt* boykottieren; * *n* Boykott *m*.

boyfriend *n* Freund *m*.

boyish *adj* jungenhaft; knabenhaft.

bra *n* BH *m*.

brace *n* Strebe *f*; Stütze *f*; Klammer *f*; Paar *n*.

bracelet *n* Armreif *m*.

bracing *adj* stärkend; erfrischend.

bracken *n* (*bot*) Farnkraut *n*.

bracket *n* Klammer *f*; Halter *m*; Konsole *f*; Gruppe *f*; Stufe *f*; * *vt* **to ~ with** auf die gleiche Stufe stellen; in eine Gruppe zusammenfassen.

brag *n* Prahlerei *f*; Prahlhans *m*; * *vi* prahlen; angeben.

braid *n* Flechte *f*; Borte *f*; * *vt* flechten.

brain *n* Gehirn *n*; Verstand *m*; * *vt* den Schädel einschlagen.

brainchild *n* Geistesprodukt *n*.

brainless *adj* dumm; gedankenlos.

brainwash *vt* jemanden einer Gehirnwäsche unterziehen.

brainwave *n* (*col*) Geistesblitz *m*.

brainy *adj* gescheit; intelligent.

brake *n* Bremse *f*; * *vt*, *vi* bremsen.

brake fluid *n* Bremsflüssigkeit *f*.

brake light *n* Bremslicht *n*.

bramble *n* Brombeerstrauch *m*.

bran *n* Kleie *f*.

branch *n* Ast *m*; Zweig *m*; Zweigstelle *f*; Arm *m*; * *vt* sich verzweigen; abzweigen; abstammen.

branch line *n* Seitenlinie *f*; (*rail*) Nebenlinie *f*.

brand *n* Marke *f*; Art *f*; Brand *m*; Brandmal *n*; * *vt* einbrennen; brandmarken.

brandish *vt* (drohend) schwingen.

brand-new *adj* (funkel)nagelneu.

brandy *n* Weinbrand *m*; Obstwasser *n*.

brash *adj* ungestüm; taktlos; frech; aufdringlich.

brass *n* Messing *n*; (*fam*) hohes Tier *n*; (*fam*) Geld *n*.

brassiere *n* Büstenhalter *m*.

brat *n* Balg *n*; Gör *n*.

bravado *n* gespielte Tapferkeit *f*; herausforderndes Benehmen *n*.

brave *adj*, **~ly** *adv* mutig; tapfer; * *vt* mutig begegnen; trotzen; * *n* Krieger *m*.

bravery *n* Mut *m*; Tapferkeit *f*.

brawl *n* laute Auseinandersetzung *f*; Schlägerei *f*; * *vi* eine laute Auseinandersetzung haben; sich schlagen.

brawn *n* Muskeln *mpl*; Sülze *f*.

bray *vi* schreien; schmettern; * *n* Schrei (*eines Esels*) *m*; Schmettern *n*.

braze *vt* hartlöten; mit Messing verzieren.

brazen *adj* Messing-; metallisch; unverschämt.

brazier *n* Kohlenpfanne *f*; Messingarbeiter *m*.

breach *n* Bruch *m*; Verletzung *f*; Bresche *f*; Kluft *f*; * *vt* brechen; verletzen.

bread *n* Brot *n*; (*fig*) Lebensunterhalt *m*; **brown ~** Mischbrot *n*; Schwarzbrot *n*.

breadbin *n* Brotkasten *m*.

breadcrumbs *npl* Paniermehl *n*.

breadth *n* Breite *f*; (*fig*) Umfang *m*.

breadwinner *n* Geldverdiener *m*.

break *vt* (zer)brechen; kaputtmachen; abbrechen; zähmen; verstoßen gegen; vernichten; mitteilen; * *vi* (aus)brechen; sich auflösen; eine Pause machen; **to ~ into** ausbrechen; einbrechen; **to ~ out** ausbrechen; * *n* Bruch *m*; Lücke *f*; Einbruch *m*; **~ of day** Tagesanbruch *m*.

breakage *n* Bruch *m*.

breakdown *n* Panne *f*; Zusammenbruch *m*; Scheitern *n*; Analyse *f*.

breakfast *n* Frühstück *n*; * *vi* frühstücken.

breaking *n* Bruch *m*; Brechen *n*.

breakthrough *n* Durchbruch *m*.

breakwater *n* Wellenbrecher *m*.

breast *n* Brust *f*.

breastbone *n* Brustbein *n*.

breastplate *n* Brustharnisch *m*; Bauchschild *m*.

breaststroke *n* Brustschwimmen *n*.

breath *n* Atem(zug) *m*; (Luft-)Hauch *m*.

breathe *vt, vi* atmen; hauchen; verschnaufen (lassen).

breathing *n* Atmung *f*; Atmen *n*; Atempause *f*.

breathing space *n* Atempause *f*; Platz zum Atmen *m*.

breathless *adj* atemlos; atemberaubend.

breathtaking *adj* atemberaubend.

breed *n* Rasse *f*; Schlag *m*; * *vt* hervorbringen; züchten; gebären; erziehen; * *vi* sich fortpflanzen; sich vermehren; brüten.

breeder *n* Züchter *m*; Brüter *m*.

breeding *n* Fortpflanzung *f*; Züchten *n*; Erziehung *f*; Manieren *pl*.

breeze *n* Brise *f*; (*fam*) Kinderspiel *n*.

breezy *adj* luftig; heiter.

brethren *npl* (*relig*) Brüder *mpl*; Glaubensgenossen *mpl*.

breviary *n* (*relig*) Brevier *n*.

brevity *n* Kürze *f*.

brew *vt* brauen; ausbrüten; * *vi* sich zusammenbrauen; * *n* Gebräu *n*.

brewer *n* Brauer *m*.

brewery *n* Brauerei *f*.

briar, brier *n* Dornstrauch *m*; Wilde Rose *f*.

bribe *n* Bestechung *f*; Bestechungsgeld *n*; Bestechungsgeschenk *n*; * *vt* bestechen.

bribery *n* Bestechung *f*.

bric-a-brac *n* Nippes *m*.

brick *n* Ziegelstein *m*; Bauklötzchen *n*; * *vt* mit Ziegelsteinen mauern.

bricklayer *n* Maurer *m*.

bridal *adj* Braut-; Hochzeits-.

bride *n* Braut *f*.

bridegroom *n* Bräutigam *m*.

bridesmaid *n* Brautjungfer *f*.

bridge *n* Brücke *f*; Steg *m*; (Nasen)Rücken *m*; **to ~ (over)** *vt* überbrücken; eine Brücke bauen über.

bridle *n* Zaum *m*; * *vt* zäumen; zügeln.

brief *adj* **~ly** *adv* kurz; knapp; * *n* Zusammenfassung *f*; Einsatzbesprechung *f*; Instruktionen *fpl*.

briefcase *n* Aktentasche *f*.

brier *n* = **briar**

brigade *n* (*mil*) Brigade *f*.

brigadier n (mil) Brigadekommandeur m.

brigand n Bandit m; Räuber m.

bright adj ~ly adv hell; leuchtend; glänzend; heiter; munter; intelligent.

brighten vt aufhellen; aufheitern; polieren; * vi sich aufhellen; aufleuchten; sich beleben; besser werden.

brightness n Helligkeit f; Glanz m; Heiterkeit f; Lebhaftigkeit f; Intelligenz f.

brilliance n Leuchten n; Glanz m; durchdringender Verstand m.

brilliant adj ~ly adv leuchtend; glänzend; hervorragend.

brim n Rand m; Krempe f.

brimful(l) adj randvoll.

bring vt (mit)bringen; einbringen; bewirken; vorbringen; **to ~ about** zustande bringen; bewirken; **to ~ forth** hervorbringen; bewirken; **to ~ up** heraufbringen; großziehen; erziehen; zur Sprache bringen.

brink n Rand m; Ufer n.

brisk adj ~ly adv flott; lebhaft; energisch; frisch.

brisket n Bruststück n.

bristle n Borste f; Stoppel f; * vi sich sträuben; zornig werden; starren; strotzen.

bristly adj borstig; stopplig; (fig) kratzbürstig.

brittle adj spröde; brüchig; reizbar.

broach vt anschneiden; anzapfen.

broad adj breit; weit; hell; liberal; derb; deutlich; allgemein.

broadbean n Saubohne f.

broadcast n Übertragung f; Sendung f; * vt, vi senden; übertragen; verbreiten; breitwürfig säen.

broadcasting n Rundfunk m; Fernsehen n; Sendung f; Übertragung f; Sendebetrieb m.

broaden vt, vi verbreitern; erweitern.

broadly adv weitgehend; allgemein.

broad-minded adj großzügig; liberal.

broadness n Breite f; Weite f; Umfang m; Derbheit f.

broadside n Breitseite f.

broadways adv der Breite nach.

brocade n Brokat m.

broccoli n Brokkoli pl.

brochure n Broschüre f; Prospekt m.

brogue n derber Straßenschuh m; irischer Akzent m; starker Dialekt m.

broil vt (auf dem Rost) braten; grillen; (fig) kochen.

broken adj zerbrochen; kaputt; gebrochen; unterbrochen; ruiniert; gezähmt; **~ English** gebrochenes Englisch n.

broker n Makler m; Vermittler m.

brokerage n Maklergeschäft n; Maklergebühr f.

bronchial adj bronchial.

bronchitis n Bronchitis f.

bronze n Bronze f; * vt bronzieren; bräunen.

brooch n Brosche f; Spange f.

brood vi brüten; grübeln; * n Brut f.

brood-hen n Bruthenne f.

brook n Bach m.

broom n Besen m; (Besen)Ginster m.

broomstick n Besenstiel m.

broth n Suppe f; Brühe f.

brothel n Bordell n.

brother n Bruder m.

brotherhood n Bruderschaft f; Brüderlichkeit f.

brother-in-law n Schwager m.

brotherly adj, adv brüderlich.

brow n Braue f; Stirn f; Vorsprung m.

browbeat vt einschüchtern; tyrannisieren.

brown adj braun; brünett; **~ paper** n Packpaier n; **~ bread** n Mischbrot n; Schwarzbrot n; **~ sugar** n brauner Zucker m; * n Braun n; * vt bräunen.

browse *vi* grasen; *(fig)* schmökern; sich umsehen.

bruise *vt* quetschen; Prellungen zufügen; kränken; * *vi* einen blauen Fleck bekommen * *n* Quetschung *f*; Prellung *f*; blauer Fleck *m*; Druckstelle *f*.

brunch *n* Brunch *m*.

brunette *n* Brünette *f*.

brunt *n* volle Wucht *f*; Hauptlast *f*.

brush *n* Bürste *f*; Pinsel *m*; Rute *f*; Scharmützel *n*; Gestrüpp *n*; * *vt* bürsten; fegen; streifen; berühren.

brushwood *n* Buschland *n*.

brusque *adj* brüsk; schroff.

Brussels sprouts *n* Rosenkohl *m*.

brutal *adj* ~ly *adv* brutal; roh.

brutality *n* Brutalität *f*; Roheit *f*.

brutalize *vt* brutal behandeln; verrohen lassen; * *vi* verrohen.

brute *n* (unvernünftiges) Vieh *n*; Untier *n*; * *adj* tierisch; unvernünftig; roh; hirnlos; hart.

brutish *adj* ~ly *adv* = brute.

bubble *n* (Seifen)Blase *f*; Schwindel *m*; * *vi* sprudeln; brodeln.

bubblegum *n* Kaugummi *m*.

bucket *n* Eimer *m*; Kübel *m*; Schaufel *f*.

buckle *n* Schnalle *f*; Spange *f*; * *vt* zuschnallen; * *vi* sich verbiegen; einknicken; zusammenbrechen.

bucolic *adj* Hirten-; ländlich; idyllisch.

bud *n* Knospe *f*; Auge *n*; Keim *m*; * *vi* knospen; keimen; heranreifen.

Buddhism *n* Buddhismus *m*.

budding *adj* knospend; angehend.

buddy *n* Kumpel *m*; Kamerad *m*.

budge *vi* sich rühren; sich bewegen.

budgerigar *n* Wellensittich *m*.

budget *n* Budget *n*; Etat *m*; Haushaltsplan *m*; Finanzen *pl*.

buff *n* Ochsenleder *n*; Lederfarbe *f*; Fan *m*.

buffalo *n* Büffel *m*; Bison *m*.

buffer *n* Puffer *m*; Prellbock *m*.

buffet *n* Büfett *n*; Theke *f*; Stoß *m*; * *vt* einen Schlag versetzen; durchschütteln; ankämpfen gegen.

buffoon *n* Possenreißer *m*; Hanswurst *m*.

bug *n* Wanze *f*; Insekt *n*; Bazillus *m*; Fanatiker(in) *m(f)*; Defekt *m*.

bugbear *n* Popanz *m*; Schreckgespenst *n*.

bugle(horn) *n* Horn *n*.

build *vt* (er)bauen; errichten; aufbauen.

builder *n* Erbauer *m*; Bauunternehmer *m*; Bauhandwerker *m*.

building *n* Gebäude *n*; (Er)Bauen *n*; Bau *m*.

bulb *n* Knolle *f*; Zwiebel *f*; Kugel *f*; (Glüh)Birne *f*.

bulbous *adj* knollig.

bulge *vi* sich (aus)bauchen; hervorquellen; * *n* (Aus)Bauchung *f*; Beule *f*.

bulk *n* Masse *f*; Umfang *m*; Volumen *n*; Großteil *m*; Hauptmasse *f*; Ladung *f*; **in** ~ lose; in großen Mengen.

bulky *adj* sehr umfangreich; sperrig.

bull *n* Bulle *m*; Stier *m*.

bulldog *n* Bulldogge *f*.

bulldozer *n* Planierraupe *f*.

bullet *n* Kugel *f*.

bulletproof *adj* kugelsicher.

bullfight *n* Stierkampf *m*.

bullfighter *n* Stierkämpfer *m*.

bullfighting *n* Stierkampf *m*.

bullion *n* Goldbarren *m*; Silberbarren *m*.

bullock *n* Ochse *m*.

bullring *n* Stierkampfarena *f*.

bull's-eye *n* Bullauge *n*; Butzenscheibe *f*; *(das)* Schwarze *(der Zielscheibe)* *n*.

bully *n* Schläger *m*; brutaler

Kerl *m*; * *vt* tyrannisieren; einschüchtern.

bulwark *n* Bollwerk *n*; Mole *f*.

bum *n* Hintern *m*; Herumtreiber *m*; Tippelbruder *m*.

bumblebee *n* Hummel *f*.

bump *n* heftiger Stoß *m*; Beule *f*; Unebenheit *f*; * *vt* (zusammen)stoßen; * *vi* holpern; rumpeln.

bumpkin *n* (*contp*) Bauer *m*; Provinzler *m*.

bumpy *adj* holprig.

bun *n* süßes Brötchen; (Haar)Knoten *m*.

bunch *n* Bündel *n*; Bund *m*; Haufen *m*; Anzahl *f*.

bundle *n* Bündel *n*; Paket *n*; Haufen *m*; * *vt* bündeln.

bung *n* Spund *m*; Stöpsel *m*; * *vt* verspunden; verstopfen.

bungalow *n* Bungalow *m*.

bungle *vt* verpfuschen; verpatzen; * *vi* pfuschen; patzen.

bunion *n* entzündeter Fußballen *m*.

bunk *n* Koje *f*.

bunker *n* Bunker *m*.

buoy *n* (*mar*) Boje *f*; Bake *f*.

buoyancy *n* Schwimmkraft *f*; Auftrieb *m*; (*fig*) Spannkraft *f*; Schwung *m*.

buoyant *adj* schwimmend; lebhaft.

burden *n* Last *f*; Ladung *f*; Bürde *f*; * *vt* belasten.

bureau *n* Schreibpult *n*; Büro *n*; Amt *n*.

bureaucracy *n* Bürokratie *f*.

bureaucrat *n* Bürokrat *m*.

burglar *n* Einbrecher *m*.

burglar alarm *n* Alarmanlage *f*.

burglary *n* Einbruch *m*.

burial *n* Begräbnis *n*; Beerdigung *f*.

burial place *n* Grabstätte *f*.

burlesque *n* Burleske *f*; Posse *f*; *adj* burlesk; possenhaft.

burly *adj* stämmig.

burn *vt vi* (ver)brennen; * *n* Verbrennung *f*; verbrannte Stelle *f*.

burner *n* Brenner *m*.

burning *adj* brennend; glühend.

burrow *n* Bau *m*; Höhle *f*; * *vi* graben; sich vergraben.

bursar *n* Quästor *m*; Finanzverwalter *m*.

burst *vi* bersten; platzen; (zer)brechen; explodieren; ausbrechen; **to ~ into tears** in Tränen ausbrechen; **to ~ out laughing** in Gelächter ausbrechen; **to ~ into** hereinplatzen; * *vt* sprengen; zum Platzen bringen; aufbrechen * *n* Platzen *n*; (Aus)Bruch *m*; Stoß *m*.

bury *vt* vergraben; begraben; beerdigen.

bus *n* Bus *m*; Omnibus *m*.

bush *n* Busch *m*, Strauch *m*; Gebüsch *n*; Schopf *m*.

business *n* Geschäft *n*; Arbeit *f*; Unternehmen *n*; Sache *f*; Angelegenheit *f*.

businesslike *adj* geschäftsmäßig; sachlich.

businessman *n* Geschäftsmann *m*.

business trip *n* Geschäftsreise *f*.

businesswoman *n* Geschäftsfrau *f*.

bus-stop *n* Bushaltestelle *f*.

bust *n* Büste *f*; Busen *m*.

bustle *vi* sich tummeln; (herum)wirtschaften; * *n* Geschäftigkeit *f*; geschäftiges Treiben.

bustling *adj* geschäftig; belebt.

busy *adj* beschäftigt; belebt; arbeitsreich; übereifrig; unruhig.

busybody *n* aufdringlicher Mensch *m*; Gschaftlhuber.

but *conj* aber, jedoch; außer, als; sondern; dennoch, trotzdem; *adv* nur, bloß.

butcher *n* Metzger *m*, Fleischer *m*, Schlachter *m*; (*fig*) Schlächter; * *vt* (ab)schlachten.

butcher's (shop) *n* Metzgerei *f*.

butchery *n* Metzgerhandwerk

n; Schlachthof *m*; (*fig*) Gemetzel *n*.

butler *n* Butler *m*.

butt *n* (dickes) Ende *n*; Kolben *m*; Stummel *m*; Stoß *m*; Hintern *m*; (*fig*) Zielscheibe *f*; * *vt* (mit dem Kopf) stoßen.

butter *n* Butter *f*; * *vt* buttern.

buttercup *n* (*bot*) Butterblume *f*.

butterfly *n* Schmetterling *m*.

buttermilk *n* Buttermilch *f*.

buttocks *npl* Gesäß *n*.

button *n* Knopf *m*; Taste *f*; * *vt* (zu)knöpfen.

buttonhole *n* Knopfloch *n*.

buttress *n* Strebepfeiler *m*; (*fig*) Stütze *f*; * *vt* (unter)stützen.

buxom *adj* drall.

buy *vt* (ein)kaufen.

buyer *n* (Ein)Käufer(in) *m*(*f*).

buzz *n* Summen *n*; Schwirren *n*; Gemurmel *n*; Gerede *n*; * *vi* summen; schwirren; (*fig*) dröhnen.

buzzard *n* Bussard *m*.

buzzer *n* Summer *m*.

by *prep* bei; an; neben; durch; über, via; vorbei; entlang; auf; spätestens bis; spätestens um; -weise; nach; von; mit; um; ~ **and** ~ nach und nach; ~ **the** ~ nebenbei bemerkt; ~ **far** bei weitem; ~ **all means** unbedingt; durchaus.

bygone *adj* das Vergangene *n*.

by-law *n* Satzung *f*; Ortsstatut *n*; Durchführungsverordnung *f*.

bypass *n* Umgehungsstraße *f*; Bypass *m*.

by-product *n* Nebenprodukt *n*.

by-road *n* Nebenstraße *f*.

bystander *n* Umstehende(r) *f*(*m*).

byte *n* (*comput*) Byte *n*.

byword *n* Sprichwort *n*; Inbegriff *m*.

C

cab *n* Taxi *n*; Führerhaus *n*.

cabbage *n* Kohl *m*.

cabin *n* Hütte *f*; Kabine *f*.

cabinet *n* Kabinett *n*; Vitrine *f*; Schrank *m*.

cabinet-maker *n* Kunsttischler *m*; Möbeltischler *m*.

cable *n* (*mar*) Kabel *n*; Tau *n*.

cable car *n* Seilbahn *f*.

cable television *n* Kabelfernsehen *n*.

caboose *n* (*mar*) Kombüse *f*.

cache *n* geheimes Lager *n*.

cackle *vi* gackern; schnattern; * *n* Gegacker *n*; Geschnatter *n*.

cactus *n* Kaktus *m*.

cadence *n* (*mus*) Kadenz *f*; Rhythmus *m*; Tonfall *m*; Gleichschritt *m*.

cadet *n* Kadett *m*.

cadge *vt* schnorren.

caesarean section, ~ operation *n* (*med*) Kaiserschnitt *m*.

café *n* Café *n*; Restaurant *n*.

cafeteria *n* Cafeteria *f*; Kantine *f*.

caffein(e) *n* Koffein *n*.

cage *n* Käfig *m*; Förderkorb *m*; * *vt* in einen Käfig sperren.

cagey *adj* verschlossen; vorsichtig.

cajole *vt* schmeicheln; beschwatzen.

cake *n* Kuchen *m*; Torte *f*; Stück *n*; Kruste *f*; * *vt* mit einer Kruste überziehen.

calamitous *adj* verheerend; katastrophal.

calamity *n* Katastrophe *f*; Misere *f*.

calculable *adj* berechenbar; kalkulierbar.

calculate *vt* berechnen; kalkulieren.

calculation *n* Berechnung *f*; Kalkulation *f*.

calculator *n* Rechner *m*.

calculus *n* Rechnung *f*; (*med*) Stein *m*.

calendar *n* Kalender *m*.

calf *n* Kalb *n*; Wade *f*.

caliber *n* Kaliber *n*.

calisthenics *npl* Gymnastik *f*.

call *vt* ; (an)rufen; herbeirufen; (ein)berufen; aufrufen; nennen; **to ~ for** rufen nach; verlangen; **to ~ on** besuchen; **to ~ attention to** Aufmerksamkeit lenken auf; **to ~ names** beschimpfen; * *n* Ruf *m*; Anruf *m*; Signal *n*; Berufung *f*; Aufruf *m*; Besuch *m*; Forderung *f*; Veranlassung *f*.

caller *n* Besucher(in) *m(f)*; Anrufer(in) *m(f)*; Rufer(in) *m(f)*.

calligraphy *n* Kalligraphie *f*.

calling *n* Rufen *n*; Beruf *m*; Berufung *f*.

callous *adj* schwielig; gefühllos.

calm *n* Ruhe *f*; Stille *f*; Gelassenheit *f*; Windstille *f*; * *adj* **~ly** *adv* ruhig; (wind)still; gelassen; * *vt* beruhigen; besänftigen.

calmness *n* Stille *f*; Ruhe *f*; Gelassenheit *f*.

calorie *n* Kalorie *f*.

calumny *n* Verleumdung *f*.

Calvary *n* Golgotha *n*; Kalvarienberg *m*.

calve *vi* kalben.

Calvinist *n* Kalvinist(in) *m(f)*.

camel *n* Kamel *n*.

cameo *n* Kamee *f*.

camera *n* Kamera *f*.

cameraman *n* Kameramann *m*.

camomile *n* Kamille *f*.

camouflage *n* Tarnung *f*; Verschleierung *f*.

camp *n* Lager *n*; * *vi* kampieren; lagern; zelten.

campaign *n* Kampagne *f*; Feldzug *m*; Wahlkampf *m*; * *vi* an einem Feldzug teilnehmen; kämpfen; im Wahlkampf stehen.

campaigner *n* Feldzugteilnehmer *m*; Kämpfer(in) *m(f)*.

camper *n* Camper(in) *m(f)*; Wohnmobil *n*.

camphor *n* Kampfer *m*.

camping *n* Zelten *n*; Camping *n*.

campsite *n* Lagerplatz *m*; Zeltplatz *m*.

campus *n* Campus *m*.

can *vi* können; dürfen; *vt* eindosen; * *n* Kanne *f*; Dose *f*; Büchse *f*; Kanister *m*.

canal *n* Kanal *m*.

cancel *vt* streichen; absagen; ausfallen lassen; widerrufen; kündigen.

cancellation *n* Streichung *f*; Absage *f*; Widerrufung *f*; Kündigung *f*.

cancer *n* Krebs *m*.

Cancer *n* Krebs *m*.

cancerous *adj* Krebs-; krebsbefallen.

candid *adj* **~ly** *adv* offen; aufrichtig; unvoreingenommen.

candidate *n* Kandidat(in) *m(f)*; Bewerber(in) *m(f)*.

candied *adj* kandiert; kristallisiert; (*fig*) zuckersüß.

candle *n* Kerze *f*.

candlelight *n* Kerzenlicht *n*.

candlestick *n* Kerzenleuchter *m*.

candour *n* Offenheit *f*; Aufrichtigkeit *f*; Unvoreingenommenheit *f*.

candy *n* Kandis *m*; Süßigkeiten *fpl*; Bonbon *n*.

cane *n* Rohr *n*; (Spazier)Stock *m*.

canine *adj* Hunde-; hündisch.

canister *n* Blechbüchse *f*; Kanister *m*.

cannabis *n* Cannabis *m*; Haschisch *n*.

cannibal *n* Kannibale *m*.

cannibalism *n* Kannibalismus *m*.

cannon *n* Kanone *f*; Geschütz *n*.

cannonball *n* Kanonenkugel *f*.

canny *adj* schlau.

canoe *n* Kanu *n*.

canon *n* Kanon *m*; Regel *f*; ~

law Kirchenrecht *n.*

canonization *n* Heiligsprechung *f.*

canonize *vt* heiligsprechen; sanktionieren.

can opener *n* Dosenöffner *m.*

canopy *n* Baldachin *m.*

cantankerous *adj* streitsüchtig.

canteen *n* Kantine *f;* Feldflasche *f.*

canter *n* Arbeitsgalopp *m.*

canvas *n* Segeltuch *n;* Segel *pl;* (Zelt)Leinwand *f;* Zelt *n;* Plane *f;* Gemälde *n.*

canvass *vt* erörtern; ausfragen; * *vi* (Stimmen) werben; diskutieren.

canvasser *n* Wahlhelfer(in) *m(f);* Handelsvertreter(in) *m(f).*

canyon *n* Felsschlucht *f.*

cap *n* Mütze *f;* Kappe *f;* Haube *f.*

capability *n* Fähigkeit *f;* Talent *n.*

capable *adj* fähig; tüchtig; imstande.

capacitate *vt* befähigen.

capacity *n* Kapazität *f;* Fassungsvermögen *f;* Fähigkeit *f;* Leistung *f;* Eigenschaft *f.*

cape *n* Umhang *m;* Cape *n;* Kap *n.*

caper *n* Kapriole *f;* Luftsprung *m;* Streich *m;* * *vi* Luftsprünge machen; herumhüpfen.

capillary *adj* kapillar; Haar-.

capital *adj* kapital; Haupt-; Tod(es)-; groß(artig); größt(er, e, es); verhängnisvoll; * *n* Hauptstadt *f;* Großbuchstabe *m;* Kapital *n.*

capitalism *n* Kapitalismus *m.*

capitalist *n* Kapitalist *m.*

capitalize *vt* kapitalisieren; groß schreiben; **to ~ on** Kapital schlagen aus.

capital punishment *n* Todesstrafe *f.*

Capitol *n* Kapitol *n.*

capitulate *vi* kapitulieren; sich ergeben.

capitulation *n* Kapitulation *f.*

caprice *n* (*mus*) Capriccio *n;* Laune *f.*

capricious *adj* ~**ly** *adv* kapriziös; launisch.

Capricorn *n* Steinbock *m.*

capsize *vi* (*mar*) kentern; umschlagen.

capsule *n* Kapsel *f.*

captain *n* Kapitän *m;* Hauptmann *m;* Führer *m.*

captaincy, captainship *n* Kapitänsrang *m;* Hauptmannsrang *m;* Führung *f.*

captivate *vt* (*fig*) gefangennehmen; fesseln; bezaubern.

captivation *n* Bezauberung *f.*

captive *n* Gefangene(r) *f(m);* * *adj* gefangen; gefesselt.

captivity *n* Gefangenschaft *f.*

capture *n* Gefangennahme *f;* Eroberung *f;* * *vt* gefangennehmen; (ein)fangen; erobern.

car *n* Auto *n;* Wagen *m.*

carafe *n* Karaffe *f.*

caramel *n* Karamel *m;* Karamelle *f.*

carat *n* Karat *n.*

caravan *n* Karawane *f;* Wohnwagen *m.*

caraway *n* (*bot*) Kümmel *m.*

carbohydrates *npl* Kohlenhydrate *npl.*

carbon *n* Kohlenstoff *m;* Kohle *f;* Kohlepapier *n.*

carbon copy *n* Durchschlag *m;* (*fig*) Ebenbild *n.*

carbonize *vt* verkohlen; karbonisieren.

carbon paper *n* Kohlepapier *n.*

carbuncle *n* Karbunkel *m;* Karfunkel *m.*

carburetor *n* Vergaser *m.*

carcass *n* Kadaver *m;* Rumpf *m;* Gerippe *n.*

card *n* Karte *f;* **pack of ~s** Kartenspiel *n.*

cardboard *n* Karton *m;* Pappe *f.*

card game *n* Kartenspiel *n.*

cardiac *adj* Herz-.

cardinal *adj* Kardinal(s)-; Haupt-; grundsätzlich; scharlachrot; * *n* Kardinal *m*; Scharlachrot *n*.

card table *n* Kartentisch *m*.

care *n* Sorge *f*; Sorgfalt *f*; Obhut *f*; Pflege *f*; * *vi* sich sorgen; mögen; Lust haben; **what do I ~?** was kümmert es mich ?; **to ~ for** *vt* sorgen für; sich kümmern um; sich etwas machen aus.

career *n* Karriere *f*; Beruf *m*; * *vi* rasen, rennen.

carefree *adj* sorgenfrei; sorglos.

careful *adj* ~ly *adv* vorsichtig; sorgfältig;.

careless *adj* ~ly *adv* unvorsichtig; sorglos; nachlässig; unbedacht; leichtsinnig; unbekümmert.

carelessness *n* Nachlässigkeit *f*; Unüberlegtheit *f*; Unachtsamkeit *f*; Leichtsinn *m*.

caress *n* Liebkosung *f*; * *vt* liebkosen; streicheln.

caretaker *n* Hausmeister(in) *m(f)*.

car-ferry *n* Autofähre *f*.

cargo *n* Fracht *f*; Ladung *f*.

car hire *n* Autoverleih *m*.

caricature *n* Karikatur *f*; * *vt* karikieren.

caries *n* Karies *f*.

caring *adj* fürsorglich.

Carmelite *n* Karmeliter(in) *m(f)*.

carnage *n* Blutbad *n*; Gemetzel *n*.

carnal *adj* ~ly *adv* fleischlich; sinnlich; sexuell.

carnation *n* Nelke *f*; Blaßrot *n*.

carnival *n* Karneval *m*; Fasching *m*; Volksfest *n*.

carnivorous *adj* fleischfressend.

carol *n* Weihnachtslied *n*.

carpenter *n* Zimmermann *m*; Tischler *m*; **~s bench** Hobelbank *f*.

carpentry *n* Zimmerei *f*; Zimmerhandwerk *n*.

carpet *n* Teppich *m*; * *vt* mit Teppich auslegen.

carpeting *n* Teppiche *mpl*.

carriage *n* Wagen *m*; Kutsche *f*; Transport *m*; Fracht *f*; Haltung *f*.

carriage-free *adj* frachtfrei.

carrier *n* (Über)Träger *m*; Spediteur *m*; Bote *m*.

carrier pigeon *n* Brieftaube *f*.

carrion *n* Aas *n*.

carrot *n* Karotte *f*; Möhre *f*.

carry *vt* (über)tragen; (über-) bringen; befördern; haben; führen; * *vi* tragen; **to ~ the day** den Sieg davontragen; **to ~ on** weitermachen; fortsetzen.

cart *n* Karre *f*; Karren *m*; Wagen *m*; * *vt* karren.

cartel *n* Kartell *n*.

carthorse *n* Zugpferd *n*.

Carthusian *n* Karthäuser(mönch) *m*.

cartilage *n* Knorpel *m*.

cartload *n* Wagenladung *f*; Fuhre *f*.

carton *n* Karton *m*; Schachtel *f*.

cartoon *n* Cartoon *m*; Zeichentrickfilm *m*.

cartridge *n* Patrone *f*; Kartusche *f*; Kassette *f*; Tonabnehmer *m*.

carve *vt* schnitzen; meißeln; tranchieren.

carving *n* Schnitzerei *f*.

carving knife *n* Tranchiermesser *n*.

car wash *n* Autowäsche *f*; Waschstraße *f*.

case *n* Kiste *f*; Koffer *m*; Behälter *m*; Gehäuse *n*; Fall *m*; Sache *f*; **in ~** im Falle.

cash *n* Bargeld *n*; * *vt* einlösen; zu Geld machen.

cash card *n* Scheckkarte *f*.

cash dispenser *n* Geldautomat *m*.

cashier *n* Kassierer(in) *m(f)*.

cashmere *n* Kaschmir *m*.

casing *n* Gehäuse *n*; Verkleidung *f*; Hülle *f*.

casino *n* Kasino *n*.

cask *n* Faß *n*.

casket *n* Schatulle *f*.
casserole *n* Kasserolle *f*.
cassette *n* Kassette *f*.
cassette player, recorder *n* Kasettenrecorder *m*.
cassock *n* Soutane *f*.
cast *vt* werfen; auswerfen; abwerfen; abgeben; gießen; formen; besetzen; * *n* Wurf *m*; Besetzung *f*; Guß(form *f*) *m*; Abdruck *m*; Gipsverband *m*; Schlag *m*.
castanets *npl* Kastagnetten *fpl*.
castaway *n* Schiffbrüchige(r) *f(m)*; Ausgestoßene(r) *f(m)*.
caste *n* Kaste *f*.
castigate *vt* züchtigen; (*fig*) geißeln.
casting vote *n* entscheidende Stimme *f*.
cast iron *n* Gußeisen *n*.
castle *n* Schloß *n*; Burg *f*; Turm *m*.
cast-off *n* abgelegtes Kleidungsstück *n*; *adj* abgelegt; ausrangiert.
castor oil *n* Rizinusöl *n*.
castrate *vt* kastrieren.
castration *n* Kastration *f*.
cast steel *n* Gußstahl *m*.
casual *adj* ~ly *adv* zufällig; gelegentlich; beiläufig; lässig; salopp.
casualty *n* Unfall *m*; Opfer *n*; **casualties** *pl* (*mil*) Verluste *pl*.
cat *n* Katze *f*.
catalogue *n* Katalog *m*; Verzeichnis *n*.
catalyst *n* Katalysator *m*.
catapult *n* Katapult *n*; Schleuder *f*.
cataract *n* Katarakt *m*; Wasserfall *m*; grauer Star *m*.
catarrh *n* Katarrh *m*; Schnupfen *m*.
catastrophe *n* Katastrophe *f*.
catcall *n* Buhruf *m*; Pfiff *m*.
catch *vt* (ein)fangen; auffangen; erwischen; einholen; ergreifen; **to ~ cold** sich erkälten; **to ~ fire** Feuer fangen; * *n* Fang *m*; Fangen *n*; (*mus*)

Kanon *m*; Haken *m*; Verschluß *m*.
catching *adj* ansteckend.
catchphrase *n* Schlagwort *n*.
catchword *n* Schlagwort *n*; Stichwort *n*.
catchy *adj* eingängig; anziehend.
catechism *n* Katechismus *m*.
catechize *vt* katechisieren; ausfragen.
categorical *adj* ~ly *adv* kategorisch.
categorize *vt* kategorisieren.
category *n* Kategorie *f*.
cater *vi* Speisen und Getränke liefern; (*fig*) befriedigen.
caterer *n* Lieferant von Speisen und Getränken *m*.
catering *n* Verpflegung *f*.
caterpillar *n* Raupe *f*.
catgut *n* (*med*) Katgut *n*; Darmsaite *f*.
cathedral *n* Kathedrale *f*; Dom *m*.
catholic *adj* katholisch; * *n* Katholik(in) *m(f)*.
Catholicism *n* Katholizismus *m*.
cattle *n* Vieh *n*.
cattle show *n* Viehausstellung *f*.
caucus *n* Wahlversammlung *f*.
cauliflower *n* Blumenkohl *m*.
cause *n* Ursache *f*; Grund *m*; Sache *f*; * *vt* verursachen; veranlassen; bereiten.
causeway *n* Damm *m*.
caustic *adj* ätzend; * *n* Ätzmittel *n*.
cauterize *vt* kauterisieren; (aus)brennen; (*fig*) abtöten.
caution *n* Vorsicht *f*; Verwarnung *f*; * *vt* (ver)warnen.
cautionary *adj* warnend; Warn-.
cautious *adj* vorsichtig; achtsam; verhalten.
cavalier *adj* arrogant; rücksichtslos; lässig.
cavalry *n* Kavallerie *f*.
cave *n* Höhle *f*.
caveat *n* (*law*) Einspruch *m*.

cavern n Höhle f.
cavernous adj voller Höhlen;
 hohl, eingefallen.
caviar n Kaviar m.
cavity n Hohlraum m; Höhle f;
 Loch (im Zahn) n.
cease vt, vi aufhören.
ceasefire n Waffenruhe f.
ceaseless adj ~ly adv unaufhörlich; unablässig.
cedar n Zeder f.
cede vt abtreten; überlassen.
ceiling n Decke f; Maximum n.
celebrate vt feiern.
celebration n Feier f; Verherrlichung f.
celebrity n Berühmtheit f;
 Ruhm m.
celery n Sellerie m.
celestial adj himmlisch; Him-
 mels-.
celibacy n Zölibat n; (sexuelle)
 Enthaltsamkeit f.
celibate adj unverheiratet; sexuell enthaltsam.
cell n Zelle f.
cellar n (Wein)Keller m.
cello n Cello n.
cellophane n Zellophan n.
cellular adj Zell-.
cellulose n (chem) Zellulose f.
cement n Zement m; Mörtel m;
 Kitt m; * vt zementieren; kitten.
cemetery n Friedhof m.
cenotaph n Ehrengrabmahl n.
censor n Zensor m.
censorious adj kritisch; krit-
 telig.
censorship n Zensur f.
censure n Tadel m; Verweis m;
 Kritik f; * vt tadeln; kritisieren.
census n (Volks)Zählung f.
cent n Cent m; (fam) Heller m.
centenarian n Hundertjäh-
 rige(r) f(m).
centenary n Jahrhundert n;
 hundertjähriges Jubiläum n;
 * adj hundertjährig.
centennial adj hundertjährig.
centre n Zentrum n; Mitte f;
 Mittelpunkt m; Zentrale f; * vt

zentrieren; in den Mittelpunkt
 stellen; * vi im Mittelpunkt
 stehen; sich konzentrieren;
 (fig) sich gründen.
centigrade adj Celsius.
centiliter n Zentiliter m.
centimetre n Zentimeter m.
centipede n Hundertfüßer m.
central adj, ~ly adv zentral;
 Haupt-.
centralize vt zentralisieren.
centrifugal adj zentrifugal.
century n Jahrhundert n.
ceramic adj keramisch.
cereals npl Getreide n.
cerebral adj Gehirn-; intellektuell; vergeistigt.
ceremonial adj zeremoniell;
 feierlich; rituell; * n Zeremoniell n.
ceremonious adj, ~ly adv
 feierlich; förmlich; umständlich.
ceremony n Zeremonie f;
 Förmlichkeiten fpl.
certain adj, ~ly adv sicher; bestimmt; gewiß.
certainty, certitude n Sicherheit f; Bestimmtheit f; Überzeugung f.
certificate n Bescheinigung f;
 Urkunde f; Zeugnis n; Gutachten n.
certification n Bescheinigung
 f; Beglaubigung f.
certified mail n eingeschrie-
 bene Sendung f.
certify vt bescheinigen; beglaubigen; versichern; für geisteskrank erklären.
cervical adj Gebärmutterhals-.
cessation n Aufhören n; Einstellung f.
cesspool n Sickergrube f; (fig)
 Pfuhl m.
chafe vt (warm)reiben; scheuern; (fig) ärgern.
chaff n Spreu f; Häcksel n.
chaffinch n Buchfink m.
chagrin n Ärger m; Verdruß
 m.
chain n Kette f; * vt (an)ketten;
 in Ketten legen.

chain reaction n Kettenreaktion f.

chainstore n Kettenladen m.

chair n Stuhl m; Sessel m; Vorsitz m; Lehrstuhl m; Sänfte f; * vt bestuhlen; den Vorsitz haben.

chairman n Vorsitzender m.

chalice n Kelch m.

chalk n Kreide f; Kalk m.

challenge n Herausforderung f; (fig) Einwand m; (fig) Aufgabe f; * vt herausfordern; fordern; in Frage stellen.

challenger n Herausforderer m.

challenging adj herausfordernd; schwierig.

chamber n Kammer f; Zimmer n.

chambermaid n Zimmermädchen n.

chameleon n Chamäleon n.

chamois leather n Fensterleder n.

champagne n Champagner m.

champion n Sieger m; Meister m; Verfechter m; * vt verfechten; eintreten für.

championship n Meisterschaft f.

chance n Chance f; Zufall m; Schicksal n; Möglichkeit f; Risiko n; **by ~** zufällig; * vt riskieren.

chancellor n Kanzler m.

chancery n Kanzlei f; Billigkeitsrecht n.

chandelier n Kronleuchter m.

change vt (ver)ändern; wechseln; (ver)tauschen; * vi sich (ver)ändern; wechseln; sich verwandeln; sich umziehen; * n (Ver)Änderung f; Wechsel m; (Ver)Wandlung f; Abwechslung f; (Aus)Tausch m; Wechselgeld n.

changeable adj unbeständig; wankelmütig.

changeless adj unveränderlich.

changing adj veränderlich; wechselnd.

channel n Kanal m; Rinne f; Furche f; (fig) Weg; * vt furchen; (fig) kanalisieren.

chant n Gesang m; Singsang m; * vt singen.

chaos n Chaos n; Durcheinander n.

chaotic adj chaotisch.

chapel n Kapelle f; Gottesdienst m.

chaplain n Kaplan m; Geistlicher m.

chapter n Kapitel n.

char vt verkohlen.

character n Charakter m; Figur f; Rolle f; Buchstabe m.

characteristic adj ~ally adv charakteristisch; typisch.

characterize vt charakterisieren.

characterless adj charakterlos.

charade n Scharade f; Farce f.

charcoal n Holzkohle f; Zeichenkohle f; Kohlezeichnung f.

charge vt (be)laden; beauftragen; anklagen; belasten; berechnen; angreifen; stürmen; * n Ladung f; Belastung f; Preis m; (mil) Angriff m; Anklage f; Verantwortung f; Schützling m.

chargeable adj anrechenbar; belangbar.

charge card n Kreditkarte f.

charitable adj ~bly adv wohltätig, karitativ; nachsichtig.

charity n Nächstenliebe f; Wohltätigkeit f; Nachsicht f; Almosen n; wohltätige Einrichtung f.

charlatan n Scharlatan m.

charm n Charme m; Zauber m; Talismann m; * vt bezaubern; verzaubern.

charming adj bezaubernd; charmant.

chart n Tabelle f; Karte f; Schaubild n.

charter n Urkunde f; Freibrief m; Charta f; Chartern n; * vt chartern.

charter flight n Charterflug m.

chase vt jagen; verfolgen; * n Jagd f; Verfolgung f.

chasm n Kluft f; Abgrund m.

chaste adj keusch; unschuldig; schlicht.

chasten vt züchtigen; (fig) läutern; (fig) dämpfen.

chastise vt züchtigen; (fig) geißeln, scharf tadeln.

chastisement n Züchtigung f; Strafe f.

chastity n Keuschheit f; Unschuld f; Schlichtheit f.

chat vi plaudern; * n Plauderei f; Schwätzchen n.

chatter vi schnattern; klappern; * n Geschnatter n; Klappern n.

chatterbox n Plappermaul n.

chatty adj gesprächig; plaudernd.

chauffeur n Chauffeur m.

chauvinist n Chauvinist m.

cheap adj, ~ly adv billig; preiswert; schäbig; ordinär.

cheapen vt verbilligen; herabsetzen.

cheaper adj billiger; preiswerter.

cheat vt betrügen; beschwindeln; * vi betrügen; schwindeln; mogeln * n Betrüger(in) m(f); Schwindler(in) m(f); Betrug m; Schwindel m.

check vt überprüfen; kontrollieren; aufhalten; zum Stehen bringen; zügeln; Schach bieten; * n Schach n; Hindernis n; Einhalt m; Kontrolle f; Überprüfung f; Karo(muster) n.

checkmate n Matt n.

checkout n Abreise f; Kasse f.

checkpoint n Kontrollpunkt m.

checkup n Überprüfung f; Vorsorgeuntersuchung f.

cheek n Wange f; Backe f; (fam) Frechheit f.

cheekbone n Wangenknochen m.

cheer n Beifall m; Hurra n; Aufmunterung f; gute Laune f; * vt Beifall spenden; zujubeln; anfeuern; aufmuntern.

cheerful adj, ~ly adv fröhlich; vergnügt; freundlich.

cheerfulness, cheeriness n Fröhlichkeit f.

cheese n Käse m.

chef n Küchenchef m.

chemical adj chemisch.

chemist n Chemiker(in) m(f); Apotheker(in) m(f); Drogist(in) m(f).

chemistry n Chemie f.

cheque n Scheck m.

cheque account n Girokonto n.

chequerboard n Schachbrett n; Damebrett n.

chequered adj kariert; bunt; (fig) bewegt.

cherish vt (wert)schätzen; in Ehren halten; hegen; zugetan sein.

cheroot n Stumpen m.

cherry n Kirsche f; Kirschrot n; * adj kirschrot.

cherrytree n Kirschbaum m.

cherub n Cherub m.

chess n Schach n.

chessboard n Schachbrett n.

chessman n Schachfigur f.

chest n Truhe f; Kiste f; Kasten m; Brust f; ~ of drawers Kommode f.

chestnut n Kastanie f; Kastanienbraun n.

chestnut tree n Kastanienbaum m.

chew vt kauen; sinnen.

chewing gum n Kaugummi m.

chic adj schick; elegant.

chicanery n Schikane f.

chick n Küken n; (sl) Biene f.

chicken n Huhn n; Hähnchen n; (fam) Feigling m.

chickenpox n Windpocken fpl.

chickpea n Kichererbse f.

chicory n Chicorée f; Zichorie f.

chide vt (aus)schelten; tadeln.

chief adj wichtigst(er, e, es); hauptsächlich; Haupt-; oberst(er, e, es) ~ly adv hauptsächlich; vor allem; * n Chef m; (Ober)Haupt n; Häuptling m.

chief executive *n* Generaldirektor *m*.

chieftain *n* Häuptling *m*; Anführer *m*.

chiffon *n* Chiffon *m*.

chilblain *n* Frostbeule *f*.

child *n* Kind *n*; **from a ~** von Kindheit an; **with ~** schwanger.

childbirth *n* Geburt *f*; Niederkunft *f*.

childhood *n* Kindheit *f*.

childish *adj* **~ly** *adv* kindlich; kindisch.

childishness *n* Kindlichkeit *f*; Kinderei *f*.

childless *adj* kinderlos.

childlike *adj* kindlich.

children *npl* Kinder *npl*.

chill *adj* kalt; frostig; kühl; * *n* Kälte *f*; Kühle *f*; Frösteln *n*; Erkältung *f*; * *vt* (ab)kühlen; abschrecken.

chilly *adj* kalt; frostig; kühl.

chime *n* Glockenspiel *n*; Geläut *n*; *(fig)* Einklang *m*; * *vi* läuten; schlagen; erklingen.

chimney *n* Schornstein *m*; Kamin *m*.

chimpanzee *n* Schimpanse *m*.

chin *n* Kinn *n*.

china(ware) *n* Porzellan *n*.

chink *n* Ritze *f*; Spalte *f*; * *vi* klimpern.

chip *vt* anschlagen; (ab)schnitzeln; * *vi* abbrechen; abbrökkeln; * *n* Splitter *m*; Schnitzel *n*; Span *n*; angeschlagene Stelle *f*; Spielmarke *f*; Pommes frites *pl*.

chiropodist *n* Fußpfleger(in) *m(f)*.

chirp *vi* zwitschern; zirpen; * *n* Gezirp *n*; Zwitschern *n*.

chirping *n* Zwitschern *n*; Zirpen *n*.

chisel *n* Meißel *m*; * *vt* meißeln.

chitchat *n* Plausch *m*; Klatsch *m*.

chivalrous *adj* ritterlich.

chivalry *n* Ritterlichkeit *f*; Rittertum *n*; Ritterstand *m*.

chives *npl* Schnittlauch *m*.

chlorine *n* Chlor *n*.

chloroform *n* Chloroform *n*.

chock-full *adj* zum Bersten voll.

chocolate *n* Schokolade *f*; Praline *f*; Schokoladenbraun *n*.

choice *n* (Aus)Wahl *f*; Auslese *f*; * *adj* ausgesucht; wählerisch.

choir *n* Chor *m*.

choke *vt* (er)würgen; ersticken.

cholera *n* Cholera *f*.

choose *vt* (aus)wählen; aussuchen; vorziehen.

chop *vt* (zer)hacken; * *n* Hieb *m*; Schlag *m*; Kotelett *n*; **~s** *pl* *(sl)* Kinnbacken *fpl*; Mund *m*; Maul *n*.

chopper *n* Hubschrauber *m*; Hackbeil *n*.

chopping block *n* Hackklotz *m*.

chopsticks *npl* Eßstäbchen *npl*.

choral *adj* Chor-.

chord *n* Saite *f*; Akkord *m*.

chore *n* (unangenehme) Aufgabe *f*; **~s** *pl* Hausarbeit *f*.

chorist, chorister *n* Chorsänger(in) *m(f)*; Chor-knabe *m*.

chorus *n* Chor *m*; Tanzgruppe *f*; Refrain *m*.

Christ *n* Christus *m*.

christen *vt* taufen.

Christendom *n* Christenheit *f*.

christening *n* Taufe *f*.

Christian *adj* christlich; *(fam)* anständig; * *n* Christ(in) *m(f)*; **~ name** Vorname *m*.

Christianity *n* Christentum *n*; Christenheit *f*.

Christmas *n* Weihnachten *n*.

Christmas card *n* Weihnachtskarte *f*.

Christmas Eve *n* Heiligabend *m*.

chrome *n* Chrom *n*.

chronic *adj* chronisch; (an)dauernd; unverbesserlich.

chronicle *n* Chronik *f*.

chronicler *n* Chronist *m*.

chronological *adj*, **~ly** *adv* chronologisch.

chronology *n* Chronologie *f*; Zeitrechnung *f*.

chronometer *n* Chronometer *n*; Zeitmesser *m*.

chubby *adj* rundlich; pummelig.

chuck *vt* werfen; (*fam*) Schluß machen mit.

chuckle *vi* glucksen.

chug *vi* tuckern.

chum *n* Kumpel *m*; Kamerad *m*.

chunk *n* Klotz *m*; Stück *n*; Batzen *m*.

church *n* Kirche *f*; Glaubensgemeinschaft *f*.

churchyard *n* Kirchhof *m*; Friedhof *m*.

churlish *adj* grob; ungehobelt; knauserig.

churn *n* Butterfaß *n*; * *vt* buttern; heftig schütteln; aufwühlen.

cider *n* Apfelwein *m*; Apfelmost *m*.

cigar *n* Zigarre *f*.

cigarette *n* Zigarette *f*.

cigarette case *n* Zigarettenetui *n*.

cigarette end *n* Zigarettenstummel *m*.

cigarette holder *n* Zigarettenspitze *f*.

cinder *n* Schlacke *f*; ~s *pl* Asche *f*.

cinema *n* Kino *n*.

cinnamon *n* Zimt *m*.

cipher *n* Ziffer *f*; Zahl *f*; Null *f*; Chiffre *f*.

circle *n* Kreis *m*; Kreislauf *m*; Rang *m*; Ring *m*; Reif *m*; * *vt* umkreisen; einkreisen; * *vi* kreisen.

circuit *n* Kreislauf *m*; Rundreise *f*; Runde *f*; Stromkreis *m*.

circuitous *adj* einen Umweg machend; weitschweifig.

circular *adj* kreisförmig; rund; * *n* Rundschreiben *n*.

circulate *vi* im Umlauf sein; kursieren; kreisen.

circulation *n* Zirkulation *f*; Kreislauf *m*; Umlauf *m*; Verbreitung *f*; Auflage *f*.

circumcise *vt* beschneiden.

circumcision *n* Beschneidung *f*.

circumference *n* (Kreis)Umfang *m*; Peripherie *f*.

circumflex *n* Zirkumflex *m*.

circumlocution *n* Weitschweifigkeit *f*.

circumnavigate *vt* umschiffen; umsegeln.

circumnavigation *n* Umschiffung *f*; (Welt)Umsegelung *f*.

circumscribe *vt* umschreiben; begrenzen.

circumspect *adj* umsichtig; vorsichtig.

circumspection *n* Umsicht *f*; Vorsicht *f*.

circumstance *n* Umstand *m*; Sachverhalt *m*; Umständlichkeit *f*; ~s *pl* Verhältnisse *npl*.

circumstantial *adj* durch die Umstände bedingt; nebensächlich; detailliert; umständlich.

circumstantiate *vt* genau beschreiben; durch Indizien beweisen.

circumvent *vt* umgehen; überlisten; vereiteln.

circumvention *n* Umgehung *f*; Überlistung *f*; Vereitelung *f*.

circus *n* Zirkus *m*; runder Platz *m*; Amphitheater *n*.

cistern *n* Zisterne *f*; Wasserbehälter *m*; Spülkasten *m*.

citadel *n* Zitadelle *f*.

citation *n* Vorladung *f*; Anführung *f*; Zitat *n*.

cite *vt* zitieren; anführen; vorladen.

citizen *n* Bürger(in) *m(f)*.

citizenship *n* Staatsbürgerschaft *f*; Bürgerrecht *n*.

city *n* (Groß)Stadt *f*.

civic *adj* Bürger-; (staats)bürgerlich; städtisch.

civil *adj* ~ly *adv* staatlich; Bürger-; bürgerlich; zivil(rechtlich); höflich.

civil defence *n* Zivilverteidigung *f*.

civil engineer *n* Bauingenieur *m*.

civilian *n* Zivilist *m*.

civility *n* Höflichkeit *f*.

civilization *n* Zivilisation *f*; Kultur *f*.

civilize *vt* zivilisieren.

civil law *n* Zivilrecht *n*.

civil war *n* Bürgerkrieg *m*.

clad *adj* gekleidet.

claim *vt* fordern; beanspruchen; in Anspruch nehmen; behaupten; * *n* Forderung *f*; Anspruch *m*; Behauptung *f*.

claimant *n* Beanspruchende(r) *f(m)*; Antragsteller(in) *m(f)*; Kläger(in) *m(f)*.

clairvoyant *n* Hellseher(in) *m(f)*.

clam *n* Muschel *f*.

clamber *vi* klettern.

clammy *adj* klamm.

clamour *n* Lärm *m*; Geschrei *n*; Tumult *m*; * *vi* schreien; lärmen; toben.

clamp *n* Klammer *f*; Klampe *f*; Zwinge *f*; * *vt* festklemmen; **to ~ down on** scharf vorgehen gegen.

clan *n* Clan *m*; Sippe *f*; Clique *f*.

clandestine *adj* heimlich; verborgen.

clang *n* Klang *m*; Geklirr *n*; * *vi* schallen; klirren; rasseln.

clap *vt* klatschen; schlagen; klopfen.

clapping *n* Klatschen *n*; Klopfen *n*; Applaus *m*.

claret *n* roter Bordeaux *m*; Rotwein *m*.

clarification *n* Klärung *f*.

clarify *vt* (er)klären; klarstellen.

clarinet *n* Klarinette *f*.

clarity *n* Klarheit *f*.

clash *vi* klirren; rasseln; zusammenstoßen; *(fig)* aneinandergeraten; nicht zusammenpassen; * *n* Geklirr *n*; Zusammenstoß *m*; Konflikt *m*.

clasp *n* Haken *m*; Schnalle *f*; Schließe *f*; Umklammerung *f*; Umarmung *f*; * *vt* ergreifen; umklammern; umarmen; zuhaken.

class *n* Klasse *f*; Kurs *m*; * *vt* klassifizieren.

classic(al) *adj* klassisch; erstklassig; * *n* Klassiker *m*.

classification *n* Klassifikation *f*.

classified advertisement *n* Kleinanzeige *f*.

classify *vt* klassifizieren; einstufen; für geheim erklären.

classmate *n* Klassenkamerad(in) *m(f)*.

classroom *n* Klassenzimmer *n*.

clatter *vi* klappern; poltern; * *n* Geklapper *n*; Getrampel *n*; Lärm *m*.

clause *n* Klausel *f*; Abschnitt *m*; Satz *m*.

claw *n* Klaue *f*; Kralle *f*; * *vt* (zer)kratzen; krallen; packen.

clay *n* Lehm *m*; Ton *m*; *(fig)* Erde *f*.

clean *adj* sauber; rein; anständig; glatt; * *vt* reinigen; säubern; putzen.

cleaner *n* Reinigung *f*; Reinigungsmittel *n*; Raumpfleger(in) *m(f)*.

cleaning *n* Reinigung *f*.

cleanliness *n* Reinlichkeit *f*.

cleanly *adj adv* reinlich.

cleanness *n* Sauberkeit *f*; Reinheit *f*.

cleanse *vt* reinigen; säubern.

clear *adj adv* klar; hell; rein; frei; glatt; * *vt* (auf)klären; (weg)räumen; roden; (be)reinigen; entlasten; abfertigen; (Hindernis) nehmen; * *vi* sich klären; sich aufhellen.

clearance *n* Räumung *f*; Leerung *f*; Rodung *f*; Lichtung *f*; (lichter) Abstand *m*; Tilgung *f*; (Zoll)Abfertigung *f*; Genehmigung *f*.

clear-cut *adj* klar (umrissen).

clearly *adv* klar; deutlich; offensichtlich.

cleaver *n* Hackmesser *n*.

clef *n* (Noten)Schlüssel *m*.

cleft *n* Spalte *f*.

clemency *n* Milde *f*; Gnade *f*.

clement *adj* mild; gnädig.

clench *vt* zusammenpressen; ballen; zusammenbeißen.

clergy *n* Klerus *m*; Geistlichkeit *f*.

clergyman *n* Geistliche(r) *m(f)*.

clerical *adj* geistlich; Schreib-; Büro-.

clerk *n* Sekretär *m*; (kaufmännische(r)) Angestellte(r) *f(m)*.

clever *adj* ~**ly** *adv* geschickt; raffiniert; gescheit; begabt.

click *vt* klicken; schnalzen; * *vi* klicken; schnalzen; zuschnappen; Gefallen aneinander finden.

client *n* Kunde *m*; Kundin *f*; Klient(in) *m(f)*.

cliff *n* Klippe *f*; Felswand *f*.

climate *n* Klima *n*.

climatic *adj* klimatisch; Klima-.

climax *n* Höhepunkt *m*.

climb *vt* erklettern; besteigen; * *vi* klettern; steigen.

climber *n* Kletterer *m*; Bergsteiger(in) *m(f)*; Kletterpflanze *f*.

climbing *n* Klettern *n*.

clinch *vt* entscheiden; vernieten; umklammern.

cling *vi* haften; kleben; hängen; sich klammern.

clinic *n* Klinik *f*.

clink *vt* klirren lassen; anstoßen; * *vi* klirren; klimpern; * *n* Klimpern *n*; Klirren *n*.

clip *vt* (be)schneiden; stutzen; scheren; lochen; (*sl*) eine knallen; * *n* Klammer *f*; Schur *f*.

clipping *n* (Zeitungs)Ausschnitt *m*; ~**s** *pl* Schnitzel *npl*; Stutzen *n*; Schur *f*.

clique *n* Clique *f*.

cloak *n* Umhang *m*; (Deck)Mantel *m*; * *vt* verhüllen; bemänteln.

cloakroom *n* Garderobe *f*.

clock *n* Uhr *f*.

clockwork *n* Uhrwerk *n*; Laufwerk *n*; **like ~** wie am Schnürchen.

clod *n* Klumpen *m*.

clog *n* Klotz *m*; Holzschuh *m*; * *vi* hemmen; verstopfen.

cloister *n* Kloster *n*.

close *vt* (ab)schließen; sperren; * *vi* (sich) schließen; enden; sich verringern; * *n* (Ab)Schluß *m*; Ende *n*; Hof *m*; Gasse *f*; * *adj* nah; dicht; eng; knapp; genau; schwül; verschlossen; * *adv* eng; nahe; dicht; ~ **by** in der Nähe; neben.

closed *adj* geschlossen; verschlossen; gesperrt; geheim.

closely *adv* genau; scharf; dicht; nah.

closeness *n* Nähe *f*; Dichte *f*; Verschlossenheit *f*; Schwüle *f*; Schärfe *f*.

closet *n* (Wand)Schrank *m*; Kabinett *n*.

close-up *n* Nahaufnahme *f*.

closure *n* Schließung *f*; Schluß *m*.

clot *n* Klumpen *m*; Klümpchen *n*.

cloth *n* Tuch *n*; Stoff *m*; (geistliche) Tracht *f*.

clothe *vt* kleiden; einhüllen.

clothes *npl* Kleidung *f*; Wäsche *f*; **bed ~** Bettwäsche *f*.

clothes basket *n* Wäschekorb *m*.

clotheshorse *n* Wäscheständer *m*; (*fam*) Modepuppe *f*.

clothesline *n* Wäscheleine *f*.

clothespeg *n* Wäscheklammer *f*.

clothing *n* Kleidung *f*; Umhüllung *f*.

cloud *n* Wolke *f*; Schwarm *m*; (*fig*) Schatten *m*; * *vt* umwölken; bewölken; einen Schatten werfen auf; * *vi* sich bewölken; sich verdunkeln.

cloudiness *n* Bewölkung *f*; Trübung *f*.

cloudy *adj* bewölkt; Wolken-; umwölkt; nebelhaft.

clout *n* Schlag *m*; Einfluß *m*.

clove *n* (Gewürz)Nelke *f*; Zehe *f*.

clover *n* Klee *m*.

clown n Clown m.

club n Keule f; Knüppel m; Schläger m; Klub m.

clue n Hinweis m; Anhaltspunkt m; Schlüssel m.

clump n Klumpen m; Büschel n; Gruppe f.

clumsiness n Ungeschicklichkeit f; Unbeholfenheit f.

clumsy adj, **clumsily** adv ungeschickt; unbeholfen; schwerfällig; taktlos.

cluster n Haufen m; Traube f; Gruppe f; * vt bündeln; * vi eine Gruppe bilden; sich scharen.

clutch n Griff m; Klaue f; Kupplung f; * vt packen; krampfhaft festhalten.

clutter vt vollstopfen; durcheinanderwerfen; * n Durcheinander n.

coach n Reisebus m; Kutsche f; Trainer m; Nachhilfelehrer m; * vt trainieren; Nachhilfeunterricht geben; instruieren.

coach trip n Busreise f.

coagulate vt gerinnen lassen; * vi gerinnen.

coal n Kohle f.

coalesce vi verschmelzen; sich vereinigen.

coalfield n Kohlenrevier n.

coalition n Koalition f; Bündnis n.

coalman n Kohlenhändler m.

coalmine n Kohlenbergwerk n.

coarse adj ~**ly** adv grob; derb..

coast n Küste f.

coastal adj Küsten-.

coastguard n Küstenwache f.

coastline n Küstenlinie f.

coat n Mantel m; Jacke f; Fell n; Überzug m; Schicht f; * vt überziehen; beschichten; bedecken.

coat hanger n Kleiderbügel m.

coating n Überzug m; Schicht f; Anstrich m.

coax vt überreden.

cob n Maiskolben m; kleines, gedrungenes Pferd n; männlicher Schwan m; Klumpen m.

cobbler n (Flick)Schuster m.

cobbles, cobblestones npl Kopfsteinpflaster n.

cobweb n Spinnwebe f.

cocaine n Kokain n.

cock n Hahn m; Anführer m; (sl) Schwanz m; Penis m; * vt aufrichten; (Ohren) spitzen; spannen.

cock-a-doodle-doo n Kikeriki n.

cockcrow n Hahnenschrei m.

cockerel n junger Hahn m.

cockfight(ing) n Hahnenkampf m.

cockle n Herzmuschel f.

cockpit n Cockpit n.

cockroach n (Küchen)Schabe f.

cocktail n Cocktail m.

cocoa n Kakao m.

coconut n Kokosnuß f.

cocoon n Kokon m.

cod n Kabeljau m; Dorsch m.

code n Codex m; Code m; Schlüssel m.

cod-liver oil n Lebertran m.

coefficient n Koeffizient m.

coercion n Einschränkung f; Zwang m; Nötigung f.

coexistence n Koexistenz f.

coffee n Kaffee m.

coffee break n Kaffeepause f.

coffee house n Kaffeehaus n; Café n.

coffeepot n Kaffeekanne f.

coffee table n Couchtisch m.

coffer n Kiste f; Truhe f; ~**s** pl Schatzkammer f; Deckenkassette f.

coffin n Sarg m.

cog n Zahnrad n.

cogency n zwingende Kraft f; Triftigkeit f.

cogent adj, ~**ly** adv zwingend; triftig.

cognac n Cognac m; Weinbrand m.

cognate adj verwandt.

cognition n Erkenntnis f; Wahrnehmung f.

cognizance n (Er)Kenntnis f; Zuständigkeit f; Gerichtsbarkeit f; Abzeichen n.

cognizant *adj* unterrichtet; (*law*) zuständig.

cogwheel *n* Zahnrad *n*.

cohabit *vi* (unverheiratet) zusammenleben; (*law*) in eheähnlichem Verhältnis leben.

cohabitation *n* Zusammenleben *n*; Beischlaf *m*.

cohere *vi* zusammenhängen.

coherence *n* Zusammenhalt *m*; Zusammenhang *m*; Klarheit *f*.

coherent *adj* zusammenhängend; verständlich; klar.

cohesion *n* Kohäsion *f*; Zusammenhalt *m*.

cohesive *adj* Kohäsions-; Binde-; zusammenhängend.

coil *n* Rolle *f*; Spirale *f*; Spule *f*; * *vt* (auf)wickeln; zusammenrollen.

coin *n* Münze *f*; * *vt* münzen; prägen.

coincide *vi* zusammentreffen; zusammenfallen; übereinstimmen.

coincidence *n* Zufall *m*; Zusammenfallen *n*; Übereinstimmung *f*.

coincidental *adj* genau übereinstimmend; zufällig.

coke *n* Koks *m*.

colander *n* Durchschlag *m*; Sieb *n*.

cold *adj*, **~ly** *adv* kalt; kühl; nüchtern; * *n* Kälte *f*; Erkältung *f*.

cold-blooded *adj* kaltblütig.

coldness *n* Kälte *f*.

cold sore *n* Gesichtherpes *m*.

coleslaw *n* Krautsalat *m*.

colic *n* Kolik *f*.

collaborate *vt* zusammenarbeiten; kollaborieren.

collaboration *n* Zusammenarbeit *f*; Kollaboration *f*.

collapse *vi* zusammenbrechen; einstürzen; * *n* Einsturz *m*; Zusammenbruch *m*; (*med*) Kollaps *m*.

collapsible *adj* zusammenklappbar; Falt-; Klapp-.

collar *n* Kragen *m*; Halsband *n*;

Kummet *n*; (Hals)Kette *f*; Kollier *n*.

collarbone *n* Schlüsselbein *n*.

collate *vt* zusammenstellen (und vergleichen); kollationieren.

collateral *adj* parallel; Seiten-; Neben-; indirekt; * *n* Nebenbürgschaft *f*.

collation *n* Vergleichung *f*; Zusammenstellung (zum Vergleichen) *n*.

colleague *n* Kollege *m*; Kollegin *f*; Mitarbeiter(in) *m(f)*.

collect *vt* (ein)sammeln; zusammentragen; abholen; versammeln.

collection *n* (An)Sammlung *f*; Eintreibung *f*; Kollektion *f*; (*fig*) Fassung *f*.

collective *adj*, **~ly** *adv* kollektiv; gesammelt; Sammel-.

collector *n* Sammler(in) *m(f)*; Einnehmer *m*.

college *n* College *n*; höhere Lehranstalt *f*; Akademie *f*.

collide *vi* kollidieren; zusammenstoßen; (*fig*) im Widerspruch stehen.

collision *n* Zusammenstoß *m*; Kollision *f*; (*fig*) Konflikt *m*.

colloquial *adj*, **~ly** *adv* umgangssprachlich; familiär.

colloquialism *n* umgangssprachlicher Ausdruck *m*.

collusion *n* (*law*) geheimes Einverständnis *n*; Verdunkelung *f*.

colon *n* Doppelpunkt *m*; (*med*) Dickdarm *m*.

colonel *n* (*mil*) Oberst *m*.

colonial *adj* Kolonial-; kolonienbildend.

colonist *n* Kolonist(in) *m(f)*; Siedler(in) *m(f)*.

colonize *vt* kolonisieren; besiedeln.

colony *n* Kolonie *f*; Siedlung *f*.

colossal *adj* kolossal; riesig.

colossus *n* Koloß *m*; Riese *m*.

colour *n* Farbe *f*; Färbung *f*; Anschein *m*; Deckmantel *m*; **~s** *pl* Fahne *f*; Flagge *f*; * *vt* färben; kolorieren; * *vi* sich (ver)färben; rot werden.

colour-blind *adj* farbenblind.

colourful *adj* farbenprächtig; bunt.

colouring *n* Färbung *f*; Farbgebung *f*; (*fig*) Schönfärberei *f*.

colourless *adj* farblos.

colour television *n* Farbfernsehen *n*.

colt *n* Fohlen *n*; (*fig*) Grünschnabel *m*.

column *n* Kolumne *f*; Spalte *f*; Kolonne *f*; Säule *f*; Pfeiler *m*.

columnist *n* Kolumnist(in) *m(f)*.

coma *n* Koma *n*.

comatose *adj* komatös; bewußtlos.

comb *n* Kamm *m*; Wabe *f*; Striegel *m*; * *vt* (durch)kämmen; striegeln.

combat *n* Kampf *m*; Gefecht *n*; **single ~** Zweikampf *m*; * *vt* (be)kämpfen.

combatant *n* Kämpfer(in) *m(f)*.

combative *adj* kampfbereit; aggressiv.

combination *n* Kombination *f*; Verbindung *f*; Vereinigung *f*.

combine *vt* verbinden; kombinieren; * *vi* sich vereinigen; sich verbünden.

combustion *n* Verbrennung *f*.

come *vi* (dran)kommen; werden; **to ~ across/upon** *vt* zufällig treffen; stoßen auf; **to ~ by** *vt* bekommen; kommen zu; vorbeikommen; **to ~ down** *vi* herunterkommen; (ein)stürzen; überliefert werden; **to ~ in for** *vt* bekommen; **to ~ into** *vt* plötzlich zu etwas kommen; erben; **to ~ round/to** *vi* wieder zu sich kommen; vorbeikommen; wiederkehren; sich wieder vertragen; **to ~ up with** *vt* einfallen lassen; auftreiben; daherkommen mit; präsentieren.

comedian *n* Komiker *m*.

comedienne *n* Komikerin *f*.

comedy *n* Komödie *f*; Komik *f*.

comet *n* Komet *m*.

comfort *n* Trost *m*; Wohltat *f*; Behaglichkeit *f*; Komfort *m*; * *vt* trösten; beruhigen.

comfortable *adj*, **~bly** *adv* bequem; komfortabel; gemütlich; angenehm.

comforter *n* Tröster *m*; Schnuller *m*.

comic(al) *adj* **~ly** *adv* komisch.

coming *n* Kommen *n*; Ankunft *f*; * *adj* kommend; (zu)künftig.

comma *n* (*gr*) Komma *n*.

command *vt* befehlen; gebieten (über); kommandieren; beherrschen; verfügen über; einflößen; erzielen; * *n* Befehl *m*; Kommando *n*; Beherrschung *f*; Verfügung *f*; (*fig*) Gewalt *f*.

commander *n* Befehlshaber *m*; Kommandant *m*.

commandment *n* Gebot *n*.

commando *n* Kommando *n*.

commemorate *vt* gedenken; feiern; erinnern an.

commemoration *n* Gedenkfeier *f*; Gedenken *n*.

commence *vt*, *vi* beginnen; anfangen.

commencement *n* Beginn *m*; Anfang *m*.

commend *vt* empfehlen; loben.

commendable *adj*, **commendably** *adv* empfehlenswert; lobenswert.

commendation *n* Empfehlung *f*; Lob *n*.

commensurate *adj* entsprechend; angemessen.

comment *n* Kommentar *m*; Bemerkung *f*; Anmerkung *f*; Stellungnahme; * *vt* bemerken; * *vi* kommentieren; (kritische) Bemerkungen machen.

commentary *n* Kommentar *m*.

commentator *n* Kommentator *m*; Berichterstatter *m*.

commerce *n* Handel *m*; Verkehr *m*.

commercial *adj* Handels-; Geschäfts-; kommerziell; Werbe-.

commiserate *vt* bemitleiden; bedauern.

commiseration *n* Mitleid *n*; Bedauern *n*.

commissariat *n* Intendantur *f*.

commission *n* Auftrag *m*; Patent *n*; Provision *f*; Kommission *f*; * *vt* beauftragen; in Auftrag geben; bestallen; in Dienst stellen.

commissioner *n* Beauftragte(r) *f(m)*; Kommissar *m*.

commit *vt* anvertrauen; einweisen; verüben; verpflichten.

commitment *n* Verpflichtung *f*; Überantwortung *f*; Verübung *f*.

committee *n* Komitee *n*; Ausschuß *m*.

commodity *n* Ware *f*; Rohstoff *m*; Vermögensgegenstand *m*.

common *adj* gemeinsam; all(gemein); Gemeinde-; alltäglich; üblich; gewöhnlich; **in ~** gemein(sam); * *n* Gemeinsamkeit *f*; Norm *f*; Gemeindeland *n*.

commoner *n* Bürgerliche(r) *f(m)*.

common law *n* Gewohnheitsrecht *n*.

commonly *adv* gewöhnlich; im allgemeinen.

commonplace *n* Gemeinplatz *m*; Alltäglichkeit *f*; * *adj* alltäglich.

common sense *n* gesunder Menschenverstand *m*.

commonwealth *n* Gemeinwesen *n*; Republik *f*; Staatenbund *m*.

commotion *n* Aufruhr *m*; Aufregung *f*; Erschütterung *f*.

commune *vt* sich (vertraulich) besprechen; zu Rate gehen.

communicable *adj* mitteilbar; übertragbar.

communicate *vt* mitteilen; übertragen; * *vi* kommunizieren; in Verbindung stehen.

communication *n* Kommunikation *f*; Mitteilung *f*; Übermittlung *f*; Übertragung *f*; Verbindung *f*.

communicative *adj* mitteil-

sam; Mitteilungs-.

communion *n* (*relig*) Kommunion *f*; Gemeinschaft *f*; Verbindung *f*.

communique *n* Kommuniqué *n*.

communism *n* Kommunismus *m*.

communist *n* Kommunist(in) *m(f)*.

community *n* Gemeinschaft *f*; Gemeinde *f*; die Allgemeinheit *f*.

community centre *n* Gemeinschaftszentrum *n*.

commutable *adj* austauschbar; umwandelbar.

commutation *n* (Aus)Tausch *m*; Umwandlung *f*; Abfindung *f*; Pendeln *n*.

commute *vt* austauschen; umwandeln; ablösen; *vi* pendeln.

compact *adj* **~ly** *adv* kompakt; dicht; * *n* Puderdose *f*; Preßling *m*; * *vt* verdichten; zusammenpressen.

compact disc *n* Compact Disc *f*.

companion *n* Begleiter(in) *m(f)*; Gefährte *m*; Gefährtin *f*; Gegenstück *n*; Handbuch *n*; Ritter *n*.

companionship *n* Gesellschaft *f*.

company *n* Gesellschaft *f*; Firma *f*; Besuch *m*; (*fam*) Genossen *pl*; (Theater)Truppe *f*; (*mil*) Kompanie.

comparable *adj* vergleichbar.

comparative *adj* vergleichend; verhältnismäßig; **~ly** *adv* verhältnismäßig; ziemlich.

compare *vt* vergleichen.

comparison *n* Vergleich *m*.

compartment *n* Abteil *n*; Abteilung *f*; Fach *n*; Kammer *f*.

compass *n* Kompaß *m*; Bereich *m*; Umfang *m*; **~es** *pl* Zirkel *m*.

compassion *n* Mitleid *n*; Mitgefühl *n*.

compassionate *adj* mitfühlend; mitleidig.

compatibility n Kompatibilität f; Verträglichkeit f.

compatible adj vereinbar; verträglich; zusammenpassend; kompatibel.

compatriot n Landmann m; Landsmännin f.

compel vt (er)zwingen; (ab)nötigen.

compelling adj zwingend; unwiderstehlich.

compensate vt kompensieren; entschädigen; ausgleichen.

compensation n Entschädigung f; Kompensation f; Ausgleich m; Vergütung f.

compere n Conférencier m; Ansager(in) m(f).

compete vi in Wettbewerb treten; konkurrieren; wetteifern; am Wettkampf teilnehmen.

competence n Kompetenz f; Fähigkeit f.

competent adj ~ly adv fähig; fachkundig; gekonnt; kompetent; ausreichend.

competition n Wettbewerb m; Wettkampf m; Konkurrenz f; Preisausschreiben n.

competitive adj konkurrierend; konkurrenzfähig; Wettbewerbs-.

competitor n Mitbewerber(in) m(f); Konkurrent(in) m(f); Teilnehmer(in) m(f).

compilation n Zusammenstellen n; Sammelwerk n.

compile vt zusammenstellen; kompilieren.

complacency n Selbstzufriedenheit f.

complacent adj selbstzufrieden; selbstgefällig.

complain vi sich beschweren; klagen; beanstanden.

complaint n Beschwerde(n) f(pl); Klage f; Beanstandung f; Reklamation f.

complement n Ergänzung f; Vollständigkeit f; volle Stärke f.

complementary adj ergänzend; komplementär.

complete adj ~ly adv komplett; vollständig; völlig; vollendet; * vt vollenden; abschließen; ausfüllen.

completion n Beendigung f; Vervollständigung f; Fertigstellung f; Ausfüllen n.

complex adj komplex; vielschichtig.

complexion n Teint m; Gesichtsfarbe f; Aussehen n.

complexity n Komplexität f; Vielschichtigkeit f.

compliance n Einwilligung f; Einhaltung f; Willfährigkeit f.

compliant adj willfährig; unterwürfig.

complicate vt komplizieren.

complicated adj kompliziert.

complication n Komplikation f.

complicity n Mitschuld f; Beihilfe f.

compliment n Kompliment n; Lob n; Empfehlung f; Gruß m; * vt ein Kompliment machen; auszeichnen.

complimentary adj Höflichkeits-; schmeichelhaft; Ehren-; Frei-; Gratis-.

comply vi sich fügen; nachkommen; befolgen.

component adj Teil-.

compose vt zusammensetzen; bilden; verfassen; komponieren; entwerfen; beruhigen; ordnen.

composed adj gefaßt; gelassen.

composer n Komponist(in) m(f); Verfasser(in) m(f).

composite adj zusammengesetzt; gemischt.

composition n Komposition f; Zusammensetzung f; Entwurf m; Schriftstück n.

compositor n (Schrift)Setzer(in) m(f).

compost n Kompost m.

composure n Fassung f; Gelassenheit f.

compound vt zusammensetzen; mischen; bilden; beilegen; tilgen; verschlimmern; * adj

zusammengesetzt; Verbund-;
* *n* Zusammensetzung *f*; Mischung *f*; Verbindung *f*; Lager
n; Gefängnishof *m*; Gehege *n*.

comprehend *vt* einschließen;
verstehen; begreifen.

comprehensible *adj* verständlich; begreiflich; **~ly** *adv* verständlicherweise.

comprehension *n* Einbeziehung *f*; Umfang *m*; Begriffsvermögen *n*; Verständnis *n*.

comprehensive *adj*, **~ly** *adv*
umfassend; Gesamt-; Begriffs-.

compress *vt* zusammenpressen; komprimieren; * *n*
Kompresse *f*.

comprise *vt* umfassen; sich
zusammensetzen aus.

compromise *n* Kompromiß *m*;
(*law*) Vergleich *m*; Zugeständnis *n*; * *vt* aufs Spiel setzen;
kompromittieren; * *vi* einen
Kompromiß schließen; (*law*)
sich vergleichen.

compulsion *n* Zwang *m*.

compulsive *adj*, **~ly** *adv*
zwanghaft; zwingend.

compulsory *adj* Zwangs-;
gezwungen; Pflicht-; obligatorisch.

compunction *n* Gewissensbisse *mpl*; Reue *f*.

computable *adj* berechenbar.

computation *n* Berechnung *f*;
Anschlag *m*.

compute *vt* berechnen; veranschlagen.

computer *n* Computer *m*; Rechner *m*.

computerize *vt* auf Computer
umstellen.

computer programing *n* (Computer) Programmierung *f*.

computer science *n* Informatik
f.

comrade *n* Kamerad(in) *m(f)*;
Genosse *m*; Genossin *f*.

comradeship *n* Kameradschaft
f.

con *vt* betrügen; reinlegen; * *n*
Schwindel *m*; Betrüger *m*.

concave *adj* konkav; hohl.

concavity *n* hohle Beschaffenheit *f*; (Aus)Höhlung *f*; Wölbung *f*.

conceal *vt* verbergen; verdecken; verheimlichen; verschleiern.

concealment *n* Verbergung *f*;
Verheimlichung *f*; Versteck *n*;
(Ver)Deckung *f*.

concede *vt* zugestehen; einräumen; gewähren; zugeben; anerkennen.

conceit *n* Einbildung *f*; Selbstgefälligkeit *f*.

conceited *adj* eingebildet;
selbstgefällig.

conceivable *adj* begreiflich;
denkbar; vorstellbar.

conceive *vt* empfangen; sich
vorstellen; ausdenken; * *vi*
schwanger werden; trächtig
werden.

concentrate *vt* konzentrieren;
zusammenziehen.

concentration *n* Konzentration *f*; Ansammlung *f*.

concentration camp *n* Konzentrationslager *n*.

concentric *adj* konzentrisch.

concept *n* Vorstellung *f*; Begriff
m; Auffassung *f*.

conception *n* Empfängnis *f*;
Begreifen *n*; Begriff *m*;
Vorstellung *f*; Konzept *n*; Idee
f.

concern *vt* betreffen; angehen;
beunruhigen; beschäftigen;
* *n* Angelegenheit *f*; Sache *f*;
Unternehmen *n*; Besorgnis *f*;
Wichtigkeit *f*.

concerning *prep* betreffend;
betreffs; hinsichtlich.

concert *n* Konzert *n*; Einvernehmen *n*.

concerto *n* Konzert *n*.

concession *n* Konzession *f*; Zugeständnis *n*; Genehmigung *f*.

conciliate *vt* versöhnen; gewinnen; in Einklang bringen.

conciliation *n* Versöhnung *f*.

conciliatory *adj* versöhnlich;
vermittelnd.

concise *adj*, **~ly** *adv* kurz; bündig; knapp.

conclude *vt* beenden; (ab)schließen; entscheiden.

conclusion *n* (Ab)Schluß *m*; Ende *n*; Entscheidung *f*; Folge *f*.

conclusive *adj*, **~ly** *adv* abschließend; endgültig; schlüssig.

concoct *vt* (zusammen)brauen; aushecken.

concoction *n* Gebräu *n*; Absud *m*.

concomitant *adj* begleitend; gleichzeitig.

concord *n* Eintracht *f*; Übereinstimmung *f*; Harmonie *f*.

concordance *n* Übereinstimmung *f*; Konkordanz *f*.

concordant *adj* übereinstimmend; harmonisch.

concourse *n* Zusammentreffen *n*; Auflauf *m*; Bahnhofshalle *f*.

concrete *n* Beton *m*; * *vt* betonieren; verbinden.

concubine *n* Konkubine *f*.

concur *vi* zusammenfallen; beipflichten; zusammenwirken.

concurrence *n* Zusammentreffen *n*; Übereinstimmung *f*; Einverständnis *n*; Mitwirkung *f*.

concurrently *adv* gleichzeitig; zusammenfallend; übereinstimmend.

concussion *n* (Gehirn)Erschütterung *f*.

condemn *vt* verurteilen; verdammen; verwerfen.

condemnation *n* Verurteilung *f*; Mißbilligung *f*.

condensation *n* Kondensation *f*; Verdichtung *f*; (*fig*) Kürzung *f*.

condense *vt* kondensieren; verdichten; kürzen; zusammenfassen.

condescend *vi* sich herablassen; geruhen.

condescending *adj* herablassend.

condescension *n* Herablassung *f*.

condiment *n* Würze *f*; Gewürz *n*.

condition *vt* zur Bedingung machen; bedingen; konditionieren; * *n* Bedingung *f*; Abmachung *f*; Zustand *m*; Kondition *f*; Lage *f*.

conditional *adj*, **~ly** *adv* bedingt; abhängig; konditional.

conditioned *adj* bedingt; geartet.

conditioner *n* (Konditions-) Trainer *m*.

condolences *npl* Beileid *n*.

condom *n* Kondom *n*.

condominium *n* Kondominium *n*.

condone *vt* verzeihen; vergeben.

conducive *adj* dienlich; förderlich.

conduct *n* (Durch)Führung *f*; Leitung *f*; Verwaltung *f*; Betragen *n*; * *vt* (durch)führen; (ge)leiten; verwalten; dirigieren.

conductor *n* Führer *m*; Leiter *m*; Schaffner *m*; Dirigent *m*; Blitzableiter *m*.

conduit *n* (Leitungs)Rohr *n*; Kanal *m*.

cone *n* Kegel *m*; Zapfen *m*.

confection *n* Konfekt *n*; Konfektionsartikel *m*.

confectioner *n* Konditor(in) *m(f)*.

confectioner's (shop) *n* Konditorei *f*; Süßwarengeschäft *n*.

confederacy *n* (Staaten)Bund *m*; Bündnis *n*; Komplott *n*.

confederate *vi* (sich) verbünden; * *adj* verbündet; Bundes-; * *n* Verbündete(r) *f(m)*; Komplize *m*; Komplizin *f*.

confer *vi* sich beraten; * *vt* verleihen; erteilen.

conference *n* Konferenz *f*; Besprechung *f*.

confess *vt*, *vi* (ein)gestehen; zugeben; beichten.

confession n Beichte f; Geständnis n; Glaubensbekenntnis n.

confessional n Beichtstuhl m.

confessor n Beichtvater m; Bekenner m.

confetti n Konfetti n.

confidant n Vertraute(r) f(m).

confide vt, vi (sich) anvertrauen; vertrauen.

confidence n Vertrauen n; Selbstbewußtsein n; Zuversicht f; vertrauliche Mitteilung f.

confidence trick n Schwindel m; Hochstapelei f.

confident adj gewiß; (selbst)sicher; zuversichtlich.

confidential adj vertraulich; Vertrauens-.

configuration n Gestalt(ung) f; Anordnung f; Aspekt m.

confine vt begrenzen; beschränken; einsperren.

confinement n Beschränkung f; Entbindung f; Haft f.

confirm vt bestätigen; bestärken; festigen; (relig) konfirmieren.

confirmation n Bestätigung f; Be(Stärkung) f; Festigung f; (relig) Konfirmation f.

confirmed adj bestätigt; bestärkt; fest; erklärt; chronisch.

confiscate vt beschlagnahmen; konfiszieren.

confiscation n Beschlagnahme f; Konfiszierung f.

conflagration n (Groß)Brand m.

conflict n Konflikt m; Kampf m.

conflicting adj widersprüchlich; im Konflikt stehen.

confluence n Zusammenfluß m; (Menschen)Auflauf m.

conform vt, vi (sich) anpassen; übereinstimmen; sich fügen.

conformity n Gleichförmigkeit f; Übereinstimmung f; Anpassung f; Konformismus m.

confound vt verwechseln; verwirren; vereiteln.

confront vt gegenüberstehen; mutig begegnen; sich stellen; konfrontieren.

confrontation n Konfrontation f; Gegenüberstellung f.

confuse vt verwechseln; verwirren; in Unordnung bringen.

confusing adj verwirrend.

confusion n Verwirrung f; Durcheinander n; Aufruhr m; Verwechslung f; Verworrenheit f.

congeal vt, vi gefrieren; gerinnen; erstarren (lassen).

congenial adj (geistes)verwandt; angenehm; zuträglich.

congenital adj angeboren; ererbt.

congested adj überfüllt; verstopft.

congestion n Stauung f; Stokkung f; Andrang m.

conglomerate vt (sich) zusammenballen; * adj (zusammen)geballt; * n Konglomerat n; Anhäufung f; (com) Mischkonzern m.

conglomeration n (An)Häufung f.

congratulate vt gratulieren; beglückwünschen.

congratulation n Glückwunsch m.

congratulatory adj Glückwunsch-.

congregate vt (sich) (ver)sammeln.

congregation n Versammlung f; (Kirchen)Gemeinde f.

congress n Kongreß m.

congressman n Kongreßabgeordneter m.

congruity n Übereinstimmung f; Angemessenheit f; Folgerichtigkeit f; Kongruenz f.

congruous adj übereinstimmend (mit); folgerichtig; passend; kongruent.

conic(al) adj kegelförmig.

conifer n Konifere f; Nadelbaum m.

coniferous adj (bot) zapfentragend; Nadel-.

conjecture *n* Vermutung *f*; Mutmaßung *f*; * *vt* vermuten; mutmaßen.

conjugal *adj* ehelich; Ehe-.

conjugate *vt* (*gr*) konjugieren.

conjugation *n* Konjugation *f*.

conjunction *n* Verbindung *f*; Konjugation *f*.

conjuncture *n* Verbindung *f*; Zusammentreffen *f*; Konjunktion *f*.

conjure *vi* beschwören; hexen; zaubern.

conjurer *n* Zauberer *m*; Geisterbeschwörer *m*.

con man *n* Betrüger *m*; Hochstapler *m*.

connect *vt* verbinden; verknüpfen.

connection *n* Verbindung *f*; Zusammenhang *m*; Beziehung *f*; Anschluß *m*.

connivance *n* stillschweigende Duldung *f*.

connive *vi* stillschweigend dulden; ein Auge zudrücken.

connoisseur *n* Kenner *m*.

conquer *vt* erobern; besiegen; unterwerfen; überwinden.

conqueror *n* Eroberer *m*; Sieger *m*.

conquest *n* Eroberung *f*; Überwindung *f*; Bezwingung *f*.

conscience *n* Gewissen *n*.

conscientious *adj*, **~ly** *adv* gewissenhaft; Gewissens-.

conscious *adj*, **~ly** *adv* bewußt; bei Bewußtsein.

consciousness *n* Bewußtsein *n*.

conscript *n* Wehr(dienst-)pflichtige(r) *f(m)*.

conscription *n* Einberufung *f*.

consecrate *vt* weihen; heiligen.

consecration *n* Weihung *f*; Heiligung *f*.

consecutive *adj* **~ly** *adv* aufeinanderfolgend; (fort)laufend; konsekutiv.

consensus *n* (allgemeine) Übereinstimmung *f*.

consent *n* Zustimmung *f*; Einwilligung *f*; * *vi* zustimmen; einwilligen.

consequence *n* Folge *f*; Konsequenz *f*; Bedeutung *f*; Einfluß *m*.

consequent *adj* (nach)folgend; resultierend; konsequent; **~ly** *adv* in der Folge; folglich; daher.

conservation *n* Erhaltung *f*; Naturschutz *m*; Umweltschutz *m*; Konservieren *n*.

conservative *adj* konservativ; erhaltend; vorsichtig.

conservatory *n* Wintergarten *m*.

conserve *vt* erhalten; bewahren; einmachen; * *n* Eingemachtes *n*.

consider *vt* nachdenken über; halten für; bedenken; erwägen; berücksichtigen; Rücksicht nehmen auf; * *vi* nachdenken; überlegen.

considerable *adj*, **~bly** *adv* beachtlich; beträchtlich; ansehnlich; erheblich.

considerate *adj*, **~ly** *adv* rücksichtsvoll; aufmerksam; taktvoll; besonnen.

consideration *n* Erwägung *f*; Überlegung *f*; Berücksichtigung *f*; Rücksicht(nahme) *f*; Grund *m*; Entgelt *n*.

considering *prep* in Anbetracht; **~ that** in Anbetracht dessen.

consign *vt* übergeben; ausliefern; anvertrauen.

consignment *n* Zusendung *f*; (Waren)Sendung *f*.

consist *vi* bestehen; vereinbar sein.

consistency *n* Konsistenz *f*; Beschaffenheit *f*; Konsequenz *f*; Übereinstimmung *f*.

consistent *adj* konsequent; übereinstimmend; vereinbar; konsistent; **~ly** *adv* durchweg; im Einklang.

consolation *n* Trost *m*.

consolatory *adj* tröstlich; Trost-.

console *vt* trösten.

consolidate *vt, vi* (ver)stärken;

festigen; verdichten; konsolidieren.

consolidation *n* (Ver)Stärkung
f; Festigung *f*; Verdichtung *f*;
Konsolidierung *f*.

consonant *adj* übereinstimmend; konsonant; harmo-
nisch; * *n* (*gr*) Konsonant *m*.

consort *n* Gemahl(in) *m*(*f*); Gefährte *m*; Gefährtin *f*; Ge-
leitschiff *n*.

conspicuous *adj*, **~ly** *adv* deutlich sichtbar; auffällig; bemerkenswert.

conspiracy *n* Verschwörung *f*.

conspirator *n* Verschwörer *m*.

conspire *vi* sich verschwören;
ein Komplott schmieden.

constancy *n* Beständigkeit *f*;
Standhaftigkeit *f*; Bestand
m.

constant *adj*, **~ly** *adv* (be)stän-
dig; unveränderlich; stand-
haft; konstant.

constellation *n* Konstellation
f; Anordnung *f*.

consternation *n* Bestürzung *f*.

constipated *adj* verstopft.

constituency *n* Wählerschaft *f*;
Wahlkreis *m*.

constituent *n* Bestandteil *m*;
Wähler(in) *m*(*f*); Vollmacht-
geber(in) *m*(*f*); * *adj* einen Bestandteil bildend; Wähler-;
verfassunggebend.

constitute *vt* ernennen; erlassen; gründen; darstellen.

constitution *n* Zusammensetzung *f*; Natur *f*; Konstitution
f; Gründung *f*; Verfassung *f*;
Satzung *f*.

constitutional *adj* anlagebed-
ingt; gesundheitsfördernd;
grundlegend; verfassungs-
mäßig; Verfassungs-.

constrain *vt* (er)zwingen; einengen.

constraint *n* Zwang *m*; Beschränkung *f*; Zurückhaltung
f.

constrict *vt* zusammenziehen;
zusammenschnüren; einen-
gen; beschränken.

construct *vt* errichten; bauen;
konstruieren.

construction *n* Konstruktion *f*;
Bau *m*; Bauwerk *n*; Auslegung
f.

construe *vt* konstruieren; bilden; auslegen.

consul *n* Konsul *m*.

consular *adj* Konsulats-; kon-
sularisch.

consulate, consulship *n* Konsulat *n*.

consult *vt* um Rat fragen; konsultieren; nachschlagen; berücksichtigen * *vi* beraten.

consultation *n* Beratung *f*;
Rücksprache *f*; Konsultation
f.

consume *vt* zerstören; verzehren; verbrauchen; vergeuden;
* *vi* (dahin)schwinden.

consumer *n* Verbraucher(in)
m(*f*).

consumer goods *npl* Konsumgüter *npl*.

consumerism *n* (kritische) Ver-
braucherhaltung *f*.

consumer society *n* Konsum-
gesellschaft *f*.

consummate *vt* vollenden; vollziehen; * *adj* vollendet.

consummation *n* Vollendung *f*;
Vollziehung *f*.

consumption *n* Verbrauch *m*;
Verzehr *m*; Konsum *m*; Zerstörung *f*; Schwindsucht *f*.

contact *n* Kontakt *m*; Kontakt-
person *f*; Berührung *f*; Verbindung *f*.

contact lenses *npl* Kontaktlinsen *fpl*.

contagious *adj* ansteckend; in-
fiziert.

contain *vt* enthalten; umfassen; zügeln; in Schach halten;
eindämmen.

container *n* Behälter *m*; Container *m*.

contaminate *vt* verunreinigen;
infizieren; vergiften; verseuchen; **~d** *adj* verunreinigt; in-
fiziert; vergiftet; verseucht.

contamination *n* Verunreinigung *f*; Vergiftung *f*; Verseuchung *f*.

contemplate *vt* betrachten; nachdenken über; erwägen.

contemplation *n* Betrachtung *f*; Nachdenken *n*; Erwägung *f*; Kontemplation *f*.

contemplative *adj* nachdenklich; kontemplativ.

contemporaneous *adj* gleichzeitig.

contemporary *adj* zeitgenössisch; gleichzeitig; gleichaltrig.

contempt *n* Verachtung *f*; Mißachtung *f*; Schande *f*.

contemptible *adj*, **~bly** *adv* verächtlich; verachtenswert; gemein.

contemptuous *adj*, **~ly** *adv* verächtlich; geringschätzig.

contend *vi* kämpfen; streiten; sich einsetzen; sich bewerben.

content *adj* zufrieden; bereit; * *vt* zufriedenstellen; zufriedengeben; * *n* Zufriedenheit *f*; Inhalt *m*; **~s** *pl* Inhalt *m*.

contentedly *adv* zufrieden.

contention *n* Streit *m*; Zank *m*; Wettstreit *m*; Behauptung *f*.

contentious *adj*, **~ly** *adv* streitsüchtig; umstritten; strittig.

contentment *n* Zufriedenheit *f*.

contest *vt* kämpfen um; wetteifern um; kandidieren für; bestreiten; anfechten; * *n* (Wett)Kampf *m*; (Wett)Streit *m*; Wortwechsel *m*; Auseinandersetzung *f*.

contestant *n* Wettkämpfer(in) *m(f)*; Anfechter(in) *m(f)*; (Mit-)Bewerber(in) *m(f)*; Kandidat(in) *m(f)*.

context *n* Zusammenhang *m*; Umgebung *f*.

contiguous *adj* angrenzend; nahe; benachbart.

continent *adj* enthaltsam; mäßig; * *n* Kontinent *m*.

continental *adj* kontinental.

contingency *n* Zufälligkeit *f*; Eventualität *f*; Bedingung *f*.

contingent *n* Kontingent *n*;

Quote *f*; * *adj*, **~ly** *adv* abhängig; möglich; (zufalls)bedingt.

continual *adj* fortwährend; unaufhörlich; dauernd; wiederholt; **~ly** *adv* fortwährend; immer wieder.

continuation *n* Fortsetzung *f*; Fortbestand *m*; Verlängerung *f*.

continue *vt* fortsetzen; beibehalten; * *vi* fortfahren; weitermachen; andauern; (ver)bleiben; fortbestehen.

continuity *n* Kontinuität *f*.

continuous *adj* **~ly** *adv* ununterbrochen; (an)dauernd; kontinuierlich.

contort *vt* verdrehen; verrenken; verzerren.

contortion *n* Verrenkung *f*; Verzerrung *f*; Verdrehung *f*.

contour *n* Kontur *f*; Umriß *m*.

contraband *n* Schmuggelware *f*; Schmuggel *m*; * *adj* Schmuggel-; illegal.

contraception *n* Empfängnisverhütung *f*.

contraceptive *n* empfängnisverhütendes Mittel *n*; * *adj* empfängnisverhütend.

contract *vt* zusammenziehen; annehmen; sich zuziehen; (ab)schließen; * *vi* sich zusammenziehen; (ein)schrumpfen; einen Vertrag schließen; * *n* Vertrag *m*; Kontrakt *m*.

contraction *n* Kontraktion *f*; Zusammenziehung *f*; Kurzwort *n*; Wehe *f*.

contractor *n* Unternehmer *m*; Lieferant *m*; Schließmuskel *m*.

contradict *vt* widersprechen.

contradiction *n* Widerspruch *m*.

contradictory *adj* widersprechend.

contraption *n* Apparat *m*.

contrariness *n* Gegensätzlichkeit *f*; Widerspenstigkeit *f*.

contrary *adj* widersprechend; gegensätzlich; widrig; verstoßend; widerspenstig; * *n*

Gegenteil *n*; **on the ~** im Gegenteil.

contrast *n* Kontrast *m*; Gegensatz *m*; * *vt* kontrastieren; vergleichen.

contrasting *adj* kontrastierend; gegensätzlich.

contravention *n* Übertretung *f*; Zuwiderhandlung *f*.

contribute *vt* beitragen; beisteuern; einbringen; spenden.

contribution *n* Beitrag *m*; Einlage *f*; Spende *f*.

contributor *n* Beitragende(r) *f(m)*; Mitwirkende(r) *f(m)*.

contributory *adj* beitragend; beitragspflichtig; mitwirkend.

contrite *adj* zerknirscht; reumütig.

contrition *n* Zerknirschung *f*; Reue *f*.

contrivance *n* Vorrichtung *f*; Plan *m*; Erfindung *f*; Findigkeit *f*; Kunstgriff *m*.

contrive *vt* erfinden; ausdenken; aushecken; bewerkstelligen.

control *n* Beherrschung *f*; Kontrolle *f*; Gewalt *f*; Steuerung *f*; Leitung *f*; * *vt* beherrschen; kontrollieren; eindämmen; regeln; leiten; lenken; steuern.

control room *n* Kontrollraum *m*.

control tower *n* Kontrollturm *m*.

controversial *adj* umstritten; kontrovers; polemisch; streitsüchtig.

controversy *n* Kontroverse *f*; Streit *m*; Debatte *f*.

contusion *n* Quetschung *f*.

conundrum *n* Scherzfrage *f*; Rätsel *n*.

conurbation *n* Ballungsraum *m*.

convalesce *vi* gesund werden; genesen.

convalescence *n* Rekonvaleszenz *f*; Genesung *f*.

convalescent *adj* rekonvaleszent; genesend; Genesungs-.

convene *vt* versammeln; einberufen; vorladen; * *vi* versammeln; zusammentreffen.

convenience *n* Bequemlichkeit *f*; Annehmlichkeit *f*; Vorteil *m*; Angemessenheit *f*.

convenient *adj* bequem; praktisch; günstig; handlich; **~ly** *adv* bequemerweise; praktischerweise; günstigerweise.

convent *n* Kloster *n*.

convention *n* Versammlung *f*; Tagung *f*; Abkommen *n*; Konvention *f*; Tradition *f*.

conventional *adj* konventionell; traditionell; vertragsgemäß.

converge *vi* zusammenlaufen; konvergieren.

convergence *n* Zusammenlaufen *n*; Konvergenz *f*.

convergent *adj* konvergent.

conversant *adj* bekannt; vertraut; bewandert.

conversation *n* Unterhaltung *f*; Gespräch *n*.

converse *vi* sich unterhalten; sprechen.

conversely *adv* umgekehrt.

conversion *n* Umwandlung *f*; Umbau *m*; Umstellung *f*; Umrechnung *f*; Bekehrung *f*; Übertritt *m*.

convert *vt* umwandeln; umbauen; umstellen; umrechnen; bekehren * *vi* umgewandelt werden; sich verwandeln; konvertieren; * *n* Bekehrte(r) *f(m)*; Konvertit(in) *m(f)*.

convertible *adj* umwandelbar; gleichbedeutend; * *n* Kabriolett *n*.

convex *adj* konvex.

convexity *n* konvexe Form *f*; Wölbung *f*.

convey *vt* (be)fördern; transportieren; übermitteln; übertragen; vermitteln.

conveyance *n* Transport *m*; (Be)Förderung *f*; Überbringung *f*; Vermittlung *f*; Übertragung *f*.

conveyancer *n* Notar *m*.

convict vt für schuldig erklären; verurteilen; * n Verurteilte(r) f(m); Strafgefangene(r) f(m); Sträfling m.

conviction n Schuldspruch m; Überführung f; Verurteilung f; Überzeugung f.

convince vt überzeugen.

convincing adj, adv überzeugend.

convivial adj gesellig; lustig.

conviviality n Geselligkeit f; unbeschwerte Heiterkeit.

convoke vt einberufen.

convoy n Geleit n; Schutz m; (Wagen)Kolonne f; Konvoi m.

convulse vt erschüttern; in Zuckungen versetzen; * vi sich krümmen.

convulsion n Krampf m; Zukkung f; Erschütterung f.

convulsive adj, ~ly adv krampfhaft; krampfartig; erschütternd.

coo vi gurren.

cook n Koch m; Köchin f; * vt kochen; (fig) zusammenbrauen; (fam) frisieren; * vi kochen.

cookbook n Kochbuch n.

cooker n Herd m; Kocher m; Kochfrucht f.

cookery n Kochen n; Kochkunst f.

cookie n Keks m; Plätzchen n; (fam) Kerl m.

cool adj, ~ly adv kühl; frisch; kaltblütig; unverfroren; * n Kühle f; Frische f; (fam) Beherrschung f; * vt (ab)kühlen.

coolness n Kühle f; Kälte f; Kaltblütigkeit f; Gelassenheit f.

cooperate vi kooperieren; zusammenarbeiten; mitwirken.

cooperation n Kooperation f; Zusammenarbeit f; Mitarbeit f.

cooperative adj kooperativ; hilfsbereit; genossenschaftlich.

coordinate vt koordinieren; aufeinander abstimmen.

coordination n Koordination f; Abstimmung f; harmonisches Zusammenspiel n.

cop n (fam) Bulle m.

copartner n Teilhaber m.

cope vi fertig werden; gewachsen sein; bewältigen.

copier n Kopierer m.

copious adj, ~ly adv reichlich; ausgiebig; weitschweifig; produktiv.

copper n Kupfer(rot) n; Kupfermünze f; (Kupfer)Kessel m.

coppice, copse n Niederwald m; Gehölz n.

copulate vi kopulieren; sich paaren.

copy n Kopie f; Abschrift f; Ausfertigung f; Exemplar n; * vt kopieren; abschreiben; nachahmen.

copybook n (Schön)Schreibheft n.

copying machine n Kopiergerät n.

copyist n Kopist m; Nachahmer m.

copyright n Urheberrecht n.

coral n Koralle f; Korallenrot n.

coral reef n Korallenriff n.

cord n Schnur f; Strick m; Strang m; Rippe f; Kord n; Klafter n.

cordial adj, ~ly adv herzlich; aufrichtig; (med) stärkend.

corduroy n Kord(samt) m.

core n Kern m; Kerngehäuse n; Innerste n; Herz n.

cork n Kork(en) m; * vt verkorken.

corkscrew n Korkenzieher m.

corn n Korn n; Getreide n; Mais m; Hühnerauge n.

corncob n Maiskolben m.

cornea n Hornhaut f (des Auges).

corned beef n Corned beef n.

corner n Ecke f; Kurve f; Winkel m; (fig) Klemme f; (fig) Monopol n.

cornerstone n Eckstein m; Grundstein m.

cornet n Kornett n; (Spitz)Tüte f; (Schwestern)Haube f.

cornfield *n* Kornfeld *n*; Getreidefeld *n*.

cornflakes *npl* Corn-flakes *pl.*

cornice *n* Gesims *n; (*Bilder-) Leiste *f; (*Schnee)Wächte *f.*

cornstarch *n* Maisstärke *f.*

corollary *n* logische Folge *f*; Folgesatz *m.*

coronary *n* Koronarthrombose *f.*

coronation *n* Krönung *f.*

coroner *n* Untersuchungsrichter *m (in Fällen gewaltsamen oder unnatürlichen Todes).*

coronet *n* Adelskrone *f*; Diadem *n*; kleine Krone *f.*

corporal *n* Unteroffizier *m*; Korporal *m*; * *adj* körperlich; persönlich.

corporate *adj* Körperschafts-; Gesellschafts-; Firmen-; gemeinsam; kollektiv.

corporation *n* Körperschaft *f*; (Aktien)Gesellschaft *f*; Zunft *f*; Innung *f*; Stadtverwaltung *f.*

corporeal *adj* körperlich; materiell.

corps *n* Korps *n*; Corps *n.*

corpse *n* Leiche *f.*

corpulent *adj* korpulent; beleibt.

corpuscle *n* (Blut)Körperchen *n*; Korpuskel *n.*

corral *n* Pferch *m*; Wagenburg *f.*

correct *vt* korrigieren; verbessern; zurechtweisen; strafen; abstellen; * *adj*, **~ly** *adv* korrekt; richtig; genau.

correction *n* Korrektur *f*; Berichtigung *f*; Richtigstellung *f*; (Ver)Besserung *f*; Bestrafung *f*; Zurechtweisung *f.*

corrective *adj* verbessernd; Korrektur-; korrektiv; Besserungs-; Straf-; * *n* Abhilfe *f*; Gegenmittel *n.*

correctness *n* Korrektheit *f*; Richtigkeit *f.*

correlation *n* Wechselbeziehung *f*; Zusammenhang *m*; Übereinstimmung *f.*

correlative *adj* wechselseitig bedingt; entsprechend.

correspond *vi* korrespondieren; übereinstimmen; entsprechen; im Briefwechsel stehen.

correspondence *n* Korrespondenz *f*; Übereinstimmung *f*; Entsprechung *f*; Briefwechsel *m.*

correspondent *adj* entsprechend; gemäß; übereinstimmend; * *n* Briefschreiber(in) *m(f)*; Geschäftsfreund *m*; Berichterstatter(in) *m(f)*; Korrespondent(in) *m(f)*; Gegenstück *n.*

corridor *n* Flur *m*; Korridor *m*; Gang *m.*

corroborate *vt* bekräftigen; bestätigen; erhärten.

corroboration *n* Bekräftigung *f*; Bestätigung *f*; Erhärtung *f.*

corroborative *adj* bestätigend; bekräftigend; erhärtend.

corrode *vt* korrodieren; zerfressen; angreifen.

corrosion *n* Korrosion *f*; Rost (-fraß) *m.*

corrosive *adj* korrodierend; zerfressend; ätzend; *(fig)* nagend; * *n* Korrosionsmittel *n*; Ätzmittel *n*; Beizmittel *n.*

corrugated iron *n* Wellblech *n.*

corrupt *vt* verderben; verleiten; korrumpieren; bestechen; untergraben; * *vi* verderben; verkommen; * *adj* korrupt; bestechlich; verfälscht; verderbt.

corruptible *adj* korrupt; bestechlich; verführbar; verderblich.

corruption *n* Korruption *f*; Bestechlichkeit *f*; Verderbtheit *f*; Verführung *f*; Verfälschung *f*; Fäulnis *f.*

corruptive *adj* verderblich.

corset *n* Korsett *n.*

cortege *n* Gefolge *n*; Prozession *f.*

cosmetic *adj* kosmetisch; Schönheits-; *(fig)* oberflächlich; * *n* Kosmetik *f*; Schönheitsmittel *n*; *(fig)* Tünche *f.*

cosmic *adj* kosmisch.
cosmonaut *n* Kosmonaut(in) *m(f)*.
cosmopolitan *adj* kosmopolitisch; weltoffen.
cosset *vt* verhätscheln.
cost *n* Kosten *pl*; Preis *m*; Schaden *m*; Nachteil *m*; * *vi* kosten; zu stehen kommen.
costly *adj* kostspielig; teuer.
costume *n* Kostüm *n*; Kleidung *f*; Tracht *f*; Badeanzug *m*.
cosy *adj*, **cosily** *adv* behaglich; gemütlich.
cottage *n* kleines Landhaus *n*; Hütte *f*.
cotton *n* Baumwolle *f*.
cotton candy *n* Zuckerwatte *f*.
cotton mill *n* Baumwollspinnerei *f*.
cotton wool *n* Watte *f*; Rohbaumwolle *f*.
couch *n* Sofa *n*; Liege *f*.
couchette *n* Platz *m* (im Liegewagen).
cough *n* Husten *m*; (*auto*) Stottern *n*; * *vi* husten; (*auto*) stottern.
council *n* Rat *m*; Ratsversammlung *f*.
councilor *n* Ratsmitglied *n*; (Stadt)Rat *m*; (Stadt)Rätin *f*.
counsel *n* Rat *m*; Beratung *f*; Ratgeber(in) *m(f)*; Anwalt *m*; Anwältin *f*.
counsellor *n* (Rechts)Berater(in) *m(f)*; Ratgeber(in) *m(f)*; Anwalt *m*; Anwältin *f*.
count *vt* zählen; (be)rechnen; mit (ein)rechnen; **to ~ on** zählen auf; sich verlassen auf; * *n* Zählung *f*; (Be)Rechnung *f*; Ergebnis *n*; (Anklage)Punkt *m*; Berücksichtigung *f*.
countdown *n* Countdown *m*.
countenance *n* Gesichtsausdruck *m*; Miene *f*; Fassung *f*; Ermutigung *f*; Unterstützung *f*.
counter *n* Ladentisch *m*; Theke *f*; Schalter *m*; Zähler *m*.
counteract *vt* entgegenwirken; zuwiderhandeln; be-

kämpfen; vereiteln.
counterbalance *vt* ausgleichen; aufwiegen; * *n* Gegengewicht *n*.
counterfeit *vt* fälschen; vortäuschen; * *adj* gefälscht; falsch.
countermand *vt* widerrufen; stornieren; abbestellen.
counterpart *n* Gegenstück *n*; Pendant *n*; Duplikat *n*.
counterproductive *adj* kontraproduktiv.
countersign *vt* gegenzeichnen; bestätigen.
countess *n* Gräfin *f*; Komteß *f*.
countless *adj* zahllos; unzählig.
countrified *adj* ländlich; bäuerlich; (*contp*) bäurisch.
country *n* Land *n*; Staat *m*; Landschaft *f*; Gelände *n*; Heimat *f*; * *adj* ländlich; Land-.
country house *n* Landhaus *n*; Landsitz *m*.
countryman *n* Landbewohner *m*; Landsmann *m*.
county *n* Grafschaft *f*; (Land-)Kreis *m*.
coup *n* Coup *m*; (Staats)Streich *m*.
coupé *n* Coupé *n*.
couple *n* Paar *n*; Koppel *f*; Verbindungsglied *n*; * *vt* (zusammen)koppeln; verbinden; paaren.
couplet *n* Verspaar *n*.
coupon *n* Coupon *m*; Gutschein *m*; Rabattmarke *f*; Tippzettel *m*.
courage *n* Mut *m*; Tapferkeit *f*.
courageous *adj*, **~ly** *adv* mutig; beherzt; tapfer.
courier *n* Kurier *m*; Eilbote *m*; Reiseleiter(in) *m(f)*.
course *n* Kurs *m*; Lauf *m*; Weg *m*; Richtung *f*; Fahrt *f*; Gang *m*; (Renn)Bahn *f*; Lehrgang *m*; Reihe *f*; **of ~** selbstverständlich; natürlich.
court *n* Hof *m*; Platz *m*; Gericht *n*; Versammlung *f*; * *vt* den Hof machen; werben um; (*fig*) heraufbeschwören.

courteous *adj*, **~ly** *adv* höflich; liebenswürdig.

courtesan *n* Kurtisane *f*.

courtesy *n* Höflichkeit *f*; Liebenswürdigkeit *f*; Gefälligkeit *f*.

courthouse *n* Gerichtsgebäude *n*.

courtly *adj* höfisch; vornehm; artig.

court martial *n* Kriegsgericht *n*.

courtroom *n* Gerichtssaal *m*.

courtyard *n* Hof *m*.

cousin *n* Cousin(e) *m(f)*; Vetter *m*; Base *f*; **first ~** leiblicher Cousin(e) *m(f)*.

cove *n* (*mar*) kleine Bucht *f*; Schlupfwinkel *m*; Wölbung *f*.

covenant *n* Abkommen *n*; Bündnis *n*; Bund *m*; Statut *n*; * *vi* einen Vertrag schließen; übereinkommen.

cover *n* Decke *f*; Deckel *m*; Umschlag *m*; Hülle *f*; Bezug *m*; Schutz *m*; Deckung *f*; Deckmantel *m*; Gedeck *n*; * *vt* bedecken; zudecken; abdecken; überziehen; einwickeln; (ver-) decken; schützen; (erschöpfend) behandeln; berichten über; beschatten; zurücklegen.

coverage *n* Deckung *f*; erschöpfende Behandlung *f*; erfaßtes Gebiet *n*; Reichweite *f*; Berichterstattung *f*.

covering *n* (Be)Kleidung *f*; Umhüllung *f*; (Fußboden)Belag *m*; Abschirmung *f*.

cover letter *n* Begleitbrief *m*.

covert *adj*, **~ly** *adv* heimlich; versteckt.

cover-up *n* Vertuschung *f*.

covet *vt* begehren.

covetous *adj* (be)gierig; lüstern; habsüchtig.

cow *n* Kuh *f*.

coward *n* Feigling *m*.

cowardice *n* Feigheit *f*.

cowardly *adj*, *adv* feig(e).

cowboy *n* Cowboy *m*; Kuhhirte *m*; (*col*) Pfuscher *m*.

cower *vi* kauern; sich ducken.

cowherd *n* Kuhhirte *m*.

coy *adj*, **~ly** *adv* schüchtern; scheu; spröde.

coyness *n* Schüchternheit *f*; Scheu *f*; Sprödigkeit *f*.

crab *n* Krabbe *f*; Krebs *m*; Nörgler(in) *m(f)*.

crab apple *n* Holzapfel *m*; **~ tree** *n* Holzapfelbaum *m*.

crack *n* Knall *m*; Schlag *m*; Knacks *m*; Sprung *m*; Spalt(e) *m(f)*; (*sl*) Kanone *f*; (*sl*) Versuch *m*; (*sl*) Witz *m*; * *vt* knallen mit; knacken (mit); zerbrechen; anbrechen; **to ~ down on** scharf vorgehen; durchgreifen; * *vi* knallen; knacken; (zer)springen; einen Sprung bekommen; überschnappen; (*fig*) zusammenbrechen; (*sl*) in die Brüche gehen.

cracker *n* Knallbonbon *m*; (*fig*) Knüller *m*.

crackle *vi* knistern; prasseln; Risse bilden.

crackling *n* Knistern *n*; Prasseln *n*; knusprige Kruste *f*.

cradle *n* Wiege *f*; (Telefon)Gabel *f*; * *vt* wiegen; betten.

craft *n* Gewerbe *n*; Handwerk *n*; Kunst(fertigkeit) *f*; Schiff *n*; Flugzeug *n*.

craftiness *n* Schlauheit *f*; Verschlagenheit *f*.

craftsman *n* (Kunst)Handwerker *m*; (*fig*) Könner *m*.

craftsmanship *n* Kunstfertigkeit *f*; (handwerkliches) Können *n*.

crafty *adj* **craftily** *adv* schlau; verschlagen.

crag *n* Felsspitze *f*; Klippe *f*.

cram *vt* (voll)stopfen; * *vi* sich vollstopfen; (*col*) pauken.

crammed *adj* vollgestopft.

cramp *n* Krampf *m*; Krampe *f*; Schraubzwinge *f*; * *vt* Krämpfe auslösen; festklammern; hemmen; einengen.

cramped *adj* verkrampft; eng; beengt.

crampon *n* Steigeisen *n*; Maueranker *m*.

cranberry n Preiselbeere f.

crane n Kran m; (zool) Kranich m.

crash vi (zusammen)krachen; zusammenbrechen; hereinplatzen; zusammenstoßen; abstürzen; * n Krach m; Zusammenstoß m; Zusammenbruch m; Absturz m.

crash helmet n Sturzhelm m.

crash landing n Bruchlandung f.

crass adj grob; krass; derb.

crate n Kiste f; Kasten m.

crater n Krater m.

cravat n Halstuch n.

crave vt ersehnen; benötigen; verlangen.

craving n heftiges Verlangen n; Sehnsucht f.

crawl vi kriechen; krabbeln; kraulen; kribbeln; (fig) sich dahinschleppen; schleichen; **to ~ with** wimmeln von.

crayfish n Flußkrebs m; Languste f.

crayon n Zeichenkreide f; Buntstift m; Pastellstift m; Kreidezeichnung f.

craze n Manie f; Verrücktheit f; Mode f; Wahn(sinn) m.

craziness n Verrücktheit f.

crazy adj verrückt; wahnsinnig; begeistert; wirr; schief; zusammengestückelt; Flicken-.

creak vi knarren; quietschen.

cream n Sahne f; Creme f; * adj Sahne-; creme(farben).

creamy adj sahnig.

crease n Falte f; Kniff m; Eselsohr n; * vt falten; kniffen; zerknittern; anschießen.

create vt (er)schaffen; verursachen; gründen.

creation n Schöpfung f; (Er)Schaffung f; Erzeugung f; Verursachung f; Gründung f; Kreation f.

creative adj schöpferisch; kreativ; Schöpfungs-; verursachend.

creator n Schöpfer m; Erzeuger

m; Urheber m; Gründer m.

creature n Kreatur f; Geschöpf n; (Lebe)Wesen n; Produkt n.

credence n Glaube m.

credentials npl Beglaubigungsschreiben n; Referenzen pl; Zeugnis n.

credibility n Glaubwürdigkeit f.

credible adj glaubwürdig.

credit n Kredit m; (Gut)Haben n; Glaube(n) m; Ansehen n; Ehre f; Anerkennung f; Verdienst m; * vt Glauben schenken; zutrauen; zuschreiben; gutschreiben.

creditable adj, **~bly** adv rühmlich; ehrenvoll; anerkennenswert; achtbar.

credit card n Kreditkarte f.

creditor n Gläubiger m.

credulity n Leichtgläubigkeit f.

credulous adj, **~ly** adv leichtgläubig; vertrauensselig.

creed n (Glaubens)Bekenntnis n; (fig) Weltanschauung f.

creek n Bach m.

creep vi kriechen; schleichen; kribbeln.

creeper n (bot) Kriechpflanze f; Kletterpflanze f.

creepy adj kriechend; gruselig.

cremate vt (Leichen) verbrennen; einäschern.

cremation n (Leichen)Verbrennung f; Einäscherung f.

crematorium n Krematorium n.

crescent adj sichelförmig; halbmondförmig; zunehmend; * n Halbmond m; Mondsichel f; Hörnchen n.

cress n Kresse f.

crest n Kamm m; Mähne f; Federbusch m; Helm(Schmuck) m; Wappen n; Gipfel m.

crested adj mit einem Kamm etc; Schopf-; Hauben-.

crestfallen adj niedergeschlagen; geknickt.

crevasse n tiefer Spalt m; Gletscherspalte f.

crevice n Riß m; (Fels)Spalte f.

crew n Mannschaft f; Gruppe f; Trupp m; Besatzung f; Belegschaft f.

crib n Krippe f; Kinderbett n; Lattengerüst n.

cricket n Grille f; Kricket n.

crime n Verbrechen n; Straftat f; Frevel m.

criminal adj, **~ly** adv kriminell; verbrecherisch; strafrechtlich; Straf-; in verbrecherischer Absicht; * n Kriminelle(r) f(m); Verbrecher(in) m(f).

criminality n Kriminalität f; Strafbarkeit f.

crimson adj karminrot; puterrot; * n Karminrot n.

cripple n Krüppel m; * vt zum Krüppel machen; lähmen; lahmlegen; kampfunfähig machen.

crippled adj verkrüppelt; gelähmt; lahmgelegt.

crisis n Krise f; Höhepunkt m.

crisp adj knusprig; kraus; steif; frisch; knackig; forsch; knapp; lebendig; klar.

crispness n Knusprigkeit f; Frische f; Forschheit f; Knappheit f; Lebendigkeit f; Schärfe f.

criss-cross adj kreuzweise; kreuz und quer.

criterion n Kriterium n; Maßstab m.

critic n Kritiker(in) m(f); Rezensent(in) m(f).

critical adj, **~ally** adv kritisch; bedenklich; prüfend.

criticism n Kritik f.

criticize vt kritisieren; rezensieren.

croak vi quaken; krächzen; (fig) unken; (col) abkratzen.

crochet n Häkelei f; * vt, vi häkeln.

crockery n Geschirr n; Töpferware f.

crocodile n Krokodil n.

crony n alter Freund m; alte Freundin f; Spezi m.

crook n (col) Gauner m; Haken m; Hirtenstab m.

crooked adj krumm; gewunden; unehrlich.

crop n (Feld)Frucht f; Ernte f; Ausbeute f; Kropf m; Reitpeitsche f; kurzer Haarschnitt m; * vt (ab)schneiden; stutzen; (ab)ernten; (ab)weiden.

cross n Kreuz(zeichen) n; Kruzifix n; Kreuzung f; Gaunerei f; * adj ärgerlich; böse; entgegengesetzt; sich kreuzend; quer; wechselseitig; widerwärtig; * vt kreuzen; bekreuzigen; durchstreichen; (fig) durchkreuzen; überqueren; überschreiten; (fig) in die Quere kommen; **to ~ over** hinübergehen; übersetzen.

crossbar n Querlatte f; Querstange f.

crossbreed n Kreuzung f; Mischrasse f.

cross-country adj querfeldein; Gelände-.

cross-examine vt ins Kreuzverhör nehmen.

crossfire n Kreuzfeuer n.

crossing n Kreuzung f; (Fußgänger)Übergang m; Überquerung f; Überfahrt f.

cross-purpose n Widerspruch m; **to be at ~s** einander mißverstehen; einander entgegenarbeiten.

cross-reference n Querverweis m.

crossroad n Querstraße f.

crotch n Schritt m; Zwickel m.

crouch vi sich ducken; hocken; kauern.

crow n Krähe f; Krähen n; * vi krähen; frohlocken; prahlen.

crowd n (Menschen)Menge f; Masse f; Haufen m; * vt zusammendrängen; hineinstopfen; bevölkern; (fig) erdrükken; * vi sich drängen.

crown n Krone f; Kranz m; Scheitel(punkt) m; Kopf m; Gipfel m; * vt krönen; überkronen.

crown prince n Kronprinz m.

crucial *adj* kritisch; entscheidend.

crucible *n* Schmelztiegel *m*; (*fig*) Feuerprobe *f*.

crucifix *n* Kruzifix *n*.

crucifixion *n* Kreuzigung *f*.

crucify *vt* kreuzigen; (*col*) verreißen.

crude *adj* ~ly *adv* roh; grob; primitiv; (*fig*) ungeschminkt; geschmacklos.

cruel *adj*, ~ly *adv* grausam; hart.

cruelty *n* Grausamkeit *f*; Mißhandlung *f*.

cruet *n* Essigfläschchen *n*; Ölfläschchen *n*; Gewürzständer *m*.

cruise *n* Kreuzfahrt *f*; * *vi* eine Kreuzfahrt machen; herumfahren.

cruiser *n* Kreuzer *m*; Kreuzfahrtschiff *n*.

crumb *n* Krümel *m*; Brösel *m*; (*fig*) Brocken *m*.

crumble *vt* zerkrümeln; zerbröckeln; * *vi* zerbröckeln; zerfallen.

crumple *vt* zerknittern; zerknüllen; (*fig*) umwerfen.

crunch *vt* knirschend (zer)kauen; zermalmen; * *n* Knirschen *n*; (*fig*) kritischer Moment *m*.

crunchy *adj* knusprig; knirschend.

crusade *n* Kreuzzug *m*.

crush *vt* (zer)quetschen; (zer)drücken; zermalmen; (*fig*) vernichten; * *n* (zermalmender) Druck *m*; Gedränge *n*; Schwärmerei *f*.

crust *n* Kruste *f*; Rinde *f*.

crusty *adj* verkrustet; barsch.

crutch *n* Krücke *f*.

crux *n* Kern *m*; springender Punkt *m*.

cry *vt*, *vi* schreien; rufen; weinen; * *n* Schrei *m*; Ruf *m*; Geschrei *n*; Weinen *n*.

crypt *n* Krypta *f*; Gruft *f*.

cryptic *adj* verborgen; geheim; rätselhaft; dunkel.

crystal *n* Kristall *m*, *n*.

crystal-clear *adj* kristallklar.

crystalline *adj* kristallin; Kristall-; (*fig*) kristallklar.

crystallize *vt*, *vi* kristallisieren; kandieren.

cub *n* Junge *n*; Bengel *m*; Anfänger *m*.

cube *n* Würfel *m*.

cubic *adj* Kubik-; kubisch; würfelförmig.

cuckoo *n* Kuckuck *m*.

cucumber *n* Gurke *f*.

cud *n*: **to chew the ~** wiederkäuen; (*fig*) nachdenken.

cuddle *vt* schmusen mit; knuddeln; * *vi* schmusen; * *n* enge Umarmung *f*.

cudgel *n* Knüppel *m*.

cue *n* Einsatz *m*; Stichwort *n*; Wink *m*; Anhaltspunkt *m*; Queue *n*.

cuff *n* Manschette *f*; Aufschlag *m*; Handschelle *f*; Schlag *m*.

culinary *adj* kulinarisch; Koch-.

cull *vt* auslesen; aussuchen; aussortieren; aussondern.

culminate *vi* den Höhepunkt erreichen; gipfeln.

culmination *n* Höhepunkt *m*; Gipfel *m*.

culpability *n* Schuldhaftigkeit *f*.

culpable *adj*, ~bly *adv* sträflich; strafbar; schuldhaft.

culprit *n* (Misse)Täter(in) *m(f)*; Schuldige(r) *f(m)*; Angeklagte(r) *f(m)*.

cult *n* Kult *m*; Sekte *f*.

cultivate *vi* kultivieren; urbar machen; bebauen; pflegen; sich widmen; sich warmhalten; zivilisieren.

cultivation *n* Kultivierung *f*; Urbarmachung *f*; Bebauung *f*; Ackerbau *m*; Züchtung *f*; Pflege *f*.

cultural *adj* kulturell; Kultur-.

culture *n* Kultur *f*; Anbau *m*; Zucht *f*; Kultiviertheit *f*; Pflege *f*.

cumbersome *adj* lästig; hinderlich; klobig; unhandlich.

cumulative *adj* kumulativ; Gesamt-; sich steigernd; zusätzlich.

cunning *adj*, **~ly** *adv* geschickt; schlau; listig; gerissen; * *n* Geschicklichkeit *f*; Schlauheit *f*; List *f*; Gerissenheit *f*.

cup *n* Tasse *f*; Becher *m*; Kelch *m*; Schale *f*; Pokal *m*.

cupboard *n* Schrank *m*.

curable *adj* heilbar.

curate *n* Hilfsgeistliche(r) *f*(*m*).

curator *n* Museumsdirektor *m*; Pfleger *m*.

curb *n* Kandare *f*; Kinnkette *f*; (*fig*) Zaum *m*; Randstein *m*; * *vt* an die Kandare nehmen; (*fig*) zügeln.

curd *n* Dickmilch *f*; Quark *m*.

curdle *vi* (*vt*) gerinnen (lassen).

cure *n* Kur *f*; (Heil)Mittel *n*; Behandlung *f*; Heilung *f*; Haltbarmachung *f*; * *vt* heilen; kurieren; abstellen; haltbar machen.

curfew *n* Ausgangssperre *f*; Sperrstunde *f*; Abendläuten *n*.

curing *n* Heilen *n*; Haltbarmachen *n*.

curiosity *n* Neugier *f*; Wißbegierde *f*; Kuriosität *f*.

curious *adj*, **~ly** *adv* neugierig; wißbegierig; gespannt; merkwürdig; komisch.

curl *n* Locke *f*; Kringel *m*; Kräuseln *n*; * *vt* locken; kräuseln; zusammenrollen; * *vi* sich locken; sich kräuseln; sich zusammenrollen.

curling iron *n*, **curling tongs** *npl* Brennschere *f*.

curly *adj* lockig; kraus.

currant *n* Korinthe *f*; Johannisbeere *f*.

currency *n* Währung *f*; Umlauf *m*; Verbreitung *f*; (Allgemein-) Gültigkeit *f*; Laufzeit *f*.

current *adj* (um)laufend; gegenwärtig; aktuell; kursierend; allgemein (bekannt); * *n* Strom *m*; Strömung *f*.

current affairs *npl* Tagespolitik *f*; aktuelle Ereignisse *npl*.

currently *adv* gegenwärtig; flüssig.

curriculum vitae *n* Lebenslauf *m*.

curry *n* Curry *m*, *n*.

curse *vt* verfluchen; verwünschen; strafen; * *vi* fluchen; * *n* Fluch *m*.

cursor *n* Cursor *m*; Positionsanzeiger *m*.

cursory *adj* flüchtig; oberflächlich.

curt *adj* kurz (angebunden); knapp; barsch.

curtail *vt* beschneiden; (ab)kürzen; einschränken.

curtain *n* Gardine *f*; Vorhang *m*; (*fig*) Schleier *m*.

curtain rod *n* Gardinenstange *f*.

curtsy *n* Knicks *m*; * *vi* knicksen.

curvature *n* Krümmung *f*.

curve *vt* biegen; krümmen; runden; * *n* Kurve *f*; Krümmung *f*; Biegung *f*; Rundung *f*.

cushion *n* Kissen *n*; Polster *n*; Bande *f*.

custard *n* Eiercreme *f*.

custodian *n* Hüter *m*; Verwalter *m*; Wächter *m*.

custody *n* Obhut *f*; Haft *f*; Aufsicht *f*; Verwaltung *f*; Sorgerecht *n*.

custom *n* Brauch *m*; Sitte *f*; Kundschaft *f*.

customary *adj* üblich; gebräuchlich; gewohnt.

customer *n* Kunde *m*; Kundin *f*.

customs *npl* Zoll *m*.

customs duty *n* Zoll *m*.

customs officer *n* Zollbeamter *m*.

cut *vt* (ab-, an-, auf-, aus-, be-, durch-, ein-, mit-, ver-, zer-, zu-) schneiden; stutzen; mähen; fällen; sägen; schleifen; einritzen; kreuzen; kürzen; herabsetzen; abbrechen; **to ~ short** unterbrechen; das Wort abschneiden; **to ~ teeth** zah-

nen; * *vi* (ein)schneiden; sägen;
kränken; * *n* Schnitt *m*; Stich
m; (*col*) Anteil *m*; (Ab-) Kürzung *f*; Senkung *f*; Schliff *m*;
Schlag *m*; **~ and dried** *adj*
routinemäßig.
cutback *n* Kürzung *f*; Rück-
blende *f*.
cute *adj* niedlich; clever.
cutlery *n* Besteck *n*.
cutlet *n* Kotelett *n*; Schnitzel *n*.
cut-rate *adj* ermäßigt; herabge-
setzt.
cut-throat *n* Halsabschneider
m; Killer *m*; * *adj* mörderisch;
halsabschneiderisch.
cutting *n* Schneiden *n*; Ausschnitt *m*; Steckling *m*; * *adj*
Schneid-; Schnitt-; schnei-
dend.
cyanide *n* Zyanid *n*.
cycle *n* Zyklus *m*; Kreis(lauf) *m*;
Periode *f*; Fahrrad *n*; * *vi* radfahren.
cycling *n* Radfahren *n*.
cyclist *n* Radfahrer(in) *m*(*f*).
cyclone *n* Zyklon *m*.
cygnet *n* junger Schwan *m*.
cylinder *n* Zylinder *m*; Walze
f; Trommel *f*.
cylindrical *adj* zylindrisch;
walzenförmig.
cymbals *n* Becken *n*.
cynic(al) *adj* zynisch; * *n* Zyniker *m*.
cynicism *n* Zynismus *m*.
cypress *n* Zypresse *f*.
cyst *n* Zyste *f*.
czar *n* Zar *m*.

D

dab *n* Klaps *m*; Klecks *m*.
dabble *vi* planschen; sich ein
wenig befassen.
dad(dy) *n* Papa *m*; Vati *m*.
daddy-long-legs *n* Weber-
knecht *m*; Schnake *f*.

daffodil *n* Narzisse *f*; Osterglocke *f*.
dagger *n* Dolch *m*.
daily *adj adv* (all)täglich; ständig; * *n* Tageszeitung *f*.
daintiness *n* Zierlichkeit *f*;
Zimperlichkeit *f*; Schmackhaf-
tigkeit *f*.
dainty *adj* **daintily** *adv* zierlich; niedlich; zart; zimperlich;
schmackhaft.
dairy *n* Molkerei *f*.
dairy farm *n* auf Milchwirt-
schaft spezialisierter Bauernhof.
dairy produce *n* Molkereipro-
dukte *npl*.
daisy *n* Gänseblümchen *n*; Mar-
gerite *f*.
daisy wheel *n* Typenrad *n*.
dale *n* Tal *n*.
dally *vi* schäkern; spielen; her-
umtrödeln.
dam *n* (Stau)Damm *m*; Mutter-
tier *n*; * *vt* stauen; eindämmen.
damage *n* Schaden(ersatz) *m*;
Verlust *m*; * schaden; (be-)
schädigen.
damask *n* Damast *m*; * *adj*
Damast-; Damaszener-.
dame *n* Freifrau *f*; (*sl*) Weibsbild *n*.
damn *vt* vedammen; verurteilen; vernichten; * *adj* verdammt; verflucht.
damnable *adj*, **~bly** *adv*
verdammungswürdig; ver-
werflich.
damnation *n* Verdammung *f*;
Verdammnis *f*.
damning *adj* erdrückend.
damp *adj* feucht; klamm; * *n*
Feuchtigkeit *f*; *pl* Schlagwet-
ter *n*; * *vt* befeuchten; dämpfen; deprimieren.
dampen *vt* befeuchten; dämpfen; feucht werden.
damper *n* Dämpfer *m*; Ofen-
klappe *f*.
dampness *n* Feuchtigkeit *f*.
damson *n* Damaszenerpflaume
f.

dance n Tanz m; * vi tanzen.
dance hall n Tanzsaal m.
dancer n Tänzer(in) m(f).
dandelion n Löwenzahn m.
dandruff n Schuppen fpl.
dandy adj prima; erstklassig.
danger n Gefahr f.
dangerous adj ~ly adv gefährlich.
dangle vi baumeln; schlenkern.
dank adj feucht; naßkalt; dumpfig.
dapper adj adrett; elegant; flink; gewandt.
dappled adj gesprenkelt; schekkig.
dare vi es wagen; sich trauen; sich unterstehen; * vt wagen; riskieren; herausfordern.
daredevil n Draufgänger(in) m(f); Teufelskerl m.
daring n (Wage)Mut m; Kühnheit f; * adj ~ly adv wagemutig; kühn; gewagt.
dark adj dunkel; düster; finster; * n Dunkelheit f; Dunkel n; Finsternis f.
darken vt verdunkeln; verfinstern; dunkler machen; verdüstern; * vi sich verdunkeln; sich verfinstern; dunkel werden; sich verdüstern.
darkness n Dunkelheit f; Finsternis f; (fig) Unklarheit f.
darkroom n Dunkelkammer f.
darling n Liebling m; * adj geliebt; entzückend.
darn vt stopfen.
dart n (Wurf)Pfeil m; Stachel m; Satz m.
dartboard n Zielscheibe f (im Darts-Spiel).
dash vi stürmen; stürzen; * vt (zer)schlagen; (zer)schmettern; schleudern; (be)spritzen; * n Schlag m; Schuß m; Spritzer m; Prise f; Anflug m; Strich m; Sprint m; Ansturm m; **at one** ~ auf einen Schlag.
dashboard n Armaturenbrett n; Spritzbrett n.
dashing adj schneidig; fesch; flott.

dastardly adj feige; heimtückisch.
data n Daten pl.
database n Datenbank f.
data processing n Datenverarbeitung f.
date n Datum n; Termin m; Verabredung f; neuester Stand m; (bot) Dattel f; * vt datieren; sich verabreden mit; (aus)gehen mit.
dated adj datiert; veraltet; überholt.
dative n Dativ m.
daub vt (ver)schmieren; (ver)streichen; (zusammen-)klecksen.
daughter n Tochter f; ~ **in-law** Schwiegertochter f.
daunting adj erschreckend; beängstigend.
dawdle vi trödeln; bummeln.
dawn n (Morgen)Dämmerung f; (Tages)Anbruch m; Morgengrauen n; * vi tagen; (herauf-)dämmern; grauen; anbrechen.
day n Tag m; Zeit f; **by** ~ bei Tag; ~ **by** ~ Tag für Tag; tagtäglich.
daybreak n Tagesanbruch m.
day laborer n Tagelöhner m.
daylight n Tageslicht n; Tagesanbruch m; ~ **saving time** n Sommerzeit f.
daytime n Tag m; Tageszeit f.
daze vt betäuben; verwirren.
dazed adj betäubt; benommen; verwirrt.
dazzle vt blenden; verblüffen.
dazzling adj blenden; strahlend; verwirrend.
deacon n Diakon m; Geistliche(r) f(m).
dead adj tot; (ab)gestorben; leblos; tief; todmüde; taub; gefühllos; todsicher; ~**wood** n totes Holz n; Ballast m; Plunder m; ~ **silence** n Totenstille f; **the** ~ npl die Toten pl.
dead-drunk adj bewußtlos betrunken.
deaden vt abtöten; abstumpfen; dämpfen; schwächen.

dead heat *n* unentschiedenes Rennen *n*.

deadline *n* Todesstreifen *m*; letzter Termin *m*; Stichtag *m*; Redaktionsschluß *m*.

deadlock *n* völliger Stillstand *m*; toter Punkt *m*.

deadly *adj* tödlich; Todes-; schrecklich; * *adv* totenähnlich; tod-; schrecklich.

dead march *n* Trauermarsch *m*.

deadness *n* Leblosigkeit *f*; Abgestumpftheit *f*; Flaute *f*.

deaf *adj* taub; schwerhörig.

deafen *vt* taub machen; betäuben; dämpfen.

deaf-mute *n* Taubstumme(r) *f(m)*.

deafness *n* Taubheit *f*; Schwerhörigkeit *f*.

deal *n* Geschäft *n*; Abkommen *n*; Kartengeben *n*; Menge *f*; Teil *m*; **a great ~** sehr viel; **a good ~** eine ganze Menge; ziemlich viel; * *vt* austeilen; geben; * *vi* Handel treiben; handeln; dealen; geben; **to ~ in/with** sich befassen mit; erledigen; fertig werden mit.

dealer *n* Händler(in) *m(f)*; Dealer *m*; Geber *m*.

dealings *npl* Umgang *m*; (Geschäfts)Verkehr *m*; Handel *m*; Handlungsweise *f*.

dean *n* Dekan *m*.

dear *adj* ~**ly** *adv* lieb; teuer.

dearness *n* hoher Wert *m*; Kostspieligkeit *f*.

dearth *n* Mangel *m*; Not *f*.

death *n* Tod *m*; Todesfall *m*; (Ab)Sterben *n*.

deathbed *n* Sterbebett *n*.

deathblow *n* Todesstoß *m*.

death certificate *n* Totenschein *m*.

death penalty *n* Todesstrafe *f*.

death throes *npl* Todeskampf *m*.

death warrant *n* Todesurteil *n*.

debacle *n* Debakel *n*; Katastrophe *f*.

debar *vt* ausschließen; (ver)hindern.

debase *vt* erniedrigen; entwürdigen; (herab)mindern; verfälschen.

debasement *n* Erniedrigung *f*; Entwürdigung *f*; Wertminderung *f*; Verfälschung *f*.

debatable *adj* fraglich; umstritten; anfechtbar.

debate *n* Debatte *f*; Diskussion *f*; * *vt* debattieren; diskutieren; erwägen; sich überlegen.

debauched *adj* verderbt; ausschweifend.

debauchery *n* Ausschweifung *f*.

debilitate *vt* schwächen; entkräften.

debit *n* Soll *n*; (Konto)Belastung *f*; * *vt* (*com*) belasten.

debt *n* Schuld *f*; Forderung *f*; **to get into ~** Schulden machen; sich verschulden.

debtor *n* Schuldner(in) *m(f)*.

debunk *vt* entlarven; vom Podest stoßen.

decade *n* Jahrzehnt *n*; Dekade *f*.

decadence *n* Dekadenz *f*; Verfall *m*.

decaffeinated *adj* koffeinfrei.

decanter *n* Karaffe *f*.

decapitate *vt* enthaupten; köpfen.

decapitation *n* Enthauptung *f*.

decay *vi* verfallen; schwinden; verwesen; (ver)faulen; * *n* Verfall *m*; Fäulnis *f*; Verwesung *f*; Zerfall *m*.

deceased *adj* verstorben.

deceit *n* Betrug *m*; Täuschung *f*; (Hinter)List *f*.

deceitful *adj* ~**ly** *adv* betrügerisch; falsch; hinterlistig.

deceive *vt* täuschen; (be)trügen.

December *n* Dezember *m*.

decency *n* Anstand *m*; Anständigkeit *f*.

decent *adj* anständig; schicklich; ~**ly** *adv* anständig(erweise).

deception *n* Täuschung *f*; Betrug *m*.

deceptive *adj* täuschend; (be)trügerisch.

decibel *n* Dezibel *n*.

decide *vt* entscheiden; bestimmen; veranlassen; * *vi* (sich) entscheiden; beschließen.

decided *adj* entschieden; entschlossen; bestimmt.

decidedly *adv* entschieden; bestimmt; zweifellos.

deciduous *adj* (*bot*) Laub-; (*jährlich*) abfallend.

decimal *adj* Dezimal-.

decimate *vt* dezimieren.

decipher *vt* entziffern; dechiffrieren; (*fig*) enträtseln.

decision *n* Entscheidung *f*; Entschluß *m*; Entschlossenheit *f*.

decisive *adj* entscheidend; ausschlaggebend; endgültig; entschlossen; **~ly** *adv* entscheidend; in entscheidender Weise.

deck *n* Deck *n*; (Karten)Spiel *n*; Laufwerk *n*; * *vt* schmücken; herausputzen.

deckchair *n* Liegestuhl *m*.

declaim *vi* deklamieren; wettern; eine Rede halten.

declamation *n* Deklamation *f*; Tirade *f*; Rede *f*.

declaration *n* (Zoll)Erklärung *f*.

declare *vt* erklären; verkünden; bekanntgeben; versichern; deklarieren.

declension *n* Deklination *f*; Neigung *f*.

decline *vt* (*gr*) deklinieren; neigen; ablehnen; ausschlagen; * *vi* sich neigen; (ver)fallen; abnehmen; ablehnen; * *n* Abnahme *f*; (*fig*) Niedergang *m*; Verfall *m*; Abhang *m*.

declutch *vi* auskuppeln.

decode *vt* entschlüsseln; dechiffrieren.

decompose *vi* zerfallen; sich zersetzen; verfaulen.

decomposition *n* Zersetzung *f*; Zerfall *m*; Verwesung *f*.

decor *n* Dekor *n*; Ausstattung *f*.

decorate *vt* schmücken; auszeichnen; renovieren.

decoration *n* Verzierung *f*; Schmuck *m*; Orden *m*; Renovierung *f*.

decorative *adj* dekorativ; Zier-; Schmuck-.

decorator *n* Maler und Tapezierer *m*; Dekorateur(in) *m(f)*.

decorous *adj* **~ly** *adv* schicklich; anständig.

decorum *n* Anstand *m*; Schicklichkeit *f*.

decoy *n* Köder *m*; Lockvogel *m*.

decrease *vt* vermindern; verringern; * *n* Abnahme *f*; Verminderung *f*; Rückgang *m*.

decree *n* Dekret *n*; Erlaß *m*; Verordnung *f*; Entscheid *m*; Fügung *f*; * *vt* verordnen; verfügen; bestimmen.

decrepit *adj* altersschwach; klapprig; baufällig.

decry *vt* schlechtmachen; herabsetzen.

dedicate *vt* weihen; widmen; übergeben.

dedication *n* (Ein)Weihung *f*; Widmung *f*; Hingabe *f*.

deduce *vt* folgern; schließen; herleiten.

deduct *vt* abziehen; absetzen.

deduction *n* Abzug *m*; Absetzung *f*; Nachlaß *m*; Subtraktion *f*; Folgerung *f*; Schluß *m*.

deed *n* Tat *f*; Handlung *f*; Urkunde *f*.

deem *vt* halten für; * *vi* denken.

deep *adj* tief(gründig); (uner-)gründlich; scharfsinnig; innig.

deepen *vt* vertiefen; tiefer machen; verstärken.

deep-freeze *n* Tiefkühltruhe *f*.

deeply *adv* tief; zutiefst; gründlich.

deepness *n* Tiefe *f*; Gründlichkeit *f*.

deer *n* Hirsch *m*; Rotwild *n*; Reh *n*.

deface *vt* entstellen; verunstalten; durchstreichen.

defacement *n* Entstellung *f*;

Verunstaltung *f*; Ausstreichung *f*.

defamation *n* Verleumdung *f*.

default *n* Unterlassung *f*; Nichterfüllung *f*; Verzug *m*; Nichterscheinen *n* vor Gericht; * *vi* seinen Verpflichtungen nicht nachkommen; im Verzug sein; versäumen; nicht (vor Gericht) erscheinen.

defaulter *n* (*law*) vor Gericht nicht Erscheinende(r) *f(m)*; säumiger Zahler *m*; Säumige(r) *f(m)*.

defeat *n* Niederlage *f*; Vereitelung *f*; Ablehnung *f*; * *vt* besiegen; (nieder)schlagen; vereiteln; zu Fall bringen.

defect *n* Defekt *m*; Fehler *m*; Mangel *m*.

defection *n* Abfall *m*; Überlaufen *n*.

defective *adj* fehlerhaft; mangelhaft; schadhaft.

defence *n* Verteidigung *f*; Schutz *m*.

defenceless *adj* schutzlos; wehrlos; (*mil*) unverteidigt; offen.

defend *vt* verteidigen; schützen.

defendant *n* Angeklagte(r) *f(m)*; Beklagte(r) *f(m)*.

defensive *adj* ~ly *adv* defensiv; Verteidigungs-; Schutz-; abwehrend.

defer *vt* verschieben; (ver)zögern.

deference *n* Ehrerbietung *f*; (Hoch)Achtung *f*; Rücksicht *f*; Nachgiebigkeit *f*.

deferential *adj* ehrerbietig; respektvoll; rücksichtsvoll.

defiance *n* Trotz *m*; Herausforderung *f*.

defiant *adj* trotzig; herausfordernd.

deficiency *n* Mangel *m*; Unzulänglichkeit *f*.

deficient *adj* unzulänglich; mangelhaft; fehlend.

deficit *n* Defizit *n*; Mangel *m*; Verlust *m*.

defile *vt* beschmutzen; beflecken; schänden.

definable *adj* definierbar; bestimmbar.

define *vt* definieren; bestimmen; umreißen; abgrenzen.

definite *adj* bestimmt; klar; festgelegt; endgültig; ~ly *adv* bestimmt; zweifellos; entschieden.

definition *n* Definition *f*; Genauigkeit *f*; Schärfe *f*.

definitive *adj*, ~ly *adv* definitiv; endgültig; entschieden; maßgeblich.

deflate *vt* Luft ablassen aus; herabsetzen; ernüchtern.

deflect *vt* ablenken; abwenden.

deflower *vt* deflorieren; entjungfern.

deform *vt* deformieren; entstellen; verunstalten.

deformity *n* Häßlichkeit *f*; Mißbildung *f*.

defraud *vt* betrügen; hinterziehen.

defray *vt* bestreiten; tragen.

defrost *vt* entfrosten; abtauen; auftauen.

defroster *n* Enteisungsanlage *f*.

deft *adj* ~ly *adv* geschickt; gewandt.

defunct *adj* verstorben; nicht mehr existierend; ehemalig.

defuse *vt* entschärfen.

defy *n* trotzen; herausfordern; sich widersetzen.

degenerate *vi* degenerieren; herabsinken; * *adj* degeneriert.

degeneration *n* Degeneration *f*; Entartung *f*.

degradation *n* Degradierung *f*; Erniedrigung *f*.

degrade *vt* degradieren; erniedrigen.

degree *n* Grad *m*; Rang *m*; Stufe *f*; (Aus)Maß *n*.

dehydrated *adj* dehydriert; Trocken-.

de-ice *vt* enteisen.

deign *vi* geruhen; belieben.

deity n Gottheit f.
dejected adj niedergeschlagen; deprimiert.
dejection n Niedergeschlagenheit f.
delay vt verzögern; hinausschieben; aufhalten; * n Verzögerung f; Aufschub m; Verspätung f.
delectable adj köstlich.
delegate vt delegieren; abordnen; übertragen; * n Delegierte(r) f(m); Abgeordnete(r) f(m).
delegation n Delegation f; Abordnung f; Übertragung f.
delete vt streichen; tilgen.
deliberate vt überlegen; * adj ~ly adv absichtlich; bewußt; wohlüberlegt; bedächtig.
deliberation n Überlegung f; Beratung f; Bedächtigkeit f.
deliberative adj beratend; überlegt.
delicacy n Delikatesse f; Köstlichkeit f; Zartheit f; Feingefühl n; Empfindlichkeit f; heikler Charakter m.
delicate adj, ~ly adv zart; fein(fühlig); empfindlich; zierlich; heikel; delikat; taktvoll; köstlich.
delicious adj ~ly adv köstlich.
delight n Vergnügen n; Freude f; Entzücken n; * vt erfreuen; entzücken; * vi sich freuen; entzückt sein; Vergnügen bereiten.
delighted adj entzückt; begeistert.
delightful adj, ~ly adv entzückend; köstlich; herrlich.
delineate vt skizzieren; zeichnen; schildern.
delineation n Entwurf m; Schilderung f.
delinquency n Kriminalität f; Pflichtvergessenheit f; Straftat f.
delinquent n Delinquent(in) m(f); Straftäter(in) m(f).
delirious adj im Delirium; phantasierend; wahnsinnig.

delirium n Delirium n; (Fieber)Wahn m; Taumel m.
deliver vt (aus)liefern; zustellen; abgeben; ausrichten; verkünden; vortragen; austeilen; befreien; erlösen; entbinden.
deliverance n Befreiung f; Erlösung f; Äußerung f.
delivery n (Aus)Lieferung f; Zustellung f; Ablieferung f; Übergabe f; Halten n; Befreiung f; Erlösung f; Entbindung f.
delude vt täuschen; verleiten.
deluge n Überschwemmung f; (Sint)Flut f.
delusion n Täuschung f; Wahn m; Irrtum m.
delve vi graben; forschen.
demagog(ue) n Demagoge m.
demand n (An)Forderung f; Verlangen n; Nachfrage f; * vt (er)fordern; verlangen.
demanding adj anspruchsvoll; fordernd; schwierig.
demarcation n Demarkation f; Abgrenzung f.
demean vt erniedrigen.
demeanour n Benehmen n; Auftreten n.
demented adj wahnsinnig; verrückt.
demise n Ableben n; Tod m; Übertragung f.
democracy n Demokratie f.
democrat n Demokrat(in) m(f).
democratic adj demokratisch.
demolish vt demolieren; abreißen; zerstören.
demolition n Demolierung f; Abbruch m; Zerstörung f.
demon n Dämon m.
demonstrable adj ~bly adv nachweislich.
demonstrate vt beweisen; zeigen; vorführen; * vi demonstrieren.
demonstration n Demonstration f; Kundgebung f; Vorführung f; Beweis m; Bekundung f.
demonstrative adj anschaulich (zeigend); demonstrativ;

betont; Gefühle offen zeigend.

demonstrator n Demonstrant(in) m(f); Vorführer(in) m(f).

demoralization n Demoralisierung f.

demoralize vt demoralisieren; entmutigen.

demote vt degradieren.

demur vi Einwendungen machen; zaudern.

demure adj ~ly adv zimperlich; prüde; ernst; gesetzt.

den n Höhle f; Bau m; (Arbeits)Zimmer n.

denatured alcohol n vergällter Alkohol m.

denial n Leugnen n; (Ver)Leugnung f; Verneinung f; abschlägige Antwort f.

denims npl Jeans pl.

denomination n Benennung f; Klasse f; Konfession f; Einheit f; Nennwert m.

denominator n (math) Nenner m.

denote vt anzeigen; bezeichnen.

denounce vt anprangern; anzeigen; denunzieren; kündigen.

dense adj dicht; begriffsstutzig.

density n Dichte f.

dent n Delle f; Beule f; * vt einbeulen.

dental adj Zahn-; zahnärztlich.

dentifrice n Zahnputzmittel n.

dentist n Zahnarzt m; Zahnärztin f.

dentistry n Zahnmedizin f.

denture npl Gebiß n; Prothese f.

denude vt entblößen; berauben.

denunciation n Denunzierung f; Anzeige f; Anprangerung f; Kündigung f.

deny vt (ver)leugnen; abstreiten; dementieren; ablehnen; versagen; verweigern; abweisen.

deodorant n Deodorant n.

deodorize vt deodorieren.

depart vi fortgehen; abreisen; abfahren; abweichen; verscheiden.

department n Abteilung f; Amt n; Dienststelle f; Ministerium n; Fach n; Ressort n; Branche f.

department store n Kaufhaus n.

departure n Abreise f; Abfahrt f; Abflug m; Ausscheiden n; Abweichung f; Hinscheiden n; (fig) Anfang m.

departure lounge n Abflughalle f.

depend vi ~ on/upon sich verlassen auf; abhängig sein von; angewiesen sein auf; ankommen auf.

dependable adj zuverlässig; verläßlich.

dependant n Abhängige(r) f(m); (Familen)Angehörige(r) f(m).

dependency n Abhängigkeit f; Schutzgebiet n; Kolonie f.

dependent adj abhängig; angewiesen; bedingt; vertrauend.

depict vt darstellen; schildern.

depleted adj erschöpft; leer; dezimiert.

deplorable adj ~bly adv beklagenswert; bedauerlich; jämmerlich.

deplore vt beklagen; bedauern.

deploy vt (mil) stationieren; entwickeln; einsetzen.

depopulated adj entvölkert.

depopulation n Entvölkerung f.

deport vt deportieren; abschieben; ausweisen; benehmen.

deportation n Deportation f; Ausweisung f; Abschiebung f.

deportment n Benehmen n; Haltung f.

deposit vt (hinter)legen; einzahlen; anzahlen; ablagern; deponieren; * n Anzahlung f; Pfand n; Hinterlegung f; Einzahlung f; Depot n; Ablagerung f.

deposition n Absetzung f; Sedimentbildung f; Ablagerung f; Hinterlegung f; Einzahlung f; eidliche Aussage f.

depositor *n* Hinterleger(in) *m(f)*; Einzahler(in) *m(f)*.

depot *n* Depot *n*; Lagerhaus *n*.

deprave *vt* verderben.

depraved *adj* verderbt; lasterhaft.

depravity *n* Verderbtheit *f*; Lasterhaftigkeit *f*; Schlechtigkeit *f*.

deprecate *vt* mißbilligen; verurteilen.

depreciate *vt* herabsetzen; geringschätzen; * *vi* sinken; sich verschlechtern.

depreciation *n* Geringschätzung *f*; Herabsetzung *f*; Entwertung *f*; Abschreibung *f*.

depredation *n* Plünderung *f*; Verwüstung *f*.

depress *vt* deprimieren; (be-)drücken; schwächen.

depressed *adj* deprimiert; niedergeschlagen; (ein)gedrückt; schwach.

depression *n* Depression *f*; Niedergeschlagenheit *f*; (Ein-)Senkung *f*.

deprivation *n* Entzug *m*; Verlust *m*; Entbehrung *f*; Benachteiligung *f*.

deprive *vt* berauben; entziehen; vorenthalten; absetzen.

deprived *adj* benachteiligt; unterprivilegiert.

depth *n* Tiefe *f*; Ausmaß *n*; Tiefgründigkeit *f*.

deputation *n* Abordnung *f*.

depute *vt* abordnen; deputieren.

deputize *vi* vertreten.

deputy *n* (Stell)Vertreter(in) *m(f)*; Abgeordnete(r) *f(m)*.

derail *vt* entgleisen lassen.

deranged *adj* (geistes)gestört; in Unordnung.

derelict *adj* verlassen; herrenlos; baufällig.

deride *vt* verlachen; verspotten.

derision *n* Hohn *m*; Spott *m*; Gespött *n*.

derisive *adj* spöttisch; höhnisch; lächerlich.

derivable *adj* ableitbar; herleitbar.

derivation *n* Ableitung *f*; Herkunft *f*.

derivative *n* Ableitung *f*; Derivat *n*.

derive *vt* herleiten; ableiten; ziehen; schöpfen; gewinnen; * *vi* abstammen; sich herleiten.

derogatory *adj* abfällig; herabsetzend; abträglich.

derrick *n* Mastenkran *m*; Bohrturm *m*; Ladebaum *m*.

descant *n* (*mus*) Diskant *m*.

descend *vi* herabsteigen; hinuntergehen; niedergehen; (ab)fallen; abstammen; herfallen; hereinbrechen; sinken; (*fig*) sich herabwürdigen.

descendant *n* Nachkomme *m*; Deszendent *m*.

descent *n* Abstieg *m*; Niedergehen *n*; Absprung *m*; Niedergang *m*; Sinken *n*; Gefälle *n*; Abstammung *f*.

describe *vt* beschreiben; schildern.

description *n* Beschreibung *f*; Schilderung *f*; Art *f*.

descriptive *adj* beschreibend; darstellend; anschaulich.

descry *vt* wahrnehmen; erspähen.

desecrate *vt* entweihen; schänden.

desecration *n* Entweihung *f*; Schändung *f*.

desert *n* Wüste; Ödland; * *adj* Wüsten-; öde.

desert *vt* verlassen; im Stich lassen; * *vi* desertieren; * *n* Verdienst *m*; verdienter Lohn *m*.

deserter *n* Deserteur *m*.

desertion *n* Verlassen *n*; Verlassenheit *f*; Desertion *f*.

deserve *vt* verdienen.

deservedly *adv* verdientermaßen.

deserving *adj* verdienstvoll; würdig.

deshabille *n* Negligé *n*.

desideratum n Erwünschte n; Bedürfnis n; Erfordernis n.

design vt entwerfen; gestalten; planen; bestimmen; * n Entwurf m; Design n; Gestaltung f; Ausführung f; Konstruktion f; Plan m; Absicht f; Anschlag m.

designate vt bestimmen; bezeichnen; ernennen.

designation n Bestimmung f; Bezeichnung f; Ernennung f.

designedly adv absichtlich.

designer n Designer(in) m(f); Erfinder(in) m(f); Konstrukteur m.

desirability n Erwünschtheit f.

desirable adj wünschenswert; erwünscht; begehrenswert.

desire n Wunsch m; Verlangen n; Begierde f; * vt wünschen; begehren; verlangen.

desirous adj begierig.

desist vi ablassen; Abstand nehmen.

desk n Schreibtisch m; Pult n; Rezeption f.

desolate adj verwüstet; einsam; verlassen; öde; trostlos.

desolation n Verwüstung f; Verlassenheit f; Öde f; Trostlosigkeit f.

despair n Verzweiflung f; Hoffnungslosigkeit f; * vi verzweifeln.

despairingly adj verzweifelt.

despatch = **dispatch**.

desperado n Desperado m; Bandit m.

desperate adj ~ly adv verzweifelt; hoffnungslos; schrecklich.

desperation n Verzweiflung f; Hoffnungslosigkeit f.

despicable adj verabscheuungswürdig; verächtlich.

despise vt verachten; verschmähen.

despite prep trotz; ungeachtet.

despoil vt plündern; berauben.

despondency n Verzagtheit f; Mutlosigkeit f.

despondent adj verzagt; mutlos; verzweifelt.

despot n Despot m.

despotic adj, ~ally adv despotisch; (fig) herrisch.

despotism n Despotismus m.

dessert n Nachtisch m; Dessert n.

destination n Bestimmungsort m; Ziel n.

destine vt bestimmen; ausersehen.

destiny n Schicksal n; Verhängnis n.

destitute adj mittellos; notleidend; bar; beraubt.

destitution n (bittere) Not f; Elend n; (völliger) Mangel m.

destroy vt zerstören; vernichten; ruinieren; töten; einschläfern.

destruction n Zerstörung f; Vernichtung f; Tötung f; Einschläferung f.

destructive adj zerstörend; vernichtend; destruktiv; zerstörerisch; schädlich.

desultory adj planlos; oberflächlich; sprunghaft; unstet.

detach vt (ab)trennen; losmachen; (los)lösen; absondern.

detachable adj abnehmbar; (ab)trennbar.

detachment n (Los)Lösung f; (fig) Abstand m; Objektivität f; (mil) Abteilung f.

detail n Detail n; Einzelheit f; Nebensache f; (mil) Kommando n; in ~ detailliert; ausführlich; * vt genau beschreiben; ausführlich berichten; (mil) abkommandieren.

detain vt aufhalten; in Haft (be)halten; nachsitzen lassen.

detect vt entdecken; wahrnehmen; aufdecken.

detection n Entdeckung f; Ermittlung f; Aufklärung f.

detective n Detektiv(in) m(f); Kriminalbeamte(r) f(m).

detector n Detektor m.

detention n Haft f; Festnahme f; Vorenthaltung f; Nachsitzen n.

deter vt abschrecken; abhalten.

detergent n Reinigungsmittel n; Waschmittel n.

deteriorate vt verschlechtern; (ver)mindern.

deterioration n Verschlechterung f; Wertminderung f.

determination n Entschlossenheit f; Bestimmung f; Feststellung f; Entscheidung f.

determine vt bestimmen; entscheiden; feststellen; beschließen.

determined adj entschlossen; entschieden; bestimmt; festgelegt.

deterrent n Abschreckungsmaßnahme f.

detest vt verabscheuen; hassen.

detestable adj abscheulich; verabscheuungswürdig.

dethrone vt entthronen.

dethronement n Entthronung f.

detonate vi detonieren; explodieren.

detonation n Detonation f; Explosion f.

detour n Umweg m.

detract vt ablenken.

detriment n Nachteil m; Schaden m.

detrimental adj nachteilig; schädlich; abträglich.

deuce n Zwei f; (col) Teufel m.

devaluation n Abwertung f.

devastate vt verwüsten; vernichten.

devastating adj verheerend; vernichtend.

devastation n Verwüstung f.

develop vt entwickeln; ausbauen; erschließen.

development n Entwicklung f; Entfaltung f; Ausbau m; Erschließung f.

deviate vi abweichen.

deviation n Abweichung f; Ablenkung f.

device n Vorrichtung f; Einfall m; Plan m; Kunstgriff m; Wahlspruch m; Muster n.

devil n Teufel m; Teufelskerl m; Reißwolf m; Handlanger m.

devilish adj, ~ly adv teuflisch; verteufelt.

devious adj verschlagen; falsch; abwegig; abgelegen.

devise vt ausdenken; ersinnen; (law) hinterlassen.

devoid adj bar; -los.

devolve vt übertragen; abwälzen.

devote vt widmen; weihen.

devoted adj ergeben; zärtlich; eifrig.

devotee n begeisterter Anhänger m; glühender Verehrer m; Fanatiker m.

devotion n Hingabe f; Ergebenheit f; Verehrung f; Frömmigkeit f.

devotional adj andächtig; fromm; Erbauungs-.

devour vt verschlingen; vernichten.

devout adj, ~ly adv fromm; andächtig; innig.

dew n Tau m.

dewy adj (tau)feucht.

dexterity n Gewandtheit f; Geschicklichkeit f.

dexterous adj gewandt; geschickt.

diabetes n Zuckerkrankheit f; Diabetes m.

diabetic n Diabetiker(in) m(f); Zuckerkranke(r) f(m).

diabolic adj ~ally adv diabolisch; teuflisch.

diadem n Diadem n.

diagnosis n (med) Diagnose f.

diagnostic adj diagnostisch; * n Symptom n; ~s (pl) Diagnostik f.

diagonal adj, ~ly adv diagonal; schräg; Kreuz-; * n Diagonale f.

diagram n Diagramm n; graphische Darstellung f.

dial n Zifferblatt n; Wählscheibe f; Skala f.

dialect n Dialekt m; Mundart f.

dialling code n Vorwahl(nummer) f.

dialogue n Dialog m; (Zwie)Gespräch n.

dialling tone *n* Wählton *m*.

diameter *n* Durchmesser *m*.

diametrical *adj* ~**ly** *adv* diametrisch; diametral; genau entgegengesetzt.

diamond *n* Diamant *m*; Raute *f*; Karo *n*.

diamond-cutter *n* Diamantschleifer *m*.

diamonds *npl* (*Kartenspiel*) Karo *n*.

diaper *n* Windel *f*; Gänseaugenstoff *m*.

diaphragm *n* Diaphragma *n*; Scheidewand *f*; Zwerchfell *n*; Membran *f*.

diarrhea *n* Durchfall *m*.

diary *n* Tagebuch *n*; Terminkalender *m*.

dice *npl* Würfel *m*; Würfelspiel *n*.

dictate *vt* diktieren; vorschreiben; (*fig*) einflößen; * *n* Diktat *n*; Gebot *n*.

dictation *n* Diktat *n*.

dictatorial *adj* diktatorisch; autoritär.

dictatorship *n* Diktatur *f*.

diction *n* (Aus)Sprache *f*; Ausdrucksweise *f*.

dictionary *n* Wörterbuch *n*; Lexikon *n*.

didactic *adj* didaktisch; belehrend.

die *vi* (ab)sterben; eingehen; verenden; (*col*) schmachten, brennen; **to ~ away** sich legen; sich verlieren; verklingen; **to ~ down** erlöschen; ersterben; verhallen; ausgehen; nachlassen.

die *n* Würfel *m*.

diehard *n* Dickschädel *m*; Reaktionär *m*.

diesel *n* Diesel *m*.

diet *n* Diät *f*; Ernährung *f*; Kost *f*; * *vi* Diät halten.

dietary *adj* Diät-.

differ *vi* sich unterscheiden; abweichen; nicht übereinstimmen.

difference *n* Unterschied *m*; Verschiedenheit *f*; Differenz *f*.

different *adj* verschieden; anders; ander(er, e, es); ~**ly** *adv* anders; verschieden; unterschiedlich.

differentiate *vt* unterscheiden; differenzieren.

difficult *adj* schwierig; schwer.

difficulty *n* Schwierigkeit *f*; Mühe *f*; Problem *n*.

diffidence *n* Schüchternheit *f*; mangelndes Selbstvertrauen *n*.

diffident *adj*, ~**ly** *adv* schüchtern; ohne Selbstvertrauen.

diffraction *n* Beugung *f*.

diffuse *vt* (*fig*) verbreiten; durchdringen; diffundieren; * *adj* diffus; zerstreut; unklar.

diffusion *n* Diffusion *f*; (*fig*) Verbreitung *f*.

dig *vt* (ein)graben; (*col*) stehen auf; * *n* (Aus)Grabung *f*; Stoß *m*; (Seiten)Hieb *m*; (*col*) Bude *f*.

digest *vt* verdauen; (*fig*) durchdenken; (*fig*) ordnen.

digestible *adj* verdaulich.

digestion *n* Verdauung *f*.

digestive *adj* verdauungsfördernd; Verdauungs-.

digger *n* (Gold)Gräber *m*; Erdarbeiter *m*; Bagger *m*.

digit *n* Finger *m*; Zehe *f*; Ziffer *f*; Stelle *f*.

digital *adj* digital; Digital-; Finger-.

dignified *adj* würdevoll; würdig.

dignitary *n* Würdenträger(in) *m(f)*.

dignity *n* Würde *f*.

digress *vi* abschweifen.

digression *n* Abschweifung *f*.

dike *n* Deich *m*; Damm *m*; Graben *m*; Grenzmauer *f*; (*sl*) Lesbe *f*.

dilapidated *adj* baufällig; klapprig.

dilapidation *n* Baufälligkeit *f*.

dilate *vt* erweitern; (aus)dehnen; * *vi* sich erweitern; sich (aus)dehnen.

dilemma *n* Dilemma *n*; Zwangslage *f*.

diligence *n* Sorgfalt *f*; Fleiß *m*.

diligent *adj*, **~ly** *adv* sorgfältig; gewissenhaft; fleißig.

dilute *vt* verdünnen; verwässern.

dim *adj*, **~ly** *adv* (halb)dunkel; trüb; matt; *(fig)* schwer von Begriff; * *vt* verdunkeln; trüben.

dime *n* Zehncentstück *n*; *(fig)* Groschen *m*.

dimension *n* Dimension *f*; Ausdehnung *f*; Ausmaß *n*.

diminish *vt* vermindern; verringern; verkleinern; *(fig)* herabsetzen; * *vi* sich vermindern; sich verringern; abnehmen.

diminution *n* (Ver)Minderung *f*; Verringerung *f*; Verkleinerung *f*; Herabsetzung *f*.

diminutive adj klein; winzig; Diminutiv-; Verkleinerungs-.

dimmer *n* Dimmer *m*.

dimple *n* Grübchen *n*.

din *n* Lärm *m*; Getöse *n*.

dine *vi* essen; speisen.

diner *n* (Speise)Gast *m*; Speiselokal *n*.

dinghy *n* Dingi *n*; Beiboot *n*; Schlauchboot *n*.

dingy *adj* schmuddelig; schmutzig; schäbig.

dinner *n* Mittagessen *n*; Abendessen *n*; Diner *n*; Festessen *n*.

dinner time *n* Essenszeit *f*.

dinosaur *n* Dinosaurier *m*.

dint *n*: **by ~ of** kraft; mittels.

diocese *n* Diözese *f*.

dip *vt* (ein)tauchen; (ein)tunken; rasch senken.

diphtheria *n* Diphterie *f*.

diphthong *n* Diphthong *m*; Doppelvokal *m*.

diploma *n* Diplom *n*; Urkunde *f*.

diplomacy *n* Diplomatie *f*.

diplomat *n* Diplomat *m*.

diplomatic *adj* diplomatisch.

dipsomania *n* Dipsomanie *f*.

dipstick *n* *(auto)* (Öl)Meßstab *m*.

dire *adj* gräßlich; schrecklich; tödlich; unheilverkündend.

direct *adj* direkt; gerade; unmittelbar; * *vt* richten; lenken; führen; anweisen; anordnen; den Weg zeigen; Regie führen.

direction *n* Richtung *f*; Führung *f*; Anweisung *f*; Anleitung *f*; Anordnung *f*; Vorschrift *f*; Anschrift *f*; Regie *f*; **~s** (*pl*) Wegbeschreibung *f*.

directly *adj* direkt; gerade; sofort.

director *n* Direktor *m*; Regisseur *m*.

directory *n* Verzeichnis *n*; Adreßbuch *n*; Telefonbuch *n*; Leitfaden *m*.

dirt *n* Schmutz *m*; Dreck *m*; Erde *f*.

dirtiness *n* Schmutzigkeit *f*; Gemeinheit *f*.

dirty *adj* schmutzig; dreckig; gemein.

disability *n* Unfähigkeit *f*; Invalidität *f*; Behinderung *f*.

disabled *adj* behindert; invalid; untauglich.

disabuse *vt* eines Besseren belehren; aufklären.

disadvantage *n* Nachteil *m*; ungünstige Lage *f*; Verlust *m*; * *vt* benachteiligen.

disadvantageous *adj* nachteilig; ungünstig.

disaffected *adj* abgeneigt; unzufrieden.

disagree *vi* nicht übereinstimmen; anderer Meinung sein; sich streiten; ablehnen; nicht bekommen.

disagreeable *adj* **~bly** *adv* unangenehm; widerlich.

disagreement *n* (Meinungs-) Verschiedenheit *f*; Unstimmigkeit *f*.

disallow *vt* nicht zugeben; nicht erlauben; nicht gelten lassen.

disappear *vi* verschwinden.

disappearance *n* Verschwinden *n*.

disappoint *vt* enttäuschen.

disappointed *adj* enttäuscht.

disappointing *adj* enttäuschend.

disappointment *n* Enttäuschung *f*.

disapproval *n* Mißbilligung *f*; Mißfallen *n*.

disapprove *vt* mißbilligen; ablehnen.

disarm *vt* entwaffnen; unschädlich machen; (*fig*) besänftigen.

disarmament *n* Abrüstung *f*; Entwaffnung *f*.

disarray *n* Unordnung *f*.

disaster *n* Unglück *n*; Katastrophe *f*.

disastrous *adj* katastrophal; verheerend; schrecklich.

disband *vt* auflösen.

disbelief *n* Ungläubigkeit *f*; Zweifel *m*.

disbelieve *vt* nicht glauben; bezweifeln.

disburse *vt* auszahlen; auslegen.

discard *vt* ablegen; ausrangieren; aufgeben.

discern *vt* erkennen; wahrnehmen; beurteilen.

discernible *adj* erkennbar; wahrnehmbar.

discerning *adj* urteilsfähig; kritisch; klug.

discernment *n* Einsicht *f*; Urteilskraft *f*.

discharge *vt* entladen; entlasten; abfeuern; ablassen; absondern; ausstoßen; befreien; freisprechen; entlassen; erfüllen; * *n* Entladung *f*; Abfeuern *n*; Abfluß *m*; Absonderung *f*; Befreiung *f*; Freisprechung *f*; Entlassung *f*; Erfüllung *f*.

disciple *n* Schüler *m*; Jünger *m*.

discipline *n* Disziplin *f*; Schulung *f*; Züchtigung *f*; * *vt* disziplinieren; schulen; bestrafen.

disclaim *vt* abstreiten; (Verantwortung) ablehnen; nicht anerkennen; widerrufen; (*law*) Verzicht leisten auf.

disclaimer *n* Verzichtleistung *f*; Widerruf *m*.

disclose *vt* bekanntgeben; enthüllen; verraten.

disclosure *n* Enthüllung *f*; Aufdeckung *f*.

disco *n* Disko *f*.

discolor *vt* verfärben.

discoloration *n* Verfärbung *f*; Fleck *m*.

discomfort *n* Unannehmlichkeit *f*; Unbehagen *n*; Beschwerde *f*.

disconcert *vt* aus der Fassung bringen; beunruhigen.

disconnect *vt* trennen; abschalten.

disconsolate *adj* ~ly *adv* untröstlich; trostlos.

discontent *n* Unzufriedenheit *f*; * *adj* unzufrieden.

discontented *adj* unzufrieden.

discontinue *vi* unterbrechen; einstellen; aufgeben; aufhören.

discord *n* Uneinigkeit *f*; Zwietracht *f*; Mißklang *m*.

discordant *adj* (sich) widersprechend; uneinig; mißtönend.

discount *n* Preisnachlaß *m*; Skonto *n*; Abzug *m*; * *vt* abziehen; unberücksichtigt lassen; mit Vorbehalt aufnehmen.

discourage *vt* entmutigen; abschrecken.

discouraged *adj* entmutigt; abgeschreckt.

discouragement *n* Entmutigung *f*; Abschreckung *f*.

discouraging *adj* entmutigend.

discourse *n* Unterhaltung *f*; Abhandlung *f*; Predigt *f*.

discourteous *adj* ~ly *adv* unhöflich; unzuvorkommend.

discourtesy *n* Unhöflichkeit *f*.

discover *vt* entdecken.

discovery *n* Entdeckung *f*; Enthüllung *f*.

discredit *vt* diskreditieren; in Verruf bringen; anzweifeln.

discreditable *adj* schändlich.

discreet *adj*, **~ly** *adv* diskret; vorsichtig.

discrepancy *n* Diskrepanz *f*; Unstimmigkeit *f*.

discretion *n* Diskretion *f*; Ermessen *n*; Belieben *n*; Vorsicht *f*.

discretionary *adj* ins freie Ermessen gestellt; beliebig; unumschränkt.

discriminate *vt* diskriminieren; unterscheiden.

discrimination *n* Diskriminierung *f*; Unterscheidung *f*; Urteilsfähigkeit *f*.

discursive *adj* weitschweifig; sprunghaft.

discuss *vt* diskutieren; sprechen über; behandeln.

discussion *n* Diskussion *f*; Besprechung *f*; Behandlung *f*.

disdain *vt* verachten; verschmähen; geringschätzen; * *n* Verachtung *f*; Geringschätzung *f*; Hochmut *m*.

disdainful *adj*, **~ly** *adv* verächtlich; geringschätzig; hochmütig.

disease *n* Krankheit *f*.

diseased *adj* krank; krankhaft.

disembark *vt* von Bord gehen lassen; ausschiffen; * *vi* von Bord gehen; sich ausschiffen.

disembarkation *n* Ausschiffung *f*; Ausladung *f*; Aussteigen *n*.

disenchant *vt* ernüchtern; desillusionieren.

disenchanted *adj* ernüchtert; desillusioniert.

disenchantment *n* Ernüchterung *f*; Desillusionierung *f*.

disengage *vt* losmachen; befreien; loskuppeln.

disentangle *vt* entwirren; befreien.

disfigure *vt* entstellen; verunstalten.

disgrace *n* Schande *f*; Ungnade *f*; * *vt* Schande bringen über.

disgraceful *adj*, **~ly** *adv* schändlich; schimpflich.

disgruntled *adj* verärgert; verstimmt.

disguise *vt* verkleiden; maskieren; verstellen; verbergen; * *n* Verkleidung *f*; Maske *f*; Deckmantel *m*; Verstellung *f*.

disgust *n* Ekel *m*; Abscheu *m*; * *vt* (an)ekeln; anwidern; empören.

disgusting *adj* ekelhaft; widerlich; abscheulich.

dish *n* (Servier)Platte *f*; Gericht *n*; **~es** (*pl*) Geschirr *n*; * *vt* (col) vermasseln; **to ~ up** auftragen; auftischen.

dishcloth *n* Spültuch *n*; Geschirrtuch *n*.

dishearten *vt* entmutigen.

dishevelled *adj* zerzaust; aufgelöst; schlampig.

dishonest *adj*, **~ly** *adv* unehrlich; unredlich.

dishonesty *n* Unehrlichkeit *f*; unredliche Handlung *f*.

dishonour *n* Unehre *f*; Schande *f*; * *vt* entehren; schänden; nicht einlösen.

dishonourable *adj*, **~bly** *adv* unehrenhaft; schändlich; ehrlos.

dishwasher *n* Tellerwäscher(in) *m(f)*; Geschirrspülmaschine *f*.

dishwater *n* Spülwasser *n*.

disillusion *vt* Ernüchterung *f*; Desillusion *f*.

disillusioned *adj* ernüchtert; desillusioniert.

disincentive *n* Abschreckungsmittel *n*; leistungshemmender Faktor *m*.

disinclination *n* Abneigung *f*.

disinclined *adj* abgeneigt.

disinfect *vt* desinfizieren.

disinfectant *n* Desinfektionsmittel *n*.

disinherit *vt* enterben.

disintegrate *vi* sich auflösen; zerfallen.

disinterested *adj*, **~ly** *adv* desinteressiert; uneigennützig; unvoreingenommen.

disjointed *adj* unzusammenhängend; (ab)getrennt.

disk *n* Scheibe *f*; (Schall)Platte
f.

diskette *n* Diskette *f*.

dislike *n* Abneigung *f*; Widerwille *m*; * *vt* nicht leiden können; nicht mögen.

dislocate *vt* verschieben; verla-
gern; ausrenken.

dislocation *n* Verschiebung *f*;
Verlagerung *f*; Verrenkung *f*;
Verwerfung *f*.

dislodge *vt* aufjagen; aufstöbern; vertreiben; * *vi* ausziehen.

disloyal *adj* ~**ly** *adv* untreu;
treulos; illoyal.

disloyalty *n* Treulosigkeit *f*;
Untreue *f*.

dismal *adj* trostlos; düster; bedrückend; gräßlich.

dismantle *vt* demontieren; auseinandernehmen; abbauen;
niederreißen; (*mar*) abwrak-
ken.

dismay *n* Entsetzen *f*; Bestürzung *f*.

dismember *vt* zerstückeln; zergliedern.

dismiss *vt* entlassen; fortschik-
ken; fallenlassen; abtun; abweisen.

dismissal *n* Entlassung *f*; Aufgabe *f*; Abtun *n*; Abweisung *f*.

dismount *vt* aus dem Sattel
heben; abwerfen; demontieren; * *vi* absteigen; absitzen.

disobedience *n* Ungehorsam
m; (Befehls)Verweigerung *f*.

disobedient *adj* ungehorsam.

disobey *vt* nicht gehorchen;
nicht befolgen; verweigern.

disorder *n* Unordnung *f*;
Durcheinander *n*; Aufruhr *m*;
Störung *f*; Erkrankung *f*.

disorderly *adj* unordenlich;
ordnungswidrig; aufrühre-
risch.

disorganization *n* Auflösung *f*;
Desorganisation *f*.

disorganized *adj* desorgani-
siert; aufgelöst.

disorientated *adj* desorien-
tiert; verwirrt.

disown *vt* nicht anerkennen;
verleugnen; ablehnen.

disparage *vt* verächtlich machen; herabsetzen; in Verruf
bringen.

disparaging *adj* verächtlich;
geringschätzig; herabsetzend.

disparity *n* Verschiedenheit *f*;
Ungleichheit *f*.

dispassionate *adj* leiden-
schaftslos; gelassen; sachlich;
objektiv.

dispatch   *vt*   (ab)senden;
(prompt) erledigen; abfertigen; * *n* (prompte) Erledigung
f; (Ab)Sendung *f*; Abfertigung
f; Eile *f*; Botschaft *f*; Bericht
m.

dispel *vt* zerstreuen.

dispensary *n* (Krankenhaus-)
Apotheke *f*.

dispense *vt* austeilen; spenden;
ausgeben; dipensieren; entbinden.

disperse *vt* verstreuen; zerstreuen; verbreiten.

dispirited *adj* mutlos; niedergeschlagen.

displace *vt* verschieben; verrücken; verdrängen; ablösen;
ersetzen; verschleppen; deportieren.

display *vt* ausbreiten; (her)zei-
gen; an den Tag legen; ausstellen; zur Schau stellen;
* *n* Entfaltung *f*; (Her)Zeigen
n; Ausstellung *f*; Zurschaustellung *f*; (Sichtbild)Anzeige
f.

displease *vt* mißfallen; ärgern;
verstimmen; beleidigen.

displeased *adj* ungehalten;
verärgert.

displeasure *n* Mißfallen *n*.

disposable *adj* (frei) verfügbar;
Einweg-; Wegwerf-.

disposal *n* Erledigung *f*; Beseitigung *f*; Entsorgung *f*; Veräußerung *f*; Verfügung *f*.

dispose *vt* (an)ordnen; veranlassen; * *vi* ~ **of** (frei) verfü-

gen; (endgültig) erledigen; loswerden; beseitigen; veräußern; abstoßen.

disposed *adj* gesinnt; geneigt.

disposition *n* Disposition *f*; Veranlagung *f*; Art *f*; Neigung *f*; Anordnung *f*; Erledigung *f*; Verfügung *f*.

dispossess *vt* enteignen; berauben.

disproportionate *adj* unverhältnismäßig; unproportioniert.

disprove *vt* widerlegen.

dispute *n* Disput *m*; Kontroverse *f*; Streit *m*; * *vt* streiten über; disputieren über; bezweifeln.

disqualify *vt* disqualifizieren; untauglich machen; für untauglich erklären.

disquiet *n* Unruhe *f*; Besorgnis *f*.

disquieting *adj* beunruhigend; besorgniserregend.

disquisition *n* Abhandlung *f*.

disregard *vt* mißachten; nicht beachten; * *n* Nichtbeachtung *f*; Mißachtung *f*.

disreputable *adj* verrufen; anrüchig.

disrespect *n* Respektlosigkeit *f*.

disrespectful *adj* ~ly *adv* respektlos; unhöflich.

disrobe *vt* entkleiden.

disrupt *vt* unterbrechen; sprengen; zerreißen.

disruption *n* Unterbrechung *f*; Sprengung *f*; Spaltung *f*.

dissatisfaction *n* Unzufriedenheit *f*.

dissatisfied *adj* unzufrieden.

dissect *vt* zerlegen; zergliedern; sezieren.

dissection *n* Zerlegung *f*; Zergliederung *f*; Sezierung *f*.

disseminate *vt* ausstreuen; verbreiten.

dissension *n* Meinungsverschiedenheit *f*; Uneinigkeit *f*.

dissent *vi* nicht zustimmen; nicht übereinstimmen; * *n*

Meinungsverschiedenheit *f*; Abweichung *f*.

dissenter *n* Andersdenkende(r) *f(m)*; Dissident *m*.

dissertation *n* Dissertation *f*; Abhandlung *f*.

dissident *n* Dissident(in) *m(f)*.

dissimilar *adj* verschieden; unähnlich.

dissimilarity *n* Verschiedenheit *f*; Unähnlichkeit *f*.

dissimulation *n* Verstellung *f*; Heuchelei *f*.

dissipate *vt* zerstreuen; vertreiben; verschwenden.

dissipation *n* Zerstreuung *f*; Verschwendung *f*; Ausschweifung *f*.

dissociate *vt* trennen; absondern; distanzieren.

dissolute *adj* ausschweifend; leichtlebig.

dissolution *n* Auflösung *f*; Zerstörung *f*.

dissolve *vt* (auf)lösen; schmelzen; * *vi* sich auflösen.

dissonance *n* Dissonanz *f*; Mißklang *m*.

dissuade *vt* abraten; abbringen.

distance *n* Entfernung *f*; Ferne *f*; Abstand *m*; Distanz *f*; **at a ~** in einiger Entfernung; von weitem; * *vt* überholen; überflügeln; distanzieren.

distant *adj* entfernt; fern; weit; kühl; distanziert.

distaste *n* Widerwille *m*; Abneigung *f*.

distasteful *adj* widerwärtig; unangenehm; zuwider.

distend *vt* (aus)dehnen; (auf-) blähen.

distil *vt* destillieren; *(Branntwein)* brennen; *(fig)* herausarbeiten.

distillation *n* Destillation *f*; Brennen *n*; Extrakt *m*; Quintessenz *f*.

distillery *n* (Branntwein)Brennerei *f*.

distinct *adj* verschieden(artig); einzeln; getrennt; klar; ein-

deutig; **~ly** adv deutlich; ausgesprochen.

distinction n Unterschied m;
Unterscheidung f; Auszeichnung f; Ruf m; Rang m; Würde f.

distinctive   adj
Unterscheidungs-; kennzeichnend; unverwechselbar; charakteristisch.

distinctness n Deutlichkeit f;
Verschiedenheit f.

distinguish vt unterscheiden;
ausmachen; auszeichnen.

distort vt verdrehen; verzerren.

distorted adj verdreht; ver-
zerrt.

distortion n Verdrehung f; Verzerrung f.

distract vt ablenken; zerstreu-
en.

distracted adj, **~ly** adj abge-
lenkt; zerstreut; außer sich.

distraction n Ablenkung f; Zerstreuung f; Zerstreutheit f;
Verzweiflung f; Wahnsinn m.

distraught adj verwirrt; verstört; außer sich.

distress n Qual f; Elend n; Not
f; Kummer m; * vt quälen; bedrücken; betrüben.

distressing adj quälend; bedrückend.

distribute vt verteilen; verbreiten; vertreiben; zustellen.

distribution n Verteilung f;
Verbreitung f; Vertrieb m; Zustellung f.

distributor n Verteiler m;
Großhändler m.

district n Distrikt m; Bezirk m;
Kreis m; Gegend f.

district attorney n Staatsanwalt m.

distrustful adj mißtrauisch;
argwöhnisch.

disturb vt stören; belästigen;
beunruhigen.

disturbance n Störung f; Beun-
ruhigung f; Unruhe f; Aufruhr
m.

disturbed adj gestört; beunruhigt.

disturbing adj störend; beunruhigend.

disuse n Nichtgebrauch m.

disused adj nicht mehr be-
nutzt; stillgelegt.

ditch n Graben m.

dither vi schwanken; bibbern.

ditto adv dito; desgleichen.

ditty n Liedchen n.

diuretic adj (med) harntrei-
bend.

dive vi tauchen; springen; sich
werfen; hechten.

diver n Taucher(in) m(f);
Kunstspringer(in) m(f).

diverge vi divergieren; ausein-
anderlaufen; abweichen.

divergence n Divergenz f; Abweichung f.

divergent adj divergierend;
abweichend.

diverse adj **~ly** adv verschieden; mannigfaltig.

diversion n Ablenkung f; Ab-
lenkungsmanöver n; Zerstreuung f; Umleitung f.

diversity n Verschiedenheit f;
Mannigfaltigkeit f.

divert vt ablenken; abbringen;
abzweigen; abbringen; umleiten; zerstreuen.

divest vt entkleiden; berauben.

divide vt (ver)teilen; trennen;
einteilen; * vi sich teilen (lassen); verschiedener Meinung
sein.

dividend n Dividende f; Ge-
winnanteil m.

dividers npl (math) Stechzirkel
m.

divine adj göttlich.

divinity n Göttlichkeit f; Gottheit f; Theologie f.

diving n Tauchen n; Kunst-
springen n.

diving board n Sprungbrett n.

divisible adj teilbar.

division n (math) Division f;
(Ver)Teilung f; Spaltung f;
Trennung f; Einteilung f; Teil
m; Abteilung f.

divisor n (math) Divisor m;
Teiler m.

divorce *n* (Ehe)Scheidung *f*; Trennung *f*; * *vi* sich scheiden lassen.

divorced *adj* geschieden; getrennt.

divulge *vt* enthüllen; preisgeben.

dizziness *n* Schwindel(anfall) *m*.

dizzy *adj* schwindlig; schwindelerregend; wirr.

DJ *n* Diskjockey *m*.

do *vt* tun; machen; schaffen; anfertigen; behandeln; erledigen.

docile *adj* fügsam; lammfromm.

dock *n* (*mar*) Dock *n*; Kai *m*; Pier *m*; (*law*) Anklagebank *f*; (*bot*) Ampfer *m*; * *vi* (an)dokken; anlegen.

docker *n* Hafenarbeiter *m*.

dockyard *n* (*mar*) Werft *f*.

doctor *n* Doktor *m*; Arzt *m*; Ärztin *f*.

doctrinal *adj* Lehr-; dogmatisch.

doctrine *n* Doktrin *f*; Dogma *n*; Lehre *f*.

document *n* Dokument *n*; Urkunde *f*; Schriftstück *n*.

documentary *adj* Dokumentar-; urkundlich.

dodge *vt* ausweichen.

doe *n* Hirschkuh *f*; Reh *n*; ~ **rabbit** weibliches Kaninchen *n*.

dog *n* Hund *m*; Rüde *m*.

dogged *adj* ~**ly** *adv* verbissen; hartnäckig; zäh.

dog kennel *n* Hundehütte *f*.

dogmatic *adj* ~**ly** *adv* dogmatisch.

doings *npl* Treiben *n*; Begebenheiten *fpl*.

do-it-yourself *n* Heimwerken *n*.

doleful *adj* traurig; trübselig.

doll *n* Puppe *f*.

dollar *n* Dollar *m*.

dolphin *n* Delphin *m*.

domain *n* Domäne *f*; Bereich *m*; Gebiet *n*.

dome *n* Kuppel *f*; Wölbung *f*; Dom *m*.

domestic *adj* häuslich; Haus(-halts)-; Familien-; Privat-; inländisch; einheimisch; Inlands-; Binnen-; innenpolitisch.

domesticate *vt* domestizieren; zähmen; kultivieren; einbürgern.

domestication *n* Domestikation *f*; Zähmung *f*; Kultivierung *f*; Einbürgerung *f*.

domesticity *n* Häuslichkeit *f*.

domicile *n* Domizil *n*; Wohnsitz *m*; Zahlungsort *m*.

dominant *adj* dominant; (vor-) herrschend; beherrschend.

dominate *vi* dominieren; (vor)herrschen.

domination *n* (Vor)Herrschaft *f*.

domineer *vi* tyrannisieren; (despotisch) herrschen.

domineering *adj* tyrannisch; herrisch; anmaßend.

dominion *n* Herrschaft *f*; (Herrschafts)Gebiet *n*.

dominoes *npl* Domino *m*, *n*.

donate *vt* schenken; stiften; spenden.

donation *n* Schenkung *f*; Stiftung *f*; Spende *f*.

done *adj* getan; erledigt; gar; fertig; abgemacht.

donkey *n* Esel *m*.

donor *n* Schenker(in) *m(f)*; Spender(in) *m(f)*; Stifter(in) *m(f)*.

doodle *vi* gedankenlos kritzeln.

doom *n* Schicksal *n*; Verhängnis *n*; Jüngstes Gericht *n*.

door *n* Tür *f*; Tor *n*; Pforte *f*.

doorbell *n* Türklingel *f*.

door handle *n* Türklinke *f*.

doorman *n* Portier *m*.

doormat *n* (Fuß)Abtreter *m*.

doorplate *n* Türschild *n*.

doorstep *n* Stufe vor der Haustür *f*; Türschwelle *f*.

doorway *n* Türöffnung *f*; Eingang *m*.

dormant *adj* schlafend; ruhend; untätig; schlummernd; latent.

dormer window *n* stehendes Dachfenster *n*.

dormitory *n* Schlafsaal *m*; Wohnheim *n*.

dormouse *n* Schlafmaus *f*; Haselmaus *f*.

dosage *n* Dosierung *f*.

dose *n* Dosis *f*; * *vt* dosieren; Dosen verabreichen.

dossier *n* Dossier *n*; Akten *fpl*.

dot *n* Punkt *m*; Tupfen *m*.

dote *vi* vernarrt sein; kindisch sein; senil sein.

dotingly *adv* vernarrt; kindisch; senil.

double *adj* (ver)doppelt; Doppel-; gekrümmt; zweideutig; falsch; * *vt* verdoppeln; doubeln; umschiffen; * *n* Doppelte *n*; Zweifache *n*; Ebenbild *n*; Doppelgänger(in) *m(f)*; Duplikat *n*; Haken *m*; (*mil*) Schnellschritt *m*; Winkelzug *m*; Double *n*; Doppel *n*.

double bed *n* Doppelbett *n*.

double-breasted *adj* zweireihig.

double chin *n* Doppelkinn *n*.

double-dealing *n* Betrug *m*.

double-edged *adj* zweischneidig.

double entry *n* (*com*) doppelte Buchführung *f*.

double-lock *vt* doppelt verschließen.

double room *n* Doppelzimmer *n*.

doubly *adj* doppelt; zweifach.

doubt *n* Zweifel *m*; Bedenken *n*; Ungewißheit *f*; * *vt* bezweifeln; mißtrauen.

doubtful *adj* zweifelhaft; im Zweifel.

doubtless *adv* zweifellos.

dough *n* Teig *m*.

douse *vt* überschütten; begießen; auslöschen.

dove *n* Taube *f*.

dovecot *n* Taubenschlag *m*.

dowdy *adj* unelegant; schlampig; schlecht gekleidet.

down *n* Tiefpunkt *m*; Daune *f*; Flaum *m*; * *prep* hinunter; **to sit ~** sich (hin)setzen; **upside ~** umgekehrt; auf den Kopf gestellt.

downcast *adj* niedergeschlagen; gesenkt.

downfall *n* Sturz *m*.

downhearted *adj* niedergeschlagen; entmutigt.

downhill *adv* bergab.

down payment *n* Anzahlung *f*.

downpour *n* Platzregen *m*.

downright *adj* ausgesprochen; glatt; völlig; offen; unverblümt.

downstairs *adv* die Treppe hinunter; (nach) unten.

down-to-earth *adj* realistisch.

downtown *adv* in der Innenstadt.

downward(s) *adv* abwärts; hinunter.

dowry *n* Mitgift *f*.

doze *vi* dösen; ein Nickerchen halten.

dozen *n* Dutzend *n*.

dozy *adj* schläfrig; verschlafen.

drab *adj* graubraun; trist.

draft *n* Skizze *f*; Entwurf *m*; Einberufung *f*.

drag *vt* schleppen; (nach)schleifen; zerren; eggen; * *n* (*mar*) Schleppnetz *n*; (*agr*) Egge *f*; Schleife *f*; Hemmschuh *m*; (*col*) (*etwas*) Langweiliges *n*; (*col*) (*etwas*) Lästiges *n*; Schleppjagd *f*; Zug *m*; (*von Männern getragene*) Frauenkleidung *f*.

dragnet *n* Schleppnetz *n*.

dragon *n* Drache(n) *m*.

dragonfly *n* Libelle *f*.

drain *vt* drainieren; trockenlegen; leeren; abgießen; ableiten; erschöpfen; * *n* Entwässerungsgraben *m*; (Straßen)Rinne *f*; Kanalisationsrohr *n*; Abfluß *m*; Aderlaß *m*.

drainage *n* Ableitung *f*; Entwässerungsanlage *f*; Kanalisation *f*; Drainage *f*.

draining board *n* Abtropfbrett *n*.

drainpipe *n* Abflußrohr *n*; Fallrohr *n*.

drake *n* Enterich *m*.

dram *n* Drachme *f*; Schluck *m*.

drama *n* Drama *n*; Schauspielkunst *f*.

dramatic *adj*, **~ally** *adv* dramatisch; Theater-.

dramatist *n* Dramatiker(in) *m(f)*; Bühnenautor(in) *m(f)*.

dramatize *vt* dramatisieren.

drape *vt* drapieren; be(hängen).

drapes *npl* Vorhang *m*.

drastic *adj* drastisch.

draught *n* Fischzug *m*; Zug *m*; (Ab)Ziehen *n*; (*mar*) Tiefgang *m*.

draughts *npl* Damespiel *n*.

draughty *adj* zugig.

draw *vt* (an)ziehen; (ab)zapfen; schöpfen; entlocken; zeichnen; entwerfen; **to ~ nigh** sich nähern.

drawback *n* Nachteil *m*.

drawer *n* Schublade *f*; Zeichner *m*.

drawing *n* Zeichnen *n*; Zeichnung *f*; Ziehung *f*.

drawing board *n* Zeichenbrett *n*.

drawing room *n* Salon *m*.

drawl *vi* schleppend sprechen.

dread *n* Angst *f*; Furcht *f*; Grauen *n*; * *vt* fürchten.

dreadful *adj*, **~ly** *adv* furchtbar; schrecklich.

dream *n* Traum *m*; * *vi* träumen.

dreary *adj* trüb(selig); langweilig.

dredge *vt* ausbaggern; (mit dem Schleppnetz) fischen.

dregs *npl* (Boden)Satz *m*; Abschaum *m*; Rest *m*.

drench *vt* durchnässen; tränken.

dress *vt* bekleiden; anziehen; dekorieren; herrichten; zurichten; verbinden; düngen; * *vi* sich anziehen; * *n* Kleid *n*; Kleidung *f*.

dresser *n* Zurichter *m*; Ankleider(in) *m(f)*; Dekora-

teur(in) *m(f)*; Anrichte *f*.

dressing *n* Ankleiden *n*; Nachbearbeitung *f*; Zubereitung *f*; Dressing *n*; Verband *m*; Dünger *m*.

dressing gown *n* Morgenmantel *m*.

dressing room *n* (Künstler-)Garderobe *f*; (Umklei-de)Kabine *f*.

dressing table *n* Frisierkommode *f*.

dressmaker *n* Schneider(in) *m(f)*.

dressy *adj* elegant; modebewußt; geschniegelt.

dribble *vi* tröpfeln; sabbern; dribbeln.

dried *adj* getrocknet; Dörr-.

drift *n* Treiben *n*; Drift *f*; Strömung *f*; Wehe *f*; Tendenz *f*; Sinn *m*; Strecke *f*; * *vi* (dahin)treiben.

driftwood *n* Treibholz *n*.

drill *n* Bohrer *m*; Bohrmaschine *f*; (*mil*) Drill *m*; Rille *f*; Furche *f*; * *vt* bohren; drillen.

drink *vt*, *vi* trinken; saufen; * *n* (alkoholisches) Getränk *n*; das Trinken *n*; Schluck *m*.

drinkable *adj* trinkbar; Trink-.

drinker *n* Trinker(in) *m(f)*; Säufer(in) *m(f)*.

drinking bout *n* Trinkgelage *n*.

drinking water *n* Trinkwasser *n*.

drip *vi* tropfen; triefen; * *n* Tropfen *n*; Tropf *m*.

dripping *n* Tropfen *n*; Tröpfeln *n*.

drive *vt* fahren; (an)treiben; lenken; * *vi* (dahin)treiben; rasen; fahren; (ab)zielen; * *n* Fahrt *f*; Treiben *n*; Schwung *m*; Neigung *f*; (An)Trieb *m*; Auffahrt *f*.

drivel *n* Geschwätz *n*; * *vi* sabbern; (dummes Zeug) schwatzen.

driver *n* Fahrer(in) *m(f)*; Treiber(in) *m(f)*; Chauffeur *m*.

driveway *n* Auffahrt *f*.

driving *n* Fahrstil *m*; Autofahren *n*; Treiben *n*.

driving instructor *n* Fahrlehrer(in) *m(f)*.

driving licence *n* Führerschein *m*.

driving school *n* Fahrschule *f*.

driving test *n* Fahrprüfung *f*.

drizzle *vi* nieseln.

droll *adj* drollig.

drone *n* Drohne *f*.

droop *vi* (schlaff) herabhängen; erschlaffen; sinken.

drop *n* Tropfen *m*; Bonbon *n*; (Ab)Fall *m*; Falltür *f*; * *vt* (herab)tropfen; fallen lassen; senken; * *vi* (herab)tropfen; triefen; (herunter)fallen; sinken; werfen; **to ~ out** aussteigen; abbrechen.

drop-out *n* Aussteiger(in) *m(f)*; Abbrecher(in) *m(f)*.

dropper *n* Tropfenzähler *m*.

dross *n* Schlacke *f*; Unrat *m*.

drought *n* Dürre *f*.

drove *n*: **in ~s** in hellen Scharen.

drown *vt* ertränken; überschwemmen; * *vi* ertrinken.

drowsiness *n* Schläfrigkeit *f*.

drowsy *adj* schläfrig.

drudgery *n* Plackerei *f*.

drug *n* Droge *f*; Medikament *n*; * *vt* unter Drogen setzen; betäuben.

drug addict *n* Drogensüchtige(r) *f(m)*.

drum *n* Trommel *f*; * *vi* trommeln.

drummer *n* Trommler(in) *m(f)*; Schlagzeuger(in) *m(f)*.

drumstick *n* Trommelstock *m*; Unterschenkel (von Geflügel) *m*.

drunk *adj* betrunken.

drunkard *n* Trinker(in) *m(f)*; Säufer(in) *m(f)*.

drunken *adj* betrunken; trunksüchtig; Sauf-.

drunkenness *n* Trunkenheit *f*; Trunksucht *f*.

dry *adj* trocken; ausgetrocknet; * *vt* (ab)trocknen; dörren; * *vi* trocknen; verdorren.

dry-cleaning *n* chemische Reinigung *f*.

dryness *n* Trockenheit *f*.

dry rot *n* Trockenfäule *f*.

dual *adj* zweifach; doppelt; Doppel-.

dual-purpose *adj* Doppel-; Mehrzweck-.

dub *vt* (zum Ritter) schlagen; (er)nennen; (*Leder*) (ein)fetten; synchronisieren.

dubious *adj* zweifelhaft; im Zweifel.

duck *n* Ente *f*; (*col*) Schatz *m*; Ducken *n*; Segeltuch *n*; * *vt* (unter)tauchen; ducken; *vi* (unter)tauchen; sich ducken.

duckling *n* Entchen *n*; Entenkücken *n*.

dud *adj* falsch; ungedeckt.

due *adj* fällig; geschuldet; verpflichtet; gebührend; angemessen; zuzuschreiben; auf Grund; * *adv* direkt; genau; * *n* Recht *n*; Anspruch *m*; Lohn *m*; Schuld *f*; Gebühr *f*.

duel *n* Duell *n*.

duet *n* (*mus*) Duett *n*; Duo *n*.

dull *adj* stumpf; langweilig; dumm; teilnahmslos; schwerfällig; dumpf; trüb; * *vt* abstumpfen; mattieren; trüben; dämpfen.

duly *adv* ordnungsgemäß; gebührend; pünktlich.

dumb *adj* ~**ly** *adv* stumm; sprachlos; (*col*) doof.

dumbbell *n* Hantel *f*.

dumbfounded *adj* verblüfft; sprachlos.

dummy *n* Attrappe *f*; (Schaufenster)Puppe *f*; Strohmann *m*; Schnuller *m*; (*col*) Blödmann *m*.

dump *n* Schutthaufen *m*; Müllkippe *f*; (Abraum)Halde *f*; (*mil*) Depot *n*; (*col*) Dreckloch *n*; * *vt* fallen lassen; hinwerfen; auskippen; (*mil*) lagern.

dumping *n* (*com*) Dumping *n*.

dumpling n Kloß m; Knödel m;
(col) Dickerchen n.
dumpy adj untersetzt; plump.
dunce n Dummkopf m.
dune n Düne f.
dung n Mist m; Dung m.
dungarees npl Overall m.
dungeon n Verließ n; Kerker m.
dupe n Angeführte(r) f(m);
Leichtgläubige(r) f(m); * vt
anführen; betrügen.
duplicate n Duplikat n; Kopie
f; * vt ein Duplikat anfertigen;
kopieren; wiederholen.
duplicity n doppeltes Vorhandensein n; (fig) Doppelzüngig-
keit f.
durability n Dauerhaftigkeit f;
Haltbarkeit f.
durable adj dauerhaft; haltbar.
duration n Dauer f.
during prep während; im Lau-
fe von.
dusk n (Abend)Dämmerung f.
dust n Staub m; * vt abstauben;
(be)stäuben.
duster n Staubtuch n; Staub-
wedel m.
dusty adj staubig.
dutch courage n angetrunke-
ner Mut m.
duteous adj = **dutiful**.
dutiful adj ~ly adv pflichtbe-
wußt; gehorsam.
duty n Pflicht f; Dienst m; Ehrerbietung f; Zoll m; Abgabe f.
duty-free adj zollfrei.
dwarf n Zwerg m; * vt klein erscheinen lassen; (fig) in den
Schatten stellen; (fig) im
Wachstum hindern.
dwell vi wohnen; leben; (fig)
verweilen.
dwelling n Wohnung f; Wohnsitz m.
dwindle vi schwinden; abnehmen; (zusammen)schrumpfen.
dye vt färben; * n Farbstoff m;
Färbung f.
dyer n Färber(in) m(f); Farbstoff m.
dyeing n Färben n.
dye-works npl Färberei f.

dying adj (er)sterbend; Ster-
be-; * n Sterben n.
dynamic adj dynamisch.
dynamics n Dynamik f; (fig)
Schwung m; (fig) Triebkraft f.
dynamite n Dynamit n; (col)
Zündstoff m.
dynamiter n Sprengstoff-
attentäter m.
dynamo n Dynamo m.
dynasty n Dynastie f.
dysentery n (med) Ruhr f.
dyspepsia n (med) Verdauungsstörung f.
dyspeptic adj an Verdauungsstörung leidend; (fig) mürrisch.

E

each pn jeder, jede, jedes; ~
other einander; sich (gegenseitig).
eager adv, ~ly adv eifrig; begierig; gespannt.
eagerness n Eifer m; Begierde
f.
eagle n Adler m.
eagle-eyed adj adleräugig;
scharfsichtig.
eaglet n junger Adler m.
ear n Ohr n; Gehör n; Öse f; Öhr
n; Ähre f; **by ~** improvisiert.
earache n Ohrenschmerzen
mpl.
eardrum n Trommelfell n.
early adj (zu) früh; Früh-; baldig; adv (zu) früh; früher;
bald; am Anfang.
earmark vt kennzeichnen; bestimmen; zurücklegen.
earn vt verdienen; einbringen.
earnest adj, ~ly adv ernst;
ernsthaft; ernstlich.
earnestness n Ernsthaftigkeit
f; Ernst m.
earnings npl Verdienst m; Einkommen n; Einnahmen fpl.

earphones *npl* Kopfhörer *m*.

earring *n* Ohrring *m*.

earth *n* Erde *f*; Land *n*; Boden *m*; Bau *m*; * *vt* erden.

earthen *adj* irden; Ton-.

earthenware *n* Steingut *n*; Töpferware *f*.

earthquake *n* Erdbeben *n*.

earthworm *n* Regenwurm *m*.

earthy *adj* erdig; weltlich; sinnlich; derb.

earwig *n* Ohrwurm *m*.

ease *n* Bequemlichkeit *f*; Ruhe *f*; Leichtigkeit *f*; Ungezwungenheit *f*; Erleichterung *f*; **at ~** bequem; ruhig; entspannt; ungezwungen; * *vt* erleichtern; beruhigen; lindern; lockern; vorsichtig bewegen.

easel *n* Staffelei *f*.

easily *adv* leicht; mühelos; bequem; durchaus; bei weitem.

easiness *n* Leichtigkeit *f*; Ungezwungenheit *f*.

east *n* Osten *m*; Orient *m*.

Easter *n* Ostern *n*.

Easter egg *n* Osterei *n*.

easterly *adj* östlich; Ost-.

eastern *adj* östlich; Ost-.

eastward(s) *adv* östlich; ostwärts.

easy *adj* leicht; mühelos; einfach; ruhig; unbesorgt; bequem; schmerzfrei; ungezwungen; **~ going** gelassen; unbeschwert.

easy chair *n* Sessel *m*.

eat *vt* essen; (zer)fressen; nagen; * *vi* essen; fressen; nagen.

eatable *adj* eßbar; genießbar; * **~s** *npl* Eßwaren *pl*.

eaves *npl* Dachgesims *n*; Traufe *f*.

eau de Cologne *n* Kölnischwasser *n*.

eavesdrop *vi* (be)lauschen; horchen.

ebb *n* Ebbe *f*; * *vi* zurückgehen; abebben.

ebony *n* Ebenholz *n*.

eccentric *adj* exzentrisch.

eccentricity *n* Exzentrizität *f*; Verschrobenheit *f*.

ecclesiastic *adj* geistlich; kirchlich; Kirchen-.

echo *n* Echo *n*; * *vi* (wider)hallen; nachbeten.

eclectic *adj* eklektisch; auswählend.

eclipse *n* Finsternis *f*; Verdunkelung *f*; * *vt* verfinstern; (*fig*) in den Schatten stellen.

ecology *n* Ökologie *f*.

economic(al) *adj* wirtschaftlich; sparsam.

economics *npl* Volkswirtschaft(slehre) *f*.

economist *n* Volkswirt *m*; guter Haushälter *m*.

economize *vt* (ein)sparen; sparsam umgehen mit; nutzbar machen.

economy *n* Sparsamkeit *f*; Wirtschaftlichkeit *f*; Wirtschaft(slehre) *f*; Einsparung *f*.

ecstasy *n* Ekstase *f*; Verzükkung *f*.

ecstatic *adj* **~ally** *adv* ekstatisch; verzückt; hingerissen.

eczema *n* Ekzem *n*.

eddy *n* Wirbel *m*; Strudel *m*; * *vi* (herum)wirbeln.

edge *n* Ecke *f*; Kante *f*; Schneide *f*; Schärfe *f*; Rand *m*; Grat *m*; Schnitt *m*; * *vt* schärfen; (um)säumen; einfassen; drängen.

edgeways, edgewise *adv* seitwärts.

edging *n* Rand *m*; Einfassung *f*; Besatz *m*.

edgy *adj* scharfkantig; nervös; gereizt.

edible *adv* eßbar; genießbar.

edict *n* Edikt *n*; Erlaß *m*.

edification *n* Erbauung *f*.

edifice *n* Gebäude *n*; Gefüge *n*.

edify *vt* (*fig*) erbauen.

edit *vt* herausgeben; redigieren; bearbeiten; kürzen; schneiden; als Herausgeber leiten.

edition *n* Ausgabe *f*; Auflage *f*.

editor *n* Herausgeber(in) *m(f)*; Redakteur(in) *m(f)*; Cutter(in) *m(f)*.

editorial *adj* Herausgeber-; redaktionell; * *n* Leitartikel *m*.

educate *vt* erziehen; unterrichten; (aus)bilden.

education *n* Erziehung *f*; (Aus)Bildung *f*; Bildungswesen *n*; Pädagogik *f*.

eel *n* Aal *m*.

eerie *adj* unheimlich.

efface *vt* wegwischen; (*fig*) (aus)löschen; zurückhalten.

effect *n* Effekt *m*; Wirkung *f*; Folge *f*; Sinn *m*; Eindruck *m*; (Rechts)Wirksamkeit *f*; ~s *npl* Effekten *pl*; persönliche Habe *f*; * *vt* bewirken; ausführen.

effective *adj* ~ly *adv* effektiv; (rechts)wirksam; eindrucksvoll; tatsächlich.

effectiveness *n* Effektivität *f*; Wirksamkeit *f*.

effectual *adj*, ~ly *adv* (rechts-) wirksam; effektiv.

effeminacy *n* Verweichlichung *f*; weibisches Wesen *n*.

effeminate *adj* verweichlicht; unmännlich; weibisch.

effervescence *n* (Auf)Brausen *n*; (Über)Schäumen *n*.

effete *adj* erschöpft; entkräftet.

efficacy *n* Wirksamkeit *f*; Effektivität *f*.

efficiency *n* Effizienz *f*; (Leistungs)Fähigkeit *f*; Wirksamkeit *f*; Wirkungsgrad *m*.

efficient *adj* effizient; (leistungs)fähig; wirksam; tüchtig.

effigy *n* Bildnis *n*.

effort *n* Anstrengung *f*; Mühe *f*; Leistung *f*.

effortless *adj* mühelos.

effrontery *n* Unverschämtheit *f*.

effusive *adj* überschwenglich.

egg *n* Ei *n*; Eizelle *f*; * **to ~ on** *vt* anstacheln; antreiben.

eggcup *n* Eierbecher *m*.

eggplant *n* Aubergine *f*.

eggshell *n* Eierschale *f*.

ego(t)ism *n* Egoismus *m*; Selbstsucht *f*; (Selbstgefälligkeit *f*).

ego(t)ist *n* Egoist(in) *m(f)*;

selbstgefälliger Mensch *m*.

ego(t)istical *adj* egoistisch; selbstgefällig.

eiderdown *n* Eiderdaunen *pl*.

eight *adj* acht; * *n* Acht *f*.

eighteen *adj* achtzehn; * *n* Achtzehn *f*.

eighteenth *adj* achtzehnt(er, e, es); achtzehntel; * *n* (der, die, das) Achtzehnte; Achtzehntel *n*.

eighth *adj* acht(er, e, es); achtel; * *n* (der, die, das) Achte; Achtel *n*.

eightieth *adj* achtzigst(er, e, es); achtzigstel; * *n* (der, die, das) Achtzigste; Achtzigstel *n*.

eighty *adj* achtzig; * *n* Achtzig *f*.

either *pn* (irgend)ein(er, e, es); beides; * *conj* (ent)weder.

ejaculate *vt* ausstoßen; ejakulieren.

ejaculation *n* Ausruf *m*; Ausstoßen *n*; Stoßseufzer *m*; Ejakulation *f*; Samenerguß *m*.

eject *vt* hinauswerfen; vertreiben; entfernen; ausstoßen.

ejection *n* Vertreibung *f*; Entfernung *f*; Ausstoßen *n*.

ejector seat *n* Schleudersitz *m*.

eke *vt* ~ **out** strecken; aufbessern; verlängern.

elaborate *vt* sorgfältig ausarbeiten; entwickeln; * *adj* sorgfältig ausgearbeitet; vollendet; kunstvoll; ~ly *adv* sorgfältig; ausführlich.

elapse *vi* verstreichen; ablaufen.

elastic *adj* elastisch; dehnbar; Gummi-.

elasticity *n* Elastizität *f*; Dehnbarkeit *f*; (*fig*) Spannkraft *f*.

elated *adj* in Hochstimmung; begeistert.

elation *n* Hochstimmung *f*; Begeisterung *f*.

elbow *n* Ell(en)bogen *m*; Krümmung *f*; Kniestück *n*; * *vt* dränge(l)n; stoßen.

elbow room *n* Ellbogenfreiheit *f*; (*fig*) Bewegungsfreiheit *f*.

elder *n* Holunder *m*; (der, die) Ältere; Älteste(r) *f(m)*; * *adj* älter(er, e, es).

elderly *adj* ältlich; älter(er, e, es).

eldest *adj* ältest(er, e, es).

elect *vt* wählen; * *adj* designiert; zukünftig; auserwählt.

election *n* Wahl *f.*

electioneering *n* Wahlkampf *m*; Wahlpropaganda *f.*

elective *adj* gewählt; Wahl-; wahlberechtigt.

elector *n* Wähler(in) *m(f).*

electoral *adj* Wahl-; Wähler-.

electorate *n* Wähler *pl.*

electric(al) *adj* elektrisch; Elektro-.

electric blanket *n* Heizdecke *f.*

electric cooker *n* Elektroherd *m.*

electric fire *n* Elektroheizgerät *n.*

electrician *n* Elektriker *m.*

electricity *n* Elektrizität *f*; Strom *m.*

electrify *vt* elektrisieren; elektrifizieren; (*fig*) begeistern.

electron *n* Elektron *n.*

electronic *adj* elektronisch; Elektronen-; **~s** *npl* Elektronik *f.*

elegance *n* Eleganz *f.*

elegant *adj* **~ly** *adv* elegant; geschmackvoll; anmutig.

elegy *n* Elegie *f.*

element *n* Element *n*; *pl* Grundlagen *pl*; (*fig*) Körnchen *n.*

elemental, elementary *adj* elementar; Ur-.

elephant *n* Elefant *m.*

elephantine *adj* Elefanten-; riesenhaft; schwerfällig.

elevate *vt* (hoch)heben; erheben; erhöhen.

elevation *n* (Hoch)Heben *n*; Erhöhung *f*; (Boden)Erhebung *f*; (An)Höhe *f*; Meereshöhe *f.*

elevator *n* Aufzug *m*; Fahrstuhl *m*; Höhenruder *n.*

eleven *adj* elf; * *n* Elf.

eleventh *adj* elft(er, e, es); elftel; * *n* (der, die, das) Elfte; Elftel *n.*

elf *n* Elf *m*; Elfe *f*; Kobold *m*; (*fig*) Zwerg *m.*

elicit *vt* entlocken; ans (Tages)Licht bringen.

eligibility *n* Eignung *f*; Berechtigung *f*; Wählbarkeit *f.*

eligible *adj* in Frage kommend; geeignet; berechtigt; qualifiziert.

eliminate *vt* eliminieren; beseitigen; entfernen; ausscheiden.

elk *n* Elch *m*; Wapiti *n.*

elliptic(al) *adj* elliptisch.

elm *n* Ulme *f.*

elocution *n* Vortragskunst *f*; Sprechtechnik *f.*

elocutionist *n* Vortragskünstler(in) *m(f)*; Sprecherzieher(in) *m(f).*

elongate *vt* verlängern.

elope *vi* ausreißen; durchbrennen.

elopement *n* Ausreißen *n*; Durchbrennen *n.*

eloquence *n* Beredsamkeit *f.*

eloquent *adj*, **~ly** *adv* beredt; redegewandt.

else *adv* sonst; weiter; ander(er, e, es).

elsewhere *adv* anderswo; woanders hin.

elucidate *vt* erklären; aufklären.

elucidation *n* Erklärung *f*; Aufklärung *f.*

elude *vt* entgehen; sich entziehen; umgehen; nicht einfallen.

elusive *adj* schwerfaßbar; ausweichend.

emaciated *adj* ausgezehrt; ausgemergelt.

emanate (from) *vi* ausströmen; ausgehen.

emancipate *vt* emanzipieren; befreien.

emancipation *n* Emanzipation *f*; Befreiung *f.*

embalm *vt* einbalsamieren; vor Vergessenheit bewahren.

embankment *n* Eindämmung

f; (Bahn)Damm *m;* Böschung *f.*

embargo *n* Embargo *n;* (Handels)Sperre *f.*

embark *vt* einschiffen; verladen; *vi* sich einschiffen; sich einlassen; anfangen.

embarkation *n* Einschiffung *f;* Verladung *f.*

embarrass *vt* verlegen machen; in Verlegenheit bringen.

embarrassed *adj* verlegen.

embarrassing *adj* unangenehm; peinlich.

embarrassment *n* Verlegenheit *f.*

embassy *n* Botschaft *f.*

embed *vt* (ein)betten; verankern.

embellish *vt* verschönern; (aus)schmücken.

embellishment *n* Verschönerung *f;* Ausschmückung *f;* Verzierung *f.*

embers *npl* Glut(asche) *f;* (*fig*) letzte Funken *m.*

embezzle *vt* veruntreuen; unterschlagen.

embezzlement *n* Veruntreuung *f;* Unterschlagung *f.*

embitter *vt* bitter(er) machen; (*fig*) verbittern.

emblem *n* Emblem *n;* Symbol *n;* Sinnbild *n.*

emblematic(al) *adj* symbolisch; sinnbildlich.

embodiment *n* Verkörperung *f.*

embody *vt* verkörpern; aufnehmen; umfassen.

embrace *vt* umarmen; umfassen; (*fig*) ergreifen; * *n* Umarmung *f.*

embroider *vt* (be)sticken; ausschmücken.

embroidery *n* Stickerei *f;* Ausschmückung *f.*

embroil *vt* verwickeln; verwirren.

embryo *n* Embryo *m;* (*fig*) Keim *m.*

emendation *n* Verbesserung *f;* Korrektur *f.*

emerald *n* Smaragd *m.*

emerge *vi* auftauchen; zum Vorschein kommen; sich erheben; sich herausstellen; hervorgehen.

emergency *n* Not(lage) *f;* Notfall *m;* unvorhergesehenes Ereignis *n.*

emergency brake *n* Notbremse *f.*

emergency exit *n* Notausgang *m.*

emergency landing *n* Notlandung *f.*

emergency meeting *n* Dringlichkeitssitzung *f.*

emery *n* Korund *m;* Schmirgel *m.*

emigrant *n* Emigrant(in) *m(f);* Auswanderer *m.*

emigrate *vi* auswandern; emigrieren.

emigration *n* Auswanderung *f;* Emigration *f.*

eminence *n* Anhöhe *f;* hohe Stellung *f;* Ruhm *m;* Eminenz *f.*

eminent *adj* eminent; hervorragend; ausgezeichnet; bedeutend; **~ly** *adv* in hohem Maße; äußerst.

emission *n* Emission *f;* Ausströmen *n;* Ausfluß *m;* Ausstoß *m.*

emit *vt* ausstoßen; ausstrahlen; ausströmen; emittieren.

emolument *n* Einkünfte *pl.*

emotion *n* Gefühl *n;* Erregung *f;* Rührung *f.*

emotional *adj* emotionell; gefühlsmäßig; gefühlsbetont; Gefühls-; rührselig.

emotive *adj* gefühlbedingt; gefühlvoll; gefühlbetont; Reiz-.

emperor *n* Kaiser *m.*

emphasis *n* Betonung *f;* Nachdruck *m;* Schwerpunkt *m.*

emphasize *vt* betonen; hervorheben.

emphatic *adj* **~ally** *adv* nachdrücklich; eindringlich.

empire *n* Reich *n;* Imperium *n;* Herrschaft *f.*

employ *vt* beschäftigen; einstellen; anwenden; verwenden.

employee n Arbeitnehmer(in) m(f); Angestellte(r) f(m).

employer n Arbeitgeber(in) m(f); Unternehmer(in) m(f).

employment n Beschäftigung f; Arbeit f; Anstellung f; Verwendung f.

emporium n Handelszentrum n; Warenhaus n.

empress n Kaiserin f.

emptiness n Leere f.

empty adj leer; hohl; * vt (aus)leeren; (aus)räumen; berauben.

empty-handed adj mit leeren Händen; unverrichteterdinge.

emulate vt wetteifern mit; nacheifern.

emulsion n Emulsion f.

enable vt ermächtigen; befähigen; ermöglichen.

enact vt erlassen; verfügen; aufführen; darstellen.

enamel n Emaille n; Glasur f; Lack m; (Zahn)Schmelz m; * vt emaillieren; glasieren; lackieren.

enamor vt verliebt machen.

encamp vi lagern; das Lager aufschlagen.

encampment n Lager(n) n.

encase vt einschließen; umhüllen.

enchant vt verzaubern; (fig) bezaubern.

enchanting adj bezaubernd; entzückend.

enchantment n Verzauberung f; Zauber m; (fig) Bezauberung f.

encircle vt umgeben; umschließen; einkreisen; umzingeln.

enclose vt einschließen; umzäunen; umfassen; beilegen.

enclosure n Einfriedung f; Umzäunung f; Anlage f.

encompass vt umgeben; (fig) umfassen.

encore n Zugabe f.

encounter n Begegnung f; Zusammenstoß m; * vt begegnen; stoßen auf; aneinandergeraten.

encourage vt ermutigen; unterstützen; fördern.

encouragement n Ermutigung f; Unterstützung f; Förderung f.

encroach vt eindringen; mißbrauchen; beeinträchtigen; schmälern.

encroachment n Übergriff m; Beeinträchtigung f; Vordringen n.

encrusted adj verkrustet; inkrustiert.

encumber vt (be)hindern; belasten.

encumbrance n Behinderung f; Belastung f; (Familien)Anhang m.

encyclical adj enzyklisch; Rund-.

encyclopedia n Enzyklopädie f.

end n Ende n; Folge f; Zweck n; Ziel n; **to this ~** zu diesem Zweck; **to no ~** vergebens; **on ~** hintereinander; -lang; hochkant; * vt beenden; * vi enden; aufhören; sterben.

endanger vt gefährden.

endear vt beliebt machen; jemandes Zuneigung gewinnen.

endearing adj gewinnend; liebenswert.

endearment n Kosename m.

endeavor vi sich bemühen; trachten; * n Bemühung f; Bestrebung f.

endemic adj endemisch; (ein)heimisch.

ending n Ende n; (Ab)Schluß m; Endung f; Beendigung f.

endive n (bot) Endivie f.

endless adj **~ly** adv endlos; unendlich; unaufhörlich; ständig.

endorse vt vermerken; indossieren; billigen; beipflichten.

endorsement n Vermerk m; Zusatz m; Giro n; Billigung f.

endow vt stiften; ausstatten.

endowment n Stiftung f; Ausstattung f; Begabung f.

endurable adj erträglich.

endurance n (Aus)Dauer f; Ertragen n; Aushalten n; Geduld f.

endure vt aushalten; ertragen; ausstehen; * vi andauern; durchhalten.

endways, endwise adv mit dem Ende nach vorn; aufrecht; gerade.

enemy n Feind(in) m(f); Gegner(in) m(f).

energetic adj energisch; wirksam.

energy n Energie f; Kraft f; Wirksamkeit f.

enervate vt entkräften; entnerven.

enfeeble vt entkräften; schwächen.

enfold vt einhüllen; umfassen.

enforce vt geltend machen; durchsetzen; aufzwingen.

enforced adj erzwungen.

enfranchise vt befreien; das Wahlrecht verleihen.

engage vt verpflichten; anstellen; in Anspruch nehmen; mieten; (mil) angreifen.

engaged adj verlobt; verpflichtet; beschäftigt; in Anspruch genommen; besetzt.

engagement n Verpflichtung f; Verabredung f; Verlobung f; Beschäftigung f; (mil) Gefecht n.

engagement ring n Verlobungsring m.

engaging adj gewinnend; einnehmend.

engender vt erzeugen; hervorrufen.

engine n Motor m; Maschine f; Lokomotive f.

engine driver n Lokomotivführer m.

engineer n Ingenieur m; Techniker m; Mechaniker m; Maschinist m.

engineering n Technik f; Ingenieurwesen n.

engrave vt (ein)gravieren; (ein)meißeln; (ein)schnitzen; (fig) einprägen.

engraving n Gravieren n; Druckplatte f; Gravierung f; Stich m; Holzschnitt m.

engrossed adj vertieft; versunken.

engulf vt verschlingen; überfluten.

enhance vt erhöhen; steigern; vergrößern.

enigma n Rätsel n.

enjoy vt Freude haben an; genießen; sich erfreuen.

enjoyable adj erfreulich; angenehm; schön; genießbar.

enjoyment n Freude f; Genuß m; Vergnügen n.

enlarge vt vergrößern; erweitern; ausdehnen.

enlargement n Vergrößerung f; Erweiterung f; Ausdehnung f.

enlighten vt (fig) erleuchten; aufklären.

enlightened adj (fig) erleuchtet; aufgeklärt; verständig.

Enlightenment n: **the age of** ~ das Zeitalter der Aufklärung.

enlist vt anwerben; einstellen; (zur Mitarbeit) gewinnen.

enlistment n (An)Werbung f; Einstellung f; Gewinnung f.

enliven vt beleben; (fig) ankurbeln.

enmity n Feindschaft f; Feindseligkeit f.

enormity n Ungeheuerlichkeit f.

enormous adj ~ly adv enorm; ungeheuer(lich); riesig.

enough adv genug; ausreichend; * n Genüge f.

enounce vt verkünden; äußern.

enquire vt = inquire.

enrage vt wütend machen.

enrapture vt hinreißen; entzücken.

enrich vt bereichern; anreichern; reich verzieren.

enrichment n Bereicherung f; Anreicherung f; Verzierung f.

enrol vt einschreiben; eintragen; (an)werben; aufnehmen; protokollieren.

enrolment n Einschreibung f; Eintragung f; Anwerbung f; Aufnahme f; Register n.

en route adv unterwegs.

ensign n (mil) Fahne f; Abzeichen n; (mar) (National)Flagge f.

enslave vt versklaven.

ensue vi (nach)folgen; sich ergeben.

ensure vt sichern; sicherstellen; sorgen für.

entail vt mit sich bringen; zur Folge haben.

entangle vt verwickeln; verstricken; verwirren.

entanglement n Verwicklung f.

enter vt eintreten (in); betreten; einsteigen; einfahren; einlaufen; eindringen in; eintragen; (an)melden; einreichen; **to ~ for** melden für; **to ~ into** sich einlassen auf; sich beteiligen an; eingehen (auf).

enterprise n Unternehmen n; Unternehmung f.

enterprising adj unternehmend; unternehmungslustig.

entertain vt unterhalten; zu Gast haben; hegen; in Betracht ziehen.

entertainer n Unterhaltungskünstler(in) m(f); Gastgeber(in) m(f).

entertaining adj unterhaltsam; amüsant.

entertainment n Unterhaltung f; Belustigung f; Bewirtung f; Gesellschaft f; Erwägung f.

enthralled adj bezaubert; gefesselt.

enthralling adj bezaubernd; fesselnd.

enthrone vt auf den Thron setzen; (fig) erheben.

enthusiasm n Enthusiasmus m; Begeisterung f.

enthusiast n Enthusiast(in) m(f).

enthusiastic adj enthusiastisch; begeistert.

entice vt (ver)locken; verleiten.

entire adj ganz; vollständig; unversehrt; voll; **~ly** adv völlig; durchaus; ganz und gar; ausschließlich.

entirety n (das) Ganze n; Vollständigkeit f; Gesamtheit f.

entitled adj Anspruch haben auf; berechtigt.

entity n Wesen n; Ding n; Dasein n.

entourage n Gefolge n.

entrails npl Eingeweide pl.

entrance n Eintritt m; Eingang m; Eintritt m.

entrance examination n Eingangsprüfung f.

entrance fee n Eintrittsgeld n; Aufnahmegebühr f.

entrance hall n Flur m; (Eingangs)Halle f.

entrance ramp n Auffahrt f.

entrant n Teilnehmer(in) m(f); Eintretende(r) f(m).

entrap vt fangen; verleiten.

entreat vt inständig bitten; ersuchen.

entreaty n inständige Bitte f; Flehen n.

entrepreneur n Unternehmer m.

entrust vt anvertrauen; betrauen.

entry n Eintritt m; Einreise f; Auftritt m; Eindringen n; Beitritt m; Einlaß m; Eingang m; Eintragung f; Meldung f.

entry phone n Sprechanlage f.

entwine vt flechten; (um)winden; (ineinander)schlingen.

enumerate vt aufzählen; spezifizieren.

enunciate vt aussprechen; erklären; aufstellen.

enunciation n Erklärung f; Aufstellung f; Aussprache f.

envelop n (ein)hüllen; einwikkeln; umgeben.

envelope vt (Brief)Umschlag m; Hülle f.

enviable adj beneidenswert.

envious adj **~ly** adv neidisch.

environment n Umgebung f; Milieu n; Umwelt f.

environmental *adj* Milieu-; Umwelt-.

environs *npl* Umgebung *f*.

envisage *vt* ins Auge fassen; sich vorstellen.

envoy *n* (Ab)Gesandte(r) *m(f)*.

envy *n* Neid *m*; * *vt* beneiden.

ephemeral *adj* Eintags-; *(fig)* kurzlebig; vergänglich.

epic *adj* episch; erzählend; heroisch; * *n* Epos *n*; Heldengedicht *n*.

epidemic *adj* epidemisch; seuchenartig; * *n* Epidemie *f*; Seuche *f*.

epilepsy *n* Epilepsie *f*.

epileptic *adj* epileptisch.

epilog(ue) *n* Epilog *m*; Nachwort *n*.

Epiphany *n* Dreikönigstag *m*.

episcopacy *n* Episkopat *n*; bischöfliche Verfassung *f*.

episcopal *adj* episkopal; Bischofs-.

episcopalian *n* Episkopale *m*; Mitglied einer Episkopalkirche *n*.

episode *n* Episode *f*; Ereignis *n*.

epistle *n* Epistel *f*; (langer) Brief *m*.

epistolary *adj* brieflich; Brief-.

epithet *n* Beiwort *n*; Beiname *m*; Attribut *n*.

epitome *n* Auszug *m*; Abriß *m*; *(fig)* Inbegriff *m*.

epitomize *vt* einen Auszug machen von; verkörpern.

epoch *n* Epoche *f*; Zeitalter *n*.

equable *adj* ~bly *adv* gleichförmig; ausgeglichen.

equal *adj* gleich(förmig); gleichberechtigt; entsprechend; fähig; ebenbürtig; * *n* Gleichgestellte(r) *f(m)*; Gleichberechtigte(r) *f(m)*; * *vt* gleichen; entsprechen; gleichkommen.

equality *n* Gleichheit *f*; Gleichberechtigung *f*; Gleichförmigkeit *f*.

equalize *vt* gleichmachen; angleichen; ausgleichen.

equalizer *n* Ausgleich *m*; Entzerrer *m*.

equally *adv* ebenso; gleich; gleichermaßen; gleichmäßig.

equanimity *n* Gleichmut *m*.

equate *vt* gleichmachen; ausgleichen; gleichsetzen.

equation *n* Gleichung *f*; Angleichung *f*; Ausgleich *m*.

equator *n* Äquator *m*.

equatorial *adj* äquatorial.

equestrian *adj* Reiter-; Reit-; beritten.

equilateral *adj* gleichseitig.

equilibrium *n* Gleichgewicht *n*.

equinox *n* Tagundnachtgleiche *f*.

equip *vt* ausrüsten; ausstatten.

equipment *n* Ausrüstung *f*; Ausstattung *f*; Einrichtung *f*; *(fig)* Rüstzeug *n*.

equitable *adj* gerecht; (recht und) billig; unparteiisch; **~bly** *adv* gerecht; gerechterweise.

equity *n* Billigkeit *f*; Unparteilichkeit *f*; Eigenkapital *n*.

equivalent *adj* gleichbedeutend; gleichwertig; äquivalent; * *n* Äquivalent *n*; Entsprechung *f*; Gegenwert *m*.

equivocal *adj* ~ly *adv* zweideutig; zweifelhaft; fragwürdig.

equivocate *vt* zweideutig reden.

equivocation *n* Zweideutigkeit *f*; Wortverdrehung *f*.

era *n* Ära *f*; Zeitalter *n*.

eradicate *vt* ausreißen; ausrotten.

eradication *n* Ausrottung *f*; Entwurzelung *f*.

erase *vt* ausradieren; (aus)löschen; tilgen.

eraser *n* Radiergummi *m*.

erect *vt* aufrichten; errichten; aufstellen; * *adj* aufgerichtet; aufrecht; gerade; erigiert.

erection *n* Errichtung *f*; Montage *f*; Erektion *f*.

ermine *n* Hermelin *n*.

erode *vt* zerfressen; erodieren; *(fig)* aushöhlen; untergraben.

erotic *adj* erotisch.

err *vi* irren; falsch sein; auf Abwege geraten.

errand *n* Auftrag *m*; (Boten-) Gang *m*; Besorgung *f*.

errand boy *n* Laufbursche *m*.

errata *npl* Errata *pl*; Druckfehlerverzeichnis *n*.

erratic *adj* (umher)wandernd; regellos; sprunghaft; unberechenbar.

erroneous *adj* irrig; irrtümlich; falsch; **~ly** *adv* irrtümlicherweise; fälschlicherweise.

error *n* Irrtum *m*; Fehler *m*; Versehen *n*.

erudite *adj* gelehrt; belesen.

erudition *n* Gelehrsamkeit *f*; Belesenheit *f*.

erupt *vi* ausbrechen; durchbrechen; (*fig*) platzen.

eruption *n* Ausbruch *m*.

escalate *vi* eskalieren; steigen.

escalation *n* Eskalation *f*.

escalator *n* Rolltreppe *f*.

escapade *n* Eskapade *f*.

escape *vt* entkommen; entwischen; entgehen; entschlüpfen; * *vi* (ent)fliehen; entkommen; entrinnen; entweichen; * *n* Flucht *f*; Rettung *f*; Entweichen *n*; Ablenkung *f*; **to make one's ~** sich aus dem Staube machen.

escapism *n* Wirklichkeitsflucht *f*.

eschew *vt* (ver)meiden; scheuen.

escort *n* Eskorte *f*; Geleit *n*; Begleitung *f*; * *vt* eskortieren; Geleit(schutz) geben; begleiten.

esoteric *adj* esoterisch; vertraulich.

especial *adj* besonder(er, e, es); vorzüglich; **~ly** *adv* besonders; hauptsächlich.

espionage *n* Spionage *f*.

esplanade *n* (*mil*) Esplanade *f*; (Strand)Promenade *f*.

espouse *vt* sich verschreiben; sich einsetzen für.

essay *n* Essay *n*; Aufsatz *m*.

essence *n* Essenz *f*; Wesen *n*.

essential *n* (das) Wesentliche; Hauptsache *f*; * *adj* wesentlich; (lebens)wichtig; destilliert; **~ly** *adv* im wesentlichen; ganz besonders.

establish *vt* festsetzen; einrichten; (be)gründen; einsetzen; etablieren; nachweisen.

establishment *n* Festsetzung *f*; Gründung *f*; Einrichtung *f*; Einsetzung *f*; Anstalt *f*; Firma *f*; Establishment *n*.

estate *n* Stand *m*; Vermögen *n*; Nachlaß *m*; Gut *n*; (Wohn)Siedlung *f*.

esteem *vt* (er)achten; (hoch-) schätzen; * *n* Wertschätzung *f*; Achtung *f*.

aesthetic *adj* ästhetisch; **~s** *npl* Ästhetik *f*.

estimate *vt* (ein)schätzen; veranschlagen; beurteilen.

estimation *n* Schätzung *f*; (Vor)Anschlag *m*; Ansicht *f*.

estrange *vt* fernhalten; entfremden.

estranged *adj* entfremdet; getrennt lebend.

estrangement *n* Entfremdung *f*.

estuary *n* Flußmündung *f*; Meeresbucht *f*.

etch *vt* ätzen; kupferstechen; radieren; (*fig*) herausarbeiten.

etching *n* Ätzen *n*; Kupferstich *m*; Radierung *f*.

eternal *adj* **~ly** *adv* ewig; unveränderlich.

eternity *n* Ewigkeit *f*.

ether *n* Äther *m*.

ethical *adj* **~ly** *adv* ethisch; moralisch.

ethics *npl* Ethik *f*; Moral *f*; Ethos *m*.

ethnic *adj* ethnisch.

ethos *n* Ethos *m*.

etiquette *n* Etikette *f*; Zeremoniell *n*; Anstandsregeln *pl*.

etymological *adj* etymologisch.

etymologist *n* Etymologe *m*.

etymology *n* Etymologie *f*.

Eucharist *n* Eucharistie *f.*

eulogy *n* Lob *n*; Lobrede *f.*

eunuch *n* Eunuch *m.*

euphemism *n* beschönigender Ausdruck *m.*

evacuate *vt* evakuieren; entleeren; räumen.

evacuation *n* Evakuierung *f*; Entleerung *f*; Räumung *f.*

evade *vt* ausweichen; vermeiden; umgehen.

evaluate *vt* (ab)schätzen; auswerten; berechnen.

evangelic(al) *adj* evangelisch.

evangelist *n* Evangelist *m.*

evaporate *vt* verdampfen lassen; eindampfen; * *vi* verdampfen; verdunsten; (*fig*) sich verflüchtigen.

evaporated milk *n* Kondensmilch *f.*

evaporation *n* Verdampfung *f*; Verdunstung *f*; (*fig*) Verflüchtigung *f.*

evasion *n* Umgehung *f*; Ausflucht *f.*

evasive *adj* ~**ly** *adv* ausweichend; schwer faßbar.

eve *n* Vorabend *m*: Vortag *m.*

even *adj* ~**ly** *adv* eben; gerade; glatt; (*fig*) ausgeglichen; gleichmäßig; gleich; unparteiisch; * *adv* sogar; selbst; noch; gerade; eben; ganz; * *vt* ebnen; glätten; * *vi*: **to ~ out** sich ausgleichen.

even-handed *adj* unparteiisch.

evening *n* Abend *m.*

evening class *n* Abendschule *f.*

evening dress *n* Abendkleid *n*; Frack *m*; Smoking *m.*

evenness *n* Ebenheit *f*; Ausgeglichenheit *f*; Gleichmäßigkeit *f*; Unparteilichkeit *f.*

event *n* Ereignis *n*; (Vor)Fall *m*; (Programm)Nummer *f*; sportliche Veranstaltung *f.*

eventful *adj* ereignisreich.

eventual *adj* schließlich; möglich; ~**ly** *adv* schließlich; endlich.

eventuality *n* Möglichkeit *f*; Eventualität *f.*

ever *adv* immer (wieder); je(mals); irgend; **for ~ and ~** für immer; auf immer und ewig; **~ since** seitdem.

evergreen *adj* immergrün; * *n* immergrüne Pflanze *f*; Evergreen *m.*

everlasting *adj* ewig; unverwüstlich.

evermore *adv* immer(fort); ewig; allezeit.

every *adj* jeder, jede, jedes; aller, alle, alles; **~ where** überall(hin); **~ thing** alles; **~ one, ~ body** jeder (einzelne).

evict *vt* zur Räumung zwingen; gewaltsam vertreiben; ausweisen.

eviction *n* Zwangsräumung *f*; Ausweisung *f.*

evidence *n* Beweis *m*; Beweismaterial *n*; (Zeugen)Aussage *f*; Zeugnis *n*; Zeuge *m*; Zeugin *f*; (An)Zeichen *n*; * *vt* beweisen; zeigen.

evident *adj* offensichtlich; augenscheinlich; klar; ~**ly** *adv* augenscheinlich; offensichtlich.

evil *adj* böse; öbel; schlecht; schlimm; * *n* Böse *n*; Übel *n*; Unheil *n*; Unglück *n.*

evil-minded *adj* bösartig.

evocative *adj* beschwörend; wachrufend.

evoke *vt* (herauf)beschwören; hervorrufen; wachrufen.

evolution *n* Evolution *f*; Entfaltung *f*; Entwicklung *f.*

evolve *vt* entfalten; entwickeln; * *vi* sich entfalten; sich entwicklen; entstehen.

ewe *n* Mutterschaf *n.*

exacerbate *vt* verärgern; verschlimmern; verschärfen.

exact *adj* exakt; genau; methodisch; * *vt* (er)fordern; verlangen; eintreiben.

exacting *adj* streng; genau; anstrengend; hart; anspruchsvoll.

exaction *n* Forderung *f*; Eintreiben *n.*

exactly *adj* exakt; genau; sorgfältig.
exactness, exactitude *n* Genauigkeit *f*; Exaktheit *f*; Sorgfalt *f*.
exaggerate *vt* übertreiben;
überbetonen.
exaggeration *n* Übertreibung
f; Überbetonung *f*.
exalt *vt* erhöhen; erheben; anregen; (lob)preisen.
exaltation *n* Erhebung *f*; Erhöhung *f*; Hochstimmung *f*.
exalted *adj* hoch; gehoben; begeistert; übertrieben.
examination *n* Untersuchung
f; Prüfung *f*; Vernehmung *f*.
examine *vt* untersuchen; prüfen; vernehmen; verhören.
examiner *n* Prüfer(in) *m(f)*.
example *n* Beispiel *n*; Vorbild
n; Muster *n*.
exasperate *vt* wütend machen;
aufbringen.
exasperation *n* Wut *f*.
excavate *vt* aushöhlen;
(aus)graben; ausschachten.
excavation *n* Aushöhlung *f*;
Ausgrabung *f*; Ausschachtung
f.
exceed *vt* überschreiten; übersteigen; übertreffen; hinausgehen über.
exceedingly *adv* außerordentlich; überaus.
excel *vt* übertreffen; überragen;
* *vi* sich hervortun; sich auszeichnen.
excellence *n* Vortrefflichkeit *f*;
hervorragende Leistung *f*.
Excellency *n* Exzellenz *f*.
excellent *adj* ~ly *adv* ausgezeichnet; hervorragend; vorzüglich.
except *vt* ausnehmen; ausschließen; sich vorbehalten;
~(ing) *prep* ausgenommen;
außer.
exception *n* Ausnahme *f*; Einwendung *f*.
exceptional *adj* Ausnahme-;
Sonder-; außergewöhnlich.
excerpt *n* Auszug *m*.

excess *n* Übermaß *n*; Exzeß *m*;
Ausschweifung *f*; Überschuß
m.
excessive *adj* ~ly *adv* übermäßig; übertrieben.
exchange *vt* (aus)tauschen;
eintauschen; (um)wechseln;
* *n* (Aus)Tausch *m*; Umtausch
m; (Um)Wechseln *n*; Börse *f*;
Wechselstube *f*; Vermittlung *f*.
exchange rate *n* Wechselkurs
m.
excise *n* Verbrauchssteuer *f*.
excitability *n* Erregbarkeit *f*;
Nervosität *f*.
excitable *adj* reizbar; (leicht)
erregbar; nervös.
excite *vt* erregen; aufregen; reizen.
excited *adj* aufgeregt; erregt.
excitement *n* Erregung *f*; Aufregung *f*; Reizung *f*.
exciting *adj* aufregend; erregend; spannend.
exclaim *vt* ausrufen; hervor-
stoßen.
exclamation *n* Ausruf *m*;
(Auf)Schrei *m*.
exclamation mark *n* Ausrufungszeichen *n*.
exclamatory *adj* exklamato-
risch; Ausrufe-.
exclude *vt* ausschließen.
exclusion *n* Ausschluß *m*; Ausschließung *f*.
exclusive *adj* exklusiv; aus-
schließend; ausschließlich;
Exklusiv-; ~ly *adv* nur; ausschließlich.
excommunicate *vt* exkommu-
nizieren.
excommunication *n* Exkom-
munikation *f*.
excrement *n* Kot *m*; Exkre-
mente *pl*.
excruciating *adj* qualvoll; unerträglich.
exculpate *vt* rechtfertigen; freisprechen.
excursion *n* Exkursion *f*; Ausflug *m*; Abschweifung *f*.
excusable *adj* entschuldbar;
verzeihlich.

excuse *vt* entschuldigen; rechtfertigen; verzeihen; * *n* Entschuldigung *f*; Rechtfertigung *f*; Ausrede *f*; Vorwand *m*.

execute *vt* ausführen; vollziehen; vortragen; hinrichten.

execution *n* Ausführung *f*; Vollstreckung *f*; Vortrag *m*; Hinrichtung *f*.

executioner *n* Henker *m*; Scharfrichter *m*.

executive *adj* ausübend; vollziehend; geschäftsführend; leitend.

executor *n* Testamentsvollstrecker *m*; Erbschaftsverwalter *m*.

exemplary *adj* exemplarisch; beispielhaft; Muster-.

exemplify *vt* veranschaulichen; eine beglaubigte Abschrift machen von.

exempt *adj* befreit; ausgenommen; frei.

exemption *n* Befreiung *f*.

exercise *n* (Aus)Übung *f*; Bewegung *f*; (*mil*) Manöver *n*; * *vi* üben; trainieren; exerzieren; sich Bewegung verschaffen; * *vt* (aus)üben; trainieren; bewegen.

exercise book *n* Schulheft *n*.

exert *vt* (ge)brauchen; anwenden; ausüben; **to ~ oneself** sich anstrengen; sich bemühen.

exertion *n* Ausübung *f*; Anwendung *f*; Strapaze *f*; Bemühung *f*.

exhale *vt* ausatmen; ausstoßen.

exhaust *n* Abgas *n*; Auspuff *m*; * *vt* erschöpfen; entleeren.

exhausted *adj* erschöpft; vergriffen.

exhaustion *n* Erschöpfung *f*; Entleerung *f*.

exhaustive *adj* erschöpfend.

exhibit *vt* ausstellen; zeigen; an den Tag legen; * *n* (law) Beweisstück *n*; Ausstellungsstück *n*.

exhibition *n* Ausstellung *f*; Zurschaustellung *f*; Vorführung *f*.

exhilarating *adj* erheiternd; erfrischend.

exhilaration *n* Erheiterung *f*; Heiterkeit *f*.

exhort *vt* ermahnen zu.

exhortation *n* Ermahnung *f*.

exhume *vt* exhumieren.

exile *n* Exil *n*; Verbannung *f*; im Exil Lebende(r) *f*(*m*); * *vt* verbannen; ins Exil schicken.

exist *vi* existieren; vorhanden sein; vorkommen; leben; bestehen.

existence *n* Existenz *f*; Vorhandensein *n*; Vorkommen *n*; Leben *n*; Dasein *n*; Bestand *m*.

existent *adj* existierend; bestehend; vorhanden; gegenwärtig.

existing *adj* = existent.

exit *n* Ausgang *m*; Ausfahrt *f*; Abgang *m*; Ausreise *f*; (*fig*) Tod *m*; * *vi* abgehen; abtreten; (*fig*) sterben.

exodus *n* Exodus *m*; Auszug *m*; (*fig*) Abwanderung *f*.

exonerate *vt* entlasten; befreien; freisprechen; entbinden.

exoneration *n* Entlastung *f*; Befreiung *f*.

exorbitant *adj* maßlos; übertrieben; astronomisch.

exorcise *vt* austreiben; bannen; exorzieren.

exorcism *n* Exorzismus *m*; Teufelsaustreibung *f*.

exotic *adj* exotisch; (*fig*) bizarr.

expand *vt* ausdehnen; erweitern; ausbreiten.

expanse *n* weite Fläche *f*; Ausdehnung *f*.

expansion *n* Ausbreitung *f*; Ausdehnung *f*; Erweiterung *f*.

expansive *adj* ausgedehnt; Expansions-; (*fig*) mitteilsam.

expatriate *vt* ausbürgern.

expect *vt* erwarten; annehmen.

expectance, expectancy *n* Erwartung *f*.

expectant *adj* erwartend; erwartungsvoll; schwanger.

expectant mother n werdende Mutter f.

expectation n Erwartung f; Aussicht f.

expediency n Ratsamkeit f; Zweckdienlichkeit f; Eigennutz m.

expedient adj ratsam; zweckdienlich; eigennützig; * n (Not)Behelf m; (Hilfs)Mittel n; ~ly adv zweckmäßigerweise.

expedite vt beschleunigen; befördern.

expedition n Expedition f; Eile f; (mil) Feldzug m.

expeditious adj ~ly adv schnell; prompt.

expel vt vertreiben; ausweisen; hinauswerfen; ausstoßen.

expend vt aufwenden; ausgeben; verbrauchen.

expendable adj entbehrlich; Verbrauchs-.

expenditure n Ausgabe f; Aufwand m; Verbrauch m; Kosten pl.

expense n = **expenditure**; Spesen pl.

expense account n Spesenkonto n.

expensive adj ~ly adv teuer; kostspielig.

experience n Erfahrung f; Erlebnis n; * vt erfahren; erleben; empfinden; erleiden.

experienced adj erfahren; erprobt.

experiment n Experiment n; Versuch m; * vi experimentieren; Versuche anstellen.

experimental adj experimentell; Versuchs-; experimentierfreudig; ~ly adv experimentell; versuchsweise.

expert adj Experte m; Expertin f; Sachverständige(r) f(m).

expertise n Expertise f; Sachkenntnis f.

expiration n Ausatmen n; (fig) Ablauf m; Ende n.

expire vi ausatmen; den Geist aushauchen; ablaufen; verfallen; erlöschen.

explain vt erklären; erläutern; rechtfertigen.

explanation n Erklärung f; Erläuterung f.

explanatory adj erklärend; erläuternd.

expletive adj ausfüllend; * n Füllsel n; Kraftausdruck m.

explicable adj erklärlich.

explicit adj, ~ly adv ausdrücklich; offen; deutlich.

explode vt zur Explosion bringen; sprengen; widerlegen; * vi explodieren; platzen; (fig) sprunghaft ansteigen.

exploit vt verwerten; ausbeuten; ausnutzen; * n (Helden)Tat f; Großtat f.

exploitation n Ausbeutung f; Ausnutzung f; Verwertung f.

exploration n Erforschung f; Untersuchung f.

exploratory adj (er)forschend; Erkundungs-.

explore vt (er)forschen; erkunden; untersuchen; sondieren.

explorer n Forscher(in) m(f); Forschungsreisende(r) f(m).

explosion n Explosion f; Ausbruch m.

explosive adj explosiv; Explosions-; * n Sprengstoff m.

exponent n (math) Exponent m; Vertreter(in) m(f).

export vt exportieren; ausführen.

export, exportation n Export m; Ausfuhr f.

exporter n Exporteur m.

expose vt aussetzen; bloßstellen; enthüllen; entblößen; zeigen; ausstellen; belichten.

exposed adj ausgesetzt; ungeschützt; exponiert.

exposition n Ausstellung f; Darlegung f; Exposition f.

expostulate vi ~ with Vorhaltungen machen; zurechtweisen.

exposure n Aussetzung f; Ausgesetztsein f; Bloßstellung f; Enthüllung f; Entblößung f; Belichtung f.

exposure meter n Belichtungsmesser m.

expound vt erklären; auslegen.

express vt ausdrücken; äußern; bedeuten; darstellen; * adj ausdrücklich; Expreß-; Eil-; * n Eilbeförderung m; Eilbote m; (rail) Schnellzug m.

expression n Ausdruck m.

expressionless adj ausdruckslos.

expressive adj ~ly adv ausdrucksvoll; Ausdrucks-.

expressly adv ausdrücklich; eigens.

expropriate vt enteignen.

expropriation n (law) Enteignung f.

expulsion n Vertreibung f; Ausweisung f; Ausschließung f.

expurgate vt (von Anstößigem) reinigen.

exquisite adj ~ly adv köstlich; erlesen; fein; intensiv.

extant adj (noch) vorhanden.

extempore adv aus dem Stegreif.

extemporize vi improvisieren.

extend vt (aus)dehnen; verlängern; vergrößern; erweitern; ausstrecken; ziehen; gewähren; * vi sich ausdehnen; sich erstrecken; reichen; hinausgehen.

extension n Ausdehnung f; Verlängerung f; Erweiterung f; Vergrößerung f; Nebenanschluß m.

extensive adj ~ly adv ausgedehnt; weitläufig; umfassend; extensiv.

extent n Ausdehnung f; Umfang m; Grad m; (Aus)Maß n.

extenuate vt abschwächen; mildern; beschönigen.

extenuating adj mildernd.

exterior adj äußerlich; Außen-; * n (das) Äußere n; Außenaufnahme f.

exterminate vt ausrotten; vernichten.

extermination n Ausrottung f; Vernichtung f.

external adj äußer(er, e, es); äußerlich; Außen-; sichtbar; auswärtig; ~ly adv äußerlich; von außen; ~s npl Äußerlichkeiten pl.

extinct adj ausgestorben; erloschen.

extinction n Aussterben n; (Aus)Löschen n; Vernichtung f.

extinguish vt (aus)löschen; vernichten.

extinguisher n Feuerlöscher m.

extirpate vt ausreißen; ausrotten.

extol vt (lob)preisen; rühmen.

extort vt erpressen; abnötigen.

extortion n Erpressung f; Wucher m.

extortionate adj erpresserisch; Wucher-.

extra adv extra; besonders; * n (etwas) Zusätzliches n; Extra n; Zuschlag m; Extrablatt n; Statist(in) m(f).

extract vt (heraus)ziehen; ausziehen; entlocken; * n Auszug m; Extrakt m.

extraction n (Heraus)Ziehen n; Auszug m; Extrakt m; Herkunft f.

extracurricular adj außerplanmäßig; außerhalb des Lehrplans.

extradite vt ausliefern.

extradition n (law) Auslieferung f.

extramarital adj außerehelich.

extramural adj außerhalb der Universität.

extraneous adj fremd; unwesentlich; Außen-.

extraordinarily adv außerordentlich; besonders.

extraordinary adj außerordentlich; ungewöhnlich; besonder(er, e, es).

extravagance n Extravaganz f; Verschwendung f.

extravagant adj, ~ly adv extravagant; verschwenderisch.

extreme adj extrem; äußerst

(er, e, es); Höchst-; außergewöhnlich; radikal; * *n* Extrem
n; (das) Äußerste *n*; **~ly** *adv*
äußerst; höchst.

extremist *adj* extremistisch;
* *n* Extremist(in) *m(f)*.

extremity *n* (das) Äußerste;
Spitze *f*; Gliedmaße *f*.

extricate *vt* herauswinden; befreien; freimachen.

extrinsic(al) *adj* äußer(er, e,
es); von außen; nicht zur Sache gehörend.

extrovert *adj* extravertiert; * *n*
extravertierter Mensch *m*.

exuberance *n* Fülle *f*; Über-
schwenglichkeit *f*.

exuberant *adj* **~ly** *adv* üppig;
reichlich; überschwenglich;
ausgelassen.

exude *vi* ausschwitzen; absondern; verströmen.

exult *vt* frohlocken; jubeln.

exultation *n* Frohlocken *n*; Jubel *m*.

eye *n* Auge *n*; Blick *m*; Öhr *n*;
Öse *f*; * *vt* betrachten; beäu-
gen.

eyeball *n* Augapfel *m*.

eyebrow *n* Augenbraue *f*.

eyelash *n* Wimper *f*.

eyelid *n* Augenlid *n*.

eyesight *n* Sehkraft *f*; Augen *pl*;
Augenlicht *n*.

eyesore *n* Schandfleck *m*.

eyetooth *n* Eckzahn *m*; Augen-
zahn *m*.

eyewitness *n* Augenzeuge *m*;
Augenzeugin *f*.

eyrie *n* Horst *m*.

F

fable *n* Fabel *f*; Sage *f*; (*fig*)
Märchen *n*.

fabric *n* Stoff *m*; Gewebe *n*;
Struktur *f*; Bau *m*.

fabricate *vt* fabrizieren; (an)fer-

tigen; (zusammen)bauen.

fabrication *n* Fabrikation *f*;
Herstellung *f*; (*fig*) Lüge *f*;
Märchen *n*.

fabulous *adj* **~ly** *adv* sagenhaft; fabelhaft.

facade *n* Fassade *f*.

face *n* Gesicht *n*; Miene *f*; (*col*)
Stirn *f*; Anblick *m*; (äußerer)
Anschein *m*; Oberfläche *f*; Vorderseite *f*; * *vt* ansehen; gegenüberstehen; blicken; liegen;
entgegentreten; ins Auge sehen; **to ~ up to** ins Auge sehen; sich mit den Tatsachen
abfinden.

face cream *n* Gesichtscreme *f*.

face-lift *n* Facelifting *m*; (*fig*)
Renovierung *f*.

face powder *n* Gesichtspuder
m.

facet *n* Facette *f*; (*fig*) Aspekt *m*.

facetious *adj* **~ly** *adv* witzig;
spaßig.

face value *n* Nennwert *m*; (*fig*)
scheinbarer Wert *m*; bare
Münze *f*.

facial *adj* Gesichts-.

facile *adj* leicht; oberflächlich;
gelassen.

facilitate *vt* erleichtern; fördern.

facility *n* Leichtigkeit *f*; Gelassenheit *f*; *pl* Gelegenheiten *fpl*;
Einrichtungen *fpl*; Anlagen
fpl; Erleichterungen *fpl*.

facing *n* (*mil*) Wendung *f*; Verkleidung *f*; Verblendung *f*;
Aufschlag *m*.

facsimile *n* Faksimile *n*; Reproduktion *f*.

fact *n* Tatsache *f*; Wirklichkeit
f; **in ~** tatsächlich; in Wirklichkeit.

faction *n* Faktion *f*; Splitter-
gruppe *f*; Zwietracht *f*.

factor *n* Faktor *m*; Umstand *m*;
(Guts)Verwalter *m*.

factory *n* Fabrik *f*.

factual *adj* tatsächlich; Tatsa-
chen-; sachlich.

faculty *n* Fakultät *f*; Fähigkeit
f; Kraft *f*; Gabe *f*.

fad n Mode f; Laune f.

fade vi (ver)welken; verblassen; sich auflösen; verklingen; schwinden.

fail vt versagen; im Stich lassen; durchfallen (lassen); * vi ermangeln; schwinden; versiegen; versagen; mißraten; scheitern; fehlschlagen; versäumen; durchfallen.

failing n Fehler m; Schwäche f.

failure n Fehler m; Ausbleiben n; Versagen n; Versäumnis n; Fehlschlag m; Scheitern n; Mißerfolg m; Nachlassen n; Durchfallen n; Versager(in) m(f).

faint vi ohnmächtig werden; * n Ohnmacht f; * adj, ~ly adv schwach; matt; zaghaft; furchtsam.

fainthearted adj feige; zaghaft; furchtsam.

faintness n Schwäche f; Mattheit f.

fair adj schön; hübsch; hell; blond; klar; frei; aussichtsreich; anständig; fair; aufrichtig; gerecht; leidlich; * adv schön; gut; sauber; günstig; anständig; fair; gerecht; aufrichtig; offen; * n Jahrmarkt m; Ausstellung f; Messe f; Basar m.

fairly adv ziemlich; leidlich; völlig; gerecht(erweise); anständig(erweise).

fairness n Schönheit f; Blondheit f; Anständigkeit f; Fairneß f; Gerechtigkeit f.

fair play n faires Spiel n.

fairy n Fee f; Elfe f.

fairy tale n Märchen n.

faith n Glaube(n) m; Vertrauen n; Treue f; Redlichkeit f.

faithful adj ~ly adv treu; aufrichtig; gewissenhaft; genau; wahrheitsgetreu; zuverlässig; gläubig.

faithfulness n Treue f; Ehrlichkeit f; Gewissenhaftigkeit f; Genauigkeit f; Glaubwürdigkeit f.

fake n Fälschung f; Schwindel m; Schwindler m; * adj falsch; gefälscht; * vt fälschen; vortäuschen; fingieren.

falcon n Falke m.

falconry n Falknerei f.

fall vi (um)fallen; (ab)stürzen; sinken; hereinbrechen; **to ~ asleep** einschlafen; **to ~ back** zurückweichen; **to ~ back on** zurückgreifen auf; **to ~ behind** zurückfallen; zurückbleiben; **to ~ down** hinfallen; herunterfallen; einstürzen; in die Knie sinken; **to ~ for** hereinfallen auf; sich verknallen in; **to ~ in** einfallen; (mil) antreten; fällig werden; sich anschließen; **to ~ short** knapp werden; **to ~ sick** krank werden; **to ~ in love** sich verlieben; **to ~ off** herunterfallen; abfallen; nachlassen; **to ~ out** herausfallen; sich streiten; * n Fall m; (Ein)Sturz m; Fallen n; Herbst m; Sinken n; Gefälle n; Untergang m.

fallacious adj ~ly adv trügerisch; irreführend; irrig.

fallacy n Trugschluß m; Irrtum m; Täuschung f.

fallibility n Fehlbarkeit f.

fallible adj fehlbar.

fallout n radioaktiver Niederschlag m.

fallout shelter n Atombunker m.

fallow adj brach; **~ deer** n Damhirsch m.

false adj ~ly adv falsch; Schein-; Fehl-.

false alarm n falscher Alarm m.

falsehood, falseness n Unwahrheit f; Lüge f; Falschheit f.

falsify vt (ver)fälschen; widerlegen.

falsity n Unwahrheit f; Lüge f.

falter vi schwanken; zaudern; stocken; versagen.

faltering adj schwankend; zögernd; stockend.

fame *n* Ruhm *m*; Berühmtheit
f.

famed *adj* berühmt.

familiar *adj* **~ly** *adv* vertraut;
bekannt; familiär; vertrau-
lich.

familiarity *n* Vertrautheit *f*;
Bekanntschaft *f*; (plumpe)
Vertraulichkeit *f*.

familiarize *vt* vertraut machen.

family *n* Familie *f*; Geschlecht
n.

family business *n* Familienbe-
trieb *m*.

family doctor *n* Hausarzt *m*.

famine *n* Hungersnot *f*; Knappheit *f*.

famished *adj* am Verhungern.

famous *adj* **~ly** *adv* berühmt;
(*col*) ausgezeichnet.

fan *n* Fächer *m*; Ventilator *m*;
Gebläse *n*; Fan *m*; * *vt* fächeln;
wedeln; anfachen.

fanatic *adj* fanatisch; * *n*
Fanatiker(in) *m(f)*.

fanaticism *n* Fanatismus *m*.

fan belt *n* Keilriemen *m*.

fanciful *adj* **~ly** *adv* phantastisch; phantasievoll.

fancy *n* Laune *f*; Phantasie *f*;
Einbildung *f*; Geschmack *m*;
Gefallen *n*; Vorliebe *f*; * *vt* sich
vorstellen; annehmen; mögen;
Lust haben.

fancy-goods *npl* Modeartikel
pl; Geschenkartikel *pl*.

fancydress ball *n* Maskenball
m.

fanfare *n* (*mus*) Fanfare *f*;
Tusch *m*.

fang *n* Reißzahn *m*; Fang *m*.

fantastic *adj* **~ally** *adv* phantastisch; absurd.

fantasy *n* Phantasie *f*; Einbil-
dungskraft *f*; Wachtraum *m*.

far *adv* weit (entfernt); fern;
* *adj* fern; weit;
(weit)entfernt; fortgeschritten; **~ and away** bei weitem;
~ off weit entfernt.

faraway *adj* (geistes)abwesend;
verträumt.

farce *n* Farce *f*; Posse *f*;
Schwank *m*; (*fig*) Theater *n*.

farcical *adj* absurd; lächerlich;
farcenhaft.

fare *n* Fahrpreis *m*; Fahrgast
m; Kost *f*.

farewell *n* Abschied *m*; **~!** *excl*
lebe(*n* Sie) wohl!

farm *n* Farm *f*; Bauernhof *m*;
landwirtschaftlicher Betrieb
m; * *vt* bebauen; bewirtschaften; züchten; * *vi* Landwirtschaft betreiben.

farmer *n* Landwirt(in) *m(f)*;
Bauer *m*; Bäuerin *f*; Farmer
m; Züchter(in) *m(f)*.

farmhand *n* Landarbeiter(in)
m(f).

farmhouse *n* Bauernhaus *n*.

farming *n* Landwirtschaft *f*;
Ackerbau *m*; Viehzucht *f*.

farmland *n* Ackerland *n*; landwirtschaftlich genutzte Fläche
f.

farmyard *n* Hof *m*.

far-reaching *adj* weitreichend;
folgenschwer.

fart *n* (*sl*) Furz *m*; * *vi* furzen.

farther *adv* weiter; mehr; außerdem; * *adj* weiter (weg);
entfernter.

farthest *adv* am weitesten; am
entferntesten; am meisten;
* *adj* weitest(er, e, es); ent-
ferntest (er, e, es); meist(er, e,
es).

fascinate *vt* faszinieren.

fascinating *adj* faszinierend.

fascination *n* Faszination *f*.

fascism *n* Faschismus *m*.

fashion *n* Mode *f*; Art und Weise *f*; Stil *m*; Manier *f*; Form *f*;
people of ~ Leute von Le-
bensart; * *vt* herstellen; formen; gestalten; machen.

fashionable *adj* **~bly** *adv* modisch; elegant; in Mode; **the ~
world** die Modewelt *f*.

fashion show *n* Mode(n)schau
f.

fast *n* Fasten *n*; * *adj* schnell;
rasch; leichtlebig; fest(ge-
macht); sicher; beständig;

* *adv* (zu) schnell; rasch; fest; stark.

fasten *vt* befestigen; festbinden; zumachen; verriegeln; (*fig*) heften; richten; * *vi* sich festmachen lassen.

fastener, fastening *n* Verschluß *m*.

fast food *restaurant n* Schnellimbiß *m*.

fastidious *adj* ~**ly** *adv* anspruchsvoll; wählerisch; heikel.

fat *adj* dick; fett; beleibt; * *n* Fett *n*.

fatal *adj* ~**ly** *adv* tödlich; fatal; verhängnisvoll.

fatalism *n* Fatalismus *m*.

fatalist *n* Fatalist(in) *m*(*f*).

fatality *n* Verhängnis *n*; tödlicher Unfall *m*; tödlicher Verlauf *m*.

fate *n* Schicksal *n*; Los *n*; Verhängnis *n*.

fateful *adj* verhängnisvoll; schicksalhaft.

father *n* Vater *m*; Pater *m*.

fatherhood *n* Vaterschaft *f*.

father-in-law *n* Schwiegervater *m*.

fatherland *n* Vaterland *n*.

fatherly *adj*; *adv* väterlich; Vater-.

fathom *n* Faden *m*; Klafter *n*; * *vt* ausloten; ergründen.

fatigue *n* Ermüdung *f*; Erschöpfung *f*; * *vt* ermüden; erschöpfen.

fatten *vt* dick machen; mästen; * *vi* dick werden; sich mästen.

fatty *adj* fettig; Fett-.

fatuous *adj* töricht; albern.

faucet *n* Hahn *m*; Zapfen *m*.

fault *n* Schuld *f*; Fehler *m*; Mangel *m*; Irrtum *m*; Defekt *m*; Verwerfung *f*.

faultfinder *n* Nörgler(in) *m*(*f*).

faultless *adj* fehlerlos; einwandfrei.

faulty *adj* fehlerhaft; defekt; falsch.

fauna *n* Fauna *f*.

faux pas *n* Fauxpas *m*.

favour *n* Gefallen *m*; Gunst *f*; Begünstigung *f*; * *vt* günstig gesinnt sein; wohlwollen; begünstigen; bevorzugen; unterstützen; beehren.

favourable *adj* ~**bly** *adv* wohlgesinnt; gewogen; günstig; vorteilhaft; gut; positiv; vielversprechend.

favoured *adj* begünstigt; bevorzugt; beliebt; favorisiert.

favourite *n* Liebling *m*; Günstling *m*; Favorit(in) *m*(*f*); * *adj* Lieblings-.

favouritism *n* Vetternwirtschaft *f*; Bevorzugung *f*; Begünstigung *f*.

fawn *n* Kitz *n*; Rehbraun *n*; * *vi* (mit dem Schwanz) wedeln; katzbuckeln; scharwenzeln.

fawningly *adv* schwanzwedelnd; schmeichlerisch; kriecherisch.

fax *n* Fax *n*; * *vt* faxen.

fear *vi* (sich) fürchten; * *n* Furcht *f*; Angst *f*; Befürchtung *f*; Sorge *f*; Ehrfurcht *f*.

fearful *adj* ~**ly** *adv* furchtbar; schrecklich; fuchtsam; angsterfüllt; ehrfürchtig.

fearless *adj* ~**ly** *adv* furchtlos; unerschrocken.

fearlessness *n* Furchtlosigkeit *f*; Unerschrockenheit *f*.

feasibility *n* Machbarkeit *f*; Durchführbarkeit *f*.

feasible *adj* machbar; durchführbar; plausibel.

feast *n* Fest(mahl) *n*; Feiertag *m*; * *vi* sich gütlich tun; sich weiden.

feat *n* Heldentat *f*; Kunststück *n*; große Leistung *f*.

feather *n* Feder *f*.

feather bed *n* Matratze *f* (mit Federfüllung).

feature *n* (Gesichts)Zug *m*; Züge *mpl*; Merkmal *n*; (Haupt)Attraktion *f*; Feature *n*; * *vt* charakterisieren; als Hauptattraktion bringen; in der Hauptrolle zeigen; aufweisen; sich auszeichnen durch.

feature film n Spielfilm m.
February n Februar m.
federal adj föderativ; Bundes-.
federalist n Föderalist m.
federate vt zu einem (Staaten)Bund vereinigen; * vi sich zu einem (Staaten)Bund zusammenschließen.
federation n Föderation f; Staatenbund m; Zusammenschluß m; Verband m.
fed-up adj: **to be ~** die Nase voll haben.
fee n Gebühr f; Honorar n; (Mitglieds)Beitrag m.
feeble adj **feebly** adv schwach.
feebleness n Schwäche f.
feed vt (ver)füttern; ernähren; unterhalten; versorgen; zuführen; nähren; **to ~ on** sich ernähren von; füttern mit; * vi fressen; sich (er)nähren; (col) futtern; * n Futter n; Nahrung f; Fütterung f; Zuführung f.
feedback n Rückkopplung f; Feedback n.
feel vt anfassen; (be)fühlen; anfühlen; (ver)spüren; empfinden; halten für; * vi (sich) fühlen; das Gefühl haben; sich anfühlen; **to ~ around** (umher)tasten; * n Gefühl n.
feeler n Fühler m.
feeling n Gefühl n; Stimmung f; Erregung f; Ansicht f.
feeling adj, **~ly** adv fühlend; Gefühls-; mitfühlend; gefühlvoll.
feign vt vortäuschen; simulieren; erfinden.
feline adj katzenhaft; Katzen-.
fellow n Kerl m; Typ m; (Zeit)Genosse m; (Zeit)Genossin f; Gefährte m; Gefährtin f; Mitmensch m; Gegenstück n; Ebenbürtige(r) f(m); Fellow m; Mitglied n.
fellow citizen n Mitbüger(in) m(f).
fellow countryman n Landsmann m; Landsmännin f.
fellow feeling n Mitgefühl n;

Zusammengehörigkeitsgefühl n.
fellow men npl Mitmenschen mpl.
fellowship n Gemeinschaft f; Kameradschaft f; Forschungsstipendium n.
fellow student n Studienkollege m; Studienkollegin f.
fellow traveller n Mitreisende(r) f(m).
felon n Verbrecher m.
felony n Verbrechen n.
felt n Filz m; Dachpappe f.
felt-tip pen n Filzstift m.
female n Frau f; Mädchen n; (contp) Weibsbild n; * adj weiblich; Frauen-.
feminine adj weiblich; Frauen-; feminin.
feminist n Feminist(in) m(f).
fen n Fenn n; Marschland n; Niedermoor n.
fence n Zaun m; Einzänung f; Hindernis n; Fechten n; * vt einzäunen; verteidigen; **~ off** abwehren; parieren; * vi fechten; (fig) Ausflüchte machen.
fencing n Fechten n; (fig) ausweichendes Verhalten; Zäune mpl; Zaunbau m.
fender n Schutzvorrichtung f; Kotflügel m; Schutzblech n; Puffer m.
fennel n (bot) Fenchel m.
ferment n Ferment n; Gärung f; (fig) Aufruhr m; * vi gären.
fern n (bot) Farn m.
ferocious adj **~ly** adv wild; grausam.
ferocity n Wildheit f; Grausamkeit f; Heftigkeit f.
ferret n Frettchen n; * vt mit Frettchen jagen; **to ~ out** aufstöbern; aufspüren.
ferry n Fähre f; * vt übersetzen; befördern.
fertile adj fruchtbar; reich.
fertility n Fruchtbarkeit f.
fertilize vt befruchten; düngen; fruchtbar machen.
fertilizer n Dünger m; Befruchter m.

fervent *adj* ~**ly** *adv* glühend; leidenschaftlich.

fervid *adj* = fervent.

fervor *n* Leidenschaft *f*; Inbrunst *f*; Glut(hitze) *f*.

fester *vi* eitern; verwesen; *(fig)* gären.

festival *n* Fest *n*; Festspiele *pl*.

festive *adj* festlich; Fest-.

festivity *n* Festlichkeit *f*; Fest(tags)stimmung *f*.

fetch *vt* (ab)holen; (her)bringen; erzielen; *(col)* fesseln.

fetching *adj* bezaubernd.

fete *n* Fest *n*.

fetid *adj* stinkend.

fetus *n* Foetus *m*.

feud *n* Fehde *f*.

feudal *adj* feudal; Lehns-.

feudalism *n* Feudalismus *m*.

fever *n* Fieber *n*; *(fig)* Erregung *f*.

feverish *adj* fiebrig; Fieber-; *(fig)* fieberhaft.

few *adj* wenige; **a** ~ einige; ein paar; ~ **and far between** dünn gesät.

fewer *adj* weniger.

fewest *adj* am wenigsten.

fiance *n* Verlobe(r) *f(m)*.

fiancee *n* Verlobte *f*.

fib *n* Flunkerei *f*; * *vi* flunkern.

fiber *n* Faser *f*; Textur *f*; *(fig)* Struktur *f*; Schlag *m*; Kraft *f*.

fiberglass *n* Fiberglas *n*.

fickle *adj* launisch; unbeständig; wankelmütig.

fiction *n* Erfindung *f*; Belletristik *f*; Romane *mpl*; Prosa *fpl*.

fictional *adj* erdichtet; erfunden; Roman-.

fictitious *adj*, ~**ly** *adv* (frei) erfunden; fiktiv; Roman-.

fiddle *n* Geige *f*; Fiedel *f*; Schwindel *m*; * *vi* geigen; fiedeln; herumfummeln; herumbasteln.

fiddler *n* Geiger(in) *m(f)*; Fiedler(in) *m(f)*; Schwindler(in) *m(f)*.

fidelity *n* Treue *f*; Genauigkeit *f*.

fidget *vi* (herum)zappeln; nervös sein.

fidgety *adj* zapplig; nervös.

field *n* Feld *n*; Gebiet *n*; Fläche *f*; Außendienst *m*.

field day *n* *(mil)* Felddienstübung *f*; (Truppen)Parade *f*; *(fig)* großer Tag; *(fig)* riesiger Spaß.

fieldmouse *n* Feldmaus *f*.

fieldwork *n* Feldarbeit *f*; praktische (wissenschaftliche) Arbeit *f*; Arbeit im Gelände.

fiend *n* Teufel *m*; Dämon *m*; Unhold *m*; Fanatiker *m*.

fiendish *adj* teuflisch; unmenschlich; höllisch.

fierce *adj* ~**ly** *adv* wild; grimmig; glühend; scharf; heftig; grell.

fierceness *n* Wildheit *f*; Grimmigkeit *f*; Schärfe *f*; Heftigkeit *f*; Grelligkeit *f*.

fiery *adj* brennend; glühend; feuerrot; feurig; hitzig; scharf; leidenschaftlich.

fifteen *adj* fünfzehn; * *n* Fünfzehn *f*.

fifteenth *adj* fünfzehnt(er, e, es); fünfzehntel; * *n* *(der, die, das)* Fünfzehnte; Fünfzehntel *n*.

fifth *adj* fünft(er, e, es); fünftel; * *n* *(der, die, das)* Fünfte; Fünftel *n*; Quinte *f*; ~**ly** *adv* fünftens.

fiftieth *adj* fünfzigst(er, e, es); fünfzigstel; * *n* *(der, die, das)* Fünfzigste; Fünfzigstel *n*.

fifty *adj* fünfzig; * *n* Fünfzig *f*.

fig *n* Feige *f*; *(fig)* Deut *m*.

fight *vt* kämpfen mit; bekämpfen; führen; sich prügeln mit; verfechten; kämpfen lassen; *vi* kämpfen; sich raufen; sich prügeln; * *n* Kampf *m*; Gefecht *n*; Streit *m*; Ringen *n*; Schlägerei *f*.

fighter *n* Kämpfer(in) *m(f)*; Schläger *m*; *(mil)* Jäger *m*.

fighting *n* Kampf *m*; Kämpfen *n*.

fig-leaf *n* Feigenblatt *n*.

fig tree *n* Feigenbaum *m*.

figurative *adj*, ~**ly** *adv* bildlich;

übertragen; symbolisch.

figure *n* Zahl *f*; Ziffer *f*; Betrag *m*; Figur *f*; Gestalt *f*; Persönlichkeit *f*; Statue *f*; Symbol *n*; ; * *vi* rechnen; vorkommen; (*col*) hinhauen; passen; **to ~ out** ausrechnen; rauskriegen; kapieren; verstehen.

figurehead *n* Galionsfigur *f*; (*fig*) Aushängeschild *n*.

filament *n* Faden *n*; Faser *f*; Filament *n*.

filch *vi* klauen; stibitzen.

filcher *n* Dieb(in) *m(f)*.

file *n* Ordner *m*; Akte *f*; Datei *f*; (*mil*) Rotte *f*; Reihe *f*; Liste *f*; * *vt* ablegen; (ein)ordnen; zu den Akten nehmen; einreichen; * *vi* **to ~ in/out** hintereinander hinein-/hinausmarschieren; **to ~ past** vorbeidefilieren.

filing cabinet *n* Aktenschrank *m*.

fill *vt* (ab)füllen; erfüllen; ausfüllen; besetzen; **to ~ in** ausfüllen; ergänzen; ins Bild setzen; informieren; ersetzen; **to ~ up** (voll)füllen; ausfüllen.

fillet *n* Filet *n*; (Haar)Band *n*; Leiste *f*.

fillet steak *n* Filetsteak *n*.

filling station *n* Tankstelle *f*.

fillip *n* (*fig*) Ansporn *m*; Schnipser *m*; Klaps *m*.

filly *n* (Stut)Fohlen *n*.

film *n* Film *m*; dünne Schicht *f*; Häutchen *n*; * *vt* überziehen; (ver)filmen; * *vi* einen Film drehen.

film star *n* Filmstar *m*.

filmstrip *n* Filmstreifen *m*.

filter *n* Filter *m*; * *vt* filtern; filtrieren; (durch)seihen.

filter-tipped *adj* Filter-.

filth *n* Schmutz *m*; Dreck *m*; Schweinerei *f*.

filthiness *n* Schmutzigkeit *f*; Unflätigkeit *f*

filthy *adj* schmutzig; dreckig; schweinisch; scheußlich.

fin *n* Finne *f*; Flosse *f*; Kühlrippe *f*.

final *adj* letzt(er, e, es); endgültig; End-; Schluß-; **~ly** *adv* endlich; schließlich; zum Schluß; endgültig.

finale *n* Finale *n*.

finalist *n* Endkampfteilnehmer(in) *m(f)*.

finalize *vt* beenden; abschließen.

finance *n* Finanzwesen *n*; *pl* Finanzen *pl*; Einkünfte *pl*.

financial *adj* finanziell; Finanz-.

financier *n* Finanzier *m*.

find *vt* (heraus)finden; feststellen; **to ~ out** entdecken; herausfinden; ertappen; **to ~ one's self** zu sich selbst finden; * *n* Fund *m*; Entdeckung *f*.

findings *npl* Befund *m*; Erkenntnisse *fpl*.

fine *adj* **~ly** *adv* fein; schön; großartig; rein; dünn; scharf; vornehm; * *n* Geldstrafe *f*; Bußgeld *n*; * *vt* zu einer Geldstrafe verurteilen.

fine arts *npl* (*die*) schönen Künste *fpl*.

finery *n* Putz *m*; Staat *m*; Eleganz *f*.

finesse *n* Finesse *f*; Spitzfindigkeit *f*; Raffinesse *f*.

finger *n* Finger(breit) *m*; * *vt* befingern; befühlen.

fingernail *n* Fingernagel *m*.

fingerprint *n* Fingerabdruck *m*.

fingertip *n* Fingerspitze *f*.

finicky *adj* pedantisch; wählerisch; affektiert.

finish *vt* (be)enden; aufhören mit; fertigmachen; erledigen; aufbrauchen; nachbearbeiten; polieren; **to ~ off** beendigen; fertigmachen; erledigen; aufbruchen; den letzten Schliff geben; **to ~ up** aufessen; * *vi*: **to ~ up** enden; schließen; aufhören.

finishing line *n* Ziellinie *f*.

finishing school *n* Mädchenpensionat *n*.

finite *adj* begrenzt; endlich.
fir (tree) *n* Tanne *f*.
fire *n* Feuer *n*; Flamme *f*; Brand *m*; Heizgerät *n*; (*mil*) Beschuß *m*; (*fig*) Leidenschaft *f*; * *vt* anzünden; (be)heizen; (ab)feuern; brennen; abschießen; zünden; * *vi* feuern; schießen; zünden; Feuer fangen.
fire alarm *n* Feueralarm *m*; Feuermelder *m*.
firearm *n* Schußwaffe *f*.
fireball *n* Brandkugel *f*; Feuerball *m*; Kugelblitz *m*.
fire department *n* Feuerwehr *f*.
fire engine *n* Feuerwehrauto *n*; Löschfahrzeug *n*; Motorspritze *f*.
fire escape *n* Feuerleiter *f*.
fire extinguisher *n* Feuerlöscher *m*.
firefly *n* Glühwurm *m*.
fireman *n* Feuerwehrmann *m*.
fireplace *n* (offener) Kamin *m*.
fireproof *adj* feuerfest.
fireside *n* (offener) Kamin *m*.
fire station *n* Feuerwache *f*.
firewater *n* Feuerwasser *n*.
firewood *n* Brennholz *n*.
fireworks *npl* Feuerwerk *n*; (*fig*) Krach *m*.
firing *n* (Ab)Feuern *n*; Zünden *n*; Feuerung *f*.
firing squad *n* Exekutionskommando *n*.
firm *adj* ~**ly** *adv* fest; hart; steif; stabil; sicher; * *n* (*com*) Firma *f*; Betrieb *m*.
firmament *n* Firmament *n*.
firmness *n* Festigkeit *f*; Beständigkeit *f*; Entschlossenheit *f*.
first *adj* erst(er, e, es); best(er, e, es); erstklassig; * *adv* zuerst; voran; zum erstenmal; eher; **at ~** anfangs; zuerst; ~**ly** *adv* erstens; zuerst (einmal).
first aid *n* Erste Hilfe *f*.
first-aid kit *n* Verbandskasten *m*.
first-class *adj* erstklassig; erster Klasse.
first-hand *adj* aus erster Hand; direkt.

First Lady *n* First Lady *f*.
first name *n* Vorname *m*.
first-rate *adj* erstklassig; ausgezeichnet.
fiscal *adj* steuerlich; Fiskal-.
fish *n* Fisch *m*; * *vi* fischen; angeln.
fishbone *n* Gräte *f*.
fisherman *n* Fischer *m*; Angler *m*.
fish farm *n* Fischzuchtanlage *f*.
fishing *n* Fischen *n*; Angeln *n*; Fischerei *f*.
fishing line *n* Angelschnur *f*.
fishing rod *n* Angelrute *f*.
fishing tackle *n* Angelgerät *n*.
fish market *n* Fischmarkt *m*.
fishmonger *n* Fischhändler *m*.
fishy *adj* fischartig; Fisch-; (*fig*) verdächtig; faul.
fissure *n* Spalte *f*; Riß *m*; Sprung *m*; (*fig*) Spaltung *f*.
fist *n* Faust *f*.
fit *n* Paßform *f*; Sitz *m*; Zusammenpassen *n*; Anfall *m*; * *adj* passend; geeignet; tauglich; fähig; angebracht; schicklich; würdig; gesund; fit; * *vt* (an)passen; ausrüsten; sitzen; angemessen sein; **to ~ out** ausrüsten; ausstatten; * *vi* passen; sitzen; angemessen sein; sich eignen; **to ~ in** einfügen; einschieben; passen; übereinstimmen.
fitment *n* Einrichtungsgegenstand *m*.
fitness *n* Gesundheit *f*; (gute) Form *f*; Eignung *f*; Tauglichkeit *f*.
fitted carpet *n* Teppichboden *m*.
fitted kitchen *n* Einbauküche *f*.
fitter *n* Einrichter *m*; Schneider(in) *m(f)*; Monteur *m*; Maschinenschlosser *m*.
fitting *adj* passend; geeignet; angemessen; schicklich; * *n* Einpassen *n*; Anprobe *f*; Montage *f*; Zubehörteil *n*; ~**s** *pl* Zubehör *n*; Einrichtung *f*.

five *adj* fünf; * *n* Fünf *f*.

fix *vt* befestigen; festsetzen; heften; fixieren; reparieren; zurechtmachen; *(fig)* verankern; *(col)* manipulieren; **to ~ up** arrangieren; unterbringen; etwas besorgen; in Ordnung bringen.

fixation *n* Fixierung *f*; Bindung *f*; Zwangsvorstellung *f*.

fixed *adj* befestigt; Fest-; stationär; gebunden; starr; *(col)* abgekartet.

fixings *npl* Geräte *npl*; Zubehör *npl*.

fixture *n* festes Inventar *n*; Installationsteil *n*; Spannvorrichtung *f*.

fizz(le) *vi* zischen; sprudeln.

fizzy *adj* zischend; sprudelnd.

flabbergasted *adj* verblüfft; platt.

flabby *adj* schlaff; schwammig.

flaccid *adj* schlaff.

flag *n* Flagge *f*; Fahne *f*; Markierung *f*; (Stein)Platte *f*; * *vi* schlaff herabhängen; *(fig)* erlahmen; nachlassen.

flagpole *n* Fahnenstange *f*.

flagrant *adj* schamlos; eklatant.

flagship *n* Flaggschiff *n*.

flair *n* Veranlagung *f*; Gespür *n*; *(col)* Eleganz *f*.

flak *n* Flak *f*; *(col)* scharfe Kritik *f*.

flake *n* Flocke *f*; (dünne) Schicht *f*; * *vi* abblättern; flocken.

flaky *adj* flockig; blätterig.

flamboyant *adj* extravagant; auffallend.

flame *n* Flamme *f*; Glanz *m*.

flamingo *n* Flamingo *m*.

flammable *adj* entflammbar; brennbar; leichtentzündlich.

flank *n* Flanke *f*; Seite *f*; * *vt* flankieren.

flannel *n* Flanell *m*; Waschlappen *m*.

flap *n* Flattern *n*; Schlag *m*; Klappe *f*; Krempe *f*; Lasche *f*; Lappen *m*; * *vt* hin und her

bewegen; schlagen mit; werfen; * *vi* flattern; klatschen; schlagen.

flare *vi* flackern; leuchten; **to ~ up** auflodern; aufleuchten; aufbrausen; * *n* plötzlicher Lichtschein; Lodern *n*; Leuchten *n*; Leuchtfeuer *n*; Leuchtkugel *f*; Schlag *m*.

flash *n* Aufleuchten *n*; Blitz *m*; Stichflamme *f*; (Augen)Blick *m*; * *vt* aufleuchten lassen; signalisieren; kurz sehen lassen; anblitzen.

flashbulb *n* Blitzlichtlampe *f*.

flash cube *n* Blitzwürfel *m*.

flashlight *n* Taschenlampe *f*; Blitzlicht *n*.

flashy *adj* protzig; auffällig.

flask *n* Thermosflasche *f*; Taschenflasche *f*; Kolben *m*.

flat *adj* flach; eben; Flach-; platt; glatt; fad(e); Pauschal-; leer; (mus) erniedrigt; * *n* Fläche *f*; Ebene *f*; Flachland *n*; (mus) B *n*; **~ly** *adv* eindeutig; kategorisch.

flatness *n* Flachheit *f*; Eintönigkeit *f*.

flatten *vt* (ein)ebnen; flach machen; dem Erdboden gleichmachen; vernichten; einen Dämpfer augsetzen.

flatter *vt* schmeicheln.

flattering *adj* schmeichelhaft.

flattery *n* Schmeichelei *f*.

flatulence *n* (med) Blähungen *fpl*.

flaunt *vt* zur Schau stellen; protzen mit.

flavour *n* Geschmack *m*; Aroma *n*; Würze *f*; *(fig)* Beigeschmack *m*; * *vt* würzen.

flavoured *adj* schmackhaft; würzig.

flavourless *adj* fad(e); ohne Geschmack.

flaw *n* Fehler *m*; Mangel *m*; Makel *m*; Defekt *m*.

flawless *adj* makellos; fehlerfrei; lupenrein.

flax *n* Flachs *m*; Lein *m*.

flea *n* Floh *m*.

flea bite n Flohbiß m.

fleck n Fleck m; Tupfen m.

flee vt fliehen vor; fliehen aus; meiden; * vi fliehen; flüchten.

fleece n Vlies n; Schur f; * vt scheren; (sl) ausnehmen; schröpfen.

fleet n Flotte f.

fleeting adj flüchtig.

flesh n Fleisch f.

flesh wound n Fleischwunde f.

fleshy adj fleischig.

flex n Kabel n; Schnur f; Beugen n; * vt biegen; beugen; anspannen.

flexibility n Flexibilität f; Biegsamkeit f; (fig) Anpassungsfähigkeit f.

flexible adj flexibel; biegsam; (fig) anpassungsfähig.

flick n Klaps m; schnelle Bewegung f; Knall m; Schnalzer m; * vt leicht schlagen; knallen mit; schnalzen mit; schnipsen.

flicker vi flackern; zucken; flimmern.

flier n Flieger m; Schwungrad n; Flugblatt n.

flight n Flug m; Fliegen n; Schwarm m; Treppe f; Flucht f.

flight attendant n Flugbegleiter(in) m(f).

flight deck n Flugdeck n; Cockpit n.

flimsy adj dünn; leichtzerbrechlich; (fig) schwach; (fig) fadenscheinig.

flinch vi zurückschrecken; (zurück)zucken.

fling vt werfen; schleudern.

flint n Flint m; Feuerstein m.

flip vt schnippen; schnellen.

flippant adj respektlos; schnippisch.

flipper n Flosse f.

flirt vi herumsausen; flirten; liebäugeln; * n Schäker(in) m(f).

flirtation n Flirten n; Flirt m; Liebäugeln n.

flit vi flitzen; huschen; flattern.

float vt treiben lassen; flößen; (mar) flottmachen; (Über-) schwemmen; in Umlauf setzen; * vi schwimmen; treiben; im Umlauf sein; * n Floß n; Prahm m; (Kork)Schwimmer m; Plattformwagen m; Wechselgeld n.

flock n Herde f; Schwarm m; Flocke f; * vi (fig) strömen.

flog vt prügeln; auspeitschen; antreiben; (col) verscheuern.

flogging n Prügel(strafe) f; Auspeitschen n.

flood n Flut f; Überschwemmung f; Schwall m; * vt (über)fluten; überschwemmen.

flooding n Überschwemmung f; Überflutung f.

floodlight n Flutlicht n.

floor n (Fuß)Boden m; Tanzfläche f; Sohle f; Stockwerk n; Börsensaal m; * vt einen (Fuß)Boden legen; zu Boden schlagen; (col) umhauen.

floorboard n Diele f.

floor lamp n Stehlampe f.

floor show n Varietévorstellung f.

flop n Plumpsen n; (col) Flop m; (col) Reinfall m.

floppy adj schlapp; schlottrig; * n Diskette f.

flora n Flora f.

floral adj geblümt; Blumen-.

florescence n Blüte f.

florid adj blühend; überladen; blumig.

florist n Blumenhändler(in) m(f).

florist's (shop) n Blumengeschäft n.

flotilla n (mar) Flotille f.

flounder n Flunder f; * vi zappeln; strampeln; sich verhaspeln; sich quälen.

flour n Mehl n; Pulver n.

flourish vi gedeihen; blühen; seine Blütezeit haben; * n Schwenken n; Schnörkel m; (mus) Tusch m; Floskel f; schwungvolle Gebärde f.

flourishing *adj* blühend; gedeihend.

flout *vt* verspotten; mißachten.

flow *vi* fließen; strömen; rinnen; wallen; entspringen; * *n* Fließen *n*; Fluß *m*; Schwall *m*; Flut *f*.

flow chart *n* Ablaufdiagramm *n*.

flower *n* Blume *f*; Blüte *f*; * *vi* blühen.

flowerbed *n* Blumenbeet *n*.

flowerpot *n* Blumentopf *m*.

flowery *adj* geblümt; (*fig*) blumig.

flower show *n* Blumenschau *f*.

fluctuate *vi* schwanken; fluktuieren.

fluctuation *n* Schwankung *f*; Fluktuation *f*.

fluency *n* Flüssigkeit *f*; (Rede-) Gewandtheit *f*.

fluent *adj* ~**ly** *adv* flüssig; fließend; gewandt.

fluff *n* Staubflocke *f*; Fussel *f*; Flaum *m*; ~**y** *adj* flaumig; flokkig; locker.

fluid *adj* flüssig; * *n* Flüssigkeit *f*.

fluidity *n* Flüssigkeit *f*.

fluke *n* (*sl*) Schwein *n*; glücklicher Zufall *m*.

fluoride *n* Fluorid *n*.

flurry *n* Windstoß *m*; Schauer *m*; Hagel *m*; Wirbel *m*; Aufregung *f*; Hast *f*.

flush *vt*: **to ~ out** (aus)spülen; aufscheuchen; * *vi* rot werden; spülen; sprießen; * *n* Erröten *n*; Röte *f*; (Wasser)Schwall *m*; Spülung *f*; (Auf)Wallung *f*; Blüte *f*.

flushed *adj* rot; erröted; erregt; erhitzt.

fluster *vt* nervös machen; durcheinanderbringen; aufregen; benebeln.

flustered *adj* nervös; durcheinander; aufgeregt; benebelt.

flute *n* Flöte *f*; Riefe *f*.

flutter *vi* flattern; zittern; * *n* Flattern *n*; Verwirrung *f*.

flux *n* (Aus)Fluß *m*; Strom *m*;

beständiger Wechsel *m*.

fly *vt* fliegen (lassen); führen; fliehen; * *vi* fliegen; fliehen; stürmen; stürzen; wehen; **to ~ away/off** fortfliegen; fortstürmen; * *n* Fliege *f*; Flug *m*; Hosenschlitz *m*.

flying *n* Fliegen *n*; Flug *m*.

flying saucer *n* fliegende Untertasse *f*.

flypast *n* Luftparade *f*.

flysheet *n* Flugblatt *n*; Überdach *n*.

foal *n* Fohlen *n*.

foam *n* Schaum *m*; * *vi* schäumen.

foam rubber *n* Schaumgummi *m*.

foamy *adj* schaumig.

focus *n* Brennpunkt *m*; Scharfeinstellung *f*; Herd *m*.

fodder *n* Futter *n*.

foe *n* Feind(in) *m(f)*; Widersacher(in) *m(f)*.

fog *n* Nebel *m*; Schleier *m*.

foggy *adj* neblig; nebelhaft; benebelt; verschleiert.

fog light *n* Nebelscheinwerfer *m*.

foible *n* Schwäche *f*.

foil *vt* vereiteln; zunichte machen; einen Strich durch die Rechnung machen; * *n* Folie *f*; Hintergrund *m*; Florett *n*.

fold *n* Falte *f*; Windung *f*; Falz *f*; Hürde *f*; Pferch *m*; * *vt* falten; verschränken; zusammenklappen; einhüllen; * *vi*: **to ~ up** zusammenbrechen.

folder *n* Mappe *f*; Schnellhefter *m*; Faltprospekt *m*.

folding *adj* Klapp-; Falt-; zusammenlegbar.

folding chair *n* Klappstuhl *m*.

foliage *n* Laub *n*; Blattwerk *n*.

folio *n* Blatt *n*; Foliant *m*.

folk *n* Leute *pl*; Volk *n*; Folk *m*.

folklore *n* Folklore *f*; Volkskunde *f*; Volkstum *n*.

folk song *n* Volkslied *n*; Folksong *m*.

follow *vt* (nach)folgen; verfolgen; nachgehen; folgen aus; **to**

~ up (weiter)verfolgen; nachgehen; * *vi* (nach)folgen; sich anschließen; sich ergeben.

follower *n* Anhänger *m*; Schüler *m*; Gefolgsmann *m*; Begleiter *m*.

following *adj* folgend(er, e, es); * *n* Gefolge *n*; Anhänger *pl*.

folly *n* Torheit *f*; Verrücktheit *f*.

foment *vt* (*med*) bähen; (*fig*) pflegen; (*fig*) schüren.

fond *adj* zärtlich; liebevoll; vernarrt; töricht; to be ~ of lieben; mögen; gern haben; **~ly** *adv* liebevoll; törichterweise.

fondle *vt* streicheln; spielen mit.

fondness *n* Zärtlichkeit *f*; Zuneigung *f*; (Vor)Liebe *f*.

font *n* (relig) Taufbecken *n*; Schrift *f*.

food *n* Essen *n*; Nahrung *f*; Verpflegung *f*; Lebensmittel *pl*; Futter *n*.

food mixer *n* Mixer *m*.

food poisoning *n* Lebensmittelvergiftung *f*.

food processor *n* Küchenmaschine *f*.

foodstuffs *npl* Lebensmittel *pl*.

fool *n* Narr *m*; Närrin *f*; Dummkopf *m*; * *vt* zum Narren halten; reinlegen; betrügen.

foolhardy *adj* tollkühn; verwegen.

foolish *adj* **~ly** *adv* dumm; töricht; albern; unklug; lächerlich.

foolproof *adj* narrensicher; todsicher.

foolscap *n* Narrenkappe *f*; *Papierformat 34,2 x 43,1 cm*.

foot *n* Fuß *m*; Infanterie *f*; Schritt *m*; Fußende *n*; **on/by** ~ zu Fuß.

footage *n* Gesamtlänge *f*; Filmmeter *pl*.

football *n* Fußball *m*.

footballer *n* Fußballspieler *m*.

footbrake *n* Fußbremse *f*.

footbridge *n* Fußgängerbrücke *f*.

foothills *npl* Ausläufer *pl*; Vorgebirge *n*.

foothold *n* Stand *m*; Tritt *m*; Halt *m*; (Ausgangs)Basis *f*.

footing *n* = footing; Sockel *m*; Fundament *n*; Grundlage *f*; Stellung *f*; Verhältnis *n*.

footlights *npl* Rampenlicht *n*.

footman *n* Lakai *m*.

footnote *n* Fußnote *f*.

footpath *n* Pfad *m*; Fußweg *m*.

footprint *n* Fußabdruck *m*.

footsore *adj* fußwund; fußkrank.

footstep *n* Schritt *m*; Fußstapfe *f*; Trittbrett *n*.

footwear *n* Fußbekleidung *f*; Schuhwerk *n*.

for *prep* für; zu; um; auf; nach; gegen; aus; vor; wegen; seit; weit; als; trotz; * *conj* denn; weil; nämlich; **as ~ me** was mich betrifft; **what ~?** wozu?

forage *n* Futter *n*; Nahrungssuche *f*; Futtersuche *f*; Überfall *m*; * *vi* (nach) Nahrung/Futter suchen; (herum)stöbern; einen Überfall machen.

foray *n* Beutezug *m*; Einfall *m*; (*fig*) Ausflug *m*.

forbid *vt* verbieten; untersagen; unmöglich machen; **God ~!** Gott bewahre!

forbidding *adj* abstoßend; bedrohlich.

force *n* Kraft *f*; Stärke *f*; Wucht *f*; Gewalt *f*; Macht *f*; (Nach-)Druck *m*; Menge *f*; Truppe *f*; **~s** *pl* Streitkräfte *pl*; Truppe *f*; * *vt* (er)zwingen; nötigen; durchsetzen; (auf)drängen; erstürmen; forcieren.

forced *adj* Zwangs-; erzwungen; gezwungen; forciert.

forced march *n* (*mil*) Gewaltmarsch *m*.

forceful *adj* energisch; kraftvoll; eindringlich; zwingend.

forceps *n* Zange *f*.

forcible *adj* **~bly** *adv* gewaltsam; zwangsweise; eindringlich.

ford *n* Furt *f*; * *vt* durchwaten.

fore *n*: **to the ~** zur Hand; im Vordergrund.

forearm *n* Unterarm *m*.

foreboding *n* (böse) Vorahnung *f*; (böses) Vorzeichen.

forecast *vt* vorhersagen; voraussagen; * *n* Vorhersage *f*; Prognose *f*.

forecourt *n* Vorhof *m*; Vorplatz *m*.

forefather *n* Ahn *m*; Vorfahr *m*.

forefinger *n* Zeigefinger *m*.

forefront *n*: **in the ~ of** in vorderster Linie.

forego *vt* vorangehen; vorhergehen.

foregone *adj* vorhergehend; früher; von vornherein feststehend.

foreground *n* Vordergrund *m*.

forehead *n* Stirn *f*.

foreign *adj* fremd; ausländisch; Auslands-; Außen-.

foreigner *n* Ausländer(in) *m*.

foreign exchange *n* Devisen *pl*.

foreleg *n* Vorderbein *n*.

foreman *n* Vorarbeiter *m*; Aufseher *m*; (law) Obmann *m*.

foremost *adj* vorderst(er, e, es); erst(er, e, es); (*fig*) herausragendst(er, e, es).

forenoon *n* Vormittag *m*.

forensic *adj* Gerichts-.

forerunner *n* Vorläufer *m*; Vorbote *m*.

foresee *vt* vorhersehen; voraussehen.

foreshadow *vt* ahnen lassen; andeuten.

foresight *n* Weitblick *m*; Voraussicht *f*.

forest *n* Wald *m*; Forst *m*.

forestall *vt* zuvorkommen; vorbeugen.

forester *n* Förster *m*; Waldbewohner *m*.

forestry *n* Forstwirtschaft *f*; Waldgebiet *n*.

foretaste *n* Vorgeschmack *m*.

foretell *vt* vorhersagen; voraussagen.

forethought *n* Voraussicht *f*; Vorbedacht *f*.

forever *adv* für immer; ständig; endlos lang.

forewarn *vt* vorher warnen.

foreword *n* Vorwort *n*.

forfeit *n* (Ein)Buße *f*; Strafe *f*; Verlust *m*; Pfand *n*; * *vt* verwirken; verlieren; einbüßen.

forge *n* Schmiede *f*; Esse *f*; Hammerwerk *n*; * *vt* schmieden; formen; erfinden; fälchen; * *vi*: **to ~ ahead** sich vorankämpfen.

forger *n* Fälscher *m*; Schmied *m*.

forgery *n* Fälschung *f*; Fälschen *n*.

forget *vt* vergessen; * *vi* vergessen.

forgetful *adj* vergeßlich; nachlässig.

forgetfulness *n* Vergeßlichkeit *f*; Nachlässigkeit *f*.

forget-me-not *n* (*bot*) Vergißmeinnicht *n*.

forgive *vt* vergeben; verzeihen.

forgiveness *n* Vergebung *f*; Verzeihung *f*.

fork *n* Gabel *f*; Gabelung *f*; * *vi* sich gabeln; **to ~ out** (*sl*) herausrücken.

forked *adj* gegabelt; gabelförmig.

fork-lift truck *n* Gabelstapler *m*.

forlorn *adj* verlassen; einsam; verzweifelt; verloren.

form *n* Form *f*; Gestalt *f*; Art *f*; Formalität *f*; Formular *n*; Formel *f*; Benehmen *n*; (Schul-) Klasse *f*; * *vt* formen; bilden; darstellen; entwerfen.

formal *adj* ~**ly** *adv* förmlich; formell; feierlich.

formality *n* Förmlichkeit *f*; Formalität *f*.

format *n* Format *n*; Gestaltung *f*; * *vt* formatieren.

formation *n* Formation *f*; Bildung *f*; Entstehung *f*; Gründung *f*; Anordnung *f*.

formative *adj* formend; bildend; gestaltend; Entwicklungs-.

former *adj* früher(er, e, es); vorhergehend; vergangen; erst (er, e, es); ehemalig(er, e, es); **~ly** *adv* früher; ehemals.

formidable *adj* furchteinflößend; ernstzunehmend; gewaltig; schwierig; eindrucksvoll.

formula *n* Formel *f*; Rezept *n*.

formulate *vt* formulieren; festlegen.

forsake *vt* verlassen; aufgeben.

fort *n* Fort *n*; Festung *f*.

forte *n* Stärke *f*.

forthcoming *adj* (in Kürze) erscheinend; bevorstehend; verfügbar; entgegenkommend.

forthright *adj* offen; direkt; freimütig.

forthwith *adv* sofort; umgehend; unverzüglich.

fortieth *adj* vierzigst(er, e, es); vierzigstel; * *n* (*der, die, das*) Vierzigste; Vierzigstel *n*.

fortification *n* Befestigung *f*; Festung *f*; (Ver)Stärkung *f*; Untermauerung *f*.

fortify *vt* befestigen; (ver)stärken; untermauern.

fortitude *n* (innere) Kraft *f*; (Seelen)Stärke *f*.

fortnight *n* vierzehn Tage *mpl*; **~ly** *adj, adv* vierzehntägig; alle 14 Tage.

fortress *n* (*mil*) Festung *f*; (*fig*) Bollwerk *n*.

fortuitous *adj* **~ly** *adv* zufällig.

fortunate *adj* glücklich; glückverheißend; **~ly** *adv* glücklicherweise; zum Glück.

fortune *n* Vermögen *n*; Reichtum *m*; (glücklicher) Zufall; Glück *n*; Schicksal *n*.

fortune-teller *n* Wahrsager(in) *m(f)*.

forty *adj* vierzig; * *n* Vierzig *f*.

forum *n* Forum *n*; Gericht *n*.

forward *adj* vorwärts; vorder (er, e, es); frühreif; fortschrittlich; vorlaut; vorschnell; bereitwillig; **~(s)** *adv* vor; nach

vorn; vorwärts; voraus; voran; * *vt* beschleunigen; fördern; schicken; (nach)senden.

forwardness *n* Frühreife *f*; vorlaute Art *f*; Voreiligkeit *f*.

fossil *adj* fossil; versteinert; (*col*) verknöchert; (*col*) vorsintflutlich; * *n* Fossil *n*; Versteinerung *f*.

foster *vt* aufziehen; in Pflege nehmen/geben; hegen; fördern.

foster child *n* Pflegekind *n*.

foster father *n* Pflegevater *m*.

foster mother *n* Pflegemutter *f*.

foul *adj* **~ly** *adv* stinkend; widerlich; schlecht; faul; schmutzig; in Kollision; abscheulich; unehrlich; unfair; **~ copy** *n* erster Entwurf *m*; * *vt* beschmutzen; verunreinigen; foulen; kollidieren mit.

foul play *n* Unsportlichkeit *f*; Gewaltverbrechen *n*; Mord *m*.

found *vt* fundar, establecer; edificar; fundir.

foundation *n* Fundament *n*; Grundlage *f*; Gründung *f*; Stiftung *f*; Grundierung *f*.

founder *n* Gründer *m*; Stifter *m*; Gießer *m*; * *vi* (*mar*) sinken, untergehen; (*fig*) scheitern.

foundling *n* Findling *m*; Findelkind *n*.

foundry *n* Gießerei *f*.

fount, fountain *n* Quelle *f*; Fontäne *f*; Springbrunnen *m*.

fountainhead *n* Quelle *f*.

four *adj* vier; * *n* Vier *f*; Vierer *m*.

fourfold *adj* vierfach.

four-poster (bed) *n* Himmelbett *n*.

foursome *n* Vierer *m*; Quartett *n*.

fourteen *adj* vierzehn; * *n* Vierzehn *f*.

fourteenth *adj* vierzehnt(er, e, es); vierzehntel; * *n* (*der, die, das*) Vierzehnte; Vierzehntel *n*.

fourth *adj* viert(er, e, es); viertel; * *n* (*der, die, das*) Vierte; Viertel *n*; Quart *f*; ~**ly** *adv* viertens.

fowl *n* Geflügel *n*; Federvieh *n*.

fox *n* Fuchs *m*.

foyer *n* Foyer *n*.

fracas *n* Aufruhr *m*; Tumult *m*.

fraction *n* Fraktion *f*; Bruch(-teil) *m*.

fracture *n* Bruch *m*; Fraktur *f*; * *vt* (zer)brechen.

fragile *adj* zerbrechlich; brüchig; gebrechlich.

fragility *n* Zerbrechlichkeit *f*; Brüchigkeit *f*; Gebrechlichkeit *f*.

fragment *n* Fragment *n*; Bruchstück *n*; Überrest *m*; Fetzen *m*.

fragmentary *adj* bruchstückhaft; fragmentarisch; zerstückelt.

fragrance *n* Duft *m*; Wohlgeruch *m*.

fragrant *adj* ~**ly** *adv* duftend; wohlriechend.

frail *adj* zerbrechlich; schwach; gebrechlich.

frailty *n* Zerbrechlichkeit *f*; Schwäche *f*; Gebrechlichkeit *f*.

frame *n* Rahmen *m*; Gestell *n*; Gerippe *n*; (Einzel)Bild *n*; Körperbau *m*; Frühbeetkasten *m*; System *n*; Verfassung *f*; * *vt* (ein)rahmen; formen; zusammensetzen; ersinnen; entwerfen.

frame of mind *n* Gemütsverfassung *f*.

framework *n* Gerüst *n*; Gebälk *n*; Gestell *n*; Gefüge *n*; Rahmen *m*.

franchise *n* Franchise *n*; Konzession *f*; Wahlrecht *n*; Bürgerrechte *pl*.

frank *adj* offen; aufrichtig; freimütig.

frankly *adv* frei heraus; offen gesagt.

frankness *n* Offenheit *f*; Freimütigkeit *f*.

frantic *adj* außer sich; verzwei-

felt; hektisch.

fraternal *adj*, ~**ly** *adv* brüderlich; Bruder-.

fraternity *n* Brüderlichkeit *f*; Zunft *f*; Bruderschaft *f*; Studentenverbindung *f*.

fraternize *vi* sich verbrüdern; fraternisieren.

fratricide *n* Brudermord *m*; Geschwistermord *m*.

fraud *n* Betrug *m*; Schwindel *m*; arglistige Täuschung *f*; (*col*) Schwindler.

fraudulence *n* Betrügerei *f*.

fraudulent *adj* ~**ly** *adv* betrügerisch; arglistig.

fraught *adj* voll; (*col*) besorgt.

fray *n* Schlägerei *f*; Streit *m*; (*mil*) Kampf *m*.

freak *n* Monstrosität *f*; Mißgeburt *f*; Laune *f*; (*sl*) Freak *m*; Fanatiker *m*.

freckle *n* Sommersprosse *f*; Fleckchen *n*.

freckled *adj* sommersprossig; gesprenkelt.

free *adj* ~**ly** *adv* frei; ohne; ungezwungen; freimütig; plumpvertraulich; freigiebig; reichlich; kostenlos; * *vt* befreien; freilassen; entlasten.

freedom *n* Freiheit *f*; Unabhängigkeit *f*.

free-for-all *n* allgemeine Diskussion *f*; Gerangel *n*.

free gift *n* Gratisprobe *f*.

freehold *n* Eigentumsrecht an Grundbesitz.

free kick *n* Freistoß *m*.

freelance *adj*, *adv* freiberuflich; freischaffend.

freemason *n* Freimaurer *m*.

freemasonry *n* Freimaurerei *f*.

freepost *n* Gebühr bezahlt Empfänger.

free-range *adj* freilaufend; Freiland-.

freethinker *n* Freigeist *m*.

freethinking *n* Freidenkerei *f*.

free trade *n* Freihandel *m*.

freewheel *vi* im Freilauf fahren.

free will *n* freier Wille *m*.

freeze *vi* (ge)frieren; erstarren; * *vt* zum Gefrieren bringen; einfrieren; erstarren lassen.

freeze-dried *adj* gefriergetrocknet.

freezer *n* Gefriergerät *f*; Gefrierfach *n*; Gefrierkammer *f*.

freezing *adj* eiskalt; Gefrier-.

freezing point *n* Gefrierpunkt *m*.

freight *n* Fracht *f*; Ladung *f*.

freighter *n* Frachter *m*; Transportflugzeug *n*.

freight train *n* Güterzug *m*.

French bean *n* Feuerbohne *f*; *pl* grüne Bohnen *pl*.

French fries *npl* Pommes frites *pl*.

French window *n* Terassentür *f*.

frenzied *adj* außer sich; rasend; hektisch.

frenzy *n* wilde Aufregung *f*; Ekstase *f*; Besessenheit *f*; Raserei *f*.

frequency *n* Frequenz *f*; Häufigkeit *f*.

frequent *adj* ~**ly** *adv* häufig; wiederholt; oft; * *vt* häufig besuchen; frequentieren.

fresco *n* Fresko *n*.

fresh *adj* ~**ly** *adv* frisch; neu; anders; (*fig*) grün; (*col*) frech; ~ **water** *n* Süßwasser.

freshen *vt*, *vi* ~ up frisch machen; erfrischen; auffrischen.

freshman *n* Erstsemester *n*; Neuling *m*.

freshness *n* Frische *f*; Neuheit *f*; Unerfahrenheit *f*.

freshwater *adj* Süßwasser-.

fret *vi* sich sorgen machen; sich ärgern; sich abscheuern.

friar *n* Mönch *m*; Bruder *m*.

friction *n* Reibung *f*; (*fig*) Reiberei *f*.

Friday *n* Freitag *m*; **Good ~** Karfreitag *m*.

friend *n* Freund(in) *m(f)*; Bekannte(r) *f(m)*.

friendless *adj* ohne Freunde.

friendliness *n* Freundlichkeit *f*; Wohlwollen *n*.

friendly *adj* freundlich; freundschaftlich; befreundet; wohlwollend.

friendship *n* Freundschaft *f*; Freundschaftlichkeit *f*.

frieze *n* Fries *m*; Zierstreifen *m*.

frigate *n* (*mar*) Fregatte *f*.

fright *n* Schreck(en) *m*; Entsetzen *n*.

frighten *vt* erschrecken; Angst einjagen.

frightened *adj* erschrocken; verängstigt.

frightening *adj* erschreckend; schreckenerregend.

frightful *adj* ~**ly** *adv* schrecklich; furchtbar.

frigid *adj* ~**ly** *adv* kalt; frostig; frigid; (*fig*) förmlich.

fringe *n* Franse *f*; Rand *m*; Ponyfrisur *f*.

fringe benefits *npl* Nebenleistungen *fpl*.

frisk *vt* wedeln mit; durchsuchen; (*col*) filzen.

frisky *adj* lebhaft; munter; ausgelassen.

fritter *vt*: **to ~ away** vertun; vertrödeln; vergeuden.

frivolity *n* Frivolität *f*; Leichtfertigkeit *f*.

frivolous *adj* frivol; leichtfertig.

frizz(le) *vt* kräuseln.

frizzy *adj* kraus; gekräuselt.

fro *adv*: **to go to and ~** auf und ab gehen.

frock *n* Kleid *n*; Kittel *m*; Kutte *f*; Gehrock *m*.

frog *n* Frosch *m*.

frolic *vi* herumtollen.

frolicsome *adj* ausgelassen; übermütig.

from *prep* von; aus; seit; von- aus.

front *n* Vorderseite *f*; Fassade *f*; Vorderteil *n*; Front *f*; Vordergrund *m*; Unverschämtheit *f*; * *adj* Front- ; Vorder-.

frontal *adj* frontal; Vorder-; Stirn-.

front door *n* Haustür *f*.

frontier n Grenze f; Grenzbereich m.

front page n Titelseite f.

front-wheel drive n (auto) Vorderradantrieb m.

frost n Frost m; Reif m; Frostigkeit f; * vt mit Reif überziehen; mattieren; mit Zuckerguß überziehen.

frostbite n Erfrierung f.

frostbitten adj erfroren.

frosted adj bereift; überfroren; matt; glasiert; mit Zuckerguß überzogen.

frosty adj frostig; eisig; mit Reif bedeckt.

froth n Schaum m; * vi schäumen.

frothy adj schaumig; schäumend; (fig) seicht.

frown vi die Stirn runzeln; * n Stirnrunzeln n; finsterer Blick m.

frozen adj (ein)gefroren; erfroren; Gefrier-; frostig.

frugal adj ~ly adv frugal; sparsam; bescheiden; einfach.

fruit n Obst n; Frucht f.

fruiterer n Obsthändler(in) m(f).

fruiterer's (shop) n Obsthändler m.

fruitful adj ~ly adv fruchtbar; (fig) erfolgreich.

fruitfulness n Fruchtbarkeit f.

fruition n Erfüllung f; Verwirklichung f.

fruit juice n Obstsaft m.

fruitless adj ~ly adv unfruchtbar; (fig) fruchtlos; (fig) erfolglos.

fruit salad n Obstsalat m.

fruit tree n Obstbaum m.

frustrate vt vereiteln; durchkreuzen; zunichte machen; hemmen; (be)hindern; frustrieren.

frustrated adj frustriert; vereitelt; gescheitert; .

frustration n Frustration f; Vereitelung f; Behinderung f; Enttäuschung f.

fry vt braten.

frying pan n Bratpfanne f.

fuchsia n (bot) Fuchsie f.

fudge n Fondant m; Weichkaramelle f.

fuel n Brennstoff m; (fig) Nahrung f.

fuel tank n Treibstofftank m.

fugitive adj flüchtig; * n Flüchtling m; Flüchtige(r) f(m).

fugue n (mus) Fuge f.

fulcrum n Drehpunkt m; (fig) Angelpunkt m.

fulfil vt erfüllen; vollbringen; abschließen.

fulfilment n Erfüllung f; Ausführung f; Abschluß m.

full adj voll; weit; rund; vollschlank; kräftig; vollständig; (fig) erfüllt; * adv völlig; ganz; direkt.

full-blown adj voll entwickelt; ausgemacht.

full-fledged adj flügge; (fig) richtig.

full-length adj lebensgroß; bodenlang; abendfüllend; ausgewachsen.

full moon n Vollmond m.

fullness n Fülle f.

full-scale adj in natürlicher Größe; großangelegt; umfassend.

full-time adj ganztägig; Ganztags-.

fully adv voll; völlig; ganz.

fulsome adj übermäßig.

fumble vi herumtasten; (herum)fummeln.

fume vi rauchen; dampfen; (fig) vor Wut schäumen; * ~s npl Dampf m; Dunst m; Rauch m.

fumigate vt ausräuchern.

fun n Spaß m.

function n Funktion f; Feier f; Veranstaltung f.

functional adj funktionell; funktionsfähig; praktisch; zweckbetont.

fund n Kapital n; Fonds m; (fig) Vorrat m; pl (Geld)Mittel pl; pl Staatsanleihen pl; * vt fundieren; finanzieren.

fundamental *adj* fundamental; grundlegend; grundsätzlich; Grund-; **~ly** *adv* im Grunde; im wesentlichen.

funeral *n* Beerdigung *f*; Bestattung *f*; Begräbnis *n*.

funeral service *n* Trauergottesdienst *m*.

funereal *adj* Begräbnis-; Trauer-; Leichen-.

fungus *n* Pilz *m*; Schwamm *m*; Fungus *m*.

funnel *n* Trichter *m*; Schornstein *m*.

funny *adj* komisch; lustig; sonderbar; merkwürdig.

fur *n* Fell *n*; Pelz *m*.

fur coat *n* Pelzmantel *m*.

furious *adj* **~ly** *adv* wütend; wild; heftig.

furlong *n* Achtelmeile *f*.

furlough *n* (*mil*) Urlaub *m*.

furnace *n* Ofen *m*; Kessel *m*; Feuerung *f*.

furnish *vt* versorgen; ausstatten; möblieren; liefern.

furnishings *npl* Einrichtung *f*; Mobiliar *n*; Zubehör *n*.

furniture *n* Möbel *pl*; Einrichtung *f*.

furrow *n* Furche *f*; Rille *f*; Rinne *f*; * *vt* pflügen; furchen; riefen; auskehlen.

furry *adj* pelzig; Pelz-.

further *adj* weiter(er, e, es); zusätzlich(er, e, es); * *adv* weiter; mehr; ferner; außerdem; * *vt* fördern; unterstützen.

further education *n* Fortbildung *f*.

furthermore *adv* ferner; überdies; außerdem.

furthest *adv* am weitesten; am meisten.

furtive *adj* **~ly** *adv* heimlich; verstohlen.

fury *n* Wut *f*; Wildheit *f*; Heftigkeit *f*; Furie *f*.

fuse *vt* einen Zünder anbringen; absichern; (*fig*) vereinigen; * *vi* durchbrennen; (*fig*) sich vereinigen; verschmelzen; * *n* Zünder *m*; Sicherung *f*.

fuse box *n* Sicherungskasten *m*.

fusion *n* Fusion *f*; Schmelzen *n*; Verschmelzung *f*; Vereinigung *f*.

fuss *n* Aufregung *f*; Ärger *m*; Wirbel *m*; Theater *n*.

fussy *adj* aufgeregt; pedantisch; wählerisch; überladen.

futile *adj* zwecklos; vergeblich; unbedeutend.

futility *n* Zwecklosigkeit *f*; Sinnlosigkeit *f*; Geringfügigkeit *f*.

future *adj* (zu)künftig; Zukunfts-; * *n* Zukunft *f*; Futur *n*.

fuzzy *adj* flaumig; kraus; verschwommen; benommen.

G

gab *n* (*col*) Gequassel *n*.

gabble *vi* schnattern; brabbeln; * *n* Geschnatter *n*; Gebrabbel *n*.

gable *n* Giebel *m*.

gadget *n* Apparat *m*; Gerät *n*.

gaffe *n* Fauxpas *m*.

gag *n* Knebel *m*; Gag *m*; * *vt* knebeln; * *vi* würgen.

gaiety *n* Fröhlichkeit *f*; Farbenpracht *f*.

gaily *adv* lustig; fröhlich; bunt.

gain *n* Gewinn *m*; Profit *m*; Vorteil *m*; Zunahme *f*; Verstärkung *f*; * *vt* verdienen; gewinnen; erreichen; erlangen; einbringen; zunehmen an.

gait *n* Gang *m*; Gangart *f*.

gala *n* Festlichkeit *f*; Galaveranstaltung *f*.

galaxy *n* Galaxie *f*.

gale *n* Sturm *m*.

gall *n* Galle *f*; Gallenblase *f*; (*col*) Frechheit *f*.

gallant *adj* tapfer; stattlich; galant; ritterlich; Liebes-.

gall bladder n Gallenblase f.
gallery n Gallerie f; Stollen m.
galley n Geleere f; Kombüse f;
Fahnenabzug m.
gallon n Gallone f.
gallop n Galopp m; * vi galoppieren.
gallows n Galgen m.
gallstone n Gallenstein m.
galore adv (col) in rauhen Mengen.
galvanize vt galvanisieren;
(feuer)verzinken; (col) elektrisieren.
gambit n Gambit n; (fig) Einleitung f.
gamble vi spielen; spekulieren;
* n Glücksspiel n; riskantes
Unternehmen n.
gambler n Spieler(in) m(f).
gambling n Spielen n.
game n Spiel n; Scherz m; Branche f; Wild n; Wildbret n; * vi
spielen.
gamekeeper n Wildhüter m.
gaming n Spielen n.
gammon n (schwachgeräucher-
ter) Schinken m.
gamut n (mus) Tonleiter f; Skala f.
gander n Gänserich m.
gang n (Arbeiter)Trupp m;
Gang f; Bande f; Clique f; Horde f.
gangrene n Wundbrand m;
Gangrän n.
gangster n Gangster m; Verbrecher m.
gangway n Fallreep n; Gangway f; Landungsbrücke f;
(Durch)Gang m; Laufbrett n.
gap n Lücke f; Loch n; Kluft f;
Spalte f.
gape vi den Mund aufreißen;
gaffen; klaffen; gähnen.
gaping adj gaffend; klaffend;
gähnend.
garage n Garage f; Reparatur-
werkstatt f.
garbage n Müll m; Abfall m.
garbage can n Mülleimer m.
garbage man n Müllmann m.
garbled adj durcheinander;

verstümmelt; (fig) unver-
ständlich.
garden n Garten m.
garden-hose n Gartenschlauch
m.
gardener n Gärtner(in) m(f).
gardening n Gärtnerei f; Gartenarbeit f.
gargle vi gurgeln.
gargoyle n Wasserspeier m.
garish adj aufdringlich; protzig; schreiend; grell.
garland n Girlande f; Kranz m;
(fig) Sammlung f.
garlic n Knoblauch m.
garment n Kleidungsstück n;
Gewand n.
garnish vt (aus)schmücken;
verzieren; garnieren; (law)
pfänden; * n Verzierung f;
Garnierung f; Ausschmük-
kung f.
garret n Dachgeschoß n; Mansarde f.
garrison n (mil) Garnison f;
* vt (mil) in Garnison legen.
garrote vt garottieren; erdrosseln.
garrulous adj geschwätzig;
redselig; weitschweifig.
garter n Strumpfband n; Sok-
kenhalter m; Strumpfhalter
m; Straps m.
gas n Gas n.
gas burner n Gasbrenner m.
gas cylinder n Gasflasche f.
gaseous adj gasförmig; Gas-.
gas fire n Gasofen m.
gash n klaffende Wunde f; tiefer Riß; Spalte f; * vt aufreißen; einschneiden.
gasket n Dichtungsmanschette
f.
gas mask n Gasmaske f.
gas meter n Gasuhr f.
gasoline n Gasäther m; Benzin
n.
gasp vi keuchen; nach Luft
schnappen; * n Keuchen n;
Laut des Erstaunens.
gas ring n Gasbrenner m.
gas station n Tankstelle f.
gassy adj gashaltig; gasartig.

gas tap *n* Gashahn *m*.
gastric *adj* gastrisch; Magen-.
gastronomic *adj* gastronomisch; feinschmeckerisch.
gasworks *npl* Gaswerk *n*.
gate *n* Tor *n*; Pforte *f*; Schranke *f*; Flugsteig *m*; Paß *m*.
gateway *n* Torweg *m*; Einfahrt *f*; (*fig*) Tor *n*.
gather *vt* (an)sammeln; versammeln; (zusammen)raffen; (*fig*) schließen; * *vi* sich versammeln; sich (an)sammeln.
gathering *n* Versammlung *f*; Zusammenkunft *f*; Sammeln *n*; Raffung *f*.
gauche *adj* linkisch; taktlos.
gaudy *adj* auffällig bunt; grell; protzig.
gauge *n* Eichmaß *n*; Meßgerät *n*; Lehre *f*; Stärke *f*; Kaliber *n*; Spurweite *f*; (*fig*) Maßstab *m*; * *vt* messen; prüfen; eichen; (*fig*) (ab)schätzen; (*fig*) beurteilen.
gaunt *adj* hager; ausgemergelt.
gauze *n* Gaze *f*; Verbandsmull *m*; Schleier *m*.
gay *adj* fröhlich; bunt; schwul.
gaze *vi* starren; * *n* (starrer) Blick *m*.
gazelle *n* Gazelle *f*.
gazette *n* Zeitung *f*; Amtsblatt *n*.
gazetteer *n* geographisches Lexikon *n*.
gear *n* Getriebe *n*; Gang *m*; Gerät *n*; Ausrüstung *f*; (*col*) Kleidung *f*; (*col*) Sachen *pl*.
gearbox *n* Getriebe *n*.
gear shift *n* Gangschaltung *f*.
gear wheel *n* Zahnrad *n*.
gel *n* Gel *n*.
gelatin(e) *n* Gelatine *f*; Gallerte *f*.
gelignite *n* Gelatinedynamit *n*.
gem *n* Edelstein *m*; Juwel *n*; (*fig*) Perle *f*.
Gemini *n* Zwillinge *pl*.
gender *n* Geschlecht *n*.
gene *n* Gen *n*.
genealogical *adj* genealogisch.

genealogy *n* Genealogie *f*; Ahnenforschung *f*; Abstammung *f*.
general *adj* allgemein; üblich; gesamt; ungefähr; General-; **in ~** im allgemeinen; **~ly** *adv* im allgemeinen; * *n* General *m*; Feldherr *m*; (*das*) Allgemeine *n*.
general election *n* Parlamentswahlen *pl*.
generality *n* allgemeine Redensart *f*; Allgemeinheit *f*.
generalization *n* Verallgemeinerung *f*.
generalize *vt* verallgemeinern; generalisieren.
generate *vt* erzeugen; hervorrufen; verursachen.
generation *n* Generation *f*; (Er)Zeugung *f*; Entstehung *f*.
generator *n* Generator *m*; Erzeuger *m*.
generic *adj* Gattungs-; allgemein.
generosity *n* Großzügigkeit *f*.
generous *adj* großzügig; reichlich; üppig.
genetics *npl* Genetik *f*.
genial *adj* freundlich; herzlich; anregend; mild.
genitals *npl* Genitalien *pl*; Geschlechtsteile *pl*.
genitive *n* Genitiv *m*.
genius *n* Genie *n*; Genialität *f*; Geist *m*.
genteel *adj* vornehm; elegant.
gentile *n* Nichtjude *m*; Nichtjüdin *f*; Heide *m*; Heidin *f*.
gentle *adj* **gently** *adv* sanft; gütig; mild; fromm; zart.
gentleman *n* Ehrenmann *m*; Herr *m*.
gentleness *n* Sanftheit *f*; Sanftmut *f*; Milde *f*; Güte *f*.
gentry *n* Oberschicht *f*; niederer Adel *m*.
gents *n* (*col*) Herrenklo *n*.
genuflexion *n* Kniebeuge *f*; Kniefall *m*.
genuine *adj* **~ly** *adv* echt; aufrichtig; natürlich; ernsthaft.
genus *n* Gattung *f*; Klasse *f*.

geographer *n* Geograph(in) *m(f)*.

geographical *adj* geographisch.

geography *n* Geographie *f*; Erdkunde *f*.

geological *adj* geologisch.

geologist *n* Geologe *m*; Geologin *f*.

geology *n* Geologie *f*.

geometric(al) *adj* geometrisch.

geometry *n* Geometrie *f*.

geranium *n* (*bot*) Geranie *f*; Storchschnabel *m*.

geriatric *adj* geriatrisch; Alters-; (*col*) uralt.

germ *n* Keim *m*; Mikrobe *f*; Krankheitserreger *m*.

germinate *vi* keimen.

gesticulate *vi* gestikulieren.

gesture *n* Geste *f*; Gebärde *f*.

get *vt* bekommen; erhalten; besorgen; erwischen; kriegen; holen; beschaffen; erreichen; lassen; veranlassen; (*col*) kapieren; * *vi* kommen; gelangen; werden; anfangen; **to ~ the better** die Oberhand gewinnen; besiegen.

geyser *n* Geysir *m*; Durchlauferhitzer *m*.

ghastly *adj* gräßlich; schrecklich; gespenstisch.

gherkin *n* Gewürzgurke *f*.

ghost *n* Gespenst *n*; Geist *m*; (*fig*) Schatten *m*.

ghostly *adj* geisterhaft; gespenstisch.

giant *n* Riese *m*; Koloß *m*; (*fig*) Gigant *m*.

gibberish *n* Geschnatter *n*; Quatsch *m*.

gibe *vi* spotten; * *n* höhnische Bemerkung *f*.

giblets *npl* Hühnerklein *n*; Gänseklein *n*.

giddiness *n* Schwindel *m*; (*fig*) Unbesonnenheit *f*.

giddy *adj* schwindlig; schwindelerregend; (*fig*) unbesonnen.

gift *n* Geschenk *n*; Spende *f*; Schenkung *f*; Gabe *f*; Talent *n*.

gifted *adj* begabt; talentiert.

gift voucher *n* Geschenkgutschein *m*.

gigantic *adj* gigantisch; riesig.

giggle *vi* kichern.

gild *vt* vergolden; (*fig*) beschönigen.

gilding, gilt *n* Vergoldung *f*; (*fig*) Beschönigung *f*.

gill *n* Kieme *f*; Lamelle *f*.

gilt-edged *adj* mit Goldschnitt; mündelsicher.

gimmick *n* Trick *m*; Masche *f*.

gin *n* Gin *m*; Wacholderschnaps *m*.

ginger *n* Ingwer *m*.

gingerbread *n* Lebkuchen *m*.

ginger-haired *adj* rothaarig.

gipsy *n* Zigeuner(in) *m(f)*.

giraffe *n* Giraffe *f*.

girder *n* Balken *m*; Träger *m*.

girdle *n* Gürtel *m*; Gurt *m*; Hüfthalter *m*.

girl *n* Mädchen *n*; (*col*) Tochter *f*.

girlfriend *n* Freundin *f*.

girlish *adj* mädchenhaft.

giro *n* Postscheckdienst *m*; (*col*) Postscheck *m*.

girth *n* Umfang *m*; Gurt *m*.

gist *n* (*das*) Wesentliche; Kern *m*.

give *vt* geben; schenken; hingeben; gewähren; von sich geben; angeben; bereiten; * *vi* (nach)geben; spenden; versagen; **to ~ away** weggeben; verschenken; verraten; **to ~ back** zurückgeben; **to ~ in** *vi* nachgeben; aufgeben; *vt* einreichen; **to ~ off** verbreiten; verströmen; **to ~ out** austeilen; **to ~ up** *vi* aufgeben; *vt* aufgeben; ausliefern.

gizzard *n* Muskelmagen *m*.

glacial *adj* eiszeitlich; eisig; Gletscher-.

glacier *n* Gletscher *m*.

glad *adj* froh; erfreut; **I am ~ to see** es freut mich zu sehen; **~ly** *adv* gern; mit Freuden.

gladden *vt* erfreuen; froh stimmen.

gladiator *n* Gladiator *m*.

glamorous *adj* bezaubernd.

glamour *n* Zauber *m*; Glanz *m*.

glance *n* (flüchtiger) Blick; * *vi* (flüchtig) blicken.

glancing *adj* streifend.

gland *n* Drüse *f*.

glare *n* greller Schein *m*; wütender Blick *m*; * *vi* grell leuchten; wütend starren; anfunkeln.

glaring *adj* grell; eklatant; (himmel)schreiend; wütend.

glass *n* Glas *n*; Spiegel *m*; **~es** *pl* Brille *f*; * *adj* Glas-.

glassware *n* Glaswaren *fpl*.

glassy *adj* gläsern; glasig; spiegelglatt.

glaze *vt* verglasen; glasieren; glasig machen.

glazier *n* Glaser *m*.

gleam *n* Schimmer *m*; * *vi* glänzen; leuchten; schimmern; funkeln.

gleaming *adj* glänzend; leuchtend; schimmernd; funkelnd.

glean *vt* nachlesen; (*fig*) zusammentragen; (*fig*) in Erfahrung bringen.

glee *n* (Schaden)Freude *f*; Ausgelassenheit *f*; Fröhlichkeit *f*.

glen *n* enges Tal *n*; Bergschlucht *f*.

glib *adj*, **~ly** *adv* schlagfertig; glatt.

glide *vi* gleiten; schweben; segelfliegen.

gliding *n* Gleiten *n*; Segelfliegen *n*.

glimmer *n* Schimmer *m*; Glimmer *m*; * *vi* glimmen; schimmern.

glimpse *n* flüchtiger Blick *m*; flüchtiger Eindruck *m*; (*fig*) Schimmer *m*; * *vt* einen flüchtigen Blick erhaschen von.

glint *vi* glitzern; glänzen.

glisten, glitter *vi* glitzern; glänzen.

gloat *vi* sich weiden; sich hämisch freuen.

global *adj* global; Welt-; umfassend.

globe *n* (Erd)Kugel *f*; Erde *f*;

Globus *m*.

gloom, gloominess *n* Düsterkeit *f*; (*fig*) gedrückte Stimmung *f*.

gloomy *adj* **~ily** *adv* düster; schwermütig; trübsinnig; hoffnungslos.

glorification *n* Verherrlichung *f*.

glorify *vt* verherrlichen; verklären; (*col*) aufmotzen.

glorious *adj* **~ly** *adv* ruhmreich; glorreich; herrlich; prächtig.

glory *n* Ruhm *m*; Ehre *f*; Stolz *m*; Herrlichkeit *f*; Pracht *f*.

gloss *n* Glanz *m*; Glosse *f*; Erläuterung *f*; * *vt* glossieren; glänzend machen; **to ~ over** beschönigen; vertuschen.

glossary *n* Glossar *n*.

glossy *adj* glänzend; Hochglanz-; (*fig*) raffiniert aufgemacht.

glove *n* Handschuh *m*.

glove compartment *n* Handschuhfach *n*.

glow *vi* glühen; leuchten; brennen; * *n* Glühen *n*; Glut *f*; Leuchten *n*; Röte *f*; Brennen *n*.

glower *vi* finster blicken.

glue *n* Leim *m*; Klebstoff *m*; * *vt* leimen, kleben.

gluey *adj* klebrig; zähflüssig.

glum *adj* bedrückt; niedergeschlagen.

glut *n* Übersättigung *f*; Überangebot *n*; Schwemme *f*.

glutinous *adj* klebrig.

glutton *n* Vielfraß *m*; Unersättliche(r) *f(m)*.

gluttony *n* Gefräßigkeit *f*; Unersättlichkeit *f*.

glycerine *n* Glycerin *n*.

gnarled *adj* knorrig.

gnash *vt*, *vi* (mit den Zähnen) knirschen.

gnat *n* (Stech)Mücke *f*.

gnaw *vt* nagen an; zernagen; zerfressen.

gnome *n* (Garten)Zwerg *m*; Gnom *m*.

go *vi* (fort)gehen; (ab)fahren; (ab)reisen; laufen; werden; umgehen; vergehen; passen; erlaubt sein; **to ~ ahead** vorangehen; Ernst machen; **to ~ away** fortgehen; **to ~ back** zurückgehen; **to ~ by** sich richten nach; urteilen nach; bekannt sein; **to ~ for** holen; machen; sich bemühen um; losgehen auf; **to ~ in** hineingehen; **to ~ off** fortgehen; losgehen; ausgehen; verderben; nicht mehr mögen; **to ~ on** weitergehen; weitermachen; vorgehen; angehen; unaufhörlich reden; **to ~ out** (hin)ausgehen; **to ~ up** hinaufgehen; steigen; hochgehen.

goad *n* Stachelstock *m*; *(fig)* Stachel *m*; Ansporn *m*; * *vt* antreiben; aufstacheln; anspornen.

go-ahead *adj* fortschrittlich; * *n (fig)* grünes Licht *n*; Initiative *f*.

goal *n* Ziel *n*; Tor *n*.

goalkeeper *n* Torhüter(in) *m(f)*.

goalpost *n* Torpfosten *m*.

goatherd *n* Ziegenhirt(in) *m(f)*.

gobble *vt* verschlingen.

go-between *n* Vermittler(in) *m(f)*; Kuppler(in) *m(f)*.

goblet *n* Kelchglas *n*; Pokal *m*.

goblin *n* Kobold *m*.

God *n* Gott *m*.

godchild *n* Patenkind *n*.

goddaughter *n* Patentochter *f*.

goddess *n* Göttin *f*.

godfather *n* Pate *m*; Patenonkel *m*.

godforsaken *adj* gottverlassen.

godhead *n* Gottheit *f*.

godless *adj* gottlos.

godlike *adj* gottähnlich; göttlich; erhaben.

godliness *n* Frömmigkeit *f*; Gottesfurcht *f*.

godly *adj* fromm; gottesfürchtig.

godmother *n* Patin *f*; Patentante *f*.

godsend *n* Geschenk des Himmels.

godson *n* Patensohn *m*.

goggle-eyed *adj* glotzäugig.

goggles *npl* Schutzbrille *f*.

going *n* (Weg)Gehen *n*; Abreise *f*; Tempo *n*.

gold *n* Gold *n*; Goldgelb *n*.

golden *adj* golden; Gold-; ~ **rule** *n* goldene Regel *f*.

goldfish *n* Goldfisch *m*.

gold-plated *adj* vergoldet.

goldsmith *n* Goldschmied(in) *m(f)*.

golf *n* Golf *n*.

golf ball *n* Golfball *m*.

golf club *n* club de golf *m*.

golf course *n* Golfplatz *m*.

golfer *n* Golfspieler(in) *m(f)*.

gondolier *n* Gondoliere *m*.

gone *adj* fort; weg; (weg)gegangen; verschwunden; tot; kaputt; vorbei.

gong *n* Gong *m*.

good *adj* gut; lieb; brav; richtig; recht; * *adv* gut; * *n* Vorteil *m*; Nutzen *m*; Wert *m*; *(das)* Gute *n*; Wohl *n*; **~s** *pl* Waren *fpl*; Güter *npl*; *(col)* Siebensachen *fpl*.

goodbye ! *excl* auf Wiedersehen! auf Wiederhören !

Good Friday *n* Karfreitag *m*.

goodies *npl* Süßigkeiten *fpl*.

good-looking *adj* gutaussehend.

good nature *n* Gutmütigkeit *f*; Freundlichkeit *f*.

good-natured *adj* gutmütig; freundlich.

goodness *n* Güte *f*; Anständigkeit *f*.

goodwill *n* Wohlwollen *n*; Bereitwilligkeit *f*; guter Wille *m*.

goose *n* Gans *f*.

gooseberry *n* Stachelbeere *f*; *(col)* Anstandswauwau *m*.

goosebumps *npl* Gänsehaut *f*.

goose-step *n* Stechschritt *m*.

gore *n* (geronnenes) Blut *n*; Keil *m*; * *vt* keilförmig zuschneiden; durchbohren; aufspießen.

gorge n Paß m; Schlucht f; Völlerei f; Schlund m; * vi schlemmen; sich vollstopfen.

gorgeous adj prächtig; großartig; wunderschön.

gorilla n Gorilla m.

gorse n Stechginster m.

gory adj blutbefleckt; blutig; (fig) blutrünstig.

goshawk n Hühnerhabicht m.

gospel n Evangelium n.

gossamer n Altweibersommer m; feine Gaze f.

gossip n Klatsch m; Schwatz m; * vi klatschen; schwatzen.

gothic adj gotisch; barbarisch; Schauer-.

gout n Gicht f.

govern vt regieren; beherrschen; leiten; verwalten; regeln; bestimmen.

governess n Gouvernante f; Erzieherin f.

government n Regierung f; Herrschaft f; Verwaltung f; Leitung f; Staat m.

governor n Gouverneur m; Direktor m; Leiter m; (col) Chef m.

gown n Kleid n; Toga f; Talar m; Robe f.

grab vt ergreifen; packen; schnappen; (fig) an sich reißen.

grace n Anmut f; Grazie f; Anstand m; Gunst f; Gnade f; Aufschub m; Tischgebet n; (mus) Verzierung f; **to say ~** das Tischgebet sprechen; * vt zieren; schmücken; ehren; auszeichnen.

graceful adj ~ly adv anmutig; graziös; würdevoll; taktvoll.

gracious adj ~ly adv gnädig; huldvoll; gütig.

gradation n Abstufung f.

grade n Grad m; (Güte)Klasse f; Rang m; Stufe f.

grade crossing n schienengleicher (Bahn)Übergang m.

gradient n Steigung f; Gefälle n; Gradient m.

gradual adj allmählich; stufen-

weise; graduell; ~ly adv nach und nach.

graduate vi graduieren; absolvieren; die Abschlußprüfung bestehen; aufsteigen; sich entwickeln; sich staffeln; allmählich übergehen.

graduation n Abstufung f; Staffelung f; Gradeinteilung f; Graduierung f; (fig) Aufstieg.

graffiti n Graffiti pl; Wandschmierereien pl.

graft n Pfropfreis n; Pfropfstelle f; Transplantat n; Transplantation f; Arbeit f; * vt pfropfen; okulieren; verpflanzen; transplantieren; (fig) aufpfropfen.

grain n Korn n; Getreide n; (fig) Spur f; Gran n; Maserung f; Strich m.

grammar n Grammatik f.

grammatical adj ~ly adv grammatisch.

gramme n Gramm n.

granary n Kornkammer f; Getreidespeicher m.

grand adj groß(artig); erhaben; grandios; vornehm; Haupt-; Gesamt-.

grandchild n Enkelkind n.

grandad n (col) Opa m.

granddaughter n Enkeltochter f; Enkelin f; **great ~** Urenkelin f.

grandeur n Größe f; Erhabenheit f; Vornehmheit f; Pracht f.

grandfather n Großvater m; **great ~** Urgroßvater m.

grandiose adj großartig; grandios; pompös; hochtrabend.

grandma n (col) Oma f.

grandmother n Großmutter f; **great ~** Urgroßmutter f.

grandparents npl Großeltern pl.

grand piano n (Konzert)Flügel m.

grandson n Enkelsohn m; Enkel m; **great ~** Urenkel m.

grandstand n Haupttribüne f.

granite n Granit m.

granny n Oma f.

grant vt gewähren; bewilligen; geben; erteilen; erfüllen; zugestehen; **to take for ~ed** für selbstverständlich halten; als gegeben ansehen; * n Bewilligung f; Erteilung f; Unterstützung f; Zuschuß m; Subvention f; Stipendium n.

granulate vt körnen; granulieren.

granule n Körnchen n.

grape n Weintraube f; Weinbeere f; **bunch of ~s** Weintraube f.

grapefruit n Grapefruit f; Pampelmuse f.

graph n graphische Darstellung f; Diagramm n; Kurve f.

graphic(al) adj **~ally** adv anschaulich; plastisch; graphisch; Schrift-.

graphics n Graphik f; graphische Darstellung f.

grapnel n (mar) Enterhaken m; Dregganker m.

grasp vt packen; (er)greifen; an sich reißen; (fig) begreifen; * n Griff m; Gewalt f; Auffassungsgabe f; Verständnis n.

grasping adj (fig) habgierig.

grass n Gras n; Rasen m; Weide f; (sl) Informant m; (sl) Petze f.

grasshopper n Grashüpfer m; Heuschrecke f.

grassland n Weide f; Grasland n.

grass-roots adj an der Basis.

grass snake n Ringelnatter f.

grassy adj grasbedeckt; Gras-.

grate n Gitter n; Rost m; * vt vergittern; reiben; raspeln; knirschen.

grateful adj **~ly** adv dankbar.

gratefulness n Dankbarkeit f.

gratification n Befriedigung f; Genugtuung f; Freude f; Genuß m.

gratify vt befriedigen; erfreuen.

gratifying adj erfreulich; befriedigend.

grating n Gitter(werk) n; Rost

m; * adj knirschend; quietschend; schrill; unangenehm.

gratis adv gratis; umsonst.

gratitude n Dankbarkeit f.

gratuitous adj **~ly** adv unentgeltlich; freiwillig; grundlos; unverdient.

gratuity n Gratifikation f; (Geld)Geschenk n; Trinkgeld n.

grave n Grab n; * adj **~ly** adv ernst; gewichtig; gesetzt; feierlich.

grave digger n Totengräber m.

gravel n Kies m; Schotter m; Geröll n.

gravestone n Grabstein m.

graveyard n Friedhof m.

gravitate vi (hin)neigen (zu); tendieren zu; hinstreben; angezogen werden; sich fortbewegen.

gravitation n Schwerkraft f; Gravitation f; Neigung f; Tendenz f.

gravity n Ernst m; Feierlichkeit f; Gesetztheit f; Schwere f; Gravitation f; Schwerkraft f.

gravy n Soße f; Bratensaft m.

graze vt abgrasen; (ab)weiden; streifen; (ab)schürfen; * vi grasen; weiden; streifen.

grease n Fett n; Schmalz n; Schmiere f; * vt (ein)fetten; (ab)schmieren.

greaseproof adj fettdicht.

greasy adj fettig; schmierig; ölig.

great adj groß; beträchtlich; lang; hoch; bedeutend; großartig; **~ly** adv sehr; höchst; außerordentlich.

greatcoat n Mantel m.

greatness n Größe f; Erhabenheit f; Bedeutung f.

greedily adv (hab)gierig.

greediness, greed n (Hab)Gier f; Gierigkeit f.

greedy adj (hab)gierig; gefräßig.

Greek n Griechisch n; Grieche m; Griechin f.

green *adj* grün; unreif; unerfahren; * *n* Grün *n*; Grünfläche *f*; ~s *pl* Blattgemüse *n*.

green belt *n* Grüngürtel *m*.

green card *n* grüne Versicherungskarte *f*.

greenery *n* Grün *n*; Laub *n*.

greengrocer *n* Obst- und Gemüsehändler *m*.

greenhouse *n* Gewächshaus *n*; Treibhaus *n*.

greenish *adj* grünlich.

greenness *n* Grün *n*; Unerfahrenheit *f*; Unreife *f*.

green room *n* Künstlerzimmer *n*.

greet *vt* (be)grüßen; empfangen.

greeting *n* Gruß *m*; Begrüßung *f*.

greeting(s) card *n* Glückwunschkarte *f*.

grenade *n* (*mil*) Granate *f*; Tränengaspatrone *f*.

grenadier *n* Grenadier *m*.

grey *adj* grau; ergraut; (*fig*) alt; * *n* Grau *n*.

grey-haired *adj* grauhaarig.

greyhound *n* Windhund *m*.

greyish *adj* gräulich.

greyness *n* Grau *n*; (*fig*) Trübheit *f*.

grid *n* Gitter *n*; Rost *m*; Netz *n*.

gridiron *n* Bratrost *m*; Gitter(werk) *n*; Netz(werk) *n*.

grief *n* Gram *m*; Kummer *m*.

grievance *n* Beschwerde *f*; (Grund zur) Klage *f*; Mißstand *m*; Groll *m*.

grieve *vt* betrüben; bekümmern; * *vi* bekümmert sein; sich grämen; trauern.

grievous *adj* ~ly *adv* schwer; schlimm; schmerzlich; bitter; bedauerlich.

griffin *n* Greif *m*.

grill *n* Grill *m*; Gegrilltes *n*; * *vt* grillen; (*col*) in die Mangel nehmen; (*col*) ausquetschen.

grille *n* Gitter *n*; (Kühler)Grill *m*.

grim *adj* grimmig; erbittert; verbissen; bitter; hart; grau-

sig; schlimm.

grimace *n* Grimasse *f*; Fratze *f*.

grime *n* Schmutz *m*; Ruß *m*.

grimy *adj* schmutzig; rußig.

grin *n* Grinsen *n*; * *vi* grinsen; feixen.

grind *vt* schleifen; wetzen; (zer)mahlen; zerreiben; schroten; knirschen; drehen; leiern; schinden.

grinder *n* (Scheren)Schleifer *m*; Schleifstein *m*; Schleifmaschine *f*; Mahlwerk *n*.

grip *n* Griff *m*; Halt *m*; (*fig*) Gewalt *f*; Greifer *m*; Griffigkeit *f*; Kulissenschieber *m*; * *vt* ergreifen; packen; fesseln.

gripping *adj* packend; fesselnd; spannend.

grisly *adj* gräßlich; schauerlich.

gristle *n* Knorpel *m*.

gristly *adj* knorpelig.

grit *n* (Streu)Sand *m*; Kies *m*; Grus *m*; (*fig*) Mut *m*; (Hafer)Schrot *m*.

groan *vi* (auf)stöhnen; ächzen; knarren; * *n* Stöhnen *n*; Ächzen *n*.

grocer *n* Lebensmittelhändler *m*.

groceries *npl* Lebensmittel *pl*.

grocer's (shop) *n* Lebensmittelgeschäft *m*.

groggy *adj* erschöpft; groggy; wacklig; taumelig.

groin *n* Leiste(ngegend) *f*.

groom *n* Pferdepfleger(in) *m(f)*; Stallbursche *m*; Bräutigam *m*; * *vt* pflegen; striegeln.

groove *n* Rille *f*; Furche *f*; Rinne *f*; Kerbe *f*; (*fig*) gewohntes Gleis *n*; (*fig*) alter Trott *m*.

grope *vt* tastend suchen; (*col*) befummeln; * *vi* tasten.

gross *adj* brutto; Gesamt-; schwer; grob; anstößig; unfein; dick; üppig; ~ly *adv* ungeheuerlich; äußerst.

grotesque *adj* grotesk.

grotto *n* Grotte *f*.

ground *n* Grund *m*; (Erd)Boden *m*; Erde *f*; Gebiet *n*; Gelände *f*; Grundbesitz *m*; Standort *m*; Stellung *f*; (*fig*) Standpunkt *m*; Grundlage *f*; Basis *f*; Ursache *f*; * *vt* niederlegen; auf Grund setzen; (*fig*) (be)gründen; stützen; einführen; grundieren; Startverbot erteilen; Hausarrest erteilen.

ground floor *n* Erdgeschoß *n*.

grounding *n* Unterbau *m*; Grundierung *f*; Stranden *n*; Einführung *f*; Grundkenntnisse *fpl*; Startverbot *n*.

groundless *adj* ~ly *adv* grundlos; unbegründet.

ground staff *n* Bodenpersonal *n*.

groundwork *n* Erdarbeit *f*; Fundament *n*; Grund *m*.

group *n* Gruppe *f*; Konzern *m*; * *vt* gruppieren.

grouse *n* Schottisches Moorhuhn *n*; Nörgelei *f*; * *vi* nörgeln; meckern.

grove *n* Wäldchen *n*; Hain *m*; Gehölz *n*.

grovel *vi* kriechen; schwelgen.

grow *vt* anbauen; anpflanzen; wachsen lassen; * *vi* wachsen; (*fig*) zunehmen; (*fig*) werden; ~ **up** aufwachsen; erwachsen werden.

grower *n* Züchter *m*; Anbauer *m*; -bauer *m*.

growing *adj* wachsend; Wachstums-.

growl *vi* knurren; grollen; * *n* Knurren *n*; Grollen *n*.

grown-up *n* Erwachsene(r) *f(m)*.

growth *n* Wachstum *n*; Wuchs *m*; Zuwachs *m*; Zunahme *f*; Trieb *m*; Anbau *m*; Gewächs *n*; Wucherung *f*.

grub *n* Made *f*; Larve *f*; (*sl*) Futter *n*.

grubby *adj* schmuddelig; madig.

grudge *n* Groll *m*; * *vt* mißgönnen; neiden; ungern geben; ungern tun.

grudgingly *adv* widerwillig; ungern; neidisch; mißgünstig.

gruelling *adj* mörderisch; zermürbend; aufreibend.

gruesome *adj* grausig; schauerlich.

gruff *adj* ~ly *adv* schroff; barsch; rauh.

gruffness *n* Schroffheit *f*; Barschheit *f*; Rauheit *f*.

grumble *vi* murren; knurren; grollen.

grumpy *adj* mürrisch; mißmutig; verdrießlich.

grunt *vi* grunzen; murren; ächzen; * *n* Grunzen *n*; Ächzen *n*.

G-string *n* (mus) G-Saite *f*; Tanga *m*.

guarantee *n* Garantie *f*; Bürgschaft *f*; Sicherheit *f*; Kaution *f*; Bürge *m*; Bürgin *f*; Kautionsnehmer(in) *m(f)*; * *vt* garantieren; (ver)bürgen für; sichern; schützen.

guard *n* Wache *f*; Wächter *m*; Wärter *m*; Bewachung *f*; Wachsamkeit *f*; Garde *f*; Schaffner *m*; Deckung *f*; Schutzvorrichtung *f*; Vorsichtsmaßnahme *f*; * *vt* bewachen; (be)schützen; (be)hüten; sichern.

guarded *adj* bewacht; vorsichtig; zurückhaltend.

guardroom *n* (mil) Wachlokal *n*.

guardian *n* Hüter *m*; Wächter *m*; Vormund *m*.

guardianship *n* Vormundschaft *f*; (*fig*) Obhut *f*.

guerrilla *n* Guerilla *f*.

guerrilla warfare *n* Guerillakrieg *m*.

guess *vt* (ab)schätzen; erraten; ahnen; vermuten; denken; annehmen; * *vi* schätzen; raten; * *n* Schätzung *f*; Vermutung *f*; Annahme *f*.

guesswork *n* Vermutungen *pl*; Raterei *f*.

guest *n* Gast *m*.

guest room *n* Gästezimmer *n*.

guffaw *n* schallendes Gelächter *n*.

guidance *n* (An)Leitung *f*; Führung *f*; Beratung *f*.

guide vt (an)leiten; führen; bestimmen; beraten; * n Führer(in) m(f); Leitfaden m; Handbuch n; Richtschnur f; Anhaltspunkt m; Wegweiser m; Führung f.

guidebook n Führer m.

guide dog n Blindenhund m.

guidelines npl Richtlinien fpl.

guild n Gilde f; Zunft f; Innung f; Vereinigung f.

guile n (Arg)List f; Tücke f.

guillotine n Guillotine f; Fallbeil n; Papierschneidemaschine f; * vt durch die Guillotine hinrichten; die Debatte befristen.

guilt n Schuld f.

guiltless adj schuldlos; unschuldig.

guilty adj schuldig; schuldbewußt.

guinea pig n Meerschweinchen n; (fig) Versuchskaninchen n.

guise n Aufmachung f; Gestalt f; (fig) Maske f; (fig) (Deck)Mantel m; (fig) Vorwand m.

guitar n Gitarre f.

gulf n Golf m; Bucht f; Abgrund m; (fig) Kluft f.

gull n Möwe f.

gullet n Schlund m; Gurgel f; Speiseröhre f.

gullibility n Leichtgläubigkeit f.

gullible adj leichtgläubig.

gully n tief eingeschnittener Wasserlauf m; Gully m; Sinkkasten m; Abzugskanal m.

gulp n Schluck m; * vi schlingen; hastig trinken; schlukken; * vt hinunterstürzen; hinunterschlingen.

gum n Zahnfleisch n; Gummi m; Klebstoff m; Gummierung f; Kaugummi m; Gummibonbon m; * vt gummieren; kleben.

gum tree n Eukalyptus m; Gummibaum m.

gun n Geschütz n; Kanone f; Feuerwaffe f; Gewehr n; Pisto-

le f; Revolver m; Spritze f.

gunboat n Kanonenboot n.

gun carriage n Lafette f.

gunfire n Geschützfeuer n.

gunman n Revolverheld m; Bewaffnete(r) f(m).

gunmetal n Rotguß m; Geschützlegierung f.

gunner n Kanonier m; Artillerist m; Bordschütze m.

gunnery n Geschützwesen n.

gunpoint n: **at ~** mit vorgehaltener Waffe; mit Waffengewalt.

gunpowder n Schießpulver n.

gunshot n Schuß m; Schußweite f.

gunsmith n Büchsenmacher m.

gurgle vi gurgeln; gluckern; glucksen.

guru n Guru m.

gush vi strömen; sich ergießen; schießen; (col) schwärmen; * n Schwall m; Strom m; Erguß m.

gushing adj (über)strömend; (col) schwärmerisch.

gusset n Zwickel m.

gust n Bö f; Windstoß m; Ausbruch m; Sturm m.

gusto n Begeisterung f; Genuß m.

gusty adj böig; stürmisch; (fig) ungestüm.

gut n Darm m; **~s** npl Eingeweide pl; Gedärme pl; Bauch m; (col) Schneid m; * vt ausweiden; ausräumen; ausbrennen; plündern.

gutter n Rinnstein m; Gosse f; (Dach)Rinne f.

guttural adj gutural; kehlig; heiser.

guy n Kerl m; Typ m.

guzzle vt saufen; fressen.

gym(nasium) n Turnhalle f.

gymnast n Turner(in) m(f).

gymnastic adj turnerisch; gymnastisch; **~s** npl Turnen n; Gymnastik f.

gynaecologist n Gynäkologe m; Gynäkologin f; Frauenarzt m; Frauenärztin f.

gyrate vi kreisen; sich drehen.

H

haberdasher n Kurzwaren-
händler m.
haberdashery n Kurzwaren-
geschäft n; Kurzwaren fpl.
habit n (An)Gewohnheit f;
Sucht f; (bot) Habitus m;
(Ordens)Kleidung f; Tracht f.
habitable adj bewohnbar.
habitat n Habitat n.
habitual adj ~ly adv gewohn-
heitsmäßig; gewohnt; ständig.
hack n Hieb m; Kerbe f; Tritt
m; Reitpferd n; Mietpferd n;
Ausritt m; (col) Schreiberling
m; * vt ausreiten; abnutzen;
(zer)hacken; gegen das
Schienbein treten; ausstehen.
hackneyed adj abgedroschen;
abgenutzt.
haddock n Schellfisch m.
haemorrhage n Blutung f.
haemorrhoids npl Hämorrhoiden pl.
hag n häßliches altes Weib f;
Hexe f.
haggard adj abgezehrt; hager;
abgehärmt; abgespannt.
haggle vi feilschen; handeln;
schachern.
hail n Hagel m; Gruß m; Ruf m;
* vt (be)grüßen; zujubeln; her-
beiwinken; * vi hageln; sich
melden; stammen; kommen.
hailstone n Hagelkorn n.
hair n Haar n; Haare pl.
hairbrush n Haarbürste f;
Haarpinsel m.
haircut n Haarschnitt m; Frisur f.
hairdresser n Friseur m; Friseuse f.
hairdrier n Fön m; Haartrock-
ner m.
hairless adj haarlos; unbe-
haart; kahl.
hairnet n Haarnetz n.
hairpin n Haarnadel f.

hairpin bend n Haarnadelkur-
ve f; Serpentine f.
hair remover n Enthaarungs-
mittel n.
hairspray n Haarspray n.
hairstyle n Frisur f.
hairy adj haarig; behaart;
Haar-; gefährlich.
hale adj gesund; kräftig; rüstig.
half n Hälfte f; Halbzeit f; * adj
halb.
half-caste adj Halbblut-.
half-hearted adj halbherzig.
half-hour n halbe Stunde f.
half-moon n Halbmond m.
half-price adj zum halben
Preis.
half-time n Halbzeit f.
halfway adv halbwegs; auf halbem Weg; bis zur Hälfte.
hall n Halle f; Saal m; Flur m;
Diele f.
hallmark n Feingehaltsstem-
pel m; (fig) Stempel m.
hallow vt heiligen; weihen.
hallucination n Halluzination
f.
halo n Heiligenschein m; Ring
m; Hof m.
halt vi anhalten; zum Stillstand
kommen; * n Halt m; Rast f;
Aufenthalt m; Stillstand m;
Haltestelle f.
halve vt halbieren.
ham n Schinken m; Hinterkeule
f; Oberschenkel m; (col) Funk-
amateur m.
hamburger n Hamburger m.
hamlet n Weiler m; Dörfchen n.
hammer n Hammer m; * vt
hämmern.
hammock n Hängematte f.
hamper n (Geschenk)Korb m;
* vt (be)hindern; stören.
hamstring vt Kniesehne f.
hand n Hand f; Seite f; Arbeiter m; (Fach)Mann m; Handschrift f; Unterschrift f; Applaus m; Zeiger m; Handbreit
f; Blatt n; at ~ nahe; in Reichweite; zur Hand; * vt aushändigen; (über)geben; (über)rei-
chen.

handbag n Handtasche f.
handbell n Handglocke f.
handbook n Handbuch n.
handbrake n Handbremse f.
handcuff n Handschelle f.
handful n Handvoll f; (col) Plage f.
handicap n Handikap n; Behinderung f; Nachteil m.
handicapped adj behindert; benachteiligt.
handicraft n (Kunst)Handwerk n; Handfertigkeit f.
handiwork n Handarbeit f; Werk n.
handkerchief n Taschentuch n.
handle n (Hand)Griff m; Stiel m; Henkel m; Klinke f; Kurbel f; (fig) Handhabe f; * vt anfassen; berühren; handhaben; umgehen mit; behandeln; erledigen; fertigwerden mit; betreuen; dressieren.
handlebars npl Lenkstange f.
handling n Berührung f; Handhabung f; Durchführung f; Behandlung f.
handrail n Handlauf m.
handshake n Händedruck m.
handsome adj ~ly adv hübsch; stattlich; gutaussehend; ansehnlich; nobel.
handwriting n Handschrift f.
handy adj zur Hand; greifbar; geschickt; handlich; praktisch; nützlich.
hang vt (auf)hängen; hängenlassen; behängen; * vi hängen; baumeln.
hanger n (Auf)Hänger m; Kleiderbügel m.
hanger-on n Anhang m; Klette f.
hangings npl Wandbehang m.
hangman n Henker m.
hangover n (col) Kater m.
hang-up n Komplex m.
hanker vi sich sehnen.
haphazard adj willkürlich; planlos.
hapless adj unglücklich; unselig.

happen vi (zufällig) geschehen; passieren; vor sich gehen; zufällig ergeben.
happening n Ereignis n; Vorkommnis n; Happening n.
happily adv glücklich; glücklicherweise.
happiness n Glück n; Glückseligkeit f.
happy adj glücklich; froh; erfreut; erfreulich; zufrieden; (col) begeistert; (col) verrückt; (col) süchtig.
harangue n Ansprache f; (flammende) Rede f; Tirade f; Strafpredigt f; * vt eine Strafpredigt halten.
harass vt belästigen; schikanieren; stören; aufreiben.
harbinger n Vorläufer m; Vorbote m.
harbour n Hafen m; Zufluchtsort m; * vt beherbergen; Zuflucht gewähren; hegen.
hard adj hart; fest; schwer; schwierig; zäh; streng; heftig; ~ of hearing schwerhörig; ~ by ganz in der Nähe; nahe bei.
harden vt (ab)härten; hart machen; verhärten; abstumpfen; * vi hart werden; erhärten; sich verhärten; abstumpfen; sich abhärten.
hard-headed adj nüchtern; realistisch; praktisch.
hard-hearted adj hartherzig.
hardiness n Zähigkeit f; Robustheit f; Winterfestigkeit f; Kühnheit f.
hardly adv kaum; hart; streng.
hardness n Härte f; Schwierigkeit f; Nüchternheit f.
hardship n Not f; Elend n; Härte f.
hard-up adj in (Geld)Schwierigkeiten; in Verlegenheit.
hardware n Eisenwaren pl; Haushaltswaren pl; Hardware f.
hardwearing adj strapazierfähig.

hardy *adj* zäh; robust; abgehärtet; winterfest; kühn.
hare *n* Hase *m*.
hare-brained *adj* verrückt.
hare-lipped *adj* hasenschartig.
haricot *n* Gartenbohne *f*.
harlequin *n* Harlekin *m*; Hanswurst *m*.
harm *n* Schaden *m*; Unrecht *m*; Übel *n*; * *vt* schaden; verletzen.
harmful *adj* nachteilig; schädlich.
harmless *adj* harmlos.
harmonic *adj* harmonisch.
harmonious *adj* ~**ly** *adv* harmonisch; wohlklingend; einträchtig.
harmonize *vt* harmonisieren; angleichen; in Einklang bringen.
harmony *n* Harmonie *f*; Akkord *m*; Wohlklang *m*; Einklang *m*.
harness *n* Geschirr *n*; Gurt *m*; Harnisch *m*; * *vt* anschirren; anspannen; nutzbar machen.
harp *n* Harfe *f*.
harpist *n* Harfenist(in) *m(f)*.
harpoon *n* Harpune *f*.
harpsichord *n* Cembalo *n*.
harrow *n* Egge *f*; * *vt* eggen; (*fig*) quälen; peinigen.
harry *vt* verwüsten; plündern.
harsh *adj* ~**ly** *adv* hart; rauh; grell; barsch; schroff; streng.
harshness *n* Härte *f*.
harvest *n* Ernte *f*; (*fig*) Früchte *pl*; * *vt* ernten; einbringen.
harvester *n* Erntearbeiter(in) *m(f)*; Mähmaschine *f*.
hash *n* Haschee *n*; (*fig*) Wiederholung *f*, Aufguß *m*; (*fig*) Durcheinander *n*.
hassock *n* Betkissen *n*; Grasbüschel *n*.
haste *n* Hast *f*; Eile *f*; **to be in** ~ in Eile sein.
hasten *vt* antreiben; beschleunigen; * *vi* (sich be)eilen.
hastily *adv* = hasty.
hastiness *n* Eile *f*; Voreiligkeit *f*.

hasty *adj* hastig; (vor)eilig; übereilt.
hat *n* Hut *m*.
hatbox *n* Hutschachtel *f*.
hatch *vt* ausbrüten; * *n* Brut *f*; Luke *f*; Durchreiche *f*.
hatchback *n* (*auto*) (Wagen mit) Hecktür *f*.
hatchet *n* Beil *n*.
hatchway *n* (*mar*) Luke *f*.
hate *n* Haß *m*; Abscheu *f*; * *vt* hassen, verabscheuen; sehr ungern tun; sehr bedauern.
hateful *adj* hassenswert; abscheulich.
hatred *n* Haß *m*; Abscheu *f*.
hatter *n* Hutmacher *m*.
haughtily *adv* = haughty.
haughtiness *n* Hochmut *m*; Arroganz *f*.
haughty *adj* hochmütig; überheblich; arrogant.
haul *vt* ziehen; zerren; schleppen; (be)fördern; (mit einem Netz) fangen; * *n* (Fisch)Zug *m*; Fang *m*; Beute *f*; Transportweg *m*.
haulier *n* Transportunternehmer *m*.
haunch *n* Hüfte *f*; *pl* Gesäß *n*, Hinterbacken *pl*; Keule *f*.
haunt *vt* spuken in; verfolgen; heimsuchen; häufig besuchen; * *n* häufig besuchter Ort *m*; Lieblingsplatz *m*; Schlupfwinkel *m*.
have *vt* haben; besitzen; bekommen; sagen; (*col*) reinlegen; dulden; müssen; lassen.
haven *n* (*fig*) (sicherer) Hafen *m*; Zufluchtsort *m*.
haversack *n* Provianttasche *f*.
havoc *n* Verwüstung *f*; Zerstörung *f*; Chaos *n*.
hawk *n* Falke *m*; Habicht *m*; Mörtelbrett *n*; * *vi* Beizjagd betreiben; hausieren; sich räuspern.
hawthorn *n* Weißdorn *m*.
hay *n* Heu *n*.
hay fever *n* Heuschnupfen *m*.
hayloft *n* Heuboden *m*.

hayrick, haystack n Heumiete f; Heuhaufen m.

hazard n Gefahr f; Risiko m; Zufall m; * vt riskieren; wagen.

hazardous adj gewagt; gefährlich; riskant; unsicher.

haze n Dunst(schleier) m; (fig) Nebel m, Schleier m.

hazel n Haselnuß f; Nußbraun n; * adj nußbraun.

hazelnut n Haselnuß f.

hazy adj dunstig; diesig; verschwommen; nebelhaft.

he pn er.

head n Kopf m; Haupt n; Spitze f; Vorstand m; Chef m; Stück n; Quelle f; Schaumkrone f; Überschrift f; Rubrik f; * vt (an)führen; leiten; betiteln; die Spitze bilden von; köpfen; **to ~ for** lossteuern auf; Kurs halten auf; sich bewegen auf... zu.

headache n Kopfschmerzen pl; (col) Problem n.

headdress n Kopfschmuck m; Frisur f.

headland n Rain m; Landzunge f.

headlight n Scheinwerfer m.

headline n Schlagzeile f; Überschrift f.

headlong adv kopfüber; (fig) Hals über Kopf.

headmaster n Direktor m; Rektor m.

head office n Hauptgeschäftsstelle f; Zentrale f.

headphones npl Kopfhörer m.

headquarters npl (mil) Hauptquartier n; (mil) Oberkommando n; Präsidium n; Zentrale f.

headroom n lichte Höhe f.

headstrong adj eigensinnig; halsstarrig.

headwaiter n Oberkellner m.

headway n Fahrt f; (fig) Fortschritt m.

heady adj berauschend; berauscht; unbesonnen.

heal vt heilen; kurieren; (fig)

versöhnen; * vi heilen; gesund werden.

health n Gesundheit f.

healthiness n Gesundheit f.

healthy adj gesund; heilsam; kräftig.

heap n Haufen m; Menge f; Halde f; * vt (über)häufen; beladen.

hear vt (an)hören; erhören; (law) verhören; (law) verhandeln; * vi hören; erfahren.

hearing n Gehör n; Hören n; Anhörung f; (law) Vernehmung f; (law) Verhandlung f.

hearing aid n Hörgerät n.

hearsay n Hörensagen n.

hearse n Leichenwagen m.

heart n Herz n; Kern m; Mut m; Zustand m; **by ~** auswendig; **with all my ~** von ganzem Herzen.

heart attack n Herzanfall m; Herzinfarkt m.

heartbreaking adj herzzerreißend.

heartburn n Sodbrennen n.

heart failure n Herzversagen n.

heartfelt adj tiefempfunden; herzlich; aufrichtig.

hearth n Herd m; Feuerstelle f; Kamin m.

heartily adv herzlich; gründlich; herzhaft.

heartiness n Herzlichkeit f; Herzhaftigkeit f.

heartless adj ~ly adv herzlos; grausam.

hearty adj herzlich; aufrichtig; gründlich; munter; herzhaft; kräftig; fruchtbar.

heat n Hitze f; Wärme f; Eifer m; (sport) Lauf m; (zool) Brunst f, Läufigkeit f, Rossen n; * vt erhitzen; aufwärmen; heizen.

heater n Heizgerät n; Heizkörper m.

heathen n Heide m; Heidin f; ~ish adj heidnisch.

heather n (bot) Heidekraut n; Erika f.

heating n Heizung f; Erwärmung f; Erhitzung f.

heatwave n Hitzewelle f.

heave vt (hoch)heben; wuchten; hieven; ausstoßen; * vi Heben n; Ruck m; Wogen n; Verwerfung f.

heaven n Himmel m.

heavenly adj himmlisch; Himmels-; herrlich.

heavily adv schwer.

heaviness n Schwere f; Gewicht n; Schwerfälligkeit f; Schwermut f.

heavy adj schwer; heftig; stark; groß; drückend; schwierig; hart; schwerfällig.

Hebrew n Hebräer(in) m(f); Israelit(in) m(f); Hebräisch n.

heckle vt (Flachs) hecheln; (fig) piesacken, zusetzen; (fig) durch Zwischenrufe aus dem Konzept bringen.

hectic adj hektisch.

hedge n Hecke f; (fig) Mauer f; * vt eine Hecke pflanzen; mit einer Hecke umgeben; (fig) einengen; (fig) abgrenzen; (ab)sichern.

hedgehog n Igel m.

heed vt beachten; Beachtung schenken; * n Beachtung f.

heedless adj ~ly adv unachtsam.

heel n Ferse f; Absatz m; Kante f; to take to one's ~s die Beine in die Hand nehmen.

hefty adj schwer; kräftig; (col) gewaltig; (col) stattlich.

heifer n Färse f.

height n Höhe f; Größe f; Höhepunkt m; Anhöhe f.

heighten vt erhöhen; (fig) vergrößern, steigern; hervorheben.

heinous adj abscheulich.

heir n Erbe m; ~ apparent rechtmäßiger Erbe m.

heiress n Erbin f.

heirloom n Erbstück n.

helicopter n Hubschrauber m.

hell n Hölle f; (col) Spaß m.

hellish adj höllisch; verteufelt.

helm n (mar) Helm m; Ruder n.

helmet n Helm m.

help vt helfen; nachhelfen; abhelfen; reichen; * vi helfen; **I cannot ~ it** ich kann nichts dafür; ich kann es nicht ändern; * n Hilfe f; Abhilfe f; (Haus)Angestellte(r) f(m); (Dienst)Personal n.

helper n Helfer(in) m(f).

helpful adj hilfsbereit; hilfreich.

helping n Portion f; Hilfe f.

helpless adj, ~ly adv hilflos; unbeholfen.

helter-skelter adv holterdiepolter.

hem n Saum m; Rand m; * vt säumen.

he-man n (sl) richtiger Mann m.

hemisphere n Hemisphäre f; Halbkugel f.

hemp n Hanf m.

hen n Henne f; Huhn f; Weibchen n.

henchman n Gefolgsmann m; (contp) Handlanger m.

henceforth, henceforward adv von nun an; fortan; künftig.

hen-house n Hühnerstall m.

hepatitis n Hepatitis f; Leberentzündung f.

her pn sie; ihr, ihre.

herald n Herold m; (fig) Verkünder m; (fig) Vorbote m.

heraldry n Heraldik f; Wappenkunde f.

herb n Kraut n; ~s pl Kräuter pl.

herbaceous adj krautig.

herbalist n Pflanzenkenner(in) m(f); Kräuterhändler(in) m(f); Kräuterheilkundige(r) f(m).

herbivorous adj pflanzenfressend.

herd n Herde f; Rudel n; Hirt(in) m(f).

here adv hier; hierher.

hereabout(s) adv in dieser Gegend.

hereafter adv künftig; in Zukunft.

hereby adv hiermit; dadurch.

hereditary adj erblich; vererbt; Erb-.

heredity n Erblichkeit f; Erbmasse f.

heresy n Häresie f; Ketzerei f.

heretic n Häretiker(in) m(f); Ketzer(in) m(f); * adj häretisch; ketzerisch.

herewith adv hiermit.

heritage n Erbe n.

hermetic adj ~ally adv hermetisch; (luft)dicht; alchimistisch.

hermit n Einsiedler m; Eremit m.

hermitage n Einsiedelei f; Einsiedlertum n.

hernia n (Leisten)Bruch m.

hero n Held m; Heros m; Halbgott m.

heroic adj ~ally adv heroisch; heldenhaft; Helden-; grandios.

heroine n Heldin f; Halbgöttin f.

heroism n Heldentum n.

heron n Reiher m.

herring n Hering m.

hers pn ihr; (der, die, das) ihrige.

herself pn sie selbst; ihr selbst; sich (selbst).

hesitant adj zögernd; unschlüssig; stockend.

hesitate vi zögern; unschlüssig sein; stocken.

hesitation n Zögern n; Unschlüssigkeit f; Stocken n.

heterogeneous adj heterogen; ungleichartig.

heterosexual adj heterosexuell; * n Heterosexuelle(r) f(m).

hew vt (be)hauen; hacken; fällen.

heyday n Höhepunkt m; Blüte(zeit) f.

hi excl hallo!

hiatus n (gr) Hiatus m; Lücke f.

hibernate vi überwintern; Winterschlaf halten.

hiccup n Schluckauf m; (col) kleines Problem n; * vi den Schluckauf haben.

hickory n Hickory m.

hide vt verbergen; verstecken; verheimlichen; abhäuten; (col) verprügeln; * n Haut f; Fell n.

hideaway n Versteck n; Zufluchtsort m.

hideous adj ~ly adv scheußlich; gräßlich.

hiding-place n Versteck n.

hierarchy n Hierarchie f; Rangordnung f.

hieroglyphic adj hieroglyphisch; unleserlich; * n Hieroglyphe f.

hi-fi n Stereoanlage f.

higgledy-piggledy adv drunter und drüber.

high adj hoch; Hoch-; erhaben; high.

high altar n Hochaltar m.

highchair n Hochstuhl m.

high-handed adj anmaßend; selbstherrlich.

highlands npl Hochland n.

highlight n Schlaglicht n; Höhepunkt m; Strähne f.

highly adj hoch; höchst; äußerst; lobend; teuer.

highness n Höhe f; Erhabenheit f; Hoheit f.

high school n High-School f.

high-strung adj reizbar; nervös.

high water n Hochwasser n.

highway n Haupt(verkehrs)straße f.

hijack vt entführen; überfallen.

hijacker n (Flugzeug)Entführer m; Räuber m.

hike vi wandern; marschieren.

hilarious adj lustig; vergnügt.

hill n Hügel m; Anhöhe f; Haufen m.

hillock n kleiner Hügel m.

hillside n (Berg)Hang m.

hilly adj hügelig.

hilt n Heft n; Griff m.

him pn ihn; ihm.

himself pn sich (selbst); selbst.

hind adj Hinter-; * n Hirschkuh f.

hinder *vt* aufhalten; (be)hindern; abhalten.

hindrance *n* Behinderung *f*; Hindernis *n*.

hindmost *adj* hinterst(er, e, es); letzt(er, e, es).

hindquarter *n* Hinterviertel *n*; Hinterhand *f*; Hinterteil *n*.

hindsight *n*: **with ~** rückblickkend.

hinge *n* Scharnier *n*; Angel *f*; (*fig*) Angelpunkt *m*.

hint *n* Wink *m*; Andeutung *f*; Hinweis *m*; Tip *m*; Anspielung *f*; (*fig*) Spur *f*; * *vt* andeuten.

hip *n* Hüfte *f*; Hagebutte *f*.

hippopotamus *n* Flußpferd *n*.

hire *vt* (ver)mieten; einstellen; (an)heuern; engagieren; * *n* Miete *f*; Lohn *m*.

his *pn* sein; seine; (*der, die, das*) seine.

Hispanic *adj* spanisch.

hiss *vt, vi* zischen.

historian *n* Historiker(in) *m(f)*; Geschichtswissenschaftler(in) *m(f)*.

historic(al) *adj* **~ally** *adv* historisch; geschichtlich.

history *n* Geschichte *f*; Werdegang *m*; Vorgeschichte *f*.

histrionic *adj* schauspielerisch; (contp) theatralisch.

hit *vt* schlagen; treffen; anfahren; rammen; stoßen (auf); finden; * *n* Schlag *m*; Hieb *m*; Treffer *m*; Hit *m*; Schuß *m*; Mord *m*.

hitch *vt* ziehen; rücken; befestigen; ankoppeln; per Anhalter fahren; * *n* Knoten *m*; Problem *n*; Haken *m*; Ruck *m*.

hitch-hike *vi* per Anhalter fahren; trampen.

hitherto *adv* bisher; bis jetzt.

hive *n* Bienenstock *m*; Bienenschwarm *n*.

hoard *n* Hort *m*; Schatz *m*; Vorrat *m*; * *vt* horten; hamstern.

hoar-frost *n* (Rauh)Reif *m*.

hoarse *adj* **~ly** *adv* heiser.

hoarseness *n* Heiserkeit *f*.

hoax *n* (Zeitungs)Ente *f*;

Schwindel *m*; Streich *m*; * *vt* einen Bären aufbinden.

hobble *vi* hinken; humpeln.

hobby *n* Steckenpferd *n*; Hobby *n*; Liebhaberei *f*.

hobbyhorse *n* Steckenpferd *n*; Schaukelpferd *n*.

hobo *n* Landstreicher *m*; Wanderarbeiter *m*.

hockey *n* Hockey *n*.

hoe *n* Hacke *f*; * *vt* hacken.

hog *n* (Haus)Schwein *n*.

hoist *vt* hochziehen; heben; hieven; hissen; * *n* (Lasten)Aufzug *m*; Winde *f*.

hold *vt* (fest)halten; zuhalten; fassen; (zurück)behalten; abhalten; veranstalten; innehaben; **to ~ on to** (sich) festhalten an; * *vi* (sich) halten; gelten; andauern; * *n* Halt *m*; Griff *m*; Gewalt *f*; Einhalt *m*; (mus) Fermate *f*; Festung *f*.

holder *n* Halter(in) *m(f)*; Inhaber(in) *m(f)*.

holding *n* Pachtgut *n*; Beteiligung *f*; Besitz *m*.

holdup *n* (Verkehrs)Stockung *f*; (bewaffneter Raub)Überfall *m*.

hole *n* Loch *n*.

holiday *n* Feiertag *m*; freier Tag *m*; **~s** *pl* Ferien *pl*.

holiness *n* Heiligkeit *f*.

hollow *adj* hohl; leer; eingefallen; * *n* Höhle *f*; Hohlraum *m*; Mulde *f*; Vertiefung *f*; * *vt* aushöhlen.

holly *n* (bot) Stechpalme *f*.

hollyhock *n* Stockrose *f*.

holocaust *n* Holocaust *m*; Massenvernichtung *f*; Katastrophe *f*.

holster *n* Halfter *n*.

holy *adj* heilig; geweiht.

holy water *n* Weihwasser *n*.

holy week *n* Karwoche *f*.

homage *n* Huldigung *f*; Anerkennung *f*; Homage *f*.

home *n* Heim *n*; Haus *n*; Wohnung *f*; Zuhause *n*; Heimat *f*.

home address *n* Privatanschrift *f*; Heimatanschrift *f*.

homeless *adj* obdachlos; heimatlos.

homeliness *n* Freundlichkeit *f*; Einfachheit *f*; Gemütlichkeit *f*.

homely *adj* freundlich; vertraut; einfach; anheimelnd.

home-made *adj* hausgemacht; selbstgemacht; einheimisch.

homesick *adj* heimwehkrank.

homesickness *n* Heimweh *n*.

hometown *n* Heimatstadt *f*.

homeward *adj* Heim-; Rück-; * *adv* heimwärts; nach Hause.

homework *n* Hausaufgaben *pl*; Heimarbeit *f*.

homicidal *adj* mörderisch; Mord-.

homicide *n* Mord *m*; Totschlag *m*.

homoeopathist *n* Homöopath(in) *m(f)*.

homoeopathy *n* Homöopathie *f*.

homogeneous *adj* homogen; gleichartig.

homosexual *adj* homosexuell; * *n* Homosexuelle(r) *f(m)*.

honest *adj* ~ly *adv* ehrlich; rechtschaffen; aufrichtig; echt; ehrbar.

honesty *n* Ehrlichkeit *f*; Rechtschaffenheit *f*; Aufrichtigkeit *f*; Ehrbarkeit *f*.

honey *n* Honig *m*; Nektar *m*; Liebling *m*.

honeycomb *n* Honigwabe *f*.

honeymoon *n* Flitterwochen *pl*.

honeysuckle *n* (*bot*) Geißblatt *n*.

honour *n* Ehre *f*; (Hoch)Achtung *f*; Auszeichnung *f*; Zierde *f*; * *vt* ehren; auszeichnen; beehren; Ehre machen; Folge leisten; honorieren; anerkennen; respektieren.

honourable *adj* ehrenwert; ehrenvoll; ehrbar; redlich.

honourably *adv* = **honourable**.

honorary *adj* Ehren-; ehrenamtlich.

hood *n* Kapuze *f*; Verdeck *n*; Haube *f*; Kappe *f*.

hoodlum *n* Schläger *m*; Ganove *m*.

hoof *n* Huf *m*.

hook *n* (Angel)Haken *m*; Sichel *f*; **by ~ or by crook** mit allen Mitteln; * *vt* (zu)haken; angeln; fangen; einen Haken versetzen.

hooked *adj* hakenförmig; Haken-; (*col*) süchtig.

hooligan *n* Rowdy *m*.

hoop *n* Reif(en) *m*; Ring *m*; Bügel *m*.

hooter *n* Hupe *f*; Sirene *f*; (*sl*) Zinken *m*.

hop *n* (*bot*) Hopfen *m*; Sprung *m*; * *vi* hüpfen; springen.

hope *n* Hoffnung *f*; Aussicht *f*; * *vi* (er)hoffen.

hopeful *adj* hoffnungsvoll; vielversprechend; ~ly *adv* = hopeful; hoffentlich.

hopefulness *n* Optimismus *m*.

hopeless *adj* ~ly *adv* hoffnungslos; verzweifelt; aussichtslos.

horde *n* Horde *f*.

horizon *n* Horizont *m*.

horizontal *adj* ~ly *adv* horizontal; waagerecht; liegend.

hormone *n* Hormon *n*.

horn *n* Horn *n*; Hupe *f*; Schalltrichter *m*; Sattelknopf *m*.

horned *adj* gehörnt; Horn-.

hornet *n* Hornisse *f*.

horny *adj* hornig; Horn-; gehörnt; geil.

horoscope *n* Horoskop *n*.

horrendous *adj* schrecklich; entsetzlich; horrend.

horrible *adj* **horribly** *adv* schrecklich; furchtbar; gemein.

horrid *adj* = horrible.

horrific *adj* schrecklich; entsetzlich; horrend.

horrify *vt* entsetzen; empören; mit Schrecken erfüllen.

horror *n* Entsetzen *n*; Schrecken *m*; Abscheu *f*; Horror *m*; Grausigkeit *f*; Greuel *m*; Scheusal *n*.

horror film *n* Horrorfilm *m*.

hors d'oeuvre *n* Vorspeise *f*.
horse *n* Pferd *n*; Bock *m*.
horseback *adv*: on ~ zu Pferd; beritten.
horse-breaker *n* Zureiter *m*; Bereiter *m*.
horse chesnut *n* Roßkastanie *f*.
horsefly *n* (Pferde)Bremse *f*.
horseman *n* Reiter *m*; Pferdezüchter *m*.
horsemanship *n* Reitkunst *f*.
horsepower *n* Pferdestärke *f*.
horse race *n* Pferderennen *n*.
horseradish *n* Meerrettich *m*.
horseshoe *n* Hufeisen *n*.
horsewoman *n* Reiterin *f*; Pferdezüchterin *f*.
horticulture *n* Gartenbau *m*.
horticulturist *n* Gartenbauexperte *m*.
hose-pipe *n* Schlauch(leitung) *f*.
hosiery *n* Strumpfwaren *pl*.
hospitable *adj* **hospitably** *adv* gastfreundlich; gastlich; (*fig*) empfänglich.
hospital *n* Krankenhaus *n*; Klinik *f*; Lazarett *n*.
hospitality *n* Gastfreundschaft *f*; Gastlichkeit *f*; (*fig*) Empfänglichkeit *f*.
host *n* Gastgeber(in) *m(f)*; (Gast)Wirt *m*; Moderator(in) *m(f)*.
hostage *n* Geisel *f*.
hostess *n* Gastgeberin *f*; (Gast)Wirtin *f*; Hostess *f*.
hostile *adj* feindlich; feindselig.
hostility *n* Feindschaft *f*; Feindseligkeit *f*.
hot *adj* ~**ly** *adv* heiß; warm; scharf; hitzig; frisch; toll; (*col*) geil.
hotbed *n* Frühbeet *n*; Brutstätte *f*.
hotch-potch *n* Eintopfgericht *n*; Mischmasch *m*.
hotdog *n* Hot dog *m*.
hotel *n* Hotel *n*.
hotelier *n* Hotelier *m*; Hotelbesitzer *m*.
hotheaded *adj* hitzköpfig.

hot-house *n* Treibhaus *n*.
hotline *n* heißer Draht *m*; Telefondienst *m*.
hotplate *n* Kochplatte *f*; Warmhalteplatte *f*.
hound *n* Jagdhund *m*.
hour *n* Stunde *f*; *pl* (Arbeits-) Zeit *f*.
hour-glass *n* Stundenglas *n*; Sanduhr *f*.
hourly *adv* stündlich.
house *n* Haus *n*; Haushalt *m*; * *vt* unterbringen; beherbergen.
houseboat *n* Hausboot *n*.
housebreaker *n* Einbrecher *m*; Abbruchunternehmer *m*.
housebreaking *n* Einbruch *m*; Abbruch *m*.
household *n* Haushalt *m*.
householder *n* Haushaltsvorstand *m*.
housekeeper *n* Haushälter(in) *m(f)*.
houskeeping *n* Haushaltsführung *f*.
houseless *adv* obdachlos; ohne Häuser.
house-warming party *n* Einzugsfeier *f*.
housewife *n* Hausfrau *f*.
housework *n* Hausarbeit *f*.
housing *n* Unterbringung *f*; Unterkunft *f*; Wohnung *f*; Wohnungsbau *m*; Wohnen *n*.
housing development *n* Wohnungsbauprojekt *n*; Wohnsiedlung *f*.
hovel *n* Schuppen *m*; (contp) Bruchbude *f*.
hover *vi* schweben; sich herumtreiben; schwanken.
how *adv* wie; ~ **do you do!** guten Tag!
however *adv* wie auch (immer); * *conj* dennoch; (je)doch; aber.
howl *vi* heulen; brüllen; * *n* Heulen *n*; Schrei *m*; Brüllen *n*.
hub *n* (Rad)Nabe *f*; (*fig*) Zentrum *n*.
hubbub *n* Stimmengewirr *n*; Tumult *m*.

hubcap n Radkappe f.

hue n Farbe f; Ton m; Schattierung f; Geschrei n.

huff n: **in a ~** verärgert; eingeschnappt.

hug vt umarmen; umklammern; sich dicht halten an; * n Umarmung f.

huge adj riesig; gewaltig; mächtig; **~ly** adv ungeheuer; ungemein.

hulk n (mar) Hulk f (abgetakeltes, altes Schiff); Koloß m.

hull n (mar) Rumpf m; (bot) Schale f, Hülle f, Hülse f.

hum vi summen; brummen.

human adj menschlich; Menschen-.

humane adj, **~ly** adv human; menschlich; humanistisch.

humanist n Humanist(in) m(f).

humanitarian adj humanitär; menschenfreundlich.

humanity n Menschheit f; Humanität f; Menschlichkeit f.

humanize vt humanisieren; menschenwürdiger gestalten; vermenschlichen.

humanly adv menschlich; human; nach menschlichen Begriffen.

humble adj bescheiden; demütig; einfach; ärmlich; * vt demütigen; erniedrigen.

humbleness n Demut f; Bescheidenheit f.

humbly adv = humble.

humbug n Humbug m; Schwindel m; Unsinn m.

humdrum adj eintönig; langweilig.

humid adj feucht; humid.

humidity n Feuchtigkeit f.

humiliate vt demütigen; erniedrigen.

humiliation n Demütigung f; Erniedrigung f.

humility n Demut f; Bescheidenheit f.

humming-bird n Kolibri m.

humour n Temperament n; Stimmung f; Laune f; Komik f; Humor m; Körperflüssigkeit

f; * vt seinen Willen lassen; hinnehmen; sich anpassen.

humorist n Humorist(in) m(f); Spaßvogel m.

humorous adj **~ly** adv humorvoll; komisch.

hump n Buckel m; Höcker m; (kleiner) Hügel m; (col) Stinklaune f.

hunch n Buckel m; Höcker m; Gefühl n; Ahnung f; **~backed** adj bucklig.

hundred adj hundert; * n Hundert n, f; Hundertschaft f.

hundredth adj hundertst(er, e, es); hundertstel.

hundredweight n Zentner m.

hunger n Hunger m; (fig) Durst m; * vi Hunger haben; hungern.

hunger strike n Hungerstreik m.

hungrily adv = hungry.

hungry adj hungrig; karg.

hunt vt jagen; hetzen; verfolgen; * vi jagen; suchen; streben; * n Jagd f; Verfolgung f; Suche f.

hunter n Jäger m; Jagdhund m; Jagdpferd n; Sprungdeckeluhr f.

hunting n Jagd f; Verfolgung f; Suche f; Jagen n.

huntsman n Jäger m; Weidmann m.

hurdle n Hürde f; Hindernis n; Geflecht n.

hurl vt schleudern.

hurricane n Hurrikan m; Wirbelsturm m; Orkan m.

hurried adj **~ly** adv eilig; hastig; schnell; übereilt.

hurry vt antreiben; hetzen; beschleunigen; übereilen; * vi eilen; hasten; sich beeilen; * n Hast f; Eile f; Hetze f.

hurt vt verletzen; verwunden; schmerzen; schaden; * n Schmerz m; Verletzung f; Wunde f; Kränkung f; Schaden m.

hurtful adj **~ly** adv verletzend; schmerzlich; schädlich.

husband *n* Ehemann *m*; Gatte *m*.

husbandry *n* Landwirtschaft *f*; (*fig*) Haushalten *n*.

hush! still! pst! * *vt* zum Schweigen bringen; beruhigen; vertuschen; * *vi* verstummen.

husk *n* Hülse *f*; Schale *f*.

huskiness *n* Heiserkeit *f*; Rauheit *f*.

husky *adj* ausgedörrt; heiser; rauh; (*col*) stämmig.

hustings *n* Wahlkampf *m*.

hustle *vt* stoßen; drängen; (an)rempeln; (an)treiben; (*col*) ergaunern.

hut *n* Hütte *f*; Baracke *f*.

hutch *n* Kasten *m*; Verschlag *m*; kleiner Stall *m*.

hyacinth *n* Hyazinthe *f*.

hydrant *n* Hydrant *m*.

hydraulic *adj* hydraulisch; Wasser-; ~s *npl* Hydraulik *f*.

hydroelectric *adj* hydroelektrisch.

hydrofoil *n* Tragfläche *f*; Tragflächenboot *m*.

hydrogen *n* Wasserstoff *m*.

hydrophobia *n* Tollwut *f*; Hydrophobie *f*.

hyena *n* Hyäne *f*.

hygiene *n* Hygiene *f*; Gesundheitspflege *f*.

hygienic *adj* hygienisch.

hymn *n* Hymne *f*; Lobgesang *m*; Kirchenlied *n*.

hyperbole *n* Hyperbel *f*; Übertreibung *f*.

hypermarket *n* Großmarkt *m*.

hyphen *n* (*gr*) Bindestrich *m*; Trennungszeichen *n*.

hypochondria *n* Hypochondrie *f*.

hypochondriac *adj* hypochondrisch; * *n* Hypochonder *m*.

hypocrisy *n* Heuchelei *f*; Scheinheiligkeit *f*.

hypocrite *n* Heuchler(in) *m(f)*.

hypocritical *adj* heuchlerisch; scheinheilig.

hypothesis *n* Hypothese *f*; Annahme *f*.

hypothetical *adj* ~ly *adv* hypothetisch.

hysterical *adj* hysterisch; (*col*) wahnsinnig komisch.

hysterics *npl* Hysterie *f*; hysterischer Anfall *m*.

I

I *pn* ich.

ice *n* Eis *n*; * *vt* gefrieren lassen; (mit Eis) kühlen; mit Zuckerguß überziehen.

ice-ax *n* Eispickel *m*.

iceberg *n* Eisberg *m*.

ice-bound *adj* eingefroren.

icebox *n* Eisfach *n*; Kühlbox *f*.

ice cream *n* Eis *n*; Eiscreme *f*.

ice rink *n* Eisbahn *f*.

ice skating *n* Eislauf *m*; Eislaufen *n*.

icicle *n* Eiszapfen *m*.

iconoclast *n* Ikonoklast *m*; Bilderstürmer *m*.

icy *adj* eisig; vereist; eiskalt.

idea *n* Idee *f*; Vorstellung *f*; Gedanke *m*; Ansicht *f*.

ideal *adj* ideal; vollendet; Muster-; ideell; idealistisch; ~ly *adv* ideal; ideell; im Idealfall; idealerweise.

idealist *n* Idealist(in) *m(f)*.

identical *adj* identisch; (genau) gleich; gleichbedeutend.

identification *n* Identifizierung *f*; (Er)Kennung *f*; Feststellung *f*; Legitimation *f*; Ausweis *m*.

identify *vt* identifizieren; gleichsetzen; erkennen; die Identität feststellen; ausweisen; legitimieren.

identity *n* Identität *f*; Gleichheit *f*; Persönlichkeit *f*.

ideology *n* Ideologie *f*.

idiom *n* Idiom *n*; Redewendung *f*; Stil *m*.

idiomatic *adj* idiomatisch.

idiosyncrasy n Eigenart f; Veranlagung f.

idiot n Idiot m; Trottel m.

idiotic adj idiotisch; blöd.

idle adj untätig; müßig; Muße-; faul; stillstehend; brachliegend; beiläufig; leer.

idleness n Untätigkeit f; Müßiggang m; Muße f; Faulheit f; Zwecklosigkeit f; Vergeblichkeit f.

idler n Müßiggänger(in) m; Faulenzer(in) m(f).

idly adv = idle.

idol n Idol n; Götze m.

idolatry n Götzendienst f; (fig) Vergötterung f.

idolize vt vergöttern; zum Idol machen.

idyllic adj idyllisch.

i.e. adv d.h..

if conj wenn (auch); falls; ob; ~ **not** wenn nicht.

igloo n Iglu n.

ignite vt (ent)zünden.

ignition n (chem) Erhitzung f; Entzünden n; Zündung f.

ignition key n Zündschlüssel m.

ignoble adj gemein; unehrenhaft; von niedriger Geburt.

ignominious adj ~ly adv schändlich; schimpflich.

ignominy n Schande f; Schimpf m.

ignoramus n Ignorant(in) m(f).

ignorance n Unwissenheit f; Unkenntnis f; Ignoranz f.

ignorant adj unkundig; unwissend; ignorant; ungebildet; unwissentlich; ~ly adv unwissentlich.

ignore vt ignorieren; nicht beachten.

ill adj schlimm; schlecht; übel; widrig; unheilvoll; schädlich; böse; krank; * n Übel n; Unglück n; Leiden n; Krankheit f; * adv schlecht; schlimm; übel; kaum.

ill-advised adj schlecht beraten; unklug; unbesonnen.

illegal adj, ~ly adv illegal; verboten; gesetzwidrig; regelwidrig.

illegality n Ungesetzlichkeit f; Gesetzwidrigkeit f; Regelwidrigkeit f; Illegalität f.

illegible adj **illegibly** adv unleserlich.

illegitimacy n Unehelichkeit f.

illegitimate adj ~ly adv unehelich; inkorrekt; illegal; gesetzwidrig.

ill feeling n Groll m; Feindseligkeit f; böses Blut n.

illicit adj verboten; unzulässig; gesetzwidrig.

illiterate adj analphabetisch; ungebildet.

illness n Krankheit f.

illogical adj unlogisch.

ill-timed adj ungelegen; unpassend.

ill-treat vt mißhandeln; schlecht behandeln.

illuminate vt erleuchten; beleuchten; erläutern; Glanz verleihen; illuminieren.

illumination n Beleuchtung f; Erleuchtung f; Erläuterung f; Glanz m; Illumination f.

illusion n Illusion f; Sinnestäuschung f; Einbildung f; Wahn m.

illusory adj illusorisch; trügerisch.

illustrate vt erläutern; veranschaulichen; illustrieren.

illustration n Illustration f; Erläuterung f; Veranschaulichung f.

illustrative adj erläuternd; veranschaulichend; illustrativ.

illustrious adj glanzvoll; erlaucht; berühmt.

ill-will n Übelwollen n; böse Absicht f.

image n Bild(nis) n; Ebenbild n; Bildsäule f; Symbol n; Metapher f.

imagery n Bilder pl; Vorstellungen pl; bildliche Darstellung f; Metaphorik f.

imaginable *adj* vorstellbar; denkbar.

imaginary *adj* imaginär; eingebildet; Phantasie-.

imagination *n* Einbildung(skraft) *f*; Phantasie *f*; Vorstellung *f*; Ideenreichtum *m*.

imaginative *adj* einfallsreich; phantasievoll; phantastisch.

imagine *vt* sich vorstellen; sich (aus)denken; sich einbilden.

imbalance *n* Unausgewogenheit *f*; Ungleichgewicht *n*.

imbecile *adj* idiotisch; vertrottelt.

imbibe *vt* trinken; schöpfen; einsaugen.

imbue *vt* durchtränken; tief färben; (*fig*) erfüllen.

imitate *vt* nachahmen; nachbilden; fälschen; nacheifern.

imitation *n* Nachahmung *f*; Nachbildung *f*; Fälschung *f*; Imitation *f*.

imitative *adj* nachahmend; imitierend; nachgemacht.

immaculate *adj* unbefleckt; makellos; tadellos; einwandfrei; fleckenlos.

immaterial *adj* unkörperlich; unwesentlich; belanglos.

immature *adj* unreif; unausgereift.

immeasurable *adj* **immeasurably** *adv* unermeßlich; grenzenlos.

immediate *adj* unmittelbar; nächst(er, e, es); unverzüglich; sofortig; umgehend; **~ly** *adv* unmittelbar; direkt; sofort; unverzüglich.

immense *adj*, **~ly** *adv* riesig; enorm; immens.

immensity *n* Riesigkeit *f*; Unermeßlichkeit *f*.

immerse *vt* (ein)tauchen; untertauchen; einbetten; vertiefen; versenken.

immersion *n* Eintauchen *n*; Untertauchen *n*; Versunkenheit *f*; Vertiefung *f*.

immigrant *n* Einwanderer *m*;

Einwanderin *f*; Immigrant(in) *m*(*f*).

immigration *n* Einwanderung *f*; Immigration *f*.

imminent *adj* unmittelbar bevorstehend; drohend.

immobile *adj* unbeweglich; starr.

immobility *n* Unbeweglichkeit *f*; Bewegungslosigkeit *f*.

immoderate *adj* **~ly** *adv* übermäßig; maßlos.

immodest *adj* unbescheiden; aufdringlich; schamlos; unanständig.

immoral *adj* unmoralisch; unsittlich.

immorality *n* Unsittlichkeit *f*; Unmoral *f*; Sittenwidrigkeit *f*.

immortal *adj* unsterblich; (*fig*) unvergänglich.

immortality *n* Unsterblichkeit *f*; Unvergänglichkeit *f*.

immortalize *vt* verewigen; unsterblich machen.

immune *adj* immun; unempfänglich; gefeit; befreit.

immunity *n* Immunität *f*; Unempfänglichkeit *f*; Befreiung *f*; Privileg *n*.

immunize *vt* immunisieren.

immutable *adj* unveränderlich.

imp *n* Kobold *m*; (*col*) Racker *m*.

impact *n* Aufprall *m*; Einschlag *m*; Impakt *m*; (Ein)Wirkung *f*; Einfluß *m*; Eindruck *m*.

impair *vt* beeinträchtigen.

impale *vt* aufspießen; durchbohren; pfählen.

impalpable *adj* unfühlbar; äußerst fein; (*fig*) kaum faßbar.

impart *vt* geben; gewähren; mitteilen; vermitteln; verleihen.

impartial *adj* **~ly** *adv* unparteiisch; unvoreingenommen; unbefangen.

impartiality *n* Unparteilichkeit *f*; Unvoreingenommenheit *f*.

impassable *adj* unpassierbar; unüberwindbar.

impasse *n* Sackgasse *f*; (*fig*) völliger Stillstand *m*; toter Punkt *m*.

impassive *adj* teilnahmslos; gleichmütig; ausdruckslos.

impatience *n* Ungeduld *f*; Unduldsamkeit *f*.

impatient *adj* ~**ly** *adv* ungeduldig; unduldsam; intolerant.

impeach *vt* in Frage stellen; (law) anklagen; (law) anfechten.

impeccable *adj* tadellos; untadelig; einwandfrei.

impecunious *adj* mittellos.

impede *vt* (be)hindern; erschweren.

impediment *n* Behinderung *f*; Hindernis *n*.

impel *vt* (an)treiben; drängen; zwingen; nötigen.

impending *adj* nahe bevorstehend; drohend.

impenetrable *adj* undurchdringlich; unergründlich; unzugänglich.

imperative *adj* gebieterisch; unumgänglich; unbedingt erforderlich; Befehls-.

imperceptible *adj* unmerklich.

imperceptibly *adv* unmerklich.

imperfect *adj* ~**ly** unvollkommen; mangelhaft; Imperfekt-; * *n* (*gr*) Imperfekt *n*.

imperfection *n* Unvollkommenheit *f*; Mangelhaftigkeit *f*; Mangel *m*; Fehler *m*.

imperial *adj* kaiserlich; Kaiser-; Reichs-; (*fig*) gebieterisch; (*fig*) königlich; (*fig*) imposant; gesetzlich.

imperialism *n* Imperialismus *m*.

imperious *adj* ~**ly** *adv* heerrisch; gebieterisch; zwingend.

impermeable *adj* undurchlässig; undurchdringbar.

impersonal *adj*, ~**ly** *adv* unpersönlich.

impersonate *vt* verkörpern; imitieren; nachahmen; sich ausgeben als.

impertinence *n* Unverschämtheit *f*; Zudringlichkeit *f*; Nebensächlichkeit *f*.

impertinent *adj* ~**ly** *adv* unverschämt; zudringlich; irrelevant; unerheblich.

imperturbable *adj* unerschütterlich.

impervious *adj* undurchlässig; undurchdringlich; unzugänglich; ungerührt.

impetuosity *n* Heftigkeit *f*; Ungestüm *n*; übereilte Handlung *f*.

impetuous *adj* ~**ly** *adv* heftig; ungestüm; übereilt; impulsiv.

impetus *n* Antrieb *m*; Anstoß *m*; Schwung *m*.

impiety *n* Gottlosigkeit *f*; Pietätlosigkeit *f*.

impinge (on) *vt* übergreifen auf; verletzen; (auf)treffen auf; sich auswirken auf.

impious *adj* gottlos; pietätlos.

implacable *adj* **implacably** *adv* unversöhnlich; unnachgiebig.

implant *vt* implantieren; einpflanzen; (*fig*) einprägen.

implement *n* Werkzeug *n*; Gerät *n*; Hilfsmittel *n*.

implicate *vt* verwickeln; in Verbindung bringen; mit sich bringen.

implication *n* Verwicklung *f*; Implikation *f*; Folgerung *f*; Auswirkung *f*; Andeutung *f*.

implicit *adj* impliziert; (stillschweigend) inbegriffen; (daraus) hervorgehend; hintergründig; vorbehaltlos; ~**ly** *adv* stillschweigend; vorbehaltlos.

implore *vt* inständig bitten; anflehen; beschwören; erflehen.

imply *vt* implizieren; (stillschweigend) einbeziehen; beinhalten; bedeuten; andeuten.

impolite *adj* unhöflich.

impoliteness *n* Unhöflichkeit *f*.

impolitic *adj* undiplomatisch; unklug.

import *vt* importieren; einführen; bedeuten; betreffen; * *n* Import *m*; Einfuhr *f*; Bedeutung *f*.

importance *n* Bedeutung *f*; Wichtigkeit *f*; Einfluß *m*.

important *adj* wichtig; bedeutend; einflußreich; wichtigtuerisch.

importation *n* Import *m*; Einfuhr *f*.

importer *n* Importeur *m*.

importunate *adj* lästig; zudringlich.

importune *vt* bedrängen; belästigen; bestürmen; hartnäckig fordern.

importunity *n* Lästigkeit *f*; Zudringlichkeit *f*; hartnäckige Forderung *f*.

impose *vt* auferlegen; aufdrängen; aufzwingen; vorschreiben.

imposing *adj* imposant; eindrucksvoll.

imposition *n* Auf(er)legung *f*; Auflage *f*; Abgabe *f*; Strafarbeit *f*; Betrug *m*.

impossibility *n* Unmöglichkeit *f*.

impossible *adj* unmöglich.

impostor *n* Betrüger(in) *m(f)*; Hochstapler(in) *m(f)*.

impotence *n* Unfähigkeit *f*; Hilflosigkeit *f*; Schwäche *f*; Impotenz *f*.

impotent *adj* ~ly *adv* unfähig; hilflos; ohnmächtig; schwach; impotent.

impound *vt* beschlagnahmen; abschleppen (lassen); (*fig*) an sich reißen.

impoverish *vt* verarmen lassen; auslaugen.

impoverished *adj* verarmt; ausgelaugt.

impoverishment *n* Verarmung *f*; Auslaugung *f*.

impracticability *n* Undurchführbarkeit *f*; Unbrauchbarkeit *f*.

impracticable *adj* unduchführbar; unbrauchbar; unpassierbar.

impractical *adj* unpraktisch; unklug; undurchführbar.

imprecation *n* Verwünschung *f*; Fluch.

imprecise *adj* ungenau.

impregnable *adj* uneinnehmbar; unerschütterlich; unangreifbar.

impregnate *vt* schwängern; befruchten; imprägnieren; (durch)tränken; durchdringen.

impregnation *n* Schwängerung *f*; Befruchtung *f*; Imprägnierung *f*; Durchdringung *f*.

impress *vt* beeindrucken; imponieren; durchdringen; tief einprägen; (auf)drücken; einprägen.

impression *n* Eindruck *m*; Nachahmung *f*; (Ab)Druck *m*; Aufdruck *m*; Vertiefung *f*; Abzug *m*; Auflage *f*.

impressionable *adj* beeinflußbar; empfänglich.

impressive *adj* eindrucksvoll; imposant; wirkungsvoll.

imprint *n* Abdruck *m*; Aufdruck *m*; Stempel *m*; (*fig*) Eindruck *m*; Impressum *n*; * *vt* (auf-)drücken; einprägen; abdrukken.

imprison *vt* inhaftieren; einsperren; einschließen.

imprisonment *n* Freiheitsstrafe *f*; Haft *f*; Inhaftierung *f*.

improbability *n* Unwahrscheinlichkeit *f*.

improbable *adj* unwahrscheinlich.

impromptu *adj* improvisiert.

improper *adj* ~ly *adv* unpassend; ungeeignet; unschicklich; ungenau.

impropriety *n* Unschicklichkeit *f*; Unrichtigkeit *f*.

improve *vt* verbessern; veredeln; steigern; * *vi* sich (ver)bessern; Fortschritte machen; sich erholen.

improvement *n* (Ver)Besserung *f*; Veredelung *f*; Steigerung *f*.

improvident *adj* sorglos; verschwenderisch.

improvise *vt* improvisieren.

imprudence *n* Unklugheit *f*; Unvorsichtigkeit *f*.

imprudent *adj* unklug; unvernünftig; unvorsichtig.

impudence *n* Unverschämtheit *f*.

impudent *adj*, **~ly** *adv* unverschämt.

impugn *vt* bestreiten; anfechten; angreifen.

impulse *n* Impuls *m*; Antrieb *m*; (An)Stoß *m*; (An)Reiz *m*; Eingebung *f*.

impulsive *adj* impulsiv; spontan; Trieb-.

impunity *n* Straflosigkeit *f*.

impure *adj* **~ly** *adv* unrein; verunreinigt; verfälscht; (*fig*) unmoralisch.

impurity *n* Unreinheit *f*; Verunreinigung *f*; Schlechtheit *f*.

in *prep* in; innerhalb; an; auf; bei; mit.

inability *n* Unfähigkeit *f*; Unvermögen *n*.

inaccessible *adj* unzugänglich; unerreichbar; unnahbar.

inaccuracy *n* Ungenauigkeit *f*.

inaccurate *adj* ungenau; unrichtig.

inaction *n* Untätigkeit *f*; Trägheit *f*; Ruhe *f*.

inactive *adj* untätig; träge; lustlos; inaktiv.

inactivity *n* Untätigkeit *f*; Trägheit *f*; Lustlosigkeit *f*; Inaktivität *f*.

inadequate *adj* unzulänglich; unangemessen.

inadmissible *adj* unzulässig; unstatthaft.

inadvertently *adv* unbeabsichtigt; versehentlich.

inalienable *adj* unveräußerlich; unübertragbar.

inane *adj* leer; (*fig*) geistlos; albern.

inanimate *adj* leblos; unbelebt; (*fig*) langweilig.

inapplicable *adj* nicht anwendbar; nicht zutreffend; ungeeignet.

inappropriate *adj* unpassend; ungeeignet; unangemessen.

inasmuch *adv* in Anbetracht der Tatsache; da; weil.

inattentive *adj* unachtsam; unaufmerksam.

inaudible *adj* unhörbar.

inaugural *adj* Einführungs-; Einweihungs-; Eröffnungs-.

inaugurate *vt* (ins Amt) einführen; einweihen; eröffnen; einleiten.

inauguration *n* Amtseinführung *f*; Einweihung *f*; Eröffnung *f*.

inauspicious *adj* ungünstig; unheilvoll.

in-between *adj* Mittel-; Zwischen-.

inborn, inbred *adj* angeboren; tief eingewurzelt.

incalculable *adj* unberechenbar; unermeßlich.

incandescent *adj* (weiß)glühend; (*fig*) strahlend.

incantation *n* Beschwörung *f*; Zauber(spruch) *m*.

incapable *adj* unfähig; hilflos; ungeeignet; untauglich.

incapacitate *vt* unfähig machen; (*law*) für geschäftsunfähig erklären.

incapacity *n* (Erwerbs)Unfähigkeit *f*; Untauglichkeit *f*.

incarcerate *vt* einkerkern; (*fig*) einschließen.

incarnate *adj* konkrete Form geben; verkörpern.

incarnation *n* Inkarnation *f*; Verkörperung *f*.

incautious *adj* **~ly** *adv* unvorsichtig.

incendiary *n* Brandbombe *f*; Brandstifter(in) *m(f)*; (*fig*) Aufwiegler(in) *m(f)*.

incense *n* Weihrauch *m*; Duft *m*; * *vt* beweihräuchern.

incentive *n* Ansporn *m*; Anreiz *m*.

inception *n* Beginn *m*; Gründung *f*.

incessant adj ~**ly** adv unaufhörlich; unablässig; ständig.

incest n Inzest m.

incestuous adj inzestuös.

inch n Zoll m; ~ **by** ~ Zentimeter um Zentimeter; (fig) allmählich.

incidence n Vorkommen n; Häufigkeit f; Verbreitung f.

incident n Vorfall m; Zwischenfall m; Nebensache f; Episode f.

incidental adj nebensächlich; Neben-; beiläufig; zufällig; verbunden (mit); ~**ly** adv nebenbei (bemerkt); übrigens; beiläufig; zufällig.

incinerator n Verbrennungsanlage f.

incipient adj einleitend; anfänglich; beginnend.

incise vt einschneiden; einkerben; einritzen.

incision n Einschnitt m.

incisive adj (ein)schneidend; (fig) scharf; (fig) prägnant.

incisor n Schneidezahn m.

incite vt anregen; anspornen; anstacheln; anstiften.

inclement adj rauh; unfreundlich; unerbittlich.

inclination n Neigung f; (Ab)Hang m.

incline vt neigen; beugen; (fig) veranlassen; * vi geneigt sein; (sich) neigen.

include vt einschließen; umfassen; aufnehmen.

including prep einschließlich.

inclusion n Einschluß m; Einbeziehung f.

inclusive adj einschließlich; inklusive.

incognito adv inkognito.

incoherence n Zusammenhanglosigkeit f.

incoherent adj ~**ly** adv unverbunden; unzusammenhängend; unverständlich.

income n Einkommen n.

income tax n Einkommenssteuer f.

incoming adj hereinkommend; neu; eingehend.

incomparable adj unvergleichbar.

incomparably adv unvergleichbar.

incompatibility n Unvereinbarkeit f; Unverträglichkeit f.

incompatible adj unvereinbar; unverträglich; inkompatibel.

incompetence n Unfähigkeit f; Inkompetenz f.

incompetent adj ~**ly** adv unfähig; unqualifiziert; inkompetent; unzulänglich.

incomplete adj unvollständig; unvollendet.

incomprehensibility n Unbegreiflichkeit f.

incomprehensible adj unbegreiflich; unfaßbar; unverständlich.

inconceivable adj unvorstellbar; undenkbar; unfaßbar.

inconclusive adj ~**ly** adv nicht überzeugend; ergebnislos.

incongruity n Unvereinbarkeit f; Ungereimtheit f.

incongruous adj ~**ly** adv nicht übereinstimmend; unvereinbar; ungereimt.

inconsequential adj inkonsequent; irrelevant; belanglos.

inconsiderate adj ~**ly** adv rücksichtslos; taktlos; unüberlegt.

inconsistency n Inkonsequenz f; Unbeständigkeit f; Unvereinbarkeit f; Widersprüchlichkeit f.

inconsistent adj inkonsequent; unbeständig; unvereinbar; widersprüchlich.

inconsolable adj untröstlich.

inconspicuous adj unauffällig; unscheinbar.

incontinence n Inkontinenz f; Zügellosigkeit f; Unaufhörlichkeit f.

incontinent adj inkontinent; zügellos; unaufhörlich.

incontrovertible adj unbestreitbar; unanfechtbar.

inconvenience n Unbequemlichkeit f; Ungelegenheit f; Unannehmlichkeit f; * vt stören; zur Last fallen; Unannehmlichkeiten bereiten.

inconvenient adj, ~**ly** adv unbequem; ungelegen; lästig.

incorporate vt vereinigen; einverleiben; aufnehmen; enthalten; einbauen; verkörpern; vi sich vereinigen; (law) eine Gesellschaft gründen.

incorporated company n rechtsfähige Gesellschaft f; Aktiengesellschaft f.

incorporation n Vereinigung f; Einverleibung f; Eintragung f.

incorrect adj, ~**ly** adv unrichtig; fehlerhaft; inkorrekt.

incorrigible adj unverbesserlich; unfügsam.

incorruptibility n Unbestechlichkeit f.

incorruptible adj unbestechlich; unverführbar; unverderblich.

increase vt vergrößern; vermehren; steigern; erhöhen; * vi zunehmen; (an)wachsen; (an)steigen; sich vermehren; * n Vergrößerung f; Zuwachs m; Zunahme f; Steigerung f; Erhöhung f; Vermehrung f.

increasing adj (an)wachsend; steigend; zunehmend; ~**ly** adv in zunehmendem Maße.

incredible adj unglaublich; unglaubwürdig.

incredulity n Ungläubigkeit f; Skepsis f.

incredulous adj ungläubig.

increment n Zuwachs m; Zunahme f.

incriminate vt beschuldigen; belasten.

incrust vt überkrusten; reich verzieren; inkrustieren.

incubate vi ausbrüten.

incubator n Brutkasten m; Inkubator m; Brutofen m.

inculcate vt einschärfen; einprägen.

incumbent adj obliegend; amtierend; lastend; (auf)liegend; * n Amtsinhaber m; (relig) Pfründeninhaber m.

incur vt sich zuziehen; sich aussetzen; geraten in.

incurability n Unheilbarkeit f.

incurable adj unheilbar; (fig) unverbesserlich.

incursion n Einfall m; Eindringen n.

indebted adj verschuldet; verpflichtet.

indecency n Unanständigkeit f; Unzucht f; Unschicklichkeit f.

indecent adj, ~**ly** adv unanständig; unzüchtig; unschicklich; ungebührig.

indecision n Unentschlossenheit f.

indecisive adj unentschlossen; unentschieden; ungewiß.

indecorous adj unschicklich; ungehörig.

indeed adv in der Tat; tatsächlich; wirklich; freilich.

indefatigable adj unermüdlich.

indefinite adj unbestimmt; unbegrenzt; unklar; ~**ly** adv auf unbestimmte Zeit; unbegrenzt.

indelible adj unauslöschlich; untilgbar; unvergeßlich.

indelicacy n Taktlosigkeit f; Unanständigkeit f; Unfeinheit f.

indelicate adj taktlos; unanständig; anstößig; unfein.

indemnify vt sicherstellen; entschädigen; Straflosigkeit zusichern.

indemnity n Sicherstellung f; Entschädigung f; Abfindung f; Straffreiheit f.

indent vt einkerben; auszakken; einrücken; mit Doppel ausfertigen; bestellen.

independence n Unabhängigkeit f; Selbständigkeit f.

independent adj ~**ly** adv unabhängig; selbständig; freiheitsliebend.

indescribable *adj* unbeschreiblich; unbestimmt.

indestructible *adj* unzerstörbar.

indeterminate *adj* unbestimmt; ungewiß; unentschieden.

index *n* Index *m*; (Inhalts)Verzeichnis *n*; Register *n*; Hinweis *m*; Zeiger *m*; Wegweiser *m*.

index card *n* Karteikarte *f*.

indexed *adj* mit einem Inhaltsverzeichnis versehen; in einem Verzeichnis aufgeführt; auf den Index gesetzt.

index finger *n* Zeigefinger *m*.

indicate *vt* zeigen auf; hinweisen auf; andeuten; angezeigt erscheinen lassen; anzeigen.

indication *n* Zeigen *n*; (An)Zeichen *n*; Hinweis *m*; Andeutung *f*; Indikation *f*.

indicative *adj* aufzeigend; andeutend; * *n* (*gr*) Indikativ *m*.

indicator *n* (An)Zeiger *m*; Blinker *m*; Indikator *m*.

indict *vt* anklagen.

indictment *n* Anklage *f*.

indifference *n* Gleichgültigkeit *f*.

indifferent *adj*, ~**ly** *adv* gleichgültig; mittelmäßig; indifferent.

indigenous *adj* einheimisch.

indigent *adj* arm; bedürftig; mittellos.

indigestible *adj* unverdaulich.

indigestion *n* Verdauungsstörung *f*; Magenverstimmung *f*.

indignant *adj* entrüstet; empört.

indignation *n* Entrüstung *f*; Empörung *f*.

indignity *n* Erniedrigung *f*; Demütigung *f*.

indigo *n* Indigo *m*.

indirect *adj* ~**ly** *adv* indirekt; mittelbar.

indiscreet *adj* ~**ly** *adv* unbesonnen; indiskret.

indiscretion *n* Unbedachtheit *f*; Indiskretion *f*.

indiscriminate *adj* nicht wählerisch; wahllos; kunterbunt; ~**ly** *adv* ohne Unterschied; wahllos; nicht wählerisch.

indispensable *adj* unentbehrlich; unerläßlich.

indisposed *adj* indisponiert; unpäßlich; abgeneigt.

indisposition *n* Indisponiertheit *f*; Unpäßlichkeit *f*; Abgeneigtheit *f*.

indisputable *adj* unstrittig; unstreitig.

indisputably *adv* = indisputable.

indistinct *adj* ~**ly** *adv* undeutlich; unscharf; unklar.

indistinguishable *adj* nicht zu unterscheiden.

individual *adj* einzeln; Einzel-; individuell; persönlich; ~**ly** *adv* einzeln; persönlich; * *n* Individuum *n*; Einzelperson *f*.

individuality *n* Individualität *f*.

indivisible *adj*, ~**bly** *adv* unteilbar.

indoctrinate *vt* indoktrinieren; unterweisen.

indoctrination *n* Indoktrination *f*; Unterweisung *f*.

indolence *n* Trägheit *f*; Indolenz *f*.

indolent *adj* ~**ly** *adv* träge; indolent; schmerzlos.

indomitable *adj* unbezähmbar; unbeugsam.

indoors *adv* im Haus; drinnen; ins Haus.

indubitably *adv* unzweifelhaft; zweifellos.

induce *vt* veranlassen; bewegen; bewirken; herbeiführen.

inducement *n* Anlaß *m*; Beweggrund *m*; Anreiz *m*.

induction *n* Herbeiführung *f*; Induktion *f*; Einführung *f*.

indulge *vt* nachsichtig sein; gewähren lassen; nachgeben; verwöhnen; genießen; * *vi* schwelgen; sich hingeben; genießen.

indulgence *n* Nachsicht *f*; Entgegenkommen *n*; Verwöhnung *f*; Schwelgen *n*; Zügellosigkeit *f*; Genuß *m*; Ablaß *m*.

indulgent *adj*, **~ly** *adv* nachsichtig.

industrial *adj* industriell; Industrie-; gewerblich; Gewerbe-.

industrialist *n* Industrielle(r) *f(m)*.

industrialize *vt* industrialisieren.

industrial park *n* Industriegebiet *n*.

industrious *adj* fleißig; arbeitsam; eifrig.

industry *n* Industrie *f*; Gewerbe *n*; Arbeit *f*; Fleiß *m*.

inebriated *vt* berauscht.

inebriation *n* Trunkenheit *f*.

inedible *adj* ungenießbar; nicht eßbar.

ineffable *adj* unbeschreiblich; unsäglich.

ineffective, ineffectual *adj* **~ly** *adv* ineffektiv; unwirksam; erfolglos; unfähig; nicht effektvoll.

inefficiency *n* Ineffizienz *f*; Unfähigkeit *f*; Unwirksamkeit *f*; Unwirtschaftlichkeit *f*.

inefficient *adj* ineffizient; (leistungs)unfähig; unwirksam; unwirtschaftlich.

ineligible *adj* unannehmbar; inakzeptabel; nicht berechtigt; nicht wählbar.

inept *adj* unpassend; verfehlt; töricht; ungeschickt; unbeholfen.

ineptitude *n* Ungeschicklichkeit *f*; Unbeholfenheit *f*; Albernheit *f*.

inequality *n* Ungleichheit *f*; Verschiedenheit *f*.

inert *adj* träge; inert.

inertia *n* Trägheit *f*.

inescapable *adj* unvermeidlich; unentrinnbar.

inestimable *adj* unschätzbar.

inevitable *adj*, **~bly** *adv* unvermeidlich.

inexcusable *adj* unentschuldbar; unverzeihlich.

inexhaustible *adj* unerschöpflich.

inexorable *adj* unerbittlich.

inexpedient *adj* nicht ratsam; unzweckmäßig.

inexpensive *adj* billig; nicht teuer.

inexperience *n* Unerfahrenheit *f*.

inexperienced *adj* unerfahren.

inexpert *adj* unerfahren; unfachmännisch; ungeschickt.

inexplicable *adj* unerklärlich.

inexpressible *adj* unaussprechlich; unbeschreiblich.

inextricably *adv* unentwirrbar; (*fig*) äußerst verwickelt; (*fig*) ausweglos.

infallibility *n* Unfehlbarkeit *f*.

infallible *adj* unfehlbar.

infamous *adj* **~ly** *adv* berüchtigt; schändlich.

infamy *n* Verrufenheit *f*; Niedertracht *f*; Infamie *f*.

infancy *n* frühe Kindheit *f*; Säuglingsalter *n*; (*fig*) Anfangsstadium *n*.

infant *n* Säugling *m*; Kleinkind *n*.

infanticide *n* Kindestötung *f*; Kindsmörder(in) *m(f)*.

infantile *adj* infantil; kindisch; kindlich; Kinder-.

infantry *n* Infanterie *f*.

infatuated *adj* betört; vernarrt.

infatuation *n* Vernarrtheit *f*; Schwarm *m*.

infect *vt* infizieren; anstecken; befallen.

infection *n* Infektion(skrankheit) *f*; Ansteckung *f*; Befall *m*.

infectious *adj* ansteckend; infektiös.

infer *vt* schließen; folgern; andeuten.

inference *n* (Schluß)Folgerung *f*; (Rück)Schluß *m*.

inferior *adj* untergeordnet; niedriger; minderwertig; Un-

ter-; * n Untergebene(r) f(m);
Unterlegene(r) f(m).

inferiority n Unterlegenheit f;
Minderwertigkeit f.

infernal adj unterirdisch; höllisch; infernalisch.

inferno n Inferno n; Hölle f.

infest vt heimsuchen; verseuchen; (fig) überlaufen.

infidel n Ungläubige(r) f(m).

infidelity n Ungläubigkeit f;
Treulosigkeit f; Untreue f.

infiltrate vt einsickern in; infiltrieren; durchtränken; unterwandern.

infinite adj ~ly adv unendlich;
grenzenlos; endlos.

infinitive n Infinitiv m.

infinity n Unendlichkeit f;
Grenzenlosigkeit f.

infirm adj schwach; gebrechlich; fragwürdig.

infirmary n Krankenhaus n;
Krankenzimmer n.

infirmity n Schwäche f; Gebrechlichkeit f; Fragwürdigkeit f.

inflame vt entzünden; entfachen; entflammen; * vi sich entzünden; entbrennen; in Wut geraten.

inflammation n Entzündung f.

inflammatory adj entzündlich;
(fig) aufrührerisch; Hetz-.

inflatable adj aufblasbar.

inflate vt aufblasen; aufpumpen; aufblähen.

inflation n Inflation f; Aufgeblasenheit f; Aufpumpen n.

inflection n Beugung f; Modulation f.

inflexibility n Unbiegsamkeit f; Unbeweglichkeit f.

inflexible adj unbiegsam; unbeweglich; nicht anpassungsfähig.

inflexibly adv = inflexible.

inflict vt zufügen; auferlegen;
verhängen; aufbürden.

influence n Einfluß m; * vt beeinflussen; bewegen.

influential adj einflußreich;
maßgeblich.

influenza n Grippe f.

influx n Zustrom m; Zufluß m.

inform vt informieren; benachrichtigen; mitteilen; erfüllen.

informal adj formlos; zwanglos; inoffiziell.

informality n Formlosigkeit f;
Zwanglosigkeit f.

informant n Informant(in)
m(f); Denunziant(in) m(f);
Spitzel m.

information n Information f;
Auskunft f; Benachrichtigung
f; Mitteilung f.

infraction n Verletzung f; Verstoß m.

infra-red adj infrarot.

infrastructure n Infrastruktur
f.

infrequent adj ~ly adv selten;
spärlich.

infringe vt brechen; verletzen;
verstoßen gegen.

infringement n Verletzung f;
Verstoß m; Eingriff m.

infuriate vt wütend machen.

infuse vt einflößen; erfüllen;
aufgießen; ziehen lassen.

infusion n Infusion f; Einflößung f; Aufguß m; Tee m.

ingenious adj, ~ly adv genial;
erfinderisch; raffiniert.

ingenuity n Genialität f; Erfindungsgabe; Findigkeit f.

ingenuous adj, ~ly adv offen(herzig); aufrichtig; naiv;
unbefangen.

inglorious adj, ~ly adv unrühmlich; schimpflich.

ingot n Barren m.

ingrained adj eingewurzelt;
eingefleischt.

ingratiate vi sich einschmeicheln.

ingratitude n Undankbarkeit
f.

ingredient n Bestandteil m;
Zutat f.

inhabit vt bewohnen; leben in.

inhabitable adj bewohnbar.

inhabitant n Bewohner(in)
m(f); Einwohner(in) m(f).

inhale vt einatmen; inhalieren.

inherent *adj* innewohnend; eigen; eingewurzelt.

inherit *vt* (er)erben; beerben.

inheritance *n* Erbschaft *f*; Vererbung *f*; Erbgut *n*.

inheritor *n* Erbe *m*.

inhibit *vt* hemmen; (ver)hindern.

inhibited *adj* gehemmt: verhindert.

inhibition *n* Hemmung *f*; (Ver-)Hinderung *f*; Untersagung *f*.

inhospitable *adj* ungastlich; unfreundlich.

inhospitality *n* Ungastlichkeit *f*.

inhuman *adj*, **~ly** *adv* unmenschlich; übermenschlich.

inhumanity *n* Unmenschlichkeit *f*.

inimical *adj* feindselig; schädlich.

inimitable *adj* unnachahmlich.

iniquitous *adj* ungerecht; frevelhaft.

iniquity *n* Ungerechtigkeit *f*; Frevelhaftigkeit *f*.

initial *adj* anfänglich; Ausgangs-; erst(er, e, es); * *n* Initiale *f*.

initially *adv* zu Anfang; zuerst; ursprünglich.

initiate *vt* einleiten; beginnen; einführen; initiieren.

initiation *n* Einleitung *f*; Initiierung *f*; Einführung *f*; Initiation *f*.

initiative *n* Initiative *f*; Anregung *f*; Unternehmungsgeist *m*.

inject *vt* injizieren; einspritzen; einflößen; einbringen.

injection *n* Injektion *f*; Spritze *f*; Einspritzung *f*.

injudicious *adj* unklug; unvernünftig; unüberlegt.

injunction *n* gerichtliches Verbot *n*; ausdrücklicher Befehl *m*.

injure *vt* verletzen; schädigen; kränken.

injury *n* Verletzung *f*; Schaden *m*; Kränkung *f*.

injury time *n* verletzungsbedingte Nachspielzeit *f*.

injustice *n* Ungerechtigkeit *f*; Unrecht *n*.

ink *n* Tinte *f*; Tusche *f*; Druckfarbe *f*.

inkling *n* Andeutung *f*; dunkle Ahnung *f*.

inkstand *n* Tintenfaß *n*.

inlaid *adj* eingelegt; Einlege-; Parkett-.

inland *adj* inländisch; Binnen-; einheimisch; * *adv* landeinwärts.

in-laws *npl* Schwiegereltern *pl*.

inlay *vt* einlegen; einbetten.

inlet *n* Eingang *m*; Einlaß *m*; schmale Bucht *f*.

inmate *n* Insasse *m*; Insassin *f*.

inmost *adj* innerst(er, e, es); (*fig*) tiefst(er, e, es).

inn *n* Gasthaus *n*; Wirtshaus *n*.

innate *adj* angeboren; innewohnend; eigen.

inner *adj* Innen-; inner(er, e, es); enger(er, e, es); verborgen.

innermost *adj* = **inmost**.

inner tube *n* Schlauch *m*.

innkeeper *n* (Gast)Wirt(in) *m(f)*.

innocence *n* Unschuld *f*; Unwissenheit *f*.

innocent *adj* unschuldig; arglos; harmlos; **~ly** *adv* in aller Unschuld.

innocuous *adj* **~ly** *adv* harmlos; unschädlich.

innovate *vt* (neu) einführen.

innovation *n* (Neu)Einführung *f*; Neuerung *f*.

innuendo *n* versteckte Anspielung *f*; Zweideutigkeit *f*.

innumerable *adj* unzählig; zahllos.

inoculate *vt* (ein)impfen.

inoculation *n* (Ein)Impfung *f*.

inoffensive *adj* harmlos; friedfertig.

inopportune *adj* unangebracht; ungelegen; zur Unzeit.

inordinately *adv* durcheinander; unmäßig; übermäßig; zügellos.

inorganic *adj* unorganisch; anorganisch.

inpatient *n* stationäre(r) Patient(in) *m(f)*.

input *n* Input *m*; Eingangsleistung *f*; Eingabe *f*.

inquest *n* gerichtliche Untersuchung *f*.

inquire *vt* sich erkundigen nach; * *vi* (nach)fragen; sich erkundigen; nachforschen; **to ~ about** sich erkundigen wegen; **to ~ after** *vt* fragen nach; sich erkundigen nach; **to ~ into** *vt* untersuchen; prüfen; erforschen.

inquiry *n* Erkundigung *f*; (An)Frage *f*; Untersuchung *f*; Ermittlung *f*.

inquisition *n* Untersuchung *f*; Inquisition *f*.

inquisitive *adj* wißbegierig; neugierig.

inroad *n* Einfall *m*; Eingriff *m*; Eindringen *n*.

insane *adj* wahnsinnig; geisteskrank; verrückt.

insanity *n* Wahnsinn *m*; Geisteskrankheit *f*; Verrücktheit *f*.

insatiable *adj* unersättlich; unstillbar.

inscribe *vt* (ein)schreiben; eintragen; mit einer Widmung versehen.

inscription *n* Inschrift *f*; Eintragung *f*; Widmung *f*.

inscrutable *adj* unerforschlich; unergründlich.

insect *n* Insekt *n*.

insecticide *n* Insektenvertilgungsmittel *n*.

insecure *adj* unsicher; ungesichert; riskant.

insecurity *n* Unsicherheit *f*.

insemination *n* Befruchtung *f*; Besamung *f*; (*fig*) Einimpfung *f*.

insensible *adj* gefühllos; bewußtlos; (*fig*) gleichgültig.

insensitive *adj* unempfindlich;

gefühllos; gleichgültig.

inseparable *adj* untrennbar; unzertrennlich.

insert *vt* einfügen; einführen; (hinein)stecken; einwerfen.

insertion *n* Einführung *f*; Einwurf *m*; Einfügung *f*; Zusatz *m*; Anzeige *f*.

inshore *adj* an der Küste; Küsten-.

inside *n* Innenseite *f*; (*das*) Innere; *pl* Eingeweide *pl*; * *adv* (dr)innen; innerhalb; hinein; herein.

inside out *adv* die Innenseite nach außen; verkehrt; umgestülpt.

insidious *adj* ~ly heimtückisch; hinterhältig.

insight *n* Einblick *m*; Einsicht *f*.

insignia *npl* Amtszeichen *n*; (Ab)Zeichen *n*.

insignificant *adj* bedeutungslos; unwichtig; unerheblich; unbedeutend; nichtssagend.

insincere *adj* unaufrichtig; falsch.

insincerity *n* Unaufrichtigkeit *f*; Falschheit *f*.

insinuate *vt* andeuten; anspielen auf.

insinuation *n* Andeutung *f*; Anspielung *f*.

insipid *adj* fad; geschmacklos; (*fig*) geistlos.

insist *vi* bestehen; beharren; betonen.

insistence *n* Bestehen; Beharren *n*; Drängen *n*; Nachdruck *m*; Hartnäckigkeit *f*.

insistent *adj* beharrlich; hartnäckig; drängend; eindringlich.

insole *n* Brandsohle *f*; Einlegesohle *f*.

insolence *n* Überheblichkeit *f*; Unverschämtheit *f*.

insolent *adj* ~ly *adv* überheblich; unverschämt.

insoluble *adj* unlöslich; (*fig*) unlösbar.

insolvency *n* Zahlungsunfähigkeit *f*; Bankrott *m*; Überschuldung *f*.

insolvent *adj* zahlungsunfähig; bankrott; überschuldet.

insomnia *n* Schlaflosigkeit *f*.

insomuch *conj* so sehr; dermaßen.

inspect *vt* untersuchen; prüfen; besichtigen; inspizieren.

inspection *n* Untersuchung *f*; Prüfung *f*; Besichtigung *f*; Inspektion *f*.

inspector *n* Inspektor *m*; Aufsichtsbeamte(r) *f(m)*; Prüfer(in) *m(f)*.

inspiration *n* Inspiration *f*; Eingebung *f*; Anregung *f*.

inspire *vt* inspirieren; anregen; erwecken; erfüllen; einatmen.

instability *n* mangelnde Stabilität *f*; (*fig*) Unbeständigkeit *f*; Labilität *f*.

install *vt* installieren; einbauen; einsetzen.

installation *n* Installation *f*; Einbau *m*; Einrichtung *f*; Anlage *f*; (Amts)Einsetzung *f*.

installment *n* Rate *f*; Fortsetzung *f*.

installment plan *n* Ratenzahlungssystem *n*.

instance *n* Beispiel *n*; Fall *m*; Instanz *f*; **for ~** zum Beispiel.

instant *adj* sofortig; augenblicklich; direkt; unmittelbar; Fertig-; **~ly** *adv* augenblicklich; sofort; * *n* Moment *m*; Augenblick *m*.

instantaneous *adj* sofortig; augenblicklich; momentan; gleichzeitig; **~ly** *adv* augenblicklich; sofort; unverzüglich.

instead (of) *pr* an Stelle von; (an)statt; statt dessen.

instep *n* Rist *m*; Spann *m*.

instigate *vt* aufhetzen; anstiften; in die Wege leiten.

instigation *n* Anstiftung *f*; Aufhetzung *f*; Anregung *f*.

instill *vt* einträufeln; (*fig*) einflößen.

instinct *n* Instinkt *m*; Trieb *m*.

instinctive *adj* **~ly** *adv* instinktiv; unwillkürlich.

institute *vt* einrichten; gründen; einsetzen; in die Wege leiten; * *n* Institut *n*; Anstalt *f*.

institution *n* Institution *f*; Einrichtung *f*; Institut *n*; Anstalt *f*; Heim *n*; Gründung *f*; Einsetzung *f*.

instruct *vt* unterrichten; schulen; informieren; anweisen; beauftragen.

instruction *n* Unterricht *m*; Schulung *f*; Unterrichtung *f*; Instruktion *f*; Anweisung *f*.

instructive *adj* aufschlußreich; lehrreich.

instructor *n* Lehrer *m*; Ausbilder *m*.

instrument *n* Instrument *n*; Werkzeug *n*; Gerät *n*; Urkunde *f*.

instrumental *adj* instrumental; dienlich; behilflich; förderlich.

insubordinate *adj* widersetzlich; aufsässig.

insubordination *n* Widersetzlichkeit *f*; Aufsässigkeit *f*; Gehorsamsverweigerung *f*.

insufferable *adj*, **~bly** *adv* unerträglich; unausstehlich.

insufficiency *n* Unzulänglichkeit *f*.

insufficient *adj* **~ly** *adv* unzulänglich; ungenügend; unfähig.

insular *adj* inselartig; Insel-; (*fig*) isoliert.

insulate *vt* isolieren; dämmen.

insulating tape *n* Isolierband *n*.

insulation *n* Isolierung *f*.

insulin *n* Insulin *n*.

insult *vt* beleidigen; * *n* Beleidigung *f*.

insulting *adj* beleidigend; unverschämt.

insuperable *adj* unüberwindlich.

insurance *n* Versicherung *f*; (Ab)Sicherung *f*.

insurance policy *n* Versicherungspolice *f*.
insure *vt* versichern.
insurgent *n* Aufrührer *m*; Rebell *m*.
insurmountable *adj* unüberwindlich.
insurrection *n* Aufstand *m*; Rebellion *f*; Revolte *f*.
intact *adj* intakt; unversehrt; ganz; unangetastet.
intake *n* Einlaß *m*; Aufnahme *f*; Zufuhr *f*.
integral *adj* integral; unerläßlich; einheitlich; vollständig; ganz; Integral-; * *n* vollständiges Ganzes *n*; Integral *n*.
integrate *vt* integrieren; eingliedern; einbeziehen; einbauen.
integration *n* Integration *f*; Eingliederung *f*; Einbeziehung *f*; Einbau *m*.
integrity *n* Integrität *f*; Rechtschaffenheit *f*; Vollständigkeit *f*.
intellect *n* Intellekt *m*; Verstand *m*.
intellectual *adj* intellektuell; geistig; Verstandes-; intelligent; verstandesbetont.
intelligence *n* Intelligenz *f*; Einsicht *f*; Verständnis *n*; Informationen *pl*; Geheimdienst *m*.
intelligent *adj* intelligent; klug; vernünftig; sinnvoll.
intelligentsia *n* Intelligenz *f*; (die) Intellektuellen *pl*.
intelligible *adj*, **~bly** *adv* verständlich.
intemperate *adj*, **~ly** *adv* unmäßig; unbeherrscht; zügellos; rauh.
intend *vi* beabsichtigen; vorhaben; bezwecken; bestimmen; meinen; bedeuten; wollen.
intendant *n* Verwalter *m*.
intended *adj* beabsichtigt; geplant; gewünscht; absichtlich.
intense *adj* intensiv; stark; heftig; konzentriert; leidenschaft-

lich; beträchtlich; **~ly** *adv* äußerst; höchst.
intensify *vt* verstärken; intensivieren.
intensity *n* Intensität *f*; Stärke *f*; Heftigkeit *f*; Leidenschaftlichkeit.
intensive *adj* intensiv; stark; heftig; gründlich.
intensive care unit *n* Intensivstation *f*.
intent *adj* **~ly** *adv* beschäftigt; aufmerksam; gespannt; erpicht; * *n* Absicht *f*; Vorsatz *m*; Ziel *n*; Zweck *m*.
intention *n* Absicht *f*; Vorhaben *n*; Vorsatz *m*; Zweck *m*; Ziel *n*.
intentional *adj* **~ly** *adv* absichtlich; vorsätzlich.
inter *vt* beerdigen; bestatten.
interaction *n* Wechselwirkung *f*; Interaktion *f*.
intercede *vi* sich einsetzen; Fürsprache einlegen.
intercept *vt* abfangen; mithören; (den Weg) abschneiden.
intercession *n* Fürsprache *f*.
interchange *n* Austausch *m*; Autobahnkreuz *n*.
intercom *n* Sprechanlage *f*.
intercourse *n* (Geschlechts-)Verkehr *m*; Umgang *m*.
interest *vt* interessieren; angehen; * *n* Interesse *n*; Beteiligung *f*; Vorteil *m*; Anspruch *m*; Zinsen *pl*.
interesting *adj* interessant.
interest rate *n* Zinssatz *m*.
interfere *vi* stören; eingreifen; sich einmischen; sich vergreifen; (*fig*) kollidieren; sich überlagern.
interference *n* Störung *f*; Einmischung *f*; Kollision *f*; Überlagerung *f*; Interferenz *f*.
interim *adj* einstweilig; vorläufig; Zwischen-; Interims-.
interior *adj* inner(er, e, es); Innen-; inländisch; intern.
interior designer *n* Innenarchitekt(in) *m(f)*.
interjection *n* (*gr*) Interjektion *f*; Zwischenruf *m*; Einwurf *m*.

interlock *vi* ineinandergreifen.

interlocutor *n* Gesprächspartner *m*.

interloper *n* Eindringling *m*; Schwarzhändler *m*.

interlude *n* Periode *f*; Unterbrechung *f*; Pause *f*; Zwischenspiel *n*; Intermezzo *n*.

intermarriage *n* Mischehe *f*.

intermediary *n* Vermittler(in) *m(f)*; Mittelsmann *m*.

intermediate *adj* dazwischenliegend; Zwischen-; Mittel-; mittelbar.

interment *n* Beerdigung *f*; Bestattung *f*.

interminable *adj* endlos.

intermingle *vt* vermischen; * *vi* sich vermischen.

intermission *n* Pause *f*; Unterbrechung *f*.

intermittent *adj* mit Unterbrechungen; aussetzend; periodisch.

intern *n* Internierte(r) *f(m)*; Assistenzarzt *m*; Assistenzärztin *f*.

internal *adj* ~**ly** *adv* inner(er, e, es); innerlich; intern; Inlands-; Innen-.

international *adj* international; Auslands-.

interplay *n* Wechselwirkung *f*.

interpose *vt* dazwischenstellen; einwerfen; einlegen; zwischenschalten; * vi dazwischentreten; vermitteln; eingreifen.

interpret *vt* auslegen; interpretieren; dolmetschen; auswerten.

interpretation *n* Auslegung *f*; Interpretation *f*; Dolmetschen *n*; Auswertung *f*.

interpreter *n* Dometscher(in) *m(f)*; Interpret(in) *m(f)*.

interregnum *n* Interregnum *n*; Zwischenregierung *f*; Pause *f*.

interrelated *adj* in Wechselbeziehung stehend; zusammenhängend.

interrogate *vt* verhören; vernehmen; befragen.

interrogation *n* Verhör *n*; Vernehmung *f*; Befragung *f*; Frage *f*.

interrogative *adj* fragend; Frage-.

interrupt *vt* unterbrechen; aufhalten; versperren.

interruption *n* Unterbrechung *f*; Störung *f*; Versperrung *f*.

intersect *vi* sich (über)schneiden; sich kreuzen.

intersection *n* Schnittpunkt *m*; (Straßen)Kreuzung *f*.

intersperse *vt* einstreuen; durchsetzen.

intertwine *vt*, *vi* (sich) verflechten; (sich) verschlingen.

interval *n* Abstand *m*; Intervall *n*; Pause *f*.

intervene *vi* eingreifen; einschreiten; sich einmischen; vermitteln; dazwischenliegen; dazwischenkommen; intervenieren.

intervention *n* Einschreiten *n*; Eingriff *m*; Einmischung *f*; Intervention *f*; Vermittlung *f*.

interview *n* Interview *n*; Einstellungsgespräch *n*; * *vt* interviewen; ein Einstellungsgespräch führen mit.

interviewer *n* Interviewer(in) *m(f)*.

interweave *vt* verweben; verflechten.

intestate *adj* ohne Hinterlassungs eines Testaments; nicht testamentarisch geregelt.

intestinal *adj* Darm-; Eingeweide-.

intestine *n* Darm *m*.

intimacy *n* Intimität *f*; Vertrautheit *f*; Vertraulichkeit *f*.

intimate *n* Vertraute(r) *f(m)*; Intimus *m*; * *adj*, ~**ly** *adv* intim; vertraut; eng; vertraulich; anheimelnd; gründlich; * *vt* andeuten; ankündigen.

intimidate *vt* einschüchtern.

into *prep* in; in... hinein; gegen.

intolerable *adj*, ~**bly** *adv* unerträglich.

intolerance *n* Intoleranz *f*;

Unduldsamkeit *f*; Überempfindlichkeit *f*.

intolerant *adj* intolerant; unduldsam; überempfindlich.

intonation *n* Intonation *f*; Satzmelodie *f*; Tonfall *m*; Singsang *m*.

intoxicate *vt* berauschen; vergiften.

intoxication *n* Rausch *m*; Vergiftung *f*.

intractable *adj* eigensinnig; hartnäckig; unlenkbar.

intransitive *adj* (gr) intransitiv.

intravenous *adj* intravenös.

in-tray *n* Eingangskorb *m*.

intrepid *adj* ~ly *adv* unerschrocken; kühn.

intrepidity *n* Unerschrockenheit *f*; Kühnheit *f*.

intricacy *n* Kompliziertheit *f*; Schwierigkeit *f*.

intricate *adj*, ~ly *adv* verschlungen; kompliziert; ausgeklügelt; schwierig.

intrigue *n* Intrige *f*; * *vi* intrigieren; * *vt* faszinieren; interessieren.

intriguing *adj* faszinierend; interessant; intrigant.

intrinsic *adj* inner(er, e, es); innewohnend; wesentlich; ~ally *adv* wirklich; eigentlich; an sich.

introduce *vt* einführen; vorstellen; bekannt machen mit; anschneiden; einleiten; ankündigen; einschleppen; einbringen.

introduction *n* Einführung *f*; Vorstellung *f*; Anschneiden *n*; Einleitung *f*; Vorwort *n*.

introductory *adj* einführend; einleitend.

introspection *n* Selbstbetrachtung *f*; Introspektion *f*.

introvert *n* introvertierter Mensch *m*.

intrude *vi* sich eindrängen; sich aufdrängen; stören.

intruder *n* Eindringling *m*; Störenfried *m*.

intrusion *n* Störung *f*; Einmischung *f*; Aufdrängen *n*.

intuition *n* Intuition *f*.

intuitive *adj* intuitiv.

inundate *vt* überschwemmen; überfluten.

inundation *n* Überschwemmung *f*; Flut *f*.

inure *vt* abhärten; gewöhnen.

invade *vt* einfallen in; eindringen in; erfüllen; überlaufen; verletzen.

invader *n* Eindringling *m*.

invalid *adj* krank; gebrechlich; invalid; arbeitsunfähig; ungültig; nicht stichhaltig; unbegründet; * *n* Invalide *m*; Kranke(r) *f*(*m*).

invalidate *vt* außer Kraft setzen; entkräften.

invaluable *adj* unschätzbar.

invariable *adj* unveränderlich; konstant; gleichbleibend.

invariably *adv* ausnahmslos; immer.

invasion *n* Invasion *f*; Einfall *m*; Einmarsch *m*; Verletzung *f*; Eingriff *m*.

invective *n* Beschimpfung *f*; Schmähung *f*.

inveigle *vt* verlocken; verleiten; verführen.

invent *vt* erfinden.

invention *n* Erfindung *f*; Phantasie *f*; Invention *f*.

inventive *adj* erfinderisch; originell; einfallsreich.

inventor *n* Erfinder(in) *m*(*f*).

inventory *n* Bestandsverzeichnis *n*; Liste *f*; Inventar *n*; Inventur *f*; Bestandsaufnahme *f*.

inverse *adj* umgekehrt; entgegengesetzt; verkehrt.

inversion *n* Umkehrung *f*; Inversion *f*.

invert *vt* umkehren; umstülpen; invertieren.

invest *vt* investieren; anlegen; einsetzen.

investigate *vt* untersuchen; Nachforschungen anstellen; erforschen; ermitteln.

investigation n Untersuchung f; Ermittlung f; (Nach)Forschung f.

investigator n Ermittler(in) m(f).

investment n Investition f; Anlage f; Beteiligung f; (mil) Belagerung f.

inveterate adj eingewurzelt; unausrottbar; eingefleischt; hartnäckig.

invidious adj verhaßt; gehässig; Neid erregend.

invigilate vi die Aufsicht führen.

invigorating adj anregend; belebend; aufmunternd.

invincible adj unbesiegbar; unüberwindlich; eisern.

invincibly adv = invincible.

inviolable adj unverletzlich; unantastbar.

invisible adj unsichtbar.

invisibly adv = invisible.

invitation n Einladung f; Aufforderung f; Bitte f; Herausforderung f; Verlockung f.

invite vt einladen; auffordern; bitten; herausfordern; verlocken; ermutigen.

inviting adj einladend; verlockend.

invoice n (com) Rechnung f.

invoke vt erflehen; anrufen; appellieren; beschwören; sich berufen auf.

involuntarily adv unfreiwillig; unabsichtlich; unwillkürlich.

involuntary adj = involuntarily.

involve vt verwickeln; hineinziehen; angehen; betreffen; mit sich bringen; verbunden sein mit; erfordern; einschließen; komplizieren; engagieren.

involved adj verwickelt; betroffen; engagiert; kompliziert; * to be ~ with zu tun haben mit; eine (enge) Beziehung haben mit.

involvement n Verwicklung f; Betroffenheit f; Kompliziert-

heit f; Beziehung f; Engagement n.

invulnerable adj unverwundbar; (fig) unanfechtbar; unangreifbar.

inward adj inner(er, e, es); innerlich; ~, ~s adv einwärts; nach innen; innerlich; insgeheim; gedämpft.

iodine n (chem) Jod n.

I.O.U. (I owe you) n Schuldschein m.

irascible adj jähzornig; reizbar.

irate, ireful adj zornig; wütend; gereizt.

iris n Iris f.

irksome adj ärgerlich; lästig; ermüdend.

iron n Eisen n; Bügeleisen n; * adj eisern; Eisen-; * vt bügeln.

ironic(al) adj ironisch; ~ly adv ironisch; ironischerweise.

ironing n Bügeln n; Bügelwäsche f.

ironing board n Bügelbrett n.

iron ore n Eisenerz n.

ironwork n Eisenbeschläge pl; ~s pl Eisenhütte f.

irony n Ironie (des Schicksals) f.

irradiate vt bestrahlen; erleuchten; (fig) verklären; (fig) erhellen.

irrational adj irrational; unvernünftig; unlogisch.

irreconcilable adj unvereinbar; unversöhnlich.

irregular adj ~ly adv unregelmäßig; ungleichmäßig; regelwidrig; ungeregelt; ungeordnet.

irregularity n Unregelmäßigkeit f; Ungleichmäßigkeit f; Vorschriftswidrigkeit f; Ungeregeltheit f.

irrelevant adj irrelevant; unerheblich; belanglos.

irreligious adj unreligiös; gottlos.

irreparable adj irreparabel; nicht wiedergutzumachen; unersetzlich.

irreplaceable *adj* unersetzlich.
irrepressible *adj* ununterdrückbar; unbezähmbar.
irreproachable *adj* untadelig; einwandfrei.
irresistible *adj* unwiderstehlich.
irresolute *adj*, **~ly** *adv* unentschlossen; unschlüssig; unbestimmt.
irresponsible *adj* unverantwortlich; verantwortungslos; (*law*) unzurechnungsfähig.
irretrievably *adv* unersetzlich; nicht wiedergutzumachen.
irreverence *n* Respektlosigkeit *f*.
irreverent *adj*, **~ly** *adv* respektlos.
irrigate *vt* bewässern; berieseln; (*med*) ausspülen.
irrigation *n* Bewässerung *f*; Berieselung *f*; (*med*) Ausspülung *f*.
irritability *n* Reizbarkeit *f*.
irritable *adj* reizbar; gereizt; nervös.
irritant *n* (*med*) Reizstoff *m*.
irritate *vt* reizen; (ver)ärgern; irritieren.
irritating *adj* ärgerlich; irritierend; Reiz-.
irritation *n* Ärger *m*; Verärgerung *f*; Reizung *f*; Irritation *f*.
Islam *n* Islam *m*.
island *n* Insel *f*.
islander *n* Inselbewohner(in) *m(f)*.
isle *n* (kleine) Insel *f*.
isolate *vt* isolieren; trennen; absondern.
isolation *n* Isolation *f*; Absonderung *f*; Abgeschiedenheit *f*.
issue *n* Ausgabe *f*; Erteilung *f*; Veröffentlichung *f*; (Streit)Punkt *m*; Problem *n*; Resultat *n*; * *vt* (her)ausgeben; erlassen; erteilen; veröffentlichen.
isthmus *n* Isthmus *m*; Landenge *f*.
it *pn* es; er; ihn; sie; sich.
italic *n* Kursivschrift *f*.

itch *n* Jucken *n*; Juckreiz *m*; (*fig*) Verlangen *n*; * *vi* jucken; kratzen.
item *n* Punkt *m*; Gegenstand *m*; Posten *m*; Einzelheit *f*; Artikel *m*; Meldung *f*.
itemize *vt* einzeln aufführen; spezifizieren; aufgliedern.
itinerant *n* Nichtseßhafte(r) *f(m)*; * *adj* reisend; umherziehend; Wander-.
itinerary *n* Reiseweg *m*; Reisebericht *m*; Reiseführer *m*.
its *pn* sein; seine; ihr; ihre.
itself *pn* sich; sich selbst; selbst.
ivory *n* Elfenbein *n*.
ivy *n* Efeu *m*.

J

jab *vt* (hinein)stechen; (hinein-) stoßen.
jabber *vi* plappern; quasseln.
jack *n* Wagenheber *m*; Bube *m*; (*col*) Kerl *m*.
jackal *n* Schakal *m*; (*fig*) Handlanger *m*.
jackboots *npl* Stulpenstiefel *mpl*; Wasserstiefel *mpl*.
jackdaw *n* Dohle *f*.
jacket *n* Jacke *f*; Jackett *n*; Hülle *f*; (Schutz)Umschlag *m*.
jack-knife *vi* zusammenklappen.
jackpot *n* Jackpot *m*; (*fig*) das große Los.
jade *n* Jade *f*.
jagged *adj* (aus)gezackt; zerklüftet.
jaguar *n* Jaguar *m*.
jail *n* Gefängnis *n*.
jailbird *n* Knastbruder *m*.
jailer *n* Gefängniswärter *m*.
jam *n* Gedränge *n*; Verstopfung *f*; Blockierung *f*; (*col*) Klemme *f*; Marmelade *f*.
jangle *vi* schrillen; klimpern; rasseln; keifen.

janitor *n* Pförtner *m*; Hausmeister *m*.
January *n* Januar *m*.
jar *vi* kratzen; quietschen; sich widersprechen; sich beißen; wackeln; zittern; (*mus*) dissonieren; * *n* Krug *m*; Topf *m*; (Einmach)Glas *n*; Kratzen *n*; Quietschen *n*; Erschütterung *f*; (*mus*) Dissonanz; Zusammenstoß *m*.
jargon *n* Jargon *m*; Kauderwelsch *n*.
jasmine *n* Jasmin *m*.
jaundice *n* Gelbsucht *f*; (*fig*) Neid *m*; Voreingenommenheit *f*.
jaunt *n* Ausflug *m*; Spritztour *f*.
jaunty *adj* flott; unbekümmert; beschwingt.
javelin *n* Wurfspieß *m*; Speer *m*.
jaw *n* Kiefer *m*; *pl* Maul *n*; *pl* Rachen *m*; (*tec*) Backen *m*; (*col*) Gerede *n*; (*col*) Moralpredigt *f*.
jay *n* Eichelhäher *m*; (*col*) Klatschtante *f*.
jazz *n* Jazz *m*.
jealous *adj* eifersüchtig; neidisch; sehr bedacht; argwöhnisch.
jealousy *n* Eifersucht *f*; Neid *m*; Argwohn *m*.
jeans *npl* Jeans *pl*.
jeep *n* Jeep *m*.
jeer *vi* höhnisch lachen; * *n* Hohngelächter *n*.
jelly *n* Gallerte *f*; Gelee *n*; Aspik *m*; Götterspeise *f*.
jelly-fish *n* Qualle *f*; (*col*) Waschlappen *m*.
jeopardize *vt* gefährden; aufs Spiel setzen.
jerk *n* Ruck *m*; Zuckung *f*; (*sl*) Trottel *m*; * *vt* ruckartig ziehen an.
jerky *adj* ruckartig; stoßweise.
jersey *n* Pullover *m*; Trikot *n*; Jersey *m*.
jest *n* Spaß *m*; Scherz *m*; Spott *m*.

jester *n* Spaßvogel *m*; (Hof)Narr *m*.
jestingly *adv* im Scherz.
Jesuit *n* Jesuit *m*.
Jesus *n* Jesus *m*.
jet *n* Düsenflugzeug *n*; Strahl *m*; Düse *f*; Jett *m*.
jet engine *n* Strahltriebwerk *n*.
jettison *vt* über Bord werfen; abwerfen; (*fig*) fallenlassen.
jetty *n* Mole *f*; Pier *m*.
Jew *n* Jude *m*.
jewel *n* Juwel *n*; Edelstein *m*.
jeweller *n* Juwelier *m*.
jewellery *n* Juwelen *pl*; Schmuck *m*.
jewellery store *n* Juwelier *m*; Schmuckgeschäft *n*.
Jewess *n* Jüdin *f*.
jewish *adj* jüdisch.
jib *n* (*mar*) Klüver *m*.
jibe *n* höhnische Bemerkung *f*.
jig *n* Gigue *f*; Einspannvorrichtung *f*.
jigsaw *n* Puzzle *n*; Dekupiersäge *f*.
jilt *vt* sitzenlassen; den Laufpaß geben.
jinx *n* Pech *n*; Unglücksbringer *m*.
job *n* Arbeit *f*; Beschäftigung *f*; Stelle *f*; Arbeitsplatz *m*; Sache *f*; Aufgabe *f*; (*col*) Ding *n*.
jockey *n* Jockey *m*.
jocular *adj* witzig; spaßig; ausgelassen.
jog *vi* trottenn; joggen.
jogging *n* Trotten *n*; Jogging *n*.
join *vt* verbinden; vereinigen; zusammenfügen; sich anschließen; eintreten in; (an)grenzen an; **to ~ in** sich anschließen; mitmachen; * *vi* sich vereinigen; sich verbinden; aneinandergrenzen.
joiner *n* Tischler(in) *m(f)*; Schreiner(in) *m(f)*.
joinery *n* Tischlerei *f*; Schreinerei *f*; Tischlerarbeit *f*; Schreinerarbeit *f*.
joint *n* Verbindung(sstelle) *f*; Verbindungsstück *n*; Gelenk *n*; Braten *m*; (*sl*) Spelunke *f*;

* adj gemeinsam; gemein-schaftlich; vereint.

jointly adv gemeinschaftlich; gemeinsam.

joint-stock company n (com) Kapitalgesellschaft f; Aktiengesellschaft f.

joke n Witz m; Scherz m; Spaß m; * vi scherzen; Witze machen.

joker n Spaßvogel m; Joker m.

jollity n Lustigkeit f; Fröhlichkeit f.

jolly adj lustig; fröhlich; vergnügt; (col) angeheitert; nett.

jolt vt einen Ruck geben; durchrütteln; (fig) aufrütteln; * n Ruck m; Stoß m; (fig) Schock m.

jostle vt anrempeln; drängeln.

journal n Tagebuch n; Journal n; Zeitschrift f.

journalism n Journalismus m.

journalist n Journalist(in) m(f).

journey n Reise f; * vt reisen.

jovial adj ~ly adv lustig; fröhlich; vergnügt.

joy n Freude f.

joyful, joyous adj ~ly adv freudig; erfreut; erfreulich.

joystick n Joystick m; Steuerknüppel m.

jubilant adj überglücklich; jubelnd.

jubilation n Jubel m.

jubilee n Jubiläum n.

Judaism n Judaismus m.

judge n Richter(in) m(f); Schiedsrichter(in) m(f); Kenner(in) m(f); * vt richten; verhandeln; beurteilen; entscheiden; (ein)schätzen.

judgment n (Gerichts)Urteil n; Beurteilung f; Urteilsvermögen n; Strafe (Gottes) f.

judicial adj ~ly adv gerichtlich; richterlich; kritisch; unparteiisch.

judiciary n Gerichtswesen n; Richterstand m.

judicious adj vernünftig; klug; umsichtig.

judo n Judo n.

jug n Krug m; Kanne f.

juggle vi jonglieren; (fig) frisieren.

juggler n Jongleur m; Schwindler m.

juice n Saft m; (fig) Kern m.

juicy adj saftig; (col) pikant; (col) knackig.

jukebox n Musikautomat m.

July n Juli m.

jumble vt durcheinanderwerfen; * n Durcheinander n; Ramsch m.

jump vi (über)springen; hüpfen; zusammenfahren; * n (Ab)Sprung m; Satz m; Hindernis n.

jumper n Pullover m.

jumpy adj nervös; schreckhaft; ruckartig.

juncture n (kritischer) Augenblick m; Verbindungsstelle f.

June n Juni m.

jungle n Dschungel m.

junior adj junior; jünger(er, e, es); Unter-.

juniper n (bot) Wacholder m.

junk n Plunder m; Schrott m.

junta n Junta f.

jurisdiction n Rechtssprechung f; Gerichtsbarkeit f.

jurisprudence n Rechtswissenschaft f.

jurist n Jurist m.

juror, juryman n Geschworene(r) f(m); Preisrichter(in) m(f).

jury n Jury f; Preisgericht n.

just adj gerecht; rechtmäßig; berechtigt; richtig; * adv gerade; (so)eben; genau; nur; einfach; ~ as ebenso wie; gerade als; ~ now gerade eben; jetzt gleich.

justice n Gerechtigkeit f; Rechtmäßigkeit f; Recht n; Rechtssprechung f; Richter m.

justifiably adv mit Recht.

justification n Rechtfertigung f; Berechtigung f.

justify vt rechtfertigen; gutheißen; justieren.

justly *adv* richtig; zu Recht;
  verdientermaßen.
justness *n* Gerechtigkeit *f*;
  Rechtmäßigkeit *f*; Richtigkeit
  f.
jut *vi*; **to ~ out** vorspringen;
  herausragen.
jute *n* Jute *f*.
juvenile *adj* jugendlich; Ju-
  gend-; unreif; infantil.
juxtaposition *n* Nebeneinan-
  derstellung *f*.

K

kaleidoscope *n* Kaleidoskop *n*.
kangaroo *n* Känguruh *n*.
karate *n* Karate *n*.
kebab *n* Kebab *m*.
keel *n* (*mar*) Kiel *m*.
keen *adj* scharf; fein; heftig;
  begeistert; versessen.
keenness *n* Schärfe *f*; Heftigkeit *f*; Begeisterung *f*; Verses-
  senheit *f*.
keep *vt* (be)halten; erhalten;
  (be)wahren; aufhalten; aufheben; unterhalten; führen; einhalten; bleiben in; * *vi* bleiben.
keeper *n* Wächter *m*; Verwalter *m*; Inhaber *m*; Halter *m*.
keepsake *n* Andenken *n*.
keg *n* kleines Faß *n*.
kennel *n* Hundehütte *f*; *pl* Hun-
  dezwinger *m*; *pl* Hundeheim
  n.
kerb *n* Bordstein *m*.
kernel *n* Kern *m*; Korn *n*.
kerosene *n* Kerosin *n*.
ketchup *n* Ketchup *m*.
kettle *n* Kessel *m*.
kettle-drum *n* (Kessel)Pauke *f*.
key *n* Schlüssel *m*; (*mus*) Tonart *f*; Taste *f*; (*fig*) Ton *m*.
keyboard *n* Tastatur *f*; Klavia-
  tur *f*; Manual *n*; Schlüssel-
  brett *n*.
keyhole *n* Schlüsselloch *n*.

keynote *n* (*mus*) Grundton *m*;
  (*fig*) Grundgedanke *m*.
key ring *n* Schlüsselring *m*.
keystone *n* Schlußstein *m*; (*fig*)
  Grundpfeiler *m*.
khaki *n* Khaki *n*, *m*.
kick *vt* treten; (mit dem Fuß)
  stoßen; loskommen von; * *vi*
  (um sich) treten; (mit dem
  Fuß) stoßen; strampeln; ausschlagen; * *n* (Fuß)Tritt *m*;
  (Rück)Stoß *m*; (Nerven)Kitzel
  m.
kid *n* (*col*) Kind *n*; Zicklein *n*;
  Kitz *n*.
kidnap *vt* kidnappen; entführen.
kidnapper *n* Kidnapper *m*;
  Entführer *m*.
kidnapping *n* Kidnapping *n*;
  Entführung *f*.
kidney *n* Niere *f*.
kill *vt* (ab)töten; umbringen;
  ermorden; schlachten; erle-
  gen; zerstören; vernichten;
  totschlagen; abwürgen.
killer *n* Mörder *m*; Killer *m*;
  Schlächter *m*; Vernichtungs-
  mittel *n*.
killing *n* Tötung *f*; Mord *m*;
  Schlachten *n*.
kiln *n* Darre *f*; Brennofen *m*;
  Kiln *m*; Trockenofen *m*.
kilo *n* Kilo *n*.
kilobyte *n* Kilobyte *n*.
kilogram *n* Kilogramm *n*.
kilometer *n* Kilometer *m*.
kilt *n* Kilt *m*; Schottenrock *m*.
kin *n* Sippe *f*; Familie *f*;
  (Bluts)Verwandtschaft *f*; **next
  of ~** (*die*) nächsten Angehöri-
  gen *pl*.
kind *adj* freundlich; liebenswürdig; nett; hilfreich; herzlich; * *n* Art *f*; Sorte *f*; Gattung
  f; Geschlecht *n*; Wesen *n*; Na-
  turalien *pl*.
kindergarten *n* Kindergarten
  m.
kind-hearted *adj* gütig; gutherzig.
kindle *vt* anzünden; entfachen;
  entflammen; wecken; * *vi*

Feuer fangen; entbrennen; entflammen.

kindliness n Güte f; Freundlichkeit f.

kindly adj gütig; freundlich.

kindness n Frendlichkeit f; Gefälligkeit f.

kindred adj (bluts)verwandt.

kinetic adj kinetisch.

king n König m.

kingdom n Königreich n; Reich n.

kingfisher n Eisvogel m.

kiosk n Kiosk m; Telefonzelle f.

kiss n Kuß m; * vt küssen.

kissing n Küssen n.

kit n Ausrüstung f; Montur f; Arbeitsgerät n; Werkzeug n; Bausatz m.

kitchen n Küche f.

kitchen garden n Küchengarten m; Gemüsegarten m.

kite n Drachen m; Gabelweihe f.

kitten n Kätzchen n.

knack n Trick m; Kniff m; Geschick n; Talent n.

knapsack n Rucksack m; Tornister m.

knave n Bube m; Schurke m.

knead vt kneten.

knee n Knie(stück) n.

knee-deep adj knietief.

kneel vi (sich hin)knien.

knell n Totengeläut n.

knife n Messer n.

knight n Ritter m; Schach: Springer m; Pferd n.

knit vt, vi tejer, stricken; (fig) verknüpfen; **to ~ the brows** die Stirn runzeln.

knitter n Stricker(in) m(f).

knitting-needle n Stricknadel f.

knitwear n Strickwaren fpl.

knob n Knauf m; Griff m; Höcker m; Stück(chen) n; Knorren m.

knock vt stoßen; schlagen; klopfen; (col) heruntermachen; (col) umhauen; * vi schlagen; klopfen; pochen; **to ~ down** umstoßen; nieder-

schlagen; überfahren; abwerfen; (col) umhauen; abreißen; herunterhandeln; * n Schlag m; Stoß m; Klopfen n.

knocker n Klopfende(r) f(m); Vertreter m.

knock-kneed adj X-beinig.

knock-out n K.o. m.

knoll n Kuppe f; Hügel m.

knot n Knoten m; Schleife f; * vt (ver)knoten; verheddern.

knotty adj knotig; astig; knorrig.

know vt wissen; können; (er)kennen; erleben; * vi wissen.

know-all n Besserwisser m.

know-how n Know-how n.

knowing adj intelligent; klug; durchtrieben; wissend; verständnisvoll; **~ly** adv = knowing; wissentlich; absichtlich.

knowledge n Wissen n; Kenntnis f.

knowledgeable adj klug; (gut)unterrichtet; kenntnisreich.

knuckle n Knöchel m.

L

label n Etikett n; Beschriftung f; Label n.

laboratory n Labor(atorium) n.

laborious adj **~ly** adv mühselig; schwierig; schwefällig; arbeitsam.

labour n Arbeit f; Mühe f; Anstrengung f; Arbeitskräfte pl; Wehen pl; **to be in ~** in den Wehen liegen; * vi (schwer) arbeiten; sich abmühen; sich mühsam fortbewegen.

labourer n Arbeiter m.

labour union n Gewerkschaft f.

labyrinth n Labyrinth n; (fig) Gewirr n.

lace *n* Spitze *f*; Borte *f*; Schnürsenkel *m*; Band *n*; * *vt*
(zusammen)schnüren; einziehen; besetzen; würzen; einen
Schuß Alkohol zugeben.

lacerate *vt* aufreißen; zerkrat-
zen; verletzen.

lack *vt* nicht haben; es fehlen
lassen an; * *vi* fehlen; * *n*
Mangel *m*.

lackadaisical *adj* lustlos;
nachlässig.

lackey *n* Lakai *m*; (*fig*) Spei-
chellecker *m*.

laconic *adj* lakonisch; wortkarg.

lacquer *n* Lack *m*; Firnis *m*;
Festiger *m*.

lad *n* junger Kerl *m*; Junge *m*.

ladder *n* Leiter *f*; Laufmasche
f.

ladle *n* (Schöpf)Kelle *f*.

lady *n* Dame *f*; Herrin *f*.

ladybird *n* Marienkäfer *m*.

ladykiller *n* Herzensbrecher *m*.

ladylike *adj* damenhaft.

ladyship *n* Ladyschaft *f*.

lag *vi* ~ behind zurückbleiben;
hinterherhinken; sich verzögern; * *vt* verschalen; isolieren.

lager *n* Lagerbier *n*.

lagoon *n* Lagune *f*.

laidback *adj* gelassen.

lair *n* Lager *n*; Höhle *f*; Versteck
n.

laity *n* Laienstand *m*; Laien *pl*.

lake *n* See *m*.

lamb *n* Lamm *n*; * *vi* lammen.

lambswool *n* Lambswool *f*.

lame *adj* lahm; (*fig*) schwach.

lament *vt* beklagen; * *vi* jammern; (weh)klagen; trauern;
* *n* (Weh)Klage *f*; Klagelied *n*.

lamentable *adj* beklagenswert;
bedauerlich; kläglich.

lamentation *n* (Weh)Klage *f*;
Lamentieren *n*.

laminated *adj* laminiert; ge-
schichtet; lamelliert.

lamp *n* Lampe *f*; Laterne *f*;
Leuchte *f*.

lampoon *n* Spottschrift *f*; (sa-

tirisches) Pamphlet *n*.

lampshade *n* Lampenschirm
m.

lance *n* Lanze *f*; (Fisch)Speer *m*;
Ulan *m*; * *vt* aufspießen; (med)
mit einer Lanzette öffnen.

lancet *n* Lanzette *f*.

land *n* Land *n*; Boden *m*; Grund
und Boden *m*; * *vt* landen; an
Land ziehen; bringen; aufhal-
sen; * *vi* landen; anlegen.

land forces *npl* Landstreitkräf-
te *pl*.

landholder *n* Grundbesitzer *m*.

landing *n* Landung *f*; Anlegen
n; Ausladen *n*; Löschen *n*; An-
legeplatz *m*; (Treppen)Absatz
m.

landing strip *n* Landebahn *f*.

landlady *n* Vermieterin *f*; Wir-
tin *f*; Grundbesitzerin *f*.

landlord *n* Vermieter *m*; Wirt
m; Grundbesitzer *m*.

landlubber *n* Landratte *f*.

landmark *n* Grenzstein *m*;
Landmarke *f*; Wahrzeichen *n*.

landowner *n* Grundbesit-
zer(in) *m(f)*.

landscape *n* Landschaft *f*.

landslide *n* Erdrutsch *m*.

lane *n* Weg *m*; Gasse *f*; (Flug-)
Schneise *f*; Fahrrinne *f*;
(Fahr)Spur *f*.

language *n* Sprache *f*; Redewei-
se *f*; Worte *pl*; Terminologie *f*.

languid *adj* ~ly *adv* matt;
schlaff; teilnahmslos; träge.

languish *vi* ermatten; erschlaffen; erlahmen; schmachten;
daniederliegen.

lank *adj* hager; mager; glatt.

lanky *adj* schlaksig; hochaufge-
schossen.

lantern *n* Laterne *f*; (*fig*) Leuchte *f*.

lap *n* Schoß *m*; Windung *f*; Vorstoß *m*; Runde *f*; Lecken *n*;
Plätschern *n*; * *vt* (ein)wickeln;
einhüllen; überlappen; (auf-)
lecken; schlecken; plätschern.

lapdog *n* Schoßhund *m*.

lapel *n* Aufschlag *m*; Revers *n*.

lapse *n* Lapsus *m*; Versehen *n*;

Fehltritt *m*; Ablauf *m*; Verfall *m*; * *vi* verstreichen; ablaufen; (ver)fallen; abgleiten; entgleisen; versäumen.

larceny *n* Diebstahl *m*.

larch *n* Lärche *f*.

lard *n* Schweineschmalz *n*.

larder *n* Speisekammer *f*.

large *adj* groß; umfassend; **at ~** auf freiem Fuße; frei; ausführlich; ganz allgemein; in der Gesamtheit; aufs Geratewohl; **~ly** *adv* größtenteils; weitgehend; reichlich; allgemein.

large-scale *adj* groß(angelegt); ausgedehnt; Groß-; in großem Maßstab.

largesse *n* Großzügigkeit *f*.

lark *n* Lerche *f*; Jux *m*; Spaß *m*.

larva *n* Larve *f*.

laryngitis *n* Kehlkopfentzündung *f*.

larynx *n* Kehlkopf *m*.

lascivious *adj* **~ly** *adv* lüstern; lasziv; schlüpfrig.

laser *n* Laser *m*.

lash *n* (Peitschen)Hieb *m*; Peischen *n*; Wimper *f*; * *vt* (aus)peitschen; peitschen mit; (*fig*) geißeln.

lasso *n* Lasso *n*.

last *adj* letzt(er, e, es); vorig(er, e, es); neuest(er, e, es); äußerst(er, e, es); * *adv* zuletzt; als letzt(er, e, es); schließlich; **at ~** endlich; schließlich; zuletzt; **~ly** *adv* zuletzt; zum Schluß; * *n* Leisten *m*; (*der, die, das*) Letzte; Ende *n*; * *vi* (an)dauern; bestehen; durchhalten; (sich) halten; (aus)reichen.

last ditch *adj* allerletzt(er, e, es); bis zum Äußersten.

lasting *adj* **~ly** *adv* dauerhaft; (an)dauernd; haltbar; nachhaltig.

last-minute *adj* in letzter Minute.

latch *n* Schnappschloß *m*; Klinke *f*.

latch-key *n* (Haus)Schlüssel *m*.

late *adj* (zu) spät; Spät-; verspätet; letzt(er, e, es); ehemalig; verstorben; (*rail*) **the train is ten minutes ~** der Zug hat zehn Minuten Verspätung; * *adv* (zu) spät; **~ly** *adv* kürzlich; in letzter Zeit; neuerdings.

latecomer *n* Zuspätkommende(r) *f(m)*; Nachzügler(in) *m(f)*.

latent *adj* latent; verborgen.

lateral *adj* **~ly** *adv* seitlich; Seiten-; lateral.

lath *n* Latte *f*; Leiste *f*.

lathe *n* Drehbank *f*; Lade *f*.

lather *n* (Seifen)Schaum *m*.

latitude *n* Breite *f*; (Bewegungs)Freiheit *f*.

latrine *n* Latrine *f*.

latter *adj* letztgenannt(er, e, es); neuer; jünger; letzt(er, e, es); später; **~ly** *adv* in letzter Zeit; neuerdings.

lattice *n* Gitter(werk) *n*.

laudable *adj* löblich; lobenswert.

laudably *adv* = laudable.

laugh *vi* lachen; **to ~ at** auslachen; lachen über; sich lustig machen über; * *n* Lachen *n*; Gelächter *n*; (*col*) Spaß *m*.

laughable *adj* lächerlich; lachhaft; komisch.

laughing stock *n* Zielscheibe des Spottes.

laughter *n* Lachen *n*; Gelächter *n*.

launch *vt* zu Wasser lassen; vom Stapel (laufen) lassen; starten; abschießen; loslassen; lancieren; sich stürzen; * *n* (*mar*) Stapellauf *m*; Abschuß *m*; Start *m*; Barkasse *f*.

launching *n* Stapellauf *m*; Abschuß *m*; Start *m*.

launching pad *n* Abschußrampe *f*; (*fig*) Sprungbrett *n*.

launder *vt* waschen.

launderette *n* Waschsalon *n*.

laundry *n* Wäsche *f*; Wäscherei *f*; Waschküche *f*.

laurel n Lorbeer m; Lorbeerkranz m.

lava n Lava f.

lavatory n Waschraum m; Toilette f.

lavender n (bot) Lavendel m.

lavish adj ~ly adv freigiebig; verschwenderisch; überschwenglich; luxuriös; * vt verschwenden; überhäufen.

law n Gesetz n; Recht n; Rechtswissenschaft f; Gericht n; Vorschrift f; (col) Bullen pl.

law-abiding adj gesetzestreu.

law and order n Recht und Ordnung.

law court n Gerichtshof m.

lawful adj ~ly adv gesetzmäßig; legal; rechtmäßig; legitim; rechtsgültig.

lawless adj gesetzlos; rechtswidrig; zügellos.

lawlessness n Gesetzlosigkeit f; Rechtswidrigkeit f; Zügellosigkeit f.

lawmaker n Gesetzgeber m.

lawn n Rasen m.

lawnmower n Rasenmäher m.

law school n Rechtsakademie f; juristische Fakultät f.

law suit n Prozeß m; (Gerichts)Verfahren n; Klage f.

lawyer n (Rechts)Anwalt m; (Rechts)Anwältin f; Rechtsberater(in) m(f); Jurist(in) m(f).

lax adj lax; locker; (nach)lässig; schlaff.

laxative n Abführmittel n.

laxity n Laxheit f; Lockerheit f; (Nach)Lässigkeit f; Schlaffheit f.

lay vt (aus)legen; (her)richten; decken; auftragen; vorbringen; auferlegen; niederlegen; aufs Kreuz legen; **to ~ claim** Anspruch erheben; * vi legen.

layabout n Faulenzer m; Tagedieb m.

layer n Schicht f; Lage f.

layette n Babyausstattung f.

layman n Laie m.

layout n Layout n; (Lage)Plan

m; Entwurf m; Anlage f.

laze vi faulenzen.

lazily adv faul; träge; langsam.

laziness n Faulheit f; Trägheit f; Langsamkeit f.

lazy adj faul; träge; langsam.

lead n Blei n; Senkblei n; Lot n; (Bleistift)Mine f; Führung f; Vorsprung m; Beispiel n; Hinweis m; Anhalspunkt m; Spur f; Hauptrolle f; Leitung f; Leine f; * vt führen; leiten; den Weg zeigen; bewegen; veranlassen; * vi führen; vorangehen.

leader n (An)Führer(in) m(f); Leiter(in) m(f); Leitartikel m; Spitzenreiter m; (bot) Haupttrieb m; Suggestivfrage f.

leadership n Führung f; Leitung f.

leading adj führend; leitend; Leit-; erst(er, e, es); Haupt-; maßgebend; ~ **article** n Leitartikel m; Lockartikel m.

leaf n Blatt n; Flügel m; Klappe f.

leaflet n Flugblatt n; Prospekt m.

leafy adj belaubt; Laub-.

league n Liga f; Bund m; Klasse f.

leak n Leck n; undichte Stelle f; Auslaufen n; * vi (mar) lekken; tropfen; (fig) durchsickern.

leaky adj leck; undicht.

lean vt neigen; beugen; lehnen; stützen; * vi sich neigen; sich lehnen; sich beugen; sich stützen; * adj mager; arm; (fig) knapp.

leap vi springen; * n Sprung m.

leapfrog n Bockspringen n.

leap year n Schaltjahr n.

learn vt, vi (er)lernen; erfahren; hören.

learned adj gelehrt; erfahren; erlernt.

learner n Anfänger(in) m(f); Lernende(r) f(m).

learning n Gelehrsamkeit f; (Er)Lernen n.

lease n Mietvertrag m; Vermietung f; Miete f; Pachtvertrag m; Verpachtung f; Pacht f; * vt pachten; mieten; leasen.

leasehold n Mietbesitz m; Pachtbesitz m; Pachtland n.

leash n Leine f; Koppel f.

least adj geringst(er, e, es); wenigst(er, e, es); **at ~** wenigstens; zumindest; **not in the ~** nicht im geringsten.

leather n Leder n.

leathery adj ledrig; zäh; lederartig.

leave n Erlaubnis f; Genehmigung f; Urlaub m; Abschied m; **to take ~** Urlaub nehmen; Abschied nehmen; sich erlauben; * vt verlassen; weggehen; abreisen; im Stich lassen; (hinter)lassen; liegenlassen; vergessen; vermachen.

leaven n Sauerteig m; Treibmittel n; * vt säuern; (auf)gehen lassen; (fig) auflockern.

leavings npl Überbleibsel pl; Abfall m.

lecherous adj geil; lüstern.

lecture n Vortrag m; Vorlesung f; Strafpredigt f; * vt einen Vortrag halten; eine Vorlesung halten; eine Strafpredigt halten.

lecturer n Vortragende(r) f(m); Lehrbeauftragte(r) f(m).

ledge n Sims m; Gesims n; Riff n; Leiste f.

ledger n (com) Hauptbuch n.

lee n (mar) Lee f; Windschattenseite f; Schutz m.

leech n Blutegel m; (fig) Klette f; Blutsauger m.

leek n (bot) Lauch m; Porree m.

leer vi anzüglich grinsen; lüstern schielen.

lees npl Bodensatz m.

leeward adj (mar) Lee-; leewärts gelegen.

leeway n Abtrift f; (fig) Rückstand m; (fig) Spielraum m.

left adj link(er, e, es); Links-; **on the ~** links.

left-handed adj linkshändig;

linkisch.

leftovers npl Reste pl.

leg n Bein n; (Unter)Schenkel m; Keule f; Etappe f.

legacy n Vermächtnis n; Erbe n.

legal adj ~ly adv gesetzlich; legal; rechtlich; gesetzmäßig; Rechts-; gerichtlich.

legal holiday n gesetzlicher Feiertag m.

legality n Legalität f; Gesetzlichkeit f; Gesetzmäßigkeit f.

legalize vt legalisieren.

legal tender n gesetzliches Zahlungsmittel n.

legate n Legat m; päpstlicher Gesandter m.

legatee n Vermächtnisnehmer(in) m(f).

legation n (päpstliche) Gesandtschaft f; Entsendung f.

legend n Legende f; Sage f.

legendary adj legendär; sagenhaft; unwahrscheinlich.

legible adj leserlich.

legibly adv = legible.

legion n Legion f.

legislate vi Gesetze erlassen.

legislation n Gesetzgebung f.

legislative adj gesetzgebend; legislativ; Legislatur-; gesetzlich.

legislator n Gesetzgeber m.

legislature n Legislative f; gesetzgebende Körperschaft f.

legitimacy n Legitimität f; Gesetzmäßigkeit f; Rechtmäßigkeit f; Ehelichkeit f; (Folge-) Richtigkeit f; Echtheit f.

legitimate adj ~ly adv legitim; gesetzmäßig; rechtmäßig; ehelich; (folge)richtig; echt; * vt legitimieren; für gesetzmäßig erklären; für ehelich erklären; sanktionieren; rechtfertigen.

leisure n Freizeit f; Muße f; ~ly adj gemächlich; gemütlich; **at ~** in aller Ruhe.

lemon n Zitrone f; Limone f.

lemonade n Limonade f.

lemon tea n Zitronentee m.

lemon tree n Zitronenbaum m.

lend *vt* (ver)leihen.

length *n* Länge *f*; Bahn *f*; Stück *n*; Dauer *f*; **at ~** ausführlich; endlich.

lengthen *vt* verlängern; ausdehnen; * *vi* sich verlängern; länger werden.

lengthways, lengthwise *adv* der Länge nach; längs.

lengthy *adj* sehr lang; langatmig.

lenient *adj* milde; nachsichtig.

lens *n* Linse *f*; Objektiv *n*; Glas *n*; Lupe *f*.

Lent *n* Fastenzeit *f*.

lentil *n* Linse *f*.

leopard *n* Leopard *m*; Panther *m*.

leotard *n* Trikot *n*; Gymnastikanzug *m*.

leper *n* Leprakranke(r) *f(m)*; Aussätzige(r) *f(m)*.

leprosy *n* Lepra *f*; Aussatz *m*.

lesbian *n* Lesbierin *f*.

less *adj* geringer; weniger; kleiner; jünger; * *adv* weniger.

lessen *vt* vermindern; verringern; herabsetzen; schmälern; * *vi* sich vermindern; abnehmen.

lesser *adj* kleiner; geringer; unbedeutender.

lesson *n* Lektion *f*; (Haus)Aufgabe *f*; (Unterrichts)Stunde *f*; Lehre *f*.

lest *conj* daß (nicht); damit nicht.

let *vt* lassen; erlauben; vermieten; verpachten; vergeben.

lethal *adj* tödlich; Todes-.

lethargic *adj* lethargisch; teilnahmslos; träge.

lethargy *n* Lethargie *f*; Teilnahmslosigkeit *f*; Trägheit *f*.

letter *n* Brief *m*; Buchstabe *m*; Type *f*.

letter bomb *n* Briefbombe *f*.

lettering *n* Beschriftung *f*; Buchstaben *pl*.

letter of credit *n* Akkreditiv *n*.

lettuce *n* Salat *m*.

leukaemia *n* Leukämie *f*.

level *adj* eben; waagerecht; gleich(bleibend); gleichmäßig; ausgeglichen; ruhig; * *n* Wasserwaage *f*; Ebene *f*; Horizontale *f*; Höhe *f*; Stand *m*; Niveau *n*; * *vt* (ein)ebnen; planieren; ausgleichen; nivellieren; anlegen; richten.

level-headed *adj* vernünftig.

lever *n* Hebel *m*; Brechstange *f*; (*fig*) Druckmittel *n*.

leverage *n* Hebelkraft *f*; (*fig*) Einfluß *m*.

levity *n* Leichtfertigkeit *f*.

levy *n* Erhebung *f*; Abgabe *f*; Beitrag *m*; (*mil*) Aushebung *f*; (*mil*) Aufgebot *n*; * *vt* erheben; auferlegen; ausheben.

lewd *adj* lüstern; obszön.

lexicon *n* Lexikon *n*; Wörterbuch *n*.

liability *n* Verpflichtung *f*; Haftpflicht *f*; Verantwortlichkeit *f*; Pflicht *f*; Verbindlichkeit *f*; Neigung *f*; Belastung *f*.

liable *adj* verantwortlich; haftpflichtig; ausgesetzt; unterworfen; anfällig.

liaise *vi* Verbindung aufnehmen; zusammenarbeiten.

liaison *n* Verbindung *f*; Zusammenarbeit *f*; Liaison *f*.

liar *n* Lügner(in) *m(f)*.

libel *n* Verleumdung *f*; Beleidigung *f*; * *vt* verleumden; beleidigen.

libellous *adj* verleumderisch.

liberal *adj* **~ly** *adv* liberal; aufgeschlossen; großzügig; frei.

liberality *n* Liberalität *f*; Großzügigkeit *f*.

liberate *vt* befreien; freilassen.

liberation *n* Befreiung *f*; Freilassung *f*.

libertine *n* zügelloser Mensch *m*; Freigeist *m*.

liberty *n* Freiheit *f*; Dreistigkeit *f*.

Libra *n* Waage *f*.

librarian *n* Bibliothekar(in) *m(f)*.

library *n* Bibliothek *f*; Bücherei *f*; Archiv *n*.

libretto *n* Libretto *n*.

licence n Erlaubnis f; Lizenz f; Zulassung f; (Handlungs)Freiheit f; Zügellosigkeit f.

licence plate n Nummernschild n.

licentious adj ausschweifend; zügellos.

lichen n (bot) Flechte f.

lick vt (ab)lecken; plätschern an; (col) verprügeln.

lid n Deckel n; Lid n.

lie n Lüge f; * vi lügen; täuschen.

lieu n: **in ~ of** an Stelle von; anstatt.

lieutenant n Stellvertreter m; Statthalter m; Leutnant m.

life n Leben n; Lebensdauer f; Biographie f; (col) Lebenslänglich n; **for ~** lebenslänglich; auf Lebenszeit; fürs ganze Leben.

lifeboat n Rettungsboot n.

life-guard n Rettungsschwimmer m; Leibgarde f.

life jacket n Rettungsweste f.

lifeless adj leblos; tot; unbelebt; ohne Leben; matt.

lifelike adj lebensecht; naturgetreu.

lifeline n Rettungsleine f; (fig) Rettungsanker m; (fig) Lebensader f; Lebenslinie f.

life preserver n Rettungsweste f; Totschläger m.

life sentence n lebenslängliche Freiheitsstrafe f.

life-sized adj lebensgroß.

lifespan n Lebenszeit f; Lebensdauer f.

lifestyle n Lebensstil m.

life support system n Life-Support-System n.

lifetime n Lebenszeit f; Leben n; Lebensdauer f.

lift vt (hoch)heben; erheben; aufmuntern; erhöhen; (col) klauen; liften.

ligament n Ligament n; Band n.

light n Licht n; Helligkeit f; Beleuchtung f; Scheinwerfer m; Ampel f; Tagesanbruch m;

Glanz m; Feuer n; Fenster n; * adj hell; licht; leicht; Unterhaltungs-; * vt anzünden; (er)leuchten; erhellen.

light bulb n Glühbirne f.

lighten vi hell werden; leichter werden; * vt erhellen; erleichtern; aufheitern.

lighter n Feuerzeug n; Prahm m.

light-headed adj leichtsinnig; leicht benommen.

lighthearted adj fröhlich; heiter, unbeschwert.

lighthouse n (mar) Leuchtturm m.

lighting n Beleuchtung f; Anzünden n.

lightly adv leicht; wenig; gelassen; leichtfertig; leichthin.

lightning n Blitz m.

lightning-rod n Blitzableiter m.

light pen n Lichtstift m.

lightweight adj leicht; leichtgewichtig.

light year n Lichtjahr n.

ligneous adj holzig.

like adj gleich; wie; ähnlich; * adv (so) wie; * vt gern haben; mögen; gern tun; * vi wollen.

likeable adj liebenswert; sympathisch.

likelihood n Wahrscheinlichkeit f.

likely adj wahrscheinlich; voraussichtlich; glaubhaft; aussichtsreich; vielversprechend.

liken vt vergleichen.

likeness n Ähnlichkeit f; Gestalt f; Abbild n; Porträt n.

likewise adv außerdem; desgleichen; ebenso.

liking n Geschmack m; Vorliebe f; Zuneigung f; Gefallen n.

lilac n Flieder m; Lila n.

lily n Lilie f; **~ of the valley** Maiglöckchen n.

limb n Glied n; (Haupt)Ast m; Arm m.

limber adj geschmeidig; beweglich; gelenkig; flexibel.

lime n Kalk m; Kalkdünger m;

Linde *f*; Limone *f*; ~ **tree** Linde *f*.

limestone *n* Kalkstein *m*.

limit *n* Grenze *f*; Beschränkung *f*; Limit *n*; * *vt* beschränken; begrenzen; limitieren.

limitation *n* Grenze *f*; Begrenzung *f*; Beschränkung *f*.

limitless *adj* grenzenlos.

limo(usine) *n* Limousine *f*.

limp *vi* hinken; humpeln; * *n* Hinken *n*; Humpeln; * *adj* schlaff; schlapp; weich.

limpet *n* Napfschnecke *f*.

limpid *adj* durchsichtig; klar.

line *n* Linie *f*; Strich *m*; Runzel *f*; Zeile *f*; Vers *m*; (*col*) Information *f*; Richtung *f*; Art und Weise *f*; Grenze *f*; Reihe *f*; Schlange *f*; Branche *f*; Leitung *f*; Leine *f*; Schnur *f*; Artikel *m*; * *vt* linieren; (zer)furchen; skizzieren; säumen; füttern; ausschlagen.

lineage *n* Abstammung *f*; Stammbaum *m*.

linear *adj* linear; geradlinig; strichförmig.

lined *adj* gefüttert; ausgeschlagen; gesäumt.

linen *n* Leinen *n*; Wäsche *f*.

liner *n* Linienschiff *n*; Verkehrsflugzeug *n*.

linesman *n* Streckenarbeiter *m*; Linienrichter *m*.

linger *vi* verweilen; (zurück-)bleiben; sich hinziehen; zögern; trödeln.

lingerie *n* Damenunterwäsche *f*.

lingering *adj* nachklingend; (zurück)bleibend; schleichend; sehnsüchtig.

linguist *n* Sprachwissenschaftler(in) *m(f)*; Sprachenkenner(in) *m(f)*.

linguistic *adj* sprachwissenschaftlich; Sprach-; linguistisch.

linguistics *n* Sprachwissenschaft *f*; Linguistik *f*.

liniment *n* Einreibemittel *n*.

lining *n* Futter *n*; Verkleidung *f*; Belag *m*.

link *n* Glied *n*; Verbindung *f*; Masche *f*; Manschettenknopf *m*; Kanal *m*; * *vt* verbinden; verknüpfen; in Verbindung bringen.

linnet *n* Hänfling *m*.

linoleum *n* Linoleum *n*.

linseed *n* Leinsamen *m*.

lint *n* Fussel *pl*; Lint *n*.

lintel *n* Sturz *m*.

lion *n* Löwe *m*.

lioness *n* Löwin *f*.

lip *n* Lippe *f*; (*col*) Unverschämtheit *f*; Mundstück *n*; Rand *n*; Tülle *f*.

lip read *vi* von den Lippen ablesen.

lip salve *n* Lippenpomade *f*.

lipstick *n* Lippenstift *m*.

liqueur *n* Likör *m*.

liquid *adj* flüssig; Flüssigkeits-; fließend; klar; feucht; * *n* Flüssigkeit *f*.

liquidate *vt* liquidieren; auflösen; beseitigen; erledigen.

liquidation *n* Liquidation *f*; Auflösung *f*; Liquidierung *f*; Beseitigung *f*.

liquidize *vt* verflüssigen; passieren.

liquor *n* Alkohol *m*; Spirituosen *pl*; Brühe *f*; Lauge *f*.

liquorice *n* Lakritze *m*; Süßholz *n*.

liquor store *n* Spirituosengeschäft *n*.

lisp *vi* lispeln; stammeln; * *n* Lispeln *n*; Stammeln *n*.

list *n* Liste *f*; Verzeichnis *n*; * *vt* verzeichnen; aufführen; registrieren.

listen *vi* (zu)hören; lauschen; horchen.

listless *adj* lustlos; teilnahmslos.

litany *n* Litanei *f*.

litre *n* Liter *n*.

literal *adj* wörtlich; genau; nüchtern; eigentlich; buchstäblich; wahr; ~**ly** *adv* wörtlich; buchstäblich.

literary *adj* literarisch; Literatur-; schriftstellerisch.

literate *adj* des Lesens und Schreibens kundig; gebildet; belesen; literarisch.

literature *n* Literatur *f*; Schrifttum *n*.

lithe *adj* geschmeidig.

lithograph *n* Lithographie *f*.

lithography *n* Lithographie *f*.

litigation *n* Prozeß *m*; (Rechts)Streit *m*.

litigious *adj* Prozeß-; strittig.

litter *n* Trage *f*; Sänfte *f*; Streu *f*; Abfall *m*; Unordnung *f*; Wurf *m*; * *vt* einstreuen; Abfall herumliegen lassen; herumliegen; werfen.

little *adj* klein; wenig; kurz; ~ **by** ~ nach und nach; allmählich; * *n* Kleinigkeit *f*.

liturgy *n* Liturgie *f*.

live *vi* leben; sich ernähren; wohnen; **to** ~ **on** leben von; sich ernähren von; **to** ~ **up to** *vt* gerecht werden; entsprechen; halten; * *adj* lebend; lebendig; aktuell; glühend; scharf; aktiv; stromführend; Live-.

livelihood *n* Lebensunterhalt *m*.

liveliness *n* Lebendigkeit *f*; Lebhaftigkeit *f*.

lively *adj* lebhaft; lebendig; aufregend; flott.

liven up *vt* beleben; in Schwung bringen.

liver *n* Leber *f*.

livery *n* Livree *f*; Tracht *f*; Mietstall *m*; (law) Übergabe *f*.

livestock *n* Vieh *n*.

livid *adj* bläulich; fahl; bleich; (col) fuchsteufelswild.

living *n* Leben *n*; Lebensunterhalt *m*; * *adj* lebend; lebendig; Lebens-.

living room *n* Wohnzimmer *n*.

lizard *n* Eidechse *f*.

load *vt* (be)laden; verladen; überhäufen; (einseitig) beschweren; * *n* Ladung *f*; Last *f*; Fuhre *f*; Belastung *f*; Leistung *f*; Massen *pl*.

loaded *adj* geladen; beladen; beschwert; präpariert; (col) stinkreich.

loaf *n* Laib *m*; Brot *n*.

loafer *n* Müßiggänger(in) *m(f)*; Faulenzer(in) *m(f)*.

loam *n* Lehm *m*.

loan *n* (Ver)Leihen *n*; Anleihe *f*; Darlehen *n*; Leihgabe *f*.

loathe *vt* verabscheuen; hassen; sich ekeln vor.

loathing *n* Abscheu *m*; Ekel *m*.

loathsome *adj* abscheulich; ekelhaft; verhaßt.

lobby *n* Eingangshalle *f*; Vorzimmer *n*; Foyer *n*; Lobby *f*; Interessengruppe *f*.

lobe *n* Lappen *m*.

lobster *n* Hummer *m*.

local *adj* lokal; örtlich; Orts-; Lokal-.

local anesthetic *n* örtliche Betäubung *f*.

local government *n* Gemeindeverwaltung *f*; Kommunalverwaltung *f*.

locality *n* Örtlichkeit *f*; Ort *m*; Gegend *f*; Lage *f*.

localize *vt* lokalisieren.

locally *adv* lokal; örtlich; am Ort.

locate *vt* ausfindig machen; aufspüren; orten; lokalisieren; einen bestimmten Platz zuweisen.

location *n* Stelle *f*; Lage *f*; Standort *m*; Ortung *f*; Lokalisierung *f*.

loch *n* See *m*; Bucht *f*.

lock *n* Schloß *n*; Verschluß *m*; Sicherung *f*; Schleuse *f*; * *vt* verschließen; zusperren; umschließen; verschränken; sichern; umfassen.

locker *n* Schließfach *n*; Spind *m*.

locket *n* Medaillon *n*.

lockout *n* Aussperrung *f*.

locksmith *n* Schlosser *m*.

lock-up *n* Garage *f*; Arrestzelle *f*.

locomotive *n* Lokomotive *f*.

locust *n* Heuschrecke *f*.

lodge *n* Hütte *f*; Sommerhaus

n; Pförtnerhaus *n*; Loge *f*; Wigwam *m*; * *vi* logieren; übernachten; stecken(bleiben).

lodger *n* Untermieter(in) *m(f)*.

loft *n* (Dach)Boden *m*; Heuboden *m*; Speicher *m*; Empore *f*.

lofty *adj* hoch(ragend); hochfliegend; erhaben; hochmütig.

log *n* (Holz)Klotz *m*; Baumstamm *m*; Log *n*.

logbook *n* (*mar*) Logbuch *n*; Fahrtenbuch *n*; Dienstbuch *n*.

logic *n* Logik *f*.

logical *adj* logisch; folgerichtig.

logo *n* Firmenemblem *n*.

loin *n* Lende *f*.

loiter *vi* bummeln; schlendern; herumlungern.

loll *vi* sich lümmeln; herabhängen.

lollipop *n* Lutscher *m*.

loneliness *n* Einsamkeit *f*.

lonely, lonesome *adj* einsam; verlassen; allein.

long *adj* (zu) lang; länglich; Längs-; weitreichend; langfristig; * *vi* sich sehnen.

long-distance *n*: ~ call Ferngespräch *n*.

longevity *n* Langlebigkeit *f*.

long-haired *adj* langhaarig; weltfremd.

longing *n* Sehnsucht *f*.

longitude *n* Länge *f*.

longitudinal *adj* Längen-; Längs-.

long jump *n* Weitsprung *m*.

long-playing record *n* Langspielplatte *f*.

long-range *adj* langfristig; auf lange Sicht; (*mil*) Fern-; Langstrecken-.

long-term *adj* langfristig.

long wave *n* Langwelle *f*.

long-winded *adj* ausdauernd; langatmig; umständlich.

look *vi* (aus)schauen; nachsehen; aussehen; **to ~ after** *vt* nachschauen; aufpassen auf; sich kümmern um; sorgen für; **to ~ for** *vt* suchen; hoffen auf; **to ~ forward to** *vt* sich freuen auf; **to ~ out for** *vt* Ausschau halten nach; aufpassen auf; sich vorsehen vor; * *n* Blick *m*; Miene *f*; *pl* Aussehen *n*.

looking glass *n* Spiegel *m*.

look-out *n* (*mil*) Ausschau *f*; Wache *f*; Ausguck *m*; (*fig*) Aussicht *f*.

loom *n* Webstuhl *m*; * *vi* undeutlich sichtbar werden; drohend aufragen; sich auftürmen.

loop *n* Schlinge *f*; Schleife *f*; Schlaufe *f*; Looping *m*.

loophole *n* Sehschlitz *m*; Schießscharte *f*; Schlupfloch *n*; Hintertürchen *n*.

loose *adj* ~**ly** *adv* lose; locker; frei; offen; weit; ~, **loosen** *vt* lösen; loslassen; befreien; lockern; losmachen.

loot *vt* erbeuten; (aus)plündern; * *n* Beute *f*.

lop *vt* beschneiden; stutzen; abästen; schlaff herunterhängen.

lop-sided *adj* schief; mit Schlagseite; unsymmetrisch; (*fig*) einseitig.

loquacious *adj* geschwätzig; redselig.

loquacity *n* Geschwätzigkeit *f*; Redseligkeit *f*.

lord *n* Herr *m*; Gebieter *m*; (*fig*) Magnat *m*; Lord *m*.

lore *n* Wissen *n*; überlieferte Kunde *f*.

lose *vt* verlieren; einbüßen; versäumen; verpassen; vergessen; abschütteln; kosten; * *vi* verlieren; unterliegen; Verluste erleiden; schwächer werden; nachgehen.

loss *n* Verlust *m*; Einbuße *f*; Schaden *m*; Schwund *m*; **to be at a ~** in Verlegenheit sein.

lost and found *n* Fundsachen *pl*.

lot *n* Los *n*; Anteil *m*; Schicksal *n*; Grundstück *n*; Partie *f*; Posten *m*; Gesellschaft *f*; Menge *f*; Haufen *m*; **a ~** viel.

lotion *n* Lotion *f*.

lottery *n* Lotterie *f*; (*fig*) Glückssache *f*.

loud *adj* ~ly *adv* laut; (*fig*) auffallend; (*fig*) aufdringlich.

loudspeaker *n* Lautsprecher *m*.

lounge *n* Wohnzimmer *n*; Salon *m*; Foyer *n*; Wartehalle *f*.

louse *n* (*pl* lice) Laus *f*.

lousy *adj* verlaust; lausig; mies.

lout *n* Flegel *m*; Rüpel *m*.

lovable *adj* liebenswert; reizend.

love *n* Liebe *f*; (*col*) Schatz *m*; **to fall in ~** sich verlieben; * *vt* lieben; liebhaben; mögen.

love letter *n* Liebesbrief *m*.

love life *n* Liebesleben *n*.

loveliness *n* Schönheit *f*; Liebreiz.

lovely *adj* (wunder)schön; reizend; (*col*) großartig.

lover *n* Liebhaber(in) *m*(*f*); Geliebte(r) *f*(*m*).

love-sick *adj* liebeskrank.

loving *adj* liebend; liebevoll; zärtlich.

low *adj* niedrig; tiefgelegen; tief; knapp; schwach; deprimiert; gering(schätzig); minderwertig; primitiv; leise; * *vi* brüllen; muhen.

low-cut *adj* tief ausgeschnitten.

lower *adj* niedriger; unter(er, e, es); Nieder-; Unter-; * *vt* niedriger machen; senken; erniedrigen; herablassen; abschwächen.

lowest *adj* niedrigst(er, e, es); unterst(er, e, es).

lowland *n* Tiefland *n*; Flachland *n*.

lowliness *n* Demut *f*; Bescheidenheit *f*.

lowly *adj* demütig; bescheiden; niedrig; nieder; unwichtig.

low-water *n* Niedrigwasser *n*.

loyàl *adj* ~ly *adv* loyal; treu (ergeben).

loyalty *n* Loyalität *f*; Treue *f*.

lozenge *n* Raute *f*; Pastille *f*.

lubricant *n* Gleitmittel *n*; Schmiermittel *n*.

lubricate *vt* gleitfähig machen; schmieren; ölen.

lucid *adj* klar; hell.

luck *n* Glück *n*; Schicksal *n*; Zufall *m*.

luckily *adv* zum Glück; glücklicherweise.

luckless *adj* glücklos; erfolglos.

lucky *adj* glücklich; Glücks-.

lucrative *adj* lukrativ; einträglich.

ludricrous *adj* lächerlich; absurd.

lug *vt* zerren; schleifen; schleppen.

luggage *n* Gepäck *n*.

lugubrious *adj* traurig; kummervoll.

lukewarm *adj* lau(warm); halbherzig.

lull *vt* einlullen; (*fig*) beschwichtigen; * *n* Pause *f*; Flaute *f*; vorübergehendes Nachlassen *n*.

lullaby *n* Wiegenlied *n*; Schlaflied *n*.

lumbago *n* Hexenschuß *m*.

lumberjack *n* Holzfäller *m*.

lumber room *n* Rumpelkammer *f*.

luminous *adj* leuchtend; strahlend; Leucht-; glänzend; brilliant.

lump *n* Klumpen *m*; Brocken *m*; Beule *f*; Höcker *m*; Geschwulst *f*; Knoten *m*; (*fig*) Masse *f*; * *vt* zusammenballen; (*fig*) zusammenfassen; (*fig*) in einen Topf werfen.

lump sum *n* Pauschale *f*.

lunacy *n* Wahnsinn *m*; Verrücktheit *f*.

lunar *adj* lunar; Mond-.

lunatic *adj* wahnsinnig; verrückt.

lunch *n* Mittagessen *n*.

lungs *npl* Lunge *f*.

lurch *n* Taumeln *n*; Schlingern *n*; Ruck *m*.

lure *n* Köder *m*; (*fig*) (Ver)Lokkung *f*; Reiz *m*; Falle *f*; * *vt* (ver)locken; verführen; ködern.

lurid *adj* fahl; gespenstisch; grell; bleich; düster; unheimlich; schauerlich.

lurk *vi* lauern; verborgen liegen; drohen; schleichen.

luscious *adj* köstlich; süß; sinnlich; üppig; herrlich.

lush *adj* saftig; üppig; reichlich.

lust *n* Lust *f*; Wollust *f*; Gier *f*; Begierde *f*; * *vi* gieren; lechzen; **to ~ after** *vi* gelüsten nach; gieren nach; lechzen nach; begehren.

lustre *n* Glanz *m*; Lüster *m*.

lustful *adj* **~ly** *adv* wollüstig; lüstern.

lustily *adv* (tat)kräftig; robust; wollüstig; lüstern.

lusty *adj* = lustily.

lute *n* Laute *f*; Kitt *m*.

Lutheran *n* Lutheraner(in) *m(f)*.

luxuriance *n* Üppigkeit *f*; Fülle *f*; Reichtum *m*; Überfluß *m*.

luxuriant *adj* üppig; fruchtbar; reich; verschwenderisch; überschwenglich.

luxuriate *vi* üppig gedeihen; schwelgen.

luxurious *adj* **~ly** *adv* luxuriös; Luxus-; verschwenderisch; genüßlich; wohlig.

luxury *n* Luxus *m*.

lying *n* Lügen *n*.

lymph *n* Lymphe *f*.

lynch *vt* lynchen.

lynx *n* Luchs *m*.

lyrical *adj* lyrisch; schwärmerisch.

lyrics *npl* (Lied)Text *m*.

M

macaroni *n* Makkaroni *pl*.

machine *n* Maschine *f*.

machine gun *n* Maschinengewehr *n*.

machinery *n* Maschinerie *f*.

mackerel *n* Makrele *f*.

mad *adj* verrückt, böse.

madam *n* gnädige Frau *f*.

madden *vt* verrückt machen, ärgern.

madly *adv* wahnsinnig.

madman *n* Verrückter *m*, Irrer *m*.

madness *n* Wahnsinn *m*.

magazine *n* Zeitschrift *f*, Illustrierte *f*.

maggot *n* Made *f*.

magic *n* Zauber *m*; * *adj* zauberhaft, magisch.

magician *n* Zauberkünstler *m*.

magistrate *n* Friedensrichter *m*.

magnanimous *adj* großmütig.

magnet *n* Magnet *n*.

magnetic *adj* magnetisch.

magnetism *n* Magnetismus *m*.

magnificent *adj* herrlich.

magnify *vt* vergrößern.

magnifying glass *n* Vergrößerungsglas *n*.

magnitude *n* Größe *f*, Ausmaß *n*.

magpie *n* Elster *f*.

mahogany *n* Mahagoni *n*.

maid *n* Dienstmädchen *n*.

maiden *n* Maid *f*.

maiden name *n* Mädchenname *m*.

mail *n* Post *f*.

mailbox *n* Briefkasten *m*.

mailing list *n* Anschreibeliste *f*.

mail order *n* Bestellung *f* durch die Post.

maim *vt* verstümmeln.

main *adj* Haupt-; **in the ~** im ganzen, im wesentlichen.

mainland *n* Festland *n*.

mainly *adv* hauptsächlich, größtenteils.

main road *n* Hauptstraße *f*.

maintain *vt* aufrechterhalten, beibehalten; instand halten; warten.

maintenance *n* Instandhaltung *f*; Wartung *f*.

maize *n* Mais *m*.

majestic *adj* majestätisch.

majesty *n* Majestät *f*.

major *adj* Haupt-; ernst; bedeutend; * *n* (*mil*) Major *m*.

majority *n* Mehrheit *f*.

make *vt* machen; ~ **for** *vt* gehen/fahren nach; ~ **up** *vt* erfinden; ~ **up for** *vt* aufholen; * *n* Marke *f*.

make-believe *n* Phantasie *f*.

makeshift *adj* behelfsmäßig.

make-up *n* Make-up *n*.

make-up remover *n* Make-up-Entferner *m*.

malaise *n* Unbehagen *n*.

malaria *n* Malaria *f*.

male *adj* männlich; * *n* Mann *m*; Männchen *n*.

malevolent *adj* überwollend.

malfunction *n* Funktionsstörung *f*.

malice *n* Bosheit *f*.

malicious *adj* böswillig, boshaft.

malign *adj* böse; * *vt* verleumden.

malignant *adj* bösartig.

mall *n* Einkaufszentrum *n*.

malleable *adj* formbar.

mallet *n* Holzhammer *m*.

malnutrition *n* Unterernährung *f*.

malpractice *n* Mißbrauch *m*.

malt *n* Malz *n*.

maltreat *vt* mißhandeln.

mammal *n* Säugetier *n*.

mammoth *adj* riesig, ungeheuer; * *n* Mammutt *n*.

man *n* Mann *m*; * *vt* (*mar*) bemannen.

manage *vt vi* führen, leiten; schaffen; zurechtkommen.

manageable *adj* handlich, fügsam.

management *n* Leitung *f*, Geschäftsführung *f*.

manager *n* Leiter *m*, Manager *m*.

manageress *n* Leiterin *f*.

managerial *adj* führend, leitend.

managing director *n* Geschäftsführer *m*.

mandate *n* Mandat *n*; Vollmacht *f*.

mandatory *n* verbindlich.

mane *n* Mähne *f*.

manfully *adv* mannhaft.

mangle *n* Mangel *f*; * *vt* verstümmeln.

mangy *adj* räudig.

manhandle *vt* grob behandeln.

manhood *n* Mannesalter *n*.

man-hour *n* Arbeitsstunde *f*.

mania *n* Manie *f*.

maniac *n* Verrückter *m*, Verrückte *f*.

manic *adj* hektisch.

manicure *n* Maniküre *f*; * *vt* maniküren.

manifest *adj* offensichtlich; * *vt* aufweisen.

manifestation *n* Erscheinung *f*.

manifesto *n* Manifest *n*.

manipulate *vt* manipulieren.

manipulation *n* Manipulation *f*.

mankind *n* Menschheit *f*.

manly *adj* männlich, mannhaft.

man-made *adj* künstlich.

manner *n* Weise *f*; Art *f*; ~**s** *pl* Manieren *pl*.

manoeuvre *n* Manöver *n*; * *vt vi* manövrieren.

manpower *n* Arbeitskräfte *fpl*.

mansion *n* Schloß *n*.

manslaughter *n* Totschlag *m*.

mantelpiece *n* Kaminsims *m*.

manual *adj* manuell; Hand-; * *n* Handbuch *n*.

manufacture *n* Herstellung *f*; * *vt* herstellen.

manufacturer *n* Hersteller *m*.

manure *n* Dünger *m*, Mist *m*.

manuscript *n* Manuskript *n*.

many *adj* viel(e); ~ **a** mancher, manche, manches; **how** ~? wie viele?.

map *n* Landkarte *f*; Stadtplan *m*; * *vt* kartieren.

maple *n* Ahorn *m*.

mar *vt* verderben.

marathon *n* Marathonlauf *m*.

marauder n Plünderer m.
marble n Marmor m, Murmel f.
March n März m.
march n Marsch m; * vi marschieren.
mare n Stute f.
margarine n Margarine f.
margin n Rand m.
marginal adj am Rande; geringfügig.
marigold n (bot) Ringelblume f.
marijuana n Marihuana n.
marinate vt marinieren.
marine adj Meeres-, See-; * n Marinesoldat m.
marital adj ehelich.
maritime adj See-.
marjoram n Majoran n.
mark n Sput f; Zeichen n; Kennzeichen n; Note f; * vt markieren; benoten.
marker n Schild n.
market n Markt m.
marketable adj marktfähig.
marketing n Marketing n, Vertrieb m.
marketplace n Marktplatz m.
market research n Markrforschung f.
market value n Marktwert m.
marksman n Scharfschütze m.
marmalade n Orangenmarmelade f.
maroon adj dunkelrot.
marquee n Festzelt n.
marriage n Ehe f; Trauung f; Heirat f.
marriage certificate n Heiratsurkunde f.
married adj verheiratet.
marrow n Knochenmark m; Speisekürbis m.
marry vt vi heiraten.
marsh n Sumpf m.
marshal n Marschall m.
marshy adj sümpfig.
martial adj Kriegs-.
martial law n Kriegsrecht n.
martyr n Martyrer m, Martyrerin f.

martyrdom n Martyrium n.
marvel n Wunder n; * vi sich wundern.
marvellous adj wunderbar, fabelhaft.
marzipan n Marzipan n.
mascara n Wimperntusche f.
masculine adj männlich.
mash vt zu Brei zerdrücken.
mask n Maske f; * vt maskieren.
masochist n Masochist m.
mason n Steinmetz m; Freimaurer m.
masonry n Mauerwerk n.
masquerade n Maskerade f.
mass n Messe f; Masse f.
massacre n Massaker n; * vt massakrieren.
massage n Massage f; vt massieren.
massive adj massiv.
mass media npl die Massenmedien pl.
mast n Mast m.
master n Herr m; Meister m; * vt meistern; beherrschen.
masterly adj meisterhaft.
masterpiece n Meisterwerk n.
mastery n Beherrschung f.
masturbate vi masturbieren.
mat n Matte f; Abtreter m.
match n Streichholz n, Spiel n; * vt passen zu.
matchbox n Streichholzschachtel f.
matchless adj unvergleichlich.
mate n Gehilfe m; Kumpel m; * vt sich paaren.
material adj materiell; * n Stoff m, Material n.
materialism n Materialismus m.
maternal adj mütterlich.
maternity n Mutterschaft f.
maternity dress n Umstandskleid n.
maternity hospital n Entbindungsheim n.
mathematical adj mathematisch.
mathematician n Mathematiker m.

mathematics *npl* Mathematik *f*.

matinee *n* Matinee *f*.

matriculation *n* Immatriculation *f*.

matrimonial *adj* ehelich, Ehe-

mat(t) *adj* matt.

matted *adj* verfilzt.

matter *n* Materie *f*; Sache *f*; Angelegenheit *f*; **what is the ~?** was ist los? **as a ~ of fact** in der Tat; * *vi* von Bedeutung sein.

mattress *n* Matratze *f*.

mature *adj* reif; * *vt vi* reifen.

maturity *n* Reife *f*.

maul *vt* übel zurichten.

mauve *adj* lila.

maxim *n* Maxime *f*.

maximum *n* Maxmium *n*; * *adj* maximal.

may *v aux* können; **~be** vielleicht.

May *n* Mai *m*.

May Day *n* der 1. Mai.

mayonnaise *n* Mayonnaise *f*.

mayor *n* Bürgermeister *m*.

mayoress *n* Bürgermeisterin *f*.

maze *n* Irrgarten *m*; Labyrinth *n*.

me *pron* mich; mir.

meadow *n* Wiese *f*.

meagre *adj* dürftig, spärlich.

meal *n* Mahlzeit *f*.

mean *adj* gemein; geizig; **in the ~time, ~while** inzwischen; **~s** *npl* Mittel *n*; * *vt vi* meinen.

meander *vi* sich schlängeln.

meaning *n* Bedeutung *f*.

meaningful *adj* sinnvoll.

meaningless *adj* bedeutungslos.

meanness *n* Geiz *m*.

meantime, meanwhile *adv* inzwischen.

measles *npl* Masern *pl*.

measure *n* Maß *n*; Maßnahme *f*; * *vt* messen.

measurement *n* Messung *f*.

meat *n* Fleisch *n*.

meatball *n* Fleischkloß *f*.

meaty *adj* fleischig.

mechanic *n* Mechaniker *m*.

mechanical *adj* mechanisch.

mechanics *npl* Mechanik *f*.

mechanism *n* Mechanismus *m*.

medal *n* Medaille *f*.

medallist *n* Medaillengewinner *m*, Medaillengewinnerin *f*.

medallion *n* Medaillon *n*.

meddle *vi* sich einmischen.

media *npl* die Medien *pl*.

median (strip) *n* Mittelstreifen *m*.

mediate *vi* vermitteln.

mediation *n* Vermittlung *f*.

mediator *n* Vermittler *m*.

medical *adj* medizinisch, Medizin-; ärztlich.

medicine *n* Medizin *f*.

medieval *adj* mittelalterlich.

mediocre *adj* mittelmäßig.

mediocrity *n* Mittelmäßigkeit *f*.

meditate *vi* meditieren.

meditation *n* Meditation *f*.

Mediterranean *adj* **the ~ (Sea)** das Mittelmeer.

medium *n* Mittel *n*; * *adj* Mittel-.

medium wave *n* Mittelwelle *f*.

medley *n* Potpourri *m*.

meek *adj* duckmäuserisch.

meet *vt* treffen; begegnen; * *vi* sich treffen.

meeting *n* Begegnung *f*.

megaphone *n* Megaphon *n*.

melancholic *adj* melancholisch.

melancholy *n* Melancholie *f*.

mellow *adj* sanft; * *vi* milder werden.

melodious *adj* melodiös.

melody *n* Melodie *f*.

melon *n* Melone *f*.

melt *vt* schmelzen lassen; * *vi* schmelzen.

melting point *n* Schmelzpunkt *m*.

member *n* Mitglied *n*.

membership *n* Mitgliedschaft *f*.

memento *n* Andenken *n*.

memo n Mitteilung f.
memoirs npl Memoiren fpl.
memorable adj denkwürdig.
memorandum n Mitteilung f.
memorial n Denkmal n.
memorise vt auswendig lernen.
memory n Gedächtnis n; Erinnerung f.
menace n Drohung f; * vt drohen.
menacing adj drohend.
menagerie n Menagerie f.
mend vt reparieren.
menial adj niedrig.
meningitis n Gehirnhautentzündung f.
menopause n Wechseljahre npl.
menstruation n Menstruation f.
mental adj geistig.
mentality n Mentalität f.
mention n Erwähnung f; * vt erwähnen.
mentor n Mentor m.
menu n Speisekarte f.
mercantile adj kaufmännisch, Handels-.
mercenary n Söldner m; adj gewinnsüchtig.
merchandise n Handelsgüter npl; Waren fpl.
merchant n Kaufmann m.
merciful adj barmherzig.
merciless adj erbarmungslos.
mercury n Quecksilber n.
mercy n Barmherzigkeit f.
mere adj bloß; ~ly adv bloß.
merge vt verbinden; fusionieren.
merger n Fusion f.
meringue n Baiser n.
merit n Verdienst m; Wert m; * vt verdienen.
mermaid n Meerjungfrau f.
merry adj fröhlich.
merry-go-round n Karussell n.
mesh n Masche f.
mesmerise vt hypnotisieren; faszinieren.
mess n Unordnung f; (mil) Messe f; ~ up vt verpfuschen.
message n Botschaft f.
messenger n Bote m.
metabolism n Metabolismus m.
metal n Metall n.
metallic adj metallisch.
metallurgy n Metallurgie f.
metaphor n Metapher f.
metaphorical adj metaphorisch.
mete out vt austeilen.
meteor n Meteor m.
meteorological adj meteorologisch.
meteorology n Meteorologie f.
meter n Meßgerät n.
method n Methode f.
methodical adj systematisch.
Methodist n Methodist m, Methodistin f.
metre n Meter m/n.
metric adj metrisch.
mettle n Mut m.
mew vi miauen.
microbe n Mikrobe f.
microphone n Mikrofon n.
microchip n Mikrochip m.
microscope n Mikroskop n.
microscopic adj mikroskopisch.
microwave oven n Mikrowellenherd m.
midday n Mittag m.
middle adj Mittel-; * n Mitte f.
middleweight n Mittelgewicht n.
middling adj mittelmäßig.
midge n Mücke f.
midget n Lilliputaner m, Lilliputanerin f.
midnight n Mitternacht f.
midriff n Taille f.
midst n Mitte f.
midsummer n Hochsommer m.
midway adv auf halbem Wege.
midwife n Hebamme f.
midwifery n Geburtshilfe f.
might n Kraft f, Macht f.
mighty adj mächtig, gewaltig.
migraine n Migräne f.
migrate vi abwandern.

migration n Abwanderung f.
mike n Mikro n.
Milan n Mailand.
mild adj mild, leicht.
mildew n Mehltau m.
mildness n Milde f.
mile n Meile f.
mileage n Meilenzahl f.
militant adj militant.
military adj militärisch, Militär-.
militate against vi entgegenwirken.
militia n Miliz f.
milk n Milch f; * vt melken.
milkshake n Milchmixgetränk n.
milky adj milchig.
Milky Way n Milchstraße f.
mill n Mühle f; * vt mahlen.
millennium n Jahrtausend n.
miller n Müller m.
millet n (bot) Hirse f.
milligram n Milligramm n.
millilitre n Milliliter m.
millimetre n Millimeter m/n.
million n Million f.
millionaire n Millionär m, Millionärin f.
millionth adj millionste(r,s).
millstone n Mühlstein m.
mime vt vi mimen.
mimic vt nachäffen.
mimicry n Nachäffung f.
mince vt durchdrehen.
mind n Sinn m; Geist m; * vi sich kümmern.
minded adj gesinnt.
mindful adj achtsam.
mindless adj sinnlos.
mine poss pron meiner, meine, mein(e)s; * n Bergwerk n; Mine f; * vt abbauen; verminen.
minefield n Minenfeld n.
miner n Bergarbeiter m.
mineral n Mineral n.
mineralogy n Mineralogie f.
mineral water n Mineralwasser n.
minesweeper n Minensuchboot n.

mingle vt mischen.
miniature n Miniatur f.
minimal adj minimal.
minimise vt auf ein Minimum beschränken.
minimum n Minimum n.
mining n Bergbau m.
minister n Minister m; Pastor m.
ministerial adj ministeriell.
ministry Ministerium n.
mink n Netz m.
minnow n Elritze f.
minor adj klein; * n Minderjähriger m, Minderjährige j.
minority n Minderheit f.
mint n (bot) Minze f; Münzanstalt f; * vt prägen.
minus adv minus.
minute adj winzig.
minute n Minute f.
miracle n Wunder n.
miraculous adj wunderbar.
mirage n Fata Morgana f.
mire n Morast m.
mirror n Spiegel m.
mirth n Heiterkeit f.
misadventure n Unfall m, Mißgeschick n.
misanthropist n Menschenfeind m.
misapprehension n Mißverständnis n.
misbehave vi sich schlecht benehmen.
miscalculate vt falsch berechnen.
miscarriage n Fehlgeburt f.
miscellaneous adj verschieden.
mischief n Unfug m.
mischievous adj durchtrieben.
misconception n falsche Auffassung f.
misconduct n Vergehen n.
misconstrue vt mißverstehen.
misdeed n Untat f.
misdemeanour n Vergehen n.
miser n Geizhals m.
miserable adj elend, trübsinnig.
miserly adj geizig.

misery n Elend n.
misfit n Außenseiter m.
misfortune n Unglück n.
misgiving n Bedenken n.
misguided adj fehlgeleitet.
mishandle vt falsch handhaben.
mishap n Mißgeschick n.
misinform vt falsch unterrichten.
misinterpret vt falsch auffassen.
misjudge vt falsch beurteilen.
mislay vt verlegen.
mislead vt irreführen.
mismanage vt schlecht verwalten.
misnomer n falsche Bezeichnung f.
misogynist n Weiberfeind m.
misplace vt verlegen.
misprint n Druckfehler m.
misrepresent vt falsch darstellen.
Miss n Fräulein n.
miss vt verfehlen; verpassen.
missal n Meßbech n.
misshapen adj mißgestaltet.
missile n Geschoß n.
missing adj fehlend; vermißt.
mission n Aufgabe f; Mission f.
missionary n Missionar m.
misspent adj vergeudet.
mist n Dunst m, Nebel m.
mistake vt verwechseln; **to be mistaken** sich irren; * n Fehler m.
Mister n Herr m.
mistletoe n (bot) Mistel f.
mistress n Herrin f; Geliebte f.
mistrust vt mißtrauen; * n Mißtrauen n.
misty adj neblig, dunstig.
misunderstand vt mißverstehen.
misunderstanding n Mißverständnis n.
misuse n Mißbrauch m; * vt mißbrauchen.
mitigate vt mildern.
mitten n Fausthandschuh m.
mix vt mischen.

mixed adj gemischt.
mixer n Kuchenmaschine f.
mixture n Mischung f, Gemisch n.
mix-up n Durcheinander n, Verwechslung f.
moan n Stöhnen n; * vi ächzen, stöhnen.
moat n Burggraben m.
mob n Horde f.
mobile adj beweglich, fahrbar.
mobile home n Wohnmobil n.
mobility n Beweglichkeit f.
mobilise vt (mil) mobilisieren.
moccasin n Mokassin m.
mock vt vi verspotten.
mockery n Spott m.
mode n Weise f.
model n Modell n; * vt modellieren.
moderate adj mäßig, gemäßigt; * vt mäßigen.
moderation n Mäßigung f.
modern adj modern.
modernise vt modernisieren.
modest adj bescheiden.
modesty n Bescheidenheit f.
modicum n bißchen n.
modification n Änderung f.
modify vt ändern.
module n Raumkapsel f.
mogul n Mogul m.
mohair n Mohair m.
moist adj feucht.
moisten vt befeuchten.
moisture n Feuchtigkeit f.
molar n Backenzahn m.
molasses npl Melasse f.
mole n Leberfleck m; Maulwurf m.
molecule n Molekul n.
molest vt bellästigen.
mollycoddle vt verhätscheln.
molten adj geschmolzen.
moment n Moment m, Augenblick m.
momentary adj vorübergehend.
momentous adj bedeutsam.
momentum n Moment n.
monarch n Monarch m.
monarchy n Monarchie f.

monastery *n* Kloster *n*.
monastic *adj* mönchisch.
Monday *n* Montag *m*.
monetary *adj* Geld-.
money *n* Geld *n*.
money order *n* Postanweisung *f*.
mongol *adj* mongoloid.
mongrel *n* Bastard *m*.
monitor *n* Monitor *m*.
monk *n* Mönch *m*.
monkey *n* Affe *m*.
monochrome *adj* schwarzweiß.
monocle *n* Monokel *n*.
monologue *n* Monolog *m*.
monopolise *vt* monopolisieren.
monopoly *n* Monopol *n*.
monotonous *adj* monoton; eintönig.
monotony *n* Monotonie *f*; Eintönigkeit *f*.
monsoon *n* (*mar*) Monsun *m*.
monster *n* Ungeheuer *n*.
monstrosity *n* Mißgeburt *f*.
monstrous *adj* unerhört.
month *n* Monat *m*.
monthly *adj* monatlich.
monument *n* Denkmal *n*.
monumental *adj* monumental.
moo *vi* muhen.
mood *n* Stimmung *f*; Laune *f*.
moody *adj* launenhaft.
moon *n* Mond *m*.
moonlight *n* Mondlicht *n*.
moor *n* Heide *f*; * *vt* (*mar*) festmachen.
moorland *n* Heidemoor *n*.
moose *n* Elch *m*.
mop *n* Mop *m*; * *vt* wischen.
mope *vi* Trübsal blasen.
moped *n* Moped *n*.
moral *adj* moralisch; ~s *npl* Moral *f*.
morale *n* Moral *f*.
morality *n* Sittlichkeit *f*.
morass *n* Sumpf *m*.
morbid *adj* krankhaft.
more *adj*, *adv* mehr; ~ **and** ~ immer mehr.
moreover *adv* außerdem.
morgue *n* Leichenschauhaus *n*.

morning *n* Morgen *m*; **good** ~ guten Morgen.
moron *n* Idiot *m*.
morose *adj* mürrisch, griesgrämig.
morphine *n* Morphium *n*.
Morse *n* ~ **Code** Morsealphabet *n*.
morsel *n* Bissen *m*.
mortal *adj* sterblich.
mortality *n* Sterblichkeit *f*.
mortar *n* Mörser *m*.
mortgage *n* Hypothek *f*; * *vt* mit einer Hypothek belasten.
mortify *vt* beschämen.
mortuary *n* Leichenhalle *f*.
mosaic *n* Mosaik *n*.
Moscow *n* Moskau *n*.
mosque *n* Moschee *f*.
mosquito *n* Moskito *m*.
moss *n* (*bot*) Moos *n*.
mossy *adj* moosig.
most *adj* meist; * *adv* am meisten; **for the** ~ **part** zum größten Teil.
mostly *adv* meistens.
motel *n* Motel *n*.
moth *n* Nachtfalter *m*.
mothball *n* Mottenkugel *f*.
mother *n* Mutter *f*.
motherhood *n* Mutterschaft *f*.
mother-in-law *n* Schwiegermutter *f*.
motherly *adj* mütterlich.
mother-to-be *n* werdende Mutter *f*.
mother tongue *n* Muttersprache *f*.
motif *n* Motiv *n*.
motion *n* Bewegung *f*.
motionless *adj* bewegungslos.
motion picture *n* Film *m*.
motivated *adj* motiviert.
motive *n* Motiv *n*.
motley *adj* bunt gemischt.
motor *n* Motor *m*.
motorbike *n* Motorrad *n*.
motorboat *n* Motorboot *n*.
motorcycle *n* Motorrad *n*.
motor vehicle *n* Automobil *n*.
mottled *adj* gesprenkelt.
motto *n* Motto *n*.

mould n Form f; * vt formen.
mouldy adj schimm(e)lig.
moult vi sich mausern.
mound n Erdhügel m.
mount vt besteigen.
mountain n Berg m.
mountaineer n Bergsteiger m.
mountaineering n Bergsteigen n.
mountainous adj gebirgig.
mourn vt betrauern.
mourner n Trauernder m, Trauernde f.
mournful adj trauervoll.
mourning n Trauer f.
mouse n (pl mice) Maus f.
mousse n Creme f.
moustache n Schnurrbart m.
mouth n Mund m; Maul n.
mouthful n Mundvoll m.
mouth-organ n Mundharmonika f.
mouthpiece n Mundstück n.
mouthwash n Mundwasser n.
mouthwatering adj lecker, appetitlich.
movable adj beweglich.
move vt bewegen; * vi sich bewegen; * n Bewegung f; Zug m.
movement n Bewegung f.
movie n Film m.
movie camera n Filmkamera f.
moving adj ergreifend.
mow vt mähen.
mower n Rasenmäher m.
Mrs n Frau f.
much adj, adv viel.
muck n Mist m; Dreck m.
mucus n Schleim m.
mud n Schlamm m.
muddle n Durcheinander n.
muddy adj schlammig.
mudguard n Schutzblech n.
muffle vt dämpfen.
mug n Becher m.
muggy adj schwül.
mule n Maultier m.
mull over vt nachdenken über.
multiple adj vielfach.
multiplication n Multiplikation f.

multiply vt multiplizieren.
multitude n Menge f.
mumble vt vi undeutlich sprechen.
mummy n Mumie f; Mutti f.
mumps npl Mumps m.
munch vt vi mampfen.
mundane adj alltäglich.
Munich n München.
municipal adj städtisch.
municipality n Stadt f mit Selbstverwaltung.
mural n WAndmalerei f.
murder n Mord m; * vt ermorden.
murderer n Mörder m.
murderess n Mörderin f.
murderous adj mörderisch.
murky adj düster, finster.
murmur n Gemurmel n;* vi murmeln.
muscle n Muskel m.
muscular adj Muskel-, muskulös.
muse vi sinnen.
museum n Museum n.
mushroom n (bot) Pilz m.
music n Musik f.
musical adj musikalisch.
musician n Musiker m, Musikerin f.
musk n Moschus m.
muslin n Musselin m.
mussel n Muschel f.
must v aux müssen.
mustard n Senf m.
muster vt aufbringen.
musty adj muffig.
mute adj stumm.
muted adj gedämpft.
mutilate vt verstümmeln.
mutilation n Verstümmelung f.
mutiny n Meuterei f; * vi meutern.
mutter vt vi murmeln.
mutton n Hammelfleisch n.
mutual adj gegenseitig.
muzzle n Schnauze f; * vt einen Maulkorb anlegen.
my poss adj mein.
myself pron selbst; mich (selbst).

mysterious *adj* geheimnisvoll, rätselhaft.

mystery *n* Geheimnis *n*, Rätsel *n*.

mystic *n* Mystiker *m*.

mystify *vt* verblüffen.

mystique *n* geheimnisvolle Natur *f*.

myth *n* Mythos *m*.

mythology *n* Mythologie *f*.

N

nab *vt* schnappen.

nag *n* Gaul *m*; * *vt vi* meckern.

nagging *adj* meckernd.

nail *n* Nagel *m*; * *vt* nageln.

nailbrush *n* Nagelbürste *f*.

nailfile *n* Nagelfeile *f*.

nail polish *n* Nagellack *m*.

nail scissors *npl* Nagelschere *f*.

naive *adj* naiv.

naked *adj* nackt.

name *n* Name *m*; * *vt* nennen.

nameless *adj* namenlos.

namely *adv* nämlich.

namesake *n* Namensvetter *m*.

nanny *n* Kindermädchen *n*.

nap *n* Nickerchen *n*.

nape *n* Nacken *m*.

napkin *n* Serviette *f*.

nappy *n* Windel *f*.

narcissus *n* (*bot*) Narzisse *f*.

narcotic *n* Betäubungsmittel *n*.

narrate *vt* erzählen.

narrative *n* Erzählung *f*.

narrow *adj* eng.

narrow-minded *adj* engstirnig.

nasal *adj* nasal.

nasty *adj* ekelhaft, fies.

nation *n* Nation *f*.

national *adj* National-.

nationalism *n* Nationalismus *m*.

nationalist *adj, n* Nationalist *m*.

nationality *n* Staatsangehörigkeit *f*.

nationalise *vt* verstaatlichen.

nationwide *adj* landesweit.

native *adj* einheimisch; * *n* Einheimischer *m*, Einheimische *f*.

native language *n* Muttersprache *f*.

Nativity *n* **the ~** Christi Geburt.

natural *adj* natürlich.

natural gas *n* Erdgas *n*.

naturalist *n* Naturkundler *m*, Naturkundlerin *f*.

naturalize *vt* eingbürgern.

nature *n* Natur *f*.

naught *n* Null *n*.

naughty *adj* unartig, ungezogen.

nausea *n* Übelkeit *f*, Ekel *m*.

nauseate *vt* anekeln.

nautical, naval *adj* nautisch, See-.

nave *n* Kirchenschiff *n*.

navel *n* Nabel *m*.

navigate *vi* navigieren.

navigation *n* Navigation *f*.

navy *n* Marine *f*.

Nazi *n* Nazi *m*.

near *prep* nahe, in der Nähe; * *adv* nah(e); * *vt* sich nähern.

nearby *adj* nahegelegen.

nearly *adv* fast, beinahe.

near-sighted *adj* kurzsichtig.

neat *adj* pur; ordentlich; gepflegt.

nebulous *adj* nebulös.

necessary *adj* notwendig.

necessitate *vt* benötigen.

necessity *n* Notwendigkeit *f*.

neck *n* Hals *m*; * *vi* knutschen.

necklace *n* Halskette *f*.

necktie *n* Schlips *m*.

née *adj*: **~ Brown** geborene Brown.

need *n* Notwendigkeit *f*, Bedarf *m*; * *vt* brauchen.

needle *n* Nadel *f*.

needless *adj* unnötig.

needlework n Handarbeit f.

needy adj notleidend.

negation n Verneinung f.

negative adj negativ; * n negativ n.

neglect vt vernachlässigen; * n Vernachlässigung f.

negligence n Nachlässigkeit f, Fahrlässigkeit m.

negligent adj nachlässig, fahrlässig.

negligible adj unbedeutend, geringfügig.

negotiate vi verhandeln.

negotiation n Verhandlung f.

negress n Negerin f.

negro n Neger m.

neigh vi wiehern.

neighbour n Nachbar m, Nachbarin f.

neighbourhood n Nachbarschaft f.

neighbouring adj benachbart, Nachbar-.

neighbourly adj nachbarlich.

neither conj ~ ... **nor** ... entweder ... noch ....

neon n Neon n.

neon light n Neonlicht n.

nephew n Neffe m.

nepotism n Nepotismus m.

nerve n Nerv m.

nerve-racking adj nervenaufreibend.

nervous adj nervös, ängstlich.

nervous breakdown n Nervenzusammenbruch m.

nest n Nest n.

net n Netz n.

netball n Netzball m.

net curtain n Store m.

Netherlands npl the ~ die Niederlande pl.

netting n Netz n.

nettle n Nessel f.

network n Netz n.

neurosis n Neurose f.

neurotic adj neurotisch.

neuter adj sächlich; * n Neutrum n.

neutral adj neutral.

neutrality n Neutralität f.

neutralise vt neutralisieren.

never adv nie, niemals, nimmer; ~ **mind** macht doch nichts.

never-ending adj endlos.

nevertheless adv trotzdem.

new adj neu.

newborn adj neugeboren.

newcomer n Neuankömmling m.

new-fangled adj neumodisch.

news npl Nachrichten pl.

newsagent n Zeitungshändler m.

newscaster n Nachrichtensprecher m.

news flash n Kurzmeldung f.

newsletter n Rundschreiben n.

newspaper n Zeitung f.

newsreel n Wochenschau f.

New Year n das Neue Jahr n.

New Year's Day n Neujahr n.

New Year's Eve Silvester n.

New Zealand n Neuseeland n.

next adj nächste(r,s); **the ~ day** am nächsten Tag.

nib n Feder f.

nibble vt knabbern.

nice adj nett; sympathisch.

niche n Nische f.

nick n Kerbe f; * vt (sl) klauen.

nickel n Nickel n.

nickname n Spitzname m; * vt den Spitznamen geben.

nicotine n Nikotin n.

niece n Nichte f.

night n Nacht f; **good ~** gute Nacht.

nightclub n Nachtklub m.

nightingale n Nachtigall f.

nightly adj nächtlich; * adv jede Nacht.

nightmare n Alptraum m.

night school n Abendschule f.

night shift n Nachtschicht f.

nighttime n Nacht f.

nihilist n Nihilist m.

nimble adj beweglich.

nine adj neun.

nineteen adj neunzehn.

nineteenth adj neunzehnte(r,s).

ninetieth *adj* neunzigste(r,s).
ninety *adj* neunzig.
ninth *adj* neunte(r,s); * *n* Neuntel *n*.
nip *vt* kneifen.
nipple *n* Brustwarze *f*.
nitrogen *n* Stickstoff *m*.
no *adv* nein; * *adj* kein(e).
nobility *n* Adel *m*.
noble *adj* adlig, edel.
nobleman *n* Adliger *m*.
noblewoman *n* Adlige *f*.
nobody *pn* niemand.
nocturnal *adj* nächtlich.
nod *n* Nicken *n* * *vi* nicken.
noise *n* Lärm *m*, Geräusch *m*.
noiseless *adj* geräuschlos.
noisy *adj* laut.
nominal *adj* nominell.
nominate *vt* ernennen, aufstellen.
nomination *n* Ernennung *f*, Aufstellen *n*.
nominee *n* Ernannter *m*, Ernannte *f*.
non-alcoholic *adj* alkoholfrei.
nonchalant *adj* gleichgültig.
nondescript *adj* nichtssagend.
none *pn* keiner, keine, kein(e)s.
nonentity *n* Null *f*.
nonetheless *adv* nichtsdestoweniger.
nonexistent *adj* nicht vorhanden.
non-fiction *n* Sachliteratur *f*.
nonplussed *adj* verblüfft.
nonsense *n* Unsinn *m*, Quatsch *m*.
nonsensical *adj* unsinnig.
non-smoker *n* Nichtraucher *m*.
nonstop *adj* Nonstop-; * *adv* ununterbrochen.
noodles *npl* Nudeln *pl*.
noon *n* Mittag *m*.
noose *n* Schlinge *m*.
nor *conj* **neither ... ~ ...** entweder ... noch ....
norm *n* Norm *m*.
normal *adj* normal.
normally *adv* normal; normalerweise.
north *n* Norden *m*; * *adj* nörd-

lich, Nord-; * *adv* nördlich, nach/im Norden.
North Africa *n* Nordafrika *n*.
North America *n* Nordamerika *n*.
northeast *n* Nortosten *m*.
northerly *adj* nördlich.
northern *adj* nördlich, Nord-.
North Pole *n* Nordpol *m*.
North Sea *n* Nordsee *f*.
northwards *adv* nach Norden.
northwest *n* Nordwesten *m*.
Norway *n* Norvegen *n*.
Norwegian *adj* norwegisch; * *n* Norweger(in) *m(f)*; Norwegisch *n*.
nose *n* Nase *f*.
nosebleed *n* Nasenbluten *n*.
nosedive *n* Sturzflug *m*.
nostalgia *n* Nostalgie *f*, Sehnsucht *f*.
nostril *n* Nasenloch *f*.
not *adv* nicht.
notable *adj* bemerkenswert, bedeutend.
notary *n* Notar *m*.
notch *n* Kerbe *f*.
note *n* Note *f*; Ton *m*; Anmerkung *f*; * *vt* zur Kenntnis nehmen; aufschreiben.
notebook *n* Notizbuch *n*.
noted *adj* bekannt.
notepaper *n* Briefpapier *n*.
nothing *n* nichts; **~ new** nichts Neues.
notice *n* Anzeige *f*, Anschlag *m*; * *vt* bemerken.
noticeable *adj* bemerkbar.
notification *n* Benachrichtigung *f*.
notify *vt* benachrichtigen.
notion *n* Idee *f*.
notoriety *n* schlechter Ruf *m*.
notorious *adj* berüchtigt.
notwithstanding *adv* trotzdem.
nought *n* Null *f*.
noun *n* (*gr*) Substantiv *m*.
nourish *vt* ernähren, nähren.
nourishing *adj* nahrhaft.
nourishment *n* Nahrung *m*.
novel *n* Roman *m*.

novelist *n* Romanschriftsteller
  m.
novelty *n* Neuheit *f*.
November *n* November *m*.
novice *n* Neuling *m*.
now *adv* jetzt, nun; **~ and then**
  hin und wieder.
nowadays *adv* heutzutage.
nowhere *adv* nirgends.
nozzle *n* Düse *f*.
nuclear *adj* nuklear, Kern-.
nucleus *n* Kern *m*.
nude *adj* nackt.
nudge *vt* mit dem Ellbogen anstoßen.
nudist *n* Nudist *m*, Nudistin *f*.
nudity *n* Nacktheit *f*.
nuisance *n* lästiger Mensch *m*,
  Quälgeist *m*.
null *adj* nichtig.
nullify *vt* für nichtig erklären.
numb *adj* gefühllos; * *vt* beta-
  üben.
number *n* Zahl *f*, Anzahl *f*; * *vt*
  numerieren.
numeral *n* Ziffer *f*.
numerical *adj* numerisch.
numerous *adj* zahlreich.
nun *n* Nonne *f*.
nuptial *adj* Hochzeits-.
nurse *n* Krankenschwester *f*;
  * *vt* pflegen.
nursery *n* Kinderzimmer *n*;
  Gärtnerei *f*.
nursery rhyme *n* Kinderreim
  m.
nursery school *n* Vorschule *f*.
nursing home *n* Privatklinik *f*.
nurture *vt* nähren.
nut *n* Nuß *f*.
nutcrackers *npl* Nußknacker
  m.
nutmeg *n* Muskat *m*.
nutritious *adj* nahrhaft.
nut shell *n* Nußschale *f*.
nylon *n* Nylon *n*.
nymph *n* Nymphe *f*.

O

oak *n* Eiche *f*; * adj Eichen(-
  holz)-.
oar *n* Ruder *n*.
oasis *n* Oase *f*.
oath *n* Eid *m*, Schwur *m*; Fluch
  m.
oatmeal *n* Haferschrot *m*.
oats *npl* Hafer *m*.
obedience *n* Gehorsam *m*.
obedient *adj* gehorsam.
obese *adj* fett(leibig).
obesity *n* Fettleibigkeit *f*.
obey *vt* *vi* gehorchen.
obituary *n* Nachruf *m*.
object *n* Gegenstand *m*; Object
  n; Ziel *n*; * *vi* dagegen sein.
objection *n* Einwand *m*, Einspruch *m*.
objectionable *adj* nicht einwandfrei; anstößig.
objective *n* Ziel *n*; * *adj* objektiv.
obligation *n* Verpflichtung *f*.
obligatory *adj* verpflichtend,
  verbindlich.
oblige *vt* zwingen; einen Gefallen tun.
obliging *adj* entgegenkommend.
oblique *adj* schräg, schief; * *n*
  Schrägstrich *m*.
obliterate *vt* auslöschen.
oblivion *n* Vergessenheit *f*.
oblivious *adj* nichr bewußt.
oblong *n* Rechteck *n*; * *adj*
  länglich.
obnoxious *adj* widerlich.
oboe *n* Oboe *f*.
obscene *adj* obszön.
obscenity *n* Obszönität *f*.
obscure *adj* unklar; undeutlich; unbekannt, obskur; düster; * *vt* verdunkeln; verbergen; verwirren.
obscurity *n* Unklarheit *f*; Dunkelheit *f*.
observance *n* Befolgung *f*.

observant *adj* aufmerksam.

observation *n* Bemerkung *f*; Beobachtung *f*.

observatory *n* Sternwarte *f*, Observatorium *n*.

observe *vt* beobachen; bemerken.

observer *n* Beobachter(in) *m(f)*.

obsess *vt* verfolgen, quälen.

obsession *n* Besessenheit *f*, Wahn *m*.

obsessive *adj* krankhaft.

obsolescence *n* Veralten *n*.

obsolete *adj* überholt, verlaltet.

obstacle *n* Hindernis *n*.

obstacle race Hindernisrennen *n*.

obstinate *adj* hartnäckig, stur.

obstruct *vt* versperren; verstopfen; hemmen.

obstruction *n* Versperrung *f*; Verstopfung *f*; Hindernis *n*.

obtain *vt* erhalten, bekommen; erzielen.

obtainable *adj* erhältlich.

obtrusive *adj* aufdringlich.

obtuse *adj* stumpf, dumpf; begriffsstutzig.

obvious *adj* offenbar, offensichtlich.

occasion *n* Gelegenheit *f*; Ereignis *n*; Anlaß *m*; * *vt* veranlassen.

occasional *adj* gelegentlich.

occupant *n* Inhaber(in) *m(f)*; Bewohner(in) *m(f)*.

occupation *n* Tätigkeit *f*; Beruf *m*; Beschäftigung *f*.

occupier *n* Bewohner(in) *m(f)*.

occupy *vt* besetzen; belegen; bewohnen.

occur *vi* vorkommen.

occurrence *n* Ereignis *n*.

ocean *n* Ozean *m*; Meer *n*.

ocean-going *adj* Hochsee-.

octagonal *adj* achteckig.

octane *n* Oktan *n*.

octave *n* Oktave *f*.

October *n* Oktober *m*.

octopus *n* Krake *f*.

odd *adj* sonderbar; ungerade; einzeln.

oddity *n* Merkwürdigkeit *f*; Kuriosität *f*.

odd jobs *npl* gelegentlich anfallende Arbeiten.

oddly *adv* seltsam.

odds *npl* Chancen *pl*; Gewinnchancen *pl*.

odious *adj* verhaßt; abscheulich.

odometer *n* Tacho(meter) *m*.

odour *n* Geruch *m*.

of *prep* von; aus.

off *adv* weg, fort; aus, ab; * *prep* von.

offence *n* Vorgehen *n*, Straftat *f*; Beleidigung *f*.

offend *vt* beleidigen.

offender *n* Gesetzesübertreter *m*.

offensive *adj* übel, abstoßend; Kampf-; verletzend.

offer * *n* Angebot *f*; * *vt* anbieten; **on ~** zum Verkauf angeboten.

offering *n* Gabe *f*.

offhand *adj* lässig; * *adv* ohne weiteres.

office *n* Büro *n*; Amt *n*.

office automation *n* Büroautomatisierung *f*.

office building *n* Bürohaus *n*.

office hours *npl* Dienstzeit *f*.

officer *n* Offizier *m*; Beamte(r) *m*.

official *adj* offiziell, amtlich; * *n* Beamte(r) *m*.

officiate *vi* amtieren.

officious *adj* aufdringlich.

off-line *adj* Off-line-.

off-peak *adj* verbilligt.

off-season *adj* außer Saison.

offset *vt* ausgleichen; * *n* Offset(druck) *m*.

offshoot *n* Zweig *m*; Randergebnis *n*.

offshore *adj* küstennah, Küsten-.

offside *adj* im Abseits; * *adv* abseits; * *n* Fahrerseite *f*.

offspring *n* Nachkommenschaft *f*; Sprößling *m*.

offstage *adv* hinter den Kulissen.

off-the-peg *adv* von der Stange.

ogle *vt* liebäugeln mit.

oh *excl* oh, ach.

oil *n* Öl *n*; * *vt* ölen.

oilcan *n* Ölkännchen *n*.

oilfield *n* Ölfeld *n*.

oil filter *n* Ölfilter *m*.

oil painting *n* Ölgemälde *n*.

oil-rig *n* Ölplatform *f*.

oil tanker *n* Öltanker *m*.

oil well *n* Ölquelle *f*.

oily *adj* ölig; ölbeschmiert.

ointment *n* Salbe *f*.

OK, okay *excl* in Ordnung, O.K.; * *adj* in Ordnung; * *vt* genehmigen.

old *adj* alt.

old age *n* Alter *n*.

old-fashioned *adj* altmodisch.

olive *n* Olive *f*.

olive oil *n* Olivenöl *n*.

omelette *n* Omelett *n*.

omen *n* Omen *n*.

ominous *adj* bedrohlich.

omission *n* Auslassung *f*; Versäumnis *n*.

omit *vt* auslassen; versäumen.

omnipotence *n* Allmacht *f*.

omnipotent *adj* allmächtig.

on *prep* auf; an; über; * *adv* an; weiters; * *adj* an; aufgedreht.

once *adv* einmal; **at ~** sofort; gleichzeitig; **~ more** noch einmal; **~ upon a time** es war einmal.

oncoming *adj* Gegen-, entgegenkommend.

one *num* eins; ein/eine/ein; *adj* einzige(r,s); *pn* eine(r,s); **~ by ~** einzeln; **~ another** einander.

one-man *adj* Einmann-.

onerous *adj* schwer(wiegend).

oneself *pn* sich; sich selbst/selber; selbst.

one-sided *adj* einseitig.

one-to-one *adj* eins-zu-eins.

one-way *adj* Einbahn-.

ongoing *adj* momentan; sich entwickelnd.

onion *n* Zwiebel *f*.

on-line *adj* On-line-.

onlooker *n* Zuschauer(in) *m(f)*.

only *adv* nur, bloß; * *adj* einzige(r,s); **an ~ child** ein Einzelkind; **not ~ ... but also** nicht nur ... sondern auch.

onset *n* Beginn *m*.

onslaught *n* Angriff *m*.

onus *n* Last *f*, Pflicht *f*.

onward(s) *adv* voran, vorwärts.

ooze *vi* sickern.

opaque *adj* undurchsichtig.

open *adj* offen; öffentlich; aufgeschlossen; * *vt* öffnen, aufmachen; eröffnen; *vi* anfangen; aufmachen; aufgeben.

opening *n* Öffnung *f*; Anfang *m*.

open-minded *adj* aufgeschlossen.

opera *n* Oper *f*.

opera house *n* Opernhaus *n*.

operate *vt* bedienen; betätigen; * *vi* laufen, in Betrieb sein; arbeiten.

operatic *adj* Opern-.

operation *n* Betrieb *m*; Operation *f*; Unternehmen *n*; Einsatz *m*.

operational *adj* einsatzbereit.

operative *adj* wirksam; operativ.

operator *n* Arbeiter *m*; Telefonist(in) *m(f)*.

ophthalmic *adj* Augen-.

opinion *n* Meinung *f*; Ansicht *f*; Stellungnahme *f*; Gutachten *n*.

opinionated *adj* starrsinnig.

opinion poll *n* Meinungsumfrage *f*.

opponent *n* Gegner *m*.

opportune *adj* passend; rechtzeitig; günstig.

opportunity *n* Gelegenheit *f*, Möglichkeit *f*.

oppose *vt* entgegentreten; ablehnen.

opposing *adj* gegnerisch; entgegengesetzt..

opposite *adj* gegenüberliegend; entgegengesetzt; * *adv* gegenüber; * *prep* gegenüber; * *n* Gegenteil *n*.

opposition *n* Widerstand *m*; Opposition *f*; Gegensatz *m*.

oppress *vt* unterdrücken.

oppression *n* Unterdrückung *f*.

oppressive *adj* repressiv; bedrückend.

opt *vi* sich entscheiden (**for** für).

optical *adj* optisch.

optician *n* Optiker *m*.

optimist *n* Optimist *m*.

optimistic *adj* optimistisch.

optimum *adj* optimal.

option *n* Wahl *f*; Option *f*.

optional *adj* freiwillig; wahlfrei.

opulent *adj* sehr reich.

or *conj* oder.

oracle *n* Orakel *n*.

oral *adj* mündlich; * *n* mündliche Prüfung *f*.

orange *n* Apfelsine *f*, Orange *f*; * *adj* orange.

orator *n* Redner(in) *m*(*f*).

orbit *n* Umlaufbahn *f*.

orchard *n* Obstgarten *m*.

orchestra *n* Orchester *n*.

orchestral *adj* Orchester-, orchestral.

orchid *n* Orchidee *f*.

ordain *vt* zum Priester weihen; verfügen; bestimmen.

ordeal *n* (schwere) Probe *f*.

order *n* Ordnung *f*; Befehl *m*; Auftrag *m*; Bestellung *f*; * *vt* befehlen; bestellen.

order form *n* Bestellschein *m*.

orderly *adj* ordentlich, geordnet.

ordinarily *adv* normalerweise.

ordinary *adj* normal, gewöhnlich.

ordnance *n* Artillerie *f*.

ore *n* Erz *n*.

organ *n* (*mus*) Orgel *f*; Organ *n*.

organic *adj* organisch.

organisation *n* Organisation *f*.

organise *vt* organisieren.

organism *n* Organismus *m*.

organist *n* Organist *m*.

orgasm *n* Orgasmus *m*.

orgy *n* Orgie *f*.

oriental *adj* orientalisch.

origin *n* Ursprung *m*, Quelle *f*; Herkunft *f*.

original *adj* ursprünglich, original; originell.

originality *n* Originalität *f*.

originate *vi* entstehen; stammen.

ornament *n* Schmuck *m*.

ornamental *adj* Zier-.

ornate *adj* reich verziert.

orphan *n* Waise *f*.

orphanage *n* Waisenhaus *n*.

orthodox *adj* orthodox.

orthodoxy *n* Orthodoxie *f*; Konventionalität *f*.

orthopaedic *adj* orthopädisch.

oscillate *vi* schwingen; schwanken.

osprey *n* Fischadler *m*.

ostentatious *adj* großtuerisch, protzig.

ostracise *vt* ausstoßen.

ostrich *n* Strauß *m*.

other *adj pn* andere(r,s); ~ **than** anders als.

otherwise *adv* anders; sonst.

otter *n* Otter *m*.

ouch *excl* aua.

ought *v aux* sollen.

ounce *n* Unze *f*.

our *adj* unser; ~**s** *pn* unsere(r,s).

ourselves *pn* uns (selbst).

oust *vt* verdrängen.

out *adv* hinaus/heraus; draußen; ~ **of** *prep* aus; außerhalb.

outback *n* Hinterland *n*.

outboard (motor) *n* Außenbordmotor *m*.

outbreak *n* Ausbruch *m*.

outburst *n* Ausbruch *m*.

outcast *n* Ausgestoßene(r) *m/f*.

outcome *n* Ergebnis *n*.

outcry *n* Protest *m*.

outdated *adj* überholt.

outdo *vt* übertrumpfen.

outdoor *adj* Außen-.

outdoors *adv* im Freien.

outer *adj* äußere(r,s).

outermost *adj* äußerst.

outer space *n* Weltraum *m*.

outfit *n* Kleidung *f*.

outfitter *n* Herrenausstatter *m*.

outgoing *adj* aufgeschlossen.

outgrow *vt* herauswachsen; ablegen.

outhouse *n* Nebengebäude *n*.

outing *n* Ausflug *m*.

outlandish *adj* eigenartig.

outlaw *n* Geächtete(r) *m*; * *vt* ächten; verbieten.

outlay *n* Auslage *f*.

outlet *n* Auslaß *m*, Abfluß *m*; Absatzmarkt *m*.

outline *n* Umriß *m*.

outlive *vt* überleben.

outlook *n* Aussicht *f*; Einstellung *f*.

outlying *adj* entlegen; Außen-.

outmoded *adj* veraltet.

outnumber *vt* zahlenmäßig überlegen sein.

out-of-date *adj* abgelaufen; altmodisch; überholt.

outpatient *n* ambulante(r) Patient *m*, ambulante Patientin *f*.

outpost *n* Vorposten *m*.

output *n* Leistung *f*, Produktion *f*; Ausgabe *f*.

outrage *n* Ausschreitung *f*; Skandal *m*; * *vt* verstoßen gegen; empören.

outrageous *adj* unerhöht.

outright *adv* sofort; ohne Umschweife; * *adj* völlig; Total-; unbeschritten.

outset *n* Beginn *m*.

outshine *vt* überstrahlen.

outside *n* Außenseite *f*; * *adj* äußere(r,s), Außen-; gering; * *adv* außen; * *prep* außerhalb.

outsider *n* Außenseiter(in) *m(f)*.

outsize *adj* übergroß.

outskirts *npl* Stadtrand *m*.

outspoken *adj* freimütig.

outstanding *adj* hervorragend; ausstehend.

outstretched *adj* ausgestreckt.

outstrip *vt* übertreffen.

out-tray *n* Ausgangskorb *m*.

outward *adj* äußere(r,s); Hin-; ausgehend; * *adv* nach außen.

outweigh *vt* überwiegen.

outwit *vt* überlisten.

oval *n* Ovalo *n*; * *adj* oval.

ovary *n* Eierstock *m*.

oven *n* Backofen *m*.

ovenproof *adj* feuerfest.

over *adv* hinüber/herüber; vorbei; übrig; wieder, noch einmal; *prep* über; **all ~** überall, vorbei; **~ and ~** immer wieder; **~ and above** darüber hinaus.

overall *adj* allgemein; Gesamt-; * *adv* insgesamt.

overalls *npl* Overall *m*.

overawe *vt* einschüchtern; überwältigen.

overbalance *vi* Übergewicht bekommen.

overbearing *adj* aufdringlich.

overboard *adv* (*mar*) über Bord.

overbook *vi* überbuchen.

overcast *adj* bedeckt.

overcharge *vt* überladen; zuviel verlangen.

overcoat *n* Mantel *m*.

overcome *vt* überwinden.

overcrowded *adj* überfüllt.

overdo *vt* verkochen; übertreiben.

overdose *n* Überdosis *f*.

overdraft *n* Überziehung *f*.

overdrawn *adj* überzogen.

overdress *vi* (sich) übertrieben anziehen.

overdue *adj* überfällig.

overestimate *vt* überschätzen.

overflow *vi* überfließen; * *n* Überschuß *m*; Überlaufrohr *n*.

overgrown *adj* verwildert.

overhang *vi* überhängen.

overhaul *vt* überholen; überprüfen; * *n* Überholung *f*.

overhead *adv* oben; * *adj* Hoch-; überirdisch, Decken-.

overheads *npl* allgemeine Unkosten *pl*.

overhear *vt* (mit an)hören.

overheat *vi* heiß laufen

overjoyed *adj* überglücklich.

overkill *n* Rundumschlag *m*.

overland *adj* Überland-; * *adv* über Land.

overlap *vi* sich überschneiden; sich teilweise decken; * *n* Überschneidung.

overleaf *adv* umseitig.

overload *vt* überladen.

overlook *vt* überblicken; übersehen.

overnight *adv* über Nacht; * *adj* Nacht-.

overpass *n* Überführung *f*.

overpower *vt* überwältigen.

overpowering *adj* überwaltigend.

overrate *vt* überschätzen.

override *vt* aufheben; übergehen.

overriding *adj* vorherrschend.

overrule *vt* verwerfen.

overrun *vt* einfallen in; überziehen.

overseas *adv* nach/in Übersee; * *adj* Übersee-, überseeisch.

oversee *vt* beaufsichtigen.

overseer *n* Aufseher *m*; Vorarbeiter *m*.

overshadow *vt* überschatten.

overshoot *vt* hinausschießen über.

oversight *n* Versehen *n*.

oversleep *vi* verschlafen.

overspill *n* Bevölkerungsüberschuß *m*.

overstate *vt* übertreiben.

overt *adj* offen(kundig).

overtake *vt vi* überholen.

overthrow *vt* stürzen.

overtime *n* Überstunden *fpl*.

overtone *n* Note *f*.

overture *n* Ouvertüre *f*.

overturn *vt vi* umkippen.

overweight *adj* zu dick.

overwhelm *vt* überwältigen.

overwhelming *adj* überwaltigend.

overwork *vt* überlasten; * *vi* sich überarbeiten; * *n* Überar-

beitung *f*.

owe *vt* schulden.

owing to *prep* wegen.

owl *n* Eule *f*.

own *vt* besitzen; * *adj* eigen.

owner *n* Besitzer(in) *m(f)*.

ownership *n* Besitz *m*.

ox *n* Ochse *f*.

oxidise *vt* oxydieren.

oxygen *n* Sauerstoff *m*.

oxygen mask *n* Sauerstoffmaske *f*.

oxygen tent *n* Sauerstoffzelt *m*.

oyster *n* Auster *f*.

ozone *n* Ozon *n*.

P

pace *n* Schritt *m*; Gang *m*; Tempo *n*; * *vt* abschreiten; * *vi* (einher)schreiten.

pacific *adj* friedlich.

pacification *n* Beruhigung *f*, Besänftigung *f*.

pacify *vt* beruhigen, besänftigen.

pack *n* Packung *f*; Meute *f*; Spiel *n*; Bande *f*; * *vt* packen; einpacken.

package *n* Paket *n*.

package tour *n* Pauschalreise *f*.

packet *n* Päckchen *n*.

packing *n* Packen *n*; Verpacking *f*.

pact *n* Pakt *m*, Vertrag *m*.

pad *n* Block *m*; Polster *n*; * *vt* polstern.

padding *n* Polsterung *f*.

paddle *n* Paddel *n*; * *vt* paddeln; * *vi* planschen.

paddle steamer *n* Raddampfer *m*.

paddock *n* Koppel *f*.

paddy field *n* Reisfeld *n*.

paediatrics *n* Kinderheilkunde *f*.
pagan *adj* heidnisch; * *n* Heide *m*, Heidin *f*.
page *n* Seite *f*; Page *m*.
pageant *n* Festzug *m*.
pageantry *n* Gepränge *n*.
pail *n* Eimer *m*.
pain *n* Schmerz *m*.
pained *adj* gequalt.
painful *adj* schmerzhaft; peinlich; mühsam.
painkiller *n* Schmerzmittel *n*.
painless *adj* schmerzlos.
painstaking *adj* gewissenhaft.
paint *n* Farbe *f*; * *vt* anstreichen; malen.
paintbrush *n* Pinsel *m*.
painter *n* Maler *m*.
painting *n* Malerei *f*; Gemälde *n*.
paintwork *n* Anstrich *m*; Lack *m*.
pair *n* Paar *n*.
pal *n* Kumpel *m*.
palace *n* Schloß *n*.
palatable *adj* schmackhaft.
palate *n* Gaumen *m*.
palatial *adj* palastartig.
pale *adj* blaß, bleich.
palette *n* Palette *f*.
paling *n* Zaumpfahl *m*; Lattenzaum *m*.
pall *n* Wolke *f*; * *vi* jeden Reiz verlieren, verblassen.
pallet *n* Pallete *f*.
palliative *n* Linderungsmittel *n*.
pallid *adj* blaß, bleich.
pallor *n* Blässe *f*.
palm *n* Handfläche *f*; Palme *f*.
Palm Sunday *n* Palmsonntag *m*.
palpable *adj* greifbar.
palpitation *n* Herzklöpfen *n*.
paltry *adj* armselig.
pamper *vt* verhätscheln.
pamphlet *n* Broschüre *f*.
pan *n* Pfanne *f*; * *vi* schwenken.
panacea *n* Allheitmittel *n*.
panache *n* Schwung *m*.
pancake *n* Pfannkuchen *m*.

pandemonium *n* Hölle *f*; Höllenlärm *m*.
pane *n* Fensterscheibe *f*.
panel *n* Tafel *f*.
panelling *n* Tafelung *f*.
panic *n* Panik *f*; * *vi* in Panik geraten.
panicky *adj* überängstlich.
panic-stricken *adj* von panischen Schrecken erfaßt.
pansy *n* Stiefmütterchen *n*.
pant *vi* keuchen; hecheln.
panther *n* Panther *m*.
panties *npl* Slip *m*.
pantihose *n* Strumpfhose *f*.
pantry *n* Vorratskammer *f*.
pants *npl* Schlüpfer *m*; Unterhose *f*.
papal *adj* päpstlich.
paper *n* Papier *n*; Zeitung *f*; Referat *n*; * *adj* Papier-, aus Papier; * *vt* tapezieren.
paperback *n* Taschenbuch *n*.
paper bag *n* Tüte *f*.
paper clip *n* Büroklammer *f*.
paperweight *n* Briefbeschwerer *m*.
paperwork *n* Schreibarbeit *f*.
par *n* Nennwert *m*; Par *n*.
parable *n* (*rel*) Gleichnis *n*.
parachute *n* Fallschirm *m*; * *vi* (mit dem Fallschirm) abspringen.
parade *n* Parade *f*; * *vt* aufmaschieren lassen; zur Schau stellen; * *vi* paradieren, vorbeimarschieren.
paradise *n* Paradies *n*.
paradox *n* Paradox *n*.
paradoxically *adv* paradoxerweise.
paragon *n* Muster *n*.
paragraph *n* Absatz *m*.
parallel *adj* parallel; * *n* Parallele *f*.
paralyse *vt* lähmen, paralysieren; lahmlagen.
paralysis *n* Lähmung *f*.
paramount *adj* oberste(r,s), höchste(r,s).
paranoid *adj* paranoid.
paraphernalia *n* Zubegör *n*.

parasite n Schmarotzer m, Parasit m.

parasol n Sonnenschirm m.

paratrooper n Fallschirmjäger m.

parcel n Paket n; * vt einpakken.

parch vt (aus)dörren.

parched adj ausgetrocknet.

parchment n Pergament n.

pardon n Verzeihung f; * vt begnadigen.

parent n Elternteil m; ~s pl Eltern pl.

parental adj elterlich, Eltern-.

parenthesis n Klammer f; Parenthese f.

parish n Gemeinde f.

parity n Umrechnungskurs m, Parität f.

park n Park m; * vt vi parken.

parking n Parken n.

parking lot n Parkplatz m.

parking meter n Parkuhr f.

parking ticket n Strafzettel m.

parlance n Sprachgebrauch m.

parliament n Parlament n.

parliamentary adj parlamentarisch, Parlaments-.

parlour n Salon m.

parody n Parodie f; * vt parodieren.

parole n on ~ auf Bewährung.

parrot n Papagei m.

parry vt parieren, abwehren.

parsley n (bot) Petersilie m.

parsnip n (bot) Pastinake f.

part n Teil m; Rolle f; Teil n; * vt trennen; scheiteln; * vi sich trennen; ~ with vt hergeben; aufgeben.

partial adj teilweise; parteiisch.

participant n Teilnehmer(in) m(f).

participate vi teilnehmen (**in** an).

participation n Teilname f; Beteiligung f.

participle n (gr) Partizip n.

particle n Teilchen n; (gr) Partikel m.

particular adj bestimmt; genau; eigen; **in** ~ besonders.

particularly adv besonders.

particulars n Einzelheiten pl; Personalien pl.

parting n Abschied m; Scheitel m.

partisan n Partisan m.

partition n Trennwand f; Teilung f; * vt aufteilen.

partly adv zum Teil, teilweise.

partner n Partner m.

partnership n Partnerschaft f.

partridge n Rebhuhn n.

party n Partei f; Party f.

pass vt vorbeigehen an +dat; vorbeifahren an +dat; weitergeben; verbringen; * vi vorbeigehen; vorbeifahren; vergehen; * n Paß m; Passierschein m; ~ **away** vi verscheiden; ~ **by** vi vorbeigehen; vorbeifahren; ~ **on** vt weitergeben.

passable adj passierbar; passabel.

passage n Gang m; Textstelle f; Überfahrt f.

passbook n Sparbuch n.

passenger n Passagier m.

passer-by n Passant(in) m(f).

passing adj vorbeifahrend; momentan.

passion n Leidenschaft f.

passionate adj leidenschaftlich.

passive adj passiv; passivisch.

Passover n Passahfest n.

passport n Reisepaß m.

passport control n Paßkontrolle f.

password n Parole f, Kennwort n.

past adj vergangen; ehemalig; * n Vergangenheit f; * prep an +dat vorbei; hinter +dat.

pasta n Teigwaren pl.

paste n Paste f; * vt kleben.

pasteurised adj pasteurisiert.

pastime n Zeitvertrieb m.

pastor n Pfarrer m.

pastry n Blätterteig m.

pasture n Weide f.

pat *vt* tätscheln.
patch *n* Fleck *m*; * *vt* flicken; ~ **up** *vt* flicken; beilegen.
pâté *n* Pastete *f*.
patent *adj* offenkundig; * *n* Patent *n*; * *vt* patentieren.
patentee *n* Patentinhaber *m*.
patent leather *n* Lackleder *n*.
paternal *adj* väterlich.
paternity *n* Vaterschaft *f*.
path *n* Pfad *m*; Weg *m*.
pathetic *adj* kläglich.
pathological *adj* pathologisch.
pathology *n* Pathologie *f*.
pathos *n* Rührseligkeit *f*.
pathway *n* Weg *m*.
patience *n* Geduld *f*.
patient *adj* geduldig; * *n* Patient(in) *m(f)*.
patio *n* Terrasse *f*.
patriotic *adj* patriotisch.
patrol *n* Patrouille *f*; Streife *f*; * *vi* patrouillieren.
patrol car *n* Streifenwagen *m*.
patrolman *n* Streifenpolizist *m*.
patron *n* Kunde *m*; Gast *m*; Förderer *m*.
patronage *n* Schirmherrschaft *f*.
patronise *vt* unterstützen; besuchen; von oben herab behandeln.
patter *n* Trappeln *n*; Prasseln *n*; * *vi* trappeln; prasseln.
pattern *n* Muster *n*.
paunch *n* Wanst *m*.
pauper *n* Arme(r) *mf*.
pause *n* Pause *f*; * *vi* innehalten.
pave *vt* pflastern.
pavement *n* Bürgersteig *m*.
pavilion *n* Pavillon *m*.
paving stone *n* Pflasterstein *m*.
paw *n* Tatze *f*; * *vt* scharren.
pawn *n* Pfand *n*; Bauer *m*; * *vt* verpfänden.
pawnbroker *n* Pfandleiher *m*.
pawnshop *n* Pfandhaus *n*.
pay *n* Bezahlung *f*, Lohn *m*; * *vt* zahlen; ~ **back** *vt* zurückzah-

len; ~ **for** *vt* bezahlen; ~ **off** *vt* abzahlen; *vi* sich bezahlt machen.
payable *adj* fällig, zahlbar.
payee *n* Zahlungsempfänger *m*.
pay envelope *n* Lohntüte *f*.
payment *n* paga *f*; Bezahlung *f*.
pay phone *n* Münzfernsprecher *m*.
payroll *n* Lohnliste *f*.
pea *n* Erbse *f*.
peace *n* Friede(n) *m*.
peaceful *adj* friedlich, ruhig.
peach *n* Pfirsich *m*.
peacock *n* Pfau *m*.
peak *n* Spitze *f*; Gipfel *m*.
peak hours *npl* Hauptverkehrszeit *f*; Hauptbelastungszeit *f*.
peak period *n* Stoßzeit *f*, Hauptzeit *f*.
peal *n* Glockenläuten *n*.
peanut *n* Erdnuß *f*.
pear *n* Birne *f*.
pearl *n* Perle *f*.
peasant *n* Bauer *m*.
peat *n* Torf *m*.
pebble *n* Kiesel *m*.
peck *n* Schnabelhieb *m*; * *vt vi* picken.
pecking order *n* Hackordnung *f*.
peculiar *adj* seltsam.
peculiarity *n* Besonderheit *f*; Eigenartigkeit *f*.
pedal *n* Pedal *n*; * *vt vi* fahren, radfahren.
pedant *n* Pedant *m*.
pedantic *adj* pedantisch.
peddler *n* Hausierer(in) *m(f)*.
pedestal *n* Sockel *m*.
pedestrian *n* Fußgänger *m*; * *adj* Fußgänger-; langweilig.
pedigree *n* Stammbaum *m*.
peek *vi* gucken.
peel *vt* schälen; * *vi* abblättern; * *n* Schale *f*.
peer *n* Peer *m*; Ebenbürtige(r) *m*; * *vi* gucken; starren.
peeved *adj* ärgerlich; sauer.
peevish *adj* verdrießlich.

peg n Pflock m; Wäschenklammer f.
pelican n Pelikan m.
pellet n Kügelchen n.
pelt n Pelz m, Fell n; * vt bewerfen; * vi schüttern.
pen n Fedelhalter m; Kuli m; Pferch m.
penal adj Straf-.
penalty n Strafe f; Elfmeter m.
penance n Buße f.
pencil n Bleistift m.
pencil case n Federmäppchen n.
pendant n Anhänger m.
pending adj noch offen.
pendulum n Pendel n.
penetrate vt durchdringen.
penguin n Pinguin m.
penicillin n Penizillin n.
peninsula n Halbinsel f.
penis n Penis m.
penitence n Reue f.
penitent adj reuig.
penitentiary n Zuchthaus n.
penknife n Federmesser n.
pennant n Wimpel m.
penniless adj mittellos.
penny n Penny m.
penpal n Brieffreund(in) m(f).
pension n Rente f.
pensioner n Rentner(in) m(f).
pension fund n Rentenfonds m.
pensive adj nachdenklich.
Pentecost n Pfingsten pl/n.
penthouse n Dachterrassenwohnung f.
pent-up adj angestaut.
penultimate adj vorletzte(r,s).
people n Volk n; * npl Leute pl; Bevölkerung f; * vt besiedeln.
pep n Schwung m; ~ **up** vt aufmöbeln.
pepper n Pfeffer m; Paprika m; * vt bombardieren.
peppermint n Pfefferminz n.
per prep pro.
per annum adv pro Jahr.
per capita adj Pro-Kopf-; * adv pro Kopf.
perceive vt wahrnehmen; verstehen.
per cent n Prozent n.
percentage n Prozentsatz m.
perception n Wahrnehmung f; Einsicht f.
perch n Stange f; Flußbarsch f.
percolator n Kaffeemaschine f.
percussion n (mus) Schlagzeug n.
peremptory adj schroff.
perennial adj wiederkehrend.
perfect adj vollkommen; perfekt; * n (gr) Perfekt n; * vt vervollkommnen.
perfection n Vollkommenheit f.
perforate vt durchlöchern.
perforation n Perforation f.
perform vt durchführen; verrichten; spielen; * vi auftreten.
performance n Durchführung f; Leistung f; Vorstellung f.
performer n Künstler(in) m(f).
perfume n Duft m; Parfüm n.
perhaps adv vielleicht.
peril n Gefahr f.
perimeter n Peripherie f.
period n Periode f; Punkt m.
periodic adj periodisch.
periodical n Zeitschrift f.
peripheral adj Rand-; * n Peripheriegerät n.
perish vi umkommen; verderben.
perishable adj leicht verderblich.
perjury n Meineid m.
perk n Vergünstigung f.
perky adj keck.
perm n Dauerwelle f.
permanent adj dauernd, ständig.
permeate vt vi durchdringen.
permissible adj zulässig.
permission n Erlaubnis f.
permissive adj nachgiebig.
permit vt erlauben, zulassen; * n Zulassung f.
perpendicular adj senkrecht.
perpetrate vt begehen.
perpetual adj dauernd, ständig.

perpetuate *vt* verewigen.
perplex *vt* verblüffen.
persecute *vt* verfolgen.
persecution *n* Verfolgung *f*.
perseverance *n* Ausdauer *f*.
persevere *vi* durchhalten.
Persian *adj* persisch; * *n* Perser(in) *m(f)*.
persist *vi* bleiben; andauern.
persistence *adj* Beharrlichkeit *f*.
persistent *adj* beharrlich; ständig.
person *n* Person *f*.
personable *adj* gut aussehend.
personal *adj* persönlich; privat.
personal assistant *n* Assistent(in) *m(f)*.
personal computer *n* Personalcomputer *m*.
personality *n* Persönlichkeit *f*.
personify *vt* verkörpern.
personnel *n* Personal *n*.
perspective *n* Perspektive *f*.
perspiration *n* Transpiration *f*.
perspire *vi* transpirieren.
persuade *vt* überreden; überzeugen.
persuasion *n* Überredung *f*; Überzeugung *f*.
persuasive *adj* überzeugend.
pert *adj* keck.
pertaining: ~ **to** *prep* betreffend +*acc*.
pertinent *adj* relevant.
perturb *vt* beunruhigen.
peruse *vt* durchlesen; prüfen.
pervade *vt* erfüllen.
perverse *adj* pervers; eigensinnig.
pervert *n* perverse(r) Mensch *m*; * *vt* verdrehen; verderben.
pessimist *n* Pessimist *m*.
pessimistic *adj* pessimistisch.
pest *n* Schädling *m*; Nervensäge *f*.
pester *vt* plagen.
pet *n* Haustier *n*; * *vt* liebkosen, streicheln; * *vi* Petting machen.
petal *n* Blütenblatt *n*.
petite *adj* zierlich.

petition *n* Bittschrift *f*.
petroleum *n* Petroleum *n*.
petticoat *n* Unterrock *m*.
petty *adj* unbedeutend; kleinlich.
petty cash *n* Portokasse *f*.
petty officer *n* Maat *m*.
petulant *adj* leicht reizbar.
pew *n* Kirchenbank *f*.
pewter *n* Zinn *n*.
phantom *n* Phantom *n*.
pharmacist *n* Pharmazeut *m*; Apotheker *m*.
pharmacy *n* Pharmazie *f*; Apotheke *f*.
phase *n* Phase *f*.
pheasant *n* Fasan *m*.
phenomenon *n* Phänomen *n*.
philanthropist *n* Philanthrop *m*.
philosopher *n* Philosopher *m*.
philosophical *adj* philosophisch.
philosophy *n* Philosophie *f*.
phlegm *n* Schleim *m*.
phlegmatic *adj* gelassen.
phobia *n* Phobie *f*.
phone *n* Telefon *n*; * *vt vi* telefonieren, anrufen; ~ **back** *vt vi* zurückrufen; ~ **up** *vt vi* anrufen.
phone book *n* Telefonbuch *n*.
phone box, phone booth *n* Telefonzelle *f*.
phone call *n* Telefonanruf *m*.
phosphorus *n* Phosphor *m*.
photocopier *n* Kopiergerät *n*.
photocopy *n* Fotokopie *f*; * *vt* fotokopieren.
photograph *n* Fotografie *f*, Aufnahme *f*; * *vt* fotografieren.
photographer *n* Fotograf *m*.
photographic *adj* fotografisch.
photography *n* Fotografie *f*.
phrase *n* Satz *m*; Ausdruck *m*; * *vt* ausdrücken, formulieren.
phrase book *n* Sprachführer *m*.
physical *adj* physikalisch; körperlich, physisch.
physical education *n* Turnen *n*.

physician *n* Arzt *m*.
physicist *n* Physiker(in) *m(f)*.
physiotherapy *n* Heilgymnastik *f*, Physiotherapie *f*.
physique *n* Körperbau *m*.
pianist *n* Pianist(in) *m(f)*.
piano *n* Klavier *n*.
pick *n* Pickel *m*; Auswahl *f*; * *vt* pflücken; aussuchen; ~ **on** *vt* herumhacken auf +*dat*; ~ **out** *vt* auswählen; ~ **up** *vi* sich erholen; * *vt* aufheben.
picket *n* Streikposten *m*.
pickle *n* Pökel *m*; * *vt* einpökeln.
pickpocket *n* Taschendieb *m*.
pick-up *n* (*auto*) Lieferwagen *m*.
picnic *n* Picknick *n*.
pictorial *adj* in Bildern.
picture *n* Bild *n*; * *vt* sich *dat* vorstellen.
picture book *n* Bilderbuch *n*.
picturesque *adj* malerisch.
pie *n* Pastete *f*; Torte *f*.
piece *n* Stück *n*.
piecemeal *adv* stückweise.
piecework *n* Akkordarbeit *f*.
pier *n* Pier *m*, Mole *f*.
pierce *vt* durchstechen.
piercing *adj* durchdringend.
piety *n* Frömmigkeit *f*.
pig *n* Schwein *n*.
pigeon *n* Taube *f*.
pigeonhole *n* Brieffach *n*.
piggy-bank *n* Sparschwein *n*.
pigheaded *adj* störrisch.
pigsty *n* Schweinestall *m*.
pigtail *n* Zopf *m*.
pike *n* Hecht *m*.
pile *n* Pfahl *m*, Haufen *m*, Stapel *m*; * *vt* aufschichten, stapeln.
piles *pl* Hämorrhoiden *fpl*;.
pile-up *n* Karambolage *f*.
pilfer *vt* stehlen, klauen.
pilgrim *n* Pilger *m*.
pilgrimage *n* Pilgerfahrt *f*.
pill *n* Pille *f*; **to be on the** ~ die Pille nehmen.
pillage *vt vi* plündern.
pillar *n* Pfeiler *m*, Säule *f*.

pillion *n* Soziussitz *m*.
pillow *n* Kopfkissen *n*.
pillow-case *n* Kopfkissenbezug *m*.
pilot *n* Pilot *m*, Pilotin *f*; (*mar*) Lotse; * *vt* führen; (*mar*) lotsen.
pilot light *n* Zundflamme *f*.
pimp *n* Zuhälter *m*.
pimple *n* Pickel *m*.
pin *n* Nadel *f*; **I have ~s and needles** mir kribbelt es; * *vt* mit einer Nadel heften.
pinafore *n* Trägerrock *m*.
pinball *n* Flipper *m*.
pincers *n* (*med*) Pinzette *f*.
pinch *vt* zwicken; (*coll*) klauen; * *vi* drücken; * *n* Zwicken *n*.
pincushion *n* Nadelkissen *n*.
pine *n* (*bot*) Kiefer *f*; * *vi*: **to ~ for** sich sehnen nach.
pineapple *n* Ananas *f*.
ping *n* Klingeln *n*.
pink *n* Rosa *n*; * *adj* rosa *inv*.
pinnacle *n* Spitze *f*.
pinpoint *vt* festlegen.
pint *n* Pint *n*.
pioneer *n* Pionier *m*.
pious *adj* fromm.
pip *n* Kern *m*.
pipe *n* Pfeife *f*; Rohr *n*; Rohrleitung *f*; ~s Dudelsack *m*.
pipe cleaner *n* Pfeifenreiniger *m*.
pipe dream *n* Luftschloß *n*.
pipeline *n* Pipeline *f*.
piper *n* Pfeifer *m*; Dudelsackbläser *m*.
piping *adj* pfeifend, schrill; * *n* Paspel *f*.
pique *n* Groll *m*.
piracy *n* Piraterie *f*; Seeräuberei *f*.
pirate *n* Pirat *m*; Seeräuber *m*.
Pisces *n* (*astrol*) Fische *pl*.
piss *vi* pissen.
pistol *n* Pistole *f*.
piston *n* Kolben *m*.
pit *n* Grube *f*; Miete *f*.
pitch *n* Pech *n*; Tonhöhe *f*; * *vt* werfen; schleudern; * *vi* (sich) lagern; hinschlagen.

pitch-black *adj* pechschwarz; stockdunkel.
pitcher *n* Krug *m*.
pitchfork *n* Mistgabel *f*.
pitfall *n* Falle *f*.
pith *n* Mark *n*.
pithy *adj* prägnant.
pitiful *adj* bedauenswert; jämmerlich.
pittance *n* Hungerlohn *m*.
pity *n* Mitleid *n*; * *vt* Mitleid haben mit.
pivot *n* Drehpunkt *m*.
pizza *n* Pizza *f*.
placard *n* Plakat *n*, Anschlag *m*.
placate *vt* beschwichtigen.
place *n* Platz *m*; Stelle *f*; Ort *m*; * *vt* setzen, stellen, legen.
placid *adj* gelassen, ruhig.
plagiarism *n* Plagiat *n*.
plague *n* Pest *f*; Plage *f*; * *vt* plagen.
plaice *n* Scholle *f*.
plain *adj* klar, deutlich; einfach, schlicht; alltäglich; * *n* Ebene *f*.
plaintiff *n* Kläger *m*.
plait *n* Zopf *m*; * *vt* flechten.
plan *n* Plan *m*; * *vt vi* planen.
plane *n* Ebene *f*; Flugzeug *n*; Hobel *m*; Platane *f*.
planet *n* Planet *m*.
plank *n* Brett *n*.
planning *n* Planung *f*.
plant *n* Pflanze *f*; Anlage *f*; Fabrik *f*, Werk *n*; * *vt* pflanzen.
plantation *n* Plantage *f*.
plaque *n* Gedenktafel *f*; Zahnbelag *m*.
plaster *n* Gips *m*; Verputz *m*; Pflaster *n*; Gipsverband *m*; * *vt* gipsen; zugipsen; verputzen.
plastered *adj* (*coll*) besoffen.
plasterer *n* Gipser *m*.
plastic *n* Plastik *n/f*; * *adj* Plastik-; plastisch, bildend.
plastic surgery *n* plastische Chirurgie *f*.
plate *n* Teller *m*; Platte *f*; Tafel *f*.

plateau *n* Plateau *n*, Hochebene *f*.
plate glass *n* Tafelglas *n*.
platform *n* Plattform *f*, Podium *n*; Bahnsteig *m*.
platinum *n* Platin *n*.
platitude *n* Plattheit *m*.
platoon *n* (*mil*) Zug *m*.
platter *n* Platte *f*.
plausible *adj* plausibel.
play *n* Spiel *n*; Theaterstück *n*; * *vt vi* spielen; ~ **down** *vt* herunterspielen.
playboy *n* Playboy *m*.
player *n* Spieler(in) *m(f)*.
playful *adj* spielerisch.
playmate *n* Spielkamerad *m*.
playground *n* Spielplatz *m*.
playgroup *n* Kindergarten *m*.
play-off *n* Entscheidungsspiel *n*.
playpen *n* Laufstall *m*.
plaything *n* Spielzeug *n*.
playwright *n* Theaterschriftsteller *m*.
plea *n* Bitte *f*; Plädoyer *n*.
plead *vt* vertreten; * *vi* dringend bitten; plädieren.
pleasant *adj* angenehm.
please *vt* gefallen +*dat*; ~! bitte!.
pleased *adj* zufrieden.
pleasing *adj* erfreulich.
pleasure *n* Freude *f*.
pleat *n* Falte *f*.
pledge *n* Pfand *n*; Versprechen *n*; * *vt* verpfänden; versprechen.
plentiful *adj* reichlich.
plenty *n* Fülle *f*.
pleurisy *n* Rippenfellentzündung *f*.
pliable *adj* biegsam.
pliers *npl* Zange *f*.
plight *n* Notlage *f*.
plinth *n* Sockel *m*.
plod *vi* trotten.
plot *n* Komplott *n*; Handlung *f*; Grundstück *n*; * *vi* sich verschwören.
plough *n* Pflug *m*; * *vt* pflügen; ~ **back** *vt* wieder in das Ge-

schäft stecken; ~ **through** *vt* durchpflügen.
ploy *n* Masche *f*.
pluck *vt* pflücken; zupfen; rupfen; * *n* Mut *m*.
plucky *adj* beherzt.
plug *n* Stöpsel *m*; Stecker *m*; Zündkerze *f*; * *vt* stopfen.
plum *n* Pflaume *f*, Zwetsch(g)e *f*.
plumage *n* Gefieder *n*.
plumb *n* Lot *n*; * *adj* senkrecht; * *adv* genau; * *vt* ausloten; sondieren.
plumber *n* Klempner *m*, Installateur *m*.
plume *n* Feder *f*; Fahne *f*.
plump *adj* ründlich, füllig.
plunder *n* Plünderung *f*; Beute *f*; * *vt* plündern.
plunge *vt* stoßen; * *vi* (sich) stürzen.
pluperfect *n* (*gr*) Plusquamperfekt *n*.
plural *n* Plural *m*, Mehrzahl *f*.
plus *n* Plus(zeichen) *n*; * *prep* plus, und.
plush *adj* feudal.
ply *vt* betreiben; * *vi* verkehren.
plywood *n* Sperrholz *n*.
pneumatic *adj* pneumatisch; Luft-.
pneumatic drill *n* Preßlufthammer *m*.
pneumonia *n* Lüngenentzündung *f*.
poach *vt* pochieren; stehlen; * *vi* wildern.
poached *adj* (egg) verloren.
poacher *n* Wilddieb *m*.
pocket *n* Tasche *f*; * *vt* einstecken.
pocketbook *n* Taschenbuch *n*.
pocket money *n* Taschengeld *n*.
pod *n* Hülse *f*.
podgy *adj* pummelig.
poem *n* Gedicht *n*.
poet *n* Dichter *m*, Poet *m*.
poetic *adj* poetisch.
poetry *n* Poesie *f*.
poignant *adj* ergreifend.

point *n* Punkt *m*; Spitze *f*; Zweck *m*; * *vt* zeigen mit; richten; * *vi* zeigen.
point-blank *adv* aus nächster Entfernung.
pointed *adj* spitz, scharf.
pointer *n* Zeigestock *m*.
pointless *adj* sinnlos.
poise *n* Haltung *f*.
poison *n* Gift *n*; * *vt* vergiften.
poisoning *n* Vergiftung *f*.
poisonous *adj* Gift-, giftig.
poke *vt* stecken; schüren.
poker *n* Schürhaken *m*; Poker *n*.
poker-faced *adj* undurchdringlich.
poky *adj* eng.
Poland *n* Polen *n*.
polar *adj* Polar-, polar.
Pole *n* Pole *n*, Polin *f*.
pole *n* Stange *f*, Pfosten *m*; Mast *m*; Pol *m*.
pole bean *n* Stangenbohne *f*.
pole vault *n* Stabhochsprung *m*.
police *n* Polizei *f*.
police car *n* Polizeiwagen *m*.
policeman *n* Polizist *m*.
police state *n* Polizeistaat *m*.
police station *n* Polizeirevier *n*, Wache *f*.
policewoman *n* Polizistin *f*.
policy *n* Politik *f*, Versicherungspolice *f*.
polio *n* Polio *f*.
Polish *adj* polnisch; * *n* Polnisch *n*.
polish *n* Politur *f*; Wachs *n*; Creme *f*; * *vt* polieren; putzen; ~ **off** *vt* erledigen.
polished *adj* glänzend; verfeinert.
polite *adj* höflich.
politeness *n* Höflichkeit *f*.
politic *adj* diplomatisch.
political *adj* politisch.
politician *n* Politiker *m*.
politics *npl* Politik *f*.
polka dot *n* Tupfen *m*.
poll *n* Abstimmung *f*; Wahl *f*; Umfrage *f*.

pollen n (bot) Blütenstaub m, Pollen m.

pollute vt verschmutzen, verunreinigen.

pollution n Verschmutzung f.

polo n Polo n.

polystyrene n Styropor n.

polytechnic n technische Hochschule f.

pomegranate n Granatapfel m.

pompom n Pompon m.

pompous adj aufgeblasen.

pond n Teich m.

ponder vt nachdenken über +acc.

ponderous adj schwerfällig.

pontiff n Pontifex m.

pontoon n Ponton m.

pony n Pony n.

ponytail n Pferdeschwanz m.

pool n Schwimmbad n; Lache f; * vt zusammenlegen.

poor adj arm; schlecht; **the ~** n die Armen pl.

pop n Knall m; Popmusik f; Limo f.

popcorn n Puffmais m.

pope n Papst m.

poplar n Pappel f.

poppy n Mohn m.

populace n Volk n.

popular adj beliebt, populär; volkstümlich.

popularise vt popularisieren.

popularity n Beliebtheit f, Popularität f.

populate vt bevölkern.

population n Bevölkerung f.

populous adj dicht besiedelt.

porcelain n Porzellan n.

porch n Vorbau m, Veranda f.

porcupine n Stachelschwein n.

pore n Pore f; * vi **~ over** vt brüten über.

pork n Schweinefleisch n.

pornography n Pornographie f.

porous adj porös; porig.

porpoise n Tümmler m.

porridge n Haferbrei m.

port n Hafen m; Hafenstadt f;

(mar) Backbord n; Portwein m.

portable adj tragbar.

portal n Portal n, Tor n.

porter n Pförtner(in) m(f); Gepäckträger m.

portfolio n Mappe f.

porthole n Bullauge n.

portion n Teil m, Stück n.

portly adj korpulent, beleibt.

portrait n Porträt n.

portray vt darstellen.

Portugal n Portugal n.

Portuguese adj portugiesisch; * n Portugiese n, Portugiesin f; Portugiesisch n.

pose n Stellung f, Pose f; * vi posieren; * vt stellen.

posh adj (coll) fein.

position n Stellung f; Lage f; Stelle f; * vt aufstellen.

positive adj positiv.

posse n Aufgebot n.

possess vt besitzen.

possession n Besitz m.

possessive adj besitzergreifend.

possibility n Möglichkeit f.

possible adj möglich.

post n Post f; Pfosten m; Stelle f; * vt anschlagen; aufgeben; aufstellen.

postage n Porto n.

postcard n Postkarte f.

postdate vt nachdatieren.

poster n Plakat n.

posterior n Hintern m.

posterity n Nachwelt f.

postgraduate n Weiterstudierende(r) mf.

posthumous adj post(h)um.

postman n Briefträger m.

postmark n Poststempel m.

postmaster n Postamtsvorsteher m.

post office n Postamt n; Post f.

postpone vt verschieben.

postscript n Postskript n.

posture n Haltung f; * vi posieren.

postwar adj Nachkriegs-.

posy n Blumenstrauß m.

pot *n* Topf *m*; Kanne *f*; *(coll)*
Hasch *f*; * *vt* eintopfen.
potato *n* Kartoffel *f*.
potato peeler *n* Kartoffelschä-
ler *m*.
potent *adj* stark; zwingend.
potential *adj* potentiell; * *n*
Potential *n*.
pothole *n* Schlagloch *n*; Höhle
f.
potion *n* Trank *m*.
potted *adj* Topf-; konzentriert.
potter *n* Töpfer *m*; * *vi* herum-
hantieren.
pottery *n* Töpferei *f*.
potty *n* Töpfchen *n*.
pouch *n* Beutel *m*.
poultry *n* Geflügel *n*.
pound *n* Pfund *n*; * *vi* pochen.
pour *vt* gießen; * *vi* strömen.
pout *vi* schmollen.
poverty *n* Armut *f*.
powder *n* Pulver *n*, Puder *m*;
* *vt* sich pudern.
powdered milk *n* Trockenmilch *f*.
powder room *n* Damentoilet-
te *f*.
powdery *adj* pulverig.
power *n* Macht *f*; Fähigkeit *f*;
Stärke *f*; * *vt* antreiben.
powerful *adj* stark; leistungsfähig; heftig, mächtig.
powerless *adj* machtlos.
power station *n* Kraftwerk *n*.
practicable *adj* durchführbar,
möglich.
practical *adj* praktisch.
practical joke *n* Streich *m*.
practice *n* Übung *f*; Praxis *f*;
Brauch *m*.
practise *vt* üben; ausüben; * *vi*
üben; praktizieren.
pragmatic *adj* pragmatisch.
prairie *n* Prärie *f*, Steppe *f*.
praise *n* Lob *n*; * *vt* loben.
praiseworthy *adj* lobenswert.
prance *vi* tänzeln.
prank *n* Streich *m*.
prattle *vi* schwatzen, plappern.
prawn *n* Garnele *f*.
pray *vi* beten.

prayer *n* Gebet *n*.
preach *vi* predigen.
preacher *n* Prediger *m*.
preamble *n* Einleitung *f*.
precarious *adj* precär.
precaution *n* Vorsichtsmaßnahme *f*.
precede *vt* vorausgehen +*dat*;
* *vi* vorausgehen.
precedence *n* Vorrang *m*.
precedent *adj, n* Präzedenzfall
m.
precinct *n* Bezirk *m*; ~s *npl*
Gelände *n*; Umgebung *f*.
precious *adj* wertvoll; preziös.
precipice *n* Abgrund *m*.
precipitate *vt* hinunterstüt-
zen; * *adj* überstürzt.
precise *adj* genau, präzis.
precision *n* Präzision *f*.
preclude *vt* ausschließen.
precocious *adj* frühreif.
preconceived *adj* vorgefaßt.
precondition *n* Voraussetzung
f.
precursor *n* Vorläufer *m*.
predator *n* Raubtier *n*.
predecessor *n* Vorgänger *m*.
predestination *n* Vorherbe-
stimmung *f*.
predicament *n* mißliche Lage
f.
predict *vt* voraussagen.
predictable *adj* vorhersagbar.
prediction *n* Voraussage *f*.
predominantly *adv* überwiegend, hauptsächlich.
predominate *vi* vorherrschen.
preen *vt* putzen.
prefab *n* Fertighaus *n*.
preface *n* Vorwort *n*.
prefer *vt* vorziehen, lieber mögen.
preferable *adj* vorzugsweise,
am liebsten.
preference *n* Vorzug *m*.
preferential *adj* Vorzugs-.
prefix *n* Präfix *n*.
pregnancy *n* Schwangerschaft *f*.
pregnant *adj* schwanger.
prehistoric *adj* vorgeschicht-
lich.

prejudice n Vorurteil n; Voreingenommenheit f; * vt beeinträchtigen.

prejudiced adj voreingenommen.

preliminary adj Vor-, einleitend.

prelude n Vorspiel n.

premarital adj vorehelich.

premature adj vorzeitig; Früh-.

premeditated adj geplant; vorsätzlich.

premier n Premier m.

premiere n Premiere f.

premise n Voraussetzung f, Prämisse f.

premises npl Räumlichkeiten fpl.

premium n Prämie f.

premonition n Vorahmung f.

preoccupied adj geistesabwesend.

prepaid adj vorausbezahlt.

preparation n Vorbereitung f.

preparatory adj Vor-.

prepare vt vorbereiten; * vi sich vorbereiten.

preponderance n Übergewicht n.

preposition n Präposition f, Verhältniswort n.

preposterous adj absurd.

prerequisite n Voraussetzung f.

prerogative n Vorrecht n.

prescribe vi vorschreiben; (med) verschreiben.

prescription n (med) Rezept n.

presence n Gegenwart f.

present adj anwesend; gegenwärtig; * n Gegenwart f; Geschenk n; * vt vorlegen; vorstellen; zeigen.

presentable adj präsentabel.

presentation n Überreichung f.

present-day adj heutig.

presenter n Moderator(in) m(f).

preservation n Erhaltung f.

preservative n Konservierungsmittel n.

preserve vt erhalten; einmachen; * n Eingemachte(s) n.

preside vi den Vorsitz haben.

presidency n Präsidentschaft f.

president n Präsident m.

presidential adj Präsidenten-; Präsidentschafts-.

press n Presse f; Druckerei f; * vt drücken; drängen; * vi drücken.

press agency n Presseagentur f.

press conference n Pressekonferenz f.

pressing adj dringend.

pressure n Druck m.

pressure cooker n Schnellkochtopf m.

pressurised adj Druck-.

prestige n Prestige n.

presumably adv vermütlich.

presume vt annehmen.

presumption n Annahme f.

presumptuous adj anmaßend.

presuppose vt voraussetzen.

pretence n Vorgabe f.

pretend vi so tun.

pretension n Anmaßung f.

pretentious adj angeberisch.

pretext n Vorwand m.

pretty adj hübsch; * adv ganz schön.

prevail vi siegen; vorherrschen.

prevailing adj vorherrschend.

prevalent adj vorherrschend.

prevent vt verhindern, verhüten.

prevention n Verhütung f.

preventive adj Schutz-.

preview n Vorschau f.

previous adj früher, vorherig.

prewar adj Vorkriegs-.

prey n Beute f.

price n Preis m.

priceless adj unbezahlbar.

price list n Preisliste f.

prick n Stich m; * vt vi stechen.

prickle n Stachel m, Dorn m.

prickly adj stachelig.

pride n Stolz m.

priest *n* Priester *m*.
priestess *n* Priesterin *f*.
priesthood *n* Priesteramt *n*.
prim *adj* prüde.
primary *adj* Haupt-.
prime *adj* erstklassig; * *vt* vorbereiten; laden.
prime minister *n* Premierminister *m*.
primeval *adj* vorzeitlich; Ur-.
primitive *adj* primitiv.
primrose *n* (*bot*) Primel *f*.
prince *n* Prinz *m*; Fürst *m*.
princess *n* Prinzessin *f*; Fürstin *f*.
principal *adj* Haupt-; * *n* Direktor *m*.
principality *n* Fürstentum *n*.
principle *n* Grundsatz *m*; Prinzip *n*.
print *n* Druck *m*; Abdruck *m*; Abzug *m*; * *vt* drucken; **out of** ~ vergriffen.
printed matter *n* Drucksacke *f*.
printer *n* Drucker *m*.
printing *n* Drucken *n*.
prior *adj* früher; * *n* Prior *m*.
priority *n* Priorität *f*.
prison *n* Gefängnis *n*.
prisoner *n* Gefangene(r) *mf*.
pristine *adj* makellos.
privacy *n* Ungestörtheit *f*; Privatleben *n*.
private *adj* privat, Privat-; geheim; * *n* einfache(r) Soldat *m*.
private eye *n* Privatdetektiv *m*.
privet *n* Liguster *m*.
privilege *n* Privileg *n*.
prize *n* Preis *m*; * *vt* (hoch)schätzen.
prize-giving *n* Preisverteilung *f*.
prizewinner *n* Preisträger(in) *m(f)*.
pro *n* Profi *m*.
probability *n* Wahrscheinlichkeit *f*.
probable *adj* wahrscheinlich.
probation *n* Probe *f*.
probe *n* Sonde *f*; Untersuchung

f; * *vt vi* erforschen.
problem *n* Problem *n*.
problematic *adj* problematisch.
procedure *n* Verfahren *n*.
proceed *vi* vorrücken; fortfahren; ~**s** *npl* Erlös *m*.
proceedings *n* Verfahren *n*.
process *n* Prozeß *m*; Verfahren *n*.
procession *n* Prozession *f*.
proclaim *vt* verkünden.
proclamation *n* Verkündung *f*.
procrastinate *vi* zaudern.
procure *vt* beschaffen.
prod *vt* stoßen.
prodigal *adj* verschwenderisch.
prodigious *adj* wunderbar; gewaltig.
prodigy *n* Wünder *n*.
produce *n* Produkte *pl*; Erzeugnis *n*; * *vt* herstellen, produzieren; erzeugen.
producer *n* Hersteller *m*, Produzent *m*; Erzeuger *m*.
product *n* Produkt *n*; Erzeugnis *n*.
production *n* Produktion *f*, Herstellung *f*.
production line *n* Fließband *n*.
productive *adj* produktiv.
productivity *n* Produktivität *f*.
profane *adj* weltlich, profan.
profess *vt* zeigen; vorgeben.
profession *n* Beruf *m*.
professional *adj* Berufs-.
professor *n* Professor *m*.
proficiency *n* Können *n*.
proficient *adj* fähig.
profile *n* Profil *n*.
profit *n* Gewinn *m*; * *vi*: **to ~ (from)** profitieren (von).
profitability *n* Rentabilität *f*.
profitable *adj* rentabel.
profiteering *n* Profitmacherei *f*.
profound *adj* tief.
profuse *adj* überreich.
programme, program *n* Program *n*; * *vt* planen; programmieren.

programmer n Programmierer(in) m(f).
programming n Programmieren n.
progress n Fortschritt m; * vi fortschreiten, weitergehen.
progression n Folge f.
progressive adj fortschrittlich, progressiv.
prohibit vt verbieten.
prohibition n Verbot n.
project n Projekt n; * vt vorausplanen; projizieren.
projectile n Geschoß n.
projection n Projektion f.
projector n Projektor m.
proletariat n Proletariat n.
prolific adj produktiv.
prologue n Prolog m; Vorspiel n.
prolong vt verlängern.
promenade n Promenade f.
prominence n (große) Bedeutung f.
prominent adj prominent; bedeutend; auffallend.
promiscuous adj lose.
promise n Versprechen n; * vt vi versprechen.
promising adj vielversprechend.
promontory n Vorsprung m.
promote vt befördern; fördern, unterstützen.
promoter n Veranstalter m.
promotion n Beförderung f; Förderung f; Werbung f.
prompt adj prompt, schnell; * adv genau; * n (computer) Meldung f; * vt veranlassen; soufflieren +dat.
prone adj hingestreckt.
prong n Zinke f.
pronoun n Fürwort n.
pronounce vt aussprechen; verkünden.
pronounced adj ausgesprochen.
pronouncement n Erklärung f.
pronunciation n Aussprache f.
proof n Beweis f; Korrekturfah-

ne f; Alkoholgehalt m; * adj sicher.
prop n Stütze f; Requisit n; * vt (ab)stützen.
propaganda n Propaganda f.
propel vt (an)treiben.
propeller n Propeller m.
propensity n Tendenz f.
proper adj richtig; schicklich.
property n Eigentum n.
prophecy n Prophezeihung f.
prophesy vt prophezeien.
prophet n Prophet m.
proportion n Verhältnis n; Teil m.
proportional adj proportional.
proportionate adj verhältnismäßig.
proposal n Vorshlag m.
propose vt vorschlagen.
proposition n Angebot n.
proprietor n Besitzer m, Eigentümer m.
propriety n Anstand m.
pro rata adv anteilmäßig.
prose n Prosa f.
prosecute vt (strafrechtlich) verfolgen.
prosecution n strafrechtliche Verfolgung f; Anklage f.
prosecutor n Vertreter m der Anklage.
prospect n Aussicht f; * vt auf Bodenschätze hin untersuchen; * vi: **to ~ (for)** suchen (nach).
prospecting n Suche f.
prospector n Sucher m.
prospectus n Prospekt m.
prosper vi blühen, gedeihen; erfolgreich sein.
prosperity n Wohlstand m.
prosperous adj reich, wohlhabend.
prostitute n Prostituierte f, Dirne f.
prostrate adj ausgestreckt.
protagonist n Hauptperson f, Held m.
protect vt (be)schützen.
protection n Schutz m.
protective adj Schutz-,

(be)schützend.
protector *n* Schützer *m*.
protégé *n* Schützling *m*.
protein *n* Protein *n*.
protest *n* Protest *m*; * *vi* protestieren.
Protestant *adj* protestantisch; * *n* Protestant(in) *m(f)*.
protester *n* Demonstrant(in) *m(f)*.
protracted *adj* sich hinziehend.
protrude *vi* (her)vorstehen.
proud *adj* stolz.
prove *vt* beweisen.
proverb *n* Sprichwort *n*.
proverbial *adj* sprichwörtlich.
provide *vt* versehen; ~ **for** *vt* sorgen für.
provided *conj*: ~ **that** vorausgesetzt, daß.
Providence *n* die Vorsehung *f*.
province *n* Provinz *f*.
provincial *adj* provinziell.
provision *n* Vorkehrung *f*; Bestimmung *f*.
provisional *adj* provisorisch.
proviso *n* Bedingung *f*.
provocation *n* Herausforderung *f*.
provocative *adj* herausfordernd.
provoke *vt* provozieren; hervorrufen.
prow *n* Bug *m*.
prowess *n* überragende(s) Können *n*.
prowl *vi* herumstreichen; schleichen.
prowler *n* Herumtreter(in) *m(f)*.
proximity *n* Nähe *f*.
proxy *n* Stellvertreter *m*; Vollmacht *f*; **by** ~ durch einen Stellvertreter.
prudence *n* Umsicht *f*.
prudent *adj* klug, umsichtig.
prudish *adj* prüde.
prune *n* Backpflaume *f*; * *vt* ausputzen.
pry *vi*: **to** ~ **into** seine Nase stecken (in +*acc*).

pseudonym *n* Pseudonym *n*, Deckname *m*.
psychiatric *adj* psychiatrisch.
psychiatrist *n* Psychiater *m*.
psychiatry *n* Psychiatrie *f*.
psychic *adj* übersinnlich.
psychoanalyse *vt* psychoanalytisch behandeln.
psychoanalysis *n* Psychoanalyse *f*.
psychoanalyst *n* Psychoanalytiker(in) *m(f)*.
psychological *adj* psychologisch.
psychologist *n* Psychologe *m*, Psychologin *f*.
psychology *n* Psychologie *f*.
pub *n* Kneipe *f*.
puberty *n* Pubertät *f*.
public *adj* öffentlich; * *n* Öffentlichkeit *f*.
public address system *n* Lautsprecheranlage *f*.
publican *n* Wirt *m*.
publication *n* Veröffentlichung *f*.
publicise *vt* bekannt machen; Publicity machen für.
publicity *n* Publicity *f*, Werbung *f*.
public opinion *n* öffentliche Meinung *f*.
publish *vt* veröffentlichen.
publisher *n* Verleger *m*.
publishing *n* Verlagswesen *n*.
pucker *vt* verziehen; kräuseln.
pudding *n* Nachtisch *m*; Pudding *m*.
puddle *n* Pfütze *f*.
puff *n* Stoß *m*; Puderquaste *f*; * *vt* blasen, pusten; paffen; * *vi* kenchen, schnaufen; paffen.
puff pastry *n* Blätterteig *m*.
puffy *adj* aufgedunsen.
pull *n* Ruck *m*; Beziehung *f*; * *vt* ziehen; abdrücken; * *vi* ziehen; ~ **down** *vt* abreißen; ~ **in** *vt* hineinfahren; anhalten; ~ **off** *vt* abschließen; ~ **out** *vi* herausfahren; aussteigen; * *vt* herausziehen; ~ **through** *vi*

durchkommen; ~ **up** *vi* anhalten; * *vt* herausreißen; anhalten.

pulley *n* Rolle *f*, Flaschenzug *m*.

pullover *n* Pullover *m*.

pulp *n* Brei *m*; Fruchtfleisch *n*.

pulpit *n* Kanzel *f*.

pulsate *vi* pulsieren.

pulse *n* Puls *m*.

pummel *vt* mit den Fäusten bearbeiten.

pump *n* Pumpe *f*; * *vt* pumpen.

pumpkin *n* Kürbis *m*.

pun *n* Wortspiel *n*.

punch *n* Locher *m*; Faustschlag *m*; Punsche *m*, Bowle *f*; * *vt* lochen; schlagen, boxen.

punctual *adj* pünktlich.

punctuate *vt* mit Satzzeichen versehen; unterbrechen.

punctuation *n* Zeichensetzung *f*.

pundit *n* Gelehrte(r) *m*.

pungent *adj* scharf.

punish *vt* bestrafen.

punishment *n* Strafe *f*; Bestrafung *f*.

punk *n* Punker(in) *m(f)*; Punk *f m*.

punt *n* Stechkahn *m*.

punter *n* Wetter *m*.

puny *adj* kümmerlich.

pupil *n* Schüler(in) *m(f)*; Pupille *f*.

puppet *n* Puppe *f*; Marionette *f*.

puppy *n* junge(r) Hund *m*.

purchase *n* Kauf *m*; * *vt* kaufen, erwerben.

purchaser *n* Käufer(in) *m(f)*.

pure *adj* rein.

purge *vt* reinigen; entschlakken.

purify *vt* reinigen.

purity *n* Reinheit *f*.

purl *n* linke Masche *f*.

purple *adj* violett; dunkelrot.

purport *vi* vorgeben.

purpose *n* Zweck *m*, Ziel *n*; **on** ~ absichtlich.

purposeful *adj* zielbewußt, entschlossen.

purr *vi* schnurren.

purse *n* Portemonnaie *n*, Geldbeutel *m*.

purser *n* Zahlmeister *m*.

pursue *vi* verfolgen; nachgeben +*dat*.

pursuit *n* Verfolgung *f*; Beschäftigung *f*.

purveyor *n* Lieferant *m*.

push *n* Stoß *m*, Schub *m*; Vorstoß *m*; * *vt* stoßen, schieben; drücken; durchsetzen; ~ **aside** *vt* beiseiteschieben; ~ **off** *vi* (*coll*) abschieben; ~ **on** *vi* weitermachen.

push-up *n* Liegestütz *m*.

put *vt* setzen, stellen, legen; ausdrücken, sagen; schreiben; ~ **away** *vt* weglegen; beiseitelegen; ~ **down** *vt* hinstellen, hinlegen; niederschlagen; einschläfern; ~ **forward** *vt* vorbringen; vorstellen; ~ **off** *vt* verschieben; ~ **on** *vt* anziehen; anschalten, anmachen; aufführen; ~ **out** *vt* ausstrecken; verbreiten; ausschalten, ausmachen; ~ **up** *vt* aufstellen; errichten; erhöhen; unterbringen.

putrid *adj* faul, verfault.

putt *n* Putten *n*; * *vt* putten.

putty *n* Kitt *m*.

puzzle *n* Rätsel *m*; Verwirrung *f*; Geduldspiel *n*.

puzzling *adj* rätselhaft, verwirrend.

pyjamas *npl* Schlafanzug *m*, Pyjama *m*.

pylon *n* Mast *m*.

pyramid *n* Pyramide *f*.

python *n* Pythonschlange *m*.

Q

quack *vi* quaken; * *n* Quaken *n*; (*sl*) Quacksalber *m*.

quadrangle n Hof m; Viereck n.
quadruple adj vierfach.
quadruplet n Vierling m.
quagmire n Morass m.
quail n Wachtel f.
quaint adj malerisch, kuriös.
quake vi beben; zittern.
Quaker n Quäker m.
qualification n Qualifikation f.
qualified adj qualifiziert.
qualify vt befähigen; * vi qualifizieren.
quality n Qualität f.
qualm n Bedenken n.
quandary n Verlegenheit f.
quantity n Quantität f, Menge f, Anzahl f.
quarantine n Quarantän f.
quarrel n Streit m; * vi sich streiten.
quarrelsome adj streitsüchtig.
quarry n Steinbruch m; Wild n.
quarter n Viertel n; Quartal n; ~ **of an hour** Viertelstunde f.
quarterly adj vierteljährlich.
quartermaster n (mil) Quartiermeister m.
quartet n (mus) Quartett n.
quartz n (min) Quarz m.
quash vt wiederrufen.
quay n Kai m.
queasy adj unwohl, übel.
queen n Königin f; Dame f.
queer adj seltsam.
quell vt unterdrucken.
quench vt löschen.
query n Frage f; * vt in Frage stellen.
quest n Suche f.
question n Frage f; * vt befragen; **out of the ~** ausgeschlossen.
questionable adj fragwürdig, zweifelhaft.
question mark n Fragezeichen n.
questionnaire n Fragebogen m.
quibble vi kritteln.
quick adj schnell.
quicken vt beschleunigen; * vi sich beschleunigen.

quicksand n Treibesand m.
quick-tempered adj jähzornig.
quick-witted adj aufgeweckt.
quiet adj leise; * n Ruhe f.
quietness n Ruhe f, Stille f.
quinine n Chinin n.
quintet n (mus) Quintett n.
quintuple adj fünffach.
quintuplet n Fünfling m.
quip n witzige Bemerkung f.
quirk n Eigenart f.
quit vt verlassen; * vi aufhören.
quite adv ganz, ziemlich; völlig.
quits adj quitt.
quiver vi zittern; * n Köcher m.
quiz n Quiz n; * vt prüfen, ausfragen.
quizzical adj neckisch.
quota n Quote f.
quotation n Zitat n.
quotation marks npl Anführungszeichen npl.
quote vt zitieren.

R

rabbi n Rabbiner m.
rabbit n Kaninchen n.
rabbit hutch n Kaninchenstall m.
rabble n Pöbel m.
rabies n Tollwut f.
race n Rasse f; Rennen n; * vt laufen lassen; * vi rennen.
racial adj Rassen-; ~**ist** adj rassistisch; * n Rassist m.
racing n Rennen n.
rack n Ständer m; * vt plagen.
racket n Krach m; Schläger m.
racy adj gewagt; spritzig
radiance n strahlende(r) Glanz m.
radiant adj strahlend.
radiate vt vi ausstrahlen.
radiation n Strahlung f.
radiator n Heizkörper m.

radical *adj* radikal.
radio *n* Radio *n*.
radioactive *adj* radioactiv.
radish *n* Rettich *m*.
radius *n* radio *f*.
raffle *n* rifa *f* (juego); * *vt* rifar.
raft *n* balsa, almadia *f*.
rafter *n* par *m*; viga *f*.
rag *n* trapo, andrajo *m*.
rage *n* Regen *m*; * *vt vi* regnen.
raid *n* incursion *f*; * *vt* invadir.
rail *n* Schiene *f*; Gelände *n*; Re-
ling *f*; ~**s** *npl* (*rail*) Geleise *pl*.
railway *n* Eisenbahn *f*.
rain *n* Regen *m*; * *vt vi* regnen.
rainbow *n* Regebogen *m*.
rainy *adj* regnerisch.
raise *vt* heben; erhohen.
raisin *n* Rasine *f*.
rake *n* Harke *f*; * *vt* harken.
rakish *adj* verwegen.
rally *vt* (*mil*) sammeln; * *vi*
Kräfte sammeln.
ram *n* Widder *m*; Ramme *f*; * *vt*
rammen.
ramble *n* Wanderung *f*; * *vi*
schwafeln.
rambler *n* Wanderer *m*.
ramp *n* Rampe *f*.
rampant *adj* wild wuchernd.
rampart *n* Schutzwall *m*.
ramshackle *adj* baufällig.
ranch *n* Ranch *f*.
rancid *adj* ranzig.
rancour *n* Verbitterung *f*.
random *adj* ziellos, wahllos; **at**
~ aufs Geratewohl.
range *n* Reihe *f*; Kette *f*; Sortiment *n*; Weite *f*; * *vt* anordnen,
aufstellen,
ranger *n* Förster *m*.
rank *n* Reihe *f*; (*mil*) Rang *m*;
Stand *m*.
rankle *vi* nagen.
ransack *vt* plündern.
ransom *n* Lösegeld *n*.
rant *vi* hochtrabend reden.
rap *vi* klopfen.
rape *n* Vergewaltigung *f*; (*bot*)

Raps *m*; * *vt* vergewaltigen.
rapid *adj* schnell, rasch.
rapidity *n* Schnelligkeit *f*.
rapist *n* Vergewaltiger *m*.
rapture *n* Entzücken *n*.
rare *adj* selten, rar.
rarity *n* Seltenheit *f*.
rascal *n* Schuft *m*.
rash *adj* übereilt; unbesonnen;
* *n* Hautausschlag *m*.
raspberry *n* Himbeere *f*.
rat *n* Ratte *f*.
rate *n* Rate *f*, Tarif *m*; Tempo *n*;
* *vt* (ein)schätzen.
rather *adv* lieber, eher; ziemlich.
ratify *vt* ratifizieren.
rating *n* Klasse *f*; Matrose *m*.
ratio *n* Verhältnis *n*.
ration *n* Ration *f*.
rational *adj* rational.
rattle *n* Rasseln *n*; Rassel *f*; * *vi*
ratteln,klappern; * *vt* ratteln
mit.
rattlesnake *n* Klapperschlan-
ge *f*.
ravage *vt* verheeren.
rave *vi* toben.
raven *n* Rabe *m*.
ravenous *adj* heißhungrig.
ravine *n* Schlucht *f*.
ravishing *adj* atemberaubend.
raw *adj* roh; wund.
ray *n* Strahl *m*.
raze *vt* dem Erdboden gleichmachen.
razor *n* Rasierapparat *m*.
reach *n* Reichweite *f*; Strecke
f; * *vt* erreichen; reichen; * *vi*
sich erstrecken.
react *vi* reagieren.
reaction *n* Reaktion *f*.
read *vt vi* lesen.
readable *adj* leserlich.
reader *n* Leser(in) *m(f)*.
readiness *n* Bereitwilligkeit *f*.
reading *n* Lesen *n*.
readjust *vt* neu erstellen.
ready *adj* bereit.
real *adj* wirklich; eigentlich;
echt.
realisation *n* Erkenntnis *f*.

realise *vt* begreifen; verwirklichen.

reality *n* Wirklichkeit *f*.

realm *n* Reich *n*.

reap *vt* ernten.

reappear *vi* wieder erscheinen.

rear *n* Rückseite *f*; Schluß *m*; * *vt* aufziehen.

rearmament *n* Wiederaufrüstung *f*.

reason *n* Grund *m*; Verstand *m*; * *vi* denken.

reasonable *adj* vernünftig.

reasoning *n* Urteilen *n*.

reassure *vt* beruhigen.

rebel *n* Rebell *m*; * *vi* rebellieren.

rebellion *n* Rebellion *f*, Aufstand *m*.

rebellious *adj* rebellisch.

rebound *vi* zurückprallen.

rebuff *n* Abfuhr *f*; * *vt* abblitzen lassn.

rebuild *vt* wiederaufbauen.

rebuke *n* Tadel *m*; * *vt* tadeln.

rebut *vi* widerlegen.

recalcitrant *adj* widerspenstig.

recall *vt* zurückrufen; sich erinnern an +*acc*; * *n* Rückruf *m*.

recant *vi* widerrufen.

recapitulate *vt vi* wiederholen.

recede *vi* zurückweichen.

receipt *n* Quittung *f*; Empfang *m*; ~s *npl* Einnahmen *pl*.

receive *vt* erhalten; empfangen.

recently *adv* neulich.

receptacle *n* Behälter *m*.

reception *n* Empfang *m*.

recess *n* Nische *f*.

recession *n* Rezession *f*.

recipe *n* Rezept *n*.

recipient *n* Empfänger *m*.

reciprocal *adj* gegenseitig.

recital *n* Vortrag *m*.

recite *vt* vortragen.

reckless *adj* leichtsinnig.

reckon *vt* rechnen, berechnen.

reckoning *n* Rechnen *n*.

reclaim *vt* zurückverlangen.

recline *vi* sich zurücklehnen.

recluse *n* Einsiedler *m*.

recognise *vt* erkennen; anerkennen.

recognition *n* Erkennen *n*; Anerkennung *f*.

recoil *vi* zurückschrecken.

recollect *vt* sich erinnern an +*acc*.

recollection *n* Erinnerung *f*.

recommend *vt* empfehlen.

recommendation *n* Empfehlung *f*.

recompense *n* Entschädigung *f*; * *vt* entschädigen.

reconcile *vt* versöhnen.

reconciliation *n* Versöhnung *f*.

reconnoitre *vt* erkunden.

reconsider *vt* von neuem erwägen.

reconstruct *vt* wiederaufbauen.

record *n* Aufzeichnung *f*; Schallplatte *f*; Rekord *m*; * *vt* aufzeichen; aufnehmen.

recorder *n* Registriergerät *n*; (*mus*) Blockflöte *f*.

recount *vt* berichten.

recover *vt* zurückerhalten; * *vi* erholen.

recovery *n* Erholung *f*; Wiedererlangung *f*.

recrimination *n* Gegenbeschuldigung *f*.

recruit *n* (*mil*) Rekrut *m*: * *vt* rekrutieren.

recruitment *n* Rekrutierung *f*.

rectangle *n* Rechteck *n*.

rectangular *adj* rechteckig.

rectify *vt* berichtigen.

rector *n* Pfarrer *m*.

recur *vi* sich wiederholen.

recurrence *n* Wiederholung *f*.

recurrent *adj* wiederkehrend.

red *adj* rot; * *n* Rot *m*.

redden *vt* röten; * *vi* sich röten.

reddish *adj* rötlich.

redeem *vt* einlösen; retten.

redeploy *vt* umverteilen.

red-hot *adj* rotglühend.

redress * *n* Entschädigung *f*; * *vt* wiedergutmachen.

redskin *n* Rothaut *f*.
red tape *n* Bürokratismus *m*.
reduce *vt* vermindern.
reduction *n* Verminderung *f*.
redundancy *n* Entlassung *f*.
redundant *adj* überflüssig.
reed *n* Schilf *n*.
reef *n* Riff *n*.
reel *n* Spule *f*, Rolle *f*; * *vi* taumeln.
refer *vi*: **to ~ to** nachschlagen in +*dat*.
referee *n* Schiedsrichter *m*.
reference *n* Referenz *f*; Verweis *m*.
refine *vt* raffinieren.
refinement *n* Kultiviertheit *f*.
reflect *vt* reflektieren; spiegeln; * *vi* nachdenken.
reflection *n* Reflexion *f*; Spiegelbild *n*.
reflex *adj* Reflex-.
reform *n* Reform *f*; * *vt* bessern.
refrain *vi*: **to ~ from** unterlassen.
refresh *vt* erfrischen.
refreshments *npl* Erfrischungen *pl*.
refrigerator *n* Kühlschrank *m*.
refuel *vt vi* auftanken.
refuge *n* Zuflucht *f*.
refugee *n* Flüchtling *m*.
refund *n* Rückvergütung *f*; * *vt* zurückerstatten.
refurbish *vt* aufpolieren.
refusal *n* Verweigerung *f*.
refuse *vt* abschlagen; * *vi* sich weigern; * *n* Abfall *n*.
refute *vt* widerlegen.
regain *vt* wiedergewinnen.
regal *adj* königlich.
regalia *npl* Insignien *pl*.
regard *n* Achtung *f*; * *vt* ansehen.
regardless *adv* trotzdem.
regenerate *vt* erneuern.
regime *n* Regime *n*.
regiment *n* Regiment *n*.
region *n* Region *f*.
register *n* Register *n*; * *vt* registrieren; eintragen.
registered trademark *n*

eingetragene(s) Warenzeichen *n*.
registrar *n* Standesbeamte(r) *m*.
registration *n* Registrierung *f*.
registry *n* Sekretariat *n*.
regret *n* Bedauern *n*; * *vt* bedauern.
regretfully *adv* mit Bedauern.
regular *adj* regelmäßig.
regularity *n* Regelmäßigkeit *f*.
regulate *vt* regeln, regulieren.
regulation *n* Vorschrift *f*; Regulierung *f*.
rehabilitation *n* Resozialisierung *f*.
rehearsal *n* Probe *f*.
rehearse *vt* proben.
reign *n* Herrschaft *f*; * *vi* herrschen.
rein *n* Zügel *m*.
reindeer *n* Ren *n*.
reinforce *vt* verstärken.
reinstate *vt* wiedereinsetzen.
reiterate *vt* wiederholen.
reject *vt* ablehnen.
rejection *n* Zurückweisung *f*.
relapse *n* Rückfall *m*.
relate *vt* erzählen; verbinden.
related *adj* verwandt.
relation *n* Verwandte(r) *mf*; Beziehung *m*.
relationship *n* Verhältnis *n*.
relative *n* Verwandte(r) *mf*; * *adj* relativ.
relax *vi* sich entspannen.
relaxation *n* Entspannung *f*.
relay *n* Staffel *f*; * *vt* weiterleiten.
release *n* Entlassung *f*; descargo *m*; * *vt* befreien; entlassen.
relent *vi* nachgeben.
relentless *adj* unnachgiebig.
relevant *adj* relevant.
reliable *adj* zuverlässig.
relic *n* Reliquie *f*.
relief *n* Erleichterung *f*; Hilfe *f*.
relieve *vt* erleichtern; entlasten.
religion *n* Religion *f*.
religious *adj* religiös.

relinquish *vt* aufgeben.
relish *n* Würze *f*; * *vt* genießen.
reluctance *n* Widerstreben *n*.
reluctant *adj* widerwillig.
remain *vi* bleiben; übrigbleiben.
remainder *n* Rest *m*.
remains *npl* Überreste *pl*.
remand *n*: **on ~** in Untersuchungshaft.
remark *n* Bemerkung *f*; * *vt* bemerken.
remarkable *adj* bemerkenswert.
remarry *vi* sich wieder verheiraten.
remedial *adj* Heil-.
remedy *n* Mittel *n*; * *vt* abhelfen +*dat*.
remember *vt* sich erinnern an +*acc*.
remembrance *n* Erinnerung *f*; Gedenken *n*.
reminder *n* Mahnung *f*.
reminisce *vi* in Erinnerungen schwelgen.
remiss *adj* nachlässig.
remission *n* Nachlaß *m*.
remit *vt* überweisen.
remittance *n* Geldanweisung *f*.
remnant *n* Rest *m*.
remorse *n* Gewissensbisse *pl*.
remorseless *adj* unbarmherzig.
remote *adj* abgelegen.
removable *adj* entfernbar.
removal *n* Beseitigung *f*; Umzug *m*.
remove *vt* beseitigen, entfernen.
remuneration *n* Vergütung *f*.
render *vt* machen; übersetzen.
rendezvous *n* Rendezvous *n*; Treffpunkt *m*.
renew *vt* erneuern.
renewal *n* Erneuerung *f*.
renounce *vt* verzichten auf +*acc*.
renovate *vt* renovieren.
renown *n* Ruf *m*.
renowned *adj* namhaft.
rent *n* Miete *f*; * *vt* mieten.

rental *n* Miete *f*.
renunciation *n* Verzicht *m*.
reorganise *vt* reorganisieren.
repair *n* Reparatur *f*; * *vt* reparieren; wiedergutmachen.
repartee *n* Witzeleien *pl*.
repatriate *vt* in die Heimat zurückschicken.
repay *vt* zurückzahlen.
repayment *n* Rückzahlung *f*.
repeal *n* Aufhebung *f*; * *vt* aufheben.
repeat *vt* wiederholen.
repel *vt* zurückschlagen; abstoßen.
repentance *n* Reue *f*.
repertory *n* Repertoire *n*.
repetition *n* Wiederholung *f*.
replace *vt* ersetzen; zurückstellen.
replenish *vt* ergänzen.
replete *adj* voll.
reply *n* Antwort *f*; * *vi* antworten.
report * *n* Bericht *m*; * *vt* berichten; melden; anzeigen; * *vi* Bericht erstatten.
reporter *n* Reporter *m*.
reprehensible *adj* tadelnswert.
represent *vt* darstellen; vertreten.
representation *n* Darstellung *f*; Vertretung *f*.
representative *n* Vertreter *m*; * *adj* repräsentativ.
repress *vt* unterdrücken.
repression *n* Unterdrückung *f*.
reprieve *n* Begnadigung *f*; * *vt* begnadigen.
reprimand *n* Verweis *m*; * *vt* einen Verweis erteilen +*dat*.
reprint *vt* wieder abdrucken.
reprisal *n* Vergeltung *f*.
reproach *n* Vorwurf *m*; * *vt* Vorwürfe machen +*dat*.
reproachful *adj* vorwurfsvoll.
reproduce *vt* reproduzieren.
reproduction *n* Reproduktion *f*.
reptile *n* Reptil *n*.
republic *n* Republik *f*.

repudiate *vt* zurückweisen.

repugnant *adj* widerlich.

repulse *vt* zurückschlagen.

repulsive *adj* abstoßend.

reputable *adj* angesehen.

reputation *n* Ruf *m*.

repute *n* hohe(s) Ansehen *n*.

request *n* Bitte *f*; * *vt* erbitten.

require *vt* brauchen; erfordern.

requirement *n* Bedarf *m*; Anforderung *f*.

requisite *n* Erfordnis *n*; * *adj* erforderlich.

rescind *vt* aufheben.

rescue *n* Rettung *f*; * *vi* retten.

research *n* Forschung *f*; * *vi* forschen; * *vt* erforschen.

resemblance *n* Ähnlichkeit *f*.

resemble *vt* ähneln +*dat*.

resent *vt* übelnehmen.

resentful *adj* nachtragend.

resentment *n* Verstimmung *f*.

reservation *n* Reservierung *f*; Vorbestellung *f*; Vorbehalt *m*.

reserve *n* Vorrat *m*; Reserve *f*; * *vt* reservieren.

reside *vi* wohnen.

residence *n* Wohnsitz *m*.

resident *n* Bewohner *m*; Einwohner *m*; * *adj* wohnhaft.

residue *n* Rest *m*; Rückstand *m*.

resign *vt* aufgeben, zurücktreten von; * *vi* zurücktreten; kündigen.

resignation *n* Kündigung *f*; Rucktritt *m*.

resin *n* Harz *n*.

resist *vt* widerstehen +*dat*.

resistance *n* Widerstand *m*.

resolute *adj* resolut, entschlossen.

resolution *n* Entschlossenheit *f*.

resolve *vt* beschliessen; * *vi* sich lösen.

resonant *adj* voll.

resort *n* Erholungsort *m*; Zuflucht *f*; **to ~ to** Zuflucht nehmen zu.

resounding *adj* nachhallend.

resource *n* Findigkeit *f*; **~s** *npl* Geldmittel *m*; Bodenschätze *pl*.

respect *n* Hinsicht *f*; Achtung *f*; **with respect to** hinsichtlich; * *vt* respektieren.

respectability *n* Ansehen *n*, Anständigkeit *n*.

respectable *adj* solide.

respectful *adj* ehrerbietig, respektvoll.

respective *adj* jeweilig.

respiration *n* Atmung *f*.

respite *n* Atempause *f*, Ruhepause *f*.

resplendent *adj* prächtig.

respond *vi* antworten; reagieren.

respondent *n* (*jur*) Beklagte *f*.

response *n* Antwort *f*; Reaktion *f*.

responsibility *n* Verantwortung *f*.

responsible *adj* verantwortlich.

responsive *adj* empfänglich.

rest *n* Ruhe *f*, Ruhepause *f*; (*mus*) Pause *f*; Stütze *f*; * *vi* ruhen, sich ausruhen.

restful *adj* erholsam, ruhig, friedlich.

restive *adj* unruhig, nervös.

restless *adj* ruhelos, unruhig.

restoration *n* Rückerstattung *f*; Restaurierung *f*; Wiederherstellung *f*.

restore *vt* wiedergeben; restaurieren; wiederherstellen.

restrain *vt* zurückhalten, unterdrücken.

restraint *n* Zurückhaltung *f*.

restrict *vt* einschränken.

restriction *n* Einschränkung *f*.

restrictive *adj* einschränkend.

result *n* Ergebnis *n*.

resume *vt* fortsetzen; wieder einnehmen.

resurrection *n* Auferstehung *f*.

resuscitate *vt* wiederbeleben.

retail *n* Einzelhandel *m*.

retain *vt* behalten.

retaliate *vt* zum Vergeltungsschlag ausholen.

retaliation n Vergeltung f.
retarded adj zurückgeblieben.
retch vi würgen.
retina n Netzhaut f.
retire vi in den Ruhestand treten; sich zurückziehen; schlafen gehen.
retired adj im Ruhestand, pensioniert.
retirement n Ruhestand m.
retort n Erwiderung f; * vi erwidern.
retrace vt zurückverfolgen.
retract vt zurücknehmen.
retrain vt umschulen.
retraining n Umschulung f.
retreat n Rückzug m; * vi sich zurückziehen.
retribution n Strafe f.
retrieve vt wiederbekommen.
retriever n Apportierhund m.
retrograde adj Rück-; rückschrittlich.
retrospective adj rückwirkend.
return n Rückkehr f; Ertrag m; * adj Rück-; * vi zurückkommen, zurückkehren; * vt zurückgeben, zurücksenden.
reunion n Wiedervereinigung f.
reunite vt wiedervereinigen.
reveal vt enthülen.
revelation n Offenbarung f.
revelry n Rummel m.
revenge n Rache f.
revenue n Einnahmen pl.
reverberate vi widerhallen.
revere vt ehren.
reverence n Ehrfurcht f.
reverent adj ehrfurchtsvoll.
reversal n Umkehrung f.
reverse n Rückseite f; Rückwärtsgang m; * adj entgegengesetzt; * vt umkehren; * vi rückwärts fahren.
review n (mil) Truppenschau f; Rezension f; Zeitschrift f; * vt mustern; rezensieren.
reviewer n Rezensent m.
revile vt verunglimpfen.
revise vt revidieren; überarbeiten.

revision n Wiederholung f; Prüfung f.
revival n Wiederbelebung f; Wiederaufnahme f.
revive vt wiederbeleben; * vi wiedererwachen.
revoke vt aufheben.
revolt n Aufstand m; * vi sich auflehnen.
revolting adj widerlich.
revolution n Umdrehung f; Revolution f.
revolutionary adj revolutionär.
revolve vi kreisen; sich drehen.
revolver n Revolver m.
revolving door n Drehtür f.
revulsion n Ekel m.
reward n Belohnung f; * vt belohnen.
rheumatism n Rheumatismus m.
rhinoceros n Nashorn n.
rhubarb n Rhabarber m.
rhyme n Reim m.
rhythm n Rhythmus m.
rib n Rippe f.
ribald adj saftig.
ribbon n Band n.
rice n Reis m.
rich adj reich.
riches npl Reichtum m.
rickets n Rachitis f.
rickety adj wackelig.
rid vt befreien.
riddle n Rätsel n.
ride n Fahrt f; Ritt m; * vt reiten; fahren; * vi fharen, reiten.
rider n Reiter m.
ridge n Kamm m; Spott m.
ridicule n Spott m; * vt lächerlich machen.
ridiculous adj lächerlich.
riding n Reiten n.
riding school n Reitschule f.
rife adj weit verbreitet.
riffraff n Pöbel m.
rifle n Gewehr n; * vt berauben.
rig n Takelung f; Aufmachung f; Bohrinsel f; * vt manipulieren.
rigging n Takelage f.

right *adj* richtig, recht; rechte(r,s); * *n* Recht *n*; Rechte *f*; * *adj* rechts; nach rechts; richtig, recht; gerade; genau; * *vt* in Ordnung bringen, korrigieren; * *excl* gut.

righteous *adj* rechtschaffen.

rigid *adj* starr, steif.

rigidity *n* Starrheit *f*.

rigmarole *n* Gewäsch *n*.

rigorous *adj* streng.

rigour *n* Strenge *f*.

rim *n* Rand *m*.

rind *n* Rinde *f*.

ring *n* Ring *m*; Kreis *m*; Klingeln *n*; * *vt vi* läufen; anrufen.

ringleader *n* Anführer *f*.

rink *n* Eisbahn *f*.

rinse *n* Spülen *n*; * *vt* spülen.

riot *n* Aufruhr *m*; * *vi* randalieren.

rioter *n* Aufrührer *m*.

riotous *adj* aufrührerisch.

rip *n* Riß *m*; * *vt vi* rreißen.

ripe *adj* reif.

ripen *vi* reifen.

rip-off *n* (*coll*): it's a ~! das ist Wucher!.

ripple *n* kleine Welle *f*; * *vi* sich kräuseln.

rise *n* Steigung *f*; Erhöhung *f*; * *vi* aufgehen; aufsteigen; steigen.

rising *n* Aufstand *m*.

risk *n* Risiko *n*; * *vt* riskieren.

risky *adj* riskant.

rissole *n* Fleischklößchen *n*.

rite *n* Ritus *m*.

ritual *n* Ritual *n*.

rival *n* Rivale *m*; * *vt* rivalisieren mit.

rivalry *n* Rivalität *f*.

river *n* Fluß *m*; Strom *m*.

rivet *n* Niete *f*; * *vt* vernieten.

road *n* Straße *f*.

road sign *n* Straßenschild *n*.

road works *npl* Straßenbauarbeiten *pl*.

roam *vi* umherstreifen.

roar *n* Brüllen *n*; * *vi* brüllen.

roast *vt* braten.

roast beef *n* Roastbeef *n*.

rob *vt* bestehlen, berauben.

robber *n* Räuber *m*.

robbery *n* Raub *m*.

robe *n* Gewand *n*; Robe *f*.

robin *n* Rotkehlchen *m*.

robust *adj* robust; gesund.

rock *n* Felsen *m*; * *vt vi* wiegen, schaukeln.

rock and roll *n* Rock and Roll *m*.

rocket *n* Rakete *f*.

rocking chair *n* Schaukelstuhl *m*.

rocky *adj* felsig.

rod *n* Stange *f*; Rute *f*.

rodent *n* Nagtier *n*.

roe *n* Reh *n*; Rogen *m*.

rogue *n* Schurke *m*.

roll *n* Rolle *f*; Brötchen *n*; Liste *f*; * *vt* rollen, wälzen; * *vi* schlingern.

roller *n* Rolle *f*, Walze *f*.

roller skates *npl* Rollschuhe *pl*.

rolling pin *n* Nudelholz *n*.

Roman *adj* römisch; * *n* Römer(in) *m(f)*.

Roman Catholic *adj* römisch-katholisch; * *n* Katholik(in) *m(f)*.

romance *n* Romanze *f*; Liebesroman *m*.

romantic *adj* romantisch.

romp *n* Tollen *n*; * *vi* herumtollen.

roof *n* Dach *n*; Gaumen *m*; * *vt* überdachen.

roofing *n* Deckmaterial *n*.

rook *n* Saatkräke *f*; Turm *m*.

room *n* Zummer *n*, Raum *m*; Platz *m*; Spielraum *m*.

rooming house *n* Mietshaus *n*.

roomy *adj* geräumig.

roost *n* Hühnerstange *f*; * *vi* auf der Stange hocken.

rooster *n* Hahn *m*.

root *n* Wurzel *f*; * *vt* wurzeln.

rope *n* Seil *n*; * *vt* festschnüren.

rosary *n* Rosenkranz *m*.

rose *n* Rose *f*.

rosebud *n* Rosenknospe *m*.

rosemary *n* Rosmarin *m*.

rosette n Rosette f.
rosy adj rosig.
rot n Fäulnis n; Quatsch m; * vi verfaulen; * vt verfaulen lassen.
rotate vi rotieren.
rotation n Umdrehung f.
rote n: by rote auswendig.
rotten adj faul; schlecht, gemein.
rotund adj rundlich.
rouble n Rubel m.
rough adj rauh; uneben; grob; stürmisch; unbequem; ungefähr.
roughen vt aufrauhen.
roughness n Rauheit f.
roulette n Roulett(e) n.
round adj rund; aufgerundet; * adv um … herum; * n Runde f; Magazin n; * vt biegen um.
roundabout n Karussell n; Kreisverkehr m.
rouse vt wecken; aufrütteln; erregen.
route n Route f, Weg m; Strecke f.
routine n Routine f; * adj üblich, routinegemäß, Routine-.
rove vi umherstreifen; durchstreifen.
row n Lärm f; Streit f; n Reihe f; * vi sich streiten; * vt vi rudern.
rowdy adj rüpelhaft.
rowing boat n Ruderboot n.
royal adj königlich, Königs-.
royalty n königliche Familie f; Tantieme f.
rub n Polieren n; Reiben n; * vt reiben.
rubber n Gummi m; Radiergummi m.
rubber band n Gummiband n.
rubber plant n Gummibaum m.
rubbish n Abfall m; Blödsinn m, Quatsch m.
rubbish bin n Mülleimer m.
rubbish dump n Müllabladeplatz m.

ruby n Rubin m; * adj rubinrot.
rucksack n Rucksack m.
rudder n Steuerruder n.
ruddy adj rötlich; verdammt.
rude adj unverschämt; hart; unsanft; grob.
rudeness n Unverschämtheit f; Grobheit f.
rudiment n Grundlage f.
rueful adj reuevoll.
ruffian n Rohling m.
ruffle vt kräuseln.
rug n Brücke f; Bettvorleger m.
rugby n Rugby n.
rugged adj zerklüftet; markig.
ruin n Ruine f; Ruin m; * vt ruinieren.
ruinous adj ruinierend.
rule n Regel f; Regierung f; Lineal n; * vt regieren; linieren; * vi herrschen.
ruler n Lineal n; Herrscher m.
rum n Rum m.
rumble vi rumpeln.
rummage vi durchstöbern.
rumour n Gerücht n.
rump n Hinterteil n.
run n Lauf m; Fahrt f; * vt laufen lassen; fahren; laufen, rennen; leiten; * vi laufen, rennen.
runaway adj flüchtig; ausgebrochen.
rung n Sprosse f.
runner n Läufer(in) m(f); Kufe f.
runner-bean n Stangenbohne f.
runner-up n Zweite(r) m/f.
runway n Startbahn f.
rupture n Bruch m.
rural adj ländlich, Land-.
ruse n Kniff m, List f.
rush n Eile f, Hetze f; * vt auf dem schnellsten Wege schaffen; * vi eilen, stürzen.
rusk n Zwieback m.
Russia n Rußland n.
Russian adj russisch; * n Russe m, Russin f; Russisch f.
rust n Rost m; * vi rosten.
rustic adj bäuerlich, ländlich.

rustle *vi* rauschen, rascheln;
* *vt* rascheln lassen; stehlen.
rustproof *adj* rostfrei.
rusty *adj* rostig.
rut *n* Radspur *f*.
ruthless *adj* rücksichtslos.
rye *n* (*bot*) Roggen *m*.

S

sabbath *n* Sabbat *m*.
sabotage *n* Sabotage *f*; * *vt* sabotieren.
saccharin *n* Saccharin *n*.
sachet *n* Briefchen *n*, Kissen *n*.
sack *n* Sack *m*; * *vt* hinauswerfen; plündern.
sacrement *n* Sakrament *n*.
sacred *adj* heilig.
sacrifice *n* Opfer *n*; * *vt* opfern.
sacrilege *n* Schändung *f*.
sad *adj* traurig.
sadden *vt* traurig machen, betrüben.
saddle *n* Sattel *m*.
saddlebag *n* Satteltasche *f*.
sadness *n* Traurigkeit *f*.
safe *adj* sicher; vorsichtig; de fiar; ~ **and sound** gesund und wohl; * *n* Safe *m*.
safe-conduct *n* freie(s) Geleit *n*.
safeguard *n* Sicherung *f*; * *vt* sichern, schützen.
safety *n* Sicherheit *f*.
safety belt *n* Sicherheitsgurt *m*.
safety pin *n* Sicherheitsnadel *f*.
sag *vi* (durch)sacken.
sage *n* (*bot*) Salbei *f*; Weise(r) *mf*.
Sagittarius *n* Schütze *m*.
sail *n* Segel *n*; * *vt* segeln; * *vi* segeln; auslaufen.
sailing *n* Segeln *n*.

sailor *n* Matrose *m*, Seemann *m*.
saint *n* Heilige(r) *mf*.
saintly *adj* heilig, fromm.
sake *n* **for the ~ of** um ... willen.
salad *n* Salat *m*.
salad bowl *n* Salatschüssel *f*.
salad dressing *n* Salatsoße *f*.
salad oil *n* Salatöl *n*.
salami *n* Salami *f*.
salary *n* Gehalt *n*.
sale *n* Verkauf *m*.
salesman *n* Verkäufer *m*.
saleswoman *n* Verkäuferin *f*.
salient *adj* bemerkenswert.
saliva *n* Speichel *m*.
sallow *adj* bleich; fahl.
salmon *n* Lachs *m*.
saloon *n* Salon *m*.
salt *n* Salz *n*; * *vt* salzen.
saltcellar *n* Salzfaß *n*.
salty *adj* salzig.
salutary *adj* nützlich.
salute *n* Gruß *m*; * *vt* salutieren.
salvage *n* Bergung *f*.
salvation *n* Rettung *f*.
same *adj pron* gleiche(r,s); derselbe/dieselbe/dasselbe.
sample *n* Probe *f*; * *vt* probieren.
sanctify *vt* weihen.
sanctimonious *adj* scheinheilig.
sanction *n* Sanktion *f*.
sanctity *n* Heiligkeit *f*.
sanctuary *n* Asyl *n*; Zufluchtsort *m*.
sand *n* Sand *m*; * *vt* schmirgeln.
sandal *n* Sandale *f*.
sandpit *n* Sandkasten *m*.
sandstone *n* Sandstein *m*.
sandwich *n* Sandwich *m/n*.
sandy *adj* sandig.
sane *adj* geistig gesund.
sanitary *adj* hygienisch.
sanity *n* geistige Gesundheit *f*.
sap *n* Saft *m*.
sapling *n* junge(r) Baum *m*.
sapphire *n* Saphir *m*.
sarcasm *n* Sarkasmus *m*.

sarcastic *adj* sarkastisch.

sardine *n* Sardine *f*.

sash *n* Schärpe *f*.

Satan *n* Satan *m*.

satchel *n* Schulmappe *f*.

satisfaction *n* Befriedigung *f*.

satisfactory *adj* zufriedenstellend.

satisfy *vt* befriedigen, zufriedenstellen; erfüllen.

saturate *vt* durchtränken.

Saturday *n* Samstag *m*, Sonnabend *m*.

sauce *n* Soße *f*, Sauce *f*.

saucepan *n* Kassrolle *f*.

saucer *n* Untertasse *f*.

saucy *adj* frech, keck.

saunter *vi* schlendern.

sausage *n* Wurst *f*.

savage *adj* wild; * *n* Wilde(r) *mf*.

savagery *n* Grausamkeit *f*.

save *vt* retten; sparen; * *prep conj* außer, ausgenommen.

saving *n* Sparen *n*, Ersparnis *f*; ~s *pl* Ersparnisse *pl*.

savings account *n* Sparkonto *n*.

savings bank *n* Sparkasse *f*.

saviour *n* Erlöser *m*.

savour *vt* schmecken.

savoury *adj* würzig, pikant.

saw *n* Sage *f*; * *vt vi* sägen.

sawdust *n* Sägemehl *n*.

sawmill *n* Sägewerk *n*.

say *vt vi* sagen.

saying *n* Sprichwort *n*.

scab *n* Schorf *m*.

scaffold *n* Schafott *n*.

scaffolding *n* Baugerüst *n*.

scald *n* Verbrühung *f*; * *vt* verbrühen.

scale *n* Schuppe *f*; Tonleiter *f*; Maßstab *m*; * *vt* erklimmen.

scallop *n* Kammuschel *f*.

scalp *n* Kopfhaut *f*.

scampi *npl* Scampi *pl*.

scan *vt* genau prüfen; absuchen; skandieren.

scandal *n* Skandal *m*.

Scandinavia *n* Skandinavien *n*.

Scandinavian *adj* skandinavisch; * *n* Skandinavier(in) *m(f)*.

scant, scanty *adj* knapp.

scantily *adv* knapp, dürftig.

scapegoat *n* Sündenbock *m*.

scar *n* Narbe *f*; * *vt* durch Narben entstellen.

scarce *adj* selten, rar.

scarcely *adv* kaum.

scarcity *n* Mangel *m*.

scare *n* Schrecken *m*; * *vt* erschrecken.

scarecrow *n* Vogelscheuche *f*.

scarf *n* Schal *m*.

scarlet *adj* scharlachrot.

scatter *vt* streuen; zerstreuen; * *vi* sich zerstreuen.

scavenger *n* Aasfresser *m*.

scenario *n* Szenario *n*.

scene *n* Ort *m*; Szene *f*.

scenery *n* Bühnenbild *n*; Landschaft *f*.

scenic *adj* landschaftlich.

scent *n* Parfüm *n*; Duft *m*; * *vt* parfümieren.

sceptical *adj* skeptisch.

schedule *n* Liste *f*; Programm *n*; Zeitplan *m*.

scheme *n* Schema *n*; Intrige *f*; Plan *m*; * *vt* planen; * *vi* intrigieren.

scholar *n* Gelehrte(r) *m*.

scholarship *n* Gelehrsamkeit *f*.

school *n* Schule *f*; * *vt* schulen.

schoolboy *n* Schüler *m*.

schoolgirl *n* Schülerin *f*.

schoolmaster *n* Lehrer *m*.

schoolmistress *n* Lehrerin *f*.

schoolteacher *n* Lehrer(in) *m(f)*.

sciatica *n* Ischias *m/n*.

science *n* Wissenschaft *f*.

scientific *adj* wissenschaftlich.

scientist *n* Wissenschaftler(in) *m(f)*.

scintillating *adj* sprühend.

scissors *npl* Schere *f*.

scold *vt* schimpfen.

scoop *n* Schaufel *f*; * *vt* herausschaufeln.

scooter *n* Motorroller *m*; Roller *m*.

scope *n* Ausmaß *n*; Spielraum *m*.

scorch *n* Brandstelle *f*; * *vt* versengen.

score *n* Punktzahl *f*; Spielergebnis *n*; Partitur *f*; zwanzig; * *vt* schießen; einritzen; * *vi* Punkte zählen.

scoreboard *n* Anschreibetafel *f*.

scorn *n* Verachtung *f*; * *vt* verhöhnen.

scornful *adj* verächtlich.

Scorpio *n* (*astrol*) Skorpion *m*.

Scot *n* Schotte *m*, Schottin *f*.

scotch *vt* unterbinden.

Scotch *n* Scotch *m*.

Scotland *n* Schottland *n*.

scoundrel *n* Schuft *m*.

Scotsman (-woman) *n* Schotte *m*, Schottin *f*.

Scottish *adj* schottisch.

scour *vt* absuchen; schrubben.

scourge *n* Geißel *f*; Qual *f*.

scout *n* (*mil*) Späher *m*; Pfadfinder *m*.

scowl *n* finstere(r) Blick *m*; * *vi* finster blicken.

scraggy *adj* dürr, hager.

scramble *n* Kletterei *f*; Kampf *m*; * *vi* klettern; sich schlagen.

scrap *n* Stückchen *n*; Kellerei *f*; Schrott *m*; * *vt* verwerfen.

scrape *n* Kratzen *n*; Klemme *f*; * *vt vi* kratzen.

scraper *n* Kratzer *m*.

scratch *n* Kratzer *m*, Schramme *f*; * *vt* kratzen.

scrawl *n* Gekritzel *n*; * *vt vi* kritzeln.

scream *n* Schrei *m*; * *vi* schreien.

scree *n* Geröll *n*.

screech *n* Schrei *m*; * *vi* schreien.

screen *n* Schutzschirm *m*; Leinwand *f*; Bildschirm *m*; * *vt* schirmen; zeigen, vorführen.

screenplay *n* Drehbuch *n*.

screw *n* Schraube *f*; * *vt* schrauben; bumsen.

screwdriver *n* Schraubenzieher *m*.

scribble *n* Gekritzel *n*; * *vt* kritzeln.

script *n* Handschrift *f*; Manuskript *n*.

Scripture *n* Heilige Schrift *f*.

scroll *n* Schriftrolle *f*.

scrub *n* Schrubben *n*; Gestrüpp *n*; * *vt* schrubben.

scruffy *adj* unordentlich.

scruple *n* Skrupel *m*.

scrupulous *adj* gewissenhaft.

scrutinise *vt* genau prüfen.

scrutiny *n* genaue Untersuchung *f*.

scuffle *n* Handgemenge *n*.

scullery *n* Spülküche *f*.

sculptor *n* Bildhauer(in) *m(f)*.

sculpture *n* Bildhauerei *f*.

scum *n* Abschaum *m*.

scurrilous *adj* unflätig.

scuttle *n* Kohleneimer *m*; * *vt* versenken.

scythe *n* Sense *f*.

sea *n* Meer *n*, See *f*; * *adj* Meeres-, See-.

seafood *n* Meeresfrüchte *pl*.

sea front *n* Strandpromenade *f*.

seagull *n* Möwe *f*.

seal *n* Seehund *m*; Siegel *n*; * *vt* versiegeln.

seam *n* Saum *m*.

seaman *n* Seemann *m*.

seamy *adj* zwielichtig.

seaplane *n* Wasserflugzeug *n*.

seaport *n* Seehafen *m*.

search *n* Suche *f*; Durchsuchung *f*; * *vi* suchen; * *vt* durchsuchen.

searchlight *n* Scheinwerfer *m*.

seashore *n* Meeresküste *f*.

seasick *adj* seekrank.

seasickness *n* Seekrankheit *f*.

seaside *n* Küste *f*.

season *n* Jahreszeit *f*; Saison *f*; * *vt* würzen.

seasonal *adj* Saison-.

seasoning *n* Gewürz *n*.

season ticket *n* Zeitkarte *f*.

seat *n* Sitz *m*, Platz *m*; Gesäß

n; * *vt* setzen.
seat belt *n* Sicherheitsgurt *m*.
seaweed *n* Seetang *m*.
seaworthy *adj* seetüchtig.
secluded *adj* abgelegen.
seclusion *n* Zurückgezogenheit *f*.
second *adj* zweite(r,s); *adv* an zweiter Stelle; * *n* Sekunde *f*.
secondary *adj* zweitrangig.
secondary school *n* Mittelschule *f*.
secondhand *adj* gebraucht.
secrecy *n* Geheimhaltung *f*.
secret *adj* geheim; * *n* Geheimnis *n*.
secretary *n* Sekretär(in) *m*(*f*).
secretion *n* Absonderung *f*.
secretive *adj* geheimtuerisch.
section *n* Teil *m*; Abschnitt *m*.
sector *n* Sektor *m*.
secular *adj* weltlich, profan.
secure *adj* sicher; fest; * *vt* sichern.
security *n* Sicherheit *f*; Pfand *n*; Wertpapier *n*.
sedate *adj* gesetzt.
sedative *n* Beruhigungsmittel *n*.
sedentary *adj* sitzend.
sediment *n* Bodensatz *m*.
sedition *n* Aufwiegelung *f*.
seduce *vt* verführen.
seduction *n* Verführung *f*.
seductive *adj* verführerisch.
see *vt vi* sehen.
seed *n* Samen *m*; * *vt* plazieren.
seedling *n* Setzling *m*.
seedy *adj* übel.
seeing *conj*: ~ that da.
seek *vt* suchen.
seem *vi* scheinen.
seeming *adj* scheinbar.
seesaw *n* Wippe *f*.
segment *n* Teil *m*; Ausschnitt *m*.
seize *vt* greifen, ergreifen, pakken.
seizure *n* Anfall *m*.
seldom *adv* selten.
select *adj* ausgewählt; * *vt* auswählen.

selection *n* Auswahl *f*.
self *pron* selbst; * *n* Selbst *n*, Ich *n*; **the ~** das Ich.
self-confidence *n* Selbstbewußtsein *n*.
self-defence *n* Selbstverteidigung *f*.
self-employed *adj* freischaffend.
self-evident *adj* offensichtlich.
self-governing *adj* selbstverwaltet.
self-interest *n* Eigennutz *m*.
selfish *adj* selbstsüchtig.
selfishness *n* Selbstsucht *f*.
self-pity *n* Selbstmitleid *n*.
self-portrait *n* Selbstbildnis *n*.
self-possessed *adj* selbstbeherrscht.
self-reliant *adj* unabhängig.
self-respect *n* Selbstachtung *f*.
self-satisfied *adj* selbstzufrieden.
self-service *adj* Selbstbedienungs-.
self-sufficient *adj* selbstgenügsam.
self-taught *adj* selbsterlernt.
sell *vt vi* verkaufen.
seller *n* Verkäufer *m*.
semblance *n* Anschein *n*.
semen *n* Sperma *n*.
semicircle *n* Halbkreis *m*.
semicolon *n* Semikolon *n*.
semiconductor *n* Halbleiter *m*.
seminary *n* Priesterseminar *n*.
senate *n* Senat *m*.
senator *n* Senator *m*.
send *vt* senden, schicken.
sender *n* Absender *m*.
senior *adj* älter; Ober-.
seniority *n* höhere(s) Alter *n*; höhere(s) Dienstgrad *m*.
sensation *n* Gefühl *n*; Sensation *f*.
sense *n* Sinn *m*; Verstand *m*; Gefühl *n*.
senseless *adj* sinnlos; besinnungslos.
sensibility *n* Empfindsamkeit *f*.

sensible *adj* vernünftig.

sensitive *adj* empfindlich.

sensual *adj* sinnlich.

sensuous *adj* sinnlich.

sentence *n* Satz *m*; Strafe *f*; Urteil *n*.

sentiment *n* Gefühl *n*; Gedenke *m*.

sentimental *adj* sentimental.

sentry *n* Wache *f*.

separate *adj* getrennt, separat; * *vt* trennen; * *vi* sich trennen.

separation *n* Trennung *f*.

September *n* September *m*.

sequel *n* Folge *f*.

sequence *n* Reihenfolge *f*.

Serbia *n* Serbien *n*.

serene *adj* heiter.

serenity *n* Heiterkeit *f*.

sergeant *n* Feldwebel *m*.

serial *n* Fernsehserie *f*; * *adj* fortlaufend

series *n* Serie *f*.

serious *adj* ernst; schwer.

sermon *n* Predigt *f*.

serrated *adj* gezackt.

servant *n* Diener(in) *m(f)*.

serve *vt* dienen +*dat*; bedienen; servieren; * *vi* dienen.

service *n* Dienst *m*; Service *m*, Bedienung *f*; Gottesdienst *m*; Inspektion *f*; * *vt* warten, überholen.

serviceable *adj* brauchbar.

service station *n* Gorßtankstelle *f*.

servile *adj* unterwürfig.

session *n* Sitzung *f*.

set *n* Satz *m*; Apparat *m*; Bühnenbild *n*; * *adj* festgelegt; bereit; * *vt* setzen, stellen, legen; ordnen; decken; * *vi* untergehen; fest werden.

settee *n* Sofa *f*.

setting *n* Hintergrund *m*.

settle *vt* beruhigen; bezahlen; begleichen; regeln; * *vi* sich einleben; sich setzen.

settlement *n* Regelung *f*; Begleichung *f*; Siedlung *f*.

settler *n* Siedler *m*.

seven *num* sieben.

seventeen *num* siebzehn.

seventh *adj* siebte(r,s); * *n* Siebtel *n*.

seventy *num* siebzig.

sever *vt* abtrennen.

several *adj* mehrere(r,s).

severe *adj* streng; schwer.

severity *n* Strenge *f*; Schwere *f*.

sew *vt* *vi* nähen.

sewage *n* Abwässer *pl*.

sewer *n* Abwasserkanal *m*.

sex *n* Sex *m*; Geschlecht *n*.

sewing machine *n* Nähmaschine *f*.

sexist *adj*, *n* Sexist(in) *m(f)*.

sexual *adj* sexuell.

sexy *adj* sexy.

shabby *adj* schäbig.

shackle *n* Fessel *f*; * *vt* fesseln.

shade *n* Schatten *m*; Schirm *m*; * *vt* beschatten; abschirmen.

shadow *n* Schatten *m*.

shadowy *adj* schattig.

shady *adj* schattenspendend.

shaft *n* Schaft *m*; Schacht *m*; Welle *f*; Strahl *m*.

shaggy *adj* struppig.

shake *vt* schütteln, rütteln; * *vi* schwanken; zittern, beben.

shaky *adj* zittrig.

shallow *adj* seicht.

sham *n* Scheim *m*; * *adj* falsch, unecht.

shambles *npl* Durcheinander *n*.

shame *n* Scham *m*; Schande *f*; * *vt* beschämen.

shamefaced *adj* beschämt.

shameful *adj* schändlich.

shameless *adj* schamlos.

shampoo *n* Shampoo(n) *n*.

shamrock *n* Kleeblatt *n*.

shanty town *n* Bidonville *f*.

shape *n* Form *f*; * *vt* formen, gestalten.

shapeless *adj* formlos.

shapely *adj* wohlproportioniert.

share *n* Anteil *m*; (*fin*) Aktie *f*; * *vt* teilen.

shareholder *n* Aktionär(in) *m(f)*.

shark n Hai m.

sharp adj scharf; spitz; (mus) erhöht; * n Kreuz n; * adv zu hoch.

sharpen vt schärfen.

shatter vt zerschmettern; * vi zerspringen.

shave n Rasur f; * vt rasieren; * vi sich rasieren.

shaver n Rasierapparat m.

shaving n Rasieren n.

shaving brush n Rasierpinsel m.

shaving cream n Rasierkrem f.

shawl n Schal m.

she pron sie.

sheaf n Garbe f.

shear vt scheren; ~s npl Hekkenschere f.

sheath n Scheide f.

shed n Schuppen m; Stall m.

sheen n Glanz m.

sheep n Schaf n.

sheepish adj verlegen.

sheepskin n Schaffell n.

sheer adj bloß, rein; steil; dünn; * adv direkt.

sheet n Bettuch n; Blatt n; Platte f.

shelf n Regal n.

shell n Schale f; Muschel f; Granate f; * vt schälen; beschießen.

shellfish n Schalentier n.

shelter n Schutz m; Bunker m; * vt schützen; * vi sich unterstellen.

shepherd n Schäfer m.

sheriff n Sheriff m.

sherry n Sherry m.

shield n Schild m; Schirm m; * vt schirmen.

shift n Verschiebung f; Schicht f; * vt rücken, verschieben.

shin n Schienbein n.

shine n Glanz m, Schein m; * vi scheinen.

shingle n Strandkies m; ~s npl (med) Gürtelrose f.

shiny adj glänzend.

ship n Schiff n; * vt verschiffen.

shipbuilding n Schiffbau m.

shipment n Schiffsladung f.

shipwreck n Schiffbruch m; Wrack n.

shirt n Hemd n.

shit excl (coll) Scheiße!.

shiver vi zittern.

shoal n Fischschwarm m.

shock n Erschütterung f; Schock m; Schlag m; * vt erschüttern; schockieren.

shoddy adj schäbig.

shoe n Schuh m; Hufeisen n; * vt beschlagen.

shoehorn n Schuhlöffel m.

shoelace n Schnürsenkel m.

shoot n Schößling m; * vt abfeuern; schießen; anschießen.

shooting n Schießerei f.

shop n Laden m, Geschäft n.

shoplifting n Ladendiebstahl m.

shopper n Käufer(in) m(f).

shopping n Einkaufen n.

shopping centre n Einkaufszentrum n.

shore n Strand m.

short adj kurz.

shortcoming n Mangel m.

shorten vt abkürzen.

short-sighted adj kurzsichtig.

shortwave n Kurzwelle f.

shot n Schuß m.

shotgun n Schrotflinte f.

shoulder n Schulter f.

shout n Schrei m; * vi schreien.

shouting n Geschrei n.

shove n Stoß m; * vt schieben, stoßen.

shovel n Schaufel f; * vt schaufeln.

show n Schau f; Ausstellung f; Vorstellung f; * vt zeigen; * vi zu sehen sein.

show business n Showbusineß n.

shower n Schauer m; Dusche f; * vi duschen.

showroom n Ausstellungsraum m.

shred n Fetzen m; * vt zerfetzen.

shrewd *adj* clever.
shriek *n* Schrei *m*; * *vi* schreien.
shrimp *n* Garnele *f*.
shrink *vi* schrumpfen.
shroud *n* Leichentuch *n*.
Shrove Tuesday *n* Fastnachtsdienstag *m*.
shrub *n* Strauch *m*.
shrubbery *n* Gebüsch *n*.
shudder *vi* schaudern.
shuffle *vt* mischen.
shun *vt* scheuen.
shunt *vt* rangieren.
shut *vt* schließen, zumachen; * *vi* sich schließen.
shutter *n* Fensterladen *m*.
shuttlecock *n* Federball *m*.
shy *adj* schüchtern.
shyness *n* Schüchternheit *f*.
sibling *n* Geschwister *n*.
sick *adj* krank; makaber.
sicken *vt* krankmachen; * *vi* krank werden.
sickle *n* Sichel *f*.
sickly *adj* kränklich, blaß.
sickness *n* Krankheit *f*.
sick pay *n* Krankengeld *n*.
side *n* Seite *m*; * *adj* Seiten-.
sidelight *n* Parkleuchte *f*.
sidelong *adj* Seiten-.
sideways *adv* seitwärts.
siding *n* Nebengleis *n*.
siege *n* Belagerung *f*.
sieve *n* Sieb *n*; * *vt* sieben.
sift *vt* sieben.
sigh *n* Seufzer *m*; * *vi* seufzen.
sight *n* Sehvermögen *n*; Blick *m*; Anblick *m*.
sightseeing *n* Besuch *m* von Sehenswürdigkeiten.
sign *n* Zeichen *n*; Schild *n*; * *vt* unterschreiben.
signal *n* Signal *n*.
signalman *n* (*rail*) Stellwerkswärter *m*.
signature *n* Unterschrift *f*.
significance *n* Bedeutung *f*.
significant *adj* bedeutend; bedeutsam.
signify *vt* bedeuten.
signpost *n* Wegweiser *m*.

silence *n* Stille *f*; Schweigen *n*; * *vt* zum Schweigen bringen.
silent *adj* still; schweigsam.
silicon chip *n* Siliciumchip *n*.
silk *n* Seide *f*.
silky *adj* seidig.
silly *adj* dumm, albern.
silt *n* Schlamm *m*, Schlick *m*.
silver *n* Silber *n*; * *adj* Silber-.
silversmith *n* Silberschmied *m*.
silvery *adj* silbern.
similar *adj* ähnlich.
similarity *n* Ähnlichkeit *f*.
simile *n* Vergleich *m*.
simmer *vi* sieden.
simpering *adj* albern.
simple *adj* einfach.
simpleton *n* Einfaltspinsel *m*.
simplicity *n* Einfachheit *f*; Einfältigkeit *f*.
simplify *vt* vereinfachen.
simulate *vt* simulieren.
simultaneous *adj* gleichzeitig.
sin *n* Sünde *f*; * *vi* sündigen.
since *adv* seither; * *prep* seit, seitdem; * *conj* seit; da, weil.
sincere *adj* aufrichtig; **yours ~ly** mit freundlichen Grüßen.
sincerity *n* Aufrichtigkeit *f*.
sinew *n* Sehne *f*.
sinful *adj* sündig, sündhaft.
sing *vt vi* singen.
Singapore *n* Singapur *n*.
singe *vt* versengen.
singer *n* Sänger(in) *m(f)*.
single *adj* einzig; Einzel-, einzeln; ledig; einfach.
singular *adj* (*gr*) Singular-; merkwürdig; * *n* (*gr*) Singular *m*.
sinister *adj* böse; unheimlich.
sink *n* Spülbecken *n*; * *vt* versenken; * *vi* sinken.
sinner *n* Sünder(in) *m(f)*.
sinus *n* Sinus *m*.
sip *vt* nippen an +*dat*.
siphon *n* Siphon *m*.
sir *n* Herr *m*.
siren *n* Sirene *f*.
sirloin *n* Lendenstück *n*.
sister *n* Schwester *f*.
sister-in-law *n* Schwägerin *f*.

sit *vi* sitzen; tagen; ~ **down** *vi* sich hinsetzen.

site *n* Platz *m*; Baustelle *f*.

sitting *n* Sitzung *f*.

sitting room *n* Wohnzimmer *n*.

situation *n* Lage *f*.

six *num* sechs.

sixteen *num* sechzehn.

sixth *adj* sechste(r,s); * *n* Sechstel *n*.

sixty *num* sechzig.

size *n* Größe *f*; Umfang *m*.

skate *n* Schlittschuh *m*; Rochen *m*; * *vi* Schlittschuh laufen.

skating *n* Eislauf *m*.

skating rink *n* Eisbahn *f*.

skeleton *n* Skelett *n*.

skeleton key *n* Dietrich *m*.

sketch *n* Skizze *f*; * *vt* skizzieren.

skewer *n* Fleischspieß *m*.

ski *n* Schi *m*; * *vi* Schi laufen.

ski boot *n* Schistiefel *m*.

skid *n* Schleudern *n*; * *vi* schleudern.

skier *n* Schiläufer(in) *m(f)*.

skiing *n* Schilaufen *n*.

skilful *adj* geschickt.

skill *n* Können *n*.

skilled *adj* geschickt; gelernt.

skim *vt* abschöpfen; gleiten über +*acc*.

skimmed milk *n* Magermilch *f*.

skin *n* Haut *f*; Schale *f*; * *vt* abhäuten; schälen.

skin diving *n* Schwimmtauchen *n*.

skinny *adj* dünn.

skip *n* Sprung *m*; * *vi* hüpfen; * *vt* übergehen.

skipper *n* Kapitän *m*.

skirmish *n* Scharmützel *n*.

skirt *n* Rock *m*.

skit *n* Parodie *f*.

skittle *n* Kegel *m*.

skulk *vi* sich herumdrücken.

skull *n* Schädel *m*.

sky *n* Himmel *m*.

skylight *n* Oberlicht *n*.

skyscraper *n* Wolkenkratzer *m*.

slab *n* Platte *f*.

slack *adj* locker; nachlässig.

slacken *vi* locker werden; nachlassen; * *vt* lockern.

slag *n* Schlacke *f*.

slam *vt vi* zuschlagen.

slander *n* Verleumdung *f*; * *vt* verleumden.

slant *n* Schräge f; Tendenz f; * *vi* schräg legen; * *vi* schräg liegen.

slanting *adj* schräg.

slap *n* Klaps *m*; * *adv* geradewegs; * *vt* einen Klaps geben +*dat*.

slash *n* Schnittwunde *f*; * *vt* (auf)schlitzen; radikal kürzen.

slate *n* Schiefer *m*; Dachziegel; * *vt* verreißen.

slaughter *n* Schlachten n; Gemetzel *n*; * *vt* schlachten; niedermetzeln.

slaughterhouse *n* matadero *m*.

Slav *adj* slawisch.

slave *n* Sklave *m*, Sklavin *f*; * *vi* schuften, sich schinden.

slavery *n* Sklaverei *f*.

slay *vt* ermorden.

sleazy *adj* schmierig.

sledge *n* Schlitten *m*.

sledgehammer *n* Schmiedehammer *m*.

sleek *adj* rassig; glatt.

sleep *n* Schlaf *m*; * *vi* schlafen.

sleeper *n* Schläfer *m*; Schlafwagen *m*.

sleeping bag *n* Schlafsack *m*.

sleeping pill *n* Schlaftablette *f*.

sleepless *adj* schlaflos.

sleepwalker *n* Schlafwandler(in) *m(f)*.

sleepy *adj* schläfrig.

sleet *n* Schneeregen *m*.

sleeve *n* Ärmel *m*.

sleigh *n* Pfredeschlitten *m*.

sleight *n*: ~ **of hand** Fingerfertigkeit *f*.

slender *adj* schlank.

slice *n* Scheibe *f*; * *vt* in Scheiben schneiden.

slide *n* Rutschbahn *f*; Diapositiv *n*; * *vt* schieben; * *vi* gleiten, rutschen.

sliding *adj* Schiebe-.

slight *adj* zierlich; geringfügig; gering; * *n* Kränkung *f*; * *vt* kränken.

slightly *adv* etwas, ein bißchen.

slim *adj* schlank; dünn; * *vi* eine Schlankheitskur machen.

slime *n* Schleim *m*.

slimming *n* Schlankheitskur *f*.

slimy *adj* glitschig; schlammig; schmierig.

sling *n* Schlinge *f*; Schleuder *m*; * *vt* schleudern.

slip *n* Flüchtigkeitsfehler *m*; Unterrock *m*; Zettel *m*; * *vt* stecken, schieben; * *vi* ausrutschen; gleiten; nachlassen.

slipper *n* Hausschuh *m*.

slippery *adj* glatt.

slipshod *adj* schlampig.

slipway *n* Auslaufbahn *f*.

slit *n* Schlitz *m*; * *vt* aufschlitzen.

slogan *n* Schlagwort *n*; Werbespruch *m*.

slope *n* Neigung *f*; Abhang *m*; * *vi*: **to ~ down** sich senken; **to ~ up** ansteigen.

sloping *adj* schräg.

sloppy *adj* schlampig.

sloth *n* Faulheit *f*.

slovenly *adj* schlampig.

slow *adj adv* langsam.

slug *n* Nachtschnecke *f*.

sluggish *adj* träge; schleppend.

sluice *n* Schleuse *f*.

slum *n* Elendsquartier *n*.

slumber *n* Schlummer *m*.

slump *n* Rückgang *m*.

slur *n* Undeutlichkeit *f*; Verleumdung *f*.

slush *n* Schneematsch *m*.

slut *n* Schlampe *f*.

sly *adj* schlau.

smack *n* Klaps *m*; * *vt* einen Klaps geben +*dat*.

small *adj* klein.

smallpox *n* Pocken *pl*.

small talk *n* Gepländer *n*.

smart *adj* elegant, schick; adrett; * *vi* schmerzen, brennen.

smash *n* Zusammenstoß *m*; *vt* zerschmettern; * *vi* zersplittern.

smattering *n* oberflächliche Kenntnis *f*.

smear *n* Fleck *m*; * *vt* beschmieren.

smell *n* Geruch *m*; Geruchssinn *m*; * *vt vi* riechen.

smelly *adj* übelriechend.

smile *n* Lächeln *n*; * *vi* lächeln.

smirk *n* blöde(s) Grinsen *n*.

smith *n* Schmied *m*.

smithy *n* Schmiede *f*.

smock *n* Kittel *m*.

smoke *n* Rauch *m*; * *vt vi* rauchen.

smoker *n* Raucher(in) *m(f)*.

smoke screen *n* Rauchwand *f*.

smoking *n*: **'no ~'** 'rauchen verboten'.

smoky *adj* rauchig; verraucht.

smooth *adj* glatt; * *vt* glätten.

smother *vt* ersticken.

smoulder *vi* schweien.

smudge *vt* beschmieren.

smug *adj* selbstgefällig.

smuggle *vt* schmuggeln.

smuggler *n* Schmuggler *m*.

smuggling *n* Schmuggel *m*.

smutty *adj* schmutzig.

snack *n* Imbiß *m*.

snack bar *n* Imbißstube *f*.

snag *n* Haken *m*.

snail *n* Schnecke *m*.

snake *n* Schlange *f*.

snap *n* Schnappen *n*; * *adj* schnell; * *vt* zerbrechen; * *vi* brechen.

snare *n* Schlinge *f*.

snarl *vi* knurren.

snatch *vt* schnappen.

sneak *vi* schleichen; * *n* (*coll*) Petze(r) *mf*.

sneer *vi* spötteln.

sneeze *vi* niesen.

sniff *vt* schnuppern; * *vi* schnüffeln.

snigger *vi* hämisch kichern.

snip n Schnippel m; * vt schnippeln.

sniper n Heckenschütze m.

snivelling adj weinerlich.

snooze vi dösen.

snore vi schnarchen.

snorkel n Schnorchel m.

snort vi schnauben.

snout n Schnauze f.

snow n Schnee m; * vi schneien.

snowball n Schneeball m.

snowdrop n Schneeglöckchen n.

snowman n Schneemann m.

snowplough n Schneepflug m.

snub vt schroff abfertigen; * n Verweis m.

snub-nosed adj stupsnasig.

snuff n Schnupftabak m.

snug adj behaglich, gemütlich.

so adv so; auch; so viele; also.

soak vt durchnassen; * vi weichen.

soap n Seife f.

soap opera n Familienserie f.

soap powder n Waschpulver n.

soapy adj seifig.

soar vi aufsteigen.

sob n Schluchzen n; * vi schluchzen.

sober adj nüchtern.

soccer n Fußball m.

sociable adj gesellig.

social adj sozial.

socialism n Sozialismus m.

socialist n Sozialist(in) m(f).

social work n Sozialarbeit f.

social worker n Sozialarbeiter(in) m(f).

society n Gesellschaft f.

sociology n Soziologie f.

sock n Socke f.

socket n Steckdose f.

sod n Rasenstück n.

soda n Soda f.

sodium n Natrium n.

sofa n Sofa n.

soft adj weich; leise.

soften vt weich machen; * vi weich werden.

softness n Weichheit f.

software n Software f.

soil n Erde f; * vt beschmutzen.

solace n Trost m.

solar adj Sonnen-.

solder vt löten; * n Lötmetall n.

soldier n Soldat m.

sole n Sohle f; Seezunge f; * adj alleinig, Allein-.

solemn adj feierlich.

solicit vt bitten um; * vi Kunden anwerben.

solicitor n Rechtsanwalt m, Rechtsanwältin f.

solid adj fest; massiv; solide; * n Festkörper m.

solidarity n Solidarität f.

solidify vi fest werden.

solitary adj einsam.

solitude n Einsamkeit f.

solo n Solo n.

soluble adj löslich; lösbar.

solution n Lösung f.

solve vt lösen.

solvent adj zahlungsfähig; n (chem) Lösungsmittel n.

some adj einige; ein paar; etwas; manche(r,s); irgendein(e); * pron einige; etwas.

somehow adv irgendwie.

someone pron jemand; acc jemand(en); dat jemandem.

something pron etwas.

sometime adv irgendeinmal.

sometimes adv manchmal.

somewhat adv etwas.

somewhere adv irgendwo; irgendwohin.

son n Sohn m.

song n Lied n.

son-in-law n Schwiegersohn m.

soon adv bald.

sooner adv früher; lieber.

soot n Ruß m.

soothe vt beruhigen; lindern.

sophisticated adj kultiviert.

soporific adj einschläfernd.

sorcerer n Hexenmeister m.

sordid adj erbärmlich.

sore n Wunde f; * adj schmerzend; wund.

sorrow n Kummer m, Leid n.

sorrowful *adj* sorgenvoll.

sorry *adj* traurig, erbärmlich; ~! Entschuldigung!.

sort *n* Art *f*; Sorte *f*; * *vt* sortieren; sichten, in Ordnung bringen.

sorting office *n* Sortierstelle *f*.

soul *n* Seele *f*; (*mus*) Soul *m*.

soulful *adj* seelenvoll.

sound *adj* gesund; sicher; vernünftig; stichhaltig; * *n* Geräusch *n*, Laut *m*; * *vt* erschallen lassen; schlagen; abhorchen; * *vi* schallen, tönen; klingen.

sound barrier *n* Schallmauer *f*.

sound effects *npl* Toneffekte *pl*.

sounding *n* (*mar*) Lotung *f*.

soundtrack *n* Tonstreifen *m*; (*mus*) Filmmusik *f*.

soup *n* Suppe *f*.

sour *adj* sauer.

source *n* Quelle *f*.

south *n* Süden *m*; * *adj* Süd-, südlich; * *adv* nach Süden, südwärts.

South Africa *n* Südafrika *n*.

South African *adj* südafrikanisch; * *n* Südafrikaner(in) *m*(*f*).

South America *n* Südamerika *n*.

South American *adj* südamerikanisch; * *n* Südamerikaner(in) *m*(*f*).

south-east *n* Südosten *m*.

southerly *adj* südlich.

southern *adj* südlich, Süd-.

South Pole *n* Südpol *m*.

southward(s) *adv* südwärts, nach Süden.

southwest *n* Südwestens *m*.

souvenir *n* Souvenir *n*.

sovereign *n* Herrscher(in) *m*(*f*); * *adj* souverän.

sow *n* Sau *f*.

sow *vt* säen.

soya bean *n* Sojabohne *f*.

space *n* Raum *m*; Platz *m*.

spacecraft *n* Raumfahrzeug *n*.

spaceman *n* Raumfahrer *m*, Raumfahrerin *f*.

spacious *adj* geräumig.

spade *n* Spaten *m*; Pik *n*; **king of ~s** Pik-König *m*.

Spain *n* Spanien *n*.

span *n* Spanne *f*; * *vt* umspannen, überspannen.

Spaniard *n* Spanier(in) *m*(*f*).

Spanish *adj* spanisch; * *n* Spanisch *n*.

spar *n* Sparren *m*; * *vi* einen Sparring machen.

spare *adj* Ersatz-; * *vt* verschonen; ersparen.

sparingly *adv* sparsam.

spark *n* Funken *m*.

sparkle *n* Funkeln *n*; * *vi* funkeln.

spark plug *n* Zündkerze *f*.

sparrow *n* Spatz *m*.

sparse *adj* spärlich.

spasm *n* (*med*) Krampf *m*.

spasmodic *adj* sprunghaft.

spatter *vt* bespritzen.

spatula *n* Spatel *m*.

spawn *n* Laich *m*; * *vi* laichen.

speak *vt vi* sprechen.

speaker *n* Sprecher(in) *m*(*f*).

spear *n* Speer *m*; * *vt* aufspießen.

special *adj* besondere(r,s).

speciality *n* Spezialität *f*.

species *n* Art *f*.

specific *adj* spezifisch.

specification *n* Angabe *f*; Bedingung *f*.

specify *vt* genau angeben.

specimen *n* Probe *f*.

speck *n* Fleckchen *n*.

spectacle *n* Schauspiel *n*.

spectator *n* Zuschauer(in) *m*(*f*).

spectre *n* Geist *m*, Gespenst *n*.

speculate *vi* spekulieren.

speculation *n* Nachdenken *n*; Grübeln *n*; Spekulation *f*.

speculative *adj* grüblerisch; spekulativ.

speech *n* Rede *f*, Sprache *f*; Reden *n*, Sprechen *n*.

speechless *adj* sprachlos.

speed *n* Geschwindigkeit *f*, Eile

f; * *vi* eilen, schnell fahren.

speedboat *n* Rennboot *n*.

speed limit *n* Geschwindigkeitsbegrenzung *f*.

speedometer *n* Tachometer *m/n*.

speedway *n* Speedwayrennen *n*.

speedy *adj* schnell, rasch.

spell *n* Weile *f*; Zauber *m*; * *vt* buchstabieren.

spelling *n* Buchstabieren *n*.

spend *vt* verwenden; ausgeben; verbringen; verbrauchen.

spendthrift *n* Verschwender *m*, Verschwenderin *f*.

spent *adj* erschöpft.

sperm *n* Sperma *n*.

spew *vi* brechen, speien.

sphere *n* Kugel *f*, Sphäre *f*; Bereich *m*.

spherical *adj* kugelförmig, sphärisch.

spice *n* Gewürz *n*; * *vt* würzen.

spick-and-span *adj* blitzblank.

spicy *adj* stark gewürzt.

spider *n* Spinne *f*.

spike *n* Dorn *m*, Spitze *f*.

spill *vt* verschütten; * *vi* sich ergießen.

spin *vt* spinnen; herumwirbeln.

spinach *n* Spinat *m*.

spinal *adj* Rückgrat-.

spindly *adj* spindeldürr.

spine *n* Rückgrat *n*.

spinning wheel *n* Spinnrad *n*.

spin-off *n* Nebenprodukt *n*.

spinster *n* unverheiratete Frau *f*.

spiral *n* Spirale *f*.

spire *n* Turm *m*.

spirit *n* Geist *m*; Stimmung *f*; Alkohol *m*; ~s *npl* Spirituosen *pl*.

spirited *adj* beherzt.

spirit level *n* Wasserwaage *f*.

spiritual *adj* geistlich.

spit *n* Bratspieß *m*; Spucke *f*; * *vi* spucken.

spite *n* Gehässigkeit *f*; **in ~ of** trotz.

spiteful *adj* gehässig.

spittle *n* Speichel *m*, Spucke *f*.

splash *n* Spritzer *m*; * *vt* bespritzen; * *vi* spritzen.

spleen *n* Milz *f*.

splendid *adj* glänzend.

splendour *n* Pracht *f*.

splint *n* Schiene *f*.

splinter *n* Splitter *m*.

split *n* Spalte *f*; Trennung *f*; * *vt* spalten; * *vi* reißen.

spoil *vt* verderben; verwöhnen.

spoke *n* Speiche *f*.

spokesman *n* Sprecher *m*.

spokeswoman *n* Sprecherin *f*.

sponge *n* Schwamm *m*; * *vt* abwaschen.

sponsor *n* Sponsor *m*; * *vt* fördern.

sponsorship *n* Finanzierung *f*.

spontaneous *adj* spontan.

spool *n* Spule *f*, Rolle *f*.

spoon *n* Löffel *m*.

spoonful *n* Löffelvoll *m*.

sport *n* Sport *m*.

sports car *n* Sportwagen *m*.

sports jacket *n* Sportjakett *n*.

sportsman *n* Sportler *m*.

sportswear *n* Sportkleidung *f*.

sportswoman *n* Sportlerin *f*.

spot *n* Punkt *m*; Fleck *m*; Stelle *f*; * *vt* erspähen.

spotless *adj* fleckenlos.

spotlight *n* Scheinwerferlicht *n*.

spotted *adj* gefleckt.

spotty *adj* pickelig.

spouse *n* Gatte *m*, Gattin *f*.

spout *n* Tülle *f*; * *vi* speien.

sprain *n* Verstauchung *f*.

sprat *n* Sprotte *f*.

sprawl *vi* ausgestreckt liegen/sitzen.

spray *n* Gischt *f*, Spray *m/n*; Sprühdose *f*; * *vi* sprühen; * *vt* zerstäuben, spritzen.

spread *n* Verbreitung *f*; * *vt* ausbreiten; verbreiten; * *vi* sich ausbreiten.

spree *n* Einkaufsbummel *m*.

sprightly *adj* lebhaft, munter.

spring *n* Sprung *m*; Feder *f*; Frühling *m*; * *vi* springen.

springtime *n* Frühling *m*.
springy *adj* federnd.
sprinkle *vt* streuen; sprenkeln.
sprout *vi* sprießen; **~s** *npl* Rosenkohl *m*.
spruce *n* Fichte *f*; * *adj* schmuck, adrett.
spur *n* Sporn *m*; Ansporn *m*; * *vt* anspornen.
spurious *adj* falsch.
spurn *vt* verschmähen.
spy *n* Spion(in) *m(f)*; * *vi* spionieren.
squabble *n* Zank *m*; * *vi* sich zanken.
squad *n* Abteilung *f*; Kommando *n*.
squadron *n* Schwadron *f*.
squalid *adj* verkommen.
squall *n* Windstoß *m*.
squalor *n* Verwahrlosung *f*.
squander *vt* verschwenden.
square *n* Quadrat *n*; Platz *m*; * *adj* viereckig.
squash *n* Squash *n*; * *vt* zerquetschen.
squat *vi* hocken; * *adj* untersetzt.
squatter *n* Hausbesetzer *m*.
squawk *vi* kreischen.
squeak *vi* quieksen; quietschen.
squeal *vi* schrill schreien.
squeamish *adj* empfindlich.
squeeze *vt* pressen, drücken.
squid *n* Tintenfisch *m*.
squint *vi* schielen.
squirrel *n* Eichhörnchen *n*.
stab *n* Stich *m*; * *vt* erstechen.
stabilise *vt* stabilisieren; * *vi* sich stabilisieren.
stable *n* Stall *m*; * *adj* stabil.
stack *n* Stapel *m*; * *vt* stapeln.
stadium *n* Stadion *n*.
staff *n* Stab *m*; Personal *n*.
stag *n* Hirsch *m*.
stage *n* Bühne *f*; Etappe *f*; Stufe *m*; * *vt* aufführen.
stagger *vi* wanken, taumeln.
stagnant *adj* stagnierend.
stagnate *vi* stagnieren.
staid *adj* gesetzt.

stain *n* Fleck *m*; * *vt* beflecken.
stainless *adj* rostfrei.
stair *n* Stufe *f*.
staircase *n* Treppenhaus *n*, Treppe *f*.
stairs *pl* Treppe *f*.
stake *n* Pfahl *m*; Einsatz *m*; * *vt* setzen.
stale *adj* alt; altbacken.
stalemate *n* Patt *n*; Stillstand *m*.
stalk *n* Stengel *m*, Stiel *m*; * *vi* jagen.
stall *n* Stand *m*, Box *n*; * *vt* abwürgen; * *vi* stehenbleiben.
stallion *n* Zuchthengst *m*.
stalwart *n* treue(r) Anhänger *m*.
stamina *n* Durchhaltevermögen *n*, Zähigkeit *f*.
stammer *n* Stottern *n*; * *vt vi* stottern.
stamp *n* Briefmarke *f*; Stempel *m*; * *vi* stampfen; * *vt* stempeln; frankieren.
stampede *n* panische Flucht *f*.
stand *n* Gestell *n*; * *vi* stehen; aufstehen; * *vt* setzen, stellen; aushalten; ausstehen.
standard *n* Norm *f*; Fahne *f*; * *adj* Normal-.
standing *adj* stehend; ständig; * *n* Dauer *f*; Ansehen *n*.
staple *n* Heftklamme *f*; * *adj* Haupt-, Grund-; * *vt* klammern.
stapler *n* Heftmaschine *f*.
star *n* Stern *m*; Star *m*.
starboard *n* Steuerbord *n*.
starch *n* Stärke *f*.
stare *vi* **to ~ at** starren auf, anstarren; * *n* starre(r) Blick *m*.
stark *adj* öde.
starling *n* Star *m*.
starry *adj* Sternen-.
start *n* Anfang *m*; Start *m*; * *vt* in Gang setzen; anlassen; * *vi* anfangen; aufbrechen; starten.
starter *n* Anlasser *m*; Starter *m*; Vorspeise *f*.

starting point n Ausgangspunkt m.

startle vt erschrecken.

startling adj erschreckend.

starvation n Verhungern n.

starve vi verhungern.

state n Zustand m; Staat m; **the S~s** die Staaten mpl; * vt erklären.

stately adj würdevoll.

statement n Aussage f.

statesman n Staatsmann m.

static n Reibungselektrizität f.

station n Bahnhof m; Wache f;
Stand m; * vt stationieren.

stationary adj stillstehend.

stationer n Schreibwaren-
händler m.

stationery n Schreibwaren pl.

station wagon n Kombiwagen
m.

statistics n Statistik f.

statue n Statue f.

stature n Größe f.

statute n Gesetz n.

stay n Aufenthalt m; * vi bleiben; wohnen; **~ in** vi zu Hause bleiben; **~ on** vi länger bleiben; **~ up** vi aufbleiben.

steadfast adj treu, standhaft.

steady adj fest, stabil; beständig; * vt festigen.

steak n Steak n; Filet n.

steal vt vi stehlen.

stealth n Heimlichkeit f.

stealthy adj heimlich.

steam n Dampf m; * vi dämpfen.

steam engine n Dampfmaschi-
ne f.

steamer n Dämpfer m.

steel n Stahl m; * adj Stahl-.

steep adj steil; * vt einweichen.

steeple n Kirchturm m.

steeplechase n Hindernisrennen n.

steer vt vi steuern; lenken.

steering n Steuerung f.

steering wheel n Lenkrad,
Steuerrad n.

stellar adj Stern(en)-.

stem n Stiel m; * vt aufhalten.

stench n Gestank m.

stencil n Schablone f.

step n Schritt m; Stufe f; * vi
treten, schreiten.

stepbrother n Stiefbruder m.

stepdaughter n Stieftochter f.

stepfather n Stiefvater m.

stepmother n Stiefmutter f.

stepsister n Stiefschwester f.

stepson n Stiefsohn m.

stereo n Stereoanlage f.

stereotype n Prototyp m; * vt
stereotypieren.

sterile adj steril; unfruchtbar.

sterling adj Sterling-; gedie-
gen; * n das Pfund Sterling.

stern adj streng; * n Heck n.

stew n Eintopf m; * vt vi schmo-
ren.

steward n Steward m.

stewardess n Stewardeß f.

stick n Stock m; Stück n; * vt
stechen, stecken; kleben; * vi
steckenbleiben.

stick-up n (coll) Raubüberfall
m.

sticky adj klebrig.

stiff adj steif; dick; stark.

stiffen vt vi versteifen.

stifle vt unterdrücken.

stifling adj drückend.

stigma n Stigma n.

stile n Steige f.

stiletto n Pfennigabsatz m.

still adj still; * adv (immer)
noch; immerhin.

stillborn adj totgeboren.

stilt n Stelze f.

stimulate vt anregen, stimulie-
ren.

stimulus n Anregung f.

sting n Stich m; * vt vi stechen.

stingy adj geizig.

stink n Gestank m; * vi stinken.

stint n Pensum n.

stipulate vt festsetzen.

stir n Bewegung f; Ruhren n;
Aufsehen n; * vt rühren; * vi
sich rühren.

stirrup n Steigbügel m.

stitch n Stich m; (med) Faden
m; * vt nähen.

stoat *n* Wiesel *n*.

stock *n* Vorrat *m*; Lager *n*; Vieh *n*; Brühe *f*; Grundkapital *n*; * *vt* führen.

stockbroker *n* Börsenmakler *m*.

stock exchange *n* Börse *f*.

stocking *n* Strumpf *m*.

stock market *n* Börse *f*.

stole *n* Stola *f*.

stomach *n* Bauch *m*; Magen *m*; * *vt* vertragen.

stone *n* Stein *m*; * *vt* steinigen; entkernen.

stone-deaf *adj* stocktaub.

stony *adj* steinig.

stool *n* Hocker *m*.

stoop *vi* sich bücken.

stop *n* Halt *m*; Haltestelle *f*; Punkt *m*; * *vt* anhalten; * *vi* aufhören; stehenbleiben; bleiben.

stoppage *n* Anhalten *n*; Verkehrsstöckung *f*; Arbeitseinstellung *f*.

stopwatch *n* Stoppuhr *f*.

storage *n* Lagerung *f*.

store *n* Vorrat *m*; Lager *n*; Warenhaus *n*, Kaufhaus *n*; * *vt* lagern.

stork *n* Storch *m*.

storm *n* Sturm *m*; * *vt* *vi* stürmen.

stormy *adj* stürmisch.

story *n* Geschichte *f*; Märchen *n*.

stout *adj* tapfer; beleibt; * *n* Starkbier *n*.

stove *n* Herd *m*; Ofen *m*.

stow *vt* verstauen.

stowaway *n* blinde(r) Passagier *m*.

straggle *vi* wuchern; nachhinken.

straggler *n* Nachzügler *m*.

straight *adj* gerade; offen; pur; * *adv* direkt, geradewegs.

straightaway *adv* sofort.

straighten *vt* gerade machen.

straightforward *adj* unkompliziert.

strain *n* Belastung *f*; * *vt* über-

anstrengen; anspannen; * *vi* sich anstrengen.

strainer *n* Sieb *n*.

strait *n* Straße *f*, Meerenge *f*.

straitjacket *n* Zwangsjacke *f*.

strand *n* Strähne *f*; Faden *m*.

strange *adj* fremd; seltsam.

stranger *n* Fremde(r) *mf*.

strangle *vt* erwürgen.

strap *n* Riemen *m*; Träger *m*; * *vt* festschnallen.

strapping *adj* stramm.

stratagem *n* Kriegslist *f*.

strategic *adj* strategisch.

strategy *n* Strategie *f*.

stratum *n* Schicht *f*.

straw *n* Stroh *n*; Strohhalm *m*.

strawberry *n* Erdbeere *f*.

stray *vi* herumstreunen; * *adj* verirrt; zufällig.

streak *n* Streiten *m*; Strähne *f*; * *vt* streifen.

stream *n* Bach *m*; Strom *m*; * *vi* strömen.

streamer *n* Wimpel *m*.

street *n* Straße *f*.

strength *n* Stärke *f*; Kraft *f*.

strengthen *vt* verstärken.

strenuous *adj* anstrengend.

stress *n* Druck *m*; Streß *m*; (*gr*) Betonung *f* * *vt* betonen.

stretch *n* Strecke *f*; * *vt* ausdehnen, strecken; * *vi* sich strecken.

stretcher *n* Tragbahre *f*.

strict *adj* streng; genau.

stride *n* lange(r) Schritt *m*; * *vi* schreiten.

strife *n* Streit *m*.

strike *n* Streik *m*; Schlag *m*; * *vt* schlagen; * *vi* streiken.

striker *n* Streikende(r) *mf*.

striking *adj* auffallend.

string *n* Schnur *f*; Saite *f*.

stringent *adj* streng.

strip *n* Streifen *m*; * *vt* abstreifen, abziehen; ausziehen; * *vi* sich ausziehen.

stripe *n* Streifen *m*.

stroke *n* Schlag *m*; Stoß *m*; (*med*) Schlaganfall *m*; Streicheln *n*; * *vt* streicheln.

stroll *n* Spaziergang *m*; * *vi* schlendern.
strong *adj* stark; fest.
strongbox *n* Kassette *f*.
stronghold *n* Hochburg *f*.
structure *n* Struktur *f*; Aufbau *m*.
struggle *n* Kampf *m*; * *vi* kämpfen.
strut *vi* stolzieren.
stub *n* Stummel *m*; Kippe *f*.
stubble *n* Stoppel *f*.
stubborn *adj* hartnäckig.
stucco *n* Stuck *n*.
stud *n* Kragenknopf *m*; Gestüt *n*.
student *n* Student(in) *m(f)*; * *adj* Studenten-.
studio *n* Studio *n*; Atelier *n*.
studious *adj* lernbegierig.
study *n* Studium *n*; Arbeitszimmer *f*; Studie *f*; * *vt vi* studieren.
stuff *n* Zeug *n*; * *vt* stopfen; füllen; ausstopfen.
stuffing *n* Füllung *f*.
stuffy *adj* schwül.
stumble *vi* stolpern.
stumbling block *n* Hindernis *n*.
stump *n* Stumpf *m*.
stun *vt* betäuben.
stunt *n* Kunststück *n*, Trick *m*.
stuntman *n* Stuntman *m*.
stupefy *vt* betäuben; bestürzen.
stupendous *adj* erstaunlich.
stupid *adj* dumm.
stupidity *n* Dummheit *f*.
stupor *n* Betäubung *f*.
sturdy *adj* robust, kräftig.
stutter *vi* stottern.
sty *n* Schweinestall *m*.
stye *n* Gerstenkorn *n*.
style *n* Stil *m*; Mode *f*.
stylish *adj* modisch.
suave *adj* zuvorkommend.
subdivide *vt* unterteilen.
subdue *vt* unterwerfen.
subdued *adj* still; gedämpft.
subject *n* Untertan *m*; Thema *n*; Fach *n*; *(gr)* Subjekt *n*; * *adj* **to be ~ to** unterworfen sein +*dat*.

subjective *adj* subjektiv.
subjugate *vt* unterjochen.
subjunctive *n* Konjunktiv *m*.
sublet *vt* untervermieten.
sublime *adj* erhaben.
submachine gun *n* Maschinenpistole *f*.
submarine *n* Unterseeboot *n*, U-Boot *n*.
submerge *vt* untertauchen.
submission *n* Gehorsam *m*; Behauptung *f*; Unterbreitung *f*.
submissive *adj* demütig.
submit *vt* behaupten; unterbreiten; * *vi* sich ergeben.
subordinate *adj* untergeordnet; * *vt* Untergebene(r) *mf*.
subpoena *n* Vorladung *f*; * *vt* vorladen.
subscriber *n* Abonnent *m*.
subscription *n* Abonnement *n*.
subsequent *adj* später, folgend.
subside *vi* sich senken.
subsidiary *adj* Neben-; * *n* Tochtergesellschaft *f*.
subsidise *vt* subventionieren.
subsidy *n* Subvention *f*.
subsistence *n* Unterhalt *m*.
substance *n* Substanz *f*.
substantial *adj* wesentlich; fest, kräftig.
substantiate *vt* begründen.
substitute *n* Ersatz *m*; * *vt* ersetzen.
substitution *n* Ersetzung *f*.
subterfuge *n* Vorwand *m*.
subterranean *adj* unterirdisch.
subtitle *n* Untertitel *m*.
subtle *adj* fein.
subtlety *n* Feinheit *f*.
subtract *vt* abziehen.
suburb *n* Vorort *m*.
suburban *adj* Vorort(s)-.
subversive *adj* subversiv.
subway *n* U-Bahn *f*; Unterführung *f*.
succeed *vi* erfolgreich sein, Erfolg haben; gelingen; * *vt* (nach) folgen +*dat*.
success *n* Erfolg *m*.
successful *adj* erfolgreich.

succession *n* Folge *f*; Nachfolge *f*.

successive *adj* aufeinanderfolgend.

successor *n* Nachfolger(in) *m(f)*.

succinct *adj* knapp.

succulent *adj* saftig.

succumb *vi*: **to ~ (to)** erliegen (+*dat*); nachgeben (+*dat*).

such *adj* solche(r,s); **as ~** an sich.

suck *vt* saugen.

suction *n* Saugkraft *f*.

sudden *adj* plötzlich.

suddenly *adv* plötzlich.

suds *npl* Seifenlauge *f*.

sue *vt* verklagen.

suede *n* Wildleder *n*.

suet *n* Nierenfett *n*.

suffer *vt vi* leiden.

suffering *n* Leiden *n*.

suffice *vi* genügen.

sufficient *adj* ausreichend.

suffocate *vt vi* ersticken.

suffrage *n* Wahlrecht *n*.

sugar *n* Zucker *m*; * *vt* zuckern.

sugar beet *n* Zuckerrübe *f*.

sugar cane *n* Zuckerrohr *n*.

sugary *adj* süß.

suggest *vt* vorschlagen.

suggestion *n* Vorschlag *m*.

suicide *n* Selbstmord *m*; **to commit ~** Selbstmord begehen.

suit *n* Anzug *m*; Farbe *f*; * *vt* passen +*dat*.

suitable *adj* passend, geeignet.

suitcase *n* Koffer *m*.

suite *n* Zimmerflucht *f*; Einrichtung *f*; (*mus*) Suite *f*.

sulk *vi* schmollen.

sulky *adj* schmollend.

sullen *adj* mürrisch.

sulphur *n* Schwefel *m*.

sultana *n* Sultanine *f f*.

sultry *adj* schwül.

sum *n* Summe *f*; Betrag *m*; Rechenaufgabe *f*; **~ up** *vt vi* zusammenfassen.

summary *n* Zusammenfassung *f*.

summer *n* Sommer *m*.

summerhouse *n* Gartenhaus *n*.

summit *n* Gipfel *m*.

summon *vt* herbeirufen; (*jur*) vorladen.

summons *n* Vorladung *f*; * *vt* vorladen.

sumptuous *adj* prächtig.

sun *n* Sonne *m*.

sunbathe *vi* sich sonnen.

sunburn *n* Sonnenbrand *m*.

Sunday *n* Sonntag *m*.

sundial *n* Sonnenuhr *f*.

sundry *adj* verschieden.

sunflower *n* Sonnenblume *f*.

sunglasses *npl* Sonnenbrille *f*.

sunlight *n* Sonnenlicht *n*.

sunny *adj* sonnig.

sunrise *n* Sonnenaufgang *m*.

sunset *n* Sonnenuntergang *m*.

sunshade *n* Sonnenschirm *m*.

sunshine *n* Sonnenschein *m*.

sunstroke *n* Hitzschlag *m*.

suntan *n* Sonnebräune *f*.

suntan oil *n* Sonnenöl *n*.

super *adj* (*coll*) prima, klasse.

superannuation *n* Pension *f*.

superb *adj* ausgezeichnet, hervorragend.

supercilious *adj* herablassend.

superficial *adj* oberflächlich.

superfluous *adj* überflüssig.

superhuman *adj* übermenschlich.

superintendent *n* Polizeichef *m*.

superior *adj* überlegen; besser; * *n* Vorgesetzte(r) *mf*.

superiority *n* Überlegenheit *f*.

superlative *adj* überragend.

supermarket *n* Supermarkt *m*.

supernatural *n* übernatürlich.

superpower *n* Weltmacht *f*.

supersede *vt* ersetzen.

supersonic *adj* Überschall-.

superstition *n* Aberglaube *m*.

superstitious *adj* abergläubisch.

supervise *vt* beaufsichtigen.

supervision *n* Aufsicht *f*.

supervisor *n* Aufsichtsperson *f*.

supine *adj* auf dem Rücken liegend.

supper *n* Abendessen *n*.

supplant *vt* ersetzen.

supple *adj* geschmeidig.

supplement *n* Ergänzung *f*; Nachtrag *m*.

supplementary *adj* ergänzend.

supplier *n* Lieferant *m*.

supply *vt* liefern; * *n* Vorrat *m*; Lieferung *f*.

support *n* Unterstützung *f*; * *vt* stützen; unterstützen.

supporter *n* Aufhänger(in) *m(f)*.

suppose *vt vi* annehmen.

supposition *n* Voraussetzung *f*.

suppress *vt* unterdrücken.

suppression *n* Unterdrückung *f*.

supremacy *n* Oberhoheit *f*.

supreme *adj* oberste(r,s).

surcharge *n* Zuschlag *m*.

sure *adj* sicher, gewiß.

surety *n* Sicherheit *f*.

surf *n* Brandung *f*.

surface *n* Oberfläche *f*.

surfboard *n* Wellenreiterbrett *n*.

surfeit *n* Übermaß *n*.

surge *n* Woge *f*; * *vi* wogen.

surgeon *n* Chirurg(in) *m(f)*.

surgery *n* Chirurgie *f*.

surgical *adj* chirurgisch.

surly *adj* verdrießlich, grob.

surname *n* Zuname *m*.

surpass *vt* übertreffen.

surplus *n* Überschuß *m*; * *adj* überschüssig.

surprise *n* Überraschung *f*; * *vt* überraschen.

surprising *adj* überraschend.

surrender *n* Kapitulation *f*; * *vi* sich ergeben.

surreptitious *adj* heimlich.

surrogate *n* Ersatz *m*.

surrogate mother *n* Leihmutter *f*.

surround *vt* umgeben.

survey *n* Übersicht *f*; * *vt* überblicken; vermessen.

survival *n* Überleben *n*.

survive *vt vi* überleben.

survivor *n* Überlebende(r) *mf*.

susceptible *adj* empfindlich.

suspect *n* Verdächtige(r) *mf*; * *adj* verdachtig; * *vt* verdächtigen.

suspend *vt* verschieben; aufhängen; suspendieren.

suspense *n* Spannung *f*.

suspension *n* Federung *f*; Suspendierung *f*.

suspension bridge *n* Hängebrücke *f*.

suspicion *n* Verdacht *m*.

suspicious *adj* verdachtig.

sustain *vt* aufrechterhalten; bestätigen.

sustenance *n* Nahrung *f*.

swab *n* (*med*) Tupfer *m*.

swagger *vi* stolzieren.

swallow *n* Schwalbe *f*; Schluck *m*; * *vt* schlucken.

swamp *n* Sumpf *m*.

swan *n* Schwan *m*.

swarm *n* Schwarm *m*.

swastika *n* Hakenkreuz *n*.

sway *vi* schwanken; schaukeln, sich wiegen; * *vt* schwenken.

swear *vi* schwören; fluchen.

sweat *n* Schweiß *m*; * *vi* schwitzen.

sweater *n* Pullover *m*.

sweatshirt *n* Sweatshirt *n*.

Swede *n* Schwede *m*, Schwedin *f*.

Sweden *n* Schweden *n*.

Swedish *adj* schwedisch; * *n* Schwedisch *n*.

sweep *n* Schornsteinfeger *m*; * *vt* fegen, kehren; * *vi* rauschen.

sweeping *adj* verallgemeinernd.

sweet *n* Nachtisch *m*; Bonbon *n*; * *adj* süß.

sweeten *vt* süßen.

sweetheart *n* Liebste(r) *mf*.

sweetness *n* Süße *f*.

swell *n* Seegang *n*; * *adj* (*coll*) todschick; * *vt* vermehren; * *vi* schwellen.

swelling n Schwellung f.
sweltering adj drückend.
swerve vt vi ausscheren.
swift n Mauersegler m; * adj geschwind, schnell, rasch.
swill n Schweinefutter n; * vt spülen.
swim vt vi schwimmen.
swimming n Schwimmen n.
swimming pool n Schwimmenbecken n.
swimsuit n Badeanzug m.
swindle vt betrügen.
swine n Schwein n.
swing n Schaukel f; Schwung n; * vt vi schwingen.
swirl vi wirbeln.
Swiss adj Schweizer, schweizerisch; * n Schweizer(in) m(f).
switch n Schalter m; Wechsel m; * vt schalten; wechseln; ~ off vt ausschalten; ~ on vt einschalten.
switchboard n Zentrale f.
Switzerland n Schweiz f.
swivel vt drehen; * vi sich drehen.
swoon vi in Ohnmacht fallen; * n Ohnmacht f.
swoop n Sturzflug m; Razzia f; * vi stürzen.
sword n Schwert n.
swordfish n Schwertfisch m.
sycamore n Bergahorn m.
syllable n Silbe f.
syllabus n Lehrplan m.
symbol n Symbol n.
symbolic adj symbolisch.
symmetry n Symmetrie f.
sympathetic adj mitfühlend.
sympathise vi mitfühlen.
sympathy n Mitleid n, MItgefühl n; Beileid n.
symphony n Sinfonie f.
symposium n Tagung f.
symptom n Sympton n.
synagogue n Synagoge f.
synchronise vt synchronisieren.
syndicate n Konsortium n.
synonym n Synonym n.
synonymous adj gleichbedeu-

tend.
syntax n Syntax f.
syringe n Spritze f.
system n System n.
systematic adj systematisch.
systems analyst n Systemanalytiker(in) m(f).

T

tab n Aufhänger m; Schild n.
table n Tisch m; Tabelle f; * vt vorlegen, einbringen.
tablecloth n Tischtuch n.
table d'hôte Tagesmenü n.
table lamp Tischlampe f.
tablespoon n Eßlöffel n.
tablet n Tablette f; Täfelchen n.
table tennis n Tischtennis n.
table wine n Tafelwein m.
tacit adj stillschweigend.
taciturn adj wortkarg.
tack n Stift m; Reißzwecke f; Heftstich m; * vt nageln; heften; * vi aufkreuzen.
tackle n Flaschenzug m; (mar) Takelage m, Tackling n; * vt anpacken; festhalten; angehen.
tact n Takt m.
tactful adj taktvoll.
tactical adj taktisch.
tactless adj taktlos.
tactics npl Taktik f.
tadpole n Kaulquappe f.
tag n Schild n, Anhänger m.
tail n Schwanz m; * vt folgen +dat.
tailor n Schneider m.
tailoring n Schneidern n.
tailor-made adj maßgeschneidert.
tailwind n Rückenwind m.
tainted adj verdorben.
take vt nehmen; machen; fassen; einnehmen; bringen; bekommen; hinnehmen; ~ away

vt wegnehmen; wegbringen; ~ **back** *vt* zurückbringen; zurücknehmen; ~ **down** *vt* abreißen; aufschreiben; ~ **in** *vt* hereinlegen; begreifen; ~ **off** *vi* starten; * *vt* wegnehmen; ausziehen; nachmachen; ~ **on** *vt* übernehmen; einstellen; ~ **out** *vt* ausführen; herausnehmen; abschließen; ~ **to** *vt* mögen; sich angewöhnen; ~ **up** *vt* aufnehmen; kürzer machen; in Anspruch nehmen.

takeoff *n* Start *m*; Nachahmung *f*.

takeover *n* Übernahme *f*.

takings *npl* Einnahmen *pl*.

talc *n* Talkumpuder *m*.

tale *n* Geschichte *f*, Erzählung *f*; **to tell ~s** Geschichten erfinden.

talent *n* Talent *n*.

talented *adj* begabt.

talk *n* Gespräch *n*; Gerede *n*; Vortrag *m*; * *vi* sprechen, reden.

talkative *adj* gesprächig.

tall *adj* groß; hoch.

tally *n* Abrechnung *f*; * *vi* übereinstimmen.

talon *n* Kralle *f*.

tame *adj* zahm.

tampon *n* Tampon *m*.

tan *n* Sonnenbräune *f*; * *vt* bräunen; * *vi* braun werden.

tang *n* Schärfe *f*.

tangent *n* Tangente *f*.

tangerine *n* Mandarine *f*.

tangible *adj* greifbar.

tangle *n* Durcheinander *n*.

tank *n* Tank *m*; Panzer *m*.

tanker *n* Tanker *m*.

tanned *adj* gebräunt.

tantalising *adj* verlockend.

tantrum *n* Wutanfall *m*.

tap *n* Hahn *m*; Klopfen *n*; * *vt* klopfen.

tape *n* Band *n*; * *vt* aufnehmen.

tape measure *n* Maßband *n*.

taper *n* Wachskerze *f*.

tape recorder *n* Tonbandgerät *n*.

tapestry *n* Wandteppich *m*.

tar *n* Teer *m*.

target *n* Ziel *n*.

tariff *n* Tarif *m*.

tarmac *n* Rollfeld *n*.

tarnish *vt* matt machen.

tarpaulin *n* Plane *f*.

tarragon *n* Estragon *m*.

tart *n* Torte *f*: (*coll*) Nutte *f*; * *adj* scharf.

tartan *n* Schottenkaro *n*.

tartar *n* Zahnstein *m*.

task *n* Aufgabe *f*.

tassel *n* Quaste *f*.

taste *n* Geschmack *m*; Geschmackssinn *m*; Vorliebe *f*; * *vt vi* schmecken.

tasteful *adj* geschmackvoll.

tasteless *adj* geschmacklos.

tasty *adj* schmackhaft.

tattoo *n* Tätowierung *m*; * *vt* tätowieren.

taunt *vt* verhöhnen.

Taurus *n* Stier *m*.

taut *adj* straff.

tawdry *adj* billig.

tax *n* Steuer *f*; * *vt* besteuern.

taxable *adj* steuerpflichtig.

taxation *n* Besteuerung *f*.

tax-free *adj* steuerfrei.

taxi *n* Taxi *n*; * *vi* rollen.

taxi driver *n* Taxifahrer *m*.

taxi rank *n* Taxistand *m*.

taxpayer *n* Steuerzahler *m*.

tax relief *n* Steuerermäßigung *f*.

tax return *n* Steuererklärung *f*.

tea *n* Tee *m*.

teach *vt vi* lehren, unterrichten.

teacher *n* Lehrer(in) *m(f)*.

teaching *n* Unterricht *m*.

teacup *n* Teetasse *f*.

team *n* Team *n*; Mannschaft *f*.

teamwork *n* Teamarbeit *f*.

teapot *n* Teekanne *f*.

tear *n* Träne *f*; Riß *m*; * *vt vi* zerreißen.

tearful *adj* weinend.

tear gas *n* Tränengas *n*.

tease *vt* necken.

tea set *n* Teeservice *n*.

teaspoon n Teelöffel m.
teat n Brustwarze f; Sauger m.
technical adj technisch; Fach-.
technicality n technische Einzelheit f.
technician n Techniker m.
technique n Technik f.
technological adj technologisch.
technology n Technologie f.
teddy (bear) n Teddybär m.
tedious adj langweilig, ermüdend.
tedium n Langweile f.
tee n Abschlagstelle f; Tee n.
teem vi wimmeln (**with** von).
teenage adj Teenager-, jugendlich.
teenager n Teenager m, Jugendliche(r) m/f.
teens npl Teenageralter n.
tee-shirt n T-Shirt n.
teethe vi zahnen.
teething troubles npl Kinderkrankheiten pl.
teetotal adj abstinent.
telecommunications npl Fernmeldewesen n.
telegram n Telegramm m.
telegraph n Telegraph m.
telephone n Telefon n.
telephone booth n Telefonzelle f.
telephone call n Telefongespräch n.
telephone directory n Telefonbuch n.
telephone number n Telefonnummer m.
telescope n Teleskop n.
televise vt durch das Fernsehen übertragen.
television n Fernsehen n.
television set n Fernseher m.
telex n Telex n; * vt per Telex schicken.
tell vt erzählen; sagen; erkennen; wissen.
teller n Kassenbeamte(r) mf.
telling adj verräterisch.
telltale adj verräterisch.

temper n Temperament n; * vt mildern.
temperament n Temperament n.
temperance n Mäßigung f.
temperate adj gemäßigt.
temperature n Temperatur f.
template n Schablone f.
temple n Tempel m; Schläfe f.
temporary adj vorläufig; provisorisch.
tempt vt verleiten; locken.
temptation n Versuchung f.
tempting adj verlockend.
ten num zehn.
tenable adj haltbar.
tenacious adj zäh, hartnäckig.
tenacity n Zähigkeit f, Hartnäckigkeit f.
tenancy n Mietverhältnis n.
tenant n Mieter m; Pächter m.
tend vt sich kümmern um.
tendency n Tendenz f.
tender adj zart; zärtlich; * n Kostenanschlag m; * vt (an)bieten.
tenderness n Zartheit f; Zärtlichkeit f.
tendon n Sehne f.
tenement n Mietshaus n.
tenet n Lehre f.
tennis n Tennis n.
tennis court n Tennisplatz m.
tennis player n Tennisspieler(in) m(f).
tennis racket n Tennisschläger m.
tennis shoes npl Tennisschuhe pl.
tenor n Tenor m.
tense adj angespannt; * n (gr) Zeitform f.
tension n Spannung f.
tent n Zelt n.
tentacle n Fühler m; Fangarm m.
tentative adj unsicher; Probe-; vorläufig.
tenth adj zehnte(r,s).
tenuous adj schwach.
tenure n Besitz m; Amtszeit f.
tepid adj lauwarm.

term n Zeitraum m; Frist f; Bedingung f; Ausdruck m; * vt nennen.

terminal adj Schluß-; (med) unheilbar; * n Endstation f; Terminal m.

terminate vt beenden; * vi enden, aufhören.

terminus n Endstation f.

terrace n Terrasse f.

terrain n Terrain n.

terrible adj schrecklich.

terrific adj fantastisch.

terrify vt erschrecken.

territorial adj Gebiets-.

territory n Gebiet n.

terror n Schrecken m; Terror m.

terrorise vt terrorisieren.

terrorism n Terrorismus m.

terrorist n Terrorist(in) m(f).

terse adj kurz, knapp.

test n Probe f; Prüfung f; * vt prüfen.

testicle n Hoden m.

testify vi aussagen.

testimony n Zeugenaussage f.

test tube n Reagenzglas n.

testy adj gereizt.

tetanus n Tetanus m.

tether vt anbinden.

text n Text m.

textbook n Lehrbuch n.

textiles npl Textilien pl.

texture n Beschaffenheit f.

than prep als.

thank vt danken +dat.

thankful adj dankbar.

thankless adj undankbar.

thanks npl danke.

Thanksgiving n Danksagung f.

that pron das; jener, jene, jenes; * rel pron der, die,das ; * conj daß; **so ~** so daß.

thatch vt mit Stroh decken.

thaw n Tauwetter n; Tauen n; * vt vi tauen; auftauen.

the art der, die, das.

theatre n Theater n.

theatregoer n Theaterbesucher m, Theaterbesucherin f.

theatrical adj Theater-, theatralisch.

theft n Diebstahl m.

their poss adj ihr, ihre; **~s** poss pron ihrer, ihre, ihres.

them pron sie (acc), ihnen (dat).

theme n Thema n.

themselves pron sich; selbst.

then adv dann; danach; **now and ~** dann und wann.

theologian n Theologe m.

theological adj theologisch.

theology n Theologie f.

theorem n Lehrsatz m.

theoretical adj theoretisch.

theorise vi Theorien aufstellen.

theory n Theorie f; **in ~** theoretisch.

therapist n Therapeut(in) m(f).

therapy n Therapie f.

there adv da, dort; dahin, dorthin.

thereabouts adv dort in der Nähe, dort irgendwo.

thereafter adv danach.

thereby adv dadurch, damit.

therefore adv deshalb, daher.

thermometer n Thermometer n.

thesaurus n Synonymwörterbuch n.

these pl pron, adj diese.

thesis n These f; Dissertation f.

they pl pron sie; man.

thick adj dick; dumm.

thicken vi dichter werden; * vt verdicken.

thickness n Dicke f; Dichte f.

thickset adj untersetzt.

thickskinned adj dickhäutig.

thief n Dieb(in) m(f).

thigh n Oberschenkel m.

thimble n Fingerhut m.

thin adj dünn, mager.

thing n Ding n; Sache f.

think vt vi denken; **~ over** vt überdenken; **~ up** vi sich dat ausdenken.

third adj dritte(r,s); * n Drittel n.

thirdly adv drittens.

third-rate *adj* minderwertig.

thirst *n* Durst *f*.

thirsty *adj* durstig; **to be ~** Durst haben.

thirteen *num* dreizehn.

thirty *num* dreißig.

this *adj* diese(r,s); * *pron* dies, das.

thistle *n* Distel *f*.

thorn *n* Dorn *m*.

thorny *adj* dornig.

thorough *adj* gründlich.

thoroughbred *n* Vollblut; * *adj* reinrassig, Vollblut-.

thoroughfare *n* Straße *f*.

those *pl pron* die (da), jene; * *adj* die, jene.

though *conj* obwohl; * *adv* trotzdem.

thought *n* Gedanke *m*; Denken *n*.

thoughtful *adj* gedankenvoll, nachdenklich.

thoughtless *adj* gedankenlos.

thousand *num* tausend.

thousandth   *adj* tausendste(r,s).

thrash *vt* verdreschen.

thread *n* Faden *m*, Garn *n*; * *vt* einfädeln.

threadbare *adj* fadenscheinig.

threat *n* Drohung *f*.

threaten *vt* bedrohen; * *vi* drohen.

three *num* drei.

three-dimensional *adj* dreidimensional.

threshold *n* Schwelle *f*.

thrifty *adj* sparsam.

thrill *n* Erregung *f*; * *vi* packen.

thriller *n* Krimi *m*.

thrive *vi* gedeihen.

throat *n* Hals *m*, Kehle *f*.

throb *vi* pochen.

throng *n* Menschenschar *f*; * *vt* sich drängen in +*dat*.

throttle *n* Gashebel *m*; * *vt* erdrosseln.

through *prep* durch; während; aus; * *adj* durchgehend; fertig; * *adv* durch.

throughout *prep* überall in

+*dat*; während; * *adv* überall; die ganze Zeit.

throw *n* Wurf *m*; * *vt* werfen; **~ away** *vt* wegwerfen; **~ off** *vt* abwerfen; **~ out** *vt* hinauswerfen; **~ up** *vt vi* speten.

throwaway *adj* Wegwerf-.

thrush *n* Drossel *f*.

thrust *n* Schubkraft *f*; * *vt vi* stoßen.

thud *n* dumpfte(r) Schlag *m*.

thug *n* Schlägertyp *m*.

thumb *n* Daumen *m*.

thumbtack *n* Reißzwecke *f*.

thump *n* Schlag *m*; Bums *m*; * *i* hämmern; * *vt* schlagen auf +*acc*.

thunder *n* Donner *m*; * *vi* donnern.

thunderbolt *n* Blitz *n*.

thunderclap *n* Donnerschlag *m*.

thunderstorm *n* Gewitter *n*.

thundery *adj* gewitterschwül.

Thursday *n* Donnertag *m*.

thus *adv* so; somit, also.

thwart *vt* vereiteln; hindern.

thyme *n* Thymian *m*.

thyroid *n* Schilddrüse *f*.

tiara *n* Diadem *n*.

tic *n* Tick *m*.

tick *n* Ticken *n*; Häkchen *n*; * *vi* ticken; * *vt* abhaken.

ticket *n* Fahrkarte *f*; Eintrittskarte *f*.

ticket collector *n* Fahrkartenkontrolleur *m*.

ticket office *n* Fahrkartenschalter *m*; Kasse *f*.

tickle *vt* kitzeln.

ticklish *adj* kitzlig.

tide *n* Gezeiten *pl*.

tidy *adj* ordentlich.

tie *n* Krawatte *f*, Schlips *m*; Band *n*; Unentschieden *n*; * *vt* binden; * *vi* unentschieden spielen; **~ down** *vt* festbinden; **~ up** *vt* anbinden; verschnüren; festmachen.

tier *n* Rang *m*.

tiger *n* Tiger *m*.

tight *adj* eng, knapp; gedrängt;

fest; streng; * *adv* fest.

tighten *vt* anziehen, anspannen; verschärfen; * *vi* sich spannen.

tightfisted *adj* knauserig.

tightrope *n* Seil *n*.

tights *npl* Strümpfhose *f*.

tigress *n* Tigerin *f*.

tile *n* Dachziegel *m*; Fliese *f*.

tiled *adj* gedeckt, Ziegel-; mit Fliesen belegt.

till *n* Kasse *f*; * *vt* bestellen; * *prep conj* bis.

tiller *n* Ruderpinne *f*.

tilt *vt* kippen, neigen; * *vi* sich neigen.

timber *n* Holz *n*; Baumbestand *m*.

time *n* Zeit *f*; Mal *n*; (*mus*) Takt *m*; * *vt* zur rechten Zeit tun, zeitlich einrichten; **in ~** rechtzeitig; mit der Zeit; (*mus*) im Takt; **from ~ to ~** gelegentlich.

time bomb *n* Zeitbombe *f*.

timeless *adj* zeitlos.

timely *adj* rechtzeitig; günstig.

time off *n* freie Zeit *f*.

timer *n* Schaltuhr *f*.

time scale *n* Zeitspanne *f*.

time zone *n* Zeitzone *f*.

timid *adj* ängstlich, schüchtern.

timing *n* Tming *n*.

tin *n* Blech *n*; Dose *f*.

tinfoil *n* Staniolpapier *n*.

tinge *n* Färbung *f*.

tingle *vi* prickeln.

tinker *n* Kesselflicker *m*.

tinkle *vi* klingeln.

tinsel *n* Rauschgold *n*.

tint *n* Farbton *m*; Anflug *m*; Tönung *f*; * *vt* (leicht) färben; tönen.

tinted *adj* getönt.

tiny *adj* winzig.

tip *n* Spitze *f*; Trinkgeld *n*; Wink *m*, Tip *m*; * *vt* kippen; antippen; ein Trinkgeld geben.

tip-off *n* Hinweis *m*; Tip *m*.

tipsy *adj* beschwipst.

tire *vt vi* ermüden, müde machen/werden.

tireless *adj* unermüdlich.

tiresome *adj* lästig.

tiring *adj* ermüdend.

tissue *n* Gewebe *n*; Papiertaschentuch *n*.

tissue paper *n* Seidenpapier *n*.

titillate *vt* kitzeln.

title *n* Titel *m*.

title deed *n* Eigentumsurkunde *f*.

titter *vi* kichern.

titular *adj* nominell.

to *prep* zu, nach; bis; vor; für.

toad *n* Kröte *m*.

toadstool *n* Giftpilz *n*.

toast *n* Toast *m*; Trinkspruch *m*; * *vt* trinken auf +*acc*; toasten.

toaster *n* Toaster *m*.

tobacco *n* Tabak *m*.

tobacconist *n* Tabakhändler *m*.

tobacconist's shop *n* Tabakladen *m*.

toboggan *n* Schlitten *m*.

today *adv* heute; heutzutage.

toddler *n* Kleinkind *n*.

toddy *n* Grog *m*.

toe *n* Zehe *f*; Spitze *f*.

together *adv* zusammen; gleichzeitig.

toil *n* harte Arbeit *f*; Plackerei *f*; * *vi* sich abmühen, sich plagen.

toilet *n* Toilette *f*; * *adj* Toiletten-.

toilet bag *n* Waschbeutel *m*.

toilet paper *n* Toilettenpapier *n*.

toiletries *npl* Toilettenartikel *pl*.

token *n* Zeichen *n*; Gutschein *m*.

Tokyo *n* Tokio *n*.

tolerable *adj* erträglich; leidlich.

tolerance *n* Toleranz *f*.

tolerant *adj* tolerant.

tolerate *vt* dulden; ertragen.

toll *n* Gebühr *f*; * *vi* läuten.

tomato *n* Tomate *f*.

tomb *n* Grab(mal) *n*.

tomboy n Wildfang m.
tombstone n Grabstein m.
tomcat n Kater m.
tomorrow adv morgen.
ton n Tonne f.
tone n Ton m; **to ~ down** vt
   mäßigen.
tone-deaf adj ohne musikalisches Gehör.
tongs npl Zange f.
tongue n Zunge f.
tongue-tied adj sprachlos, stumm.
tongue-twister n Zungenbrecher m.
tonic n (med) Stärkungsmittel
   n.
tonight adv heute abend.
tonsil n Mandel f.
too adv auch.
tool n Werkzeug n.
toolbox n Werkzeugkasten m.
toot vi tuten; hupen.
tooth n Zahn m.
toothache n Zahnschmerzen
   pl.
toothbrush n Zahnbürste f.
toothpaste n Zahnpasta f.
toothpick n Zahnstocher m.
top n Spitze f; Gipfel m; Wipfel
   m;   Kreisel   m;   * adj
   oberste(r,s); * vt an erster
   Stelle stehne auf +dat; **to ~ off**
   vt auffüllen.
top floor n oberste(s) Stockwerk n.
top-heavy adj kopflastig.
topic n Thema n.
topical adj aktuell.
topless adj oben ohne.
top-level adj auf höchster Ebene.
topmost adj oberste(r,s).
topple vt vi stürzen, kippen.
top-secret adj streng geheim.
topsy-turvy adv durcheinander.
torch n Taschenlampe f.
torment n Qual f; * vt quälen.
torrent n Sturzbach m.
torrid adj heiß.
tortoise n Schildkröte f.

tortoiseshell n Schildplatt m.
tortuous adj gewunden.
torture n Folter f; * vt foltern.
toss vt schleudern.
total n Gesamtheit f; * adj Gesamt-, total.
totalitarian adj totalitär.
totter vi wanken.
touch n Berührung f; Tastsinn
   m; * vt berühren; leicht anstoßen; rühren.
touch-and-go adj riskant.
touchdown n Landen n.
touched adj gerührt.
touching adj rührend.
touchy adj empfindlich.
tough adj zäh; schwierig; * n
   Schlägertyp m.
toughen vt zäh machen; abhärten.
toupee n Toupet n.
tour n Tour f; * vi umherreisen.
touring n Umherreisen n.
tourism n Tourismus m.
tourist n Tourist(in) m(f).
tourist office n Verkehrsamt n.
tournament n Tournier n.
tow vt schleppen.
toward(s) prep gegen; nach.
towel n Handtuch n.
toweling n Frottee n/m.
towel rack n Handtuchstange
   f.
tower n Turm m.
towering adj hochragend.
town n Stadt f.
town clerk n Stadtdirektor m.
town hall n Rathaus n.
towrope n Abschlepptau n.
toy n Spielzeug n.
toyshop n Spielwarengeschäft
   n.
trace n Spur f; * vt nachziehen,
   durchpausen, aufspüren.
track n Spur f, Weg m; Gleis n;
   * vt verfolgen.
tracksuit n chandal m.
tract n Landstrich m; Traktat
   n.
tractor n Traktor m.
trade n Handel m, Gewerbe f;
   * vi handeln.

trade fair *n* Messe *f*.
trade mark *n* Warenzeichen *n*.
trade name *n* Handelsbezeichnung *f*.
trader *n* Händler *m*.
tradesman *n* Händler *m*.
trade union *n* Gewerkschaft *f*.
trade unionist *n* Gewerkschaftler *m*.
trading *n* Handel *m*.
tradition *n* Tradition *f*, Brauch *m*.
traditional *adj* traditionell.
traffic *n* Handel *m*, Verkehr *m*.
traffic jam *n* Verkehrsstauung *f*.
traffic lights *npl* Ampel *f*.
tragedy *n* Tragödie *f*.
tragic *adj* tragisch.
trail Spur *f*; Rauchfahne *f*; Pfad *m*, Weg *m*; * *vt* verfolgen; folgen +*dat*; * *vi* schleifen; hinterhinken.
trailer *n* Anhänger *m*; Wohnwagen *m*; Vorschau *f*.
train *n* Zug *m*; Schleppe *f*; Folge *f*; * *vt* ausbilden; abrichten; * *vi* trainieren.
trained *adj* geschult; ausgebildet.
trainee *n* Lehrling *m*.
trainer *n* Trainer *m*; Ausbilder *m*.
training *n* Training *f*; Ausbildung *f*.
trait *n* Zug *m*, Merkmal *m*.
traitor *n* Verräter *m*.
tramp *n* Landstreicher *m*; * *vi* stampfen.
trample *vt* niedertrampeln.
tranquil *adj* ruhig, friedlich.
tranquiliser *n* Beruhigungsmittel *n*.
tranquility *n* Ruhe *f*.
transact *vt* abwickeln.
transaction *n* Abwicklung *f*; Geschäft *n*.
transcend *vt* übersteigen.
transcription *n* Transkription *f*.
transfer *n* Übertragung *f*; Umzug *m*; Transfer *m*; * *vt* verle-

gen; versetzen; übertragen; überweiswen.
transform *vt* umwandeln.
transformation *n* Umwandlung *f*.
transfusion *n* Transfusion *f*.
transient *adj* kurzlebig.
transit *n* Durchgang *m*.
transition *n* Übergang *m*.
transitional *adj* Übergangs-.
translate *vt* übersetzen.
translation *n* Übersetzung *f*.
translator *n* Übersetzer(in) *m(f)*.
transmission *n* Übertragung *f*.
transmit *vt* übertragen.
transmitter *n* Sender *m*.
transparency *n* Durchsichtigkeit *f*.
transparent *adj* durchsichtig.
transpire *vi* sich herausstellen.
transplant *vt* verpflanzen; * *n* Transplantat *n*.
transport *n* Transport *m*; * *vt* transportieren.
trap *n* Falle *f*; * *vt* in einer Falle locken.
trapdoor *n* Falltür *f*.
trappings *npl* Aufmachung *f*.
trash *n* Plunder *m*; Mist *m*.
trash can *n* Mülleimer *m*.
travel *vi* Reisen *n*; * *vi* reisen.
travel agency *n* Reisebüro *n*.
travel agent *n* Reisebürokaufmann(frau) *m(f)*.
traveller *n* Reisende(r) *mf*.
traveller's cheque *n* Reisescheck *m*.
travelling *n* Reisen *n*.
travel sickness *n* Reisekrankheit *f*.
trawler *n* Fischdampfer *m*, Trawler *m*.
tray *n* Tablett *n*.
treacherous *adj* verräterisch.
treachery *n* Verrat *m*.
tread *n* Schritt *m*, Tritt *m*; * *vi* treten.
treason *n* Verrat *m*.
treasure *n* Schatz *m*; * *vt* schätzen.

treasurer n Schatzmeister m.

treat n besonderer Freude f; * vt behandeln; **to ~ sb to sth** jdm etw spendieren.

treatise n Abhandlung f.

treatment n Behandlung f.

treaty n Vertrag m.

treble adj dreifach; * vt verdreifachen.

treble clef n Violinschlüssel m.

tree n Baum m.

trek n Treck m; * vi trecken.

trellis n Gitter n.

tremble vi zittern; beben.

trembling n Zittern n; * adj zitternd.

tremendous adj gewaltig, kolossal; prima.

tremor n Zittern n; Beben n.

trench n Graben m; (mil) Schützengraben m.

trend n Tendenz f.

trendy adj modisch.

trepidation n Beklommenheit f.

tress n Locke f.

trestle n Bock m.

trial n Prozeß m; Versuch m, Probe f.

triangle n Dreieck n; (mus) Triangel f.

triangular adj dreieckig.

tribal adj Stammes-.

tribe n Stamm m.

tribulation n Mühsal f.

tribunal n Gericht n.

tributary n Nebenfluß m.

tribute n Zeichen n der Hochachtung.

trick n Trick m; Stich m; * vt überlisten, beschwindeln.

trickery n Tricks pl.

trickle n Tröpfeln n; * vi tröpfeln.

tricky adj schwierig; kitzlig.

tricycle n Dreirad n.

trifle n Kleinigkeit f; Trifle m.

trifling adj geringfügig.

trigger n Drücker m; **~ off** vt auslösen.

trill n Triller m; * vi trillern.

trim adj gepflegt; schlank; * n

Verfassung f; Verzierung f; * vt schneiden; stutzen; besetzen; trimmen.

trimmings npl Verzierung f, Verzierungen pl; Zubehör n.

Trinity n Dreieinigkeit f.

trinket n kleine(s) Schmuckstück n.

trip n (kurze) Reise f; Ausflug m; Stolpern n; * vi trippeln; stolpern; **~ up** vi stolpern; einen Fehler machen.

tripe n Kutteln pl; Mist m.

triple adj dreifach.

triplets npl Drillinge pl.

triplicate n **in ~** in dreifacher Ausfertigung.

tripod n Stativ n.

trite adj banal.

triumph n Triumph m; * vi triumphieren.

triumphant adj triumphierend.

trivia npl Trivialitäten pl.

trivial adj trivial.

trolley n Handwagen m.

trombone n Posaune f.

troop n Trupp m; **~s** npl Truppen pl.

trophy n Trophäe f.

tropical adj tropisch.

trot n Trott m; * vi trotten.

trouble n Ärger m; Sorge f; Mühe f; Unruhen pl; * vt stören.

troubled adj beunruhigt.

troublemaker n Unruhestifter m.

troubleshooter n Vermittler m.

troublesome adj lästig.

trough n Trog m; Rinne f, Kanal m.

trousers npl Hose f.

trout n Forelle f.

trowel n Kelle f.

truce n Waffenstillstand m.

truck n Lastwagen m; offene(r) Güterwagen m.

truck driver n Lastwagenfahrer m.

truculent adj trotzig.

trudge *vi* sich (mühselig) dahin-schleppen.
true *adj* wahr; echt; treu.
truffle *n* Trüffel *f/m*.
trump *n* Trumpf *m*.
trumpet *n* Trompete *f*.
trunk *n* Stamm *m*; Rumpf *m*; Truhe *f*; Rüssel *m*.
truss *n* Bruchband *n*; * *vt* fesseln.
trust *n* Vertrauen *n*; Treuhand-vermögen *n*; * *vt* vertrauen.
trusted *adj* treu.
trustee *n* Vermögensverwalter *m*.
trustful *adj* vertrauensvoll.
trusting *adj* vertrauensvoll.
trustworthy *adj* vertrauens-würdig.
truth *n* Wahrheit *f*.
truthful *adj* ehrlich.
try *n* Versuch *m*; * *vt* versuchen; probieren; unter Anklage stellen; * *vi* sich bemühen; ~ **on** *vt* anprobieren; ~ **out** *vt* ausprobieren.
trying *adj* schwierig.
tub *n* Wanne *f*.
tube *n* Röhre *f*, Rohr *n*; Tube *f*.
tubing *n* Schlauch *m*.
Tuesday *n* Dienstag *m*.
tuft *n* Büschel *m*.
tug *n* Schleppendampfer *m*; * *vt* *vi* schleppen.
tuition *n* Unterricht *m*.
tulip *n* Tulpe *f*.
tumble *n* Sturz *m*; * *vi* fallen, stürzen.
tumbledown *adj* baufällig.
tumbler *n* Trinkglas *n*.
tummy *n* Bauch *m*.
tumour *n* Geschwulst *f*.
tumultuous *adj* stürmisch.
tuna *n* Thunfisch *m*.
tune *n* Melodie *f*; * *vt* (*mus*) stimmen.
tuneful *adj* melodisch.
tuner *n* Klavierstimmer(in) *m(f)*.
tunic *n* Waffenrock *m*.
tuning fork *n* Stimmgabel *f*.
tunnel *n* Tunnel *m*; * *vi* einen Tunnel anlegen.
turbulent *adj* stürmisch.
tureen *n* Terrine *f*.
turf *n* Rasen *m*; Sode *f*; * *vt* mit Grassoden belegen.
turgid *adj* geschwollen.
Turk *n* Türke *m*, Türkin *f*.
Turkey *n* Türkei *f*.
turkey *n* Puter *m*, Truthahn *m*.
Turkish *adj* türkisch; * *n* Türkisch *n*.
turmoil *n* Aufruhr *m*; Tumult *m*.
turn *n* Umdrehung *f*; Nummer *f*; Schock *m*; * *vi* drehen; umdrehen, wenden; umblättern; ~ **down** *vt* ablehnen; ~ **in** *vi* ins Bett gehen; ~ **off** *vi* ausschalten; ~ **on** *vt* anschalten; ~ **out** *vi* sich erweisen.
turning *n* Abzweigung *f*.
turnip *n* Steckrübe *f*.
turnover *n* Umsatz *m*.
turnstile *n* Drehkreuz *n*.
turntable *n* Plattenteller *m*.
turpentine *n* Terpentin *n*.
turquoise *n* Türkis *m*.
turret *n* Turm *m*.
turtle *n* Schildkröte *f*.
tusk *n* Stoßzahn *m*.
tussle *n* Balgerei *f*.
tutor *n* Privatlehrer *m*; Tutor *m*.
tuxedo *n* Smoking *m*.
twang *n* Näseln *n*.
tweezers *npl* Pinzette *f*.
twelfth *adj* zwölfte(r,s).
twelve *num* zwölf.
twentieth *adj* zwanzigste(r,s).
twenty *num* zwanzig.
twice *adv* zweimal.
twig *n* dünne(r) Zweig *m*.
twilight *n* Zwielicht *n*.
twin *n* Zwilling *m*.
twine *n* Bindfaden *m*.
twinge *n* Stechen *n*.
twinkle *vi* funkeln.
twirl *n* Wirbel *m*; * *vt* *vi* wirbeln.
twist *n* Drehung *f*; * *vt* drehen; verbiegen; verdrehen; * *vi* sich drehen.

twit *n* (*coll*) Idiot *m*.
twitch *n* Zucken *n*; * *vi* zucken.
two *num* zwei.
two-door *adj* zweitürig.
two-faced *adj* falsch.
twofold *adj adv* zweifach, doppelt.
two-seater *n* Zweisitzer *m*.
twosome *n* Paar *f*.
tycoon *n* Magnat *m*.
type *n* Typ *m*; Art *f*; Type *f*; * *vt vi* machineschreiben, tippen.
typecast *adj* auf eine Rolle festgelegt.
typeface *n* Schrift *f*.
typescript   *n* maschinegeschriebene(r) Text *m*.
typewriter *n* Schreibmaschine *f*.
typewritten *adj* maschinegeschrieben.
typical *adj* typisch.
typing *n* Maschineschreiben *n*.
typist   *n* Maschinenschreiber(in) *m(f)*.
tyrannical *adj* tyrannisch.
tyrant *n* Tyrann *m*.
tyre *n* Reifen *m*.
tyre pressure *n* Reifendruck *m*.

U

ubiquitous *adj* überall zu findend; allgegenwärtig.
udder *n* Euter *n*.
ugh *excl* hu.
ugliness *n* Häßlichkeit *f*.
ugly *adj* häßlich; böse, schlimm.
ulcer *n* Geschwür *n*.
ultimate *adj* äußerste(r,s), allerletzte(r,s).
ultimately *adv* schließlich, letzten Endes.
ultimatum *n* Ultimatum *n*.
ultrasound *n* Ultraschall *m*.

umbilical cord *n* Nabelschnur *f*.
umbrella *n* Schirm *m*.
umpire *n* Schiedsrichter *m*; * *vt vi* schiedsrichtern.
umpteenth *num* zig; **for the ~ time** zum X-ten Mal.
unaccompanied *adj* ohne Begleitung.
unaccountably *adv* unerklärlich.
unaccustomed *adj* nicht gewöhnt.
unanimous *adj* einmütig; einstimmig.
unarmed *adj* unbewaffnet.
unassuming *adj* bescheiden.
unattached *adj* ungebunden.
unattended *adj* unbeaufsichtigt; unbewacht.
unauthorised *adj* unbefugt.
unavoidable *adj* unvermeidlich.
unawares *adv* unversehens.
unbalanced *adj* unausgeglichen; gestört.
unbearable *adj* unerträglich.
unbelievable *adj* unglaublich.
unbend *vt* geradebiegen; * *vi* aus sich herausgehen.
unbiased *adj* unparteiisch.
unbreakable *adj* unzerbrechlich.
unbroken *adj* ununterbrochen; ungebrochen.
unbutton *vt* aufknöpfen.
uncalled-for *adj* unnötig.
uncanny *adj* unheimlich.
unceasing *adj* unaufhörlich.
unceremonious *adj* brüsk.
uncertain *adj* unsicher; ungewiß.
uncertainty *n* Ungewißheit *f*.
unchanged *adj* unverändert.
unchecked *adj* ungeprüft; ungehindert.
uncivilised *adj* unzivilisiert.
uncle *n* Onkel *m*.
uncomfortable *adj* unbequem, ungemütlich.
uncommon *adj* ungewöhnlich; außergewöhnlich.

uncompromising *adj* kompromißlos, unnachgiebig.

unconcerned *adj* unbekümmert; gleichgültig.

unconditional *adj* bedingungslos.

unconscious *adj* bewußtlos; unbeabsichtigt; * *n* the ~ das Unbewußte.

uncontrollable *adj* unkontrollierbar.

unconventional *adj* unkonventionell.

uncouth *adj* grob.

uncover *vt* aufdecken.

undecided *adj* unschlüssig.

undeniable *adj* unleugbar.

under *prep* under; * *adv* darunter.

under-age *adj* minderjährig.

underclothes *npl* Unterwäsche *f*.

undercoat *n* Grundierung *f*.

undercover *adj* Geheim-.

undercurrent *n* Unterströmung *f*.

undercut *vt* unterbieten.

underdeveloped *adj* Entwicklungs-, unterentwickelt.

underdog *n* Unterlegene(r) *mf*.

underdone *adj* nicht gar, nicht durchgebraten.

underestimate *vt* unterschätzen.

undergo *vt* durch machen; sich unterziehen +*dat*.

undergraduate *n* Student(in) *m(f)*.

underground *n* U-Bahn *f*; * *adj* Untergrund-.

undergrowth *n* Gestrüpp *n*, Unterholz *n*.

underhand *adj* hinterhältig.

underlie *vt* zugrundeliegen +*dat*.

underline *vt* unterstreichen; betonen.

undermine *vt* untergraben.

underneath *adv* darunter; * *prep* unter.

underpaid *adj* unterbezahlt.

underprivileged *adj* benach-

teiligt, unterpriviligiert.

underrate *vt* unterschätzen.

undershirt *n* Unterhemd *n*.

underside *n* Unterseite *f*.

understand *vt vi* verstehen.

understandable *adj* verständlich.

understanding *n* Verständnis *n*; * *adj* verständnisvoll.

understatement *n* Untertreibung *f*.

undertake *vt* unternehmen; * *vi* to ~ to do sth sich verpflichten, etw zu tun.

undertaking *n* Unternehmen *n*; Verpflichtung *f*.

underwater *adj* Unterwasser-; * *adv* unter Wasser.

underwear *n* Unterwäsche *f*.

underworld *n* Unterwelt *f*.

underwriter *n* Assekurant *m*.

undesirable *adj* unerwünscht.

undisputed *adj* unbestritten.

undo *vt* öffnen, zumachen.

undoing *n* Verderben *n*.

undoubted *adj* unbezweifelt.

undoubtedly *adv* zweifellos, ohne Zweifel.

undress *vt* ausziehen; * *vi* sich ausziehen.

undue *adj* übermäßig.

undulating *adj* wellenförmig; wellig.

unearth *vt* ausgraben; ans Licht bringen.

unearthly *adj* nachtschlafen.

uneasy *adj* unruhig; ungut.

uneducated *adj* ungebildet.

unemployed *adj* arbeitslos.

unemployment *n* Arbeitslosigkeit *f*.

unending *adj* endlos.

unerring *adj* unfehlbar.

uneven *adj* uneben; ungleichmäßig.

unexpected *adj* unerwartet.

unfailing *adj* nie versagend.

unfair *adj* ungerecht, unfair.

unfaithful *adj* untreu.

unfamiliar *adj* ungewohnt; unbekannt.

unfashionable *adj* nicht in

Mode.

unfasten *vt* öffnen, aufmachen.

unfavourable *adj* ungünstig.

unfeeling *adj* gefühllos, kalt.

unfinished *adj* unvollendet.

unfit *adj* ungeeignet; nicht fit.

unfold *vt* entfalten; auseinanderfalten; * *vi* sich entfalten.

unforeseen *adj* unvorhergesehen.

unforgettable *adj* unvergeßlich.

unforgivable *adj* unverzeihlich.

unfortunate *adj* unglücklich, bedauerlich.

unfortunately *adv* leider.

unfounded *adj* unbegründet.

unfriendly *adj* unfreundlich.

ungainly *adj* linkisch.

ungrateful *adj* undankbar.

unhappiness *n* Unglück *n*.

unhappy *adj* unglücklich.

unharmed *adj* unversehrt.

unhealthy *adj* ungesund.

unheard-of *adj* unerhört.

unhurt *adj* unverletzt.

uniform *n* Uniform *f*; * *adj* einheitlich.

uniformity *adj* Einheitlichkeit *f*.

unify *vt* vereinigen.

uninhabited *adj* unbewohnt.

unintentional *adj* unabsichtlich.

union *n* Vereinigung *f*; Bund *m*, Union *f*; Gewerkschaft *f*.

unique *adj* einzig(artig).

unison *n* Einstimmigkeit *f*.

unit *n* Einheit *f*.

unite *vt* vereinigen; * vi sich vereinigen.

United   Kingdom   *n* Vereinigte(s) Königreich *n*.

United Nations (Organisation) *n* Vereinte Nationen *fpl*.

United States (of America) *npl* Vereinigte Staaten *mpl* (von Amerika).

unity *n* Einheit *f*; Einigkeit *f*.

universal *adj* allgemein.

universe *n* Weltall *n*.

university *n* Universität *f*.

unjust *adj* ungerecht.

unkempt *adj* zerzaust, ungepflegt, verwahrlost.

unkind *adj* lieblos, gefühllos, grausam.

unknown *adj* unbekannt.

unlawful *adj* ungesetzlich.

unlawfulness *n* Ungesetzlichkeit *f*.

unleash *vt* entfesseln.

unless *conj* es sei denn.

unlicensed *adj* unbefugt, unerlaubt.

unlike *adj* verschieden; **not ~** nicht unähnlich.

unlikelihood *n* Unwahrscheinlichkeit *f*.

unlikely *adj* unwahrscheinlich.

unlimited *adj* unbegrenzt, unbeschränkt.

unload *vt* entladen.

unlock *vt* aufschließen.

unluckily *adv* unglücklicherweise.

unlucky *adj* unglücklich, unglückbringend.

unmanageable *adj* nicht zu handhaben.

unmarried *adj* unverheiratet.

unmask *vt* entlarven.

unmistakable *adj* unverkennbar.

unmitigated *adj* ungemildert, ganz.

unnatural *adj* unnatürlich.

unnecessary *adj* unnötig.

unobtrusive *adj* unauffällig.

unofficial *adj* unoffiziell.

unpack *vt* auspacken.

unpalatable *adj* bitter.

unparalleled *adj* beispiellos.

unpleasant *adj* unangenehm.

unplug *vt* den Stecker herausziehen von.

unpopular *adj* unbeliebt; unpopulär.

unprecedented *adj* beispiellos.

unpredictable *adj* unvorhersehbar; unberechenbar.

unqualified *adj* unqualifiziert.

unquestionably *adv* fraglos.
unravel *vt* ausfasern, entwirren.
unreal *adj* unwirklich.
unrealistic *adj* unrealistisch.
unreasonable *adj* unvernünftig; übertrieben.
unrelated *adj* ohne Beziehung; nicht verwandt.
unrelenting *adj* unerbittlich.
unreliable *adj* unzuverlässig.
unremitting *adj* unermüdlich.
unrest *n* Unruhe *f*; Unruhen *fpl*.
unroll *vt* aufrollen.
unruly *adj* undiszipliniert; schwer lenkbar.
unsafe *adj* nicht sicher.
unsatisfactory *adj* unbefriedigend; unzulänglich.
unsavoury *adj* widerwärtig.
unscathed *adj* unversehrt.
unscrew *vt* aufschrauben.
unscrupulous *adj* skrupellos.
unsettled *adj* rastlos; wechselhaft.
unshaven *adj* unrasiert.
unsightly *adj* unansehnlich.
unskilled *adj* ungelernt.
unspeakable *adj* unsagbar; scheußlich.
unstable *adj* instabil.
unsteady *adj* unsicher; unregelmäßig.
unsuccessful *adj* erfolglos.
unsuitable *adj* unpassend.
unsure *adj* unsicher.
unsympathetic *adj* gefühllos.
untapped *adj* ungenützt.
unthinkable *adj* unvorstellbar.
untidy *adj* unordentlich.
untie *vt* aufschnüren.
until *prep conj* bis; ~ **now** bis jetzt.
untimely *adj* vorzeitig.
untold *adj* unermeßlich.
untoward *adj* widrig.
unused *adj* unbenutzt.
unusual *adj* ungewöhnlich.
unveil *vt* enthüllen.
unwavering *adj* standhaft, unerschütterlich.

unwelcome *adj* unwillkommen; unerfreulich.
unwieldy *adj* sperrig.
unwilling *adv* widerwillig.
unwind *vt* abwickeln; * *vi* sich entspannen.
unwise *adj* unklug.
unworkable *adj* undurchführbar.
unwrap *vt* auspacken.
unwritten *adj* ungeschrieben.
up *adv* oben; * *prep* ~ **sth** oben auf etw *dat*; auf etw *dat*.
upbringing *n* Erziehung *f*.
update *vt* auf den neuesten Stand bringen.
upheaval *n* Umbruch *m*.
uphill *adj* ansteigend; mühsam; * *adv* bergauf.
uphold *vt* unterstützen.
upholstery *n* Polster *n*; Polsterung *f*.
upkeep *n* Instandhaltung *f*.
upon *prep* auf.
upper *n* Oberleder *n*; * *adj* obere(r,s), höhere(r,s).
upper-class *adj* vornehm.
uppermost *adj* oberste(r,s), höchste(r,s).
upright *adj* aufrecht.
uprising *n* Aufstand *m*.
uproar *n* Aufruhr *m*.
uproot *vt* ausreißen.
upset *n* Aufregung *f*; * *vt* umwerfen; aufregen; * *adj* aufgeregt; verdorben.
upshot *n* Endergebnis *n*.
upside-down *adv* verkehrt herum.
upstairs *adv* oben; nachoben; * *adj* obere(r,s), Ober-; * *n* obere(s) Stockwerk *n*.
upstart *n* Emporkömmling *m*.
uptight *adj* nervös; verklemmt.
up-to-date *adj* modisch, modern; neueste(r,s).
upturn *n* Aufschwung *m*.
upward *adj* nach oben gerichtet.
upwards *adv* aufwärts.
urban *adj* städtisch, Stadt-.
urbane *adj* höflich.

urchin n Schlingel m; Seeigel m.

urge n Drang m; * vt **to ~ sb to do sth** jdn (dazu) drängen, etw zu tun.

urgency n Dringlichkeit f.

urgent adj dringend.

urinal n (med) Urinflasche f; Pissoir n.

urinate vi urinieren.

urine n Urin m, Harn m.

us pn uns.

usage n Gebrauch m.

use n Gebrauch m; Zweck m; * vt gebrauchen.

used adj Gebrauch-.

useful adj nützlich.

usefulness n Nützlichkeit f.

useless adj nützlos, unnütz.

user n Benutzer m.

user-friendly adj benutzerfreundlich.

usher n Platzanweiser m.

usherette n Platzanweiserin f.

usual adj gewöhnlich, üblich; **as ~** wie üblich.

usually adv gewöhnlich.

usurp vt an sich reißen.

utensil n Gerät n.

uterus n Gebärmutter f.

utilise vt benützen.

utility n Nützlichkeit f; öffentliche(r) Versorgungsbetrieb m.

utmost adj äußerste(r,s).

utter adj äußerste(r,s), höchste(r,s), völlig; * vt äußern, aussprechen.

utterance n Äußerung f.

utterly adv äußerst, absolut, völlig.

V

vacancy n offene Stelle f; freies Zimmer n.

vacant adj leer, frei.

vacate vt aufgeben, räumen.

vacation n Ferien fpl.

vaccinate vt impfen.

vaccination n Schutzimpfung f.

vaccine n Impfstoff m.

vacuum n Vakuum n.

vacuum cleaner n Staubsauger m.

vacuum flask n Thermosflasche f.

vagina n Scheide f.

vagrant n Landstreicher m.

vague adj vage, unklar.

vain adj vergeblich, eitel.

valet n Kammerdiener m.

valiant adj tapfer, mutig, heldenhaft.

valid adj gültig.

valley n Tal n.

valour n Tapferkeit f.

valuable adj wertvoll.

valuables npl Wertgegenstände fpl.

valuation n Bewertung f.

value n Wert m; * vt schätzen.

value added tax Mehrwertsteuer f.

valued adj geschätzt.

valve n Ventil n; Hahn m; Klappe f.

vampire n Vampir m.

van n Lieferwagen m.

vandal n Vandale m.

vandalise vt mutwillig beschädigen.

vandalism n Vandalismus m.

vanguard n Spitze f.

vanilla n Vanille f.

vanish vi verschwinden.

vanity n Eitelkeit f.

vanity case n Kosmetikkoffer m.

vantage n Vorteil m.

vantage point n Aussichtspunkt m.

vapour n Dampf m.

variable adj veränderlich, wechselhaft.

variation n Schwankung f.

varicose veins npl Krampfadern fpl.

varied *adj* verschiedenartig.

variety *n* Abwechslung *f*.

variety show *n* Varietévorstellung *f*.

various *adj* verschieden.

varnish *n* Lack *m*; * *vt* lackieren.

vary *vt* abändern; *vi* schwanken.

vase *n* Vase *f*.

vast *adj* riesig.

vat *n* Bottich *f*, Faß *n*.

vault *n* Gewölbe *f*; Tresorraum *m*; Sprung *m*; * *vt*, *vi* springen.

veal *n* Kalbfleisch *n*.

veer *vi* (*mar*) abdrehen.

vegetable *n* Gemüse *n*.

vegetable garden *n* Gemüsegarten *m*.

vegetarian *adj* vegetarisch; * *n* Vegetarier(in) *m(f)*.

vegetate *vi* vegetieren.

vegetation *n* Vegetation *f*.

vehemence *n* Heftigkeit *f*.

vehement *adj* heftig.

vehicle *n* Fahrzeug *n*.

veil *n* Schleier *m*; * *vt* verschleiern, verhüllen.

vein *n* Vene *f*.

velocity *n* Geschwindigkeit *f*.

velvet *n* Samt *m*.

vending machine *n* Automat *m*.

vendor *n* Verkäufer *m*.

veneer *n* Furnier *n*.

venerable *adj* ehrwürdig.

venerate *vt* verehren.

veneration *n* Verehrung *f*.

venereal *adj* ~ **disease** Geschlechtskrankheit *f*.

vengeance *n* Rache *f*.

venison *n* Reh(fleisch) *n*.

venom *n* Schlangengift *n*.

venomous *adj* giftig.

vent *n* Luftloch *m*; Luftschlitz *m*.

ventilate *vt* lüften.

ventilation *n* Lüftung *f*.

ventilator *n* Ventilator *m*.

ventriloquist *n* Bauchredner *m*.

venture *n* Unternehmen *n*; * *vt* wagen, riskieren.

venue *n* Treffpunkt *m*; Tagungsort *m*; Schauplatz *m*.

veranda(h) *n* Veranda *f*.

verb *n* (*gr*) Verb *n*.

verbal *adj* verbal, mündlich, wörtlich.

verbatim *adj* wörtlich; * *adv* Wort für Wort.

verbose *adj* wortreich.

verdict *n* Urteil *n*.

verification *n* Nachprüfung *f*.

verify *vt* überprüfen.

veritable *adj* echt, wirklich.

vermin *n* Ungeziefer *n*.

vermouth *n* Wermut *m*.

versatile *adj* vielseitig.

verse *n* Strophe *f*; Vers *m*.

version *n* Fassung *f*.

versus *prep* gegen.

vertebra *n* Wirbel *m*.

vertebrate *adj* Wirbel-.

vertical *adj* senkrecht, vertikal.

vertical take-off aircraft *n* Senkrechtstarter *m*.

vertigo *n* Schwindel *m*.

verve *n* Schwung *m*.

very *adj* genau; * *adv* sehr.

vessel *n* Schiff *n*; Gefäß *n*.

vest *n* Unterhemd *n*.

vestige *n* Spur *f*.

vestments *n* Meßgewand *n*.

vestry *n* Sakristei *f*.

vet *n* Tierarzt *m*.

veteran *adj*, *n* Veteran *m*.

veterinary *adj* tierärztlich.

veto *n* Veto *n*; * *vt* verbieten; durch ein Veto zurückweisen.

vex *vt* irritieren, ärgern.

vexed *adj* verärgert.

via *prep* über.

viable *adj* lebensfähig; durchführbar.

viaduct *n* Viadukt *m*.

vial *n* redoma, ampolleta *f*.

vibrate *vi* vibrieren, schwingen, beben.

vibration *n* Vibration *f*, Schwingung *f*.

vicar *n* Pfarrer *m*.

vicarage Pfarrhaus *n*.

vicarious *adj* nachempfunden.
vice *n* Laster *n*; Schraubstock *m*.
vice-chairman *n* stellvertretender Vorsitzender *m*.
vice-president *n* Vizepräsident *m*.
vice versa *adv* umgekehrt.
vicinity *n* Nähe *f*.
vicious *adj* bösartig, gemein.
victim *n* Opfer *n*.
victimisation *n* Schikane *f*.
victimise *vt* schikanieren.
victor *n* Sieger *m*.
victorious *adj* siegreich.
victory *n* Sieg *m*.
video cassette *n* Videokassette *f*.
video tape *n* Videoband *n*.
video tape recorder *n* Videorecorder *m*.
viewer *n* Betrachter *m*.
vie *vi* wetteifern.
Vienna *n* Wien *n*.
view *n* Besichtigung *f*; Aussicht *f*; Ansicht *m*; * *vt* ansehen; betrachten.
viewfinder *n* Sucher *m*.
viewpoint *n* Gesichtspunkt *m*.
vigil *n* Wache *f*.
vigilance *n* Wachsamkeit *f*.
vigilant *adj* wachsam.
vigorous *adj* energisch.
vigour *n* Energie *f*, Vitalität *f*.
vile *adj* widerwärtig.
vilify *vt* verleumden.
villa *n* Villa *f*.
village *n* Dorf *n*.
villager *n* Dorfbewohner *m*, Dorfbewohnerin *f*.
villain *n* Schurke *m*.
vindicate *vt* rechtfertigen, geltend machen.
vindictive *adj* rachsüchtig, nachtragend.
vine *n* Weinstock *m*.
vinegar *n* Essig *m*.
vineyard *n* Weinberg *m*; Weingarten *m*.
vintage *n* Weinlese *f*.
viola *n* (*mus*) Bratsche *f*.
violate *vt* verletzen; übertreten.

violation *n* Verletzung *f*; Übertretung *f*.
violence *n* Gewalt *f*.
violent *adj* gewaltsam.
violet *n* (*bot*) Veilchen *n*.
violin *n* (*mus*) Violine *f*, Geige *f*.
violinist *n* Geiger *m*, Geigerin *f*.
violoncello *n* (*mus*) Cello *n*.
viper *n* Giftschlange *f*.
virgin *n* Jungfrau *f*; * *adj* jungfräulich.
virginity *n* Jungfräulichkeit *f*.
Virgo *n* Jungfrau *f*.
virile *adj* viril, männlich.
virility *n* Virilität *f*, Männlichkeit *f*.
virtual *adj* eigentlich, praktisch.
virtue *n* Tugend *f*.
virtuous *adj* tugendhaft.
virulent *adj* bösartig.
virus *n* Virus *m*.
visa *n* Visum *n*.
vis-à-vis *prep* gegenüber.
viscous *adj* zähflüssig.
visibility *n* Sichtbarkeit *f*.
visible *adj* sichtbar.
vision *n* Sehkraft *f*; Vision *f*.
visit *vt* besuchen; * *n* Besuch *m*.
visiting card *n* Visitenkarte *f*.
visitor *n* Besucher *m*, Gast *m*.
visor *n* Visier *n*.
vista *n* Aussicht *f*.
visual *adj* visuell.
visual aids *n* Anschauungsmaterial *n*.
visualise *vt* vorstellen.
vital *adj* lebenswichtig, vital.
vitality *n* Vitalität *f*.
vital statistics *npl* Maße *pl*.
vitamin *n* Vitamin *n*.
vitiate *vt* beeinträchtigen.
vivacious *adj* lebhaft.
vivid *adj* hell, leuchtend.
vivisection *n* Vivisektion *f*.
vocabulary *n* Wortschatz *m*.
vocal *adj* Stimm-, Gesang-.
vocation *n* Berufung *f*; Begabung *f*; Beruf *m*.
vocational *adj* Berufs-.

vociferous *adj* lautstark.
vodka *n* Wodka *m*.
vogue *n* Mode *f*.
voice *n* Stimme *f*; * *vt* äußern.
void *adj* leer; * *n* Leere *f*.
volatile *adj* flüchtig, überschäumend.
volcanic *adj* vulkanisch.
volcano *n* Vulkan *m*.
volition *n* Willenskraft *f*.
volley *n* Geschützsalve *f*.
volleyball *n* Volleyball *m*.
volt *n* Volt *n*.
voltage *n* Spannung *f*.
voluble *adj* redselig.
volume *n* Band *m*; Volumen *n*; Lautstärke *f*.
voluntary *adj* freiwillig.
volunteer *n* Freiwillige(r) *m*; * *vi* sich freiwillig melden.
voluptuous *adj* wollüstig.
vomit *vt* erbrechen; *vi* sich übergehen.
vomiting *n* Erbrechen *n*.
voracious *adj* gierig.
vote *n* Abstimmung *f*, Stimme *f*; * *vt*, *vi* wählen.
voter *n* Wähler *m*.
voting *n* Abstimmung *f*, Wählen *n*.
voucher *n* Gutschein *m*.
vow *n* Gelübde *f*; * *vt* geloben.
vowel *n* Vokal *m*.
voyage *n* Seereise *f*.
vulgar *adj* vulgar, ordinär.
vulgarity *n* Gewöhnlichkeit *f*.
vulnerable *adj* verletzbar, anfällig.
vulture *n* Geier *m*.

W

wad *n* Bündel *n*; Stoß *m*; Pakken *m*.
waddle *vi* watscheln.
wade *vi* waten.

wafer *n* Waffel *f*; Hostie *f*.
waffle *n* Waffel *f*; Geschwafel *n*; * *vi* schwafeln.
waft *vt vi* wehen.
wag *vt* wedeln mit; * *vi* wedeln.
wage *n* Lohn *m*.
wage earner *n* Lohnempfänger(in) *m(f)*.
wager *n* Wette *f*; * *vt vi* wetten.
waggle *vt* wedeln mit; * *vi* wedeln.
wag(g)on *n* Fuhrwerk *n*; Wagen *m*; Waggon *m*.
wail *n* Wehgeschrei *n*; * *vi* wehklagen, jammern.
waist *n* Taille *f*.
waistcoat *n* Weste *f*.
waistline *n* Taille *f*.
wait *n* Wartezeit *f*; * *vi* warten.
waiter *n* Kellner *m*.
waiting list *n* Warteliste *f*.
waiting room *n* Wartezimmer *n*.
waitress *n* Kellnerin *f*.
waive *vt* verzichten auf.
wake *vt* wecken; * *vt* aufwachen; * *n* Totenwache *f*; (*mar*) Kienwasser *n*.
waken *vt* aufwecken.
Wales *n* Wales *n*.
walk *n* Spaziergang *m*; Gang *m*; Weg *m*; * *vi* gehen; spazierengehen; wandern.
walker *n* Spaziergänger *m*; Wanderer *m*.
walkie-talkie *n* tragbare(s) Sprechfunkgerät *n*.
walking *n* Gehen *n*; Wandern *n*.
walking stick *n* Spazierstock *m*.
walkout *n* Streik *m*.
walkover *n* (*sl*) leichte(r) Sieg *m*.
walkway *n* Fußweg *m*.
wall *n* Wand *f*; Mauer *f*.
walled *adj* von Mauern umgeben.
wallet *n* Brieftasche *f*.
wallflower *n* (*bot*) Goldlack *m*.
wallow *vi* sich wälzen.
wallpaper *n* Tapete *f*.

walnut *n* Walnuß *f*.
walrus *n* Walroß *n*.
waltz *n* Walzer *m*; * *vi* Walzer tanzen.
wan *adj* bleich.
wand *n* Zauberstab *m*.
wander *vi* (herum)wandern.
wane *vi* abnehmen.
want *n* Mangel *m*; * *vt* brauchen; wollen; nicht haben.
wanton *adj* mutwillig, zügellos.
war *n* Krieg *m*.
ward *n* Station *f*; Bezirk *m*; Mündel *n*.
wardrobe *n* Garderobe *f*; Kleiderschrank *m*.
warehouse *n* Lagerhaus *n*.
warfare *n* Kriegsführung *f*.
warhead *n* Sprengkopf *m*.
wariness *n* Vorsicht *f*.
warm *adj* warm; herzlich; * *vt* *vi* wärmen; ~ **up** *vt* aufwärmen; * *vi* warm werden.
warm-hearted *adj* warmherzig.
warmth *n* Wärme *f*; Herzlichkeit *f*.
warn *vt* warnen.
warning *n* Warnung *f*.
warning light *n* Warnlicht *n*.
warp *vt* verziehen.
warrant *n* Haftbefehl *m*.
warranty *n* Garantie *f*.
warren *n* Labyrinth *n*.
warrior *n* Krieger *m*.
Warsaw *n* Warschau *n*.
warship *n* Kriegsschiff *f*.
wart *n* Warze *f*.
wary *adj* mißtrauisch.
wash *n* Wäsche *f*; * *vt* waschen; abwaschen; * *vi* (sich) waschen.
washable *adj* waschbar.
washer *n* Dichtungsring *m*.
washing *n* Wäsche *f*.
washing machine *n* Waschmaschine *f*.
washing-up *n* Abwasch *m*.
wash-out *n* Reinfall *m*.
washroom *n* Waschraum *m*.
wasp *n* Wespe *f*.
wastage *n* Verlust *m*.

waste *n* Verschwendung *f*; Abfall *m*; * *adj* überschüssig, Abfall-; * *vt* verschwenden; vergeuden.
wasteful *adj* verschwenderisch; aufwendig.
waste paper basket *n* Papierkorb *m*.
waste pipe *n* Abflußrohr *n*.
watch *n* Wache *f*; Uhr *f*; * *vt* ansehen; beobachten; * *vi* zusehen.
watchdog *n* Wachthund *m*.
watchful *adj* wachsam.
watchmaker *n* Uhrmacher *m*.
watchman *n* Wächter *m*.
watchword *n* Kennwort *n*, Parole *f*.
water *n* Wasser *n*; * *vt* gießen; bewässern; tränken; * *vi* tränen.
water closet *n* Wasserklosett *n*.
watercolour *n* Aquarell *n*; Wasserfarbe *f*.
waterfall *n* Wasserfall *m*.
water heater *n* Heißwassergerät *n*.
watering can *n* Gießkanne *f*.
water level *n* Wasserstand *m*.
waterlily *n* Scerose *f*.
water line *n* Wasserlinie *f*.
waterlogged *adj* voll Wasser; mit Wasser vollgesogen.
water main *n* Hauptwasserleitung *f*.
watermark *n* Wasserzeichen *n*.
water melon *n* Wassermelone *f*.
waterproof *adj* wasserdicht.
watershed *n* Wasserscheide *f*.
watertight *adj* wasserdicht.
waterworks *npl* Wasserwerk *n*.
watery *adj* wäss(e)rig.
watt *n* Watt *n*.
wave *n* Welle *f*; Winken *n*; * *vt* schwenken; winken mit; * *vi* winken; wehen.
wavelength *n* Wellenlänge *f*.
waver *vi* schwanken.
wavy *adj* wellig.

wax n Wachs n; Siegellack m; Ohrenschmalz n; * vt wachsen; * vi zunehmen.

waxworks n Wachsfigurenkabinett n.

way n Weg m; Art und Weise f; Richtung f; Gewohnheit f.

waylay vt auflauern.

wayward adj eigensinnig.

we pron wir.

weak adj schwach.

weaken vt schwächen; * vi schwächer machen.

weakling n Schwächling m.

weakness n Schwäche f.

wealth n Reichtum m; Fülle f.

wealthy adj reich.

wean vt entwöhnen.

weapon n Waffe f.

wear vt tragen; haben; abnutzen; * vi halten; (sich) verschleißen; ~ **away** vt verbrauchen; * vi schwinden; ~ **down** vt zermürben; ~ **off** vi sich verlieren; ~ **out** vt verschleißen; erschöpfen; * n Verschleiß m.

weariness n Müdigkeit f; Überdruß m.

wearisome adj ermüdend.

weary adj müde; * vi überdrüssig werden.

weasel n Wiesel n.

weather n Wetter n; * vt verwittern lassen; überstehen.

weather-beaten adj verwittert.

weather-cock n Wetterhahn m.

weather forecast n Wettervorhersage f.

weather vane n Wetterfahne f.

weave vt weben.

weaver n Weber(in) m(f).

weaving n Webkunst f.

web n Netz n; Schwimmhaut f.

wed vt heiraten.

wedding n Hochzeit f.

wedding day n Hochzeitstag m.

wedding dress n Hochzeitskleid n.

wedding present n Hochzeitsgeschenk n.

wedding ring n Trauring m, Ehering m.

wedge n Keil m; * vt festklemmen.

wedlock n Ehe f.

Wednesday n Mittwoch m.

wee adj klein, winzig.

weed n Unkraut f; * vt jäten.

weedkiller n Unkrautvertilgungsmittel n.

weedy adj schmächtig.

week n Woche f.

weekday n Wochentag m.

weekend n Wochenende n.

weekly adj wochentlich.

weep vi weinen.

weeping willow n Trauerweide f.

weigh vt vi wiegen.

weight n Gewicht n.

weight-lifter n Gewichtheber m.

weighty adj gewichtig; schwerwiegend.

welcome n Willkommen n, Empfang m; * vt begrüßen.

weld vt schweißen.

welder n Schweißer(in) m(f).

welfare n Wohl n; Fürsorge f.

welfare state n Wohlfahrtsstaat m.

well n Brünnen m; Quelle f; * adj gesund; * adv gut; **as ~** auch; **as ~ as** wosohl als auch; ~ **done!** gut gemacht!.

well-behaved adj wohlerzogen.

well-being n Wohl n.

well-bred adj wohlerzogen.

well-built adj kräftig gebaut.

well-deserved adj wohlverdient.

well-dressed adj gut gekleidet.

well-known adj bekannt.

well-mannered adj wohlerzogen.

well-meaning adj wohlmeinend; gutgemeint.

well-off adj gut situiert.

well-to-do adj wohlhabend.

well-wisher n Gönner m.

Welsh adj walisisch; * n Walisisch n.

Welshman n Waliser m.

Welshwoman n Waliserin f.

wench n Mädchen n.

west n Westen m; * adj West-, westlich; * adv westwärts, nach Westen.

westerly adj westlich.

western adj westlich, West-.

westward(s) adv westwärts.

wet adj naß.

wet suit n Taucheranzug m.

whack n Schlag m; * vt schlagen.

whale n Wal m.

wharf n Kai m.

what adj welche(r,s); was für ein(e); * pron was; * excl wie, was.

whatever pron was (immer auch).

wheat n Weizen m.

wheatgerm n Weizenkeim m.

wheedle vt beschwatzen.

wheel n Rad n; Leknrad n; Scheibe f; * vi schieben.

wheelbarrow n Schubkarren m.

wheelchair n Rollstuhl m.

wheel clamp n Parkkralle f.

wheeze vi keuchen.

when adv wann; * conj wenn; als; wo ... doch.

whenever adv wann (auch) immer; jedesmal wenn; * conj wenn.

where adv wo; wohin; ~ from woher.

whereabouts adv wo; * n Aufenthaltsort m.

whereas conj während, wo ... doch.

whereby pron woran, wodurch, womit, wovon.

whereupon conj worauf, wonach; daraufhin.

wherever adv wo (immer).

wherewithal npl nötige Mittel pl.

whet vt anregen.

whether conj ob.

which adj welche(r,s); * pron welche(r,s); wer; rel pron der; die das; was.

whiff n Hauch m.

while n Weile f; * conj während.

whim n Laune f.

whimper n Wimmern n; * vi wimmern.

whimsical adj launisch.

whine n Gewinsel n, Gejammer n; * vi heulen, winseln.

whinny vi wiehern.

whip n Peitsche f; (pol) Fraktionsführer m; * vt peitschen.

whipped cream n Schlagsahne f.

whirl n Wirbel m; * vt vi (herum)wirbeln.

whirlpool n Wirbel m.

whirlwind n Wirbelwind m.

whiskers npl Barthaare pl.

whisky n Whisky m.

whisper n Flüstern n; * vt vi flüstern.

whistle n Pfiff m; Pfeife f; * vt vi pfeifen.

white n Weiß n; Eiweiß n; * adj weiß.

white elephant n Fehlinvestition f.

white lie n Notlüge f.

whiten vt weiß machen; * vi weiß werden.

whiteness n Weiße f.

whitewash n Tünche f; Ehrenrettung f; * vt weißen, tünchen; reinwaschen.

whiting n Weißfisch m.

Whitsun n Pfingsten n.

whitish adj weißlich.

who pron wer; (acc) wen; (dat) wem; * rel pron der/die/das.

whoever pron wer/wen/wem auch immer.

whole adj ganz; * n Ganze(s) n.

wholehearted adj rückhaltlos.

wholemeal adj Vollkorn-.

wholesale n Großhandel m; * adj Großhandels-.

wholesome adj bekömmlich, gesund.

whom *pron* (*acc*) wen; (*dat*) wem; * *rel pron* (*acc*) den/die/das; (*dat*) dem/der/dem.

whooping cough *n* Keuchhusten *m*.

whore *n* Hure *f*.

why *adv* warum, weshalb; * *conj* warum, weshalb; * *excl* na so was; also dann.

wick *n* Docht *m*.

wicked *adj* böse.

wickedness *n* Bosheit *f*.

wicker *n* Korbgeflecht *n*.

wide *adj* breit; weit.

wide-awake *adj* hellwach.

widen *vt* erweitern.

wide open *adj* weit geöffnet.

widespread *adj* weitverbreitet.

widow *n* Witwe *f*.

widowed *adj* verwitwet.

widower *n* Witwer *m*.

width *n* Breite *f*, Weite *f*.

wield *vt* schwingen, handhaben.

wife *n* Frau *f*, Ehefrau *f*, Gattin *f*.

wig *n* Perücke *f*.

wiggle *vt* wackeln mit; * *vi* wakkeln.

wild *adj* wild; heftig; verrückt.

wilderness *n* Wildnis *f*, Wüste *f*.

wildlife *n* Tierwelt *f*.

wilful *adj* vorsätzlich; eigensinnig.

will *v aux* werden; * *vt* wollen; * Wille *f*; Testament *n*.

willing *adj* gewillt, bereit.

willingness *n* Bereitwilligkeit *f*.

willow *n* Weide *f*.

willpower *n* Willenskraft *f*.

wilt *vi* welken.

wily *adj* gerissen.

win *n* Sieg *m*; * *vt vi* gewinnen.

wince *n* Zusammenzucken *n*; * *vi* zusammenzucken.

winch *n* Winde *f*.

wind *n* Wind *m*; * *vt* winden; wickeln; * *vi* sich winden; ~ **up** *vt* aufziehen.

windfall *n* unverhoffte(r)

Glücksfall *m*.

winding *adj* gewunden.

wind instrument *n* Blasinstrument *n*.

windmill *n* Windmühle *f*.

window *n* Fenster *n*.

window box *n* Blumenkasten *m*.

window cleaner *n* Fensterputzer *m*.

window ledge *n* Fenstersims *m*.

window pane *n* Fensterscheibe *f*.

window sill *n* Fensterbank *f*.

windpipe *n* Luftrohre *f*.

wind power *n* Windenergie *f*.

windscreen *n* Windschutzscheibe *f*.

windscreen washer *n* Scheibenwaschanlage *f*.

windscreen wiper *n* Scheibenwischer *m*.

windy *adj* windig.

wine *n* Wein *m*.

wine cellar *n* Weinkeller *m*.

wine glass *n* Weinglas *n*.

wine list *n* Weinkarte *f*.

wine merchant *n* Weinhändler *m*.

wine tasting *n* Weinprobe *f*.

wing *n* Flügel *m*; Schwinge *f*.

winger *n* Flügelstürmer *m*.

wink *n* Zwinkern *n*; * *vi* zwinkern, blinzeln.

winner *n* Gewinner *m*; Sieger *m*.

winning post *n* Ziel *n*.

winter *n* Winter *m*.

winter sports *npl* Wintersport *m*.

wintry *adj* Winter-, winterlich.

wipe *vt* wischen.

wire *n* Draht *m*; Telegramm *n*; * *vt* telegrafieren.

wiring *n* elektrische Leitungen *pl*.

wiry *adj* drahtig.

wisdom *n* Weisheit *f*; Klugheit *f*.

wisdom tooth *n* Weisheitszahn *m*.

wise *adj* klug, weise.

wisecrack *n* Witzelei *f*.

wish *n* Wunsch *m*; * *vt* wünschen.

wishful *adj* sehnsüchtig.

wisp *n* Strähne *f*; Wölkchen *n*.

wistful *adj* sehnsüchtig.

wit *n* Verstand *m*; Witz *m*; Witzbold *m*.

witch *n* Hexe *f*.

witchcraft *n* Hexerei *f*.

with *prep* mit.

withdraw *vt* zurückziehen; abheben; zurücknehmen; * *vi* sich zurückziehen.

withdrawal *n* Zurückziehung *f*; Abheben *n*; Zurücknahme *f*.

withdrawn *adj* verschlossen.

wither *vi* welken.

withhold *vt* to ~ sth (from sb) (jdm) etw vorenthalten.

within *prep* innerhalb; * *adv* innen.

without *prep* ohne.

withstand *vt* aushalten, widerstehen.

witness *n* Zeuge *m*, Zeugin *f*; * *vt* beglaubigen.

witness box *n* Zeugenbank *f*.

witticism *n* witzige Bemerkung *f*.

witty *adj* witzig, geistreich.

wizard *n* Zauberer *m*.

wobble *vi* wackeln, schwanken.

woe *n* Leid *n*, Kummer *m*.

woeful *adj* jammervoll.

wolf *n* Wolf *m*; **she ~** Wölfin *f*.

woman *n* Frau *f*.

womanly *adj* weiblich.

womb *n* Gebärmutter *f*.

women's libber *n* Frauenrechtlerin *f*.

wonder *n* Wunder *m*, Erstaunen *n*; * *vi* sich wundern.

wonderful *adj* wunderbar.

wont *n* Gewohnheit *f*.

woo *vt* den Hof machen, umwerben.

wood *n* Wald *m*; Holz *n*.

wood carving *n* Holzschnitzerei *m*.

woodcut *n* Holzschnitt *m*.

woodcutter *n* Holzfäller *m*; Holzschnitzer *m*.

wooded *adj* bewaldet.

wooden *adj* hölzern.

woodman *n* Förster *m*; Holzfäller *m*.

woodpecker *n* Specht *m*.

woodwind *n* Blasinstrumente *pl*.

woodwork *n* Holzwerk *n*; Holzarbeiten *pl*.

woodworm *n* Holzwurm *m*.

wool *n* Wolle *f*.

woollen *adj* Woll-.

woollens *npl* Wollsachen *pl*.

woolly *adj* wollig; schwammig.

word *n* Word *n*; Bescheid *m*; * *vt* formulieren; **in other ~s** anders gesagt.

wording *n* Wortlaut *m*; Fassung *f*.

word processing *n* Textverarbeitung *f*.

word processor *n* Textverarbeitungsgerät *n*.

wordy *adj* wortreich.

work *n* Arbeit *f*; Werk *n*; * *vi* arbeiten; funktionieren; wirken; **~ out** *vi* aufgehen; klappen; * *vt* lösen; ausarbeiten.

workable *adj* bearbeitbar; ausführbar.

workaholic *n* Arbeitssüchtige(r) *m/f*.

worker *n* Arbeiter(in) *m(f)*.

workforce *n* Arbeitschaft *f*.

working class *n* Arbeiterklasse *f*.

working-class *adj* Arbeiter-.

workman *n* Arbeiter *m*.

workmanship *n* Arbeit *f*, Ausführung *f*.

workshop *n* Werkstatt *f*.

world *n* Welt *f*.

worldly *adj* weltlich, irdisch.

worldwide *adj* weltweit.

worm *n* Wurm *m*.

worn-out *adj* abgenutzt; völlig erschöpft.

worried *adj* besorgt, beunruhigt.

worry *n* Sorge *f*; * *vt* beunruhigen; * *vi* sich sorgen.

worrying *adj* beunruhigend.

worse *adj* schlechter, schlimmer; * *adv* schlimmer, ärger; * *n* Schlimmere(s) *n*, Schlechtere(s) *n*.

worship *n* Verehrung *f*; * *vt* anbeten.

worst *adj* schlimmste(r,s), schlechteste(r,s); * *adv* am schlimmsten, am ärgsten; * *n* Schlimmste(s) *n*, Ärgste(s) *n*.

worth *n* Wert *m*; * *adj* wert.

worthless *adj* wertlos; nichtnutzig.

worthwhile *adj* lohnend, der Mühe wert.

worthy *adj* wert, würdig.

would-be *adj* Möchtegern-.

wound *n* Wunde *f*; * *vt* verwunden, verletzen.

wrangle *n* Streit *m*; * *vi* sich zanken.

wrap *vt* entwickeln.

wrath *n* Zorn *m*.

wreath *n* Kranz *m*.

wreck *n* Wrack *n*; Ruine *f*; * *vt* zerstören.

wreckage *n* Trümmer *pl*.

wren *n* Zaunkönig *m*.

wrench *n* Schraubenschlüssel *m*; Ruck *m*; * *vt* reißen, zerren.

wrest *vt* reißen.

wrestle *vi* ringen; **~r** *n* Ringer(in) *m(f)*.

wrestling *n* Ringen *n*.

wretched *adj* elend; verflixt.

wriggle *vi* sich winden.

wring *vt* wringen.

wrinkle *n* Falte *f*, Runzel *f*; * *vt* runzeln; * *vi* sich runzeln; knittern.

wrist *n* Handgelenk *n*.

wristwatch *n* Armbanduhr *f*.

writ *n* gerichtliche(r) Befehl *m*.

write *vt vi* schreiben; **~ down** *vt* aufschreiben; **~ off** *vt* abschreiben; **~ up** *vt* schreiben.

writer *n* Schriftsteller *m*.

writhe *vi* sich krümmen.

writing *n* Schreiben *n*; Schift *f*; **in ~** schriftlich.

writing paper *n* Schreibpapier *n*.

wrong *adj* falsch; unrecht; * *n* Unrecht *n*; * *vt* Unrecht tun.

wrongful *adj* unrechtmäßig.

wrongly *adv* falsch; zu Unrecht.

wry *adj* ironisch.

X

Xmas *n* Weihnachten *fpl*.

X-ray *n* Röntgenstrahl *m*; * *vt* röntgen.

xylophone *n* Xylophon *n*.

Y

yacht *n* Jacht *f*.

yachting *n* Segelsport *m*.

Yank, Yankee *n* Ami *m*.

yard *n* Hof *m*; Yard *n*.

yarn *n* Garn *n*.

yawn *vi* gähnen; * *n* Gähnen *n*.

yawning *adj* gähnend.

year *n* Jahr *n*.

yearbook *n* Jahrbuch *n*.

yearly *adj* jährlich.

yearn *vi* sehnen.

yearning *n* Sehnen *n*.

yeast *n* Hefe *f*.

yell *vt*, *vi* schreien; * *n* Schrei *m*.

yellow *adj* gelb; * *n* Gelb *n*.

yelp *vi* kläffen, jaulen; * *n* Kläffen *n*, Jaulen *n*.

yes *adv* ja; * *n* Ja *n*.

yesterday *adv* gestern; **the day before ~** vorgestern.

yet *conj* dennoch; * *adv* noch.

yew *n* Eibe *f*.

yield *vt* liefern; abwerfen; einbringen; * *vi* nachgeben; * *n* Ertrag *m*; Ernte *f*; Zinsertrag *m*.

yoga *n* Joga *n*.

yoghurt *n* Joghurt *m*.

yoke *n* Joch *n*.

yolk *n* Eidotter *n*, Eigelb *n*.

yonder *adv* dort drüben, da drüben.

you *pron* (*nominative*) Sie; du, ihr; (*accusative*) Sie; dich, euch; (*dative*) Ihnen; dir, euch.

young *adj* jung.

youngster *n* Jugendlicher *m*, Jugendliche *f*.

your *poss adj* Ihr; dein, euer.

yours *poss pron* Ihrer, Ihre, Ihres; deiner, deine, deines, eurer, eure, eures.

youth *n* Jugend *f*.

youthful *adj* jugendlich.

youthfulness *n* Jugendlichkeit *f*.

English and German Verbs

Unregelmässige Englische Verben

	Präteritum	Partizip des Perfekts		Präteritum	Partizip des Perfekts
arise	arose	arisen	do [he/she/it does]		
awake	awoke	awaked,		did	done
awoken			draw	drew	drawn
be [I am; you/we/they are, he/she/it			dream	dreamed,	dreamed
is, *Gerundium* being]				dreamt	dreamt
	was, were	been	drink	drank	drunk
bear	bore	borne	drive	drove	driven
beat	beat	beaten	dwell	dwelt,	dwelt,
become	became	become		dwelled	dwelled
begin	began	begun	eat	ate	eaten
behold	beheld	beheld	fall	fell	fallen
bend	bent	bent	feed	fed	fed
beseech	besought,	besought,	feel	felt	felt
beseeched	beseeched		mistake	mistook	mistaken
beset	beset	beset	fight	fought	fought
bet	bet, betted	bet, betted	find	found	found
bid	bade, bid	bade, bid,	flee	fled	fled
		bidden	fling	flung	flung
bite	bit	bitten	fly [he/she/it flies]		
bleed	bled	bled		flew	flown
bless	blessed	blessed,	forbid	forbade	forbidden
		blest	forecast	forecast	forecast
blow	blew	blown	forget	forgot	forgotten
break	broke	broken	forgive	forgave	forgiven
breed	bred	bred	forsake	forsook	forsaken
bring	brought	brought	forsee	foresaw	foreseen
build	built	built	freeze	froze	frozen
burn	burnt,	burnt,	get	got	got, gotten
	burned	burned	give	gave	given
burst	burst	burst	go [he/she/it goes]		
buy	bought	bought		went	gone
can	could	(been able)	grind	ground	ground
cast	cast	cast	grow	grew	grown
catch	caught	caught	hang	hung,	hung,
choose	chose	chosen		hanged	hanged
cling	cling	clung	have [I/you/we/they have,		
come	came	come	he/she/it has, *Gerundium* having]		
cost	cost	cost		had	had
creep	crept	crept	hear	heard	heard
cut	cut	cut	hide	hid	hidden
deal	dealt	dealt	hit	hit	hit
dig	dug	dug	hold	held	held

439

	Präteritum	Partizip des Perfekts		Präteritum	Partizip des Perfekts
hurt	hurt	hurt	shake	shook	shaken
keep	kept	kept	shall	should	-
kneel	knelt, kneeled	knelt, kneeled	shear	sheared	sheared, shorn
know	knew	known	shed	shed	shed
lay	laid	laid	shine	shone	shone
lead	led	led	shoot	shot	shot
lean	leant, leaned	leant, leaned	show	showed	shown, showed
leap	leapt, leaped	leapt, leaped	shrink	shrank	shrunk
learn	learnt, learned	learnt	shut	shut	shut
			sing	sang	sung
leave	left	left	sink	sank	sunk
lend	lent	lent	sit	sat	sat
let	let	let	slay	slew	slain
lie [Gerundium lying]			sleep	slept	slept
	lay	lain	slide	slid	slid
light	lighted, lit	lighted, lit	sling	slung	slung
lit			smell	smelt, smelled	smelt, smelled
lose	lost	lost	sow	sowed	sown, sowed
make	made	made			
may	might	-	speak	spoke	spoken
mean	meant	meant	speed	sped, speeded	sped, speeded
meet	met	met			
mow	mowed	mowed, mown	spell	spelt, spelled	spelt, spelled
must	(had to)	(had to)	spend	spent	spent
overcome	overcame	overcome	spill	spilt, spilled	spilt
pay	paid	paid			
put	put	put	spin	spun	spun
quit	quitted	quitted	spit	spat	spat
read	read	read	split	split	split
rid	rid	rid	spoil	spoilt, spoiled	spoilt
ride	rode	ridden	spread	spread	spread
ring	rang	rung	spring	sprang	sprung
rise	rose	risen	stand	stood	stood
run	ran	run	steal	stole	stolen
saw	sawed	sawn	stick	stuck	stuck
say	said	said	sting	stung	stung
see	saw	seen	stink	stank	stunk
seek	sought	sought	stride	strode	stridden
sell	sold	sold	strike	struck	struck
send	sent	sent	strive	strove	striven
set	set	set	swear	swore	sworn
sew	sewed	sewn	sweep	swept	swept

	Präteritum	Partizip des Perfekts		Präteritum	Partizip des Perfekts
swell	swelled	swelled, swollen	wake	woke	woken
			wear	wore	worn
swim	swam	swum	weave	wove,	wove,
swing	swung	swung		weaved	weaved
take	took	taken	wed	wed,	wed,
teach	taught	taught		wedded	wedded
tear	tore	torn	weep	wept	wept
tell	told	told	win	won	won
think	thought	thought	wind	wound	wound
throw	threw	thrown	withdraw	withdrew	withdrawn
thrust	thrust	thrust	withhold	withheld	withheld
tread	trod	trodden	withstand	withstood	withstood
understand	understood	understood	wring	wrung	wrung
upset	upset	upset	write	wrote	written

German Verbs

Regular verbs
machen *to make*
present participle machend
present indicative
   ich mache
   du machst
   er/sie/es macht
   wir machen
   irh macht
   sie/Sie machen
past imperfect
   ich machte
   du machtest
   er/sie/es machte
   wir machten
   ihr machtet
   sie/Sie machten

past participle gemacht
present subjunctive
   ich mache
   du machest
   er mache
   wir machen
   ihr machet
   sie machen
past subjunctive
   iche machte
   du machtest
   er/sie/es machte
   wir machten
   ihr machtet
   sie/Sie machten

The past perfect and past subjunctive tenses are formed with **haben,** *the future and conditional tenses with* **werden**

Auxiliary verbs
haben *to have*
present participle hatte
present indicative
   ich habe
   du hast
   er/sie/es hat
   wir haben
   irh habt
   sie/Sie haben
past imperfect
   ich hatte
   du hattest
   er/sie/es hatte
   wir hatten
   ihr hattet
   sie/Sie hatten

past participle gehabt
present subjunctive
   ich habe
   du habest
   er/sie/es habe
   wir haben
   ihr habet
   sie/Sie haben
past subjunctive
   iche habte
   du habtest
   er/sie/es habte
   wir habten
   ihr habtet
   sie/Sie habten

sein *to be*
past participle gewesen
present indicative
   ich bin
   du bist
   er/sie/es ist

   wir sind
   ihr seid
   sie/Sie sind

past imperfect
- ich war
- du warst
- er/sie/es war
- wir waren
- ihr wart
- sie/Sie waren

present subjunctive
- ich sei
- du sei(e)st
- er/sie/es sei
- wir seien
- ihr seiet
- sie/Sie seien

past subjunctive
- ich wäre
- du wär(e)st
- er/sie/es wäre
- wir wären
- ihr wär(e)t
- sie/Sie wären

werden *to become*
present participle werdend
past participle worden

present indicative
- ich werde
- du wirt
- er/sie/es wird
- wir werden
- ihr werdet
- sie/Sie werden

present subjunctive
- ich werde
- du werdest
- er/sie/es werde
- wir werden
- ihr werdet
- sie/Sie werden

past imperfect
- ich wurde
- du wurdest
- er/sie/es wurde
- wir wurden
- ihr wurdet
- sie/Sie wurden

past subjunctive
- ich würde
- du würdest
- er/sie/es würde
- wir würden
- ihr würdet
- sie/Sie würden

Irregular and semi-irregular verbs

(Verbs that take the auxiliary **sein** are marked with an asterisk)

Infinitive (indicative)	Preterite	Past Participle
backen (du bäckst, er bäckt)	backte, buk	gebacken
befehlen (du befiehlst, er befiehlt)	befahl	befohlen
beginnen	begann	begonnen
beißen	biß	gebissen
bergen (du birgst, er birgt)	barg	geborgen
*bersten (du birst, er birst)	barst	geborsten
bewegen	bewog	bewogen
biegen	bog	gebogen
bieten	bot	geboten
binden	band	gebunden
bitten	bat	gebeten
blasen (du bläst, er bläst)	blies	geblasen
*bleiben	blieb	geblieben
bleichen	blich	geblichen

Infinitive (indicative)	Preterite	Past Participle
braten (du brätst, er brät)	briet	gebraten
*brechen (du brichst, er bricht)	brach	gebrochen
brennen	brannte	gebrannt
bringen	brachte	gebracht
denken	dachte	gedacht
dingen	dang	gedungen
dreschen (du drischst, er drischt)	drasch	gedroschen
*dringen	drang	gedrungen
dunken (es dünkt)	deuchte	gedeucht
dürfen (ich darf, du darfst, er darf)	durfte	gedurft
empfehlen (du empfiehlst, er empfiehlt)	empfahl	empfohlen
*erlöschen (du erlischst, er erlischt)	erlosch	erloschen
erschallen	erscholl	erschollen
*erschrecken (du erschrickst, er erschrickt)	erschrak	erschrocken
essen (du ißt, er ißt)	aß	gegessen
*fahren (du fährst, er fährt)	fuhr	gefahren
*fallen (du fällst, er fällt)	fiel	gefallen
fangen (du fängst, er fängt)	fing	gefangen
fechten (du fichtst, er ficht)	focht	gefochten
finden	fand	gefunden
flechten (du flichtst, er flicht)	flocht	geflochten
*fliegen	flog	geflogen
*fliehen	floh	geflohen
fließen	floß	geflossen
fressen (du frißt, er frißt)	fraß	gefressen
frieren	fror	gefroren
*gären	gor	gegoren
gebären (du gebierst, sie gebiert)	gebar	geboren
geben (du gibst, er gibt)	gab	gegeben
*gedeihen	gedieh	gediehen
*gehen	ging	gegangen
*gelingen	gelang	gelungen
gelten (du giltst, er gilt)	galt	gegolten
*genesen	genas	genesen
genießen	genoß	genossen
*geschehen (es geschieht)	geschah	geschehen
gewinnen	gewann	gewonnen
gießen	goß	gegossen
gleichen	glich	geglichen
*gleiten	glitt	geglitten
glimmen	glomm	geglommen
graben (du gräbst, er gräbt)	grub	gegraben
greifen	griff	gegriffen

Infinitive (indicative)	Preterite	Past Participle
halten (du hältst, er hält)	hielt	gehalten
hängen	hing	gehangen
hauen	haute	gehauen
heben	hob	gehoben
heißen	hieß	geheißen
helfen (du hilfst, er hilft)	half	geholfen
kennen	kannte	gekannt
kiesen	kor	gekoren
*klimmen	klomm	geklommen
klingen	klang	geklungen
kneifen	kniff	gekniffen
kommen	kam	gekommen
können (ich kann, du kannst, er kann)		
	konnte	gekonnt
kreischen	krisch	gekrischen
*kriechen	kroch	gekrochen
küren	kor	gekoren
laden (du lädst, er lädt)	lud	geladen
lassen (du läßt, er läßt)	ließ	gelassen
*laufen (du läufst, er läuft)	lief	gelaufen
leiden	litt	gelitten
leihen	lieh	geliehen
lesen (du liest, er liest)	las	gelesen
*liegen	lag	gelegen
lügen	log	gelogen
mahlen	mahlte	gemahlen
meiden	mied	gemieden
melken (du melkst, er melkt)	melkte	gemolken
messen (du mißt, er mißt)	maß	gemessen
*mißlingen	mißlang	mißlungen
mögen (ich mag, du magst, er mag)	mochte	gemocht
müssen (ich muß, du mußt, er muß)	mußte	gemußt
nehmen (du nimmst, er nimmt)	nahm	genommen
nennen	nannte	genannt
pfeifen	pfiff	gepfiffen
pflegen	pflog	gepflogen
preisen	pries	gepriesen
*quellen (du quillst, er quillt)	quoll	gequollen
raten (du rätst, er rät)	riet	geraten
reiben	rieb	gerieben
*reißen	riß	gerissen
*reiten	ritt	geritten
*rennen	rannte	gerannt
riechen	roch	gerochen
ringen	rang	gerungen
*rinnen	rann	geronnen

Infinitive (indicative)	Preterite	Past Participle
rufen	rief	gerufen
salzen	salzte	gesalzen
saufen (du säufst, er säuft)	soff	gesoffen
saugen	sog	gesogen
schaffen	schuf	geschaffen
schallen	scholl	geschallt
scheiden	schied	geschieden
scheinen	schien	geschienen
scheißen	schoß	geschossen
schelten (du schiltst, er schilt)	schalt	gescholten
scheren	schor	geschoren
schieben	schob	geschoben
schießen	schoß	geschossen
schinden	schindete	geschunden
schlafen (du schläfst, er schläft)	schlief	geschlafen
schlagen (du schlägst, er schlägt)	schlug	geschlagen
*schleichen	schlich	geschlichen
schleifen	schliff	geschliffen
schleißen	schliß	geschlissen
schließen	schloß	geschlossen
schlingen	schlang	geschlungen
schmeißen	schmiß	geschmissen
*schmelzen (du schmilzt, er schmilzt)		
	schmolz	geschmolzen
schnauben	schnob	geschnoben
schneiden	schnitt	geschnitten
schrecken (du schrickst, er schrickt)		
	schrak	geschreckt
schreiben	schrieb	geschrieben
schreien	schrie	geschrie(e)n
schreiten	schritt	geschritten
schweigen	schwieg	geschwiegen
*schwellen (du schwillst, er schwillt)		
	schwoll	geschwollen
*schwimmen	schwamm	geschwommen
*schwinden	schwand	geschwunden
schwingen	schwang	geschwungen
schwören	schwor	geschworen
sehen (du siehst, er sieht)	sah	gesehen
senden	sandte	gesandt
sieden	sott	gesotten
singen	sang	gesungen
*sinken	sank	gesunken
sinnen	sann	gesonnen
*sitzen	saß	gesessen
sollen (ich soll, du sollst, er soll)	sollte	gesollt

Infinitive (indicative)	Preterite	Past Participle
spalten	spaltete	gespalten
speien	spie	gespie(e)n
spinnen	spann	gesponnen
spleißen	spliß	gesplissen
sprechen (du sprichst, er spricht)	sprach	gesprochen
*sprießen	sproß	gesprossen
*springen	sprang	gesprungen
stechen (du stichst, er sticht)	stach	gestochen
stecken	stak, stekte	gesteckt
stehen	stand	gestanden
stehlen (du stiehlst, er stiehlt)	stahl	gestohlen
*steigen	stieg	gestiegen
*sterben (du stirbst, er stirbt)	starb	gestorben
stieben	stob	gestoben
stinken	stank	gestunken
stoßen (du stößt, er stößt)	stieß	gestoßen
streichen	strich	gestrichen
*streiten	stritt	gestritten
tragen (du trägst, er trägt)	trug	getragen
treffen (du triffst, er trifft)	traf	getroffen
*treiben	trieb	getrieben
*treten (du trittst, er tritt)	trat	getreten
triefen	troff	getroffen
trinken	trank	getrunken
trügen	trog	getrogen
tun	tat	getan
verderben (du verdirbst, er verdirbt)		
	verdarb	verdorben
verdrießen	verdroß	verdrossen
vergessen (du vergißt, er vergißt)	vergaß	vergessen
verlieren	verlor	verloren
verloschen (du verlischst, er verlischt)		
	verlosch	verloschen
*wachsen (du wächst, er wächst)	wuchs	gewachsen
wägen	wog	gewogen
waschen (du wäschst, er wäscht)	wusch	gewaschen
weben	wob	gewoben
*weichen	wich	gewichen
weisen	wies	gewiesen
wenden	wandte	gewandt
werben (du wirbst, er wirbt)	warb	geworben
*werden (du wirst, er wird)	wurde,	geworden
(as auxiliary, see above)		worden
werfen (du wirfst, er wirft)	warf	geworfen
wiegen	wog	gewogen
winden	wand	gewunden

Infinitive (indicative)	Preterite	Past Participle
wissen (ich weiß, du weißt, er weiß)	wußte	gewußt
wollen (ich will, du willst, er will)	wollte	gewollt
wringen	wrang	gewrungen
zeihen	zieh	geziehen
ziehen	zog	gezogen
zwingen	zwang	gezwungen